THE PEOPLE'S POWER
American Government and Politics Today

THE PEOPLE'S POWER

American Government and Politics Today

Charles P. Sohner
El Camino College

Scott, Foresman and Company
Glenview, Illinois   Brighton, England

To Michelle

Picture Credits

Part One, Parade: Roger Lubin © 1972, Jeroboam
Part Two, Angela Davis: Paul Sequeira
Part Three, Convention: Ken Regan, Camera Five
Part Four, Senate Commerce Committee hearing: Paul
 Conklin
Part Five, City Council, Syracuse-Hamilton County, Kansas:
 Tim Kantor, Rapho Guillumette Pictures
Part Six, Demonstrator: Michael Abramson, Jeroboam

Library of Congress Catalog Number 72-85610
ISBN: 0-673-07646-6

Copyright © 1973 by
Scott, Foresman and Company, Glenview, Illinois.
Philippines Copyright 1973 by Scott, Foresman and
Company.
All Rights Reserved.
Printed in the United States of America.

Regional offices of Scott, Foresman and Company are
located in Dallas, Texas; Glenview, Illinois; Oakland,
New Jersey; Palo Alto, California; Tucker, Georgia; and
Brighton, England.

Preface

It is easy for an author to believe that his work has its own reason for being. He likes to assume that it should be read, as the mountain should be climbed, simply because it is there. But the prospective reader deserves more of an accounting.

This book was written primarily to examine American politics from the perspective of the people. It emphasizes those aspects of the political system which affect them most directly and over which they can exert the most influence. Its rationale can be summarized in a simple truism: American government involves Americans. It is they who pay the taxes to finance their government; it is they who are called into battle to protect its interests; it is they whose faith and loyalty give it the legitimacy necessary to exercise authority effectively. Even with all its power, the government must solicit the support of the people to cope with crime, resist racism, prevent pollution, and demonstrate generally that democracy works.

This book, therefore, was designed to meet the most basic political needs of the average citizen. The author sees these as falling largely in two categories: Americans need to understand the nature, extent, and importance of their constitutionally guaranteed rights and they need to know the channels through which they can exert maximum influence on government policy. For these reasons, three of the eleven chapters in this book are devoted to civil rights (Part Two) and three others to pressure groups, political parties, and the campaign techniques designed to affect voting decisions (Part Three). In addition, notably unlike other introductory American politics texts, this one devotes three chapters to local governments (Part Five). Through their authority to control land use, their responsibility for mass transit facilities, their administration of the public schools, and myriad other activities, they have a more profound impact upon the daily life styles of their citizens than any other political level. If the people cannot control local governments, a belief that popular influence is decisive at any other level of government may be largely a delusion.

The emphasis on such topics is further justified because this text was not written for future members of exalted political elites. It assumes that more of its readers will be litigants than lawyers, pressure group members than corporate or union officials, and city council members than congressmen. This probability prevails for both university and community college students.

Nevertheless, the following pages ignore neither political ideas nor governmental organization. On the contrary, Part One begins with a description of fundamental concepts in empirical and normative theory and then proceeds to apply them to the American political system. Part Four consists of an integrated and concise account of the legislative, executive, and judicial branches of government at both the national and state levels. Here there are enough essential facts regarding both structure and process to free the instructor for the more discretionary elaboration and commentary that transform teaching from ritualistic recitation to creative art. To make it easier for readers to find information on particular states, counties, and cities, this data is separately indexed.

Part Six, concluding the book, contains three chapters on public policy. The first of these, dealing with government regulation of people's behavior in the areas of population growth, ecology, drugs, sex, and gambling, considers some social issues too long ignored in most basic texts. Another is concerned with current economic issues such as the distribution of wealth, inflation and unemployment, poverty and welfare, industrial disputes, and consumer protection. The last chapter discusses the framework of American foreign policy.

Together, the six parts of this volume provide a basic text for an introductory course in American politics. Each is relatively autonomous and may be omitted without a significant loss of comprehension regarding any of the other parts. Needless technical terms are avoided and the length permits supplementary reading. In short, the book is designed to enhance people's sense of political efficacy by imparting the knowledge needed to understand and hence to influence the governments created to serve them. Consequently, much of this work may recommend itself also to broad programs of social science education and to private groups attempting to mobilize political participation.

The concept of power has been employed to unify the book both because the author believes it provides the surest key to a comprehension of the whole political process and because it lends coherence to the treatment of diverse subjects. It is defined in Chapter 1, along with other analytical options, and continuously reappears to interpret phenomena throughout the text. Since power blocs clash, conflicting interests inevitably surface in these pages, related to the major political issues of the 1970s.

The reader should be alerted to the fact that the author does not write from a position of olympian detachment. As a teacher at the community college and state college and university levels, he has been a government employee for nearly twenty years. As a party official and former candidate for a state legislature, he has felt the exhilaration of partisan battle. By his selection of material and interpretations, he has betrayed his own values and priorities. The accompanying manual of test items indicates general areas both stressed and omitted in each chapter. Among the former, for example, are geographic factors, ethnic politics, women's liberation, functions of freedom, campaign organization, criminal procedure and punishment, local government finance, and "victimless crimes." While the reader is invited to identify his biases (which shouldn't be difficult), the author has tried to be fair and tolerant, to keep his facts straight, and to remain within the academic tradition. These too are among the values he cherishes.

The merits of this book are due in large measure to those who have helped me so generously. In both personal and professional ways, they include Will Scoggins, Gus Shackelford, Helmut Bader, and Nadine Hata. I am indebted to Professors Fred I. Greenstein and Charles Press for their encouragement and criticisms, as I am to Lance Widman, Edgar Love, Don Haley, Bob Putzel, and Dick Schwarzman among my El Camino colleagues. Two others, Jeannette Campiglia and Tom Wilson, devoted many hours and great skill to helping me translate political science into comprehensible English. How my wife, to whom this book is dedicated, could type the entire manuscript and provide sage editorial criticism while at the same time shielding me from the realities of daily life is more to be admired than understood.

I was also the beneficiary of invaluable institutional assistance. From the Dean's office at El Camino College came the tolerance and assistance of George Merrill and Helen Puckett. Scott, Foresman has far exceeded its publication commitment, thanks to the enthusiasm and expertise of Peter Quass and the wisdom and kindness of the late George Vlach. Finally, if future editors can be mass produced, let them be made in the mold of Nancy Kannappan. Authors will be chastened, but the kind of editorial diligence, practicality, intelligence, and uncompromising standards which she personifies will produce far better books.

Inescapably, however, the flaws of this text lie neither in my stars nor in those who have assisted me, but in myself.

Charles P. Sohner

Contents

PART THREE: POLITICAL BEHAVIOR

PART ONE

AMERICAN POLITICS IN PERSPECTIVE

Iron rusts in the atmosphere; trees bend in the wind; and nothing exists in a vacuum. That is why this book begins with a look at the broad environment within which American politics operates. Chapter 1 discusses the basic nature of politics and government, primarily in terms of power, and it contrasts the United States government with other systems. Chapter 2 explores some of the factors that make our government unique—the land, the people, the culture, the Constitution, and our own particular historical experience. In short, we begin with these chapters because politics in America requires some understanding of both the nature of politics and the nature of America.

Chapter **1**

The Nature of Politics
What's It All About?

Families, and communities, and indeed free nations, rest not on law and not on force but on a certain indispensable faith and confidence, mixed with some affection and much charity, each person for his fellow man.

Walter Lippmann

Aristotle, often called the father of political science, wrote that man is a political animal. There is considerable dispute about whether this was a compliment or an insult. A public opinion poll has revealed that most American parents do not want their children to enter politics; yet at the same time they seem to reserve their greatest admiration for Washington, Lincoln, and other political leaders. Is politics a "dirty game" or a "noble calling?" Let us begin the study of American government by noting that there are several different views of politics and several ways of studying it. At the end, readers may formulate their own answers to the above question.

THE STUDY OF POLITICS

Politics refers to government action and anything designed to affect it.[1] It involves a bewildering array of official decisions, ranging from building sidewalks to bombing cities. Since complexity is always

---

1 "Politics" has a diversity of meanings. See, for example, Austin Ranney's discussion of the term in *The Governing of Men,* 3rd ed. (N.Y.: Holt, Rinehart & Winston, Inc., 1971), pp. 4–6.

confusing, perhaps that is why politics is viewed with such mixed emotions. The study of these activities, now called political science, once seemed helplessly entangled with philosophy, economics, history, law, even religion—all subjects with which it is still concerned. But political science today tends to concentrate mostly on the state.

The State

The state, here, refers not to New York or California; *the state is the largest area under common control*—currently an entire nation. The nation-state, as it is sometimes called, is often defined as: (1) a fixed territory, (2) with a more or less permanent population, (3) ruled by a reasonably stable government, (4) which possesses the final power to make decisions, a power known as sovereignty. Yet because the state seems to encompass so much, many political scientists limit their scholarly appetites primarily to a study of government.

Government

Government is not so broad a concept as the state and excludes much that is significant about politics. For example, private organizations such as pressure groups exert great influence on important government decisions. On the other hand, the concept of government is too broad if it encompasses the administration of such organizations as churches or yacht clubs in which political scientists are seldom interested. They are concerned, instead, with *governments which make and administer the decisions of the state.* It is these which possess sovereignty.

Sovereignty

At first, the idea of sovereignty seems somewhat vague and intangible. Its essence, however, is relatively simple: It is the *ultimate power to make final decisions affecting all the inhabitants of the state.* This concept of power has had the most important influence upon the study of politics in the last forty years and is explored more fully in the following pages.

POLITICS AS POWER

Power means the capacity to alter socially significant behavior. It makes people do things which they might not do, or stops them from doing things which they might do. In other words, power involves a relationship between people which is based on dominance and submission. All the topics considered in this book can be interpreted in terms of power—how it is distributed, how it is obtained, and how it is used.

Power as Force

The most obvious source of government power is its preponderance of physical force. Governmental dominance in this area is almost a monopoly, for although private citizens may possess guns, they are subject to whatever restrictions are legally imposed. By contrast, other social institutions seem weak. A church can make rules but can only expel or excommunicate those who defy them. An employer, too, can issue orders but can at most fire the rebellious employee. Only government can use physical coercion to compel compliance to its commands.

Power as Influence

Fortunately for human dignity, government can usually gain obedience without resort to force. Schattschneider points out that only "about 5 percent of all state and local government employees are police officers" and concludes that "the internal relations of American government are not characteristically forceable."[2] Instead, government often can obtain the ends it seeks by the use of influence—a more subtle approach that involves both rewarding people with what they want (tax exemptions, medals, or defense contracts, for example) and threatening to deprive them of what they have (such as drivers' licenses, teaching credentials, or prison paroles).

Of course the capacity to bestow rewards and impose deprivations is not limited to government. Other institutions exert influence, both in their own private sphere, as when a business promotes one employee rather than another, and also in the broad political sphere, as when a union denounces a senator in its weekly newspaper. Since the process of giving (bestowing rewards) and taking (imposing deprivations) may involve honor, affection, or money, nearly everyone has at least some influence over at least a few people.

Power as Authority

No government could long survive if it had to rely exclusively upon force and influence. Policemen and prisons are too few and money and honor too scarce. Instead, most governments endure because they possess authority—that most remarkable kind of power with which people voluntarily comply because they believe it necessary, just, and therefore legitimate. If there is anything which merits description as a "law" of politics, it is that when a government loses the faith and confidence of its people, it must increase the force necessary to maintain its rule. When too much confidence is lost, there eventually comes a time

---

2 E. E. Schattschneider, *Two Hundred Million Americans in Search of a Government* (N.Y.: Holt, Rinehart & Winston, Inc., 1969), pp. 19–21.

when too little force is available to sustain continued power. Laws are obeyed, finally, because people believe they should be. It is this which converts power into authority, producing voluntary obedience.

Yet governments must share authority, as well as influence, with other institutions. The moral doctrines of a church, the examples of parents, or the impressions left by the TV screen or printed page persuade many of their correctness, more to be obeyed than questioned. For some, authority is the law, the command of the state; but for others, it is religious beliefs, family traditions, or the Columbia Broadcasting System.

Political Resources: Tools of Power

In order to exercise any kind of power—force, influence, or authority—an individual or institution must possess certain tools or capabilities. If these are used to affect government policy, they are often called political resources.

Type of Power	Political Resources
Force	Military weapons
	Police equipment
	Home-made bombs
	Riots (and revolution)
	Assassination
Influence	Votes
	Money (taxes, loans and subsidies, campaign contributions)
	Jobs (patronage)
	Honor (medals)
	Restrictions (or privileges)
	Respect (or contempt)
	Services (road repairs, fire protection)
Authority	Constitution (and laws and court decisions)
	Appeals to conscience (fasts, demonstrations)
	Holy Scriptures (and church command)
	Tradition (custom and habit)
	Family example (and early indoctrination)
	Propaganda (radio, TV, advertising, books)
	Education (schools, knowledge, expertise)
	Intelligence (reason, logic)
	High status (upper class)
	Respected role (parent, President)

Usually, both the kind of power brought into play and the particular resources used will be determined by the nature of a particular situation. In coping with a criminal, for example, government will employ force and use police equipment. But many times a tactical choice must be made. In protesting compulsory busing to achieve racial integration ordered by a school board, a group might blow up the buses (force), elect a new school board (influence), or challenge the school board decree in court (authority). When such a choice is available, the easiest course—but not necessarily the most effective—is often to invoke authority, because it entails less risk than force and is usually less costly than influence.

OTHER VIEWS OF POLITICS

Not all political scientists are pleased with this type of emphasis upon power. They acknowledge power to be an important component of politics, but insist that one must understand its other ingredients to appreciate the many functions performed by modern political systems.

Politics as Compromise

In our pluralistic society, one notable for its numerous and diverse groups, politics is often viewed largely as an instrument of compromise among them. Between white and black, the religious and the agnostic, labor and management, some sort of agreement must be reached. If we are to avoid civil war, there must be both an accommodation of interests and an agreement to disagree peacefully.

This conception of politics has been given a bad time by some in recent years. Compromise has been equated with a betrayal of principles, unethical deals, and a cynical sellout for the purpose of gaining power. Yet compromise reflects a tradition both long and strong in American politics. Jefferson, among the most idealistic of men, wrote that "We must be contented to secure what we can get. . . . It takes time to persuade men to do even what is for their own good."[3] Henry Clay of Kentucky won his place in history books as "the Great Compromiser," forestalling North-South conflict by authoring the Missouri Compromise of 1820 and the Compromise of 1850. John C. Calhoun justified in theory the kind of compromise which his Kentucky colleague had practiced. Calhoun developed the concept of the *concurrent majority*, by which the government would adopt only policies which had the support of a majority within each of the major sections or interest groupings of the nation.

More recently, the political importance of compromise has been reflected in the attempt of both the Republican and Democratic

---

3 Saul K. Padover, *Thomas Jefferson On Democracy* (N.Y.: Penguin Books, Inc., 1939), p. 154.

parties to gain power through the formation of coalitions of several and often differing groups. From the English playwright, George Bernard Shaw, comes one of the best defenses of compromise. He criticized a Labour Party parliamentary candidate who insisted on expressing his unpopular pacifist opinions and lost the election.

When I think of my own unfortunate character, smirched with compromise, rotted with opportunism, mildewed by expedience, . . . I do think Joe might have put up with just a speck or two on those white robes of his for the sake of the millions of poor devils who cannot afford any character at all because they have no friend in Parliament. Oh, . . . these superior persons. Who is Joe anyhow that he should not risk his soul occasionally like the rest of us?[4]

Just as Shaw asked that a candidate compromise a little in order to be elected to a position enabling him to serve the people best, so the voter is often asked to compromise. He is asked to choose the "lesser of two evils." He is reminded by honest and dedicated campaign workers that "God isn't running this year."

But compromise can also be defended as a positive good. It provides the cement, the social cohesion, which holds together diverse groups in peace, if not in total harmony. It is a sort of ransom with which we buy off bloodshed, the visible manifestation of an unseen humility, an admission that one might be wrong. However, unfortunately, crisis situations do not always permit the considerable time necessary to negotiate a compromise. Also, compromise presupposes that all groups involved have some underlying common interest, some political resources, and some reason to trust one another. If these conditions do not exist, compromise politics, the *quid pro quo* (this for that) won't work.

Politics As Continuity And Change

Another conception of politics emphasizes mediation between the forces of stability and the forces of change. Some stability is essential and is related to our psychological needs for security and predictability. If you are a barber, for example, you need confidence that commercial hair cuts will not be declared illegal tomorrow. If you are Jewish, you want the assurance that police will not suddenly impose a curfew forcing Jews off the streets after dark.

Yet if stability is necessary, it is equally true that change is inevitable. The invention of new machines, like the train or airplane, has led governments to subsidize their development, to regulate the fares charged, and to establish requirements for the licensing of pilots. Changes in the relative influence of various groups have produced such legislation as that prohibiting racial discrimination in theaters and hotels. A shift in values and moral codes has forced legal alterations in regulations governing nudity, drinking, and abortion.[5]

4 Quoted in Stephen Bailey, Howard D. Samuel, and Sidney Baldwin, *Government in America* (N.Y.: Henry Holt and Company, 1957), p. 543.
5 Alvin Toffler, *Future Shock* (N.Y.: Random House, Inc., 1970).

Many look to government to limit the scope of these changes, channel their direction, minimize their violence, aid their victims, and maintain, through it all, some comforting strains of continuity, a few strands of the yesterdays which molded our habits and shaped our minds. Sometimes, of course, changes have been bathed in the blood of violence. It was thus that we displaced the native Indians, won our independence, settled the western frontier, ended slavery, and secured the rights of working people to organize unions.

Politics as Group Dominance: Varieties of Elitism

A variety of political observers with little else in common agree that politics is the process through which governments are dominated by some sort of privileged minority, or elite class. Marxists or communists believe that politics is the process by which this "ruling class" maintains its advantages relative to the rest of the population. They assert, moreover, that the ruling class is always an economic one consisting of those persons who own the farms and factories, the means of production, in any nation. They point to the use of police and even armies to protect the ownership of private property and to preserve the unequal distribution of wealth.

This theory was shared by non-Marxists such as Charles Beard, the American historian who interpreted the Constitution of the United States as a document designed to protect the economic interests of those who wrote it, a view challenged by subsequent scholarship.[6] Considerably later sociologist C. Wright Mills criticized contemporary American politics because of its alleged control by a small "power elite" consisting primarily of corporation officials and military leaders.[7]

Other writers, sometimes called "democratic elitists," also assert that modern government is dominated by an "establishment" power structure consisting of relatively few leaders from business, unions, the professions, and the universities. Members of this establishment are believed to have so overwhelming a predominance of long-established prestige, money, specialized abilities, and other political resources, as well as such close agreement on fundamental political issues, that they are virtually impossible to dislodge from their seats of power. Yet far from deploring this state of affairs, elitists believe it is not

---

6 Charles A. Beard, *An Economic Interpretation of the Constitution* (N.Y.: The Macmillan Company, 1913). For divergent views, see Robert E. Brown, *Charles Beard and the Constitution* (Princeton, N.J.: Princeton University Press, 1955), Edmund S. Morgan, *The Birth of the Republic, 1763–89* (Chicago: University of Chicago Press, 1956), Forrest McDonald, *We the People: The Economic Origins of the Constitution* (Boston: Houghton Mifflin Company, 1965), and Jackson Turner Maine, *The Anti-Federalists: Critics of the Constitution, 1781–1788* (Chapel Hill: University of North Carolina Press, 1961).
7 *The Power Elite* (N.Y.: Oxford University Press, 1956). For diverse views on this issue, note the opinions of Dahl, Domhoff, Janowitz and others in Normal L. Crockett, ed., *The Power Elite in America* (Lexington, Mass.: D. C. Heath & Company, 1970).

only inevitable but in some respects beneficial. They support their position by such arguments as these:

1) Political resources such as money, knowledge, and access to the mass media are—and always will be—unequally distributed;

2) The complexity of modern problems requires that policy decisions come from those who possess specialized training rather than from an ill-informed majority;

3) Most citizens are indifferent to most public issues and unaware of their implications; such apathetic ignorance helps stabilize the political system by minimizing passionate dissent and maximizing the chances for the peaceful compromise of existing differences;

4) The mass of the people are more intolerant than the highly educated elites and often tend to support selfish demagogues who seek to violate the rights of unpopular minorities;

5) Even if the government is democratically organized, it is influenced decisively by pressure groups that are not democratically controlled;

6) Democracy requires only that the governing elite be held accountable for its performance at the next election.

In contrast to the elitists, other scholars known as pluralists maintain that political power is actually shared by many different groups interested in different policy areas; each group helps control decisions on matters of its special concern, and all interact both in occasional competition and intermittent alliance with one another. In a very general way, however, both the elitists and pluralists would agree that there is a governing class even in the most democratic of nations.[8]

Politics as Enforced Morality

Still another interpretation of the political process holds it to be a method by which rules of moral behavior may be formalized, enforced, and passed on to future generations. Often these rules have religious roots—in the Judeo-Christian tradition in the case of the United States. Although all politics is affected by the values and customs of society, it is often hard to distinguish their secular from their ecclesiastical origins. Both, certainly, have influenced government policy. When established codes of behavior based on the influence of church, family, or society break down, law becomes the ultimate source of moral authority. For if individuals are to be prevented from hurting their fellow men, some form of social control seems essential.

Governmental policies may reflect the teachings of a dominant church group. National prohibition of the manufacture, sale, or transportation of alcoholic beverages in the United States between 1919 and 1933 is a major example, as are state laws restricting business

8 Peter Bachrach, *The Theory of Democratic Elitism* (Boston: Little, Brown and Company, 1967).

operations on Sundays and gambling, abortion, and prostitution all week long. The classic illustration of the impact of religious views on politics is the government of Geneva, Switzerland, by a *theocracy,* or religious elite, dominated by John Calvin, a leader of the Protestant Reformation. In seventeenth-century New England, the government of the Massachusetts Bay Colony also bore the strong imprint of Calvinist theology. Even in the midst of the 1972 presidential campaign, two authors noted that Gallup polls have shown the Reverend Billy Graham to be the second most-admired man in America and suggested that the winning candidate would be the one whose values seem closest to his.[9]

Politics as Systems Analysis

The fifth and final conception of politics to be noted is the attempt to understand the political system without the preconceptions (or biases) implicit in the other views. According to *systems analysis* government is an institution through which certain pressures (public demands and expectations) are transformed into official programs and policies. Borrowing the language of economics and mechanics, the pressures are sometimes called "inputs" and the resulting effects are termed "outputs;" the government is thus a processing machine.[10]

The activities of parties and interest groups help channel the inputs entering the political system, while laws, executive actions, and court decisions are the outputs. Usually, any kind of governmental output alters the later needs, opinions, and other inputs into the political system through a "feedback" process. If policy outputs fail to cope with the inputs adequately (in other words, if the people aren't satisfied with government action), the maintenance of the whole system may be in jeopardy. As a general objective, advocates of systems analysis seek to establish a better understanding of the relationship between the environmental influences on government and the policies which government pursues. This approach is diagrammed in Figure 1.

GROWING POWER OF THE STATE

Whatever people believe to be the fundamental nature of politics, there is wide agreement that the state, compared with other social institutions such as the family, church, or business, has assumed increasing importance. The modern national government provides the ultimate police power necessary for the protection of life and property. It has received much of the devotion once given to religion, assumed the direction and support of education once in the hands of church or family, and provided welfare services once dispensed by private groups. There seems now to be as much government regulation of business as business control over government, and the use of over one fourth of the gross national product is determined by government allocation. In short, the

9 *Los Angeles Times,* July 22, 1972, p. 23.
10 David Easton, *The Political System* (N.Y.: Alfred A. Knopf, Inc., 1953).

Figure 1   Politics Viewed by Systems Analysis

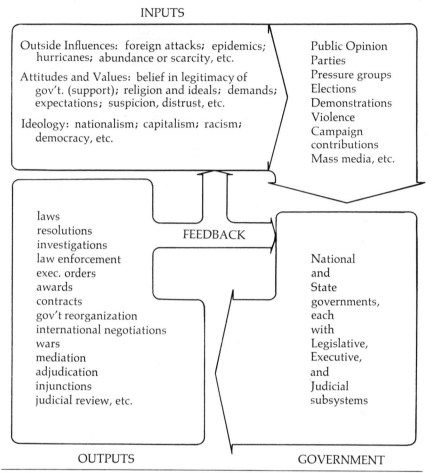

INPUTS

Outside Influences: foreign attacks; epidemics; hurricanes; abundance or scarcity, etc.

Attitudes and Values: belief in legitimacy of gov't. (support); religion and ideals; demands; expectations; suspicion, distrust, etc.

Ideology: nationalism; capitalism; racism; democracy, etc.

Public Opinion
Parties
Pressure groups
Elections
Demonstrations
Violence
Campaign contributions
Mass media, etc.

laws
resolutions
investigations
law enforcement
exec. orders
awards
contracts
gov't reorganization
international negotiations
wars
mediation
adjudication
injunctions
judicial review, etc.

FEEDBACK

National
and
State
governments,
each
with
Legislative,
Executive,
and
Judicial
subsystems

OUTPUTS   GOVERNMENT

Note that systems analysis is based on a "cause and effect" assumption. Each influence (or input) encourages the government to take some action (or output) which alters (by feedback) the subsequent influences.

so-called negative state, which "governed best" when it "governed least," has been replaced by the positive state, engaged in innumerable activities.

This is not to say that government has become the most powerful of all social institutions, but only that it is heading most rapidly in that direction. The family still has the capacity to shape the personalities of infant children in a way unlikely to be seriously rivaled, but its stability has been jeopardized by rising divorce rates, new life styles, and the generation gap. Devotion to one's employer seems little more than a nostalgic myth, and the rejection of one's ancestral religion seldom causes more than a mild reproach. In fact, all institutional loyalties have lost much of their former sanctity. Yet despite the renewed popularity of

Figure 2   The Role of Government in American Life

PRIVATE		GOVERNMENT
Gross National Product	20%	Purchased by government (1966)
Total U.S. Land Area	34%	Owned by federal government (1962)
The National Non-Farm Economy	20%	Regulated by federal agencies (1950)
All Loans To Farmers	72%	Extended by federal government (1963)
National Income	23%	Net tax revenue of government (1962)
All Debt In U.S.	30%	Net debt owed by government (1966)
Gross Corporate Profit	47%	Federal corporate taxes (1962)
Personal Income	22%	Personal taxes (1966)
All Unemployed Workers	43%	Received government unemployment (1962)
All Employed Workers	16%	Employed by government (1965)
Total Building	34%	Public construction (1966)
Bank Deposits	86%	Insured by federal government (1963)
All Medical Research	60%	Financed by federal government (1967)
Commercial Investment Holdings	54%	U.S. Government obligations (1966)
Outstanding House Mortgage Debt	34%	FHA and VA guaranteed mortgages (1965)
Revenues of State and Local Governments	15%	Federal aid (1965)
Electric Power	11%	Produced in federal-owned plants (1962)
Scientific Research	66%	Financed by federal government (1962-63)
Atomic Energy Research	99%	Financed by federal government (1954)
All Schools and Colleges	77%	Financed by government (1967)
All Medical Care Expenditures	25%	Paid by government (1965)
All Welfare Payments	88%	Paid by government (1965)

Source: Reprinted with permission of Benziger Bruce & Glencoe, Inc. (Beverly Hills, California), a Division of The Macmillan Company from *Pattern Of American Government* by Harvey M. Karlan. Copyright © The Glencoe Press 1968.

civil disobedience and political protest (in part itself a consequence of increasing state power), disloyalty to one's country or repudiation of its form of government is now the supreme and inexcusable heresy.

ORGANIZATION OF THE STATE: VARIETIES OF GOVERNMENT

The distinctive and characteristic features of American politics can sometimes be seen most clearly in contrast with other types of political systems. Such comparative analysis usually focuses on power.

Possessors of Power

Aristotle classified governments usefully, but somewhat crudely, into three broad categories based on who possessed ultimate power within them: government by one person, a few, or many. Today these types are most frequently labeled dictatorship, aristocracy (or elitism) and democracy.

Dictatorship   Governmental power controlled by one person was once found most commonly in the hands of hereditary kings, as in Saudi Arabia today. But such absolute monarchies are a dying political species, and the few remaining thrones are usually occupied by persons, like Queen Elizabeth of Great Britain, who "reign but do not rule." They are constitutional monarchs who perform ceremonial functions as head of state but do not run the government. One-man rule in modern times has usually been exercised by a dictator such as Castro in Cuba, Franco in Spain, or Hitler in Germany, often swept into power on a wave of violence.

Aristocracy   Rule by a small, privileged minority of the population is sometimes called an elite, an aristocracy (when benevolent), or an oligarchy (when self-serving). It has many forms and holds most of the world's people in its sway. Indeed, it is probable that pure dictatorships may not exist at all, since even a dictator is dependent upon his servants, advisers, and especially his secret police and armed forces for continued power.

Some oligarchies have been based upon race, as in the Union of South Africa, Rhodesia, and certain areas of the American South, or upon membership in a dominating elite political party, as in the Soviet Union today. Others, like the military juntas ruling in Greece and numerous countries in Asia, Africa, and South America, are aristocracies of career army officers. Theocracy, as noted earlier, is rule by a religious elite; it dominated Geneva, Switzerland, for a time as well as the early years of the Massachusetts colony. Another common form has been plutocracy, government by the wealthy few, and there are also countless aristocracies of age and sex that have rewarded old men with political dominance. Among all the varieties of minority rule, government by the wise and just is conspicuously rare.

Democracy   Governments chosen by and responsive to a majority of the adult population are called democracies. Most have emerged rather recently and they are still limited to relatively few nations. The term democracy was originally used to describe rule directly by the people—*direct democracy,* in which all participate, as in the ancient Greek city-state or New England town meeting. This was contrasted with a republic—*representative democracy,* in which actual rule was exerted by representatives elected by the people. Such a distinction is less significant than an underlying issue suggested earlier: Is any kind of real majority rule possible if various elites possess most political resources?

The Extent of Power

Broadly speaking, government power is either limited or unlimited. Since both types have been found among democracies, aristocracies and dictatorships, one must separate the question of how many people control the government from that of the scope or extent of government power.

Constitutionalism   Government power is limited where the governors as well as the governed must follow the "rules of the game" and where certain rights are guaranteed to minorities, even against the majority. Because written constitutions, like ours in America, usually contain "bills of rights" designed to protect individual freedom, governments which acknowledge such limitations upon their own power are often referred to as "constitutional" ones even where, as in England, there is no single document called a constitution. Pluralists, who emphasize the importance of distributing power among many different groups, sometimes contend that a government is constitutional only to the degree that it recognizes the autonomy (self-government) of private organizations within its jurisdiction.

Totalitarianism   Governments which reject any limitations upon their authority, either by law or practice, are called authoritarian, despotic, tyrannical, or totalitarian ones, the latter term implying a monopoly of decision-making power to the exclusion of all voluntary groups. Today such regimes severely limit individual freedom and depend upon rigid censorship and control of mass media, a secret police, and the prohibition of all political parties except the one controlling the government. The regimes of Greece, Haiti, the Soviet Union, and the People's Republic of China seem to fit this definition fairly closely.

Territorial Distribution of Power

Especially in large nations the distribution of power between the government of the whole country and the governments of the smaller parts into which it is divided is of considerable importance. There are three possible relationships between central and regional governments.

Unitary governments   Most common, especially in relatively small countries or those having a very homogeneous population with similar characteristics, is the *unitary* system. In this form the regional or local governments have only those powers which the central or national government chooses to give them. England, France, Italy, and China are leading examples of unitary systems. Moreover, if each of the fifty states in the United States is viewed as a separate political system, they too are unitary, since cities, counties, townships, and other units of local government have only the power which the various state governments delegate to them.

Confederations   The opposite of a unitary system is a *confederation.* Here, the central or national government possesses only those powers which the regional governments choose to give it. The first national constitution in America was called the Articles of Confederation, for the central government was dependent upon the thirteen states for all the authority it exerted. Confederations have become rather rare. With the possible exception of Yugoslavia and some Arab states, the

Figure 3   Methods of Distributing Power Territorially

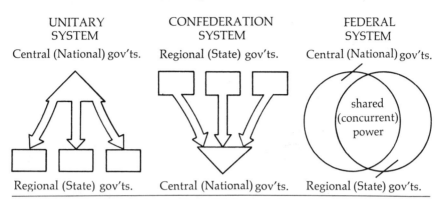

Note: The nature of the federal system in the U.S. is described more fully in Chapter 2. The exact division between national and state powers has occasioned bitter political controversy.

leading—but weak—example is the United Nations, functioning at the international level.

    Federalism   The third plan for distributing power territorially within a nation is *federalism,* an American invention first implemented in our present Constitution. In this system the central (national or federal) government and the regional (state) governments each have certain powers independent of one another and allocated by the Constitution itself. There is often cooperation between the two, but in the event of a conflict, the national government normally prevails. In addition to this country, the system is found primarily in other large nations such as Brazil, Canada, Mexico, Australia, West Germany, India, the Soviet Union, and because it is so heterogeneous even if small, Switzerland.

Functional Distribution of Power

    Every government performs two kinds of functions: It makes rules and it enforces them. The former, entailing the passage of laws, is a legislative function; the second, involving the administration of laws, is an executive function. The relationship between those who pass the laws and those who enforce them may take two broad forms.

    Parliamentary governments   If the same group is largely involved in the performance of both functions, one may say that there is a *fusion of power,* usually called a *parliamentary* system. Such is the case in Great Britain, Canada, West Germany, and Italy, among many other nations. In this form of government, the prime minister or premier, as the chief executive is called, must be a member of the legislative body as must all members of his cabinet. Usually, he is the head of the largest political party, or coalition of parties, in the legislature and holds office only as long as he has the support of a majority of the lawmakers.

    Presidential governments   In contrast, if one group is responsible for passing laws and another group for their enforcement, a *separation of powers* exists, often called a *presidential* system. This is the case in the United States, where the president and members of his cabinet are prohibited from serving simultaneously in Congress, and where he serves for a fixed term of four years, whether he has the support of a majority in Congress or not. In accordance with the separation of powers principle, there is a separate judicial branch as well. The same three branches—legislative, executive, and judicial—similarly separated, comprise each of the fifty state governments.

The separation of powers is modified substantially in the American system, however, by formal and informal powers, known as a system of *checks and balances,* which each branch can exert upon the other two—such as the Supreme Court's power to declare legislative or executive actions unconstitutional or the President's power to select judges, subject to confirmation by the Senate. France, Mexico, the Philippines, and various South American countries have presidential systems modified to one degree or another and roughly comparable to the American one. *The United States has a representative, democratic, constitutional, federal, presidential form of government.* But many other combinations of the preceding characteristics are possible.

The Purpose of Power

The language of politics remains fairly cool when discussing the forms of government described above. Nonetheless, it heats to the boiling point when the subject changes to the basic purposes of government and the philosophies on which they rest—how to interpret the pursuit of justice or the national welfare. Conservatives who view untested policies with cautious skepticism are sometimes denounced as "fascist pigs" and liberals who criticize the existing society may be branded as "commie traitors." And so, a word of caution: Labels are less important than the actual policies or personalities to which they are applied, and every group works for government policies which will advance its own interests. Yet because we use words and labels to communicate with one another, there should be some agreement on their definition.

Labels of the left   Political views are frequently described in the oversimplified terms of liberal *vs.* conservative, radical *vs.* reactionary, or left wing *vs.* right wing.

A liberal is usually believed to be one who wants change, reform, or innovation, inspired through tolerance for a wide diversity of viewpoints, including new and heretical ones. In modern times, however, self-styled liberals usually favor not only freedom of expression for differing opinions, but also a strong, active government that often limits the economic freedom of businessmen in the interests of consumers and employees, and supports government policies to improve the lot of the poor and the victims of discrimination. Especially since the 1930s, the Democratic party in America usually has been associated with such views, to the dismay of some very conservative Democrats. As a result it has developed voter support primarily among industrial workers, low-income groups and such oppressed minorities as blacks and Mexican-Americans.

The term radical is often associated with extreme liberalism and describes one who wishes great changes, frequently accomplished through violent protest or revolution. Sometimes those who want a drastic reversal of liberal policies are also called radicals, although this use of the term is rather confusing. Leftists, or left-wingers, represent a broad category often encompassing everyone from mild liberals to revolutionary Communists. The so-called New Left which gained prominence in the late 1960s, is characterized by its youth, its distrust of orthodox liberal politicians, and by a proclivity for confrontation politics, often involving illegal demonstrations. The Progressive Labor Party, the Black Panthers, and the Students for a Democratic Society (SDS) are all parts of the New Left. They tend to be anticapitalist, but often view the communist bureaucracy of the Soviet Union with equal suspicion.

The Old Left, defined very broadly, includes politicians committed to the mid-century New Deal philosophy, along with democratic socialists who favor government ownership of basic industries such as those producing electricity, mineral resources, and steel. Members of the Communist Party are committed to the doctrines of Karl Marx as interpreted by the Soviet Union. They tend to encourage participation in the traditional compromise which characterizes American electoral politics, however, while retaining the old goal of government ownership of the entire economy attained—where necessary—by violence.

Labels of the right   At the other end of the political spectrum are conservatives, reactionaries, or right-wingers. A conservative is one who wishes to conserve and perpetuate existing values and institutions. He is usually a bit skeptical of abstract logic or pure rationality, preferring instead to depend upon experience and tradition, the "tried and true," as a guide for future action. Conservatives also tend to rely primarily upon individual initiative, private enterprise capitalism, and state and local responsibility to solve social problems. They harbor a sustained distrust of comprehensive government welfare programs as a policy that destroys the freedom and self-reliance necessary for both personal integrity and national strength. Many believe that President Nixon betrayed his initial dedication to these principles. The Republican Party has typically been associated with such ideas. Its main sources of support have been businessmen and independent farmers, both with a considerable stake in existing success and therefore committed to a continuation of things pretty much as they are.

Just as radicals are considered extreme liberals, so reactionaries may be described as ultra-conservatives. They are not content with resisting new innovations but fight for a return to what they believe to be the good old days. Rightists, or right-wingers, are terms referring to a broad group that includes moderate conservatives, as well as reactionaries, and extends from organizations like the Young Americans for Freedom (YAF) to the John Birch Society and the American Nazi Party. This rightist extreme usually endorses censorship, toughness toward criminals, superpatriotism, and sometimes racial or religious bigotry.

Oddly enough, a look at the far edges of left and right reveals certain similarities in the two extremes: Both are hostile to human freedom, the left in the interests of greater equality, the right for purposes of suppressing immorality and alien ideas. Nonetheless, liberals and conservatives view the world from somewhat different perspectives. The liberal sees men as basically rational and cooperative once education has freed them from ancient superstitions and a decent standard of living has liberated them from the brutalizing effects of poverty. Both are government responsibilities. The conservative sees men as potentially impulsive and combative unless conditioned to cherish established values and restrained by firm control. These also are tasks of government.

It is important to note, however, that most Americans are not ideologically oriented. If pressed, they tend to describe themselves as middle-of-the-road, but they seldom think in terms of liberal and conservative and, with characteristic practicality, are most interested in policies that work, no matter what labels they bear. It is not surprising, then, that the government's economic and social policy is really a mixed one, a compromise between the right and the left. It is clearly moving away from individualism, however, toward a greater reliance upon collectivism, which includes economic controls, welfare programs, and socialism. Even the large private corporation is also a kind of collectivist entity whose impact on the individual may rival that of the government.

THE STUDY OF POLITICS

How can one best study a subject as complex as this? At first political science emphasized the careful analysis of political institutions and their legal foundations. Considerable stress was placed on constitutional law as enunciated in America by the Supreme Court, while the organization of Congress, political parties, and executive agencies also received much attention.

In the 1950s another approach known as behavioralism appeared more frequently in the research of political scientists. It stressed the politically significant behavior of individuals and groups more than formal structures, abstract theory, and legal authorization. Behavioralism was characterized by (1) a reliance on ideas and empirical findings derived from such other social sciences as psychology, anthropology and sociology; (2) the statistical measurement of the frequency of political actions; (3) an emphasis on the root causes and conditioning factors which may explain political phenomena; and (4) an attempt to develop a "value-free," objective, morally neutral method of political analysis.

The trend today seems away from behavioralism too, toward a sort of eclecticism combining both old and new approaches. Most particularly, there is an insistence that research be relevant to current issues and that it be related to values, to ethical standards of right and wrong. In other words, a systematic description of what *is* (empirical theory) should be associated with a conception of what *ought to be* (normative theory). With that in mind, this book will include a little of history, philosophy, law, institutions, political behavior, and other ingredients as well.

Chapter **2**

The Americans
Land, Legacy, and Political Culture

God has not been preparing the English-speaking and
Teutonic peoples for a thousand years for nothing. . . . No!
He has made us . . . adept in government that we may
administer government among savage and senile
peoples. . . . And of all our race He has marked the American
people as His chosen nation to finally lead in the
regeneration of the world.
Senator Albert J. Beveridge

Americans now live in the oldest republic in the world. We have a rich political heritage—if less divinely inspired than Senator Beveridge so arrogantly asserted—and a long-established Constitution. Indeed, ours is the largest and most heterogeneous country ever to attempt to operate as a democracy. The land and history, the basic constitutional principles, the people, with their values and beliefs—all of these have shaped the contemporary American political culture. They help determine, in other words, the way we think and act in politics.

GEOGRAPHICAL INFLUENCES

Robert Frost, one of America's great literary figures, was the first person ever asked to read a poem at a presidential inauguration. Squinting out into the reflected glare of the winter sun, he spoke not of John F. Kennedy, about to take the oath of office, but of the United

States itself. "The land was ours," the old poet rasped, "before we were the land's."[1] The words sink in slowly. We understand owning the land. Only later, gradually, do we realize that the land we own begins to mold us, determine our actions, change our thinking. The very word, "land," is synonymous with country or nation in several languages. Where we live, how far apart, the way we make our money—even how we govern ourselves depends, at least in part, on the land.

Size and Location

The most obvious geographical fact about America is that it is large. When a country is large, it is almost essential that its governmental authority be decentralized. It would be absurd to regulate the speed limits in Hawaii from a Washington office. Where government services and controls are widely dispersed, then efficiency and adaptability also require dispersal of the power to make policy. This is a major justification for the federal system.

The immense size of America has contributed to its relative security, as well as to its decentralized authority. Even were an enemy army to establish an invasion beachhead on our shores, the logistical problems of supply lines thousands of miles long make successful occupation wildly improbable.

Location seems to be a geographic factor at least as important as size, although the advent of ICBM's (intercontinental ballistic missiles), making every point on the earth's surface vulnerable to attack from every other point, may have reduced its significance. America's location between oceans 3000 miles wide on the east and 6000 miles wide on the west promoted a foreign policy usually described as *isolationism.* Until this century we made few international commitments and joined no military alliances. Geographic remoteness from international power centers inhibited foreign invasion from Europe or Asia and permitted national attention to be devoted to the occupation and development of a rich, vast, and largely virgin continent. As the French, Germans, or Russians would surely testify, the advantages of a country beyond the reach of alien infantrymen are enormous.

The world is smaller now, diminished by the technology of modern communication, transportation, and weaponry. Isolationism fell victim to this new reality, with its death marked by the graves of American soldiers killed in two World Wars and in Korea and Vietnam. The emergence of the missile age has required a reevaluation of America's international position. Although sea power, so forcefully advocated by Admiral Alfred T. Mahan at the close of the last century, remains an important consideration, the air routes over the Arctic polar region have

1 From "The Gift Outright" from *The Poetry of Robert Frost,* edited by Edward Connery Lathem. Copyright 1942 by Robert Frost. Copyright © 1969 by Holt, Rinehart and Winston, Inc. Copyright © 1970 by Lesley Frost Ballantine. Reprinted by permission of Holt, Rinehart and Winston, Inc.

surpassed it in significance. The United States, isolated for so long by its location in the Western Hemisphere, now finds itself an air neighbor to the other great powers of the Northern Hemisphere. In terms of American defense, the change is not a happy one. While our security can be jeopardized from nearly anywhere, we have insufficient power to protect our interests everywhere. In the Middle East, Asia, and Europe, hard choices must be made.

Since ancient times, most significant world changes seem to have sprung from moderate climates. The United States is favored in this respect, too. Except for northern Alaska and southern Hawaii, it is located in the temperate zone. With less energy required for the physical necessities of getting warm or cooling off, more seems available for other endeavors.

Resources: People of Plenty

The political significance of America's geographic size and location has been dwarfed by the importance of its enormous riches. In quantity, variety, and accessibility of natural resources we have been favored—perhaps too much so, because the very abundance of these resources may have encouraged the rapid and wasteful depletion of far too high a proportion of them. The extensive river systems, the level of rainfall, the availability of reasonably flat farm land, and the length of the growing season also have contributed to economic wealth.

The United States grows a surplus of wheat, corn, rice, meat, and dairy products, and is a leading producer of copper, lead, sulfur, coal, iron, natural gas, petroleum, and magnesium, although known reserves of some of these minerals can support current use for only a limited future. In a world where wealth is often measured by industrialization, the U.S. manufacturing output far outstrips that of the Soviet Union, Japan, and Germany—its chief competitors.

To compare America's wealth with that of other nations, one must rely on reported production statistics for various commodities, and especially on the gross national product (GNP) per capita. This shows the value of all goods and services produced in a country if its total were divided equally among its inhabitants. Figure 4 summarizes some of this data for purposes of international comparison. Such figures demonstrate the enormous disparities between the "have" and the "have not" nations, between the American island of plenty and its surrounding sea of poverty. It is hardly surprising that the United States occasionally becomes the object of envious hatred among the destitute majorities of Asia or Latin America.

Apart from this, affluence has another important political implication. Statistical analysis demonstrates that democracy flourishes most consistently in relatively wealthy nations while poor nations, it seems, tend to trade majority rule and personal freedoms for promises of

Figure 4   Comparative National Wealth

	GNP per capita		Electricity		Steel		Wheat	
Rank	Nation	Amount	Nation	Volume[2]	Nation	Volume[3]	Nation	Volume[4]
1	U.S.	$4,664	U.S.	1,552	U.S.	141	U.S.S.R.	85
2	Sweden	$3,315	U.S.S.R.	689	U.S.S.R.	122	U.S.	44
3	Canada	$2,997	Japan	316	Japan	91	China	30
4	Switz.	$2,965	U.K.	238	W.Ger.	50	India	21
5	Denmark	$2,860	W.Ger.	221	U.K.	30	Canada	21
6	France	$2,783	Canada	190	France	25	France	16
7	Norway	$2,528	France	132	Italy	18	Austral.	12
8	W.Ger.	$2,512	Italy	97	China	17	Turkey	12
9	Austral.	$2,476	E.Ger.	65	Poland	12	Italy	11
10[1]	Belgium	$2,372	Sweden	58	Czech.	12	Argen.	8

[1]Other GNP figures: U.K. $1,976; Japan $1,626; U.S.S.R. $890; Mexico $566; Kenya $136; India $84. [2]In trillions of kilowatt-hours. [3]In millions of short tons. [4]In millions of short tons. Source: U.S. Bureau of the Census, *Statistical Abstract of the United States: 1971.* For U.S.S.R. GNP, *Los Angeles Times,* Nov. 21, 1968, Part II, p. 5.

economic security and material enrichment.[2] David M. Potter, in *People of Plenty,* pins down the relationship between prosperity and politics in the peculiar American experience. He argues that our economic surplus made it possible to improve the lot of the poor without substantially hurting the rich. The prevailing belief that equality could be attained by "leveling up" as well as by "leveling down" has made revolution less attractive to America's poor and reliance upon the democratic processes more appealing.[3] Nevertheless, the trend of the 1970s is toward increasing concern with redistribution of existing wealth and a disenchantment with economic growth.

HISTORICAL INFLUENCES

Our roots are sunk deep in the past. American government had already passed through three clear stages before the adoption of our present Constitution: the colonial, Revolutionary, and Confederation periods. Each of these contributed important characteristics to our present system.

Colonial Development

In spite of Spanish, Dutch, French, and American Indian influences, American history is essentially a child of English imperial expansion. From the establishment in 1607 of Jamestown, Virginia, to

2 Seymour M. Lipset, *Political Man* (Garden City, N.Y.: Anchor Books, Doubleday & Company, Inc., 1963), pp. 31–45.
3 David M. Potter, *People of Plenty* (Chicago: University of Chicago Press, 1954), pp. 111–27.

the founding in 1733 of Savannah, Georgia, England had created the thirteen colonies which became the nucleus of the United States of America. Thus, the American Revolution was a revolt against an English rule which had lasted for about a century and a half. During that time certain characteristics became so entrenched that they persist, in one form or another, to the present time.

Common law One of these enduring characteristics is the English common law tradition, which now prevails in all American states except Louisiana, still reflecting its French origins. The common law was developed before the birth of legislative bodies by judges who traveled from place to place settling disputes in a common, or uniform, manner. The judges employed a combination of old Roman legal ideas, Catholic doctrines, prevailing customs which defined what was "just," and their own ethical sensitivity. Strong reliance was placed upon precedents, or previous decisions in similar cases, to give the law consistency and continuity.

The common law established rules of court *procedure* that we still regard as essential to a fair trial. It insisted that the burden of proof in criminal cases be placed upon the prosecution and that defendants have such rights as trial by jury and access to legal counsel. It also determined certain *substantive* grounds of injury, such as contract violations or property damage, which enabled one person to sue another to gain compensation for losses.

Governmental institutions The colonial period laid the foundations for many later institutions. The separation of legislative and executive officials into distinct branches of government, the establishment of bicameral (two-house) legislatures, and the creation of towns, counties, and other units of local rule were among the most important of these.

Representative government At the time of the Revolution, eight of the thirteen colonies were royal ones. Their governors, and often members of the upper houses of bicameral legislatures were chosen—directly or indirectly—by the English king. But the Crown permitted members of the lower houses to be chosen by the voters so that government was representative at least of the people allowed to vote. The other colonies had even more elected representation. The effects of this system had immense significance.

First, in these elected houses native Americans such as Thomas Jefferson and James Madison gained the political experience and leadership training necessary to govern the nation effectively once independence had been won. This kind of training ground was sadly deficient in former Dutch, French, and Spanish colonies and may help to explain the difficulty with which stable governments have been established in those areas. Second, the election of legislators gradually created a desire for the election of still other government officials.

State loyalty Because the first thirteen states existed before there was an American national government, people focused their loyalty on the states in which they lived and only later, grudgingly, did they transfer it to the nation as a whole. When English colonial policy became harsh and restrictive in the 1760s and 1770s, Americans developed an increasing hatred for national authority and a conviction that decentralized government was the best government. Such attitudes help account for the extreme weakness of the central government provided under the Articles of Confederation, and the subsequent ambiguous compromise between national and state power represented in the federalism of our Constitution.

The continuing vigor of antinational states' rights sentiment is manifested in the support for Barry Goldwater in 1964 and George Wallace in 1968 and 1972. Devotion to decentralized, regional rule is far from dead. This preference is reflected when we speak (misleadingly but lovingly) of "states' rights," but refer (far more ominously) to "national power."

To be sure, national patriotism now supersedes state loyalty in the hearts of most Americans. Some hope that the next step, long and still more hazardous, will be the further expansion of our allegiance to embrace the entire human race. Yet, our global involvement since World War II has produced a reaction which looks inward, to unsolved problems at the state, and especially at the community, level. When presidential candidate George McGovern summoned America to "come home," some interpreted it as a new isolationism while others heard it as a plea for the kind of participatory democracy that would enable people to control their own destinies at the local level. But his real intention seemed to be to strengthen the national government, though to employ its resources more for domestic than for international purposes. Most Americans, like citizens of other lands, accept governmental action at the level best calculated to meet their needs.

Revolution and Confederation

Although the Revolution spanned only six years, its legacy would affect American government for many decades.

Independence It has been nearly two centuries since Thomas Jefferson wrote that "these United Colonies are, and of Right ought to be Free and Independent States." The freedom from imperialistic control thus proclaimed in the Declaration of Independence remains pertinent today because the American experience has similarities to the struggles against foreign colonialism that recently have swept across Africa and Asia. These revolts have often entailed subversive conspiracies (such as led by Samuel Adams), inflammatory prose (written here by Tom Paine, one of the most skilled propagandists in history), and guerrilla warfare (utilized in America by General Nathaniel Green and others). As in the American Revolution, predominantly agricultural regions have struggled against a more industrialized foe.

In any event, the American example became a source of

encouragement for oppressed peoples everywhere. In the 1820s, when Latin Americans sought to free themselves from Spanish imperialism, the United States gave support through the Monroe Doctrine, warning against repressive foreign intervention. Nearly a century later, President Woodrow Wilson enunciated the right of national self-determination as one of our aims in World War I.

In recent years, however, American dedication to the cause of independence has been compromised by our far-ranging economic interests, alliances with colonial powers, and fears that "wars of national liberation" are merely instruments of communist imperialism. The embarrassment of our dilemma was underscored in 1946 when Ho Chi Minh quoted from Thomas Jefferson in proclaiming the independence of Vietnam from French rule.

A revolutionary heritage? There is an ageless struggle between the forces of authority and stability on one side and those of freedom and progress on the other. The American Revolution represented a victory for the latter. This triumphant treason created a radical political tradition that has been deeply troublesome to the conservative defenders of established institutions.

Some writers argue, with considerable merit, that the events of the 1770s were not a true revolution because their purpose and effect were not significantly to alter the existing relationships among social classes in America—already a basically middle-class country.[4] Assessed in terms of other characteristics of revolutions—violence, the creation of new political institutions, speed of change—there certainly was a revolution, but against an external, not internal, enemy.

New American governments As independence became the major and most dramatic objective of the Revolution, its success required the establishment of new state constitutions and an American national government. During the Revolutionary War, the colonies drafted new constitutions as independent states. These first state constitutions, in reacting strongly against what was thought to have been the excessive power of the old royal governors, weakened the authority of the new state governors, especially with respect to money matters and appointment powers. As a result, many believe that state governors still have too little authority to meet their responsibilities effectively.

At the national level, the Second Continental Congress, consisting of delegates chosen by the various colonies, functioned to direct the war effort, but it did not have a legally secure status. Hence a committee was appointed to draft a formal constitution. This, the Articles of Confederation, was approved by all thirteen state legislatures and went into effect in 1781. In the distribution of authority throughout its far-flung territory, the British Empire was a unitary system of government, in which colonies had only that authority which the central

4 Louis Hartz, "Democracy without a Democratic Revolution," *American Political Science Review* 46 (June 1952): 321–42.

government chose to give to them. Since the American colonists came to equate a strong centralized government with arbitrary and even tyrannical power, not surprisingly they overreacted and created through the Articles of Confederation a system in which the territorial distribution of authority was arranged in exactly the opposite way. As is characteristic of a confederation, the central government was limited to that authority given it by the thirteen states.

Under the Articles, the national government, although generally quite weak, was delegated some important responsibilities. It could establish a postal system, make treaties, maintain a navy, and govern all territories outside the jurisdiction of the various states. In the long run (if its eight-year existence can be so named), the powers the national government lacked were more significant than those which it possessed. Since it could neither tax nor enlist troops into the army, it was dependent upon the states for both money and manpower—two prime ingredients of any political system. It could not prevent the states from coining money or prohibit the erection of tariffs or other trade barriers between states.

The structure of the national government under the Articles consisted only of a one-house, or unicameral, legislature in which each state had one vote regardless of population. Not only did the Confederation possess no independent executive branch and no court system, but any amendment that might strengthen it required the unanimous approval of all thirteen state legislatures. Predictably, the Articles were never amended.

Failure of the Confederation   The Confederation government had the misfortune of a wartime birth and a postwar infancy in an era later described as "the critical period" in American history. Both the state governments and the Congress had incurred heavy debts during the Revolution, and the poor farmers, forced to foot the tax bill, were already hard pressed to make their mortgage payments. They staged bitter and sometimes violent demonstrations. In 1786 the militia was called out to counter angry demands for the printing of more paper currency in New Hampshire and to suppress Shays' Rebellion in Massachusetts, an uprising designed to prevent the courts from ordering farm foreclosures.

There were other problems also. The Confederation Congress could not guarantee American territory against British and Spanish encroachments, and it was unable to get the states to make the contributions necessary to meet its own financial responsibilities, in particular to the troops and other war claims. It was difficult to find foreign markets to supplant those temporarily lost in England, and state-imposed trade barriers simultaneously reduced the volume of goods sold within the country. Finally, there was a pervasive fear among bankers, land speculators, and other creditors that many states would follow the example of Rhode Island and adopt an inflationary currency policy to enable the poor to repay their debts in money worth less than that which they initially borrowed. Confronted with the inability of the Confederation to cope with these crises, it is little wonder that some prominent politicians began to explore the possibility of creating a stronger national government.

THE CONSTITUTION
The Constitutional Convention

While meeting for the supposed purpose of improving the Articles of Confederation, most of the fifty-five delegates to the convention assembled in Philadelphia quickly agreed to start from scratch in drafting a new document. They were partially motivated by a recognition that it would be impossible to get the unanimous state approval required to amend the Articles, and were emboldened to broaden their mandate by a decision to bar the press and public from their deliberations.

The delegates   The men who wrote our Constitution left the imprint of their minds, personalities, and vested interests upon it. As a group, they possessed certain characteristics which seem, in retrospect, most significant: (1) Their average age was only forty-two, and their youth may have contributed to their innovative vigor and sympathy for expanded national power. (2) They were an exceptionally well-educated group, with practical backgrounds covering a broad spectrum of public life. Many had served in diplomatic and military posts, seven as state governors, and thirty-nine in Congress. In short, they were seasoned politicians, adept in the skills of compromise and tactical maneuver.[5] (3) The delegates represented a relatively wealthy professional and commercial elite. Although small, independent farmers constituted a huge majority of the population, they found themselves almost unrepresented in the most vital gathering of the day. (4) Conservatism is often defined to include a distrust of the mass of the people, and by this standard, delegates were largely conservative. Elbridge Gerry, more liberal than most, asserted that the "evils were experience flow from the excess of democracy," and Edmund Randolph of Virginia argued that "our chief danger arises from the democratic parts of our (state) constitutions."[6]

The agreements   With relative ease the delegates agreed to write a new constitution in which the power of the national government would be enlarged to include the authority to tax, raise an army, regulate interstate and foreign commerce, regulate the value of currency, and control navigable rivers. The result, of course, was to diminish the relative power of the states.

This reallocation of authority required a more elaborate structure for the national government. There, to guard against despo-

5 Stanley Elkins and Eric McKitrick, "The Founding Fathers: Young Men of the Revolution," *Political Science Quarterly* 76 (June 1961): 202–16, and John P. Roche, "The Founding Fathers: A Reform Caucus in Action," *American Political Science Review* 55 (December 1961): 799–816.
6 Cited in J. Mark Jacobson, *The Development of American Political Thought: A Documentary History* (N.Y.: D. Appleton-Century Co., 1932), pp. 41 and 43.

tism, a separation of powers with built-in checks and balances was established. It was decided that the legislative branch should be bicameral, an independent chief executive should be established, and a national court system should be created. But there were important controversies still to be resolved.

The disputes   Early in the proceedings, the Virginia delegation introduced a draft constitution which provided that representation in both houses of a bicameral legislature be based on population. The small states feared that if they were outvoted in the legislative branch they would be helpless victims of large-state tyranny. From New Jersey came an alternative proposal for a unicameral Congress with one vote for each state. The deadlock between proponents of the Virginia Plan and the New Jersey Plan was finally broken by the acceptance of Benjamin Franklin's compromise as proposed by the Connecticut delegation. Now generally known as the Great Compromise, it provided a bicameral Congress, giving each state two votes in the upper house, the Senate, while apportioning seats in the lower chamber, the House of Representatives, on a population basis.

Growing directly out of the Great Compromise was another major dispute concerning direct taxes, which were to be apportioned among the states, like seats in the House of Representatives, according to population. The South did not want slaves fully counted in determining its tax burdens; the North did not want slaves fully counted in determining the number of representatives southern states could have. Eventually a compromise emerged by which each slave was counted as three fifths of a person for both purposes.

Still another controversy, concerning the term of office and manner of electing the chief executive, resulted finally in the electoral college, one of the strangest political inventions ever devised.[7]

Ratification

The ratification process was not an easy one. Those opposing the Constitution drew their strength largely from the small farmers who were generally untroubled by state trade barriers and delighted with inflated state currency that expedited the payment of their debts. Yet these were the very conditions to which the commercial and financial interests favoring the new Constitution objected most strongly. In any event, the opponents of ratification leveled three main attacks upon the Constitution: (1) It was a tool of wealthy interests to be used against the small farmers. (2) It created a danger of tyranny by transferring too much power from the states to the national government. (3) It contained no Bill of Rights to protect the individual citizens.

The supporters responded in a series of eighty-five essays appearing first in New York newspapers and later in book form. Written

7 See Chapter 10.

by Alexander Hamilton, James Madison, and John Jay, *The Federalist* (or *The Federalist Papers*) evaluated the weaknesses of the Articles and made a penetrating and highly favorable analysis of the proposed Constitution. Not only did this work win supporters for ratification but it is today regarded as one of America's most notable contributions to the literature of political theory.

Another and possibly crucial factor in getting the Constitution approved was the admission by its supporters that a Bill of Rights was desirable and their pledge to add one by amending the Constitution once it had been ratified.

The "Wonderful Work": Seven Pillars of Wisdom

The seven articles of the Constitution established a basic organization of government which was without precedent in any nation then in existence and which has survived for nearly two centuries. Before evaluating it, a distinction must be made between constitutional and statutory law. The former is the highest and most binding law and is normally confined to four topics: the creation of major governmental agencies, a description of the authority these agencies possess, amendment procedures permitting necessary changes, and a series of limitations upon governmental power (usually called a Bill of Rights). Statutory law, in contrast, is that passed by appropriate legislative bodies in exercising the authority granted them by the Constitution.

One of the frequent and unfortunate characteristics of state constitutions is that they include numerous provisions for specific government policies which are most appropriately statutory in nature. These tend to tie the hands of the state legislatures and make constitutional amendments necessary whenever certain policy changes seem desirable. The framers in Philadelphia avoided this pitfall. They wrote a Constitution consisting only of a preamble and seven articles—brief, essential, flexible.

The Constitution has endured longer than any other in any nation in recorded history. More significantly, it has proved responsive to the needs of whatever group has gained control of the government which it established. In the 1790s, for example, wealthy commercial interests used the new government to take taxes from the farmers to finance a newly created National Bank which loaned money to manufacturers. Yet in the nineteenth century that same government, yielding to farm pressures, built canals and gave away land to encourage agricultural expansion. In this century, industrial labor was able to extract from it minimum wage laws and social security benefits. Like the delicate machinery in a fine car, the political system created by the Constitution has responded to the desires of the driver, occasionally changed direction, and proceeded at varying speeds.

Constitutional amendments　If a constitution can be altered

Figure 5   An Outline of the Constitution

Preamble:	*Attributes Constitution to "We the People"*
	States purposes of Constitution
	Contains no enforceable provisions
Article I:	*Legislative Branch*
	Bicameral Congress: Senate and House of Representatives
	Membership and methods of selection
	Legislative procedures
	Powers and limitations on powers
	Limitations on state governments
Article II:	*Executive Branch*
	President and Vice President
	Selection by electoral college
	Conditions of service
	Powers
Article III:	*Judicial Branch*
	Supreme Court and provision for lower courts
	Selection and service for judges
	Powers
	Trial by jury guaranteed
	Treason defined
Article IV:	*Intergovernmental Relations*
	Obligations of states to one another
	Admission of new states
	Obligations of national government to states
Article V:	*Amendment Procedures*
Article VI:	*Supremacy of Constitution*
	Assumption of prior debts
	Prohibition of religious qualifications for public office
Article VII:	*Procedure for Ratifying Constitution*

too easily, its authority as the basic law is diminished and it cannot provide needed stability and continuity; if, on the other hand, it is too difficult to amend, its own rigidity may doom it to an early death. The authors of our Constitution provided four alternative amendment methods in Article V. Of these, proposal by two-thirds vote of Senate and House of Representatives, with ratification by three quarters of the state legislatures, has been used for all amendments but the Twenty-first. Altogether the document written in 1787 has been changed only sixteen times since the first ten amendments providing the Bill of Rights were added in 1791. Nothing speaks more eloquently of the work of the framers. The subject matter of the amendments and the dates they became effective are shown in Figure 6.

Figure 6   An Outline of Amendments to the Constitution

Amendment	Subject	Year of Ratification
1	Guarantees freedom of expression Prohibits establishment of religion	1791
2	Protects states' power to maintain armed militias (national guard)	1791
3	Prohibits housing soldiers in private homes	1791
4	Protects right to privacy from unreasonable searches and seizures	1791
5	Limits criminal prosecution (grand jury) Prohibits two trials for same crime (double jeopardy) Prohibits forced confessions (self-incrimination) Guarantees due process of law Limits power to take private property (eminent domain)	1791
6	Criminal trial procedures guaranteeing rights: To a speedy and public trial To an impartial jury To cross-examine witnesses To subpoena witnesses To legal counsel	1791
7	Guarantees jury trial in civil cases	1791
8	Prohibits excessive bail and fines Prohibits cruel and unusual punishments	1791
9	Guarantees rights not otherwise described	1791
10	Protects powers reserved to the states	1791
11	Reduces judicial power of national courts, modifying Article III (adopted to counteract Supreme Court decision)	1798
12	Changes method of electing Vice President, modifying Article II	1804

More than sixty years elapsed before the Civil War amendments were adopted, largely to protect black people against oppressive legislation passed by white-controlled state legislatures.

| 13 | Prohibits slavery | 1865 |

14	Establishes citizenship by birth in U.S.	1868
	Guarantees due process of law against state interference, incorporating most of Bill of Rights as limitations upon state as well as national power	
	Prohibits denial by states of equal protection of the laws	
	(adopted partially to counteract Supreme Court decision)	
15	Prohibits denial of right to vote because of race	1870

After another forty years, Amendments Sixteen through Nineteen were adopted within seven years. Although dissimilar in content, they were all products of the Progressive movement which, early in this century, urged experimentation and reform in all levels of government.

16	Permits national income tax levied without regard to state population, modifying Article I (adopted to counteract Supreme Court decision)	1913
17	Requires U.S. Senators be elected directly by voters, modifying Article I	1913
18	Prohibits manufacture, sale, or transportation of alcoholic beverages	1919
19	Prohibits denial of right to vote because of sex	1920
20	Reduces period of time between election and start of term for national officials	1933
21	Repeals Amendment Eighteen	1933
22	Limits President to two terms	1951
23	Gives Washington, D.C., electoral votes in presidential elections	1961
24	Prohibits denial of right to vote because of failure to pay taxes	1964
25	Establishes procedure to select Vice President to fill vacancy in that office	1967
	Establishes procedures for Vice President to become Acting President in the event of presidential disability	
26	Prohibits denial of right to vote because of age to those eighteen or more	1971

The "unwritten constitution" If one interprets a constitution to mean whatever determines the fundamental scope or structure of government authority (as the British do, for example), then there is more to the United States Constitution than its short text. Under such a definition, our Constitution has other sources, some of which (again as in the English case) are unwritten.

First, there are institutions and procedures that have become deeply entrenched through custom and tradition. These include the two-party system, pressure groups, the President's cabinet, and the congressional committee system for handling legislation. They are as important as many provisions of the Constitution itself, and may be altered in practice through the years.

Second, certain actions by the state governments have had so profound an effect upon national politics as also to be of constitutional importance. The selection of presidential electors by the voters rather than by state legislatures, the abolition of property ownership as a voting requirement, and the nomination of congressional candidates by primary elections rather than party conventions are all results of state action.

Third, various parts of the Constitution have been supplemented through statutory elaboration by acts of Congress. Article III gives Congress the authority to create lower courts and Article II, at least implicitly, allows it to create executive departments. The result has been a government bureaucracy of intricate complexity and immense power. To the bones of constitutional structure, statutory elaboration has attached awesome muscles. Some would argue that it has added considerable fat as well.

Fourth, presidential action has occasionally altered the emphasis of certain parts of the Constitution, and perhaps even distorted their intent. Thus, various Presidents have used their constitutional authority as commander in chief of the armed forces to render the congressional power to declare war almost irrelevant.

Finally, the American Supreme Court, gradually entrenching itself as the final interpreter of the Constitution, has made decisions of constitutional significance. "The Constitution," as a former Chief Justice of the United States Supreme Court once wrote, "is what the judges say it is."[8] And the judges may—and do—reverse their own interpretations.

BASIC CONSTITUTIONAL PRINCIPLES
Federalism: The Middle Way

The framers of the Constitution were confronted with a dilemma: The existing Confederation, in which the states had ultimate power, was not working well; yet the people feared a strong, unitary

---

8 Saul K. Padover, *The Living U.S. Constitution* (N.Y.: Mentor Books, The New American Library Inc., 1953), p. 58.

system, such as that of the British empire, in which the national government was the source of all authority. They devised a practical compromise which provided a middle way between these extremes. This is the system of federalism, perhaps America's greatest political invention. Federalism gives authority to both the national and state governments. It forbids either from usurping the power of the other, yet provides a wide arena for cooperation and steadily expanding joint action.

The division of powers The authority of the national government stems largely from Article I, Section 8 of the Constitution. Although this deals with the powers of Congress, it involves the executive and judicial branches as well, since they administer legislation once enacted and apply it in individual cases. In the first seventeen paragraphs of Article I, Section 8 are the *enumerated powers* expressly delegated to Congress (and also called *delegated* or *expressed* powers) while the eighteenth grants broad and vague authority to make laws "which shall be necessary and proper" to carry out the powers specifically listed. Action based on this "necessary and proper" clause is often called an exercise of *implied powers.*

The United States Supreme Court formalized the doctrine of implied powers in a decision written by our third and most influential Chief Justice, John Marshall, in the case of *McCulloch* v. *Maryland* in 1819. This concept has become the major constitutional justification for the immense expansion of national authority that has since taken place.

Such enumerated powers as those to tax and to regulate interstate commerce have had a much greater impact on our lives than others because so many implied powers have been found to be "necessary and proper" to carry them out. The power to tax, for example, implies the power to spend, and hence justifies such programs as Medicare to pay the hospital costs of the elderly, monetary grants-in-aid to state and local governments, farm price supports, and cash subsidies to corporation-owned airlines and ships. Similarly, the power to regulate interstate commerce implies the authority to pass congressional legislation concerning racial discrimination in restaurants, kidnapping, minimum hourly wages, and consumer protection. Some observers feel that the "necessary and proper" clause has by now been so stretched in its interpretation that they call it the "elastic" clause.

While the national government possesses the powers just mentioned, the Tenth Amendment states that all other powers, unless specifically prohibited elsewhere in the Constitution, "are reserved to the States respectively, or to the people." Traffic regulations, marriage and divorce requirements, the operation of the public schools, building codes, gambling laws, the licensing of lawyers and doctors, the control of crime—all these are exercises of the *reserved powers* of the states. They are not so dramatic as tragedies in Vietnam or triumphs in space exploration, but they provide the day-to-day necessities of civilized life. It should be noted that the authority of the states (as unitary systems) extends also to local governments, which have only the powers given to them by the states.

Cooperative federalism As the national government has expanded its activities, it has intruded into matters of state jurisdiction. The result has been the growth of the area of *concurrent powers,* exercised jointly by national and state authorities. Thus, federalism has become a sharing, as well as a division, of power.

In recent years, grants-in-aid have become an increasingly important area of cooperative federalism. This form of financial assistance appropriates national tax revenue to state and local governments and permits Congress to help finance activities which it generally would have no constitutional authority to initiate. Few expenditures in our history have risen so rapidly as these. In 1964, they amounted to a little over ten billion dollars and within six years, by 1970, had increased about 150 percent, to an estimated nearly twenty-four billion dollars. The major activities assisted by grants-in-aid are shown in Figure 7.

There are two major strings usually attached to these grants. One is that the state or local governments receiving them put up some minimum of funds to help finance the same projects, and the other is that they meet nationally determined standards in administering the program receiving assistance.

While such grants accounted for only 8.2 percent of state and local revenues in 1942, this had more than doubled in the next twenty-five years, reaching 16.7 percent in 1969: In nine states, over 25 percent of government revenue came from this source, and quite significantly, five of these were among the poorest fifth of all states in per capita

Figure 7   Federal Aid to State and Local Governments in 1970

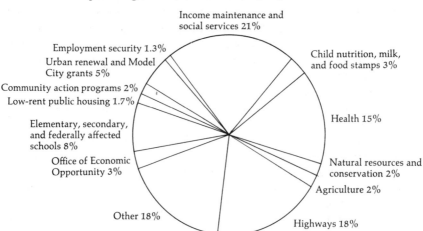

Grants-in-aid and shared revenue for selected programs in percentages of the total aid of $23,955,000.00

Income maintenance and social services 21%

Employment security 1.3%
Urban renewal and Model City grants 5%
Community action programs 2%
Low-rent public housing 1.7%
Elementary, secondary, and federally affected schools 8%
Office of Economic Opportunity 3%
Other 18%

Child nutrition, milk, and food stamps 3%
Health 15%
Natural resources and conservation 2%
Agriculture 2%
Highways 18%

Source: U.S. Bureau of the Census, *Statistical Abstract of the United States: 1971,* p. 401.

personal income. At the opposite extreme, seven of the ten richest states were among the ten for which national funds accounted for the smallest percentage of revenue. The grants-in-aid program, it seems, tends to aid poor states more than rich ones.[9]

President Nixon has instituted a far-reaching program of revenue sharing that would augment most of these grants with national tax money given to state and local governments to be used largely at their own discretion. Revenue sharing has three broad purposes. First, it is an attempt to save local governments hovering on the brink of bankruptcy; second, it seeks to decentralize control over the expenditure of public funds by transferring budgetary decisions from the national government to the states, counties, and cities; and finally, it shifts some of the financial burden of state and local government services from local property tax sources to more equitably extracted income taxes.

Intergovernmental relations: the jealous partners   Numerous relationships among many governments obviously require certain ground rules, some of which are provided in Article IV of the Constitution. This sets forth three obligations of the states to one another. As people move from state to state more easily and in larger numbers, the importance of these interstate obligations has increased greatly. (1) The "full faith and credit" clause requires each state to honor the contracts, deeds, marriages, wills, and court orders (including financial settlements) authorized by the legal processes of all other states. (2) The "privileges and immunities" clause prohibits states from unjustly discriminating against citizens of other states. They may, however, charge students from other states higher college and university tuition fees on the grounds that they have not helped to pay the state taxes which largely finance these institutions. They may also require newly resident professionals (such as doctors or lawyers) to satisfy their particular standards. (3) Each state should return escaped criminal suspects to the states from which they fled. This is the process of rendition, often called extradition, but it is one which national courts have declared they are powerless to enforce, since no constitutionally guaranteed individual rights are at stake.

Article IV also requires that the national government assume three obligations to the states. The first of these obligations guarantees "a republican form of government," but the Supreme Court has held that whether a state has this kind of government is a "political question" which must be determined by Congress or the President. With incredible good fortune, the second obligation, protection of the states against invasion, has never been tested.

In actual practice, by far the most important of the national responsibilities to the states has been the protection against domestic violence whenever states have asked for such assistance. Racial conflict

9 The statistics cited in this paragraph are taken from U.S. Bureau of the Census, *Statistical Abstract of the United States: 1971*, pp. 314, 402, and 405.

on the streets of Detroit and Newark, for example, led President Lyndon Johnson to send in army units at state request. Considerably more controversial has been the presidential dispatch of troops in violation of the wishes of state officials. President Cleveland sent troops into Chicago in 1894 to end a railroad strike and resume mail transportation. Similarly, President Eisenhower dispatched armed forces to Little Rock, Arkansas, in 1957, and President Kennedy to the University of Mississippi in 1963, to avert violence which threatened to block racial integration in the schools. On all three of these occasions, however, national action was justified not by Article IV dealing with intergovernmental relations but by Article II authorizing the President to see to it that laws (including federal court orders) "be faithfully executed."

Cooperation between state governments has become increasingly meaningful. As Article I, Section 10 is interpreted, states may make interstate agreements known as compacts with the approval of Congress. Dozens of these are now in effect, and those involving oil conservation and convicts on probation or parole include most of the states. Most compacts deal with such matters as interstate boundaries, the allocation of river water, interstate bridges, forest fire prevention, and cooperative use of state-supported medical and dental schools. The Port of New York Authority, involving the states of New Jersey and New York, is the biggest business enterprise created by an interstate compact and one of the largest in the world.

Assessment   The federal division of power, like any compromise, possesses both assets and liabilities which deserve brief enumeration. Some advantages of the system are: (1) It permits unity on matters affecting the whole nation, such as foreign policy, while permitting diversity with respect to more personal matters such as gambling and abortion laws. (2) By dividing power between national and state officials it provides a possible barrier to dictatorship. (3) States may act as "social laboratories" in which new policies can be tested without damaging other states. (4) Policies may be tailored more readily to local conditions and interests. (5) State officials can gain experience which will prepare them to perform comparable functions in the national government with greater effectiveness. (6) Federalism permits the election of a large number of people, engaged personally in a kind of participatory democracy.

Offsetting these are several liabilities: (1) Federalism perpetuates unequal opportunities, since rich states can provide better schools, hospitals, and other services than poor states. (2) A division of power means mutual suspicion and jealousy and sometimes a bitter dispute over where national power ends and state power begins. (3) It encourages delay in the solution of problems by fostering "buck-passing" between national and state officials. (4) Differences among state laws in such fields as traffic regulations provide a source of embarrassment and confusion to citizens who travel across the country. (5) Fragmentation of authority makes it easier for powerful pressure groups concentrated in particular geographic areas to gain unwarranted influence. (6) State boundaries, the offspring of historical circumstance, have rendered many states too small, and others too large, for maximum administrative efficiency.

Separation of Powers: Ambition *vs.* Ambition

Although the Founding Fathers intended to create a stronger national government, they had mixed feelings, for they took a dim view of human nature and feared that more centralized power heightened the danger of its abuse. Their solution was to increase the authority of the national government but at the same time to separate it among three groups of officials—legislative, executive, and judicial—each of which was empowered to check the other two. "Ambition," in Madison's words, was "made to counteract ambition."[10] All fifty state governments are structured in much the same way.

The three branches The separation of powers provided in Articles I, II, and III of the Constitution is a separation both of personnel and of function. In terms of personnel, no one (with the exception of the Vice President) can serve in more than one branch at a time; in terms of function, each branch was assigned dominance in its particular realm: Congress was to pass laws; the President was to enforce and administer them; the courts were to interpret them in individual circumstances and punish those who violated them. The idea was borrowed from Montesquieu, a French theorist who had urged a separation of powers to give each group of officials enough independent authority to limit the power of the other two.

Checks and balances American constitutional theory assumes the three branches to be equal in authority. To assure this in practice, the framers gave each one certain checks with which to balance the power of the other two. This modifies the separation of powers principle substantially, since each branch shares some of the functions of the other two; considerable cooperation among all three is required, therefore, if the government is to function effectively. The Senate, for example, must approve presidential appointments and treaties, the President may veto acts of Congress, and the courts may declare actions of the other two branches unconstitutional.

Judicial review Perhaps the most controversial and unique of the interbranch checks is this last one, known as the power of judicial review. The Constitution does not give the courts this authority, and there is some disagreement over whether most of the framers intended that they should have it. Hamilton, however, in No. 78 of *The Federalist*, supported judicial review and others agreed. The issue was of no practical

---

10 *The Federalist* No. 51. Exact authorship is undetermined, and it is possible that it was written by Hamilton rather than Madison.

importance until 1803 when, in *Marbury* v. *Madison,* the Supreme Court declared a congressional law unconstitutional for the first time. The Court's opinion, written by Chief Justice Marshall, relied largely on the "supremacy" clause of Article VI of the Constitution to justify its decision. That provision states that "This constitution, and the laws . . . which shall be made in pursuance thereof . . . shall be the supreme law of the land . . ." Marshall asserted, quite simply, that the law in question came in conflict with the Constitution and was hence invalid. There were those who contended passionately that it was unconstitutional to declare a law unconstitutional, but they cried out in vain. As the Court's prestige increased, the precedent established in *Marbury* v. *Madison* became more deeply entrenched. Judicial review has now been used to invalidate nearly one hundred national and over seven hundred state laws, as well as dozens of executive acts committed by officials ranging from rookie policemen to the President of the United States. It has made American courts the most powerful in the world, is a central component in the system of checks and balances, and ranks with federalism as one of this nation's most ingenious governmental innovations.

Assessment   The separation of powers possesses several merits. First, like federalism, it helps to prevent the concentration of too much power in the hands of too few people. Second, it creates stability and continuity by guaranteeing fixed and often overlapping terms of office for congressmen and the President. Finally, it helps to balance the sometimes conflicting claims of majority rule and minority rights by permitting both the periodic election of the two "political" branches as well as lifetime tenure, immune from majority pressure, for judges in the third branch.

There are, however, liabilities as well. First, if the various branches are controlled by opposing political parties, governmental delay and even deadlock may result. Second, responsibility is so dispersed that the people may become confused, wondering who is to blame for what.

Both federalism and separation of powers relate to government structure, and both fragment government authority, the first territorially and the second functionally. The other two constitutional principles to be examined, freedom and democracy, involve not the structure of government but its relationship to the people whom it governs.

Freedom: The People's Rights

Freedom of speech, press, and assembly as well as freedom from unjust convictions and arbitrary imprisonment had been established by the common law and the English Parliament long before American independence. The Revolution, indeed, was fought in part to protect these freedoms more effectively. One of the chief reasons for dividing governmental machinery between national and state authorities and among three distinct branches was to limit the capacity of government officials to impinge upon the freedom of individual citizens. Several provisions of the original Constitution along with Amendments One through Nine, Thirteen, and Fourteen entrench freedom as a major principle in American society.

Natural rights The idea that citizens have the rights to possess the property for which they labor and to express their individuality in action and opinion goes back to ancient Greece and Rome. This concept was refined by a famous English philosopher, John Locke, who wrote that mankind lived initially in a "state of nature" governed only by "natural law." This natural law, Locke argued, was the product of universal and unchanging reason, and it endowed the individual with "natural rights" to life, liberty, and property. In order to protect these rights more efficiently, people formed a "social compact," or contract, which created government. Granting Locke's basic assumptions, it follows logically that if the government does not protect these natural rights, the people may revolt against it and form one which will. With only minor modifications, this was the justification for revolution which Jefferson wrote into the Declaration of Independence.

Assessment There are, of course, other arguments in behalf of freedom. It stems logically from a belief in the ultimate value of the individual and the development of his or her potential; it is necessary to control the arrogance of government officials; and it is indispensable to the search for truth upon which the creative advance of civilization depends.

Governments actually play complex roles in relation to individual freedom. They may, as Locke hoped, protect freedom from the murderer or bully or crook, or they may themselves be the biggest bullies of all. Restrictions on government power and the protection of liberty are, in this case, two sides of the same coin. All in all, the friends of freedom should remember that it can be jeopardized by both private and public power. In very effective ways, the pressures of social conformity and the demands of employers or families can erode the freedom of individual men and women most seriously. But the power of the state can imprison or kill. All this is not to endorse unrestricted freedom; each one of us must lower his voice occasionally so that another may be heard. In an increasingly congested, interdependent society, some degree of discipline, restraint, and order is necessary. It is the price society demands for efficiency, fairness, and perhaps even for survival.

Democracy: the People's Power

In its modern context, the simplest definition of democracy is majority rule. As such, this is the most recently established of the major principles of American politics. It requires two obvious conditions: that a majority of the people be permitted to vote and that they or their elected representatives be permitted to determine government policy. In the early decades of American government, however, suffrage (the right to vote) was restricted by property-ownership requirements in some states, and racial and sexual impediments persisted long after that. Further, even those who could vote were permitted to elect few of the real decision-makers. The Constitution set up a national government in which U.S. Senators were selected by state legislatures until the ratification of Amendment Seventeen in 1913; the President was elected by an electoral college which, in most states, was also chosen by state legislatures until the 1820s; judges were, and still are, appointed. Only the House of Representatives—one half of one of the three branches—was initially subject to direct popular control.

Since most of these procedural barriers have now been swept away, can we conclude that democracy will permanently flourish? Not necessarily. Democracy is not a hardy, garden-variety perennial that one can plant and then forget. Instead, it is a rare species, so delicate that it withers quickly outside a supporting environment.

Social supports   A democratic society is one in which families, churches, factories, and schools embody democratic principles. From these major social institutions individual citizens derive their attitudes and values. If social institutions are controlled dictatorially or discourage respect for minorities and human dignity, then prospects are dim for political democracy. The inability of Germany to maintain a democratic government prior to World War II, for example, has been attributed in part to the attitudes developed in the traditionally authoritarian German family. Conversely, the growth of democracy in America has been associated to some degree with the fact that many early New England churches were democratically controlled by local congregations. Some form of participatory democracy in the home, classroom, and office bolsters the chance for successful democracy in city hall and in Washington, D.C.

Economic supports   It was observed earlier that democracies seem to flourish best in fairly wealthy countries, where there is not a constant struggle for mere existence. Normally, people can't get the information they need to make intelligent political decisions unless they can read, and they can't read unless they live in a country rich enough to provide free public schools. In modern times, of course, a wealthy nation is a highly industrialized one, and although literacy, education, and industrialization may exist without democracy, democracy seldom exists without them. A large middle class appears to provide the stability requisite for democracy. If a nation is divided chiefly between the very rich and very poor, there will be no moderating force, with a stake in the system, to effect the compromises necessary to avoid violence.

Psychological supports   Analysts of individual behavior have focused their attention on psychological factors which may help to explain the relationship between democratic attitudes and certain personality characteristics. Among the traits thought to be associated with democracy are self-esteem (a good feeling about oneself which enables one to believe that others are "good folks" also), an open ego (warm, trusting, and friendly), and a multi-valued orientation rather than an obsessive preoccupation with a single interest for which one might sacrifice democratic procedures.

Cultural supports Crucial to the survival of democracy is a culture in which its basic values are widely shared. If a society is sharply divided about such fundamental principles as religious freedom, racial tolerance, or the protection of personal property, the issue may be settled by bullets rather than by ballots. In other words, democracy can tolerate disagreements on minor issues because there is fundamental agreement on major ones.

The cultural value most central to democracy is the belief in the dignity and worth of the individual. Majority rule itself pays tribute numerically to the equal importance of each individual in the group. But the equal worth of each human being is not merely a convenient mathematical assumption for counting votes: Because it involves the assumption that all citizens are equal before the laws, it also commits us to equal justice under the laws. We want people to vote because that is the best way yet devised to guarantee that their interests will be the ultimate concern of the government. Democracy, then, is more than a procedural device to decide who will rule. It is a substantive dedication to the enhancement of human dignity. The individual is not merely a means, but an end as well.

Democracy and freedom Democracy cannot survive without a commitment to freedom. Therefore, majority rule should not (though it sometimes does) override minority rights. For unless the majority permits the minority freedom of expression, people may be doubly deprived—deprived of knowledge that may be necessary to a wise decision on public policy, and also deprived of that choice between alternatives which permits the rejection of one proposal or one official in favor of another. Without a choice, without alternative policies and personnel, the people have no way to keep the government accountable to their wishes. Moreover, as long as today's minority is free to become tomorrow's majority, it is likely to accept the verdict of the voters without resorting to violence.

Assessment Even under the best of circumstances, democracy is not a simple system. Sometimes the freedom of the individual conflicts with the will of a majority; sometimes the substance of justice must await the due process of democratic procedures; and sometimes liberty conflicts with the legal equality of all citizens. Each generation must meet these contradictions in some form. To do so, procedurally, at a minimum there must be universal suffrage and popularly elected policy-makers as the means to attain majority rule. Substantively, there must be a commitment to individual dignity and well-being as the ultimate ends of government policy. These must be both supplemented with and limited by a devotion to minority rights, for individual freedom is essential to a real choice by an enlightened majority.

In America, democracy must accommodate itself to federalism and to the separation of powers, both of which fragment power. Although this protects freedom by limiting power, it also requires a majority of the people to elect more representatives, perhaps, than they can intelligently evaluate. As a result, a vigilant press, competitive parties, and effective pressure groups must act on behalf of the public as watchdogs to help hold officials accountable for their performance and responsible to the voters.

The social, economic, psychological, and cultural conditions of democracy indicate that it is not merely a political system: It is a pattern of relationships in the home, a luxury product of an affluent economy, a set of collective personality patterns prone to mutual trust, and a state of mind both widely shared and deeply dedicated to common values of human worth.

The critics of democracy sometimes contend that it is so lofty an ideal, confounded by such imposing difficulties, that it can never be attained. To some, it is little more than a delusion nurtured by small elites to conceal their own political dominance. Others admit that democracy is feasible but undesirable: It works too slowly and debases cultural standards to the lowest common denominator.

The proponents of democracy counter these allegations on both theoretical and practical levels. Theoretically, they assert that if democracy is visionary, it at least is a vision that summons the best and noblest of human aspirations. Practically, they concede that democracy is an ideal that is realized only by degrees. But they point out that the societies that are most democratic are those that came out on top in both World Wars, are most productive, and fulfill most completely the individual's need for recognition and significance.

DEMOGRAPHIC INFLUENCES

Four demographic features have persisted for so long and intensified to such a degree that they are the most significant characteristics of the American population: numbers, the westward movement, urbanization, and diversity.

Numbers: Plenty of People

The American population has increased more spectacularly than that of any nation in history. From the nearly four million recorded in the first official census count in 1790, it rose to more than 204 million in 1970. The current trend, however, is toward a much lower rate of increase.

Our vast geographic area is capable of sustaining a large population with relatively little crowding. While uninhabitable mountain and desert regions make population density figures misleading, it nonetheless is significant that the United States has an average of about 57 inhabitants per square mile, compared with 200 in China, 239 in France, 426 in India, 245 in West Germany, and 720 in Japan. At the other

Charles Gatewood.

Young people, aware of the relationship between population and pollution, urge fewer babies, fewer cars.

extreme are 29 in the Soviet Union, 23 in Argentina, and 5 in Canada. The world average is 68.

By a coincidence convenient to human memory, America ranks fourth in both population and area among the world's nations. Although numbers alone cannot make a nation a formidable power, they are an important element in its total strength. Large numbers of combat troops are still military assets of considerable consequence, as we recently were reminded in Korea and Vietnam. Moreover, for economic diversification and a reasonable degree of national self-sufficiency there must be some minimum population to exploit the available resources most advantageously.

But exceptional growth is not an unmixed blessing, and partially counteracts the nation's geographic assets. Automobiles pollute the air, industrial wastes contaminate rivers and oceans, and an increasing population demands that government permit the leveling of hillsides for housing tracts and the construction of resort areas on previously unspoiled mountain slopes or lake shores. Although population density is relatively light, commercial, residential, and recreational needs already imperil the environment to a substantial degree. Despite these problems, world population growth will bring increasing pressures upon America to liberalize its immigration policy, since the distribution of the three-and-a-half billion people on earth is far from equitable.

Distribution: A Violent Frontier

As the American people have moved from East to West, the center of population has shifted gradually from Maryland in 1790 to a point in southwestern Illinois, not far from St. Louis, in 1970. This massive migration has been carried on in the face of many formidable obstacles, both physical and human. Its political implications have been almost as numerous. The lure of the West exerted pressures upon the government to facilitate movement by subsidizing roads, canals, and railroads, reducing the price of land on the frontier, and driving Indians from their ancestral homes.

Population has pulled political power with it. Between 1900 and 1973, for example, 55 of the 435 seats in the House of Representatives were transferred from other parts of the country to western states. California alone gained thirty-five, Washington and Arizona four, Hawaii, Colorado, New Mexico, and Oregon two, and Alaska, Idaho, Montana, and Utah each added one.[11] The shift of power was best dramatized on January 20, 1969, when one native Californian, former Chief Justice Earl Warren, swore in another, Richard Nixon, as President of the United States.

When Americans had spanned the entire continent, there followed changes in foreign policy. It seemed to many that our long Pacific coastal boundary required that we become a major power in that most vast of oceans. We acquired the Philippines and Hawaii, constructed the Panama Canal to increase both commercial and naval access to the Pacific, and developed a growing interest in Asia. In a sense, then, the westward movement has taken the United States to the Far East, and veterans of Vietnam know some of the consequences.

The frontier thesis   As Americans shoved west, lured by cheap land or furs, timber or gold, they moved into that uncharted, perilous, promising domain that historians call the frontier. This, of course, was not a fixed and static place. It was the rugged, ragged cutting edge at the western limits of a civilization that was essentially European in origin and style. As the first settlers pushed the frontier steadily back, mowing down like a giant reaper the trees and Indians and wild game which obstructed their advance, they brought their European civilization with them. Their language, the faith of their fathers, their customs and laws—all were transplanted wherever they built their homes.

11 The source of statistical data here and elsewhere in "Demographic Influences" is U.S. Bureau of the Census, *Statistical Abstract of the United States: 1971*. These figures were computed from the table on p. 357.

Yet in the process of carrying an old culture to a new environment, that culture underwent a number of gradual but important changes. According to Frederick Jackson Turner, the western wilderness promoted individualism, equality, and democracy. Faced with unknown hazards, the settlers had to develop self-reliance in order to survive. They were equally good targets, regardless of social rank, race, or family wealth, for Indian arrows or a dozen other misfortunes. These common problems, Turner argued, generated the sense of brotherhood and mutual respect out of which American democracy developed.

The frontier also contributed to a kind of political stability. Whereas European malcontents and radicals posed a constant threat of revolt, the free land of the American frontier acted as a safety valve, enticing the most discontented and rebellious citizens to start new societies in the West rather than overthrow the old ones in the East.

The effects of the frontier were not always so laudable. They included a kind of crude materialism, a proclivity for violence, and a distrust of authority. In any case, both the good and the bad of the frontier seem to have persisted in modern society. Many Americans, imbued with the values of individual self-reliance, oppose most government welfare programs; "law and order" are threatened by rising crime and widespread violence; the nation is regularly accused of a preoccupation with material goods rather than broader cultural values. Yet for all its psychological impact, it is generally agreed that the actual frontier had about vanished by 1890. Later historians have contended that Turner overstated his case, but few would doubt that as Americans moved westward they became—at least in part—products of that free and lawless land which for so long was their environment.

Urbanization

A popular song of World War I asked, "How ya gonna keep 'em down on the farm, after they've seen Paree?" The answer was—whether they had seen Paris or not—that you couldn't. In fact, the steady process of urbanization began long before World War I; by 1970, 74 percent of the population was urban. The massive shift away from rural areas is as momentous as the westward movement and has the same essential cause: the continuing, consuming desire for economic improvement. The movement from rural to urban areas was, in most instances, a shift from farms to factories. Its effects had political and legal implications that no student of government can ignore.

First, it reduced the percentage of the labor force which was self-employed and increased the portion working for someone else. This led to the eventual passage of minimum-wage, workmen's-compensation, child-labor, and union-recognition laws.

Second, it created new industries which demanded and received governmental subsidies, tax advantages, and tariffs on imported goods to afford protection from foreign competition.

Figure 8   Population Growth

	Population Growth 1960–70
Central cities	6.4%
Outside central cities (suburbs)	26.7%
Nonmetropolitan areas	6.8%
Entire nation	13.3%

Source: U.S. Bureau of the Census, *Statistical Abstract of the United States: 1971*, p. 16.

Third, it increased the population density in cities, thrusting upon local governments grave new problems in such areas as zoning, public health, transportation, recreation facilities, and air pollution.

While the majority of the American people had moved to urban areas by 1920, there remain enormous differences among the states. As recently as 1970, for example, eight states were still predominantly rural. Vermont led (or trailed) the list, with only 32.2 percent of its population living in urban areas, while at the other extreme were New Jersey with 88.9 percent and California with 88.6 percent.

Until recent years, urbanization conjured up thoughts of the big city—bright and bursting with opportunity. Yet the latest population figures reveal that significant population growth is occurring not in the central cities of large metropolitan areas but in the suburban fringe cities which surround them. In fact, the major metropolises, beset by crime, pollution, and the sheer ravages of age, may be losing their vitality altogether.

Diversity: A Mixed Blessing

Franklin D. Roosevelt once mischievously teased the ancestral pride of the conservative ladies who comprise the Daughters of the American Revolution by addressing them as "My fellow immigrants." His remark contained an element of truth, for if not immigrants, our citizens are the descendants of immigrants. Even the ancestors of the Indians were probably Asians who made their way across the Bering Straits.

America: a group portrait   Americans were reasonably homogeneous only until the arrival of European invaders in the sixteenth century. Even before that, the Indian tribes displayed remarkable diversity in language and life style. The Spanish, English, Dutch, and French settlers contributed still more variety during the early colonial period, and a multiracial society was guaranteed with the importation of African laborers beginning in 1619. Thereafter, each year brought new immigrants, all carrying, duty free, their ancestral prejudices and varied ethnic backgrounds: These differences exerted a profound impact on the political behavior of Americans. The demands of blacks have led to a

Figure 9   Major American Ethnic Groups

Group	Number	Percentage
English, Scotch, Welsh	31,006,000	15.3
German	25,661,000	12.7
Negro	22,810,000	11.2
Irish	16,325,000	8.0
Italian	8,733,000	4.3
French	5,189,000	2.6
Mexican	5,073,000	2.5
Polish	4,941,000	2.4
Spanish, Puerto Rican, Cuban, other Latin American	3,883,000	1.9
American Indians, Japanese, Chinese, other nonwhite	2,412,000	1.2
Russian	2,132,000	1.1
Austrian, Canadian, Swedish, other white	59,467,000	29.3
Not reported	15,216,000	7.5
Total	202,848,000	100.0

Source: Adapted from *Congressional Quarterly Weekly Report*, March 11, 1972, p. 532. Reprinted by permission of Congressional Quarterly,Inc. Figures are based on a Census Bureau sampling taken in March 1971.

white backlash; political organizations formed by Indians, Mexican-Americans, Chinese-Americans and other groups have mushroomed rapidly; and "bloc voting" by various ethnic groups has persisted to elect (and defeat) many a candidate. To understand American politics, therefore, one should know what sorts of people inhabit the country in the 1970s. What color are they? Where did they come from?

Immigration policy   The composition of the American population did not come about by sheer accident. Although no significant prohibitions were placed on immigration into the country during its first century of independence, black Americans had previously been brought here in chains and shackles, countless Indians were killed, and numbers of Chinese were brought to the United States under exploitative contracts to lay railroad tracks. In 1882, with the transcontinental railroad completed, a combination of racial prejudice and fear on the part of native white factory workers that they might lose their jobs to Asian laborers led to a prohibition of further immigration imposed by the Chinese Exclusion Act. No nation had ever before been subjected to any restriction whatever.

The Immigration Restriction Act of 1921 was the first to place general limitations on the number of new immigrants. Inspired by the antiforeign fervor generated during World War ɪ, it established the

national origin quota system. This was designed—as amended in 1924—
to keep the proportion of new immigrants from various nations the same
as the proportion who had come from those countries before 1890. It was
justified as a measure to assist the assimilation of new arrivals into
American society, but discriminated against non-Protestants, since large
numbers of Catholics and Jews had emigrated after 1890 from countries
such as Russia, Poland, and Italy.

This religious prejudice was augumented by racial bigotry as
well. Orientals were prohibited from becoming citizens as a result of
additional legislation passed in 1924, and immigration was prohibited for
persons ineligible for citizenship. Most astonishing of all, the system
which fixed immigration quotas for each country on the basis of the
national origins of American residents prohibited the classification of
Negroes as being of African origin.

Not until 1965 was the national origin quota system abandoned and the American welcome mat largely cleansed of the stains of
ethnic bias. The new law establishes a maximum of 170,000 immigrants
each year who may enter the United States from outside the Western
Hemisphere. No more than 20,000 of this number may be admitted from
any one country, and preference is given to those who have either
relatives in the United States or special occupational skills needed by the
American economy. The 1965 Act includes another controversial change
in previous policy. Before its passage, immigrants from nations in the
Western Hemisphere were admitted "quota free" in unlimited numbers.
But present policy limits to 120,000 per year the number entering from
these areas, in addition to the 170,000 from the rest of the world.

The melting pot   Early in our history, a French immigrant
lauded "that strange mixture of blood . . . melted into a new race of
men, whose labors and posterity will one day cause great changes in the
world."[12] He thus became one of the first to propound the now famous
melting pot thesis. The diversity of the American population has no
doubt exceeded his most enthusiastic expectation, and the nation is far
richer for it. Zubin Mehta, the Asiatic Indian, has given us great music;
Albert Einstein, the German Jew, brought us genius in physics; George
Washington Carver, the Afro-American, contributed brilliance in agricultural chemistry; Amadeo P. Giannini, of Italian origin, founded the
Bank of America, largest in the world. The list is nearly endless.

Yet this is only part of the story. Although we have welded
the talents, skills, and values of many peoples into a rich and unique
amalgam, we have yet to create an alloy of happy fellowship. While
conceding that some ethnic groupings (notably German-Americans)
have diminished in solidarity, two leading scholars have concluded that
the melting pot has melted very little, and that racial and religious

12 Michel Guillaume St. Jean de Crevecoeur, *Letters from an American Farmer,* excerpted
in Oscar Handlin, *Immigration as a Factor in American History* (Englewood Cliffs, N.J.:
Prentice-Hall, Inc., 1959), p. 149.

groups—especially in New York City—retain immense political importance.[13] Thus we are confronted with a culture enriched by the creativity of diversity, yet impoverished by its accompanying rivalries.

Summary   *Population growth,* although producing a density substantially less than in many other nations, is creating an increasingly serious problem of pollution. At the same time, however, it has enabled the economic diversification and military potential necessary to a major rank among world powers.

The *westward movement* has enhanced the political power of the Pacific states and helped Asia rival Europe as a focus of the attention of foreign policy planners. The frontier period has diluted revolutionary tendencies, and contributed to the materialism, equality, democracy, individualism, and lawlessness of American society. *Urbanization* has been economically inspired, for the most part, by the lure of new jobs created by the Industrial Revolution, and has placed dramatic new demands upon governments.

Within the *ethnic diversity* of American society, northern Europeans predominate, with British descendants constituting a plurality, and those of German ancestry next in numbers. Despite overtly discriminatory immigration policies from 1882 to 1965, ours is a richly heterogeneous society. But under the melting pot there are flames of resentment as well as the warmth of fellowship.

IDEOLOGICAL INFLUENCES

The American political system operates within a context of related ideas and values which help to determine political behavior. Such ideological influences are part of the political culture. A leader identified with this ideology will most likely enjoy the widespread respect that is an essential ingredient of authority.

Americanism

Loyalty to the nation has become the overriding allegiance in much of the globe. Most Americans will forsake conflicting obligations to family, occupation, church, or political creed in order to defend their country. This loyalty is not merely the result of a threat of imprisonment; nationalism involves the identification of individual interests with the welfare of the entire country. Such an identification is strengthened by common language, traditions, and ethnic backgrounds—and yet Americans, spread over a large geographic area, possess a wide variety of racial, religious, political, and linguistic backgrounds. Why, then, are we so patriotic?

First, most Americans came to view their new homeland as

---

13 Nathan Glazer and Daniel P. Moynihan, *Beyond the Melting Pot* (Cambridge, Mass.: The M.I.T. Press, 1963).

an immense improvement over the rigid class structures and economic destitution of the lands from which they came. Second, the very barriers to a common loyalty have inspired extraordinary and generally successful attempts to overcome them. Thus, free public education deliberately sought to Americanize the immigrants' children by teaching them English, American history and customs, and a reverence for such symbols as the flag, the national anthem, and the patriotic mythology surrounding Washington, Jefferson, and other heroes. A 1958 survey reported that 56.7 percent of the people believed that "freedom does not give anyone the right to teach foreign ideas in our schools."[14]

In addition, the geographical divisions separating the eastern and western parts of the nation were bridged by Senator Henry Clay's "American System," providing roads, canals, and high tariffs to satisfy both sections. Even the tragedy of Civil War, nearly severing the South from the North, was diminished by the intentional postwar glorification of both Robert E. Lee, a saintly Southerner, and Abraham Lincoln, the noble Northerner. To seal the reunification bargain, the North, in 1877, quietly acquiesced in the resumption of power by the old white southern aristocracy, the violation of black voting rights, and the imposition, in the 1890s, of a rigid system of racial segregation. Lincoln himself had enunciated his priorities quite clearly: "If I could save the Union without freeing any slave," he wrote to Horace Greeley in 1862, "I would do it; and if I could save the Union by freeing all the slaves, I would do it." The great Emancipator thereby showed himself also the great nationalist. No price was too great, it seemed, to reclaim that most valued of ideals, a reunited union and an invigorated sense of national solidarity.

In America, as in all countries, the glorification of nationalism affects the conduct of American politics. First, it allows public officials to divert attention from the validity of their own ideas by associating them with patriotic pride. Thus President Nixon pleaded for support of his Vietnam policy in April 1970 by reminding a nation-wide television audience that in the "proud history" of America we had never lost a war and he did not intend that we should lose this one. His appeal was a strategically shrewd one. A 1964 poll showed 56 percent of the American people committed to the idea, "The United States should maintain its dominant position as the world's most powerful nation at all costs . . ."[15]

Second, nationalism helps to create a general public confidence in the government, investing it with a legitimacy and authority which reduces the force necessary to gain compliance with its policies. Third, patriotic devotion to the nation contributes to internal cohesion and compromise. It appeals to altruistic rather than selfish impulses and

14 Lloyd A. Free and Hadley Cantril, *The Political Beliefs of Americans* (N.Y.: Clarion Books, Simon & Schuster, Inc., 1968), p. 93.
15 Herbert McClosky, "Consensus and Ideology in American Politics," *American Political Science Review* 58 (June 1964): 361–82.

encourages labor and business, black and white, the devout and the atheist, to submerge their differences on behalf of the common good.

Fourth, and unfortunately, it increases the possibility of international conflict. Love of country can too easily become xenophobia, a fearful hatred of foreign peoples, as was skillfully accomplished in Nazi Germany. The cause of the fatherland or the mother country can flood the recruiting offices with volunteers, but the cause of the brotherhood of man has no armies. It too needs volunteers.

Capitalism

While nationalism is perhaps the dominant ideology in almost every country, capitalism has had a uniquely powerful influence on the American political system. Briefly described, capitalism is an economic system based on the ownership of business by private individuals or corporations, rather than by government. In 1776, Adam Smith argued in *The Wealth of Nations* that prosperity resulted from a government policy of *laissez-faire*, one that placed few legal restrictions upon the free competition of private business firms. A dozen generations of American capitalists have enthusiastically agreed that this would produce a division of labor resulting in a higher standard of living for the entire society. The law of supply and demand, a kind of "unseen hand" governing the economy, was believed to result in the manufacture of the variety of goods consumers wished to buy because only that would maximize sales and therefore profits as well. Moreover, each company would be forced to produce the best possible product at the lowest possible price, at the risk of losing customers to its competitors. Governmental activity could then be confined largely to the protection of life and property, and each individual left to confront life with little more than his own cleverness and initiative.

Capitalist theory was also nurtured by the Protestant ethic. Although the Catholic Church has prospered from its immense property holdings, it was the Protestants who glorified and even sanctified private profits. Specifically, the disciples of John Calvin had argued that the accumulation of earthly wealth was a probable indication of that grace of God which predestined one for eternal salvation. This religious conception, providing a sharp impetus to hard work, simple living, frugality, and business shrewdness, was implanted in colonial New England, from which it exerted a formidable influence upon all of early America.

Private capitalism was further bolstered in the last half of the last century by the ideas of social Darwinism. This theory held that the capitalistic competition for markets and jobs resulted in the "survival of the fittest." Society would be improved because its inferior members— the weak, lazy, stupid, and decadent—would be gradually eliminated through a process of natural selection; that is, they would reproduce less rapidly than the fittest. For political programs, the implication was clear: Government should neither restrain the successful nor assist the weak. It is little wonder that the United States lagged far behind Germany, France, and England in instituting such social security programs as unemployment compensation, retirement pensions, or Medicare.

Although modern times have forced numerous and substantial modifications in American capitalism, it remains the dominant theme in an economy now "mixed" with limited government ownership. A few years ago, 79 percent of the American people were found to agree with the statement, "We should rely more on individual initiative and not so much on government welfare programs."[16]

Racism

The Commission on Civil Disorders, appointed by President Lyndon B. Johnson in 1967, received considerable criticism for its conclusion that riots in Los Angeles, Detroit, Newark, and other cities were essentially the result of white racism.[17] But racism has been a pervasive and persistent ingredient of American attitudes throughout our history.

American Indians The first victims of racism in America were the first people encountered by the Europeans. The Indian population in what is now the United States is estimated to have been over a million at the time Columbus arrived in the New World. It has been substantially reduced by broken treaties, contamination with disease germs, bloody massacres by the United States cavalry, intentional inducements to chronic alcoholism, and a continual displacement to poorer lands farther West.

These first discoverers of America had initially received the white intruders with general hospitality. But after several centuries of deceit and betrayal, they fought back with vengeance and tenacity. By that time, of course, the odds against them were overwhelming and armed Indian resistance ended in 1890 at Wounded Knee, South Dakota, where several hundred Sioux, including many women and children, were killed.

Afro-Americans The first blacks were brought from Africa in 1619 as indentured servants, but their status soon degenerated into one of the most brutal systems of slavery the world has ever known. In many states it was against the law to teach slaves to read or write; some profitable plantations derived most of their income from commercial slave-breeding; theologians debated whether blacks possessed souls; and 3437 blacks were lynched between 1882 and 1951.[18]

Asian-Americans Discrimination against Asians in immigration and naturalization laws already has been noted. In addition, several massacres of Chinese occurred, and it was not until 1952 that

16 Free and Cantril, op. cit., p. 30.
17 *Report of the National Advisory Commission on Civil Disorders,* (N.Y.: Bantam Books, Inc., 1968), p. 203.
18 *Negro Year Book* (N.Y.: Wm. H. Wise & Co., Inc., 1952), p. 277.

immigrants from the world's most populous nation could be employed by state, county, or municipal governments in California. Japanese were also targets of those who feared the "yellow peril." They were segregated in San Francisco public schools in 1906 and, worst of all, 110,000 Americans of Japanese ancestry were herded into "relocation centers" during World War II, although not one had been found to be disloyal.

White ethnics   The list goes on and on, embracing Mexicans, Irish, Jews, Italians, Slavs, and others. Most of these ethnic groups, one might reasonably object, *are* white; how could they be fair game for racism? The answer is partly that racism has an insatiable appetite for new groups to devour and partly that the concept of the white race was compressed to a category so small as to exclude practically anyone the categorizers didn't like. In 1924, just nine years before Hitler, the most notorious modern racist, rose to power in Germany, a widely used American sociology text asserted that immigrants of those days "belong to a different race from ours. They belong to the Slavic and Mediterranean subraces which have not shown the capacity for self-government . . . which the peoples of northern and western Europe have shown." It is not surprising that the author also opposed black voting and viewed the "negro problem" as "essentially the same as the Indian problem or the problem of any backward people or race . . . inferior in culture and possibly also inferior in nature."[19]

Equality

In spite of the inequalities of racism, Americans have cherished the ideal of equality in very meaningful ways. In 1776 when Thomas Jefferson, a slave owner, asserted it to be "self-evident" that "all men are created equal," even a commitment to white, largely Anglo-Saxon equality was a truly revolutionary concept. Alexis de Tocqueville, an observant and witty Frenchman who visited America in the 1830s, was as impressed by the social equality which he observed here as he was astonished by our capitalistic obsession with material possessions or amused by our pugnaciously patriotic nationalism.

We demonstrated the commitment to equality by prohibiting titles of nobility in Article I of our Constitution and by guaranteeing "equal protection" of state laws in Amendment Fourteen. Equality thus has major implications for the legal processes of government. Jurors, judges, legislators, and voters each have an equal vote in making the decisions entrusted to them. Yet several opinion surveys reveal considerable confusion, uncertainty, and even opposition regarding the concept of equality.

A major study reported 58 percent agreement with the statement that "we have to teach children that all men are created equal

19 Charles A. Ellwood, *Sociology and Modern Social Problems,* rev. ed. (N.Y.: American Book Company, 1924), pp. 233 and 265–66.

but almost everyone knows that some are better than others."[20] Clearly we are not equal if equality means identity. People differ widely in strength, virtue, skill, ambition, and intelligence. On the other hand, all share membership in the human species: They are all similar in their biological desires for food, drink, and sex; all require shelter and warmth; all have emotional needs for approbation and respect; all must endure whatever genetic attributes, infant environment, and racial identity have been their gratuitous endowment; all, finally, must confront their inevitable mortality. Increasingly, each is dependent upon the other—butcher, mortician, plumber, and lawyer—in industrialized societies demanding ever more specialized division of labor. Equality assumes the similarities outweigh the differences.

The belief in equality springs from a variety of roots. We were, in fact, more equal in material conditions than people in other nations; the open frontier with its available land and the absence of an old feudal aristocracy were immensely important in this respect. A rapidly developing literary heritage also stressed the equality theme, with Melville, Whitman, and Twain its major contributors; the individualist philosophy of Emerson and Thoreau enhanced it too. In addition, while some religious ideas have been used to justify extreme inequalities, there are others which have opposite effects. The concept of the brotherhood of man is often rooted in a belief in the universal fatherhood of God, and the family analogy is comfortable and persuasive. Finally, equality is also part of the humanist tradition. Eugene V. Debs, an American socialist, said in 1919: "(Y)ears ago I recognized my kinship with all living things, and I made up my mind that I was not one bit better than the meanest of the earth . . . While there is a lower class, I am in it; while there is a criminal element, I am of it; while there is a soul in prison, I am not free."[21] He was sent to a federal penitentiary for opposing American involvement in World War i.

Pragmatism

While Americans are not well known for their philosophical speculation, they are internationally renowned for their practical accomplishments. They take frank pride in being "doers," not "thinkers." It is therefore appropriate that this country's most notable contribution to philosophy is pragmatism, which glorifies its most characteristic traits. Pragmatism stresses the belief that the truth of an idea is best tested by its results. Abstract conceptions have validity, pragmatists contend, only in terms of their practical consequences.

This philosophy, developed and refined in the early years of the twentieth century by Charles Peirce, William James, and John Dewey, is not so much a conscious belief embraced by the people as it is

20 McClosky, loc. cit.
21 Quoted in Ray Ginger, *The Bending Cross* (New Brunswick, N.J.: Rutgers University Press, 1949), p. 374.

an operational definition of their attitudes and behavior patterns. Its basic sources go back to an earlier period when American frontiersmen were forced to devise practical expedients to cope with their immediate, and often unexpected, needs. Gradually, a faith in the process of trial and error largely replaced more dogmatic doctrines. Pointing out that there is a discrepancy between what Americans say they believe and the actual programs they favor, two prominent pollsters concluded that "what seems to make the system continue to function as effectively as it does is its distinctly American pragmatism."[22]

Although short on political philosophers, America has been long on skillful practical politicians. The pragmatic orientation stands out clearly in almost every part of the political system. Our major political parties are not ideologically oriented, for the most part, but consist of expedient and sometimes shifting group coalitions formed to win elections. The legislative process is marked by a sort of consensus politics born of the lawmaker's concessions to his conscience, his colleagues, and his constituents. Even the courts, led by the great justices Holmes and Brandeis, have applied a sort of legal pragmatism which "follows the election returns" under the guise of sociological jurisprudence—the theory stressing the law's role as a problem solver. Finally, the "mixed economy" of America, part government owned or regulated and part privately controlled, reflects the same practical preoccupation with final results rather than formal doctrine. Our preference for democracy itself manifests a practical, empirical concern with existing realities. As Winston Churchill said, democracy is the worst form of government—except for all the others that have ever been tried. Democratic politics is above all the art of the possible. Theoretically, it is not very neat; morally, it is sometimes corrupt. But, meeting the pragmatic and typically American test, it usually works.

Political Culture, Past and Future

The symbolic importance of the Constitution demonstrates the influence of intangible elements in the maintenance of America's evolving nationhood, for human beings cannot live by bread alone. They need emblems and ideals, common hopes and shared habits, in order to endure. It is the combination of all of these that constitutes what is called political culture, and this involves the many influences and principles we have already discussed. It includes, therefore, our special brand of patriotism, our preference for capitalism, our entanglements with racism, our respect for equality, and our tendency to practicality. It is grounded on a devotion to freedom and democracy, reinforced by a tradition of self-reliant individualism, materialism and a lawless sort of antiauthoritarianism. Some of it embraces the remnants of Puritan moralism and an emphasis on hard work.

22 Free and Cantril, op. cit., p. 178.

"Courtesy Chicago Historical Society."

Campaign antics have long enlivened American democracy. Here a supporter of
the losing presidential candidate plays donkey for the triumphant backer of the
winner, Grover Cleveland, in 1892.

       Popularly accepted myths, legends, heroes, and traditions all
contribute to political culture by emotionally tying the individual to the
vast multitude that shares a common citizenship in the whole nation.
Thus, the elaborate etiquette surrounding the display of "Old Glory," a
national Father who "never told a lie," and a martyr who regretted that
he had "but one life to give" for his country all became pillars of support
for the nationalism inherent in the developing political culture of the new
America. The skeptic may be right in charging that some of these
phenomena are irrational, irrelevant, even fraudulent. But they contributed immeasurably to the growth and solidarity of a nation.[23]

23 An illuminating account of some "fictions" that have infused our political culture is in
the preface to Forrest McDonald, *E Pluribus Unum: The Formation of the American
Republic, 1766–1780* (Boston: Houghton Mifflin Company, 1965).

The evolution of a common American political culture is dynamic and continuing. The War of 1812 produced the national anthem, the Uncle Sam symbol, and the successful defiance—for the second time—of English military might. Some twenty years later it was strengthened by the administration of Andrew Jackson, who linked the welfare of the lower middle class to national prosperity much as Washington and Hamilton had performed the same feat with respect to the commercial elite. Union victory in the Civil War was important in reaffirming the primacy of national rather than sectional loyalties. In the last century, America fell in love with its own prosperity and power. As we aspired to the world leadership we finally attained, we incorporated a devotion to an unexcelled standard of living and unmatched military might into our national self-image. How long can reality sustain the illusion?

Our political culture today is in a state of flux, in part because those with a substantial stake in society assimilate its values more readily than the poor, the ethnic minorities, and the alienated youth who proclaim allegiance to a real but poorly defined counterculture. Changes also result from the technological challenges and realignments of international power which no country can now escape. History provides little solace for nations seeking immortality. Whether the United States, as we know it, will survive, depends on whether its political culture can be diffused more evenly among our people and whether it can adjust to the pervasive changes which characterize our time on earth.

Conclusion to Part One

The American political system is a variation on universal political themes. To illustrate this, the first chapter has defined the world-wide nature of politics, and the second has described the geographical, historical, social, and cultural forces that have made American politics unique.

If we interpret these in terms of power, we see some of the paradoxes presented by our historical development. The Revolution signified rebellion, change, and freedom—a challenge to authority—but the Constitution adopted thirteen years later symbolized stability, order, and authority itself. The protection of individual rights, federalism, and the separation of powers have limited power more than in almost any other country, yet our national government has continuously increased its centralized authority. Furthermore, while government authority has become more concentrated, political influence has also been more widely diffused through the gradual extension of voting rights and direct elections.

There are other complexities as well: White dominance has declined but racism persists; the westward movement dispersed power geographically but urbanization has concentrated it; and political resources such as money remain unequally distributed even as votes and education are more equally allocated than ever before. The American people exert an enormous impact on the use of government power, but they have yet to control it.

Bibliography

Chapter 1

The Nature of Politics: What's It All About?

Dahl, Robert A., *Modern Political Analysis,* 2nd. ed. (Englewood Cliffs, N.J.: Prentice-Hall, Inc., 1970).

Easton, David, *The Political System: An Inquiry into the State of Political Science* (N.Y.: Alfred A. Knopf, Inc., 1953).

Ebenstein, William, *Today's Isms,* 6th ed. (Englewood Cliffs, N.J.: Prentice-Hall, Inc., 1970).

Eulau, Heinz, *The Behavioral Persuasion in Politics* (N.Y.: Random House, Inc., 1963).

Lasswell, Harold D. and Abraham Kaplan, *Power and Society* (New Haven, Conn.: Yale University Press, 1950).

Murphy, Robert E., *The Style and Study of Political Science* (Glenview, Ill.: Scott, Foresman and Company, 1970).

Ranney, Austin, *The Governing of Men,* 3rd ed. (New York: Holt, Rinehart & Winston, Inc., 1971).

Chapter 2

The Americans: Land, Legacy, and Political Culture

Beard, Charles A., *An Economic Interpretation of the Constitution of the United States* (N.Y.: The Macmillan Company, 1913).

Brown, Robert E., *Charles Beard and the Constitution* (Princeton, N.J.: Princeton University Press, 1956).

Corwin, Edward S., and Jack W. Peltason, *Understanding the Constitution,* rev. ed. (N.Y.: The Dryden Press, Inc., 1958).

DeTocqueville, Alexis, *Democracy in America,* trans. by Phillip Bradley (N.Y.: Alfred A. Knopf, Inc., 1945).

Farrand, Max, *The Framing of the Constitution of the United States* (New Haven, Conn.: Yale University Press, 1913).

Free, Lloyd A. and Hadley Cantril, *The Political Beliefs of Americans* (N.Y.: Clarion Books, Simon & Schuster, Inc., 1968).

Grodzins, Morton, *The Federal System* (Englewood Cliffs, N.J.: Prentice-Hall, Inc., 1960).

Hamilton, Alexander, *et al., The Federalist* (N.Y.: Everyman's Library, E. P. Dutton & Co., Inc., 1929).

Hofstadter, Richard, *The American Political Tradition* (N.Y.: Alfred A. Knopf, Inc., 1959).

Kammen, Michael G., ed., *Politics and Society in Colonial America* (N.Y.: Holt, Rinehart & Winston, Inc., 1967).

Lipset, Seymour M., *Political Man,* (Garden City, N.Y.: Anchor Books, Doubleday & Company, Inc., 1963).

Myers, Henry A., *Are Men Equal?* (Ithaca, N.Y.: Cornell University Press, 1945).

Potter, David M., *People of Plenty* (Chicago: University of Chicago Press, 1954).

Roche, John P., ed., *Origins of American Political Thought* (N.Y.: Torchbooks, Harper & Row, Publishers, 1967).

Smith, Adam, *The Wealth of Nations* (N.Y.: Everyman's Library E. P. Dutton & Co., Inc., 1957).

Steinfield, Melvin, ed., *Cracks in the Melting Pot* (Beverly Hills, Calif.: Glencoe Press, 1970).

U.S. Bureau of the Census, *Statistical Abstract of the United States,* published annually (Washington, D.C., 1971).

PART TWO

THE PEOPLE'S RIGHTS

Even in a democracy, relatively few people hold positions of government power, but everyone is affected by government actions. In Part Two, we examine ways in which we have tried to prevent those in possession of government power, the rulers, from destroying the rights and freedoms of the ruled.

It makes no difference how just the laws are, or how scrupulously they preserve the rights and freedoms of individual citizens, if they are applied in an arbitrary or excessive manner. There is a distinction, in other words, between the law itself and the way it is enforced, between the substance or content of a government decree, and the procedure by which it is carried out. The Constitution places limits on both by guaranteeing substantive and procedural rights alike. A law prohibiting all brothers from talking to one another, for example, would be a bad law substantively, no matter how fairly it might be enforced. Similarly, a good law prohibiting drunken driving would be procedurally intolerable if the home of every licensed driver were searched each night for alcoholic beverages. The First Amendment freedoms discussed in Chapter 4 are substantive rights to which the Supreme Court once seemed to give a preferred position. Amendments Four through Eight in Chapter 5 deal primarily with procedural requirements imposed upon police practices and the conduct of trials. Judicial interpretation now makes little distinction as to the relative importance of these two types of constitutional protections. To be either substantively or procedurally just, law in a democracy must apply equally to all citizens. None can be arbitrarily favored or disfavored. Chapter 6 discusses equal justice under law.

Chapter **3**

Freedom of Expression
First Things First

[W]hen men have realized that time has upset many fighting faiths, they may come to believe, even more than they believe the very foundations of their own conduct, that the ultimate good desired is better reached by free trade in ideas—that the best test of truth is the power of the thought to get itself accepted in the competition of the market. . . . That at any rate is the theory of our Constitution. It is an experiment, as all life is an experiment.

Oliver Wendell Holmes

It is no coincidence that the First Amendment to the Constitution protects the freedoms central to democracy: religion, speech, press, assembly, and petition. These were believed to be the very lifeblood of an enlightened society, and the authors of the Bill of Rights were simply putting first things first.

Most of these specific freedoms are dependent upon one another. Freedom of religion, for example, entails the freedom to assemble in church congregations; freedom of speech without freedom of assembly is nothing but the right to talk to oneself; and freedom of the press is often necessary to petition the government effectively (meaning to protest or request official action). This interrelatedness enables us to refer to all five of these rights as freedom of expression. Clearly a democracy requires such freedom in order that citizens may form their own opinions, propose and evaluate policies and personnel, and then organize for political action supporting or opposing the government of the day.

THE DOUBLE STANDARD FADES

Before considering specific provisions of the Bill of Rights, it would be well to distinguish those rights guaranteed against only the national government from those protected against both the national and state governments.

Although it doesn't say so, the Bill of Rights (Amendments One through Ten) was adopted to protect individuals only from the arbitrary power of the national government. The Civil War changed all that. Contemplating the potential menace presented by white-dominated southern states to the rights of newly freed blacks, a northern-controlled Congress proposed the Fourteenth Amendment to limit the powers of all state governments—north or south—to abuse any individual citizens— white or black. The words of that amendment were broad and sweeping: "No State shall . . . deprive any person of life, liberty, or property, without due process of law . . ." What, precisely, did these words mean?

Not much, for quite a while. The *Slaughter House Cases* of 1873 declined to interpret the Fourteenth Amendment as aiding the individual against the state governments.[1] Not until 1925 did the Supreme Court, in *Gitlow* v. *New York,* hold that the "due process" clause protected at least part of the First Amendment (freedom of speech) against interference by the state governments as well as by the national government.[2] Since that decision, many other cases have produced Court opinions placing more and more of the rights in the first nine amendments under protection against state as well as national threat. The Supreme Court, in effect, has used the due process provision of the Fourteenth Amendment to incorporate most of the Bill of Rights into a broad barricade against state, as well as national, power.

But the justices on the Court have disagreed on how to determine which rights are protected by the Fourteenth Amendment against the states and which are not. Clearly, any guideline establishes a double standard of superior and inferior rights. Some justices, notably the late Hugo Black, would abolish that double standard altogether and apply the whole Bill of Rights to the states. Most have adhered to the rule of Justice Cardozo, who said in *Palko* v. *Connecticut*[3] that any provision in the Bill of Rights that was essential to "a scheme of ordered liberty" limited all governments, state as well as national.

The *Palko* rule is obviously a subjective one, and some justices who endorse it have held several provisions of the Bill of Rights to be necessary to ordered liberty which Cardozo, who devised the doctrine, thought not to be. In any event, the Court has now made the rights in Amendments One, Four, most of Five and Six, Eight, and possibly Nine applicable to the states as well as the national government.

1 16 Wall. 36 (1873).
2 268 U.S. 652 (1925).
3 302 U.S. 319 (1937).

THE SEPARATION OF
RELIGION AND POLITICS

Religion has permeated nearly every aspect of American life. It has influenced our literature, music, art, and recreational activities. Among twelve leading nations the U.S. ranks highest in belief in God and a life after death.[4] For more than a decade, over 40 percent of our people have attended a religious service each week.[5] Even without an established church such as is found in many other countries, the United States may be one of the most religious nations in the world. The young "Jesus people" are the offspring of a strong tradition.

Freedom from Religion:
The "Establishment" Clause

In view of its pervasive influence, it is not surprising that religion has exerted a strong impact upon our government. Thirty-seven states have "blue laws" which require the closing of business establishments on Sundays, the armed forces employ chaplains, and legislative bodies throughout the nation begin each day's session with prayer. Even our official currency affirms that "In God We Trust," although the behavior of many citizens indicates a stronger belief in the money than in the motto.

It is more difficult to assess the likely future of religion as a factor in American politics. The election of John F. Kennedy as our first Catholic president in 1960 may signal either an increase in tolerance or a diminished importance attached by voters to religious matters. Such a decline may be inferred from the fact that church attendance has dropped by 7 percent since 1958 and by 15 percent among adults between twenty-one and twenty-nine years of age. On the other hand, political issues continue to surface, such as abortion or aid to Israel, which have unmistakable religious overtones. Richard Nixon, a perceptive interpreter of public opinion, has been the first President to hold religious services in the White House.

The secular state   Yet American government is commanded by the Constitution to remain neutral on religious issues. Although some examples above indicate official endorsement of theological principles, they have either been upheld by the courts on nonreligious grounds, as in the Sunday-closing laws,[6] or have not yet produced cases forcing the Supreme Court to rule on their constitutionality. It can be argued,

---

4 George Gallup, *Los Angeles Times*, Dec. 28, 1968, p. 19. Note that 98 percent of the people said they believe in God, up 4 percent since 1948, and 73 percent in life after death, up 5 percent.
5 *Los Angeles Times*, March 20, 1972, p. 9.
6 See, especially, *Gallagher* v. *Crown Kosher Super Market of Massachusetts*, 366 U.S. 617. Supreme Court decisions are usually documented this way. "U.S." refers to *United States Reports*, the official volumes containing the full text of Court opinions. The first number indicates the volume and the last the page on which the case begins.

Figure 10   American Religious Preferences[1]

Denomination	Percentage of Population	Denomination	Percentage of Population
Protestant	66.2	Roman Catholic	25.7
Baptist	19.7	Jewish	3.2[2]
Methodist	14.0	Other religions	1.3
Lutheran	7.1	No religion	2.7
Presbyterian	5.6	Not reported	0.9
Others	19.8		

[1]Based upon 1957 responses to the only government census of religious preference.
[2]About 40 percent of all American Jews live in New York City where they constitute about one fourth of the population.
Source: "American Religious Preferences" from *This U.S.A.* by Ben J. Wattenberg with Richard M. Scammon. Copyright © 1965 by Ben J. Wattenberg. Reprinted by permission of Doubleday & Company, Inc. and A.D. Peters & Co.

however, that the framers of the Constitution wished to create a political system which was essentially secular, or nonreligious in nature.

In the first place, the Constitution makes no mention of a Supreme Being. Secondly, Article VI clearly stipulates that "no religious Test shall ever be required as Qualification to any Office or public Trust under the United States." Finally, the First Amendment opens with the words "Congress shall make no law respecting an establishment of religion . . ."

The phrasing of this "establishment" clause is significant. It does not simply prohibit an established church—an officially favored one receiving tax support—but goes further to ban legal aid for all churches and for religion in general. There are two major reasons for this categorical rejection of government assistance. Most important is that European history was marred by innumerable and tragic wars fought over what help government was to give, and to whom, in support of religious principles. This our American forebears wished to avoid. A second reason for the insistence upon government neutrality in religious matters was the antipathy which some of our early leaders felt toward the organized churches of the day.

In addition to the constitutional restrictions, religious influence in America is partially neutralized by the immense diversity of beliefs. The expression of almost any religious sentiment is bound to antagonize some people holding contrary views, and candidates for office are well advised to remember that more than sixty separate church denominations have memberships in excess of 50,000 people in the United States.

Confusion on the Court   The Supreme Court of the United States, as final arbiter of what government can and cannot do, has been faced with many hard decisions regarding how much encouragement laws can give to organized religion without violating the First Amendment's prohibition of religious "establishment." Upon occasion it has ruled that this merely prevents some legal preference for one religion over another. But the difficulty the judges confront is indicated by their frequent inability to agree with one another. In 1947, in the case of *Everson* v. *Board of Education of Ewing Township, N.J.,*[7] the Court upheld by a 5–4 vote the constitutionality of a school district providing bus transportation for pupils attending parochial schools as well as for those attending public schools. In 1968, a six-member majority approved a New York law supplying textbooks for parochial school children. In this case, *Board of Education* v. *Allen,* the Court distinguished state aid primarily for the benefit of students from that which constitutes direct assistance to religion.[8] Three years later federal aid to construct church-owned classrooms not used for religious instruction was approved 5–4 but state subsidies for teachers' salaries in church schools was invalidated 8–1. Seven justices sustained the constitutionality of property tax exemptions for church property in 1968.[9]

In *Zorach* v. *Clauson,* a 6–3 decision in 1952, the Court held that public school students could be released part of the regular school day for the purpose of receiving religious instruction in the church or synagogue of their choice.[10] Only four years earlier the Court ruled that released-time programs for religious purposes were a violation of the "establishment" clause if the religious instruction took place on public school property.[11] It is extremely doubtful that the Supreme Court has heard its last case regarding the "establishment" clause. President Nixon has pledged himself to seek greater tax support for parochial schools than ever before proposed.

Prayer in the schools   The most controversial recent cases involving government aid to religion have dealt with religious observances conducted as a part of the daily routine in public schools. The leading case is *Engel* v. *Vitale* in which the Supreme Court decided that a nondenominational prayer written by the New York State Board of Regents and recited in every public school classroom was unconstitutional—even though no student was required to join in saying the prayer. Justice Hugo Black, who wrote the majority opinion, believed that the prayer constituted a kind of state-endorsed religious activity prohibited by the "establishment" clause of the First Amendment. It is not "the business of government," he wrote, "to compose official prayers."[12] Standing alone, Justice Potter Stewart wrote a dissenting opinion stating that he saw nothing unconstitutional in "letting those who want to say a prayer to say it."[13]

7 330 U.S. 1.
8 392 U.S. 236.
9 *Tilton* v. *Richardson,* 403 U.S. 672 (1971), *Lemon* v. *Kurtzman,* 403 U.S. 602 (1971), and *Walz* v. *Tax Commission of City of New York,* 397 U.S. 664 (1970).
10 343 U.S. 306.
11 *Illinois ex rel McCollum* v. *Board of Education,* 333 U.S. 203.
12 370 U.S. 425. The case illustrates our religious diversity, as it was brought by five parents—two Jews, a Unitarian, a member of the Ethical Culture Society, and a nonbeliever.
13 370 U.S. 445. The prayer itself was quite short: "Almighty God, we acknowledge our dependence upon Thee, and we beg Thy blessings upon us, our parents, our teachers, and our country."

Only a handful of decisions in our entire history have been met with attacks as bitter as those which assaulted the majority opinion in the *Engel* case. Even though Justice Black took great pains to point out that he saw nothing objectionable in *studying* religion, or in nondevotional or nonworship activities such as singing Christmas carols, over a hundred congressmen introduced constitutional amendments specifically to permit prayer in the public schools.

The following year, 1963, the Supreme Court handed down two more decisions consistent with its ruling in *Engel.* In one, *Abington School District* v. *Schempp,* a Pennsylvania law requiring portions of the King James Version of the Bible to be read in all public schools each` morning was declared unconstitutional, and in the other, *Murray* v. *Curlett,*[14] a Maryland law authorizing classroom use of the Lord's Prayer met the same fate. Such laws established not merely religion, but the Christian religion. While outraged criticism followed the *Engel* decision, the *Schempp* and *Murray* decisions were defied. An estimated 30 percent of all public schools had required religious observances prior to 1962 and as late as 1966 nearly 13 percent were continuing them in deliberate, determined disobedience of the supreme law of the land.[15]

Freedom of Religion: The·"Free Exercise" Clause

In addition to prohibiting the establishment of religion, the First Amendment also contains another clause guaranteeing "the free exercise thereof." The "establishment" and "free exercise" clauses together appear to guarantee government neutrality, neither assisting or encouraging religion, on the one hand, nor punishing or preventing it, on the other.

Yet, just as the "establishment" clause is not absolute, so also the "free exercise" clause has exceptions. Here we approach a vital but lamentable principle of our human existence: Society is so complex and our values so often contradictory that there is no freedom guaranteed in the Constitution which can be absolute—all have permissible limitations.

The limits of "free exercise"   In 1878 the Supreme Court placed some limits on freedom of religion by upholding a law prohibiting polygamy in what was then the territory of Utah, even though the Mormon religion at that time endorsed plural marriages.[16] Similarly, there seems little doubt that states can prohibit practices such as human torture or sacrifice or the use of drugs such as LSD, even though they may be sanctioned by religious groups. In a 1905 case, a Massachusetts law compelling vaccinations against smallpox was upheld, regardless of

14 The two cases were decided together. 374 U.S. 203.
15 Prof. Richard B. Dierenfield's figures, in Charles H. Sheldon, ed., *The Supreme Court: Politicians in Robes* (Beverly Hills, Calif.: Glencoe Press, 1970), p. 84.
16 *Reynolds* v. *U.S.,* 98 U.S. 145.

contrary religious convictions.[17] Most of these instances involved the use of the so-called *police power* of the states (a substantial portion of the powers reserved by the Tenth Amendment) to protect the health, safety, morals, and welfare of the people. Unfortunately, sometimes such legitimate authority runs counter to religious freedom for a portion of the population and a conflict arises between two parts of the Constitution. Under such circumstances judges, forced to decide which of the conflicting provisions shall prevail, really earn their money.

The extent of "free exercise"   While freedom of religion is not absolute, the Supreme Court has guaranteed it wide latitude. A relatively small church, the Jehovah's Witnesses, has brought about thirty cases to the Supreme Court and as a result has produced official recognition of the rights to distribute religious literature without a permit, to expound religious views even to people offended by them, to sell religious tracts without payment of the license fees often required by municipalities, and to refuse to salute the flag on grounds of religious doctrine.[18] A 1972 decision upheld the right of members of the Amish church to prohibit their children from attending high school.[19] These cases produced sharp disagreement among Supreme Court justices and in a few instances represent reversals of previous decisions. Like all human beings, judges change their minds. When they do, the authoritative meaning of constitutional provisions changes also.

Religion, Conscience, and the Draft

No issue has troubled young Americans of this generation more than the undeclared war in southeast Asia, especially if they were about to be drafted into the army fighting it. Of the 22.7 million men registered under selective service regulations in 1970, some ten thousand conscientious objectors, more than three times the number in 1965, were working on civilian projects required by the selective service system, and another 28,000 had been classified as available for such work.[20] Adding to the significance of these numbers is the fact that as many as 30,000 draft-age men had fled to Canada and other countries to escape induction and that 450 went to federal penitentiaries in violation of selective service laws in 1970 compared to only 173 in 1965.[21] More men applied for conscientious objector classification in 1970 than in either World War I or World War II.

Conscientious objection   American draft laws, the first of which was enacted during the Civil War, have always been opposed by

---

17 *Jacobson* v. *Massachusetts,* 197 U.S. 25.
18 *Lovell* v. *Griffin,* 303 U.S. 444 (1938); *Cantwell* v. *Connecticut* 310 U.S., 296 (1940); *Murdock* v. *Pennsylvania,* 319 U.S. 105 (1943); *West Virginia State Board of Education* v. *Barnette,* 319 U.S. 624 (1943).
19 *Wisconsin* v. *Yoder,* 92 S.Ct. 1526 (1972).
20 U.S. Bureau of the Census, *Statistical Abstract of the United States: 1971,* p. 257.
21 Ibid., p. 151. See the estimate of columnist Stewart Alsop, *Newsweek,* July 20, 1970, p. 88.

some citizens on the ground that they represent the sort of tyranny which many immigrants came to this country to escape. Yet these laws have recognized that no person shall be compelled to serve in the armed forces if "by reason of religious training and belief [he is] conscientiously opposed to participation in war in any form." Such training and belief has been most characteristic of the so-called peace churches, *i.e.*, the Church of the Brethren, Friends (Quakers), Jehovah's Witnesses, and a great many Methodist congregations, although it has been claimed by members of many other denominations as well. If the selective service system believes "c.o." claims to be valid, it compels alternative nonmilitary service in the armed forces, or civilian work of a humanitarian nature. In every war, some people have been imprisoned because they have denied the legitimacy of any sort of government-compelled service at all.

The courts and the "c.o."   The courts have been forced to consider four vital constitutional issues regarding the conscientious objector: (1) Is exemption from military combat service on grounds of religious belief an unconstitutional violation of the "establishment" clause prohibiting aid to religion? (2) Is denial of draft exemption because a man's objection is moral, but not religious, a violation of the "free exercise" clause? (3) What is religion? (4) Is one, on either religious or moral grounds, entitled to draft exemption if he opposes specific wars (*e.g.*, Vietnam), but not all war?

Three decisions have dispelled considerable uncertainty. In the 1965 *Draft Act Cases,* often cited as *United States* v. *Seeger,*[22] the nation's highest court unanimously ruled that religious belief might include not only a belief in a Supreme Being or God, but also a belief which is equal to it in genuine importance in the lives of those who hold it. Perhaps an even more important decision, extending this ruling, was handed down in 1970. Here the court decided that a sincere opposition to war based entirely on philosophic, moral, and sociological grounds warranted "c.o." classification, because of the "establishment" clause, just as much as opposition rooted in more traditional religious doctrine.[23] Finally, selective opposition to particular wars was declared legally invalid in 1971.[24]

FREEDOM OF SPEECH, PRESS, ASSEMBLY, AND PETITION

The constitutionally guaranteed freedoms of speech, press, assembly, and petition are closely related, yet each has distinguishing characteristics. Freedom of speech has sometimes been suppressed on the grounds that it might produce violence, but some nonverbal acts have been protected as "symbolic" speech. Freedom of the press is guaranteed

22 380 U.S. 163.
23 *Welsh* v. *U.S.,* 398 U.S. 333.
24 *Gillette* v. *U.S.,* 401 U.S. 437 (1971).

to a great degree by preventing censorship, although motion pictures, theoretically, have not been freed from that control. Freedom of assembly, in certain circumstances, cannot occur without prior permission; yet such permission cannot be denied arbitrarily nor in a discriminatory fashion. Freedom of petition, entailing the right to request or protest government action, is increasingly exercised by pressure group lobbyists.

Freedom of Speech

Private citizens can restrict speech in whatever way they wish in their own homes, offices, and factories. The First Amendment is a protection against government interference. Even here, however, speech has consequences affecting other people, and its freedom is not unlimited.

Restrictions on free speech   Justice Oliver Wendell Holmes, a phrasemaker who had few peers, once asserted that no man has the right to shout "fire" falsely in a crowded theater. In other words, one man's freedom of speech should not endanger another man's safety. In the same vein, he once remarked that "your right to swing your arms ends where my nose begins."

Yet it is easier to devise clever epigrams than it is to apply the First Amendment to situations in which impassioned speakers hurl inflammatory charges at angry crowds. Should violence erupt, who is at fault? The person employing his freedom of speech to provoke and denounce, sometimes without justification? Or the listeners, whose anger may flow only from their own hotheaded intolerance? The answers have not been easy, for we are again confronted with a constitutional contradiction: an individual right (Amendment One) *vs.* the authority of the state to prevent riots (implicit in Amendment Ten). Sometimes, constitutional *law* and public *order* may thus conflict.

Verbal attacks upon the government pose a more serious problem than those upon private individuals. Should those who would destroy our freedoms be entitled to use them for that purpose? Should freedom of speech be protected for those who use it to urge the overthrow of the government? Again there is a clash of principles—this time between freedom of expression and the legitimate power of national self-preservation. In 1798 Congress passed the Alien and Sedition Acts, the latter of which made it a crime, in effect, to criticize public officials. During World War I, it enacted Espionage and Sedition Acts which prohibited virtually any statement which was designed to interfere with military success. In 1940, moreover, the Smith Act made teaching or advocating the violent overthrow of the government illegal, declared the Communist Party to be committed to that very purpose, and made joining it with knowledge of that aim to be illegal also. Ten years later, the McCarran, or Internal Security Act of 1950, was passed over President Truman's veto. It created a Subversive Activities Control Board to designate organizations as subversive if it found them to be loyal to a foreign government or advocating the violent overthrow of our own. Membership in such groups was required to be registered with the Board each year. Some believe these laws betray a surprising fear that the advantages of our form of government are so few that appeals for its forceful destruction might enlist many eager recruits. Others consider these laws vital to national security in times of great peril. Whatever the truth, the application of such statutes has revealed the difficulty of balancing freedom of expression and government power.

Rights reclaimed   In resolving the dilemmas presented by freedom of speech, the Supreme Court has drawn some very fine lines—some would say nearly invisible ones—in distinguishing speech that is constitutionally protected from that which is not. In 1942 it held that calling a policeman a "damned Fascist," and "God-damned rack-eteer" was so likely to invite violence as to lose its First Amendment protection.[25] Yet seven years later, by the narrowest of margins, it reversed a breach of the peace conviction of a speaker who denounced Jews and other minorities in highly offensive terms. Should violence break out, as it did in the latter situation, the Court apparently believed that the violent ones, and not the speaker, should be punished.[26] Another significant case involved a speaker who denounced the President and the mayor of Syracuse, New York, as "bums," and in addition urged that Negroes should "rise up in arms and fight" for equal rights. By a 5–3 vote, the Court upheld the "disorderly conduct" conviction of the Syracuse orator.[27] But it reversed the "breach of the peace" conviction against 187 blacks who marched to the South Carolina state capital carrying banners proclaiming "Down with Segregation," and chanting "We Shall Not Be Moved." Only Justice Clark dissented.[28]

Most cases involving free speech *vs.* public order have resulted from state and local prosecutions. But a new element was added in 1968 when Congress first entered the riot-control business. It passed legislation which made it a national crime to cross state boundaries for the purpose of inciting a riot, and under which demonstration leaders at the 1968 Democratic national convention were convicted.

The Supreme Court first passed on the constitutionality of subversion laws in 1919, in *Schenck* v. *U.S.*,[29] in which the "clear and present danger" doctrine was developed. The issue involved a man convicted of urging draft evasion during World War I. In an opinion written by Justice Holmes, the court based its decision on three assump-

25 *Chaplinski* v. *New Hampshire,* 315 U.S. 568. "Resort to epithets or personal abuse," the Court said, "is not in any proper sense communication of information or opinion safe-guarded by the Constitution."
26 *Terminiello* v. *Chicago,* 337 U.S. 1. Justice Douglas, for the Court majority, observed that ". . . A function of free speech . . . is to invite dispute. It may indeed best serve its high purpose when it induces a condition of unrest, creates dissatisfaction with conditions as they are (and) strike(s) at prejudices and preconceptions."
27 *Feiner* v. *New York,* 340 U.S. 315 (1951).
28 *Edwards* v. *South Carolina,* 372 U.S. 229 (1963). The dissenting opinion observed that "to say that the police may not intervene until the riot has occurred is like keeping out the doctor until the patient dies."
29 249 U.S. 47. Schenck's conviction was upheld.

tions: (1) The Constitution guarantees freedom of expression but not freedom of action; (2) expression is often designed to provoke action; (3) when expression creates "a clear and present danger" that illegal action will occur, it loses its constitutional protection. This "clear and present danger" doctrine, while not consistently followed by the Court, has influenced almost all its decisions in the last half century in cases involving verbal attacks upon the government or its policies. Under this Court standard, freedom of expression is protected by the First Amendment up to that point when it results in an obvious (clear) and immediate (present) threat of "substantive evil" (illegal action) that the state has the power to prohibit.

Although criticized by those who believe that freedom of speech and press are absolute rights never to be infringed, this "clear and present danger" test, in actual application, has protected a wider area of expression than almost any of the alternative standards that have been suggested from time to time in other cases. In *Gitlow* v. *New York*,[30] for example, the Court utilized what has come to be known as the "bad tendency" (or "dangerous tendency") doctrine. Over the dissents of Justices Holmes and Brandeis, this held that free expression lost its constitutional protection if it created a tendency toward illegal acts.

The necessity of drawing the delicate line between personal freedom and state power was presented again in 1950 by the prosecution of the eleven top leaders of the Communist Party under the Smith Act provision prohibiting advocacy of violent revolution. The Supreme Court majority, in *Dennis* v. *U.S.*,[31] upheld the conviction of these defendants under a diluted version of the "clear and present danger" test, sometimes called the "grave and probable" doctrine. This made it sufficient cause to limit free expression if it created a probable danger of some grave evil. In the following years, more than seventy other Communists were convicted under the Smith Act, but in 1957 such prosecutions ceased when the Supreme Court held in *Yates* v. *U.S.*[32] that the First Amendment protected all political expression except that which urges "one to *do* something . . . rather than merely to *believe* in something." This emphasis upon incitement to action rather than abstract advocacy moves the Court closer to the "clear and present danger" test as originally propounded by Holmes.

Just as the *Yates* case defused the Smith Act as a weapon for jailing Communists or other alleged subversives, so the Internal Security Act of 1950 was rendered largely useless when the Court held that its ultimate registration requirement compels people to testify against themselves in violation of the Fifth Amendment.[33] Since the old 1798 Sedition Act was enforced for only two years, and the World War I legislation is

30 268 U.S. 652 (1925).
31 341 U.S. 494.
32 354 U.S. 298.
33 *Albertson* v. *Subversive Activities Control Board,* 382 U.S. 70 (1965). This constitutional provision is examined in greater detail in the next chapter. The Internal Security (or McCarran) Act is also known as the Subversive Activities Control Act.

operative only in time of declared war, no significant congressional legislation designed to suppress subversive propaganda is now being enforced.

This does not mean that the government is helpless; it can still prosecute those who cross state lines to incite riots, or those who bomb banks, derail troop trains, dodge the draft, sabotage weapon production, spy, and engage in other overt acts of rebellion. It does mean that the Supreme Court in many instances has defended the First Amendment from abuse by the other two branches and, at least partially, has reclaimed for all Americans some of the rights which are too quickly threatened by paranoid patriots who would sacrifice freedom under the guise of protecting it.

Symbolic speech   Whereas antiriot or antisubversion laws tend to restrict freedom of speech, the courts have recently accepted a doctrine which tends to expand it. This is the concept that silent, nonverbal communication can be used as a vehicle for the transmission of ideas in a sort of symbolic speech protected by the First Amendment.

The idea of symbolic speech has been used in a number of relatively minor cases, such as those in which California courts have held that nude dancers in public bars are engaged in a kind of freedom of expression which exempts them from prosecutions for lewd conduct. In a case involving not only civil rights, but more specifically student rights as well, the Supreme Court held in *Tinker* v. *Des Moines* that the wearing of black arm bands to class as a gesture of antiwar sentiment is protected by the First Amendment even in the face of prohibitive action by school authorities. This 1969 decision[34] tended, in some slight degree, to offset a decision one year earlier that the public burning of a draft card was not a constitutionally permissible exercise of freedom of expression.[35] The extent of constitutionally protected symbolism is still largely undetermined.

Freedom of the Press

From a practical point of view, it is difficult to censor what is said, verbally, in advance of its utterance. Yet this is a distinct possibility with respect to the written word. The constitutional meaning of freedom of the press, therefore, has been clarified to a substantial degree by the case of *Near* v. *Minnesota*,[36] which ruled that censorship before publication, or what is called "prior restraint," is normally unconstitutional, and can be undertaken only to prevent revelations endangering national security such as the description of future troop movements. Possible abuse of this press freedom can be prevented, the court argued, because publishers can be sued or perhaps prosecuted *after* publication, for instance for libel or obscenity.

34 *Tinker* v. *Des Moines Independent Community School District,* 393 U.S. 503.
35 *United States* v. *O'Brien,* 391 U.S. 367.
36 283 U.S. 697 (1931).

The prohibition of "prior restraint" of the press was further strengthened by the 1971 Pentagon Papers case involving a secret history of the Vietnam War. Here, the Court ruled 6–3 that the government could not suppress the publication of documents provided to newspapers by Daniel Ellsberg. But some observers believe that freedom of the press was weakened in 1972 by a 5–4 decision requiring journalists to divulge confidential news sources when questioned by grand juries. All news reporters—for the press, radio, and television—are further frustrated by the excessive application of "secret" classifications to official documents, the closed sessions of many legislative committees, and other government actions carried on privately. Freedom of the press is of little value without free access to significant information.

The movies go to court In 1952 the Supreme Court expanded the constitutional guarantee of freedom of the press to encompass motion pictures, previously considered entertainment rather than serious communication. It has not, however, extended to them the protection of no "prior restraint." Movies can, therefore, be censored in advance,[37] although only a few states have done so. In addition, the court has refused to permit the banning of films either on the ground that they were "sacrilegious" (treating religion with "contempt, mockery, scorn and ridicule") or because they depict "sexual immorality (adultery, in this case) as desirable."[38] To date, the court has approved of film censors but paradoxically has reversed every act of censorship which has been brought to its attention.

Freedom of the press vs. trial by jury Just as the "free exercise" clause may conflict with the prohibition of the establishment of religion, or freedom of speech may interfere with the power to control domestic violence, so too, freedom of the press may interfere with the right to trial by an impartial jury, guaranteed in Amendment Six. If newspapers, radio, and television inflame readers' emotions and reveal selective information or allegations about a pending trial, it may be impossible to find jurors who can deliberate with calm and open minds and render a verdict based only on evidence disclosed in court.

The English tend to solve this problem by contempt of court actions against the press. Thus far, American courts have tended to nullify the conviction of those found guilty by juries potentially brainwashed by earlier publicity.[39] On the constitutional level, conflicting rights must somehow be compromised; on a practical level we need a press capable of exercising responsible restraint.

Freedom of the press vs. slander and libel: what price a good

---

37 *Times Film Corp.* v. *Chicago,* 365 U.S. 43 (1961). The vote was 5–4.
38 *Burstyn* v. *Wilson* 343 U.S. 495 (1952) and *Kingsley Pictures* v. *Regents of the University of New York,* 360 U.S. 684 (1959). The vindicated film in this case was a screen adaptation of *Lady Chatterley's Lover.*
39 Two major cases in point involve a former aide to the U.S. Senate, *Estes* v. *Texas,* 381 U.S. 532 (1965) and a well-known doctor accused of murdering his pregnant wife, *Sheppard* v. *Maxwell,* 384 U.S. 333 (1966). On this topic, see the discussion by Henry J. Abraham, *Freedom and the Court* (N.Y.: Oxford University Press, Inc., 1967), pp. 127–32.

name? A person's reputation is his most valuable possession. At stake may be his job, his friends, even his family. Slander and libel laws are designed to protect individuals from irresponsible accusations. Slander is an oral, and libel a written, statement which maliciously injures the reputation of another person. Although there are criminal laws prohibiting such statements, they result in few prosecutions; most court cases are brought under state civil codes which permit the person allegedly injured to sue the person who purportedly made the damaging statement for a specified amount of money. This amount may compensate a person for suffering and loss, and may also include punitive damages designed to teach the offender a lesson.

As a general rule, the truth of the alleged statement is an adequate defense for the beleaguered defendant, especially in criminal cases, although there are occasions in which even this will not help him. If, for example, one person charges another with some scandalous action (e.g., "Smith is always half-drunk"), the person so insulted and maligned may collect money, even if he *is* half-drunk, in the absence of any proof that the accusation served any useful purpose or was motivated by anything other than purely personal malice. Correspondingly, a false statement does not necessarily make one vulnerable to a successful libel suit if the statement was made without spite or deliberate deception.

Now, if one is threatened with a slander or libel suit, that fact will surely act as a restraint upon one's freedom of expression. Yet the courts have held that laws in this area do not violate the First Amendment because they were a part of the common law long before that amendment was proposed and would doubtlessly have been prohibited expressly if that had been the intention of those who wrote the Bill of Rights.

There is less danger of being successfully sued for libel if you criticize a public figure than if you make allegations against a generally unknown citizen. Former President Harry Truman is said to have remarked to one complaining about attacks on government officials, "If you can't stand the heat, stay out of the kitchen." The Supreme Court, in effect, has adopted the same logic with respect to libel suits involving public figures in general. This is the essence of the Court's decision in *New York Times* v. *Sullivan*,[40] in which a libel judgement in favor of a Montgomery, Alabama, city official was set aside on the grounds that "erroneous statement is inevitable in free debate" and that discussion of public issues "should be uninhibited, robust, and wide open." In *Associated Press* v. *Walker*[41] the Court expanded this same doctrine to protect those who write of prominent citizens who engage in debate on vital public controversies. A 1971 decision extended the protection against

---

40 376 U.S. 254 (1964).
41 388 U.S. 130 (1967). In another case decided with this one, *Curtis Publishing Co.* v. *Butts,* the Supreme Court upheld a $460,000 libel suit won in a lower court by Butts, athletic director of the University of Georgia, against the *Saturday Evening Post,* a magazine which had accused him of giving pregame information to the University of Alabama football team.

slander suits to a radio station that made unintentionally false charges against a little-known person whose business was the object of a police raid.

All of this does not mean that the Court has declared open season on anyone involved with some matter of public concern. As former Chief Justice Warren observed in the *Walker* case, "Freedom of the press . . . does not include absolute license to destroy lives or careers."

Obscenity: The Uncertain Crime   The reserved powers of the states, guaranteed by the Tenth Amendment, always have been assumed to include the "police power" necessary to protect, among other things, public morality. Thus, the states tended to punish the sale or distribution of sexually explicit books and pictures since early in the last century. In 1873 the national government joined the crusade against obscene materials by banning them from the mails. Although the exact definition of obscenity was rather vague, American courts usually followed the Hicklin obscenity test which hinged upon "whether the tendency of the matter . . . is to deprave and corrupt those whose minds are open to such immoral influences and into whose hands a publication of this sort may fall."

Not until 1957 did the Supreme Court confront the incompatibility of obscenity laws and freedom of expression. Although the case, *Roth* v. *United States*,[42] upheld a conviction for sending obscene materials through the mail, and even though Justice Brennan's majority opinion asserted that "obscenity is not within the area of constitutionally protected speech or press," it had the effect of permitting open distribution of materials previously confined to men's locker rooms or the back alleys of Paris.

It had this effect because first, the *Roth* decision explicitly repudiated the Hicklin doctrine which barred everyone from access to publications which might have an undesirable influence on anyone. Second, it established a new test of obscenity: "whether to the average person, applying contemporary community standards, the dominant theme of the material taken as a whole appeals to prurient interest." Thus obscenity was made a dynamic concept, shaped always by the changing standards recognized by "average" people. "Prurient interests" is defined in such a way as to involve only "lustful thoughts," or "a shameful or morbid interest in nudity, sex or excretion."[43] It in no way includes violence, greed or other indications of immorality.

The permissive society   The *Roth* case was the crack in a censorship wall which has since been widened to an open door. In 1959, for example, the Court held that a book seller could not be convicted unless he knew he was selling an obscene publication,[44] and seven years

---

42 354 U.S. 476 (1957).
43 The definitions are cited and discussed in Eberhard and Phyllis Kronhausen, *Pornography and the Law* (N.Y.: Ballantine Books, Inc., 1959), pp. 147–48.
44 *Smith* v. *California*, 361 U.S. 147.

later, in *Memoirs* v. *Massachusetts*,[45] it was decided that no publication could constitutionally be deemed obscene unless it was "utterly without redeeming social value." The most permissive decision of all came in 1969 in the case of *Stanley* v. *Georgia,* in which the Supreme Court upheld the right of a man to possess admittedly pornographic films in his own home. In 1971, however, a divided Court upheld prohibitions against the mailing or importation[46] of obscene materials.

Only one case has significantly tightened the state's control over obscenity since the Roth decision in 1957. In *Ginzburg* v. *U.S.*,[47] with four judges each filing individual dissents, the Court upheld an obscenity conviction on the grounds that works were *advertised* in a way which appealed to prurient interests, even though the publications themselves were not obscene.

Freedom of Assembly

Freedom of speech and press have generally enjoyed fewer restrictions than freedom of assembly. This is because assembly often entails large crowds and/or such physical demonstrations as marches and picketing. Local governments, therefore, may require permits or licenses for rallies and parades so long as they are granted on an impartial basis under local regulations which prohibit arbitrary administrative discretion. A permit application for a peace march, in other words, must be treated the same as one for an armed forces parade. Either may be denied if a busy highway would have to be closed during a workday rush hour, or either may be granted. But they cannot be treated differently, nor could they be refused on capricious, unreasonable grounds.

The Court also has held that if freedom of assembly is unconstitutionally denied by a licensing agency such as a park department or police commission, the legal remedy is to seek a court order requiring the license rather than assemble without it.[48]

A more difficult problem in this area, and one which divided the Court badly, was posed when thirty-two students from Florida A. & M. University entered the jail grounds in Tallahassee to protest both racial segregation in the prison and the earlier arrest of some fellow students. Police arrested the protesters under a "malicious trespass" law. At issue was whether trespass laws may be applied to restrict assembly on public as well as private property. In a 5–4 vote, the Court held that they could.[49]

Picketing, a particularly important form of assembly in labor disputes, generally has been held to be constitutionally protected if the

45 383 U.S. 413 (1966). The "Memoirs" are those of a "Woman of Pleasure," a book more commonly known as *Fanny Hill.*
46 89 S. Ct. 1243.
47 383 U.S. 463 (1966).
48 *Poulos* v. *New Hampshire,* 345 U.S. 395 (1953).
49 *Adderley* v. *Florida,* 385 U.S. 39 (1966).

picketers do not block the entrances of the institution picketed. The Court has ruled, however, that a shopping center may bar distributors of antiwar leaflets from its premises, but not labor pickets.

Freedom of Petition

The First Amendment right to "petition the Government for a redress of grievances" was designed to guarantee the people some access to government officials, some medium of communication with those in charge. Increasingly, large groups of citizens hire professional lobbyists to contact officials in their behalf, and most recent court cases involving the right to petition have arisen from congressional attempts to regulate lobbying activity.[50] The right to petition guaranteed in the First Amendment is not related to the initiative petitions by which some states permit propositions to be placed on the ballot for approval by the voters.

THE FUNCTIONS OF FREEDOM

It is disturbing that the strong emphasis on freedom of expression found in both the Constitution and many court decisions seems to have relatively little support among the American people. Surveys during the past two decades indicate that about three fourths would not allow groups to organize peaceful antigovernment demonstrations, 60 percent would prohibit speeches against churches or religion, 45 percent would forbid socialists from publishing newspapers, 40 percent would ban peaceful anti-Vietnam war demonstrations, and 36.7 percent believed that "a man oughtn't to be allowed to speak if he doesn't know what he's talking about."[51]

Few Americans know much about the Bill of Rights (21 percent according to a 1945 poll)[52] and even fewer are familiar with the Declaration of Independence (only one person out of fifty signed it in the form of a typed petition in 1970).[53] There seems to have been a failure of political socialization, an inability of families, schools, and other institutions to teach new generations the political values and traditions of the old ones. The importance of freedom of expression clearly requires renewed emphasis.

50 For a good discussion of this subject, see the editor's essay in Robert F. Cushman, ed., *Cases in Civil Liberties* (N.Y.: Appleton-Century-Crofts, 1968), pp. 490–92. This casebook is one of the best, containing condensations of many Supreme Court decisions, along with interesting editorial commentary.
51 Herbert McCloskey, "Consensus and Ideology in American Politics," *American Political Science Review* 58 (June 1964): 367.
52 Robert E. Lane and David O. Sears, *Public Opinion* (Englewood Cliffs, N.J.: Prentice-Hall, Inc., 1964), p. 61.
53 *Los Angeles Times,* July 5, 1970, p. 2. Two called it "Commie junk," one "the work of a raver," another "rubbish," and yet another "meaningless."

Human Dignity: Are Natural Rights Self-Evident?

The Declaration of Independence contends that it is a self-evident truth that governments were created to protect, among other things, the natural right to liberty. The chief trouble arising from this natural rights philosophy is that it cannot be empirically proved; no one can feel or see the rights that are claimed. Yet whether or not there is a natural right to liberty the *theory* of natural rights elevates the individual human being to a position of supreme importance. It assumes that he *has* rights, that the state is supposed to protect them, and that society exists for the purpose of enhancing his dignity, rather than he for the purpose of serving its needs. Indeed, if there were no natural rights of man (and there may not be), we would surely have to invent them if we are to save the individual human being from all the governments, churches, families, corporations, and movements ever ready to sacrifice him to some "greater good."

The characteristic of democracy which most sets it apart from communist or fascist regimes is the belief that there is no greater good than the dignity and nobility of the individual. Love and compassion may lead him to sacrifice himself for other individuals, but his essential integrity and worth must never be bartered away by others in behalf of some abstract class, creed, or flag. Freedom is important, then, because without it the individual is stripped of his basic dignity and subject to the control of those more interested in class consciousness, national honor, the one true faith or racial pride.

The belief in natural rights philosophy may be essential to freedom, just as freedom is necessary to human dignity. But it is a belief that cannot be proved. Like confidence in God's mercy, a belief in man's dignity requires an act of faith.

Social Progress: The Search for Truth

In the last century, the case for individual freedom has relied largely on the value of its social contributions, rather than on its protection of individual rights. This line of reasoning was expressed most influentially by the great English philosopher John Stuart Mill in his long essay, *On Liberty*. Mill defended freedom of expression as necessary to the search for truth on which human progress depends. Through the clash and combination of differing viewpoints, he believed, new insights are possible. Even the expression of bad ideas is socially valuable, he argued, because they stimulate the further improvement of good ones, make the truth easier to ascertain by comparison with them, and by their challenge convert dead dogmas too easily taken for granted into living faiths rationally understood and more vigilantly defended. Moreover, it is often difficult to distinguish truth from falsity, good ideas from bad ones. Socrates and Jesus, perhaps the two most honored figures in the

Western World, were put to death because the authorities—and remarkably enlightened ones at that—believed their ideas to be blasphemous and subversive. Galileo was forced to retract a scientific truth of surpassing importance (the belief that the earth revolves around the sun) in order to escape the same fate. Even the wisest of men occasionally suppress the wrong ideas and would-be censors would do well to heed Mill's reminder that "all silencing of discussion is an assumption of infallibility."

In the century and more since its publication, *On Liberty* has been vindicated many times. Yesterday's "dangerous heresies," such as biological evolution or birth control, have become accepted parts of today's "truth." Freedom is clearly a prerequisite for maximum progress.

Personal Improvement and Intellectual Growth

In a free society, there are many opinions among which men and women are asked to choose. Such choices are often difficult, and require the maximum use of our intellectual capacities. But the very freedom which makes choice necessary, also affords us the practice which makes wise choice possible. Just as a child learns to walk by standing, stepping, and falling, over and over, learning from his mistakes, so we learn to make wise choices by choosing over and over, learning finally from our bad ones.

John Dewey, the famous pragmatist, was primarily an educational philosopher. As such, he was also a leading defender of freedom as essential to personal growth and mental development. "Learning by doing," as his theory was often described, is impossible in a totalitarian society where choice is impossible and one may do only what he is ordered to do. Freedom, on the other hand, exercises the mental muscles.

Varieties of Freedom

This discussion thus far has focused upon but one kind of freedom—the absence of governmental or social restraint. Vital as this is, freedom is too slippery and complex a concept to be confined in so narrow a definition. The truth is that there are several different conditions which various people call "freedom." One, certainly, is the lack of external control just mentioned. Another, not so pertinent to politics, is the absence of compulsive drives, as when one is "free" of nicotine or alcohol. These are essentially negative freedoms; they are freedom *from* something. Equally important is freedom of opportunity—a more positive aspect that involves the freedom to make a choice among two or more realistically available alternatives.

One more point is relevant: One person's freedom limits another's. The freedom to have a party extending until 3:00 A.M. in a crowded apartment building destroys the freedom of other tenants to sleep; the freedom to manufacture or drive a car may restrict the freedom to breathe clean air; the freedom to sell your house to whom you wish (say a white family) limits the freedom of others (say a black family) to buy a house they can afford. Dewey put the matter plainly:

"There is no such thing as the liberty or effective power of an individual, group, or class, except in relation to the liberties, the effective powers, of *other* individuals, groups and classes. . . . (L)iberty is always a *social* question, not an individual one."[54]

The fact that freedoms come in conflict poses society's most difficult dilemma: Whose freedom is to prevail? There is no easy answer or pat formula, but two suggestions may be in order. One is the traditional democratic solution of counting noses: Restrict the freedom of the minority in the interests of the majority. The other, more difficult to apply, is to determine which of the conflicting freedoms is most important. It is a subjective test. Try applying it to the examples cited earlier. In any event, chances are that government will finally decide.

54 John Dewey, *Philosophy of Education* (Totowa, N.J.: Littlefield, Adams Company, 1956), pp. 112–13.

Chapter **4**

The Defendant's Rights
Criminal Justice in America

*Solon, asked how justice could be secured in Athens, replied,
"If those who are not injured feel as indignant as those who
are."*

What happens to the citizen who is arrested? This chapter is
mainly devoted to the procedural rights guaranteed him in Amendments
Four through Eight. But as a preliminary, there is a more general
provision in the Fifth Amendment which is of fundamental significance:
"No person shall . . . be deprived of life, liberty, or property, without
due process of law . . ."

As we have seen, the "due process" clause in the Fourteenth
Amendment has been interpreted to mean that most of the provisions of
the Bill of Rights limit state governments as well as the national government. Yet the fact that the Bill of Rights itself, in Amendment Five, has a
clause almost identical in wording suggests that "due process" has
further meaning. Our whole legal history, however, reveals that few
phrases in the Constitution are so difficult to define.

Its origins lie obscured in the ancient common law of England; as recently as 1952, due process was described by the Supreme
Court in such general terms as "civilized conduct," "a sense of justice,"
and "the community's sense of fair play and decency."[1] The concept of
due process has both substantive and procedural aspects—it limits the
content of laws as well as the procedures by which they are enforced.

---

1 *Rochin* v. *California,* 342 U.S. 165 (1952).

Substantively, laws may not be so vague that no one is sure of their purpose nor so arbitrary and capricious that they cannot be defended on reasonable grounds. Procedurally, the rulers cannot attain their objectives by using just any means they may find convenient against the ruled. In *Rochin* v. *California,* the 1952 case just referred to, the Court dealt with a denial of procedural due process. It decided that morphine, a narcotic, could not be used to convict a drug suspect because it was obtained by pumping his stomach despite his vigorous resistance.

The "due process" clause comes very close, then, to providing constitutional affirmation that we are a government of laws and not of men. Although it is true that laws are made, enforced, and administered by men and women, the authority of these officials is limited by legal and constitutional restrictions. They do not have unlimited power merely because they won an election, wear a badge, or wield a gavel. To put it in theoretical terms, the agents of the law must not be permitted to violate the law; in practical terms, officials must neither use more force than is necessary to perform their duties, nor presume to enlarge those duties. This is what makes us a constitutional democracy.

SUBSTANTIVE SAFEGUARDS IN THE ORIGINAL CONSTITUTION

Although most of the rights that protect the person accused of crime are procedural, to be found in the Bill of Rights, there are also three provisions of the original Constitution that insure substantive rights because they limit what the legislature can do in dealing with crime.

The old adage that "ignorance of the law is no excuse" is obviously not applicable to laws not yet passed. The citizen cannot be expected to behave today in anticipation of what may be declared illegal tomorrow. This elementary logic underlies the prohibition against *ex post facto* laws. Such laws make some action a crime that was not a crime when the action was performed, or make it easier to convict someone of a crime committed previously, or retroactively increase criminal punishment.[2] They are fortunately unconstitutional. Motorists, for example, could not be arrested for driving without seat belts on January 1, if the law requiring them was not passed until January 2. Article I, Section 9 forbids Congress from passing such laws and Article I, Section 10 extends this prohibition to the states.

"Equal justice under law" is one of humanity's highest aspirations and is the motto inscribed on the Supreme Court building in Washington, D.C. A society that has one law for the rich and another for the poor, one for me and another for you, is clearly unjust. The ban on *bills of attainder,* laws which inflict punishment on specific persons or groups without a conviction in court, was meant to prohibit such unequal

2 The leading case in this matter is an old one, *Calder* v. *Bull,* 3 Dallas 386 (1798).

justice. They are specifically forbidden in Article I, Sections 9 and 10. Laws withholding salary from three allegedly subversive government employees and prohibiting Communists from serving as officers of labor unions have been declared unconstitutional bills of attainder even though they were not criminal statutes in the usual sense of that term.[3] The claim that the relocation of Japanese-Americans in World War II concentration camps constituted a bill of attainder (while no action was taken against German-Americans) was not upheld by the courts.

A writ is a court order and a writ of *habeas corpus* is intended to prevent arbitrary imprisonment. The writ, in effect, requires public officials holding a person in custody to either "put up or shut up"—to release him, charge him with some criminal act, or demonstrate in some way why he should be held. If a writ of habeas corpus is issued, the suspect will be released on bail (an amount of money deposited with the court) pending a trial, or held in custody under some specific legal provision.

The Constitution contains no provision relating this writ to the states, but Article I, Section 9 provides that the national government shall not suspend it "unless when in Cases of Rebellion or Invasion the public Safety may require it." Since the Civil War, the writ has been suspended only in Hawaii when martial law (military rule) was invoked during World War II. The Supreme Court, however, has declared this permissible only if the regular civilian courts are unable to function.[4]

PROTECTING THE SUSPECT

The common law required the government to assume persons to be innocent of criminal charges until it had proved them guilty. But this noble ideal needed to be translated into specific day-to-day practices. Some of these protect persons who are simply "suspicious characters"; others protect them should they become actual defendants in a criminal case.

Policing the Police: The Right to Privacy

"A man's house is his castle," says an old English proverb. But if the police are to be given maximum authority to capture criminals it is certain that they will occasionally batter down the castle walls. The two horns of the dilemma, adequate power for the police and reasonable privacy for the people, deserve brief examination.

The thin, blue line   Confronted with a soaring crime rate, society looks more and more to the police as a barricade against the apparent barbarism that seems to threaten it. Certainly, the police are the first line of defense against the criminal hordes, and a thin blue line

3 *U.S.* v. *Lovett,* 328 U.S. 303 (1946) and *U.S.* v. *Brown,* 381 U.S. 437 (1965).
4 *Ex parte Milligan,* 4 Wall 2 (1866) and *Duncan* v. *Kahanamoku,* 327 U.S. 304 (1946) are perhaps the most important judicial interpretations.

they are, expected to enforce the laws yet insulted by cries of "pig" and continuously accused of needless brutality.

The lot of the "cop" appears to be getting worse. Underpaid and often undereducated, his profession is among the most dangerous in the world. In 1968 patrolmen's pay in big cities averaged about $7500 a year, only two-thirds that of union plumbers and far less than they received thirty years earlier relative to those in other occupations. But police salaries rose about 9 percent between 1969 and 1970. Whereas over half of the police recruits in New York City were college graduates in 1940, this proportion had fallen to about 5 percent in less than thirty years and reflected trends in other cities as well.[5]

As police pay and preparation have become comparatively poorer, their jobs have become more difficult. Between 1960 and 1966 the number of law enforcement officers rose about 20 percent, but the crime rate during the same period increased 62 percent.[6] While there has been some dispute about the reliability of official crime statistics, records show a 144 percent increase in the rate of serious crime between 1960 and 1970. Policemen themselves were often the victims: 48 were killed in 1960, 88 in 1964, and 125 in 1969. A 1971 Harris poll showed that more people feared crime in the streets (55 percent) than at any time in six years, even though the annual increase in the rate of crime had dropped from 17 to 7 percent since 1968.

As crime continued to increase, so did its political importance. In 1968 Congress passed a Safe Streets Act establishing a Law Enforcement Assistance Administration (LEAA) to supervise financial grants from the national government to aid in the "war on crime." President Nixon persuaded Congress to pass an Omnibus Crime Control Act in 1970, and by 1972 LEAA grants were more than eleven times larger than in 1969.[7] Increasingly fearful voters turned to law-and-order candidates. In 1971 the mayors of Philadelphia, Detroit, and Minneapolis were former police officials. Many citizens demanded that society stop "coddling crooks," "handcuffing the cops," and even that we "curb the courts" in their leniency toward criminal defendants. As a result of President Nixon's judicial appointments it was clear by 1972 that the courts were getting the message. But there is another side to the story, called privacy.

The Fourth Amendment: protecting the castle   The Constitution does not explicitly mention privacy, but it is a value long enshrined

5 Jerome H. Skolnick, *The Politics of Protest:* A report to the National Commission on the Causes and Prevention of Violence (N.Y.: Clarion Books, Simon & Schuster, Inc., 1969), pp. 151–54 and 384. Low educational backgrounds are noted also for new policemen in Berkeley, California, and Washington, D.C.

6 *Report of the National Advisory Commission on Civil Disorders* (N.Y.: Bantam Books, Inc., 1968), p. 269. Sometimes known as the Kerner Commission, the group responsible for this report was appointed by President Johnson to study the causes of big city riots.

7 Fred P. Graham, "A Contemporary History of American Crime," Hugh Davis Graham and Ted Robert Gurr, *Violence in America* (N.Y.: A Signet Book, The New American Library, Inc., 1969), pp. 460–78. See also U.S. Bureau of the Census, *Statistical Abstract of the United States: 1971,* pp. 140 and 143, and *Crime and the Law* (Washington, D.C.: Congressional Quarterly, Inc., 1971), pp, 2, 30, and 54.

Figure 11   The Increase in Crime, 1960-1970

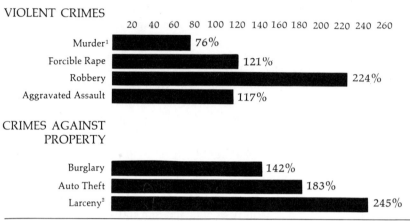

VIOLENT CRIMES

CRIMES AGAINST
PROPERTY

Source: U.S. Bureau of the Census, *Statistical Abstract of the United States: 1971*, p. 140.
[1]Includes non-negligent manslaughter. [2]$50 and over.

in American tradition. Justice Brennan spoke for the Supreme Court
majority when he wrote that "The overriding function of the Fourth
Amendment is to protect personal privacy and dignity against unwarranted intrusion by the State."[8]

But what intrusions are unwarranted? It is a hard question,
and even the Fourth Amendment provides little more than loose guidelines in formulating an answer. "The right of the people," it stipulates,
"to be secure . . . against unreasonable searches and seizures, shall not
be violated, and no Warrants shall issue, but upon probable cause, . . .
and particularly describing the place to be searched, and the persons or
things to be seized."

Clearly, the provision involving warrants, which are court
permits authorizing police action, is designed to limit the procedures
used by law enforcement officers. It is also generally agreed that a search
or seizure (including an arrest) accomplished without a warrant is
unreasonable *except* in one of the following circumstances:

1) The crime is committed in the presence of the policeman
(or person making a "citizen's arrest");

2) There is "probable cause" to believe that a felony (or
major crime) has been committed, and there is no time to get a warrant;

3) There is probable cause to make an arrest and a search of
the person is necessary to seize weapons which might endanger the
arresting officer or to prevent the destruction of evidence.

On many occasions, these rules are easy enough to apply. If
a patrolman hears a gun shot from inside an apartment followed by a
bloodcurdling scream, most reasonable men would admit he has probable cause to believe a crime has been committed and that it would be

8 *Schmerber* v. *California*, 384 U.S. 757 (1966).

folly to prohibit his immediate entry into the building—warrant or not. Yet there are borderline cases in which decisions about what is reasonable, about what constitutes probable cause to suspect crime, would confound the wisest of judges, let alone the policemen who must make instantaneous choices in an atmosphere of perilous excitement. If the officer decides there is no probable cause, a criminal may escape; if he decides there is, a court may disagree and release the suspect.

Three Supreme Court cases decided in 1968 indicate some of the complexities involved. In the major one, *Terry* v. *Ohio*,[9] police "stop and frisk" procedures were upheld with respect to a suspect whose behavior indicated he might be about to hold up a store. The detective "patted down" the outside of the suspect's clothes, felt a revolver, removed it, and arrested him for carrying a concealed weapon. Similarly, the Court approved another frisking without a warrant when a policeman discovered burglar tools on a suspect who was tiptoeing down an apartment hall and began to run when a door was slammed. These cases indicate Court approval of at least modified searches when there was enough cause to suspect criminal activity, although no reasonable or probable grounds for arrest. Yet the Court reversed a conviction on the grounds that the mere fact that the defendant had talked to known drug addicts did not justify his being searched (successfully) for narcotics.[10]

Most arrests take place without a warrant,[11] although this part of the Bill of Rights now limits state and local officers as well as the national government.[12] Moreover, an "exclusionary rule" has been propounded which prohibits materials unconstitutionally seized from being used as evidence in criminal court prosecutions.[13] No warrant is needed for a search of an automobile or other moving vehicle if there is probable cause for an arrest,[14] but even when there are sufficient grounds for an arrest without a warrant inside a house, the police must confine their search to the suspect and the area within his reach. Warrants must usually specify items to be seized, although officers entering a home with a warrant to search for one object (for example, forged checks) may seize something else (draft cards belonging to others), but only if possession of the latter is itself a crime.[15] The implication for drug or marijuana users is clear and ominous.

Finally, it is well to remember that police entry into a private dwelling, even without a warrant, is permissible if it can be justified in terms of "practical considerations of everyday life."[16] Loud noises or

9 392 U.S. 1 (1968).
10 The cases were *Peters* v. *New York*, involving burglary, and *Sibron* v. *New York*, narcotics. 20 L. Ed. 2d 917 (1968).
11 Paul W. Tappan, *Crime, Justice and Correction* (N.Y.: McGraw-Hill Book Company, 1960), p. 329.
12 *Wolf* v. *Colorado*, 338 U.S. 25 (1949), and *Mapp* v. *Ohio*, 367 U.S. 643 (1961).
13 *Weeks* v. *U.S.*, 232 U.S. 383 (1914) and *Mapp*, loc. cit.
14 *Carroll* v. *U.S.*, 267 U.S. 132 (1925).
15 *Harris* v. *U.S.*, 331 U.S. 145 (1947).
16 In this connection, see *Johnson* v. *U.S.*, 333 U.S. 10 (1948) and, more importantly, *Brinegar* v. *U.S.*, 338 U.S. 160 (1949).

suspicious smells emanating from a late night party, for example, are probably sufficient to justify such action. With respect to general criminal investigation in Washington, D.C., and suspected drug offenses throughout the nation, Congress has authorized the issuance of "no knock" warrants which permit police to enter a building without prior warning if they believe evidence would otherwise be destroyed or personal safety endangered.

Taking the Fifth: self-incrimination   Closely related to the Fourth Amendment, is a provision in Amendment Five which specifies that "No person . . . shall be compelled in any criminal case to be a witness against himself . . ." This protection against compulsory self-incrimination has become one of the best known of our constitutional rights, and one may "take the Fifth" in refusing to answer any questions about oneself whether they are posed by policemen, prosecuting attorneys, legislative committees, or any other government officials. An exception in which persons *may* be compelled to testify about their own activities occurs when they are offered immunity from prosecution involving related criminal behavior.

Police brutality: the "third degree"   Although a refusal to reveal facts about one self is obviously a protection of privacy, it may also jeopardize one's safety while being questioned by police. A clear purpose of the Fifth Amendment is to prevent law enforcement officers from extracting confessions by force, the so-called "third degree," yet such techniques seem to persist in the privacy of a few police station back rooms in spite of the constitutional prohibition. Forced confessions once involved physical torture, replaced in many instances with psychological pressures including the loss of sleep, deprivation of tobacco, use of bright lights, and promises of leniency if the suspect confesses. Police training manuals have also advised the use of such deception as false claims that an alleged accomplice had confessed or that nonexistent evidence has been obtained.[17]

Pretrial procedure   The usual procedure in an arrest varies somewhat from state to state but it always entails *detention* by an officer, often only for the purpose of asking questions.[18] Next, assuming the answers are unsatisfactory to the policeman, the suspect is *arrested* and transported to the police station. There one is *booked,* with name recorded, and thus saddled with a "police record." Within a certain period after arrest and booking, averaging from forty-eight to seventy-two hours, the suspect is brought before a magistrate, or judge, for a *preliminary examination.* During the period between the booking and examination most police questioning takes place, and "as many as 40 percent of those arrested are released without being charged before a

17 Fred E. Inbau and John E. Reid, *Criminal Interrogation and Confessions* (Baltimore: The Williams & Wilkins Co., 1962), p. 28.
18 Questionable police practices sometimes occur at this point. See Diane Schroerluke, *Police Personnel Complaints and Redress Remedies* (Berkeley, Calif.: American Civil Liberties Union, Berkeley-Albany Chapter, 1970). Mimeographed.

magistrate.[19] Finally, one may be *arraigned* and ordered to stand trial either through a complaint from a private citizen, the police, or the prosecuting attorney, or else through action of a grand jury.

In the long process described above, the police have viewed the opportunity to obtain pretrial confessions as essential to effective crime control. In defense of suspect questioning, they have asserted that about 80 percent of all felony convictions result largely from confessions.[20] Then what legal guarantees does the suspect have in protecting himself against attempts to extract confessions? The answer lies in a series of recent court decisions regarding the right of the suspect to remain silent.

The Supreme Court held in 1964 that the Fifth Amendment's prohibition of forced self-incrimination applies to both state and national government.[21] Most significantly, in *Miranda* v. *Arizona*,[22] it was decreed that any confession obtained was inadmissible evidence unless the suspect was first informed of his constitutional rights to remain silent and to obtain legal counsel. The *Miranda* decision has been much criticized. The case against the right to refuse to testify against oneself is that it tends to protect the guilty and restricts the police too severely. The argument in its defense is not only that it protects the individual from invasion of privacy and painful police coercion, but also that it encourages difficult and detailed police investigation. An Indian policeman put it well when he said "It is far pleasanter to sit comfortably in the shade rubbing red pepper in some poor devil's eyes than to go about in the sun hunting up evidence."[23] But perhaps the strongest argument for the right to remain silent is that it helps to prevent the conviction of innocent people. In 1964, in New York City alone, three men confessed to murders, under police questioning, of which they were later proved innocent.[24]

The defense of the Fifth Amendment is not meant to suggest that policemen are clever fiends intent upon sending innocent people to jail. On the contrary, they are members of understaffed institutions expected to solve more crimes than they can adequately investigate. Both their prestige and potential for promotion are dependent on producing, as nearly as possible, a probable culprit for every crime. Under these circumstances, they try to get the quickest confession from the most probable suspect. The people need protection from the police not because they are evil but because they are—like all officials to whom we grant vast powers—human.

Technological tyrants   The framers of the Constitution no

19 Ed Cray, *The Big Blue Line* (N.Y.: Coward-McCann, Inc., 1957), p. 73, and A. C. Germann, Frank D. Day, and Robert R. J. Gallati, *Introduction to Law Enforcement* (Springfield, Ill.: Charles C Thomas, Publisher, 1962), pp. 164–65.
20 Cray, op. cit., p. 70 and note 8, p. 231.
21 *Malloy* v. *Hogan*, 378 U.S. 1.
22 384 U.S. 436 (1966).
23 Cited in Robert F. Cushman, ed., *Cases in Civil Liberties* (N.Y.: Appleton-Century-Crofts, 1968), p. 242.
24 Cray, op. cit., pp. 77–82.

doubt believed that the prohibitions on unreasonable searches (Amendment Four) and forced confessions (Amendment Five) were sufficient to protect the privacy and dignity of innocent suspects. But they reckoned without knowledge of the twentieth-century technology which has produced such skilled snoopers as electronic eavesdropping devices and chemical blood tests.

The Supreme Court met the problem of telephone wiretaps in 1928 in the case of *Olmstead* v. *U.S.* and held, 5 to 4, that they were constitutionally acceptable because they involved no seizure of material things nor any physical trespass.[25] Since then, electronic listening has had a stormy history and is no less controversial today than it was forty years ago. In 1934 Congress declared the practice illegal, but in 1941 the law was interpreted by the U.S. Justice Department (which includes the Federal Bureau of Investigation) to permit the use of wiretaps if the information gained were not used in court. Law enforcement officials contended it provided valuable "leads" to other information which was admissible in court.

In 1961 and 1967[26] the Court began a retreat from the *Olmstead* ruling and held that the Fourth Amendment's prohibition against seizing things extended to intangible things such as conversations. The constitutionality of wiretapped evidence was rejected entirely in *Katz* v. *U.S.*[27] which involved an F.B.I. listening device attached outside a public telephone booth. Here the Court ruled that conversations were not only things but that their seizure without a warrant was normally unconstitutional even though (as in this case) the search involved no physical entrance, penetration or trespass. Although the *Katz* decision seemed to overrule the old *Olmstead* doctrine, only a short time later, in the summer of 1968, Congress passed the Omnibus Crime Control and Safe Streets Act which appeared to repeal the old 1934 law outlawing electronic eavesdropping. The new legislation authorized judges to issue warrants permitting the use of wiretapping and listening devices, or "bugs" as they are called in the trade, and in addition permitted the use of certain confessions in ways which some thought to violate the *Miranda* ruling cited earlier. Clearly, in its eagerness to fight crime, Congress was responding to political pressures and was all too eager to pass the buck back to the Courts for delicate decisions involving constitutionality.

At last report, the bugging business was flourishing, although presumably with the blessings of court warrants. New York officials authorized 191 wire taps in 1969 and U.S. Attorney General John Mitchell revealed that midway through 1970 the national government had obtained permission for "more than double . . . the previous year's total of 33."[28] The Nixon administration suffered a setback in 1972,

25 277 U.S. 438 (1928). In dissent, Justice Holmes called wire tapping a "dirty business."
26 *Silverman* v. *U.S.*, 365 U.S. 505, and *Berger* v. *New York*, 388 U.S. 41.
27 389 U.S. 347 (1967).
28 "The Assault on Privacy," *Newsweek,* July 27, 1970, p. 17.

however, when a unanimous Court declared the use of wiretaps in domestic security cases to be unconstitutional unless court authorization had been first obtained. The government had argued that when the safety of the nation was menaced internally, no warrants were necessary to obtain evidence in this way.[29]

There are other weapons in the total technological arsenal poised against individual privacy. Blood tests to determine whether motorists are drunk do not involve unreasonable search and seizure because they entail emergency situations in which it is reasonable to suspect that the alcoholic content of the blood would diminish during the time required to obtain a warrant. Nor do they constitute compulsory self-incrimination, the Court has held, since they consist of "physical evidence" rather than "testimony" or some "communicative act or writing." On the same grounds, traffic officers may require suspects to "assume a stance, to walk, or to make a particular gesture."[30]

The threat of government intrusion upon private affairs is heightened by the use of computers that are capable of recording, combining, and exchanging information about individual citizens almost instantly. The Army has the criminal and "loyalty" records of seven million servicemen, contractors, and civilian employees on file, as well as data on anti-Vietnam war protesters such as folk singer Joan Baez and pediatrician Benjamin Spock. Even the Internal Revenue Service in the Treasury Department has been active in the peering-and-peeking business with regard not only to tax records but also to "militant and subversive" books individual citizens have borrowed from public libraries.

We are confronted, it seems, with a sort of pollution of our privacy often associated more with totalitarian dictatorship, and unparalleled in our history. It is not only government agencies which have pried into our conversations, criminal records, political attitudes, and reading habits. They have been joined in their intrusions upon our personal lives by private peekers such as the Pacific Telephone and Telegraph Company which monitored 27 million phone calls in 1965, the Retail Credit Company of Atlanta which has files on seventy million installment buyers, and psychological testing experts who inform employers about the bed-wetting histories and sexual attitudes of job applicants.[31]

These threats to privacy cannot be thwarted by the Constitution alone, for they are products of an increasingly urbanized, congested, economically interdependent society. But whatever their origins, they threaten the integrity of individual citizens who may wish, in Thoreau's words, to "march to the beat of a different drum." They threaten also the progress and ingenuity of a nation whose greatness has required the resourceful inventiveness of people who were a little bit strange. Ein-

29 *Los Angeles Times,* June 20, 1972, p. 1.
30 *Schmerber* v. *California,* 384 U.S. 757 (1966).
31 "The Assault on Privacy," op. cit., p. 16.

stein, for example, seldom wore socks. The computers might go crazy with that one.

A constitutional "catch-all": Amendment Nine   One of the least-invoked guarantees of the Constitution is Amendment Nine which assures us in mysteriously general terms that the people have other rights in addition to those specifically mentioned. At least by implication, it seems to rival the broad guarantees of due process discussed above. Nonetheless, most Americans would probably agree that it is a valuable safeguard, and that citizens should indeed enjoy rights other than those specified in the Constitution. One expects to be able to choose his occupation, for example, or the color of his shoes, without government interference. Yet a constitution which attempted to enumerate all such rights would be both interminably long and patently absurd. Hence, the Ninth Amendment. The most important case involving matters such as this is *Griswold* v. *Connecticut*,[32] which declared unconstitutional a state law prohibiting the use of birth control devices. The decision elicited six different opinions, including one endorsed by three justices who asserted that such a law impinged upon a right of marital privacy such as the Ninth Amendment was designed to guarantee.

The Difficult Choice

As we have seen, to help protect the citizen from the occasional excesses of police procedure, Amendment Four forbids unreasonable searches and seizures, Amendment Five prohibits compulsory self-incrimination, and Amendment Nine guarantees additional, unspecified rights. Moreover, both the Fifth and Fourteenth Amendments require national and state officials respectively to employ "due process of law" in their contacts with private citizens.

When confronted with these constitutional handicaps in their attempts to enforce the laws, the police naturally become frustrated. After careful study, one finally must confront the sad truth that crime detection and personal privacy are sometimes incompatible. Although the police search, arrest, and question many innocent people, often with casual indifference to their constitutional rights, many more who are subjected to the same treatment are indeed guilty. In short, if we want all criminals captured, the rights of some innocent people will be sacrificed; but if we want the rights of all innocent people preserved, some criminals will escape. It is a hard choice, to be sure, on balance well handled by the courts. No one ever claimed that it was easy to run a society which promised "liberty and justice for all."

PROTECTING THE ACCUSED

Thus far we have been concerned with those constitutional provisions which protect the people in their homes, on the street, or in

32 381 U.S. 479 (1965).

the police station. We come now to the nation's courtrooms and the rights of those who must stand trial as criminal defendants.

Prelude to Prosecution

It is said that the wheels of the gods grind slowly, but they grind exceeding fine. The same could be said of American justice, in spite of both the constitutional requirement of a speedy trial and public accusations of inadequate fineness or fairness.

Trial without error   To be a defendant in a criminal trial is a terrible and traumatic experience. It forces the accused person to endure social embarrassment, entails time sacrificed to prepare a defense, and often costs money necessary to hire a good lawyer. Ideally, then, no one should be tried unless he or she is guilty. This ideal, like most others, can never be fully attained, but the American legal system tries at least to make sure that no one is tried without good cause.

The Fifth Amendment deals with this by providing that no person can be tried for a serious crime except through "indictment of a grand jury." A grand jury is a group of one to two dozen citizens, which can issue formal criminal accusations—known as *indictments*—to bring suspects to trial, if the evidence against them, presented by the police and prosecuting attorneys, indicates probable guilt. In practice, the grand jury seems to be most important in cases involving criminal charges against government employees and those otherwise favored by the power or prestige of their positions.

In many states, however, grand juries have been abolished, or are important only in investigating local government agencies such as the welfare department or coroner's office. The reference to them in the Fifth Amendment is one of the few provisions of the Bill of Rights which the Supreme Court has not held to limit state as well as national action. Even in the most serious of crimes, therefore, states may bring persons to trial either through grand jury indictments or through charges brought by prosecuting attorneys known as bills of information, or *true bills*.

No excessive bail   Anglo-American law insists that no person be considered guilty of a crime unless guilt has been proved in a court of law. The burden of proof is on the government prosecutors. The defendant has no obligation to prove his innocence.

This presumption of innocence raises a difficult problem. Since a suspect is presumed innocent until proven guilty, he should not have to languish in jail until his trial. Yet if he is released, he must be provided with some motivation to appear for the trial rather than to run away. Therefore, *bail* is required—an amount of money which must be deposited with the court in return for which the defendant may be released from jail until the trial begins. If he shows up for the trial the bail money is returned; but if he has "jumped bail" and evaded prosecution, a warrant for his arrest is immediately issued by the judge.

Amendment Eight prohibits excessive bail, an amount which

generally depends on the seriousness of the alleged crime and the previous record of the defendant. Suggestions that the amount of bail be influenced by the wealth of the accused have been judicially ignored. But if one can't raise bail, it is usually possible to go free by paying a fee to a bail bondsman who then posts the bail. Occasionally, judges allow an accused person to be released without bail on his *own recognizance,* or in the event the crime was quite serious, deny the accused bail and retain him in prison until the trial.

One of the controversial aspects of the crime-control law that Congress enacted for Washington, D.C. in 1970 is a "preventive detention" provision that permits judges to hold defendants without bail for sixty days if they believe the defendants might commit a crime if released. The constitutionality of such an unprecedented departure from our tradition is yet to be tested.

A Fair Trial

The Sixth Amendment contains as impressive a list of defendants' rights as can be found anywhere in the world.

How fast is speedy?   The first command of the Sixth Amendment is that "the accused shall enjoy the right to a speedy . . . trial." The longer it takes to bring a man to trial the less reliable will be the memory of key witnesses and the greater likelihood that they will have died or disappeared. But how fast is speedy? In an age of increasing crime and overworked courts, the only reasonable answer is, "as soon as possible." Courts have usually held that this constitutional requirement has been met if there has been no deliberate delay in bringing a case to trial although in some areas they have set six-month limits. In 1970 there were over 140 people in Washington, D.C., jails who had been awaiting trial for over a year.[33] To facilitate the demand for speed, criminal cases are given precedence over civil ones and statutes of limitations have been passed prohibiting prosecutions, except in murder cases, if no arrest warrant has been issued within a specified period of time, usually from one to seven years, after the crime has been committed.

How exposed is public?   The Sixth Amendment also demands public trials, on the assumption that secret, or "star chamber," proceedings are less apt to be fair than those illuminated by the floodlights of publicity. But judges can clear the courtroom if spectators behave in ways which jeopardize the serious and thoughtful decorum necessary to ascertain the truth. To maintain such an atmosphere, photographs of the trial and live radio and television coverage are almost always banned.

Confrontation   The accused has the additional right "to be confronted with the witnesses against him," on the theory that his

33 Richard L. Strout, "The District's Crime Bill," *The Christian Science Monitor,* July 24, 1970, p. 14. Such conditions contributed to the Washington prison revolt in 1972.

accusers, testifying under penalty of perjury (lying under oath), and subject to cross-examination by the defense counsel, will be more likely to tell the truth.

This provision has prohibited second-hand hearsay testimony and created two additional problems. First, it limited the use of secret witnesses (sometimes called "faceless informers" or "stool pigeons") by the prosecution. If such persons were forced to appear in court, they might be murdered later by criminals who had confided in them. The testimony of these witnesses, often paid by the police, is sometimes of dubious validity anyway, although it is often of real value in the capture, if not the actual conviction, of dangerous criminals.

Another problem involving the right to confront witnesses is raised by defendants whose wild behavior makes it difficult or even impossible to continue their trials. It gained national attention in 1969 when Federal District Court Judge Julius Hoffman ordered Bobby Seale, a defendant in the case involving incitement to riot at the 1968 Democratic National Convention, to be chained and gagged because of his insulting and disruptive courtroom shouts. Although Judge Hoffman apparently believed he could not constitutionally remove Seale from his own trial, the Supreme Court later ruled, in another case, that such action is permissible under certain extreme circumstances.[34]

The right to subpoena witnesses   Since the prosecution may summon witnesses in an attempt to prove guilt, Amendment Six gives the accused the right "to have compulsory process for obtaining witnesses in his favor." Subpoenas are the compulsory process available. They are court orders requiring people upon whom they are served to appear in court and answer questions (not involving their own possible guilt) regarding the alleged crime. If the person subpoenaed does not testify, the judge may rule him in contempt of court and punish him, without trial, by fine or imprisonment.

The right to legal counsel   No Sixth Amendment right has been more strengthened or expanded by recent court decisions than the right to professional legal advice. In 1963 *Gideon* v. *Wainwright* applied it to state as well as federal courts.[35] Then, in 1964, the Court ruled in *Escobedo* v. *Illinois*[36] that legal counsel had to be provided when the defendant requested it at the time of his arrest, and not solely for trial. The *Miranda* decision required the police not only to inform the defendant of his right to remain silent, as mentioned regarding the Fifth Amendment, but also to tell him, before questioning, of his right to be represented by an attorney. A 1972 decision required that legal counsel be made available to anyone threatened with even a single day in jail.

But how can the accused obtain legal counsel? He may, of course, hire his own lawyer. The *Miranda* decision also insisted that he

34 *Illinois* v. *Allen,* 397 U.S. 337 (1970).
35 372 U.S. 335. An intriguing account of the case appears in Anthony Lewis, *Gideon's Trumpet* (N.Y.: Random House, Inc., 1964).
36 378 U.S. 478.

must be informed that an attorney will be provided for him if he cannot afford to hire one. This is done in two different ways. In federal courts, and in most state courts, a judge will appoint some local attorney to represent the indigent defendant. Alternatively, especially in major cities, public defenders offices have been created and staffed by full-time lawyers who are recruited and paid on the same basis as those working in the prosecuting attorney's offices. These public defenders, devoted exclusively to representing the poor, seem to provide a higher caliber of legal counsel than is otherwise available in such cases.

No double jeopardy   With only a few exceptions, criminal defendants may be tried only once for a single act. This is the result of the Fifth Amendment's assurance that no person shall be "twice put in jeopardy of life or limb." The exceptions are: (1) Persons in the armed services are subject both to military law and civilian law. There are situations, therefore, permitting both a military court martial and a prosecution in a regular state court for the same offense. (2) If, for example, one robs a bank of funds insured by the national government, he has broken both national and state laws and theoretically could be tried in both national and state courts. In practice this seldom happens. (3) One may be tried twice for the same crime if convicted the first time as a result of some unconstitutional procedure and on appeal, a higher court orders a second one. Hence convicted criminals are not always set free on some technicality, as is often supposed, when the Supreme Court or some other appellate tribunal finds that the conviction was obtained in an unconstitutional manner.

Trial by jury   Trial by jury is mentioned three times in the Constitution. Article III establishes it, Amendment Six specifies an impartial jury, and Amendment Seven extends the right from criminal cases to civil cases involving more than $20. Sir William Blackstone, an eighteenth-century English legal scholar, wrote in his famous *Commentaries* that ". . . the trial by jury ever has been, and I trust ever will be, looked upon as the glory of the English law."[37]

Yet jury trials are not mandatory; they are simply a right the accused may exercise, except in petty cases, if he wishes to do so. Either a judge or a jury may render a verdict and the defendant has the choice. If judges are corrupt or hopelessly prejudiced, as during the colonial period in America, then trial by jury is indispensable. But if judges are believed to be honest, competent, and fair—which seems to be the prevailing view today—then trial by jury is not essential to procedural fairness. In fact, the right of trial by jury has been utilized less and less. Judges now render the verdict in 40 percent of criminal cases going to trial.[38] As long as jury trials exist, however, the constitutional requirement of impartiality is of vital importance, and that guarantee is enforced in a number of ways:

37 Quoted by Justice Black, *Reid* v. *Covert*, 354 U.S. 1.
38 Justice Harlan, in dissent, *Duncan* v. *Louisiana*, 20 L. Ed. 2d 491 (1968).

1) If the defendant in a case has received so much adverse publicity that it would be impossible to find enough jurors who are not already biased against him, then the judge should issue a *change of venue,* an order transferring the trial to some area where there has been less coverage of the case by TV, radio, and the press.

2) No group may be systematically excluded from jury duty because of race, sex, nationality, or attitude toward capital punishment (the death penalty).

3) Attorneys for both defense and prosecution may disqualify prospective jurors after questioning each of them. These *voir dire* examinations permit an unlimited number of disqualifications for adequate cause, and usually from five to thirty peremptory challenges for which no explanation need be given.

In 1970 the Supreme Court upheld the constitutionality of Florida's six-member jury, repudiating a centuries-old tradition that juries must consist of twelve persons. A more important issue was whether juries could hand down a verdict in criminal cases by less than the unanimous vote prescribed by common law custom. It was resolved in 1972 when all four justices appointed by President Nixon were joined by one other in a 5–4 decision sustaining the Louisiana law that permitted convictions by a 9–3 margin. Only Oregon, Montana, and Oklahoma allowed similar verdicts but defendants throughout the country feared that other states would join them.[39]

OF CRIME AND PUNISHMENT: VENGEANCE, DETERRENCE, REHABILITATION

Once the criminal suspect has been searched, arrested, interrogated, and formally charged with a crime, he is an accused person. As such, he has certain constitutional protections spelled out primarily in the Sixth Amendment but also in the double jeopardy and grand jury provisions of Amendment Five and the prohibition of excessive bail in Amendment Eight. But, in spite of all this, what happens to him if he is convicted?

Americans, perhaps like other peoples, aren't quite sure what to do with their criminals. The oldest theory was that they should be punished in a manner commensurate with their crime; this follows the Old Testament rule of "an eye for an eye, a tooth for a tooth." It is a concept rooted in revenge.

An alternative criterion for punishment rests upon the assumption that its purpose is not for revenge but to discourage or deter others from committing crime. Those holding this opinion often believe that the harsher the penalty, the more effective the deterrent.

---

39 *New York Times,* May 28, 1972, p. 6. The ruling affected only state court procedures; federal court verdicts must still be unanimous.

The newest theory is that convicts should be punished only to the degree that is necessary to reform them, to make sure that their rehabilitation is sufficient for safe release into the society at large.

The Criminals: A Group Biography

Before discussing what to do with criminals, it would be well to find out who they are. That is not easy because less than one fourth of all crimes lead to arrests, and many of these do not result in convictions.[40] We do know, however, that cities of over 250,000 population have crime rates from two to six times higher than those with populations under 10,000.[41] Moreover, judging from the persons arrested by the police we can see some characteristics of the "typical" criminal. In 1969, five out of six persons charged with a serious crime were male, three out of four were under twenty-four years of age, and more than six out of ten were white. Although no exact statistics are available, it seems nearly certain that an overwhelming number were poor.

How did they go wrong? Beware of the single, simple explanation. Among the possible "causes" for crime are poverty, permissiveness, television violence, overcrowding, racism, a lawless social heritage, leniency of the courts, inept police work, broken homes, increased (and expensive) drug addiction, and inadequate gun control laws. Whatever the reasons, the crime crisis is urgent.

"To Keep and Bear Arms:" A Right or a Wrong?

One of the most misunderstood provisions of the Constitution is Amendment Two, which seems to guarantee "the right of the people to keep and bear arms." It is also one which many people believe to be related to the high crime rate in America. The fact is that this right was actually designed to guarantee to the states the authority to maintain their own military and police forces. This is indicated by the opening words of the Second Amendment, seldom quoted, which refer to "A well regulated Militia, being necessary to the security of a free state . . ." Only the national guard, sheriffs' deputies, and other law enforcement officers, therefore, have a right to carry guns.

While many people sincerely believe that private citizens *should* be allowed to own firearms, this issue is essentially a political one on which the Constitution maintains a silent neutrality. Only after the assassinations of President John F. Kennedy, Dr. Martin Luther King, and Senator Robert Kennedy, did gun control become a major public controversy. President Lyndon B. Johnson requested more stringent national restrictions than had ever been proposed previously, and the

40 Reo M. Christenson, *Challenge and Decision,* 3rd ed. (N.Y.: Harper & Row, Publishers, 1970), pp. 216–17.
41 U.S. Bureau of the Census, *Statistical Abstract of the United States: 1971,* p. 142.

resulting legislation placed severe restrictions upon the mail order and other interstate sale of firearms. It also prohibited the sale of guns to convicts and minors, but did not require that gun owners be licensed or that the firearms themselves be registered.

Outside of Congress, the National Rifle Association, a powerful private pressure group, and extremist groups on both the left and right, the Black Panthers and the predominantly Caucasian Minutemen, all insist that they need guns for hunting, target shooting, or self-defense. Opposing them are several prominent police officials, the U.S. Conference of Mayors, Common Cause, Americans for Democratic Action, and various union and church groups.

The issue of gun control touches emotions rooted in the soil of our unique history. Americans have been a frontier people, accustomed to rely on self-defense and fond of glorifying the cowboy, sheriff, or even the crook who shot first and asked questions later. That the issue will not soon disappear is suggested by the facts that gun controls are weaker here than in any other major nation and that private ownership of hand guns quadrupled between 1962 and 1968. The most reliable estimates indicate that there are at least thirty-five million rifles, thirty-one million shotguns, and twenty-four million hand guns in civilian possession.[42]

Types of Sentences

No cruel and unusual punishment   Although the Constitution contains many provisions aimed at helping criminal defendants, it includes only one for the person finally convicted—the Eighth Amendment's prohibition against cruel and unusual punishments. The courts have not found it easy to say precisely what such punishments are, but their decisions indicate a belief that the severity of sentences should be related to the seriousness of the crime.

In *Robinson* v. *California*,[43] the Court ruled that *any* criminal punishment for being a narcotics addict was cruel and unusual. While a state may punish possession or use of narcotics, addiction was held to be an illness, not a crime. In *Powell* v. *Texas*,[44] however, the conviction of a chronic alcoholic for being drunk in a public place was sustained.

Capital punishment   In the darkest days of World War II, Winston Churchill paid tribute to the British air force by asserting that never before in human history had so many owed so much to so few. Before June 29, 1972, never in American history had as many as six hundred people owed their lives to a single court decision. Those saved were not freedom-loving citizens resisting tyranny; they were 517 mur-

---

42 The National Commission on the Causes and Prevention of Violence, *To Establish Justice, to Insure Domestic Tranquility* (Toronto: Bantam Books, Inc., 1970), p. 158.
43 370 U.S. 660 (1962).
44 20 L. Ed. 2d 1254 (1968).

derers, 79 rapists, and 4 armed robbers. What had happened, of course, is that the death penalty had been declared unconstitutional in the case of *Furman* v. *Georgia*[45]—at least as applied to all persons then on death row. They were an intriguing group: 329 blacks, 257 whites, 10 Mexican-Americans, 2 Puerto Ricans, and 2 Indians.

The historic decision was announced in conflicting voices: The vote was 5–4, nine different opinions were written, and the long-term impact was far from certain. Justices William Brennan and Thurgood Marshall seemed to believe the death penalty to be a cruel and unusual punishment under almost any circumstances. Justices Potter Stewart, Byron White, and William O. Douglas objected to the arbitrary and uncertain standards by which some felons were doomed to death and others guilty of the same offenses were given lesser sentences. The four dissenters were the Nixon appointees, voting together as they had on other 5–4 decisions which permitted less than unanimous jury verdicts and denied the right of reporters to conceal their sources of information from grand juries. Although the decision spared the lives of those already sentenced to death, most justices seemed willing to withhold judgment on capital punishment in situations in which the judge or jury was permitted less discretion in imposing the death sentence. Because the future is in doubt, the opposing arguments require mention.

Those who defend the ultimate penalty claim that it serves as a deterrent to murder and assert that it has been sanctioned by centuries of religious tradition and legal precedent. Critics argue that the death penalty is immoral, an affront to human dignity, and of questionable importance as a deterrent, since in eleven of the fifteen states where it was abolished, the homicide rate was below the national average. Perhaps certainty and speed of convictions would be more of a deterrent than the stiffness of the sentence. Finally, opponents of capital punishment allege that it has been inequitably imposed, selecting a disproportionately large number of its victims from the poor, the black, and the male.

Imprisonment   Until recently, there was general agreement that the easiest way to deal with the convicted criminal was to lock him up. Yet by the end of September 1971, prison violence in state penitentiaries at San Quentin, California, and Attica, New York, had resulted in nearly fifty deaths, claiming inmates and guards alike. Suddenly penal problems became a major social and political controversy. Although black militancy and political radicalism may have contributed to these tragedies, they focused belated attention on such issues as overcrowding, abuse by prison guards, inadequate facilities for recreation and job training, and the general brutalization of inmates. Of the jails maintained by local governments in 1970, 86 percent had no facilities for exercise, 89 percent lacked education, 49 percent lacked medical care, and 26 percent were without provisions for visitors. In addition to spawning acts of

45 92 S.Ct. 2726 (1972).

dangerous desperation, imprisonment has two other disadvantages: It is expensive and it fails to rehabilitate the criminal.

In part, its expense is due to the number of people imprisoned, more than 360,000 in 1970, or about one person out of every 570 in the nation. It can be attributed, also, to relatively long sentences imposed in this country in comparison with most other Western nations.[46] For the more than 8000 federal prisoners released for the first time in 1970, the average time served was almost twenty months. The per prisoner cost of all government correctional programs amounted to more than $4000 per year, an amount capable of maintaining a family of four above the poverty level outside prison.[47]

Even this price would be cheap enough if imprisonment rehabilitated the criminal. Yet the evidence indicates that this is not the case. One expert notes that "Two thirds of the men and women now imprisoned are repeaters,"[48] and another asserts that in Oklahoma those convicts receiving short sentences actually committed proportionately fewer crimes upon their release than those who had been imprisoned longer.[49]

All too often, it seems, prolonged imprisonment simply allows criminals to develop more efficient techniques by exchanging ideas with one another, or it contributes to homosexuality by cutting them off from contact with the opposite sex. In any event, since "85 percent of the nation's crime is committed by repeaters,"[50] a reexamination is required of the usefulness of imprisonment as an effective anticrime device. The major alternatives to jail seem to be probation or parole.

Probation and parole In most states, judges may release convicted persons on probation, rather than sending them to prison. This entails certain restrictions on their travel, associates, and behavior during a specified period, and places them under the supervision of a probation officer. Parole is a similar arrangement by which persons already in prison are given a conditional release requiring them to fulfill certain requirements and report periodically to parole agents.

Probation and parole have clear advantages over long imprisonment in that they permit the convict to earn a living, enjoy normal sex relations, support a family, and minimize correctional expenses for the taxpayer. Their success is somewhat difficult to assess, but seems related to the types of persons selected for such treatment and the adequacy of their supervision. Of prisoners paroled in New York, New

46 *Crime and the Law,* op. cit., pp. 11–14, (the prisoner figure includes 21,000 in federal prisons, 185,000 in state prisons, and 160,000 in local jails) and Hoyt Gimlin, "Street Crimes in America," *Editorial Research Reports on Challenges for the 1970's* (Washington, D.C.: Congressional Quarterly, Inc., 1970), p. 78.
47 Computed from U.S. Bureau of the Census, *Statistical Abstract of the United States: 1971,* p. 148, and previously cited data.
48 Gimlin, loc. cit.
49 Ronald L. Goldfarb, *Washington Post,* reprinted in *Los Angeles Times,* July 26, 1970, Section G, p. 1. See also Christenson, op. cit., p. 216.
50 Christenson, op. cit., p. 221.

Jersey, and California, between 40.5 and 50.9 percent had violated the conditions of their parole within three to five years.[51]

Justice for Juveniles

Beginning with Illinois in 1899, all states have authorized special methods of dealing with alleged delinquents under the age of 18. They were intended to spare children the embarassment and disgrace which accompany criminal proceedings against adults, and to save them "from a downward career." But the realities of juvenile court operations often left minors as helpless pawns who could be assured only of the "right" to whatever form of custody the court felt best, without the benefit of constitutional guarantees enjoyed by adults as a matter of course.

These conditions were suddenly changed by the Supreme Court in 1967. *Re Gault*[52] involved a fifteen-year-old Arizona boy who was on probation because he had been with another boy who stole a lady's purse and who, nearly two years earlier, had stolen a baseball glove from another boy. The appeal to the Supreme Court resulted from an allegedly obscene phone call for which young Gault was sentenced to up to six years in a so-called "industrial school." Had he been an adult (at least three years older), his maximum sentence for the crime, were he guilty, would have been imprisonment for two months. In an eight to one decision, the Court reversed the sentence and decreed that juveniles, as well as adults, were entitled to notification of charges against them, legal counsel, the right to refuse to testify against themselves, and the right to confront and cross-examine their accusers—all constitutional guarantees that had been denied to Gault and his parents. The Court took great pains, however, to affirm its belief that juveniles should be accorded special treatment, so long as such treatment does not deprive defendants of the procedures essential for "due process of law."

51 Tappan, op. cit., p. 749.
52 387 U.S. 1 (1967).

Chapter 5

Equal Justice Under Law
Of Dreams Deferred

What happens to a dream deferred?

Does it dry up
like a raisin in the sun?
Or fester like a sore—
And then run?
Does it stink like rotten meat?
Or crust and sugar over—
like a syrupy sweet?

Maybe it just sags
like a heavy load.

Or does it explode? *
                    Langston Hughes

      Human equality is the underlying and often unspoken assumption supporting many rights guaranteed in the Constitution. Freedom of the press, for example, is not restricted only to writers who belong to the Democratic Party, and the right of trial by jury is available to women as well as men. This chapter is devoted to the broad concept of equality itself, and the gap that still exists between that ideal and the practical realities of every day American life.

*Copyright 1951 by Langston Hughes. Reprinted from *Selected Poems of Langston Hughes* by permission of Alfred A. Knopf, Inc.

EQUAL PROTECTION OF THE LAWS: JUSTICE IN BLACK AND WHITE

Following the "due process" clause in the Fourteenth Amendment is another crucial clause, the one that stipulates that no state shall "deny to any person within its jurisdiction the equal protection of the law." In the last quarter of a century, no part of the Constitution has had a more explosive impact on American life than this one.

A Color-blind Constitution

We have already noted that in 1873 the Supreme Court declined to interpret the Fourteenth Amendment as aiding the individual against the state governments. In 1883, the Court also ruled unconstitutional much of the 1875 Civil Rights Act which had penalized discrimination in places of public accommodation.

Separate but equal Some years later, in 1896, the Court held in *Plessy* v. *Ferguson*[1] that a Louisiana law requiring separate but equal railroad coaches for white and black passengers did not deny Negroes their constitutional right to equal protection. The result of this "separate but equal" doctrine was to enable the spread of "legal" segregation of blacks and whites in almost every area of southern life—in schools, theaters, restaurants, court houses, rest rooms, and marriage chapels, as well as in railroad coaches. Only Justice John Marshall Harlan, in a lonely dissenting opinion, sounded a cry largely unheeded for over half a century. "Our Constitution," he wrote, "is color-blind."

A segregated nation Whether or not the Constitution was color-blind, most white Americans had no such eye trouble. While the South relied chiefly on legally compelled segregation to keep the races apart, the North was more subtle. White businessmen simply refused to serve blacks or to employ them in any positions of prestige or prominence.

The ranks of America's leading opera companies, for example, were closed to black singers until Camilla Williams appeared in a New York City Center production in 1946, and the next year Jackie Robinson became the first black to play on a major league baseball team.[2] Blacks and whites were segregated from the cradle to the grave, from birth in segregated neighborhoods to burial in segregated cemeteries.

The "separate but equal" rule which the Supreme Court endorsed in 1896 was remarkably effective in permitting states to ensure

1 163 U.S. 573.
2 Edgar A. Toppin, "Breaching the Old Walls of Prejudice," *The Christian Science Monitor*, June 5, 1969, p. 12. This article is one of an excellent series by a professor of history at Virginia State College.

the racial dominance of white people. In 1899, the Court approved the maintenance of a high school for whites only on the plea that the county in question could not afford another one for blacks;[3] in 1927 it sanctioned the requirement that a Chinese student attend a school for colored children rather than one for whites closer to her home;[4] and not until 1940 were school boards required to pay black teachers as much as white ones of equal training and experience.[5]

Most shameful of all was the role of American government, which declined to lead or even set an example. While a number of blacks had served in positions of some prominence in the half-century following emancipation, President Woodrow Wilson's inauguration in 1913 marked a discouraging setback for the supporters of equal opportunity. The number of black presidential appointees dropped from thirty-one to nine and the segregation of offices and toilet facilities was suddenly introduced for employees of the Post Office, the Treasury, and the Navy. The armed forces were not integrated until the administration of President Harry S. Truman (1945–53).[6] Finally, at the pinnacles of power, no cabinet position escaped Caucasian control until 1966, when President Lyndon B. Johnson designated Robert C. Weaver as Secretary of the newly created Department of Housing and Urban Development. The next year Thurgood Marshall became the first black on the Supreme Court. Mexican-Americans, Asian-Americans, and American Indians are still waiting.

The decline of compulsory segregation   The "equal protection of the laws" clause persisted, however, as a rebuke to the hypocrisy of prevailing legal standards. Back in 1886 the Supreme Court used it to declare the application of San Francisco business licensing laws to be an unconstitutional discrimination against Chinese laundry operators.[7] Much later, it was invoked to permit black people to vote in Democratic party primary elections,[8] serve on juries,[9] and attend previously all-white state law schools.[10]

But it was not until 1954 that the Fourteenth Amendment began to fulfill its initial promise of racial justice, when the case of *Brown v. Board of Education of Topeka*[11] repudiated the "separate but equal" doctrine. The *Brown* decision produced profound changes in American society. In the first place, its immediate purpose was to declare racial segregation in the public schools to be an unconstitutional violation of the "equal protection of the laws" clause of Amendment Fourteen. Second, it established a precedent, soon followed, for ending compulsory

3 *Cumming* v. *County Board of Education,* 175 U.S. 528.
4 *Gong Lum* v. *Rice,* 257 U.S. 78.
5 *Allston* v. *School Board,* 112 Fed. 2d 992.
6 Leslie H. Fishel, Jr., and Benjamin Quarles, eds., *The Negro American* (Glenview, Ill.: Scott, Foresman and Company, 1967), pp. 390, 484–85.
7 *Yick Wo* v. *Hopkins,* 118 U.S. 356.
8 *Nixon* v. *Condon,* 286 U.S. 73 (1932).
9 *Norris* v. *Alabama,* 294 U.S. 587 (1935).
10 *Sweatt* v. *Painter,* 339 U.S. 629 (1950).
11 347 U.S. 483.

racial segregation in all government facilities, such as public parks, beaches, prisons, and municipally owned buses.

Third, the decision constituted a moral victory for blacks, which inaugurated a period of rapidly rising expectations embodied in the civil rights movement led by Martin Luther King. During the next few years blacks made major gains, but by 1955 the gap between expectation and change transformed hope into disillusionment and converted much of the civil rights movement into a crusade for "Black Power." A fourth effect of the *Brown* decision, although perhaps a temporary one, was to increase tensions between the South, where racial prejudice had been most obvious, and the rest of the nation. In 1957 President Eisenhower sent troops into Little Rock, Arkansas, to enforce a court order requiring the integration of a local high school and five years later, President Kennedy responded the same way to insure the enrollment of James Meredith, the first black ever admitted to the University of Mississippi.

The Court's desegregation command is still the subject of bitter dispute and diverse interpretations. Its application has been extended to certain districts in the North and West where segregation in the schools reflects the racial composition of residential neighborhoods. The Supreme Court has yet to review fully these cases of *de facto* segregation, and in view of the busing controversy, it would be well to examine the reasoning of the Court in its unanimous opinion.

The case involved situations in which white and black children were attending schools that were legally segregated, but without any significant differences "with respect to buildings, curricula, . . . and other 'tangible' factors." If the black schools were admittedly as good as the white ones, how could the mere fact of segregation violate the equal protection clause? The Court conceded that there was little historical evidence indicating that the framers of the Fourteenth Amendment intended it to ban segregation in the public schools, since few existed at the time it was written. But the contemporary effect of segregation, the Court contended, creates among black children "a feeling of inferiority as to their status in the community that may affect their hearts and minds in a way unlikely ever to be undone." This feeling of inferiority, moreover, adversely "affects the motivation of a child to learn."

The conclusion of the Court has been most bitterly criticized on the basis that it rested more on a number of studies by psychologists and sociologists, cited in the decision, than it did on historical records or legal precedent. Nonetheless, there seems little doubt that when segregated schools were first established, they were created by white state legislators and white school board members who in fact did believe that blacks were inferior. Moreover, there were at least a few cases, at the graduate-school level, in which the Supreme Court had held segregation unconstitutional even before the *Brown* decision.

But the most important evidence supporting the Court ruling came twelve years after it was handed down, in *Racial Isolation in the*

Public Schools, a report issued by the United States Commission on Civil Rights.[12] This report, based largely on a 1966 study of thousands of black students in the ninth and twelfth grades,[13] concluded that racial segregation in schools tends to lower students' achievement and restrict their aspirations. The chief reason for the improved academic progress of black students in integrated schools seems to be the superior educational backgrounds of their classmates' parents and the resultingly higher occupational goals of the classmates themselves.

One of the major barriers to interracial understanding has been a fantastic array of traditions, rumors, fantasies, and fears centering around sex. The importance of this whole matter to the vast majority of Americans is indicated in a nation-wide poll showing that whereas only 21 percent of white people would object to using the same rest rooms as blacks, a whopping 88 percent would oppose their teen-aged child dating them.[14] In 1968, moreover, an international Gallup Poll found that American opposition to white-nonwhite marriage, 72 percent, was highest among the thirteen nations surveyed.[15] Judicial interpretation of the Constitution, of course, should not depend on public opinion, and in 1967, a unanimous Supreme Court declared state laws prohibiting racial intermarriage (miscegenation) to be an unconstitutional violation of both the "equal protection" and "due process" clauses of the Fourteenth Amendment.[16]

Racial Politics

The historical record indicates that if constitutional prohibitions are to be enforced, and if private individuals are to be prevented from discriminatory behavior, then court decisions must be supplemented by legislative and executive action. But the potential of such political action for solving a particular problem is determined largely by the attitudes of those who elect the politicians. The issue of civil rights, therefore, begins with the nature and extent of prejudice among the people. If prejudice influences politics—and surely it seems to—the explanations for it point to contradictory conclusions regarding its future importance. With respect to the condescending portrayals of minority groups in history books and the mass media, substantial changes have been made which should diminish antagonism and promote harmony. The psychological need for belonging to a group—"we" vs. "they"—and the need to bolster bruised egos by looking down on someone "worse" are deep-seated and enduring, however.

12 U.S. Commission on Civil Rights, *Racial Isolation in the Public Schools* (Washington, D.C.: U.S. Government Printing Office, 1967).
13 James Coleman, *et al., Equality of Educational Opportunity* (Washington, D.C.: U.S. Government Printing Office, 1966).
14 *Newsweek,* August 22, 1966, p. 26.
15 *Los Angeles Times,* Nov. 11, 1968, p. 6. Sweden with 67 percent, was highest in approval. "A slight majority" of American Negroes approved of mixed marriages, "but as many as three in ten disapproved."
16 *Loving* v. *Virginia,* 388 U.S. 1.

Economic considerations are also discouraging. After World War II, two researchers found that veterans who slid downward in socioeconomic status (those who had to take poorer jobs, for example) were more prejudiced than those who were more successful.[17] In view of this finding it is not surprising that nearly twenty years later a new survey found that racial prejudice was most prevalent among the troubled "middle Americans" who were hardest hit by inflation, high taxes, and rising unemployment. "The more precarious a family's hold on economic security," the study revealed, "the more menaced it feels by . . . black militancy."[18]

Most of these people felt that blacks had greater opportunities than they did, and only a quarter of them favored increased racial integration of the public schools. Although traditionally aligned with the Democratic party, they are prime targets for President Nixon's appeal to the "silent majority." They are worried about losing their jobs—who can blame them?—and blacks often seem to threaten these jobs most severely. Politically, candidates such as Louise Day Hicks in Boston and Lester Maddox in Georgia hover over them, eager to peck the political flesh of desperate men. Racial prejudice may have its price after all: economic prosperity for white America.

In any event, statistics produced by public opinion polls show an unmistakable increase in tolerance toward ethnic minorities. Between 1967 and 1969, to cite but one example, the percentage of the American people who would vote for a Jew for President jumped from 82 to 86, and those willing to vote for a Negro climbed even more, from 54 to 67.[19]

State action   While the Fourteenth Amendment's "equal protection" clause prohibited state discrimination, it did nothing to compel private institutions to afford equal treatment. Yet by 1947, without court compulsion, eighteen states had prohibited discrimination because of race in places of public accommodation such as privately owned restaurants, hotels, and theaters.[20] This, apparently, was racism's most vulnerable barrier and the first one to be cracked—but not the last. By 1962 twenty-one states had passed laws forbidding racial discrimination in employment, beginning with New York in 1945, and in 1963 discrimination in at least a portion of the housing market had been barred in nineteen states and fifty-five cities, including New York City, Pittsburgh, and Toledo.[21] However, a 1972 Supreme Court decision

17 Bruno Bettelheim and Morris Janowitz, "Prejudice," *Scientific American* (October 1950): 11–13.
18 *Newsweek,* October 6, 1969, p. 32, 45. The Archie Bunker stereotype is a bit unfair in the opinion of several recent observers.
19 These figures are from Gallup polls reported in the *Los Angeles Times,* June 4, 1967, Section G, p. 2, and April 3, 1969, p. 31.
20 Gustavus Myers, *History of Bigotry in the United States,* ed. by Henry M. Christman (N.Y.: Capricorn Books, G. P. Putnam's Sons, 1960), p. 443.
21 United States Commission on Civil Rights, *Freedom to the Free* (Washington, D.C.: U.S. Government Printing Office, 1963), pp. 132–33, 144.

upheld the power of a state to issue liquor licenses to private lodges (the Moose, in this case) which refused to serve black guests.[22]

Population changes and political power These state prohibitions against racial discrimination, sometimes badly enforced, were imposed in northern and western states. This may be explained largely by the steady exodus of black people from the South to other sections of the country, and from rural areas to urban ones. World War II accelerated the move. The percentage of all blacks in the nation who resided in the eleven southern states dropped from 77 in 1940 to 53 in 1970. By the latter year, each of the four cities with the largest black population—New York, Chicago, Detroit, and Philadelphia—were northern ones. Most of the emigrants who left southern rural areas seem to have moved to these and other cities. The 1960 census revealed that for the first time in American history a higher percentage of blacks than whites had urban homes.[23]

One effect of these population changes was to increase black political power. Not only were voting restrictions fewer in the North and West than in the South, but the black voters were more heavily concentrated in cities, and hence better able to elect black candidates and influence the passage of civil rights laws. As a result of the 1970 congressional elections there were eleven blacks in the House of Representatives, more than at any time since the Reconstruction period following the Civil War. All were Democrats from big cities, and none were from the eleven southern states. Perhaps most prominent among them was Rep. Shirley Chisholm of New York, the first black woman ever elected to Congress and a 1972 candidate for the Democratic presidential nomination. In the Senate was Edward W. Brooke, Republican from Massachusetts, who in 1967 became the first black to sit in that august body in this century. Such encouraging progress should not obscure the fact that even now blacks, with 11 percent of the population, have less than 3 percent of the members of Congress. The situation at the state level is similar. In 1970, 174 blacks were serving in thirty-four state legislatures; they held the most seats in Illinois, Missouri, Georgia, Ohio, and Michigan.[24]

Other ethnic minorities have fared little better than blacks, at least in national politics. There were four congressmen of Asian parentage, all from Hawaii (including Rep. Patsy T. Mink, a woman), and five Mexican-Americans, (two each from New Mexico and Texas, and one from California). Of this group, seven were Democrats, and two Republicans.

Congressional action After decades of inaction, Congress finally enacted a civil rights law in 1957, followed by others in the next decade. The 1957 act created the United States Commission on Civil

22 The case involved K. Leroy Irvis, a Pennsylvania legislator. *New York Times,* June 18, 1972, p. 6.
23 U.S. Bureau of the Census, *Statistical Abstract of the United States: 1971,* pp. 16, 21–24, 27.
24 *Congressional Quarterly Guide to Current American Government* (Fall 1970), p. 138.

Rights and authorized it to investigate voting discrimination prohibited by the Fifteenth Amendment as well as alleged violations of the "equal protection of the laws" clause of the Fourteenth. It also prohibited attempts to prevent persons from voting, empowered the U.S. Attorney General to intervene in voting-rights cases, and banned discrimination in jury selection.

The Civil Rights Act of 1960 outlawed the possession of explosives designed to blow up a vehicle or building and allowed the federal courts, in suits filed by the Attorney General, to declare persons qualified to vote. Although two laws thus pushed a congressional foot in the discrimination door, it was the passage of the 1964 legislation that seemed to unhinge it completely. This legislation followed the spectacular and often violent events of the early 1960s which dramatized the need for further congressional action.

The record of those events, written in bravery and blood, still commands respectful attention. In February 1960, students from the North Carolina Agricultural and Technical College began a "sit-in" at a Greensboro, North Carolina, lunch counter where blacks had been refused service. In spite of their arrest, the movement rapidly reached out across the South, sometimes in the form of widely publicized "Freedom Rides." In 1961, for example, when black and white bus passengers defied the local requirements of seating segregation in a journey across Alabama and into Mississippi, riots broke out, a bus was burned, and the riders were attacked by enraged whites. On April 23 1963, William Moore, a white civil rights marcher, was shot to death in northeast Alabama. In May, protest marches were launched in Birmingham seeking an end to discrimination in public accommodations and access to better jobs. The demonstrators were confronted with police dogs and fire hoses, and a few days later bombs were thrown in attempts to kill Rev. Martin Luther King, Jr., and his brother, Reverend A. D. King. On June 12, Medgar Evers, the head of the National Association for the Advancement of Colored People in Mississippi, was fatally wounded by a gunman outside his home in Jackson.

Against this background of tension and fear, President Kennedy, on June 19, 1963, submitted to Congress the proposal which was the basis for the Civil Rights Act of 1964. It was passed by Congress exactly one year later. The events of the intervening twelve months elicit memories both painful and important. In August, 200,000 people streamed into Washington, D.C., in the largest civil rights demonstration in history; in September, four black girls were killed by a bomb exploded in a Birmingham Sunday School. "It was," as the *Congressional Quarterly* observed, "the 21st time in eight years that Negroes had been the victims of bombings in Birmingham, and like the previous cases, the crime went unsolved."[25] In October, congressional committees debated

25 Shirley M. Seib, ed., *Revolution in Civil Rights,* 3rd ed. (Washington, D.C.: Congressional Quarterly, Inc., 1967), p. 11.

the most recent civil rights proposals, but on November 22, the man who made them was assassinated. Five days later his successor, President Lyndon B. Johnson, urged Congress to pass the pending legislation to honor his memory. Without these tear-stained traumas, the most sweeping civil rights legislation of this century might never have been enacted.

Its time had come   On eleven occasions between 1938 and 1962, civil rights legislation was defeated because the Senate, normally permitting unlimited debate on a bill, refused to invoke the *cloture* rule to shut off further discussion and bring the matter to a vote. Therefore, even after the House of Representatives had passed the 1964 bill by an overwhelming margin, there was fear that it would be talked to death by a filibuster on the floor of the Senate. Just as depressing to supporters of the bill was the possibility that it would die in the Senate Judiciary Committee, traditionally exercising jurisdiction over such matters, before the entire Senate had an opportunity even to consider it. Bills are normally referred to the appropriate committee before they are considered by either house, and in the preceding ten years the Judiciary Committee, under the chairmanship of Senator James Eastland of Mississippi, had been the graveyard for no fewer than 120 out of the 121 civil rights bills referred to it.

Senate passage was assured by sending the bill to the Commerce Committee and by imposing limitations on debate. It was the first time in history that cloture had been voted on a civil rights bill. Nine days after the vote on cloture (71 to 29), the Senate passed the bill itself, 73 to 27. As the late Senator Everett Dirksen (R–Ill.), essentially conservative and flamboyantly colorful, put it, nothing is more powerful than "an idea whose time has come."

The Civil Rights Act of 1964   The idea whose time had come was a complex law divided into eleven parts, called titles. Two are of particular importance. Title II prohibits discrimination based on race, color, religion, or national origin in restaurants, gas stations, theaters, stadiums, hotels, and similar "public accommodations." Title VII forbids discrimination in employment practices based on race, color, religion, sex, or national origin by employers with twenty-five or more workers. Other provisions make a sixth-grade education sufficient proof of literacy for purposes of state voting requirements; cut off federal financial assistance from programs, including schools, which practice discrimination; and allow the U.S. Attorney General to bring suit against schools defying court decisions on desegregation.

The battle for the ballot   The Fifteenth Amendment, adopted in 1870, prohibited voting requirements based on race. Yet many states, especially in the South, displayed remarkable ingenuity in getting around it. Laws imposed ridiculously complex "literacy tests" as a prerequisite for voting and "white primary" elections excluded blacks from the selection of party candidates. Poll taxes also kept poor people (including most blacks) from the ballot boxes, and simultaneously laws had "grandfather clauses" which suspended certain other voting requirements if one's grandfather had been able to vote. Over the years several of these devices were invalidated, but they had all done their share to make the southern polling booth off limits to most blacks prior to 1965. Earlier civil rights laws changed this situation very little, and President Johnson, therefore, asked for additional legislation in this area. Assisted by a vastly expanded liberal Democratic majority resulting from the 1964 elections, Congress responded favorably with the Voting Rights Act of 1965. Its major provision permitted the national government to appoint voting examiners who, in effect, could register persons to vote in any area where there was a state literacy requirement and less than 50 percent of the persons of voting age had actually voted in the last election. It also prohibited poll taxes as voting requirements in state elections, thereby supplementing the Twenty-fourth Amendment to the Constitution which had forbidden poll taxes in the election of national officials.

The Voting Rights Act is perhaps the most effective civil rights legislation ever passed. As a result, the percentage of blacks registered to vote in the eleven southern states zoomed from 36 to 65 between 1964 and 1968.[26] While there were only thirty-six black state legislators in the entire nation in 1960, their number had grown to 205 after the 1970 elections, and Arkansas was left as the only state in the South with an all-white legislative branch. Lounds County, Alabama, exemplifies the dramatic change: In the spring of 1965, it had not a single black registered voter; in the fall of 1970, it elected a black sheriff.[27]

Further congressional action   Ironically, civil rights laws also stimulated more violent bigotry. In 1964 three young men, Michael Schwerner and Andrew Goodman (white) and James Chaney (black) were killed in Mississippi as a result of their civil rights activities. The next year, the Rev. James Reeb and Mrs. Viola Liuzzo (both white) were murdered for similar reasons in Alabama. In 1966, James Meredith— who had gained fame as the first black person admitted to the University of Mississippi—was wounded in the course of a voter registration campaign. On April 4, 1968, Martin Luther King, Jr., was assassinated in Memphis, Tennessee, while attempting to gather support for the strike of that city's predominantly black rubbish collectors. The death of Rev. King, winner of the Nobel Peace Prize and the most influential black man in America, helped to precipitate two important developments; militant black demands shifted from racial integration to "Black Power," discussed in the following chapter, and Congress passed another civil rights law.

The Civil Rights Act of 1968 contained several provisions, including harsh penalties for those who cross state lines to incite a riot or who interfere with a person's exercise of his civil rights. What seemed most significant when the law was passed was a fair housing provision

26 U.S. Bureau of the Census, *Statistical Abstract of the United States: 1971,* p. 365.
27 *Los Angeles Times,* November 29, 1970, Sec. F, p. 8.

which prohibited racial discrimination in the sale or rental of nearly 80 percent of all housing units in the nation. Less than three months after the enactment of this legislation, however, a Supreme Court decision rendered the housing section obsolete by holding that an old law passed over a hundred years earlier barred discrimination in disposing of all property.[28] The civil rights legislation passed in 1970 extended and broadened the 1965 Voting Rights Act.

Racial Realities

Any attempt to assess intelligently the attitudes attributed to either race in the 1970s requires some facts regarding the conditions of minority life.

Employment In spite of persistent obstacles, nonwhite Americans (mostly black) seem to be making important advances in getting better jobs. Between 1957 and 1970, for example, the percentage of whites working in professional and technical jobs increased 4.0 percent while their nonwhite counterparts increased 5.4 percent. More impressive is the fact that the percentage of whites engaged in clerical occupations rose 2.8 percent while the nonwhite figure went up 7.2 percent.[29] Perhaps the employment provisions of the 1964 Civil Rights Act are beginning to pay off, although progress in this area is far from consistent. An officially authorized study of the U.S. Department of Housing and Urban Development has revealed that as late as October 1970, that agency discriminated against blacks in the promotion of its own employees.[30] Moreover, the Nixon administration's "Philadelphia plan" to provide minority jobs in the construction industry has fallen short of initial expectations.

Police treatment It is almost impossible to assess changes, if any, in the behavior of police toward racial minorities. This issue has been a hot one for a long time and it caught fire with the somewhat extravagant charges of police brutality hurled by several militant groups in 1970. The Black Panther Party especially declared war on the police, and "off the pigs" (kill the cops) became a call to arms for radical groups, both white and black.

Charges of racial prejudice among law enforcement officers have had no effect upon congressional legislation thus far, but have led to demands for police review boards, staffed by civilians, in major metropolitan centers. In 1966, Mayor John Lindsay established such an agency in New York City, only to have it abolished four months later by an overwhelming vote of the people in a referendum election. The police

28 *Jones* v. *Mayer Co.*, 392 U.S. 409 (1968).
29 Computed from U.S. Bureau of the Census, *Statistical Abstract of the United States: 1971*, p. 223.
30 *Los Angeles Times*, Oct. 22, 1971, p. 20.

themselves led the attack against it. In St. Louis, where such an agency exists, it has also produced police hostility.[31]

Education Ten years after compulsory racial segregation in the public schools was declared unconstitutional, over 90 percent of the black students in seventeen southern and border states were still attending all-black schools.[32] Progress had been so slow primarily because the Supreme Court ordered desegregation to be accomplished "with all deliberate speed," recognizing that practical problems—worse in some districts than in others—would take time to solve. The result was that additional law suits were required to integrate school districts that refused to do so voluntarily.

The years since 1964 have seen changes of immense magnitude. Spurred by threats to cut off federal financial assistance and additional court decisions that condemned too much deliberation and too little speed, the pace of southern desegregation accelerated so quickly that by 1970 there was more school integration in the South than in the nation as a whole. The proportion of black students attending schools that had a white majority was nearly 40 percent in the eleven states of the deep South but only about 33 percent throughout the entire nation.[33]

This situation is one of the most ironic in the tormented history of American race relations. Its explanation lies primarily in the fact that the *Brown* desegregation case applied only to *de jure* segregation (required by law and confined primarily to the South), but not to *de facto* segregation (based upon residential housing patterns and most common in the North and West).

The school segregation controversy has now shifted to two relatively new focal points: Is *de facto* segregation also unconstitutional and is compulsory busing of students a legitimate means of overcoming it? On the first issue, a California judge insisted that there was little difference between *de jure* and *de facto* segregation in Los Angeles because the school board had drawn school attendance boundaries and located new schools in a way which resulted in an all-white enrollment in 120 of the district's 428 elementary schools and an over 80 percent black enrollment in another 64 schools.[34] The issue seems still in doubt. On the matter of forced busing, President Nixon has taken a negative view, lauding the concept of the "neighborhood school," although in 1971 the Supreme Court upheld such busing, at least on a limited basis.

Under election-year pressures, Congress enacted a law in 1972 which reflected the President's recommendations, although in drastically diluted form. It postponed the authority of the courts to order involuntary busing for purposes of racial balance. Since about 40 percent of all students take a bus to school anyway, the controversy seemed laden with racist implications. There were no impassioned pleas for

31 Jerome H. Skolnick, *The Politics of Protest* (N.Y.: Ballantine Books, Inc., 1969), pp. 278–81.
32 U.S. Bureau of the Census, *Statistical Abstract of the United States: 1970,* p. 118.
33 *Los Angeles Times,* June 18, 1971, p. 4.
34 Los Angeles County Commission on Human Relations, *Report of the Housing Committee to the Commission,* June 5, 1967, p. 6. (Mimeographed).

Bruce Roberts from Rapho Guillumette Pictures.

Cross-town busing in Charlotte, North Carolina, 1971.

Figure 12   White Parent Opinion on School Integration

Percent Objecting to Children Attending Integrated Schools

	Northern	Southern
With a few Negroes		
1963	10%	61%[1]
1970	6%	16%
With half Negroes		
1963	33%	78%
1970	24%	43%
With Negro majorities		
1963	53%	86%
1970	51%	69%

[1] Gallup calls the rapid drop in southern opposition, revealed in this column "one of the most dramatic shifts in the history of public opinion polling, bringing North and South closer together on this issue (as one can see by reading across the 1970 columns) than at any other time in recent years." While this shows considerable progress, a poll taken in 1969 showed that 44 percent of the American people believed that school integration was going "too fast." Ibid., Aug. 17, 1969, Sec. F, p. 8.

Source: Gallup Poll, *Los Angeles Times,* May 3, 1970, Sec. H, p. 4. Reprinted by permission of the American Institute of Public Opinion (The Gallup Poll).

tedious trips to crime-infested neighborhoods, but those who valued racial harmony asked two questions that were hard to ignore. Why was there no white opposition to the busing that maintained school segregation for so many years? More important, how else can black and white children overcome centuries of racial antagonism, if segregated neighborhoods prevent them from knowing one another?

Mexican-Americans are the second largest racial minority in America, and their problems are most obvious in the field of public education. Of the 1.4 million Chicano school children in Colorado, Texas, New Mexico, Arizona, and California, nearly half (635,000) are attending predominantly Mexican-American schools. Moreover, while Chicano pupils comprise 17 percent of the public school enrollment in these five southwestern states, Mexican-Americans account for only 10 percent of the school board members, 4 percent of the teachers, and 3 percent of the school principals.[35] In California, "Spanish surname persons" (mostly Chicano) achieved a median educational level of 8.6 years in 1960, compared with 10.5 for nonwhites (mostly black), and 12.1 for Anglo-American (white).[36] In five southwestern states, the U.S. Civil Rights Commission reported in 1972 that 80 percent of Mexican-American students were receiving education which showed little respect for their culture or the Spanish language, and which was inadequate to their needs. American Indians are confronted with educational disadvantages that are even greater. Ten percent of those over age fourteen have never been to school at all and more than half never completed the eighth grade.

Housing   School segregation outside the South is largely a reflection of discriminatory housing patterns. These have persisted in spite of the fact that local ordinances prohibiting blacks from inhabiting certain residential areas were declared unconstitutional in 1917.[37] In addition, "restrictive covenants" barring blacks, Orientals, and Jews from certain neighborhoods, through private deed restrictions, were invalidated in 1948.[38]

These legal advances did little to forestall increasing residential segregation in cities throughout the nation. Predominantly black areas have become more overwhelmingly black, and white regions even whiter, in such cities as Buffalo, New York; Louisville, Kentucky; Evansville, Indiana; and Raleigh, North Carolina. The black population of central cities (those at the heart of metropolitan regions) increased 31.6 percent between 1960 and 1970, while the white population dropped 1.3 percent.[39]

35 U.S. Civil Rights Commission, United Press International release, *Los Angeles Times*, August 21, 1970, p. 11.
36 A Report of the California State Advisory Committee to the U.S. Commission on Civil Rights, *Education and the Mexican-American Community in Los Angeles County*, April 1968, p. 3. (Mimeographed).
37 *Buchanan* v. *Warley*, 245 U.S. 60.
38 *Shelley* v. *Kraemer*, 334 U.S. 1.
39 U.S. Bureau of the Census, *Statistical Abstract of the United States: 1971*, p. 16.

Explanations for this growing segregation, with blacks in the big cities and whites elsewhere, are tentative and complex. For one thing, the end of the plantation or tenant farm system has abolished the need for rural blacks to live near white landowners. In urban areas, electric dishwashers and similar laborsaving devices, along with industrial mechanization, have also diminished the need for large numbers of black workers living close by. Very generally, one might conclude that automation—on the farm, in the home, and in the factory—has reduced the necessity for a large black labor force and therefore has permitted increased residential segregation. Phrased differently, what economic necessity no longer demands, racial prejudice has prohibited.[40]

From a white point of view, higher living standards have permitted moves to more expensive, cleaner, less crowded, more modern suburban environments. Black concentration in the central cities is viewed, correspondingly, as an inevitable consequence of older, cheaper housing units attracting generally poorer inhabitants.

In the final analysis, it is hard to separate racial prejudice and the disappearance of economic necessity as causes of housing segregation. If one is wealthy enough, by and large, one can afford to be a practicing segregationist.

While it is generally true that modern technology has contributed to residential segregation, another factor has helped to produce the same result. This one, however, is based upon a belief that is almost totally false: It is generally assumed that if a black family moves into a white neighborhood, property values will fall. Except for a brief period in which white home owners, inspired by this myth, try quickly to sell their houses, this is simply not true. A study of 10,000 home sales over a five-year period in San Francisco, Oakland, and Philadelphia, revealed that property values are usually at least as high in racially integrated areas as in all-white ones.[41] The contrary belief is often fostered by real estate salesmen, called "block-busters," who spread the rumor in order to sell more houses.

Institutional racism   When governmental commissions or sociologists speak of "white racism," they are talking about more than the effects of individual racial prejudice. In fact, there is considerable evidence that such bigotry is declining, and it surely would be unjust to attribute it to all whites. Instead, the experts are referring to "institutional racism," a situation in which significant social differences exist between racial groups. This condition may exist without any prejudice,

40 J. William Stinde, a perceptive Los Angeles land developer has observed that the recent availability of cheap used cars has permitted both the economic exploitation of black labor and increasing residential segregation. He notes that the percentage of black-occupied housing units in the south Los Angeles ghetto without auto use dropped by 29.5 percent between 1960 and 1965. U.S. Bureau of the Census, Current Population Reports, Series P–23, No. 18, *Characteristics of the South and East Los Angeles Areas: November 1965* (Washington, D.C.: U.S. Government Printing Office, 1966), pp. 36–37, and conversations with the author.
41 Luigi Laurenti, *Property Values and Race* (Berkeley, Calif.: University of California Press, 1960).

or even any racial discrimination, and may be illustrated by three examples: (1) Predominantly white public schools in large cities are usually in better condition and more modern than others, not because of discrimination but because racial minorities in search of cheaper housing live in older neighborhoods, with older schools; (2) Proportionately more battle casualties are suffered by minority groups because their members have less education to gain them draft exemptions or noncombat army jobs; (3) Nonwhites are often the first to be fired during times of recession, not because of lack of ability or employer prejudice, but because they have been the most recently hired, and union contracts protect the seniority of older workers. Other important differences, stemming chiefly from institutional racism, are shown in Figure 13. A racist society is one that permits such differences to continue.

Figure 13   Racial Differences

	Infant Death Rate[1]		Median School Years Completed		Unemployment Rate		Median Family Income	
	1960	1968	1960	1970	1960	1970	1960	1969
White	22.9%	19.2%	10.9	12.2	4.9%	4.5%	$5835	$9794
Non-white	43.2	34.5	8.2	10.1	10.2	8.2	3233	5999

[1] Per 1000 live births

Source: U.S. Bureau of the Census, *Statistical Abstract of the United States: 1971,* pp. xviv, xxv, xxvi, and 53; and *Los Angeles Times,* July 16, 1970, p. 22.

EQUAL PROTECTION OF THE LAWS: ONE MAN, ONE VOTE

One of the nation's leading authorities on constitutional law has observed that "Negroes would probably constitute a minority of those who have invoked the equal protection clause against discriminatory treatment."[42] Indeed, the largest group to benefit from this provision is not racial but geographic—those who live in and around the nation's major cities.

Rural Dominance

Farm interests have dominated American government for most of our history. This was quite proper until urban dwellers began to outnumber the rural population shortly before 1920, but the situation persisted until the 1960s and still does, to some degree.

Legislative apportionment   Perhaps the chief reason for the

42 Robert F. Cushman, *Cases in Civil Liberties* (N.Y.: Appleton-Century-Crofts, 1968), p. 541.

excess political power of rural areas lies in the way in which seats in Congress and the state legislatures are distributed, or apportioned.

The United States Senate, with two members per state, gives the farmers an enormous advantage because the small states, mostly rural, have as many votes as bigger ones with huge metropolitan centers. The fifty-two senators from the twenty-six states with the fewest people represent fewer people than the four senators from California and New York.[43] This imbalance, or malapportionment, of Senate seats seems destined to get worse. Nothing can be done about it since the only provision of the Constitution which cannot be amended, according to Article V, is the one which guarantees an equal number of senators from each state.

Seats in the upper houses of the state legislatures have also been apportioned to benefit rural areas since most state constitutions allocated state senate seats among counties or other local units of government in a way similar to that in which U.S. senators' seats were allocated among the states in our federal union. Such representation schemes produced a number of state senates in which urban majorities fared even worse than in the U.S. Senate. In Nevada, for example, senators from the two largest urban counties, with 62 percent of the population, amounted to only 12 percent of the total membership of the state senate. Similarly, urban counties with over half of the state population had only 38 percent of the state senate seats in New Jersey, 24 percent in Florida and Delaware, and 10 percent in California.[44]

The state legislatures themselves have had the responsibility for drawing the boundaries of districts from which members of their own lower houses are elected. They determine as well the boundaries for congressional districts, from which members of the U.S. House of Representatives are chosen. Since these legislatures were initially under farm control, it is not surprising that they apportioned these districts—or refused to reapportion them—in such a way as to keep their own jobs and, on occasion, to help to insure the election of some of their members to Congress. Consequently, even as rural areas were losing thousands of people to the lure of the city and suburban life, they were able to retain most of their legislative seats.

The failure of the state legislatures to pass reapportionment laws to insure that equal numbers of people would elect equal numbers of lawmakers produced predictably bizarre results. In Tennessee, which had not changed the district boundaries for over sixty years, legislators from Nashville represented districts averaging over 54,000 people in 1961, while a representative from a rural area represented only 3948 people—along with 8611 cows and 4739 pigs and horses.[45] Less than 29 percent of the people could elect a majority of the members in the

43 Glendon Schubert, ed., *Reapportionment* (N.Y.: Charles Scribner's Sons, 1965), p. 169.
44 Gordon E. Baker, *Rural versus Urban Political Power* (Garden City, N.Y.: Doubleday & Company, Inc., 1955), p. 16.
45 Editorial, *New Republic*, January 29, 1962; p. 3.

Tennessee General Assembly. The situation in many other states was similar, and often worse. In Vermont, 11.6 percent of the population could elect over 50 percent of the members in the lower house of the legislature, as could 12 percent in Florida, 18.5 in Kansas and Delaware, and 22.6 in Georgia.[46] Congressional districts as drawn by state legislatures revealed the same sort of population disparities. In 1962 thirteen states had at least one congressional district over twice the population of its smallest one.

Gerrymandering   State legislators have been in the habit of drawing election district boundaries to their own advantage for at least a century and a half. During that time, the weirdly shaped results have been known as *gerrymanders,* after Governor Elbridge Gerry of Massachusetts who signed a reapportionment bill in 1812 containing a district whose shape resembled a legendary animal called the salamander. More will be said of this in Chapter 10.

Not until 1946 did the Supreme Court face the issue of the constitutionality of a gerrymander which created districts with huge population differences, each selecting a single official. The case before it involved obvious bias in favor of agricultural regions: Southern Illinois, mostly rural, elected proportionately more congressmen than the larger populations of northern Illinois concentrated in and around the Chicago metropolitan area. The high court decided it could do nothing about it. In Justice Frankfurter's words, the apportionment issue was a "political thicket," a nonjusticiable question that the Constitution intended to be decided not by the courts but by the popularly elected legislative and executive branches.[47]

". . . People, not trees or acres"   But sixteen years later in *Baker* v. *Carr,*[48] the Court ruled that legislative apportionment *was* an issue properly subject to judicial attention. If equal numbers of voters could not elect equal numbers of legislators, they could scarcely expect the constitutionally guaranteed "equal protection of the laws." The *Baker* case involved the lower house of the Tennessee legislature, and was interpreted by lower courts to require that at least one house of all state legislatures had to be chosen from equally populated districts.

Two years later, there followed *Wesberry* v. *Sanders* in which the Court voted, 6–2, that state legislatures must also apportion congressional districts in a way that permitted equal numbers of voters to elect equal numbers of members of the House of Representatives.[49] Completing the process, the Court concluded its 1964 session by ruling that the "equal protection" clause required *both* houses of a state legislature to be elected from districts with approximately the same

---

46 Schubert, op. cit., p. 82.
47 *Colegrove* v. *Green,* 328 U.S. 549 (1946).
48 369 U.S. 186 (1962).
49 376 U.S. 1 (1964). *Wesberry* did not impose the equal population rule on the basis of the "equal protection" clause of Amendment Fourteen, but on the basis of Article I, Section 2, which requires that members of the House Representatives be elected "by the People"—presumably in equal numbers.

population. The key case, *Reynolds* v. *Sims,* produced the "one man, one vote" formula which held that a person's vote in any district should have as much influence in electing a candidate as any other person's vote in any other district. Or as Chief Justice Warren put it: "Legislators represent people, not trees or acres."[50]

Just as the *Baker, Wesberry,* and *Reynolds* cases required substantial equality in the populations which elected certain national and state officials, so *Avery* v. *Midland County,* a case from Texas, demanded the same standards in the selection of "a city council, school board, or county governing board."[51]

In 1962, Justice Frankfurter indicated in his *Baker* dissent that this initial reapportionment decision simply would not be obeyed. He confidently predicted that the Court ruling was "merely empty rhetoric, sounding a word of promise to the ear, sure to be disappointing in the hope."[52] Yet Frankfurter, for all his cynical realism, was dramatically wrong. Eight years after his pessimistic prediction, ninety-five of America's ninety-nine state legislative bodies had been reapportioned to meet the "one man, one vote" standard.[53] Similar progress seems indicated in congressional districting. The result is a substantial increase in the political power of the cities and suburbs.

Equal Protection in other Areas

The importance of the "equal protection" clause of Amendment Fourteen extends beyond questions of race or legislative apportionment. Under this constitutional provision, various courts have also held that states may not designate males over females in the administration of wills, require jail sentences of those too poor to pay fines, or keep the names of candidates who can't afford filing fees off the ballot. Most important, perhaps, is that courts in California, Minnesota, Texas, and New Jersey have ruled that public schools can no longer be financed primarily by a local property tax because such a scheme denies equal educational opportunity to students in poor districts.

50 377 U.S. 533.
51 390 U.S. 474 (1968).
52 *Baker* v. *Carr,* 81 S.Ct. 691, at 739.
53 George B. Merry, "U.S. Census Promises Fresh Wave of Redistricting," *The Christian Science Monitor,* July 23, 1970, p. 1. Only the South Carolina and Alaska lower houses and both houses of the Oregon legislature were apportioned so fairly before 1962 as to require no change. There are only ninety-nine legislative bodies at the state level because Nebraska has a unicameral legislature.

Conclusion to Part Two

The Constitution exalts the free mind and commits the government to no creed but tolerance. As a result, it guarantees the freedom in which a new idea or an unpopular cause may grow and even flourish. It also provides the protection of fair procedure for the defendant confronting the awesome power of criminal prosecution, and it seeks to guarantee equal legal treatment. Yet fairness and equality, in life as well as in law, proceed not only from official policy but from the widely shared conviction that all humanity is precious. Unless the constitutional safeguards protect each of us, no matter how despised or even truly despicable, the rights of all of us someday may be in jeopardy.

Like all great constitutional standards, those described in the last three chapters are sometimes abused in the rough and tumble of legislative and executive processes. Their chief protection, therefore, has come primarily from the courts. More than most of us, judges have recognized that if the rights of the people are to be preserved, the power of government must be limited.

Bibliography

Chapter 3

Freedom of Expression: First Things First

Abraham, Henry J., *Freedom and the Court* (N.Y.: Oxford University Press, Inc., 1967).
Chafee, Jr., Zechariah, *Free Speech in the United States* (New York, Atheneum Publishers, 1969).
Cushman, Robert F., ed., *Cases in Civil Liberties* (N.Y.: Appleton-Century-Crofts, 1968).

Meiklejohn, Alexander, *Free Speech and Its Relation to Self-Government* (N.Y.: Harper & Row, Publishers, 1948).
Mill, John Stuart, *On Liberty* (Chicago: Gateway Edition, Henry Regnery Co., 1955).
Sheldon, Charles H., ed., *The Supreme Court: Politicians in Robes* (Beverly Hills, Calif.: Glencoe Press, 1970).

Chapter 4

The Defendant's Rights: Criminal Justice in America

Campbell, James S., *et al., Law and Order Reconsidered,* A Staff Report to the National Commission on the Causes and Prevention of Violence (N.Y.: Bantam Books, Inc., 1970).
Cray, Ed, *The Big Blue Line* (N.Y.: Coward-McCann, Inc., 1967).
Crime and the Law, (Washington, D.C.: Congressional Quarterly Service, 1971).
Tellman, David, *The Defendant's Rights* (N.Y.: Holt, Rinehart & Winston, Inc., 1958).
Germann, A. C., Frank D. Day, and Robert R. J. Gallati, *Introduction to Law Enforcement* (Springfield, Ill.: Charles C Thomas, Publisher, 1962).
Inbau, Fred E., and John E. Reid, *Criminal Interrogation and Confessions* (Baltimore: The Williams and Wilkins Co., 1962).
Tappan, Paul W., *Crime, Justice and Correction* (N.Y.: McGraw-Hill Book Company, 1960).

Chapter 5

Equal Justice Under Law: Of Dreams Deferred

Baker, Gordon E., *Rural versus Urban Political Power* (Garden City, N.Y.: Doubleday & Company, Inc., 1955).
Fishel, Jr., Leslie H., and Benjamin Quarles, eds., *The Black American* (Glenview, Ill.: Scott, Foresman and Company, 1970).
Myers, Gustavus, *History of Bigotry in the United States,* ed. by Henry M. Christman (N.Y.: Capricorn Books, G. P. Putnam's Sons, 1960).

Schubert, Glendon, ed., *Reapportionment* (N.Y.: Charles Scribner's Sons, 1965).
Seib, Shirley M., ed., *Revolution in Civil Rights,* 3rd ed. (Washington, D.C.: Congressional Quarterly , Inc., 1967).
Silberman, Charles, *Crisis in Black and White* (N.Y.: Random House, Inc., 1964).
U.S. Commission on Civil Rights, *Racial Isolation in the Public Schools,* vol. 1 (Washington, D.C.: U.S. Government Printing Office, 1967).

PART THREE

POLITICAL BEHAVIOR

A democracy does what a majority of the people wants it to do. Effective methods of communication, therefore, are indispensable to democratic government, so a majority on any particular issue can inform government officials of its wishes. The next three chapters describe the most effective communication channels available in American politics. Chapter 7 stresses the importance of concerted group action, suggesting how opinions are formed and how pressure groups transmit those opinions to the government through various kinds of lobbying techniques. Chapter 8 deals with political parties, the groups which are formed specifically for the purpose of electing officials, and which help to formulate policy alternatives. Since communication is a two-way process, Chapter 9 considers the campaigns in which politicians attempt to win the people's favor, and the voting process by which majorities are won at the polls. In all three of these chapters, we thus deal with behavior that links the citizens to the government and transmits policy preferences back and forth between the people and the politicians.

Chapter **6**

The People's Influence
Public Opinion and Pressure Groups

*If there is no struggle, there is no progress. Those who
profess to favor freedom, and yet deprecate agitation, are men
who want crops without plowing up the ground. They want
the rain without thunder and lightning. . . . Power concedes
nothing without a demand. It never did and never will.*
Frederick Douglass

Power is a two-way street. Government can alter the behavior of the people, and in a democracy the people can alter the direction of government policy as well. But what do the people want and how can they get it? This chapter may give some clues.

THE DYNAMICS OF PUBLIC OPINION

Democracy has been described as a government chosen by and responsive to a majority of the adult population. This is simply another way of saying that it rests upon public opinion, defined as the beliefs shared by large numbers of people regarding some issues of public importance.

Political Socialization:
The Transfer of Opinion

How do people acquire their opinions? How are the attitudes and values that make up their political culture transferred from one generation to the next? Answers to these questions lie in the study of political socialization, a relatively new research area.

The family   Even while many people (mostly parents) are worrying about the "generation gap," there is considerable evidence that most persons—at least in political matters—have views substantially similar to those of their elders. One study, for example, disclosed that only 12 percent of the people whose parents were both Democrats identified themselves as Republicans, and only 16 percent of those whose parents were both Republicans were traitorous enough to become Democrats.[1] The influence of the older generation, moreover, is apparent at an early age. Greenstein found that by the age of ten over 60 percent of a group of Connecticut children were able to express a party preference, even though only "little more than a third . . . could name even one (leader) of either of the two major parties."[2]

Any political ideas tend either to stabilize the status quo by perpetuating established values, or to promote change by challenging the existing order of things. There is little doubt that ideas obtained in the family, or at least somewhere before the child reaches high school, are primarily of the former variety. Children seem to have viewed the United States government as the next best thing to Disneyland and have attributed to government officials qualities of power and goodness usually imputed only to saints. A study of pupils in grades three through eight in the Chicago area revealed that from 70 to 84 percent of them agreed that "The government usually knows what is best for the people."[3] The Connecticut research mentioned earlier disclosed that nearly all children view the President and mayor very favorably. The President, somewhat typically, was thought by a fifth-grade girl to "stop bad things before they start," and a fourth-grade boy believed that the mayor "helps everyone to have nice homes and jobs."[4]

In view of this general acceptance of "the best of all possible worlds," one scholar concluded that the "early family socialization process is . . . one of the most important factors making for the resistance to social and political change."[5] Adult dissatisfaction with the Vietnam war, however, has forced a reexamination of some of these conclusions. A study released in 1971 confirms family influence on children's political views, but shows, as a result, that 45 percent of elementary school pupils doubted that the President always tells the truth about the conflict in southeast Asia.[6]

1 Angus Campbell, Gerald Gurin, and Warren E. Miller, *The Voter Decides* (N.Y.: Harper & Row, Publishers, 1954), p. 99.
2 Fred I. Greenstein, *Children and Politics* (New Haven: Yale University Press, 1965).
3 David Easton and Jack Dennis, "The Child's Image of Government," *The Annals of the American Academy of Political and Social Science* 361 (September 1965).
4 Fred I. Greenstein, "The Benevolent Leader: Children's Images of Political Authority," *The American Political Science Review* 54 (December 1960): 934–43.
5 Gabriel A. Almond, "A Functional Approach to Comparative Politics," Gabriel A. Almond and James S. Coleman, eds., *The Politics of Developing Areas* (Princeton: Princeton University Press, 1960), p. 27.
6 *Los Angeles Times,* October 17, 1971, Sec. F, p. 2. The research was under the direction of Professor Howard Tolley.

The schools   It is generally agreed that compulsory school attendance affects political socialization, and that it does so in a way which bolsters the prevailing norms, or standards, of our society. This simply indicates that the schools do what we want them to do. "Nationalistic values," as two observers have written, "permeate the entire school curriculum . . ."[7]

After examining teaching materials used in Los Angeles County, Will Scoggins, a leading labor historian, concluded that "the United States as portrayed in high-school social studies textbooks would seem very near paradise for a man who was blind to economic and social facts."[8] The texts most commonly used are more objective than was once the case, however. A study by Edgar Litt indicated that students in three Boston area high schools showed greater support of democratic ideals as a result of a semester course in civics, but the effects of the course depended in considerable part on the nature of the community in which it was taught.[9] School influence far exceeds the impact of textbooks and subject matter, of course. In extracurricular activities and patriotic rituals it infuses the minds of the students with the political attitudes and values of their elders. That's what the socialization process is all about.

Peer groups   But individual Americans do not simply respond passively to the programming of organized institutions such as family and school. They seek and usually share the opinions of their friends and fellow workers—those whom sociologists call their peers. One study showed that 88 percent of those whose three best friends were Republicans voted Republican, and 85 percent of those whose best friends were Democrats voted Democratic.[10] It is difficult to tell, of course, whether our choice of friends determines our political views, or whether our political views determine our choice of friends. In either event, the desire to belong, to be accepted, may convert one's social circle into a sort of filter, straining out those ideas that are either unacceptable or unknown to the group as a whole.

The Mass Media: Information Dissemination

Newspapers, magazines, radio, television, and other methods of mass communication are also sources of political socialization. Although their impact is not so personal or intimate as that of a family member, teacher, or friend, they reach a far larger audience.

Newspapers   Thomas Jefferson wrote to a friend in 1816

7 Richard E. Dawson and Kenneth Prewitt, *Political Socialization* (Boston: Little, Brown and Company, 1969), p. 147.
8 *Labor in Learning* (Los Angeles: U.C.L.A., Institute of Industrial Relations, 1966), p. vii.
9 Edgar Litt, "Civic Education, Community Norms, and Political Indoctrination," *American Sociological Review* 28 (February 1963): 69–75.
10 V. O. Key, Jr., *Politics, Parties, and Pressure Groups,* 5th ed. (N. Y.: Thomas Y. Crowell Company, 1964), p. 120.

that "Where the press is free, and every man able to read, all is safe."[11] Yet recent experience suggests that perhaps newspapers are not quite so important as Jefferson believed. The evidence, at least, seems mixed. On the one hand, the paid circulation of daily papers is over sixty-two million.[12] President Nixon has sent personal letters praising editorials he admires,[13] and, in an earlier day, when he had just been defeated for the California governorship, he blamed the press for his loss. President Kennedy was so unhappy with the *New York Times'* coverage of the Vietnam war that he suggested to the publisher that its reporter in that country be assigned elsewhere.[14] Important officeholders have more or less regular press conferences, and the legendary "fearless reporter" is believed to have struck frequent terror into the hearts of corrupt local politicians. It was the work of newspaper reporters that revealed the medical history of Senator Thomas Eagleton, which led to his withdrawal from the vice-presidential race in 1972. In addition, newspapers can influence people indirectly because they are widely read by "opinion makers" such as politicians, authors, teachers, and clergymen.

On the other hand, radio and television have replaced the newspapers as a prime source of information for many Americans; consequently, the impact of the press on election results is of doubtful importance. One indication of this is that although most newspapers usually endorse Republican party candidates editorially, the Democrats controlled Congress for all but four years between 1930 and 1972. In 1960, John F. Kennedy was elected president with the support of less than one third of the nation's daily newspapers, and even these had only 16 percent of the total daily circulation.[15] But while most editorial writers support Republican candidates, the working reporters who write the front-page stories tend to favor the Democratic party[16] and may—as President Nixon once implied—slant their stories to reflect that bias.

Three trends in the newspaper field require brief mention. First, the total number of papers declined by over seven hundred between 1950 and 1971[17] largely because of increased operating costs and the resulting mergers—prevalent in other industries as well.

Second, an increasing percentage of newspaper space is filled by syndicated material sold to hundreds of papers throughout the country and proportionately less is devoted to locally produced journalism. The result may be that the public receives more information about national and international affairs but less about state and local political issues. The same news stories written by reporters for the Associated

11 Saul K. Padover, ed., *Thomas Jefferson On Democracy* (N. Y.: Pelican Books, Penguin Books Inc., 1946), p. 89.
12 U. S. Bureau of the Census, *Statistical Abstract of the United States: 1971*, p. 490.
13 *Time,* August 31, 1970, p. 45.
14 David Halberstam, *The Making of a Quagmire* (N. Y.: Random House, Inc., 1965), p. 268. Halberstam was the reporter in question.
15 *New York Times,* November 4, 1960, p. 24.
16 Seymour Martin Lipset, *Political Man* (Garden City, N.Y.: Anchor Books, Doubleday & Company, Inc., 1963), pp. 339–40. This was true both in the mid-1930s and mid-1950s.
17 U.S. Bureau of the Census, *Statistical Abstract of the United States: 1971*, p. 491.

Press (AP) and United Press International (UPI) appear in papers all over the country. A similar situation exists with respect to the work of editorial cartoonists and political columnists.

Third, there has been a notable decrease in locally owned newspapers, not only because there are fewer newspapers but because many of those that remain are owned by the same corporation. These newspaper chains often control other mass media outlets as well. The most famous is that founded by William Randolph Hearst which "includes 12 newspapers, 14 magazines, three television stations, six radio stations, a news service, a photo service, a feature syndicate, and Avon paperbacks."[18] Another communications octopus is the Knight chain which owns papers in Miami, Detroit, Akron, and Charlotte.

All of these developments are parts of the same problem: more and more people are acquiring information and attitudes from fewer and fewer sources. To some extent, the same problem exists with respect to magazines.

Television and radio Television and radio stations are licensed by the Federal Communications Commission and neither has been given the special freedom guaranteed to the press by the First Amendment. Both television and radio are required by the Federal Communications Commission to give equal time to different candidates for the same office and to honor the *fairness doctrine* in presenting both sides of important issues. It is generally agreed that television now reaches more people than any other medium. It is the only one of the mass media that reaches the child early enough and often enough to rival his family in shaping values and molding opinions. It first gained political notice in 1948, and by 1960 it had become the most important single vehicle for campaign propaganda. It is widely credited with a decisive role in determining the outcome of the 1960 Kennedy-Nixon presidential race since the two candidates met in four nationally televised face-to-face debates. After the first of these confrontations, public opinion polls show that Kennedy picked up 4 percent of the probable vote and thereby took a narrow lead which he never lost.[19]

A survey completed in the mid-1960s reveals that television is the chief source of information for most people and that they have considerable confidence in its reliability.[20] In view of the pervasive impact of this newest of media (98 percent of all American homes had at least one set in 1971),[21] it is not surprising that a philosopher should emerge to try to explain its significance. "A new form of 'politics' is emerging," wrote Marshall McLuhan,

18 G. William Domhoff, *Who Rules America?* (Englewood Cliffs, N.J.: Prentice-Hall, Inc., 1967), p. 81.
19 See Hugh A. Bone and Austin Ranney, *Politics and Voters* (N.Y.: McGraw-Hill Book Company, 1963), p. 38, Table 8.
20 James D. Barber, *Citizen Politics* (Chicago: Markham Publishing Co., 1969), pp. 124–25.
21 U.S. Bureau of the Census, *Statistical Abstract of the United States: 1971*, p. 677.

and in ways we haven't yet noticed. The living room has become a voting booth. Participation via television in Freedom Marches, in war, revolution, pollution, and other events is changing *everything*.[22]

There are signs, however, that television's impact is not unlimited. The general public is becoming aware that this medium is even more monopolized than newspapers. Three networks, NBC, CBS, and ABC, have a virtual stranglehold on national and international news. One may reject, therefore, the views of David Brinkley, Walter Cronkite, and Howard K. Smith (all liberal to moderate in their interpretations), and still claim that his own personal attitudes are ·"correct." Vice President Agnew has attacked TV news reporters as "a tiny enclosed fraternity of privileged men" who are "supersensitive, self-annointed, supercilious electronic barons of opinion." His view that the mass media in general, and television in particular, have an anticonservative bias is shared by a significant percentage of the general population.[23]

Additionally, the opinions and attitudes developed over a lifetime form a sort of selective sieve that permits us to see primarily that which we wish to see, whether on television or in direct observation. Thus, we often do not perceive those impressions which might challenge our values or beliefs to an emotionally disturbing degree.

Whereas the family, school, and peer group largely tend to reinforce prevailing opinions and thereby strengthen the *status quo,* this is not so much the case with the mass media. Although the latter have a conservative bias in behalf of maintaining the conditions under which they presently exist, they are also committed, by their essential function, to report the new and different. Nevertheless, at least one expert believes that political opinions are so firmly rooted in social and psychological influences that newspapers, radio, and television serve mostly to reinforce existing attitudes.[24]

Public Opinion and Political Activity

Public opinion has political significance when it is translated into overt behavior. This could be negative, as in not voting or in expressing cynicism about the whole political process. If widespread, such alienation might severely diminish respect for government and hence the authority it exercises.

Normally, however, public opinion results in various kinds of positive behavior, each with a different degree of impact on the political system. For example, the individual may vote, urge friends to vote, write letters to the press and public officials, "walk a precinct" for a

22 Marshall McLuhan and Quentin Fiore, *The Medium Is the Massage* (N.Y.: Bantam Books, Inc., 1967), p. 22.
23 *Newsweek,* November 9, 1970, pp. 22–25.
24 Joseph T. Klapper, *The Effects of Mass Communication* (N.Y.: The Free Press, 1960), pp. 8–15.

political candidate, join a pressure group, make a campaign contribution, or run for office. What the individual does will be determined not only by his or her political resources (time, money, role, skills) but also by the intensity of his or her opinions about public matters. Consequently, the intensity of public opinion is as important a dimension as its content. If Jones thinks Smith would be a good governor, but doesn't believe this with much intensity or conviction, he may not even bother to vote. But if Green believes this very strongly she will not only vote for Smith but campaign for him with vigor. Politicians resort to highly emotional appeals more to increase the intensity of convictions than to change them. Public opinion polls often acknowledge the importance of this factor by asking their respondents whether they "strongly favor," "mildly favor," "mildly oppose," or "strongly oppose" a particular candidate or proposal. The distinctions indicate the kind of behavior which is likely to ensue.

The influences which determine the intensity of public opinion are the same as those which determine its content (family, friends, press, and so forth), plus an additional one—a sense of political efficacy. In other words, if one believes that what one does can make a difference, one is more likely to do it than if it seems that it will not matter anyway. A sense of political efficacy appears to be related both to social status and personality characteristics.

GROUP POLITICS

The United States has a population so vast that the voice of the individual can easily get lost. In fact, were it not so, government agencies would be widely and properly denounced for yielding to the wishes of a single person. Most political participation, therefore, is a collective phenomenon, because groups of individuals—bound together by mutual need and common interests—attempt to influence government policy.

Just as the people influence the government largely through group politics, so also government policy concerns itself almost entirely with groups, with types of activity, instead of with the individual citizen. Therefore, the analysis of group politics is essential to an understanding of modern democracy.

The Types of Groups

One must first distinguish those groups that are politically meaningless from those that are politically relevant. The former are sometimes called *categoric* and are based on certain shared characteristics that have little political importance. People with red hair or people with sisters are examples in point. By contrast, politically relevant groups are based on some common *interest* as a result of which their members are affected by certain government policies in much the same way. Indians, veterans, and doctors are interest groups. Students of politics are concerned with interest groups, which in turn can be subdivided into unorganized (or informal) and organized (or formal) groups.

The importance of organization   Unorganized groups tend to be relatively impotent in influencing the important conditions that affect their lives. Children, the insane, and poor people are examples, exerting little political clout. Indeed, some of the most important political changes throughout our history have come about when previously unorganized groups "got themselves together" through formal organization. Slavery was ended only after those opposed to it formed abolition societies, the work day was shortened after laborers unionized, and civil rights laws were passed after minority groups organized.

This raises a question which is of the utmost tactical importance: What ingredients must be added to simple group membership for effective group organization? Six factors seem paramount:

1) Group consciousness: The members must realize that they are a group with common interests and common wants.

2) Leadership: At least a few members must possess the knowledge, intelligence, dedication, efficiency, persuasiveness, and popularity to create the organization and articulate its goals.

3) Communication: There must be a way for the members to communicate with each other, either through meetings or through mimeographed pamphlets, newspapers, radio, or television.

4) Money: It may not take much, but there must be financial resources to defray leadership expenses and the cost of whatever communications media are used.

5) Hope: An air of hopelessness blights the prospects for effective group action. Any sign of possible improvement—any "light at the end of the tunnel"—may engender what has been called a revolution of rising expectations and inspire more consolidated group effort.

6) Ideology: Most people will sacrifice very little—even organizational dues—on behalf of a common cause unless it can be justified by some idea or doctrine. It may be as simple as "brotherhood" or "justice," but it is necessary to legitimize the organization, to assure the members that it is "right."

The important organized interests discussed later in this chapter possess in varying degree these basic characteristics.

Membership groups and reference groups   For a long time foreign observers have been commenting on the strong tendency of Americans to seek group associations. These associations may be personal ones that involve membership in organizations such as unions, or clubs, or they may be vicarious ones that the individual respects and identifies with (feels he is similar to), even though he may not belong to them. The former are *membership groups* and the latter *reference groups*. The influence of a group in which one is a member is more or less direct but the importance of reference groups requires a few more words.[25] A reference group is one from which a person derives his values or standards, whether he belongs to it or not. For the most part, individuals adopt the opinions of reference groups because they admire people in those groups, fulfill certain emotional needs to "belong" in that manner, or hope to obtain personal advantage as a result. Some white people, for example, support predominantly black organizations, while many blacks adopt the values of white society; rising young business executives model their opinions on those of the top management of the companies for which they work.

Primary groups and secondary groups In some groups, people have regular face-to-face relationships with each other. These *primary groups* include the family, the local parish congregation, and one's job associates. As a rule, such primary groups have a greater influence on our political ideas than the *secondary groups* of which we are also members, but which are bigger, more impersonal, and may involve little or no personal contact. The United States Chamber of Commerce, the Catholic Church, and the National Rifle Association are examples of secondary groups. In this sort of classification, the small (primary group) is often mightier than the large (secondary group).

Ingroups and outgroups There seems to be a natural inclination to divide people into "we" and "they" or—as the sociologists would put it—into ingroups and outgroups. One generally views with indifference, suspicion, or hostility the "outs" to which one does not belong, but shares the opinions of the "ins" to which one does. Although this sort of division is nearly universal, it may spring less from a natural inclination than from the conscious attempts of each group to instill a feeling of loyalty among its own members. Figure 14 depicts the various kinds of groups.

Economic Pressure Groups

In politics, as in nearly everything else, the wheel that squeaks the loudest gets the grease. *Pressure groups are organized interest groups that attempt to influence government policy,* and are among the biggest wheels in the American political machine. Their squeaks rarely go ungreased by some sort of government service. Among the major pressure groups are those that represent the chief elements of the American economy—business, labor, agriculture, and the professions.

The nation's business Of those who speak for business, the National Association of Manufacturers (NAM) and the U.S. Chamber of Commerce are the most prominent. The NAM, founded in 1895, consists of large industrial corporations—what might loosely be called big business—and the Chamber of Commerce, established in 1912,

25 Heinz Eulau, *The Behavioral Persuasion in Politics* (N.Y.: Random House, Inc., 1963), pp. 53–54.

Figure 14   Types of Groups

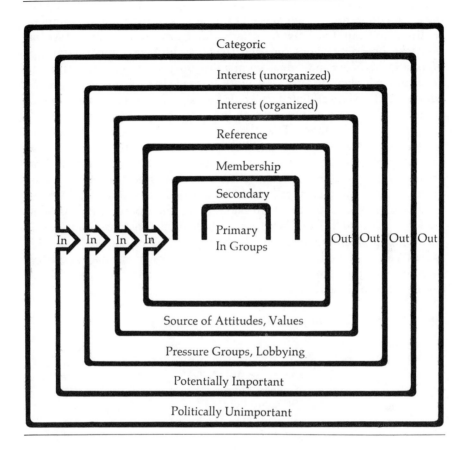

is made up chiefly of retail merchants, or small business firms.[26] While these two groups occasionally differ, they share a basic conservatism that leads them to join in opposition to most welfare programs, to the relatively high taxes necessary to pay for such benefits, and to most proposals made by labor unions.

Each kind of business also normally maintains its own specialized pressure group. Among the many examples, the American Petroleum Institute has assisted oil companies and mineral producers in obtaining depletion allowances that have resulted in lower taxes; the National Association of Real Estate Boards has lobbied hard for government-guaranteed loans for house buyers; and the Association of American Railroads has fought for authorization from the Interstate Commerce Commission to raise freight rates. There is often a clash of competing economic interests between specific groups. The natural gas industry and

---

26 Harmon Zeigler, *Interest Groups in American Society* (Englewood Cliffs, N.J.: Prentice-Hall, Inc., 1964).

electric power companies are inevitable foes, for example, with more stringent government regulation of one giving the other an advantage in the competition for a larger share of the stove and oven market. Similarly, the American Trucking Association and the Air Transport Association take opposing views on such issues as highway construction appropriations. Most individual companies do not attempt to influence government policy directly, but work instead through pressure groups with which they are affiliated. It would be naive, however, to assume that America's corporate giants exert no influence on government policy.

The unions   The first enduring labor alliance was the American Federation of Labor (AFL) formed in 1886. It was an association of highly skilled workers, such as carpenters and machinists, organized into trade, or craft, unions—the aristocracy of the labor movement, as some have called it. Not until half a century later, in the midst of America's Great Depression, were the poorer and unskilled workers unionized. The Congress of Industrial Organizations (CIO), was a group of unions each of which included all production workers, skilled and unskilled alike, who were employed in any one industry. Leading examples are the United Steel Workers and the International Brotherhood of Electrical Workers.

Figure 15   America's Largest Corporations

1969 Rank	Company	Net Profits[1]
1	American Tel. & Tel.	2,199
2	General Motors	1,711
3	Standard Oil (N.J.)	1,048
4	Int. Business Mach.	934
5	Texaco	770
6	Gulf Oil	611
7	Ford Motor	547
8	Standard Oil (Calif.)	454
9	Sears, Roebuck	441
10	Mobil Oil	435
11	Eastman Kodak	401
12	Du Pont, E.I.	356
13	Standard Oil (Ind.)	321
14	Shell Oil	291
15	General Electric	278
16	General Tel. & Elec.	237
17	International Tel.	234
18	Atlantic Richfield	227
19	United States Steel	217
20	Proctor & Gamble	187

[1] In millions of dollars.
Source: *The New York Times Encyclopedic Almanac* 1971, p. 637. Note: Five of the ten largest are oil companies, due in part to the tax depletion allowance mentioned in the text. Each of the three largest have net profits exceeding the total revenue of 27 states in 1969. U.S. Bureau of the Census, *The Statistical Abstract of the United States: 1971*, p. 410.

After some twenty years of rivalry, mutual animosity between the craft unions and the industrial unions declined enough that a single giant labor federation could be formed in 1955 by a merger of the AFL and CIO. Although it encompassed more than a hundred groups, neither the Teamsters Union nor the United Auto Workers, now the two largest in the entire nation, belong to the AFL-CIO. Other independent unions are various railroad brotherhoods, the United Mine Workers, and the International Longshoremen's and Warehousemen's Union.

There are now about twenty million union members in America, constituting approximately one quarter of the total labor force.[27] Automation has cut heavily into the jobs available in many of those industries which were once most effectively unionized, such as newspaper printers and typesetters, sheet metal workers, and musicians. Offsetting this downward trend, however, is union growth among farm laborers, white-collar workers, and government employees such as social workers and teachers. The old distinction between craft and industrial unions has become blurred and some unions are ignoring their traditional jurisdictional boundaries in much the same way as business conglomerates are now diversifying their activity. Thus, the Teamsters Union, which initially consisted of wagon and truck drivers almost exclusively, now embraces many warehouse and processing employees, taxi drivers, airline workers, and people in other occupations as well.

Unions have been largely liberal: They have worked persistently for larger pensions and medical care through the social security program, passage of civil rights laws, higher miminum wages and lower maximum hours, and more expenditures for public schools. Union leadership is divided and somewhat confused regarding its proper role. Some officials, like George Meany, president of the AFL-CIO, seem content to concentrate on such bread-and-butter issues as higher wages and job security for those already unionized. As part of the "establishment," they dine at the White House and usually support the administration's foreign adventures. In contrast, men like the late Walter Reuther of the UAW and Cesar Chavez of the United Farm Workers have had a broader vision of organizing the dispossessed and powerless.

The voices of the farmer   The major agricultural pressure group is the American Farm Bureau Federation, founded in 1919 and possessing a reported membership of about a million and a half. Its members are concentrated largely in the corn and cotton belts of the Midwest and South and include many of the richest farmers with the largest agricultural acreage in the nation. It has enjoyed unusually close relations with agricultural agencies in both the national and state governments.[28] The National Grange, the oldest of the major farm groups, is

27 Estimates based largely on data in U.S. Bureau of the Census, *Statistical Abstract of the United States: 1971,* pp. 233–34. Much of the material in this section reflects the erudition and insight of Paul Perlin, a former member of the Executive Board of the International Longshoremen's and Warehousemen's Union.
28 Theodore Lowi, "How the Farmers Get What They Want," *The Reporter,* May 21, 1964.

Figure 16   America's Largest Unions

Union	Members[1] 1964	1968
Teamsters[2]	1,507	1,755
Automobile workers[2]	1,168	1,473
Steelworkers	965	1,120
Machinists	808	903
Electrical (IBEW)	806	897
Carpenters	760	793
Laborers[2]	432	553
Retail clerks	428	552
Garment, ladies'	442	455
Hotel and restaurant	445	459
Clothing workers	377	386
Meatcutters	341	500
Building services	320	389
Engineers, operating	311	350
Communications workers	294	357
Electrical (IUE)	271	324
Plumbers	256	297
State, county	235	364
Railway and steamship clerks[2]	270	280
Musicians	275	283
Mine workers, District 50[2]	210	232
Painters	199	200
Government (AFGE)	139	295
Letter carriers	168	210
Railroad trainmen[2]	185	185

[1] In thousands
[2] All unions except these are affiliated with the AFL-CIO.
Source: U.S. Bureau of the Census, *Statistical Abstract of the United States: 1971,* p. 234.

strongest in the East and has about half the membership of the Farm Bureau.

The National Farmers Union is the smallest of these three groups with about 250,000 members, most of whom live in the wheat, dairy, and cattle country of Wisconsin, Minnesota, Montana, Colorado, and the Great Plains states. This group is substantially more liberal, and hence more receptive to government intervention in farm affairs, than the more moderate Grange or the increasingly conservative Farm Bureau. Just as these organizations frequently differ with one another on questions of government policy, so also do the more specialized agricultural groups, such as the American Livestock Association, the National Apple Institute, and the National Wool Growers Federation.[29]

The chief concerns of nearly all farm organizations are government-guaranteed prices, acreage restrictions, and tariffs on for-

29 Key, op. cit., pp. 31–40.

eign imports. Even on these issues, however, their divergent views reflect opposing economic interests. Corn farmers naturally want high grain prices and poultry farmers low ones. Similarly, citrus growers may favor free international trade, because of their large export market, while dairy farmers or beef producers may want rigid restrictions because of the competitive threat of foreign imports.

Two overriding and related issues now confront American agriculture: the displacement of the small, privately owned family farm by far larger, corporately owned, "factories in the field," and the remarkably rapid growth of the United Farm Workers Organizing Committee, AFL-CIO, in unionizing agricultural laborers. In the near future, agriculture may be dominated by business corporations as farm employers, with workers largely organized in unions.

The professions   Jobs in America have usually been classified into occupational and professional categories, although this distinction may be more one of status considerations than of economic, educational, or ethical differences. At any rate, many professional organizations are enormously influential pressure groups.

Most lawyers belong to the American Bar Association (ABA) and through that organization exert considerable influence on such matters as the appointment of judges, court organization and procedure, and—to a lesser extent—changes in certain legal codes. The American Medical Association (AMA), representing an even greater percentage of the nation's medical doctors, successfully opposed tax-supported medical care (Medicare) for more than fifteen years and continues to restrict the supply of doctors and exert influence on health legislation.

Like the ABA and AMA, there are groups of barbers, morticians, insurance salesmen, cosmetologists, teachers, and many others who are permitted by state laws to establish entrance requirements for new members of their professions. Again like the ABA and AMA, most of them tend to be somewhat conservative where protecting their own interests is concerned.

Ethnic Solidarity: Lumps in the Melting Pot

Economic interests have been forced to share the stage of group politics with many organizations representing Americans of various races and national origins.

"If you're white, you're all right"   Prowhite groups can be divided into those based on prejudice and those designed to promote the interests of particular ethnic groups. Both have little influence at the national level and scarcely more in state and local politics. The former include the Ku Klux Klan, formed after the Civil War and of some influence as late as the 1920s, the American Nazis, the white Citizens' Councils that led the more sophisticated southern attack on racial integration in the 1950s and 1960s, and the Christian Nationalist Crusade

Burt Glinn © 1970 Magnum Photos.

Many Americans enthusiastically support their country's policies, both foreign and domestic, although many others urge basic changes.

led by the Rev. Gerald L. K. Smith of California.[30] These organizations are nearly always antiblack, usually anti-Jewish, often anti-Catholic, and seldom capable of acting effectively in the arena of nation-wide pressure politics.

Those groups that seek to advance their own group more than to attack others have more respectability than those based on bigotry. One of the most militant is the Jewish Defense League which has staged demonstrations against the anti-Semitism practiced in the Soviet Union. Irish-American groups have traditionally held St. Patrick's Day parades and Polish-Americans have organized Pulaski Day dinners.[31] A common denominator of many such groups in recent years has been a desire to counteract the growing influence of black organizations, in order to retain their share of job training and college scholarship

30 For a general survey of racist groups, consult Gustavus Myers, *History of Bigotry in the United States,* ed. and rev. by Henry M. Christman (N.Y.: Capricorn Books, Random House, Inc., 1960). For more detailed recent information, see George Thayer, *The Farther Shores of Politics* (N.Y.: A Clarion Book, Simon and Schuster, Inc., 1968), Part One.
31 Edgar Litt, *Ethnic Politics in America* (Glenview, Ill.: Scott, Foresman and Company, 1970), p. 64.

programs. A National Confederation of American Ethnic Groups has been established for this purpose.[32]

There is little doubt that the last ten years have seen an increase in ancestral pride, especially vocal among the descendants of those Americans from southern and eastern Europe whose ancestors arrived in the United States most recently, often to be derided as "hunkies" and "wops." White ethnics such as these are not free of prejudice—who among us is?—but they reveal a genuine fear that they somehow may be lost in the continuing shuffle of a competitive economy and status system in which they have only recently found a reasonably prosperous place. They learned that whites from the old American families are somewhat more "all right" than those who arrived more recently. Having been scorned by the upper classes, they now feel caught in a vise tightened by the increasing militancy of the lower classes—the racial minorities who covet the respectability that Americans of Irish, Italian, Polish, Slovak, Greek, and Russian ancestry have struggled so hard to attain.

"If you're brown, stick around"   The five million Mexican-Americans, most of whom have some Indian ancestry, constitute the second-largest racial minority in the United States. In a sense, theirs is a double disability: They are often identifiable by their physical characteristics, and their Spanish language environment, especially in areas near the Mexican border, makes it difficult for them to learn English. Throughout the Southwest they attend schools whose teachers and administrators are, for the most part, alien to their culture, ignorant of their language, and often indifferent to their aspirations.[33] In Los Angeles, where more persons of Mexican ancestry live than in any metropolis except Mexico City and Guadalajara, there is a substantial amount of residential segregation. The "Chicano barrios," or Mexican-American neighborhoods, are characterized by lower incomes, higher unemployment, and poorer medical care than in the county as a whole.

In recent years Chicanos have developed new organizational weapons in their struggle for equal opportunity and new leaders to provide inspiration and direction in waging it. In Denver, Rodolfo "Corky" Gonzalez, a colorful and articulate ex-boxer, formed the Crusade for Justice to help meet the needs of Colorado's substantial Chicano population. In south Texas, where Mexican-Americans are a majority in twenty-six counties, a political party, *La Raza Unida* (the United People), has elected two mayors. In Crystal City, the "spinach capital" of the nation, it won a majority on both the city council and school board.[34] In California's rich San Joaquin Valley, Cesar Chavez, the nonviolent head of the United Farm Workers Organizing Committee, AFL-CIO, has

---

32 *Newsweek,* October 6, 1969, p. 36.
33 See Chapter 5, p. 118.
34 Frank del Olmo, "Chicano Group Seeks Control of South Texas," *Los Angeles Times,* August 23, 1970, Sec. F, p. 3.

brought more gains for migratory laborers in five years than they had achieved in the preceding fifty.

Older organizations, such as California's Community Service Organization, established in 1947, or the American G.I. Forum, founded in Texas in 1948, function much like other pressure groups which wish to work by traditional methods and in fairly close alliance with sympathetic Anglos. Although the Mexican-American Political Association (MAPA) and the Political Association of Spanish-Speaking Organizations (PASSO) have much in common with these groups, they are newer and emphasize the election of Mexican-Americans to office in California and Texas respectively.[35] Finally, there are radicals who favor militant direct action or even revolutionary measures. The Brown Berets in California and the native Indian *Alianza Federal de los Pueblos Libres* (Federal Alliance of Free City States) in New Mexico, although quite small, are leading examples.[36]

Behind these disagreements on tactics there is another barrier to Mexican-American unity that involves a problem of identity. As a group, they differ about what to call themselves—Mexican-Americans, Chicanos, Spanish-Americans, browns, or something else. This psychological confusion reflects very real and sometimes deep divisions among the people themselves. Some have been in this country for many generations, while 17 percent are foreign born; some speak little Spanish, while 47 percent speak little English;[37] some are legal entrants into the United States, while others are *wetbacks* who crossed the border illegally; and some are relatively prosperous while many are very poor. Yet with few exceptions, they are united by a common religion, a common cultural heritage, and a common problem: aloof toleration by, or active hostility from, the dominant Anglo society. At best, they have been permitted to "stick around."

Some of the problems confronting Mexican-Americans, concentrated in the southwestern states, are similar to those of the one and three-quarter million Puerto Ricans living principally in New York, and the 565,000 Cubans residing mainly in Florida. All persons of Latin American origin average three years less schooling and a 30 percent smaller family income than other Americans. In October 1971, a "Brown Power" conference attempted to map a common political program on

35 Ralph Guzman, "Politics and Policies of the Mexican-American Community," Eugene P. Dvorin and Arthur J. Musner, eds., *California Politics and Policies* (Reading, Mass.: Addison-Wesley Publishing Co., Inc., 1966), pp. 373–81.
36 The members of the *Alianza*, along with others of Indian ancestry in New Mexico, are often called Hispanos. In many cases their forebears lived in what is now New Mexico as long ago as 1540 when the Spanish explorer Coronado became the first European to set foot in this region. For an account of the *Alianza* and Reies Lopez Tijerina, its dynamic and unorthodox leader, see Carroll Cagle, "The Great Land Grab Game," *The Black Politician* 1 (April 1970): pp. 17–21.
37 *The World Almanac and Book of Facts* 1972 Edition (N.Y.: Newspaper Enterprise Association, Inc., 1971), p. 656, and U.S. Bureau of the Census, *Statistical Abstract of the United States: 1971*, p. 29.

which Americans of both Mexican and Puerto Rican ancestry could unite.[38] One of the difficulties it confronted was a disagreement on the ultimate ends to be sought. Some cherish the traditional American dream of full integration into the mainstream of Anglo society; others, disillusioned by prejudice or fearful of losing unique characteristics of their own heritage, wish to progress as a separate and largely autonomous subculture within the nation as a whole.[39]

"**If you're black, get back**" Some of the difficulties confronting blacks in America have been depicted in Chapter 5.[40] The present discussion is confined to a consideration of the organizations that cope with such difficulties. The significance of the subject transcends the black community, since the strategies they have used have inspired many members of other minorities to seek solutions to their own problems in similar ways.

The first important civil rights organization to work in behalf of racial justice was the National Association for the Advancement of Colored People (NAACP), founded in 1909. In many ways, the group was an organizational reaction to the doctrines of Booker T. Washington, the black educator who opposed, on tactical grounds, work toward integration and social equality. To W. E. B. Du Bois and other leaders of the NAACP, on the contrary, these goals seemed the minimum essentials of individual dignity and social justice. The organization's most important contribution has been its legal leadership in getting segregation laws declared unconstitutional.

The National Urban League, formed in 1910, has been concerned as much with equal opportunity in housing and employment as with governmental policy. In recent years, Roy Wilkins, executive director of the NAACP, and the late Whitney M. Young, Jr., holding the same post for the Urban League, have epitomized the moderate and responsible leadership that has linked the white liberal to the black community, and the black community to the decision-makers who hold government power.[41]

In 1941 the Fellowship of Reconciliation, a predominantly white organization consisting primarily of religious pacifists, broadened its antiwar preoccupation to embrace the cause of racial harmony. For this purpose, it organized the Congress of Racial Equality (CORE) which developed nonviolent civil disobedience as an effective technique for fighting racial segregation. In the mid-1960s CORE lost much of its initial white pacifist support because it abandoned nonviolence in the face of increasingly brutal reactions by white racists. Simultaneously, it

38 *Los Angeles Times,* October 22, 1971, p. 18.
39 The separatist movement is described by del Olmo, loc. cit.
40 See pp. 115–120.
41 For background information on the NAACP and Urban League, see Arna Bontemps, *One Hundred Years of Negro Freedom* (N.Y.: Dodd, Mead & Co., 1961), Chs. 9–13, and Langston Hughes, *Fight for Freedom, the Story of the NAACP* (N.Y.: Berkley Publishing Corporation, 1962).

suffered defections by many blacks to similar groups and more militant organizations.[42]

Prior to the assassination of Rev. Martin Luther King in 1968, the Southern Christian Leadership Conference (SCLC) was, in large measure, a reflection of his magnetic leadership. He was a scholar influential among intellectuals and a preacher effective in mobilizing the indignation of the multitude. The SCLC, influenced by CORE, was born in 1957 after the Montgomery bus boycott, touched off when Mrs. Rosa Parks was denied a vacant seat in the front of a bus in December 1955. Subsequently, through massive marches, illegal sit-ins, and placid perseverance in the face of billy clubs, electric cattle prods, and police dogs, the SCLC succeeded in capturing the essence of that which seemed "best" in the civil rights movement.

The Student National (formerly Non-Violent) Coordinating Committee (SNCC, or "Snick") was founded in 1960 and moved rapidly from moderate militancy to left-wing agitation. The organization began as a sort of junior CORE, helping to register black voters. Under the leadership of Stokely Carmichael, it was the first leading civil rights group to embrace the slogan and ideology of "Black Power." This idea, also propounded with great vigor and effectiveness by Malcolm X, the former Black Muslim leader, signaled the temporary abandonment of racial integration as a major black objective. Instead, it sought the election of black officials to represent black ghettoes and black ownership of businesses that have predominantly black customers.[43]

At the left-wing extreme is the Black Panther party, formed in Oakland, California, in 1966. It is not a party in the usual sense, since it nominates no candidates for office. But it is deeply political in its commitment to a modified Marxist philosophy and has formulated a specific program that includes full employment, the exemption of black men from military service, and a United Nations-supervised plebiscite to determine "the will of black people as to their national destiny."[44] Panther tactics have ranged from a free breakfast program for ghetto children to armed confrontations with police and prison officials. The group has been badly damaged by a leadership split between Eldridge Cleaver, in exile in Algeria, and Huey Newton.

By 1969 most blacks displayed greater racial pride than ever before, but rejected the tactics and goals of extremist groups; 63 percent believed equality was possible without violence, 74 percent favored integration, and 70 percent felt that blacks had made progress in the preceding five years.[45] There was also a change among whites. Their

42 For a brief summary of post-World War II civil rights organizations, see *Report of the National Advisory Commission on Civil Disorders* (N.Y.: Bantam Books, Inc., 1968), pp. 223–36.
43 The most detailed and sophisticated analysis is in Stokely Carmichael and Charles V. Hamilton, *Black Power* (N.Y.: Vintage Books, Random House, Inc., 1967).
44 The full, ten-point program of the Panthers is found in every issue of its weekly newspaper, *The Black Panther,* and is reprinted in William M. Chace and Peter Collier, eds., *Justice Denied* (N.Y.: Harcourt Brace Jovanovich, Inc., 1970), pp. 534–37.
45 *Newsweek,* June 30, 1969, p. 19.

stereotype of the superstitious and cowardly Negro had been destroyed, a victim of the civil rights and "Black Power" movements of the 1960s. The choice of an integrated and united America, or separate and mutually suspicious racial blocs is still before us.[46] It requires both races to choose the first alternative, but either one can compel the second. Blacks will "get back" no longer.

The red agony   Informed observers have little doubt that the native Indians now suffer greater deprivations than any other ethnic group.

The indicators of Indian suffering are appalling. Their life expectancy is 44 years, compared with 71 for white Americans. The average income for each Indian family living on a reservation—and more than half do—is only $1,500. The average years of schooling are 5.5, well behind that of both the black and the Mexican-American. Some officials rate 90 percent of reservation housing as substandard. Unemployment ranges from 20 percent on the more affluent reservations to 80 percent on the poorest.[47]

These statistics apply to a total reservation population of over 425,000— more than the populations of Oklahoma City, or Portland, Oregon. What is even more depressing is that the red man has been unable to form groups sufficiently strong to bring about any substantial changes in this situation. The reasons for this lack of organization include geographic dispersion, ignorance, feelings of futility, a pronounced shyness common among Indian cultures, and the disunity fostered by fragmentation among nearly three hundred tribes. One should derive no comfort from a notion that the Indians, although poor and disorganized, are happy. On the contrary, among young Indians the suicide rate is three times the national average.[48]

There are some bright clouds on the horizon, although they are few and faint. For the first time in this century, President Johnson appointed an Indian to head the Bureau of Indian Affairs, and President Nixon has followed suit. Furthermore, in 1970 Mr. Nixon asked Congress to appropriate an additional $250 million for Indian economic development, to grant Indians more control over reservation affairs, and to rescind the "termination" policy of the 1950s designed to lure Indians off the reservations.[49]

More importantly, there have been signs of organizational activity among Indians themselves. In 1961, 460 Indians from ninety tribes met to issue a "Declaration of Indian Purpose";[50] an Indian Patrol has been formed in Minneapolis in an attempt to minimize police mistreatment; La Donna Harris, the part-Comanche wife of a United

46 For several different points of view expressed by prominent blacks, see "Which Way Black America?," a special issue of *Ebony* magazine, August 1970.
47 *Time,* February 9, 1970, p. 16.
48 *Los Angeles Times,* July 5, 1970, Sec. G. p. 3.
49 *Christian Science Monitor,* July 14, 1970, p. 13.
50 Wilcomb E. Washburn, ed., *The Indian and the White Man* (Garden City, N.Y.: Anchor Books, Doubleday & Company, Inc., 1964), pp. 400–407.

Paul Conklin.

Navajo men learn stone masonry in a self-help housing program in Arizona.

States senator, has organized a group called "Oklahoma for Indian Opportunity" to attract antipoverty funds from the national government; and there is a Congress of American Indians headquartered in Washington, D.C. An increased impatience and a growing militancy is apparent among a portion of the Indian population, directed in part against the loss of water rights on Indian land. The most dramatic manifestation of the new activism was the Indian seizure of Alcatraz Island, site of a former federal prison, in 1969. One thing seems sure: The problem will not go away. A high birth rate has resulted in a 50 percent increase in the Indian population during the last ten years.

Asian-Americans; a "yellow peril?"   Americans of Asian ancestry—Japanese, Chinese, Filipinos, and Koreans, in order of their numerical strength in this country—generally have stayed out of politics. Their lack of involvement can be attributed to many factors, including a fear of white retribution and their small numbers. Even in the San Francisco-Oakland region, with its world famous Chinatown, Chinese-Americans constitute only about 2 percent of the population.[51] (In Hawaii, however, the situation is different. There, Asian-Americans

51 Hon. Alfred H. Song, California State Assemblyman, "Politics and Policies of the Oriental Community," in Dvorin and Misner, op. cit., p. 389, Table 14–3. One exception is Ken Nakaoke, a Japanese-American who served as mayor of Gardena, California, a Los Angeles suburb.

comprise over three quarters, and Japanese-Americans about two thirds, of the state legislature.)

An additional reason for the political inactivity of Asian-Americans is their fragmentation into Chinese, Japanese, Filipino, and other communities, geographically isolated from one another and each with relatively unique problems and dissimilar outlooks. They came to the United States during different time periods, entered various occupations in different proportions, and to some degree reflected in their mutual suspicions the rivalries that existed between the nations from which they came. The Chinese, who arrived first, reacted to white bigotry by attempting to maintain their cultural traditions intact, and gradually tended to specialize in wholesale and retail trade. The Japanese arrived later, tried hard to adapt to American cultural norms, and engaged in agriculture much more frequently. Filipinos, the last to come in significant numbers, are racially distinct from Chinese and Japanese, and work in disproportionately large numbers as migratory farm laborers and in domestic capacities.

The result of all these factors has been the emergence of very few pressure groups specifically for the purpose of articulating the peculiar needs and desires of Asian-Americans. By far the most important organization is the Japanese American Citizens League (JACL), founded in 1930, which maintains direct lobbying relationships with officials in Washington.[52] The situation, especially among young, college-educated Asians, is changing however, particularly in the direction of greater militancy and increasing unity among nonwhite minorities. In 1970 their activism was expressed in its most extreme form by the Red Guards, a San Francisco-based, communist-oriented organization whose members have denounced the traditional Six Companies that have long dominated Chinese economic and social activity in America.[53] The Six Companies grew out of associations of family-based clans and control a substantial number of restaurants, banks, and sweatshop factories. The sharpened sense of kinship among all Americans of Asian descent has led the Wah Ching, a group of Hong Kong-born Chinese, to work with the Asian-American Political Alliance[54] as well as with blacks and browns in the Third World Liberation Front, which is committed to the overthrow of white colonialism wherever it is found—either in foreign imperialism or domestic oppression.[55]

While nearly all Asian-Americans identify totally with the United States, they remember the World War ii internment of Japanese-Americans in concentration camps, and they realize the uneven nature of their present prosperity. As recently as 1960, Filipinos in

52 Bill Hosokawa, *Nisei: The Quiet Americans* (N.Y.: William Morrow & Co., Inc., 1969), pp. 198–99, and passim.
53 Min Yee, "Chinatown in Crisis," *Newsweek*, February 23, 1970, pp. 57–58.
54 Kenneth Lamott, "The Awakening of Chinatown," Los Angeles Times *West Magazine*, January 4, 1970, pp. 7–15.
55 Amy Uyematsu, "The Emergence of Yellow Power in America," *Gidra* 1 (October 1969): pp. 10–11.

California had a median income of $2925, Chinese $3803, Japanese $4388, and Caucasians $5109—in spite of the fact that a higher percentage of both Chinese and Japanese had completed college than had whites.[56] In San Francisco's Chinatown the rate of substandard housing is over three times the city average and the rate of suicide is three times the national average. The situation there is not likely to improve for some time, because more than 33,000 Chinese, largely poor people from Hong Kong, have arrived since immigration quotas were abandoned by Congress in 1965.[57] In 1972 Chinatown was beset by a serious wave of extortion and violent crime.

Despite considerable improvement in their overall public image, Asian-Americans still encounter occasional social ostracism (especially with respect to intermarriage), some housing discrimination, and a competitive disadvantage in obtaining semiskilled and skilled industrial jobs. In the opinion of some observers, American economic competition with Japan could produce repercussions of prejudice against Japanese-Americans. Nonetheless, there has been immense improvement in the lot of most Asian-Americans—largely achieved by their own tenacity and hard work—since the days when whites viewed them as part of a vast and menacing "yellow peril." Because problems still exist, the nation cannot, in good conscience, ignore their plight.

Figure 17 Leading States in Minority Population

Rank	Indians	Japanese	Chinese	Mexicans	Negroes
1	Oklahoma	Hawaii	California	California	New York
2	Arizona	California	Hawaii	Texas	Illinois
3	California	Washington	New York	New Mexico	Texas
4	New Mexico	Illinois	Illinois	Arizona	California
5	No. Carolina	New York	Massachusetts	Colorado	Georgia

Source: Computed from U.S. Bureau of the Census, *Statistical Abstract of the United States: 1971*, pp. 27 and 31, *The New York Times Encyclopedic Almanac,* 1971, p. 288, and *The World Almanac and Book of Facts,* 1972 Edition (N.Y.: Newspaper Enterprise Association, Inc., 1971), p. 149.

"Sexual Politics": The Women's Liberation Movement

Few social movements in our history have received so much publicity as that which has accompanied the struggle of the female majority to attain equal rights. With steady persistence, the fiery feminists have gained a grudging acknowledgement that American society, like others, is dominated by men.

Along with nationalism, racism, and the other ideological influences that have shaped our politics, sexism is an important ingredient of modern society. Consider the following facts regarding the three branches of the national government:

56 Uyematsu, op. cit., p. 9.
57 Yee, loc. cit.

© George W. Gardner, 1972.

Gloria Steinem, in the forefront of the effort to increase women's representation in politics.

1) In early 1972 there was only one woman among the one hundred United States senators (Margaret Chase Smith, R–Maine), and there never have been over twenty women among the 435 members of the House of Representatives;

2) There has never been a woman President or Vice President, and during our entire history only two women have ever served in the President's cabinet.

3) There has never been a woman on the Supreme Court of the United States and of 8750 judges—at all levels of government—only three hundred are women.

In the teaching profession (and it is important to note that most teachers are government employees) women represent 88 percent of the total at the elementary school level, yet only 22 percent of all principals. At the high school and college levels their plight is even worse. Such statistics can be piled up almost endlessly. Women are only 7 percent of doctors, 3 percent of lawyers, and 1 percent of engineers. More depressing is evidence that the situation has been getting worse. In

Figure 18   Median Earnings of Men and Women, by Occupation of
Longest Job Held, During the Year 1969

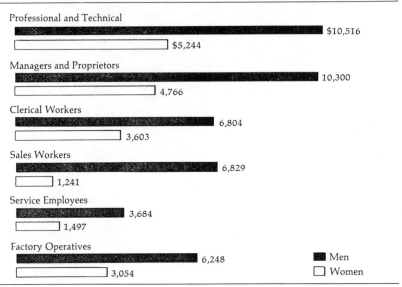

Professional and Technical
— $10,516
— $5,244

Managers and Proprietors
— 10,300
— 4,766

Clerical Workers
— 6,804
— 3,603

Sales Workers
— 6,829
— 1,241

Service Employees
— 3,684
— 1,497

Factory Operatives
— 6,248   ■ Men
— 3,054   □ Women

Source: U.S. Bureau of the Census, *Statistical Abstract of the United States: 1971*, p. 229.

the field of dentistry, women have slipped from 3 to 1 percent in the last
half-century and in university teaching from 30 to about 20 percent in
little more than thirty years.[58] From 1961 to 1972, the number of women
in Congress dropped from nineteen to thirteen.

Worst of all, working women make less money than men
who have similar jobs, and the discrepancy is widening. According to the
Women's Bureau of the U.S. Department of Labor, the median income of
working women was 63.9 percent of that of their male counterparts in
1955, but had slipped to 58.9 percent in 1970.[59] Yet the percentage of
women in the total labor force has increased; in 1970, 53 percent of single
women and 41 percent of married women were working outside their
homes.[60]

In 1848 the first organized attempt to improve the status of
women culminated in a women's rights convention in Seneca Falls,
N.Y., but progress was slow, and it was not until 1869 that the right to
vote was first won in Wyoming, and not until 1920 that the Nineteenth
Amendment forbade sex discrimination in voting booths throughout the
nation. After the long decades of effort and agitation—even the arrest of
women who chained themselves to the White House fence—the extension of voting rights to women inaugurated a period of general apathy
regarding the relative roles of the sexes. For forty years only the National

58 *Time,* August 31, 1970, p. 17, and Dorothy Townsend, "Women's 'Lib' Groups Plan
Nationwide Strike," *Los Angeles Times,* August 23, 1970, Sec. C., pp. 1 and 5.
59 *Congressional Quarterly Weekly Report,* March 18, 1972, p. 599.
60 U.S. Bureau of the Census, *Statistical Abstract of the United States: 1971,* p. 212.

Federation of Business and Professional Women's Clubs and a few smaller groups worked actively, although with dignified discretion, for equal opportunity. A turning point came in 1963 with the publication of Betty Friedan's *The Feminine Mystique,* and in 1966 this was followed by the formation of NOW, the National Organization for Women. Within a few years more militant groups such as Bread and Roses, Female Liberation, and SALT (Sisters All Learning Together) were established. Of these, NOW is the largest, least militant, and most broadly based— what some have called the NAACP of women's liberation.

In 1970 the movement gained impetus from the passage of a constitutional amendment by the House of Representatives (approved by the Senate the following year), and from a women's one-day strike. The proposed amendment provides that "equality of rights under the law shall not be denied or abridged . . . on account of sex" and was promptly ratified by a number of states. The strike, primarily symbolic in nature, was called to mark the fiftieth anniversary of women's suffrage, and demanded abolition of abortion laws, free child-care centers, and equal employment at equal pay. In 1971 the National Women's Political Caucus was formed in Washington, D.C., to encourage the election and appointment of more women to public office.

Groups in the Government

Pressure groups are usually thought of as private organizations seeking government action, or trying to prevent it. But governments themselves consist of people and these, like other citizens, often have conflicting interests. The result is that there are pressure groups within the government as well as outside it.

Government employees Among the more important government groups are the American Federation of State, County, and Municipal Employees, the American Federation of Government Employees, and unions for letter carriers, teachers, firefighters, and social workers. Some of these are among the most rapidly growing unions in the AFL-CIO, and tend to be among the most militant. While the right of public employees to strike against the government is the subject of heated dispute, the fact is that they are striking with increasing frequency. Postal workers, school teachers, air traffic controllers, college professors, and occasionally even policemen and nurses have all engaged in work stoppages of one kind or another—sometimes under the guise of mass sick-ins. From 1958 through 1965, there were no more than fifty work stoppages by government employees in any single year, but in 1966 the figure was 142, and in 1968 it climbed to 254.[61]

Level against level Not only do government employees lobby against their employers (with work stoppages only a fraction of that activity), but governments lobby against governments as well. The

61 *American Teacher,* May 1970, p. A–6.

National League of Cities attempts to get increased assistance from the state and national governments, and it is sometimes joined by the Council of State Governments in seeking to influence Washington policy makers. Moreover, a number of states and large cities have lobbyists working for them in Washington.[62] Even at the same level of government, various federal departments and agencies vie with one another for appropriations and other benefits bestowed by legislative bodies.

The Politics of Shared Attitudes

Since life consists of more than money-making, race, and sex, many pressure groups are concerned with the wide variety of other interests that enrich life but may also lead to conflict with others' interests.

Religious groups The constitutional provision banning the establishment of religion does not prohibit church organizations from attempting to influence public policy. The largest of these is the National Council of Churches, which was formed in 1950 and includes most major Protestant denominations. It has supported reduced American military action abroad and civil rights and Medicare legislation at home. On the conservative side, both theologically and politically, is the American Council of Christian Churches, a much smaller organization. Other Protestant groups are the Women's Christian Temperance Union, long a proponent of the prohibition of alcoholic beverages, and the Friends Committee on National Legislation, a Quaker organization promoting pacifism, foreign economic aid, and a liberal domestic program. Roman Catholics often express their views on political questions through such groups as the Social Action Department of the National Catholic Welfare Conference and Jews, ever alert to the problems of anti-Semitism, through the Anti-Defamation League of B'nai B'rith and the American Jewish Congress. All are predominantly liberal in orientation. While these and many other religious groups are still interested in matters of public morals, most of them now have concerns far broader in scope.[63]

Veterans' groups After World War I, returning servicemen formed the American Legion, one of the nation's most influential lobbies, with a membership now exceeding two and one-half million. The Veterans of Foreign Wars, about half the size of the Legion, is the second largest such group, with the Disabled American Veterans ranking third. The major objectives of all three involve pensions, educational assistance, and other GI benefits, although the Legion has also lobbied for larger military appropriations, a more militant foreign policy, and a continuation of the Subversive Activities Control Board.

62 Congressional Quarterly Service, *Legislators and the Lobbyists,* 2nd ed., (Washington, D.C., Congressional Quarterly, Inc., 1968), p. 63. The states are California, Florida, Illinois, Indiana, Maryland, Massachusetts, New York, Ohio, Pennsylvania, Texas, and West Virginia; the cities are New York, Los Angeles, San Francisco, Boston, Dallas, New Orleans, San Diego, and Seattle.
63 Key, op. cit., pp. 116–21 and Thayer, op. cit., pp. 217–61.

After World War II, two new organizations sprang up, both relatively small, to challenge their older counterparts. They are the moderate AMVETS (American Veterans of World War II and Korea), and the liberal American Veterans Committee. Both have placed more emphasis upon assistance to those in need than on blanket increases to all veterans. There are also smaller ex-servicemen's groups based on the common bonds of religion and ethnic origin: the Catholic War Veterans, Jewish War Veterans, Polish Legion of American Veterans, and Italian-American War Veterans.[64] Finally, the Retired Officers Association has been extremely active in recent years.

Foreign policy groups   A wide variety of small but often influential organizations are interested in altering America's international outlook. Some, such as the Fellowship of Reconciliation and the American Friends Service Committee, are committed to pacifism to one degree or another. Others, such as the Council for a Livable World and the Committee for a Sane Nuclear Policy (known often as SANE), have worked for a relaxation of world tensions through disarmament. The United Nations Association and the United World Federalists seek a stronger world organization, and other groups have arisen from passionate opposition to the Vietnam War, including the National Mobilization Committee, The Resistance, and Another Mother for Peace. In contrast to these are the highly nationalistic Daughters of the American Revolution, and other groups with heavy commitments to the interests of some foreign country. Examples include the "China lobby" of the 1950s, dedicated to strengthening the Nationalist Chinese regime on Formosa; the National Council of American-Soviet Friendship in the 1940s; and the German-American Bund of the 1930s.

Ideological groups   Organizations like the Communist party, National States' Rights party, and Socialist Workers party seldom nominate candidates for office. When they do, campaign activity is more for propaganda purposes than in genuine hope for victory in the polling booths. Most such groups that are wedded to a particular ideology, however, make no pretense of being separate political parties, but instead either engage in lobbying activity or, occasionally, employ illegal and sometimes violent techniques. At the far right are the Minutemen and the more respectable John Birch Society, nearly obsessed with a fear of internal communist subversion. Closer to the center, but still conservative, are the Americans for Constitutional Action and the Liberty League.

All of these groups have roughly analogous counterparts on the left end of the political spectrum. Most radical are the young Weathermen, with liberal groups such as the Americans for Democratic Action, the Urban Coalition, and Common Cause less distant from the center.

---

64 Membership figures for these and other groups, along with the addresses of their national headquarters, may be found in *The New York Times Encyclopedic Almanac*, 1972, pp. 334–38 and 576.

Single-issue groups   Many other groups have interests involving one or only a few issues. Among these are the Sierra Club and other conservation groups leading the ecological crusade; the American Civil Liberties Union, which concentrates on defending First Amendment rights (but has recently taken left-wing stands on public issues), and public service law firms, such as that organized by Ralph Nader for the defense of consumer interests against careless manufacturers and ineffective government regulation. Still more specialized are the American Cancer Society, National Rifle Association, Gay (homosexual) Liberation Front, American Automobile Association, and countless others. Wherever people are united by a common goal affected by government policy, a pressure group is likely to be found. Altogether, 269 organizations attempting to influence legislation were registered with Congress in 1969.[65]

Although pressure groups are as varied as they are numerous, they usually share certain common characteristics. Many of them are national in scope, but with local affiliates; they often serve their members in other ways than influencing government policy; and they usually work against, though sometimes with, other pressure groups on specific issues. Unfortunately, some are governed rather undemocratically and therefore do not always express the wishes of their membership.

LOBBYING TECHNIQUES

We come now to what is perhaps the most important question of this chapter: How can the groups just described obtain their objectives? There are three broad choices available. Pressure can be exerted through access, confrontation, or violence.

The Politics of Access: Traditional Methods

Most pressure groups in the United States exert influence on government policy by gaining access to government officials. This involves a communication process called lobbying, and the pressure group spokesmen who engage in it are termed lobbyists, although some prefer more elegant titles such as legislative counsels or advocates. The fragmentation of governmental authority inherent in both federalism and the separation of powers gives lobbyists many different points of potential access at which they can direct their influence.

The lobbyists   The public image of the lobbyist falls somewhere between that of a dope pusher and a sideshow barker at a carnival. It is almost totally erroneous. Lobbyists are probably as honest (or dishonest) as teachers or butchers, and a good deal better informed about the major issues of the day. They come from all walks of life, but their

---

65 *Congressional Quarterly Guide to Current American Government* (Fall 1970), p. 107.

backgrounds frequently fall into three broad categories: pressure group members who have worked their way up in their organizations, lawyers who have a legal specialty coinciding with the interests of a particular group, and former public officials who have been defeated in seeking reelection.[66] Whatever their background, it is imperative that they know the problems of the groups they represent. A lobbyist for the Farm Bureau, for example, probably knows more about international wheat prices, the average size of farms, and the amount of money spent on agricultural research than most of the members of Congress. Equally important, lobbyists for the larger pressure groups are assisted by Washington office staffs that include statisticians, attorneys, and whatever other specialists may be needed. It would be a foolish lawmaker indeed who did not avail himself of the information that lobbyists are eager to make available about the problems a proposed bill is designed to solve.

In human terms, the most effective kind of access to public officials is through personal trust and friendship, and this results in a considerable amount of socializing between lobbyists and legislators. There is nothing necessarily corrupt about lobbyists taking congressmen out to lunch or to a weekend yachting cruise on the Potomac River. While lobbyists often entertain legislators, their purpose is not bribery but a discussion of pending legislation at greater length and in a more informal atmosphere than is possible in offices or capitol building lobbies (the origin of the term "lobbyist"). In any event, few public officials will trade their votes for a pitcher of martinis or a few days of fun: Most are too honest; some have a higher price. One other point needs to be made. Some lobbyists work only for a single pressure group, often one with which they have had a lifetime association, while others are for hire and may represent as many as twenty-five different organizations.

Legislative contacts   A more significant legislative contact comes through committee testimony or the authorship of bills. In both state legislatures and Congress, bills are referred to appropriate legislative committees, where open public hearings usually will be held; lobbyists are among the most frequent witnesses giving testimony at such hearings. It is there, perhaps, that pressure groups perform their two most valuable services to our political system: They contribute to more enlightened legislation by transmitting their specialized knowledge, and they act as direct channels of communication between the thousands of group members for whom they speak and the most powerful government decision-makers in our national and state capitols. The benefits to the groups themselves are fairly obvious: Committee testimony permits lobbyists to argue for or against the bills in which they are most interested before those legislators most likely to determine passage or defeat.

66 Between 1946 and 1967, twenty-three former senators and ninety former representatives served as lobbyists for one or more pressure groups. *Legislators and the Lobbyists,* op. cit., pp. 45–49.

Occasionally, lobbyists will not only affect the passage of bills, but also will assist in writing them. The Association of American Railroads drafted legislation exempting freight rate agreements from antitrust laws, for example, and unions shaped part of the language written into the National Industrial Recovery Act in 1933. Most legislators, especially those who are not lawyers, do not personally write the bills they introduce. They are too busy, or lack the technical vocabulary required. As a result, even though the idea for some new legislation is their own, they may seek assistance in drafting the exact language from sympathetic lobbyists who have been urging such legislation anyway.

Campaign contributions   Much of the money required for political campaigns comes from pressure groups. They contribute not because it will guarantee that the candidate, if elected, will always vote the way they wish, but because it will at least assure access to him. Few lawmakers slam down the receiver when they get a phone call from the group that contributed $5000 to the last campaign.

There are, however, certain general principles that govern financial contributions from pressure groups. For one, help is given to individual candidates rather than political party organizations. The reason for this is that lobbies wish to retain some influence regardless of which party controls the government. In the 1970 congressional races, the Committee on Political Education (COPE), speaking for the AFL-CIO, endorsed 341 Democrats, one Independent, and nineteen Republicans.[67] In a few instances, the same pressure group may quietly contribute funds to two opposing candidates, if the views of both are acceptable, just to cover its bets.

Another rule governing campaign contributions is that pressure groups support their friends, rather than trying to buy off their enemies. There are two reasons for this. If a contribution is made in the hope of changing the vote of a legislator on some important bill, then the fine line between bribery and campaign support becomes even more blurred and criminal prosecution might result. A second consideration is that it often costs little more to elect a candidate who agrees with you than to bribe one who doesn't.

A last principle of financial donation is to give preference to the incumbent when in doubt. He has already compiled a voting record, which is a better indication of his intentions than the promises of the challenger, and he usually has a better chance of winning simply because he has the greater publicity accorded to one already in office. Moreover, his experience and seniority will probably make him a more effective ally than a green, first-term legislator.

Mobilizing the public   In addition to legislative contacts and campaign contributions, pressure groups try to influence government officials indirectly through the manipulation of public opinion. This

67 *The Washington Lobby* (Washington, D.C.: Congressional Quarterly, Inc., 1971), pp. 49–50.

can be done by urging group members to write or wire their state legislators or congressmen, asking them to vote a certain way on a particular bill. In 1971 various environmental protection groups, led by Friends of the Earth, launched such a campaign to defeat the appropriation of additional money to finance the costly supersonic transport plane. Senator Clinton Anderson (D–N.M.), a former supporter of the SST, changed his vote because, he said, "I read my mail."[68] Or a more ambitious attempt can be made to gain support from the broader public through advertising campaigns in the mass media, usually designed by professional public relations firms. These appeals are more often calculated to win general sympathy than to influence action on a particular bill.

    Executive and judicial influence Lobbying is usually associated with attempts to influence the passage of laws, but it also may involve access to the executive agencies that enforce laws and the courts that apply them. Pressure group influence upon executive or administrative officials seems most pronounced in the case of business and professional organizations. Television representatives keep a close eye on the Federal Communications Commission, for example, especially when they are under attack. In 1971 CBS broadcast a controversial documentary critical of Defense Department public relations programs. The FCC, in this instance, defended the network when it was accused of distortion and bias by certain congressmen and administration officials. The American Medical Association is widely credited with preventing the appointment of a liberal doctor, John F. Knowles, to the post of Assistant Secretary of the Department of Health, Education and Welfare in 1969.

    Lobbyists pay only a little less attention to the judicial branch. Few political battles in recent history have equaled the intensity of the successful attempts by labor unions and civil rights groups to block Senate confirmation of two of President Nixon's appointments to the Supreme Court. AFL-CIO President George Meany denounced the nomination of Court of Appeals Judge G. Harrold Carswell as a "slap in the face" to blacks, and the lobbyist for the NAACP gave highly critical testimony before the Senate Judiciary Committee considering the appointment. Most lobbying activity directed toward the courts, however, entails the submission of written arguments known as *amicus curiae* ("friend of the court") briefs by parties not directly involved in a case. These are often used to persuade judges that a particular law or executive act is unconstitutional. Two pressure groups have enjoyed noteworthy success in this respect: the NAACP in its struggle against racial segregation and, to a lesser extent, the ACLU in its opposition to restrictions upon individual freedom.[69] Between 1945 and 1960, the Supreme Court ruled as the NAACP wished in fifty cases, including one that declared

68 Ibid., p. 108.
69 Henry J. Abraham, *The Judicial Process* (N.Y.: Oxford University Press, Inc., 1962), pp. 209–12.

racially discriminatory real estate deeds to be unenforceable. In this one, no fewer than twenty-five *amicus curiae* briefs were accepted by the Court. In 1972 the ACLU was successful in persuading a Court of Appeals to strike down a provision of the Hatch Act which barred government employees from engaging in campaign politics.

Reservations and regulations   The case for the traditional lobbying techniques described above seems to be fairly persuasive. They contribute to the democratic ideal of popular control over government by providing a link between millions of group members and government officials; they help to educate legislators; and in addition they can infuse fresh ideas into the stagnant waters of stand-pat politics. Yet access politics poses some real perils. While the power of most pressure groups tends to be counterbalanced by the power of others, with some opposing each measure that others favor, this is not always the case. Some interests don't get represented, and others get overrepresented. Even when opposing groups are equally well organized, one side is often much better financed than its opposition.

There are no foolproof remedies for these problems, in part because of the First Amendment's guarantee of the right to petition the government. But Congress has shown some sensitivity to the situation.

Figure 19   Pressure Groups Spending $50,000 per Year for Six or More Years (1946–1966) on Lobbying Activity

Group	Number of Years
AFL-CIO	20
American Legion	20
American Farm Bureau Federation	18
National Housing Conference	17
United Federation of Postal Clerks	17
National Assn. of Real Estate Boards	15
U.S. Savings and Loan League	15
International Assn. of Machinists, District Lodge No. 44	14
National Farmers Union	14
American Medical Assn.	13
Assn. of American Railroads	13
National Assn. of Electric Companies	13
National Assn. of Letter Carriers	12
National Education Assn.	11
American Trucking Assns.	10
National Assn. of Home Builders	10
International Brotherhood of Teamsters	8
National Federation of Independent Business	7
Brotherhood of Locomotive Firemen and Enginemen	6
Central Arizona Project Assn.	6

Source: *Legislators and the Lobbyists,* 2nd ed., (Washington, D.C., Congressional Quarterly, Inc., 1968), p. 34. Reprinted by permission of Congressional Quarterly, Inc. Omitted are groups that did not report spending over $50,000 since 1959.

It has prohibited the use of corporation profits and union dues for direct campaign contributions, and it passed a Regulation of Lobbying Act in 1946 which requires lobbyists to register and file financial reports four times a year. Although this act has many loopholes and few enforcement provisions, it brought to light far more data regarding traditional pressure group politics than had ever before been available.

The AMA alone spent over one million dollars in each of three years, and the AFL-CIO, Farm Bureau, Committee for Constitutional Government, and National Association of Electric Companies each have spent more than half a million dollars in a single year.[70] Access politics is an expensive business.

The Politics of Confrontation: Lobbies in the Streets

When traditional lobbying seems to work so well, why would certain groups resort to raucous street demonstrations which often entail confrontations with the police? One answer is that the usual pressure group tactics are sometimes unsuccessful,[71] and another lies in the ideological preferences of specific groups.

Challenge and change Confrontation techniques may seem desirable if a group is small, poor, or disenfranchised. If it is small, few lawmakers will pay much attention to what it wants. This preoccupation with numbers is one of the characteristics of a democratic society. Election statistics or group membership figures reveal quantity rather than quality. Thus, 51 percent of the voters with a mild preference for a particular candidate will defeat an opponent strongly favored by the other 49 percent.

Yet a group can sometimes compensate for its meager numbers by dramatic actions that demonstrate the intensity of its convictions. To do this successfully, it must gain a wide audience for its grievances and prick the conscience of the majority. It must appeal, in other words, to a kind of moral authority. Thus, although opposition to the Vietnam war was small in 1967, a series of rallies, teach-ins, and other activities was instrumental in attracting wide television and newspaper publicity that by 1968 had helped reverse the tide of public opinion.

If a group has sufficient funds, even if it is small, it stands a good chance of utilizing the old-fashioned type of access lobbying with some effectiveness. A poor group, on the other hand, regardless of its size, is forced to rely upon dramatic demonstrations—what has been called the politics of confrontation—to influence government policy. Vivid illustrations of such actions were the sit-ins and mass marches employed by the civil rights movement of the early 1960s, and the fasts of Cesar Chavez, leader of the farm workers, in later years.

---

70 *Legislators and the Lobbyists,* op. cit., pp. 28–31.
71 Lewis Anthony Dexter, *How Organizations are Represented in Washington* (Indianapolis: The Bobbs-Merrill Co., Inc., 1969), especially Ch. 7.

George Ballis, Black Star.

Cesar Chavez leads agricultural workers in a strike.

A third kind of group that usually finds access politics ineffective is one that is disenfranchised—whose members cannot vote. Recognizing this, women demanding the right to vote in the early part of this century utilized picketing and widely publicized protest demonstrations to win the sympathy of those who were already enfranchised. Students, many of whom were too young to go to the polls, have used similar techniques in trying to advance their causes.

Change has come about in our political system not only through pressures exerted in the private offices of lobbyists and legislators, but also in response to street demonstrations, sit-ins, strikes, and fasts. Such activities counterbalance quantities of people and dollars with personal commitment, risk, and exposure. It is unlikely that the Civil Rights Act of 1964 could have been enacted without them.

Civil disobedience The significance of confrontation politics lies in its possible effectiveness for groups that find the more orthodox methods of access politics to be impossible or unproductive. One form that confrontation politics may take is civil disobedience—a deliberate violation of the law that entails nonviolent acts designed to bring about social change and usually involving willingness to accept whatever punishment the law may prescribe for the disobedience.

Civil disobedience, both as a theoretical concept and as a consciously contrived tactic, owes much to Henry David Thoreau. In 1849 the American essayist published a short book, *On Civil Disobedience,* justifying his refusal to pay a tax in protest against the Mexican War. In it he argued that it was morally wrong to obey an unjust law and insisted that the citizen must measure government policy against the dictates of his own conscience. Justifiably or not, civil disobedience has played a supporting role on the American political stage. The successful sit-down strikes of auto workers in 1937 were carried on in defiance of a court injunction. More recently, this tactic was popularized by Rev. Martin Luther King, who was inspired in part by the example of Mahatma Gandhi in India. CORE, SNCC, and the SCLC defied segregation laws in the struggle for civil rights; thousands of young men have chosen federal penetentiaries rather than the U.S. Army. Nothing dramatizes the depths of one's convictions more convincingly than the willingness to risk imprisonment for them.

The Politics of Violence: From the Barrel of a Gun

The outcome of the 1968 presidential race may well have been decided on June 5 of that year—five months before the general election. It was then that Sirhan B. Sirhan assassinated Senator Robert F. Kennedy on the night of his victory in California's presidential primary. A single bullet nullified millions of ballots.

A decade of death Senator Kennedy's death marked the culmination of one of the bloodiest decades in our history, and led President Johnson to appoint a Commission on the Causes and Prevention of Violence. There was much for it to study. Since 1960 Medgar Evers, head of the Mississippi NAACP, President John F. Kennedy, Malcolm X (leading "Black Power" spokesman) George Lincoln Rockwell (American Nazi party boss) and Martin Luther King, Jr., had also been killed. Race riots had left thirty-four dead in Los Angeles, twenty-three in Newark, and forty-three in Detroit. Dozens of other cities were ravaged by similar, smaller riots, and the 1968 Democratic National Convention brought bloody encounters to the streets of Chicago. Violence, both political and nonpolitical was increasing steadily. By 1969 the murder rate had reached 7.2 per 100,000 people in the United States, compared with 3.3 in West Germany, 2.6 in Israel, 2.2 in Japan, 0.6 in Sweden, and 0.4 in England and Wales.[72] A comparative international study revealed that in the 1960s the U.S. ranked twenty-fourth among

72 *The New York Times Encyclopedic Almanac,* 1972, p. 231.

114 nations in "total magnitude of strife" and first among the seventeen Western democracies.[73]

The 1970s were off to a tragic start with the deaths of two students in Jackson, Mississippi, and four at Kent State University in Ohio, at the hands of law enforcement officers. A few months later, four persons, including a judge, were killed in a jail break attempt in northern California, and forty-two died in the Attica, New York, prison revolt. In 1972 Governor George Wallace came within inches of death from another assassin's bullet.

The quest for causes   What has gone wrong? How can this tragic toll be explained in a nation whose Constitution is designed, in part, "to insure domestic tranquility?" The answers are entangled in a complex web of history and contemporary social movements. Some of the historical roots of American violence may be our revolutionary heritage, the brutal legacy of slavery, our lawless frontier tradition, the attempt to exterminate native Indians, frictions generated by ethnic and racial diversity, unusually intense conflict in the annals of labor-management relations, and the population pressures accompanying urbanization. American violence has also been explained in terms of the polarization of opinion regarding the Vietnam war, the relative ease with which guns can be acquired, increasing permissiveness in bringing up children, the lurid depiction of violence in the mass media, a rapid rise in the aspirations of the disadvantaged, the psychological necessity of oppressed peoples to prove their manhood, archaic prison conditions, and the fears and frustrations entailed in rapid social change.

Some of these factors are peculiarly American while others are characteristic of much of the modern world. Those that seem indigenous suggest that violence is a product of cultural conditioning in the United States, while the more universal factors suggest that human beings are biologically equipped with hostile impulses that make them, along with ants and rats, one of the most violent species in the animal kingdom. Although the human capacity for cruelty is terrifying, its potential for compassion and reason is encouraging. The challenge lies in creating a culture more conducive to the latter than the former. Whatever its causes or motivation, the resort to brute force challenges the authority of government, the stability of society, and the fundamental democratic doctrine of human dignity.

From a practical political standpoint, a crucial issue is this: Does violence work? It obviously succeeded in securing independence from England by the Revolution and in preserving the nation while freeing the slaves by the Civil War. Yet in these situations the tactical advantages or military strength were on the winning side. When those who resort to violence are outgunned, outmanned, and out-maneuvered—militant students or ghetto blacks, for example—they lose.

73 Hugh Davis Graham and Ted Robert Gurr, *Violence in America* (N.Y.: A Signet Book, The New American Library, Inc., 1969), pp. 775–76. This is an official report to the presidential commission on violence.

On college campuses, it is the students who usually get killed. In big city riots, it is the blacks who suffer 90 percent of the casualties.

Yet to a great extent, the politics of violence remains a mystery not subject to simple analysis. In totalitarian states such as the Soviet Union, it is almost certain to be totally unsuccessful; in free societies such as ours, ironically, it may result in some beneficial change. In both instances, the violent ones will die, but in America, their death commands attention, however briefly, to the grievances which led to such terrible acts of desperation. Who can say whether the voting age was lowered and student freedom increased because—or in spite—of youthful acts of rebellion? Who can be sure that educational and job opportunities for blacks have been expanded because—or in spite—of the bloodshed on city sidewalks? But if violence buys progress, it does so at a price both tragic and incalculably high. In addition to death, it tends to produce a backlash of resentment and repression directed against those whom the public believes to have instigated it; freedom and justice then become trampled in the rush for law and order. Moreover, most violence is counterproductive, even when it may appear successful. Perhaps this is because it brutalizes, or at least desensitizes, those who resort to it. Thus, the French Revolution led to a Reign of Terror and the Russian Revolution produced the Stalin dictatorship. Violence has an insatiable appetite, devouring friend and foe alike. It may come to liberate, but it stays to dominate.

Chapter **7**

Government by the People
Political Parties

I have great confidence in the common sense of mankind in general.

Thomas Jefferson

People cannot expect to get what they want from government simply by supporting their favorite pressure groups. Important as these organizations are, citizens can maximize their political influence only by also engaging in political party activity and voting as intelligently as they can.

PARTY SYSTEMS

Political parties play a crucial role in governments all over the world. Nevertheless, they aren't even mentioned in the Constitution; Washington and Madison opposed the formation of parties as a matter of principle, fearing that people might develop greater loyalty to them than to the nation as a whole. Yet even before Washington left the presidency, the seeds of the first two parties had already been planted.

The Functions of Parties

Political parties would not have lasted so long or spread so widely if they did not perform useful functions that are central to the democratic process. These deserve enumeration.

Candidate recruitment When national party conventions meet to select candidates for President and Vice President, the typical nominating speaker traditionally refers to his favorite as "the man who . . ." will do wondrous things, without mentioning his name until the end of the speech. This oratory points up one of the major functions of political parties: They act as political talent scouts, nominating the candidates who will run in the general election. If the parties did not, the voters might be confronted with incredible confusion and perhaps dozens of candidates for some offices but none for the others.

Figure 20   Pressure Groups and Parties: How They Differ

1. Pressure groups are chiefly interested in influencing government policies.	1. Parties are chiefly interested in controlling government personnel.
2. Pressure groups aid any person or party who promotes their goals.	2. Parties select candidates, conduct campaigns, and staff government.
3. Citizens may support several pressure groups.	3. Citizens support one party or are independent.
4. Pressure groups are not accountable for actions to general public.	4. Parties are accountable for actions to general public at elections.
5. Pressure groups represent minority factions concerned with specific policies related to a few interests.	5. Parties seek majorities comprised of aggregations which must achieve broad compromises related to many interests.
6. Pressure groups devise and publicize new policy proposals.	6. Parties advocate or carry out policies already popular.
7. Pressure group organization is subject to few democratic legal controls.	7. Party organization is subject to many democratic legal controls.
8. Pressure group unity is usually based on shared interests and characteristics within population segments (women, factory workers, etc.).	8. Party unity is usually based on shared ambitions and broad attitudes within geographic areas (districts, states, etc.).
9. Pressure groups operate by many techniques sometimes involving extra-legal demonstrations.	9. Parties operate almost entirely by seeking election victories.

Campaign conduct   Parties not only select nominees for office but also organize their campaigns. They obtain the money for campaign advertising and help determine campaign strategies. All this makes democracy exciting, and in the process of generating so much heat, sometimes light is shed on the major issues confronting the nation, although most candidates tend to be as vague as possible to avoid antagonizing voters.

Policy alternatives and peaceful change   One major problem confronting every political system is how to change government policies (or personnel) without resorting to bloody rebellion. When free elections permit a choice between two or more political parties, that problem may be largely solved, especially if the parties represent genuine policy alternatives. When the voters chose McKinley, the Republican, over Bryan, the Democrat, in the presidential election of 1896 they were opting for high tariffs and the gold standard, and when they elected

Lyndon Johnson rather than Barry Goldwater in 1964, they chose civil rights legislation, Medicare, federal aid to education, and (they were told) nonintervention in Vietnam. Thus party competition at the polling booths permits the voters a peaceful choice among policies as well as personalities; it then enables a peaceful transfer of power.

Sometimes in the U.S., however, the major parties pursue a middle course so desperately that their policy pronouncements are virtually indistinguishable. They often do this because they believe the voters favor a moderate position; they may also do it when social conflicts are acute and the parties seek to reconcile these conflicts by a compromise satisfactory to a majority.

The existence of competing parties also helps to keep them fairly honest. In their competition for votes, each watches the other, perhaps less like a hawk than a vulture. The result is a system of political checks and balances which is just as important as the governmental one.

Policy coordination   The separation of powers among various agencies of the national government, and the division of powers between the national and state governments can cause friction and rivalry. But if several governmental branches or levels are in the hands of the same party, that party can help bridge the gaps among them and coordinate government activities on behalf of the same policies. On the other hand, if different parties dominate different parts of government, competition among them may result in a political deadlock, as happened on welfare reform and other issues involving President Nixon and the Democratic-controlled Congress. Vigorous action, therefore, usually requires the legislative and executive branches under the control of the same party.

Citizen involvement   Political parties provide an institutional link between the voters and the government. Because their committees and conventions include both public officials and private citizens, parties, like pressure groups, give people some direct and personal access to the centers of governmental power. At the same time, they provide government officials additional opportunities to gauge public opinion and strengthen their popular support. Parties also link government and people in the imperfect but important mechanism by which government is held accountable to the citizens.

Latent functions   Finally, some less apparent functions of parties are of importance. They define problems and structure the views of voters who identify with them. Likewise they provide a relevant reference for the political behavior of individual citizens who seek government services, jobs, or contracts.

The Number of Parties

Much is revealed about the stability and the democratic character of a modern political system by the number of parties which operate within it. We can distinguish three variations.

One-party politics   Some nations, such as the U.S.S.R. and Spain, have only one major party because it is illegal to form another one. Obviously, choice, accountability, and free political activity are minimal in such nations. Occasionally, however, one party will dominate the government because of peculiar historical circumstances and in spite of the existence of several other weak parties. This is the case in Mexico, India, and parts of the United States.

Two-party politics   Taken as a whole, America has a two-party system. But this does not mean that there are only two parties, nor that this situation prevails to an equal degree everywhere in the nation. It does mean that only the Republican and Democratic parties have a realistic chance of obtaining congressional majorities or electing a President.

How has such a situation come about? For one thing, an example of a two-party system had been established in Great Britain even before the Revolution. For another, congressmen and most state legislators are elected by simple pluralities rather than majorities, from *single-member* rather than from larger *multi-member* districts. As a result, candidates who finish second or third lose, which tends to discourage vigorous campaigns by small third parties. (By contrast, in some Western European nations where three or four candidates are elected from each of several large, multi-member districts, small parties have a chance to elect a lawmaker who finishes third or fourth.) Finally, the Constitution requires that the President be elected by a majority vote (over 50 percent) in the electoral college, and this also discourages small parties.

Once established, our two-party system has been sustained both by the habits of the people and by practical political realities. Most voters are Republicans or Democrats largely because their parents were. The relative strength of the two leading parties varies substantially from place to place. In only about half the states do they compete on a relatively equal basis,[1] although recent trends seem to indicate growing Democratic strength in such hitherto Republican strongholds as Maine and Vermont, while Republicans have begun to crack the traditionally Democratic "solid South." Nonetheless, a survey of the party affiliations of state legislators in 1971 revealed that political systems in many states are still close to the one-party variety. The Republicans dominated legislatures 116 to 49 in Kansas, and 118 to 62 in Vermont. And if the South is no longer solid, it remains remarkably firm. There, Democrats controlled state legislatures by a margin of 139 to 2 in Alabama, 142 to 2 in Louisiana, and 169 to 12 in Texas.[2] In presidential races, however, neither party can take the South for granted.

Most congressional districts reveal a lack of genuine competition. Two leading scholars have estimated that from 75 to 80 percent of

1 V. O. Key, Jr., *Politics, Parties, and Pressure Groups,* 5th ed. (N.Y.: Thomas Y. Crowell Company, 1964), pp. 284–87.
2 *Congressional Quarterly Guide to Current American Government* (Spring 1971), p. 18.

all seats in the House of Representatives are "safe" for one party or the other.[3] Yet the central fact remains that the two-party system has dominated national politics during nearly all of our history. As state and local issues become more similar in all sections of the country, this trend will probably spread to these levels.

Multi-party politics Since there are numerous possible opinions on political issues, many nations where there is considerable personal freedom have three or more relatively strong parties. Multi-party systems have a major disadvantage, however. By fragmenting political groups along doctrinaire lines, political compromise is more difficult, and an unstable situation often results in which no single party has a legislative majority. Hence several parties form an uneasy coalition in order to pass laws or support the executive effectively. In some parliamentary systems, such as Italy, this has caused frequent changes in executive leadership.

The Types of Parties

Aside from sheer habit, why do voters support a particular party? As a partial answer, three major types of parties, each with a distinctive appeal, may be identified.

Charismatic parties Some political parties are formed largely to support a popular and magnetic candidate—one who is said to have "charisma." That quality is an intangible one, entailing the capacity to inspire confidence and enthusiastic devotion among large numbers of people. It is hard to define, but, like sex appeal, most people know it when they see it.

Few American parties have been primarily charismatic. Those that have come closest to it, such as Theodore Roosevelt's short-lived Progressive party in 1912, have been unable to get their leaders elected. Nevertheless, there is no doubt that both Franklin D. Roosevelt in the 1930s and Dwight D. Eisenhower in the 1950s possessed some charismatic appeal. It may well be that charisma will be more important in the future than in the past because of the dramatic vividness with which television can project the personalities of leading candidates into millions of living rooms. There is a danger in this, for charismatic leadership, like romantic love, can obscure real issues and divert attention from the hard problems ahead.

Doctrinaire parties While a few parties have rested on charismatic leadership, many have been based on a political principle, doctrine, or ideology. Thus, the German Nazi party was founded on the doctrine of anti-Semitic Aryan supremacy, communist parties on anti-

3 William J. Keefe and Morris S. Ogul, *The American Legislative Process: Congress and the States* (Englewood Cliffs, N.J.: Prentice-Hall, Inc., 1968) pp. 109–14.

capitalist Marxism, the Prohibition party on opposition to alcoholic beverages, and socialist parties on a belief that certain industries should be nationalized (owned and operated by the government).

The major political parties in the United States are not doctrinaire. Both include citizens as well as public officials who hold widely diverse points of view. Nonetheless, the Democrats, with the notable exception of many in the South, tend to be vaguely liberal in orientation. Either they may be slightly more permissive with respect to personal behavior, or they may favor a larger role for the government in overcoming poverty or prejudice, or both. But many bread-and-butter Democrats are conservative on such issues as abortion and drugs. Republicans, in not-so-sharp contrast, are generally conservative. They are inclined to favor tighter controls on personal morality and to stress the importance of individual responsibility rather than government action in overcoming social problems. Since most Americans are nonideological moderates, it is widely held that if either party becomes too doctrinaire, as when Barry Goldwater espoused a rigidly conservative brand of Republicanism in 1964, the other party will probably win. Many attributed George McGovern's defeat in 1972 to his excessively liberal image.

Broker parties   If American parties are primarily neither charismatic nor doctrinaire, what are they? The answer is phrased in different ways. They are pragmatic, interested in winning elections; they are consensus oriented, attempting to gain enough agreement on as few issues among as many groups as is required to get a majority of the votes; they are willing to "rise above principle" in order to get into office; they are flexible, bending their positions with the changing winds of public opinion.

In other words, American parties are broker parties. A broker is essentially a middleman, one who helps people get together for a mutually beneficial deal on which he too can make a profit. Thus real estate brokers bring buyers and sellers together and stockbrokers bring investors and business corporations together. In this sense, the Republican and Democratic parties are political brokers, compromising diverse and often conflicting demands. The Democratic coalition welded together in the 1930s is a classic example of broker politics. It included blacks, Southerners, the unions, urban ethnic groups, and the big city political "bosses." Each party tries to assemble a combination of voters from various geographic sections, from ethnic and religious groups, and from diverse occupations, ages, and income categories that will add up to a majority on election day. To do this, they will put together as attractive a "package" as they can, including as charismatic a candidate as possible and as many proposed government programs as necessary without binding themselves to a specific ideological principle.

A number of important results stem from the broker nature of the two major parties:

1) Since both Republicans and Democrats usually appeal to

a wide variety of groups, they tend to unify the country, rather than to divide it as Washington and Madison had feared.

2) In their search for a majority of votes, the two parties often appeal to the same groups (especially small businessmen, farmers, and skilled workers), and thus the party programs may sound very much alike. This Tweedledum and Tweedledee effect has often led third parties to argue, with some justification but little success, that they provide the only meaningful alternatives.

3) On the other hand, the similarities between the Republicans and Democrats have persuaded many pressure groups that they can work reasonably well with either party and therefore need not form one of their own.

4) Whenever a new third party has increased rapidly in popularity, especially when it has received more votes than had been expected, at least one of the two major parties has shifted its position closer to that of the brash young upstart, thereby thwarting the growth of the latter.

5) The most frequently criticized effect of the broker nature of American parties is that it makes it more difficult to hold the government responsible to the people. Because this serious charge involves a central mechanism for maintaining democracy, it deserves a careful analysis.

Democracy, Responsibility, and Parties

By definition, a democracy should provide a government responsible to a majority of the people. But the word "responsible" has a double meaning. It means that the people should be able to hold government officials *accountable* for their conduct, reelecting them if they deserve it and "turning the rascals out" if they don't. It also means that government officials should be *reliable* in the sense that they do what the people expected them to do when they elected them. But genuine responsibility, in terms of either accountability or reliability, is hard to come by in American government.

Accountability   The principal difficulty in holding elected officials accountable is that there are simply too many of them. In the 1970 general election, the present author was confronted with a ballot listing thirty-six candidates running for eleven national and state offices, plus four more seeking local judgeships. He knew nothing about sixteen of the candidates, except for their party affiliations listed on the ballots. For the judicial candidates, he lacked even that knowledge. Unfortunately, this situation is somewhat typical of conditions throughout the country. Voters are more than voters; they are also employees, family members, bowlers, Elks, and stamp collectors. They have neither the time, the information, nor the desire to hold all public officials accountable.

Reliability   The failure of public officials to be reliable may be caused by unrealistic voter demands or by conflicting pressures on the official. For instance, the voters may expect more government programs and also a tax cut, or the newly elected congressman may discover that a tax cut will truly endanger important government activities. But if the congressman votes for a tax cut, it is still possible that such a bill will be defeated in either the House or Senate or vetoed by the President. Even if the taxes imposed by the national government were reduced, this could be more than offset by increases in state taxes.

The point is that power is so widely dispersed among so many officials in American government that no one of them (with the possible exception of the President in the area of international relations) is easily able to accomplish what a majority of voters want done. The elected official is thwarted in his attempts to carry out the wishes of the people by at least four characteristics of our political system: bicameral legislatures, allowing one house to oppose the other; the separation of powers, permitting one branch to frustrate the efforts of another; federalism, enabling the national and state governments to pass the buck back and forth so as to create a political stalemate; and the constitutional principles of individual freedom and legal equality thwarting the intentions of an intolerant majority. Those who framed the Constitution, fearful of concentrating too much power in the hands of too few people, distributed authority so widely that few officials can fairly be charged with unreliability for not doing what they said they would try to do.

Party responsibility Since the voter is expected to elect more officials than he possibly can keep track of, and since power is fragmented among them so as to pit one against another, many argue that the political parties are responsible for government action. If particular officials are not fully responsible for what finally happens, why not hold the winning party at the last election responsible? Although voters may know little of the individual candidates for whom they vote, at least the ballot usually indicates the party to which those candidates belong.

But complete party responsibility would require that all candidates of the same party favor the same government policies, and that there be some methods of party discipline to persuade all party members to vote the same way on important bills. For broker parties, by definition consisting of loose coalitions embracing widely divergent views, this situation simply does not exist. In 1967, for instance, *Congressional Quarterly* reported that a conservative coalition of Republicans and southern Democrats in the House of Representatives repeatedly defeated the Democratic President, Lyndon Johnson, on many of his key proposals. This occurred in the face of a sixty-one member Democratic majority in that chamber. Although southern Democrats were most notable in their defection to the opposition party, eight northern Democrats voted with the Republicans on at least 54 percent of the crucial roll calls.[4]

One is forced to conclude that substantial numbers of voters

4 *Congressional Quarterly Guide to Current American Government* (Spring 1968), pp. 88 and 91.

are probably frustrated by voting for Republican candidates, hoping for a conservative government, or for Democratic candidates, hoping for a liberal one. The major parties in American politics impose no effective loyalty tests, nor can they control their own members.

Yet to emphasize legislators who vote against their party's majority tends to distort the picture. The fact remains that most Democrats are liberal and most Republicans are conservative, and one major survey shows this distinction to be considerably more pronounced among party leaders than among the rank and file party members.[5] Were there no ideological differences whatever between the parties, candidates might just as well run without party labels. But democracy requires some basis for determining what—as well as whom—most people prefer. Imperfect as it is, the party system permits us to conclude, after most elections, that a majority prefers either the conservative ideas propounded by most leading Republicans or the liberal ideas advocated by most prominent Democrats. And when, in the same election, the voters choose a Republican President and a Democratic-controlled Congress— as they did in 1956 and again in 1968 and 1972 —the only victor is a party system that is essentially irresponsible.

PARTIES IN AMERICA

As we have seen, two major parties have been dominant in America during most of its history. We must now examine their evolution and organization.

Party Origins: The Major Parties

The first important parties were the Federalists, led by Alexander Hamilton and John Adams, and the anti-Federalists, or Democratic-Republicans, championed by Thomas Jefferson and James Madison. The Federalists favored a strong national government, drew support from commercial interests, and were pro-English, while the Democratic-Republicans favored state power, were supported by farmers, and were pro-French.

By the early 1820s, initial party loyalties had disintegrated, largely because of a split among the Federalists regarding the War of 1812. The next decade witnessed a new political alignment in which the supporters of Andrew Jackson constituted what is now known as the Democratic party, while his opponents formed what was called the Whig party. As the Civil War moved ominously closer, the issue of whether to permit slavery in the western territories killed the Whigs, who were badly divided on the matter. The northern ex-Whigs were chiefly responsible for the present-day Republican party. And so the situation

5 Herbert McClosky, *et al.*, "Issue Conflict and Consensus among Party Leaders and Followers," *American Political Science Review* 54 (June 1960): 406–27.

remains, more than a century later. So entrenched was the dominance of the two parties in 1972 that only two of the 535 members of Congress had been elected without the benefit of nomination by either party.

Between 1861 and 1933, the Republicans occupied the White House for fifty-six years and the Democrats, during the administrations of Grover Cleveland and Woodrow Wilson, for only sixteen. Since 1933, however, Democratic Presidents have held office for twenty-eight years and Republicans, led by Dwight Eisenhower and Richard Nixon, for twelve. Democrats boast of guiding the nation through two World Wars and the Great Depression, while enacting legislation providing for minimum hourly wages, union recognition, pensions and Medicare through the social security program, guaranteed price supports for farm crops, and enforcement of black voting rights. The "Grand Old Party" (GOP), as the younger Republican party is inappropriately called, claims credit for ending slavery, acquiring Alaska, Hawaii, and Puerto Rico, building the Panama Canal, passing pure food and conservation laws, ending the Korean conflict, constructing the St. Lawrence Seaway, and withdrawing ground combat forces from Vietnam.

In the 1972 campaign most Democratic candidates argued for income supplements for the poor, national health insurance, closing tax loopholes for corporations, and reduced military expenditures, while Republicans generally defended the Nixon program of revenue sharing with state and local governments, a high level of defense spending, expanded aid for law enforcement, and opposition to compulsory school busing for racial integration. On a few issues, the two parties offered clear-cut alternatives, but on many more their differences were the more customary disagreements about the relative priority of various national needs.

Neither party has remained entirely loyal to the principles for which it initially stood. Broker parties, if they are to survive, cannot afford that moral luxury. They must be flexible, often in the face of strong challenges from minor third parties.

Winning Causes and Losing Candidates: Minor Parties

Like pressure groups, third parties in America have influenced our politics in a number of important respects. Most important, they have been among the first to champion new causes. Many of these were later adopted by the Republicans and Democrats—once their popularity had been demonstrated. The People's (or Populist) party, perhaps the most significant minor party in our history, provides the best example. Formed in 1892, the Populists were among the first to advocate the popular election of U.S. senators, women's suffrage, a flexible expansion of currency, and other liberal reforms. When they won three governorships and elected half a dozen congressmen, mostly at the

Figure 21   Party Platforms, 1972
How Some of the Republican and Democratic Planks Contrast

	Democrats	Republicans
Vietnam War	Immediate complete withdrawal of all U.S. forces in Indochina, all P.O.W.'s to be returned. No more military aid to Indochina.	Withdrawal 4 months after internationally supervised cease-fire in effect in Indochina and all prisoners returned.
Amnesty	Amnesty after war to draft resisters who refused to serve.	No amnesty to those who evaded military service.
Defense	Reduce military spending where consistent with national security and reduce overseas forces and bases.	No meat-ax slashes, but prudent reductions in defense spending; will not let America become second-class power.
Foreign Policy	Reemphasis on UN and Congress. Help to Israel; pursue with U.S.S.R. mutual force reductions in Europe; reduce military aid in Latin America; opposition to policies of regimes in Rhodesia, Greece, Portugal, and South Africa.	Maintenance of strength in Europe and Mediterranean, but seek agreement with Warsaw Pact nations for mutual reduction of forces; increased contacts with China and Eastern · Europe; help to Israel; opposition to policies of regime in Cuba.
Taxes	Tax reform to distribute cost of government more fairly, close loopholes such as special favors for oil industry, capital gains, fast depreciation, and expense accounts.	Tax reform to include revenue sharing, fair distribution of tax burden, simplification, but no sharp increase in middle-income taxes.
Welfare	Income security program, guaranteeing an income substantially above poverty level. Expansion of public employment to guarantee jobs for all.	No government guaranteed income. Reform of welfare system, provision of day care.
Labor	Minimum wage of $2.50; no compulsory arbitration.	Discourage location of plants in foreign countries.
Education	Increased federal aid and equalization of spending among school districts.	Channeling aid to education so as to enable parental choice of public or nonpublic schools, as through income tax credits.
Desegregation and Busing	Desegregation to be pursued by various means including busing.	End de jure segregation, but no busing for racial balance.
Health Care	Establish system of universal national health insurance to cover all Americans.	No nationalized compulsory health insurance. Support comprehensive health insurance financed by employers, employees, and federal government.
Housing	Provide financing for decent homes. Promote free choice in housing through development of new communities with diversified housing and enforcement of fair housing laws.	Housing programs aimed at decent homes for all, but not for use of housing or community-development programs to impose arbitrary housing patterns on unwilling communities.

expense of the Democrats, the Democratic National Convention in 1896 nominated William Jennings Bryan, a Populist hero, for the presidency, and adopted a platform that advocated many Populist ideas.

The Socialist party also has had an effect on the policies of its far larger rivals. Organized in 1901, it was years ahead of them in its call for a graduated income tax, unemployment compensation, and old-age pensions. Such reforms would surely have come anyway, but one suspects the process was hastened by the 900,000 votes cast for Eugene V. Debs, the Socialist presidential candidate in 1912 and again in 1920. Four years later, the Socialists joined various farm groups, the AFL, and the independent railroad brotherhoods to support the newly created Progressive party. Under the leadership of Senator Robert M. ("Fighting Bob") La Follette, a liberal Republican from Wisconsin, the party urged government support for agriculture, collective bargaining for labor unions, and other proposals to which the Democratic New Deal was destined to give birth in the next decade. The Progressive ticket garnered 16.6 percent of the popular vote—a figure not since surpassed by any third party candidate.

Closely related to the policy innovation associated with minor parties is their effect in determining what ideas are considered to be politically extreme. When Alabama Governor George Wallace ran for President, for instance, he took positions on school desegregation and on law and order that made the policies of the Republicans in these areas seem quite moderate in comparison. In shifting the center of the political spectrum to the right in 1968, Governor Wallace not only forced both the Democrats and Republicans to advocate more conservative positions, but also led both major parties, in their fear of losing votes to him, to focus their campaigns on the issues (mostly law and order) which he was emphasizing.

It is probably safe to assume that any time a third party threatens to get over 5 percent of the vote, and Wallace received 13.5 percent, it will have considerable impact on the two major contenders. One does not necessarily throw away one's vote, therefore, if it is cast for minor party candidates. They cannot win, but their ideas may prevail.

One other effect of third parties must be noted: If they take most of their votes away from one major party, they may well guarantee victory for the other. In 1912, for example, dissident Republicans formed a Progressive party to support the candidacy of Theodore Roosevelt, who had failed in his attempt to get the GOP nomination. As a result, the Democratic candidate, Woodrow Wilson, was elected.

Party Organization

Parties in the United States, at least in comparison with those in England and Western Europe, are highly decentralized. National party organizations have small staffs with little control over state parties, and state parties, in turn, have little control over the organizations at the county or city level. Yet the national parties are major cogs in the machinery of American politics.

National conventions: the people's choice?   The national parties' most remarkable activity is the staging of national conventions. Every four years some four thousand delegates to the Republican and Democratic national conventions nominate the two presidential candidates between whom more than seventy million voters make a choice. More remarkable still, they congregate in a colorfully raucous atmosphere, arranged in part for maximum television impact, and often resembling a carnival more than a convention.

How these delegates are chosen is clearly a matter of fundamental importance. It is also one of incredible complexity, since no two states select convention delegates in exactly the same way. In some the procedure is determined by state law and in others it is decided upon by the state committee of each party. There are about ten states in which Republican delegates are chosen differently than Democratic delegates. With a few exceptions, however, two general methods are employed: Delegates are either elected by the voters in presidential primaries or they are chosen by party conventions at the state or district levels.

Even among the twenty-three states that have presidential primaries, there are wide variations in procedure. The election of convention delegates may be separate from a presidential preference poll in which voters can indicate their personal choice for their party's nomination. In New Jersey and West Virginia, for example, the result of the preference poll is not binding on the state's delegates, while in Indiana and Oregon it is. Another important distinction among the primary states is the extent to which the delegates elected to the national convention are pledged in advance to vote for a particular presidential candidate. New York does not even permit the presidential preference of the prospective delegate to appear on the ballot. In Florida, those seeking to become delegates may list themselves as favoring a certain presidential contender but if elected to the convention, they may vote for someone else. Delegates from New Hampshire are elected as either pledged to a particular candidate, favoring a candidate, or expressing no preference. In Wisconsin, only the names of the presidential candidates appear on the ballot and delegates supporting the winner are pledged to vote for him at the convention. Most presidential primaries select at least a few of the delegates from districts into which the states are divided, but in South Dakota, the District of Columbia, and California all the delegates are chosen in "winner-take-all," at-large elections. As a result, when George McGovern led the field in the 1972 California primary with 45 percent of the vote, he garnered all 271 delegates from that state in spite of the indignant protests of Hubert Humphrey, with 40 percent of the total.

Among states in which district or state conventions select delegates to the national convention, there is little uniformity in the methods by which convention membership is chosen. Some such as

Colorado and Texas, allow wide voter participation while Kansas and a few others are far less democratic. Illinois selects some of its delegates by state convention and some by primary, and a few other states use a similar combination of methods. If the student of national conventions thinks the whole matter of delegate selection is somewhat confusing, he has learned the most outstanding point about it. Complicating matters still more, many states change their selection methods with bewildering frequency.

The number of delegates to which each state is entitled at a national convention is not governed by law but is determined by rules adopted by each party. Although the Republicans and Democrats differ from one another in the apportionment of convention delegates, both use formulas based on state population, but reward those states where they have enjoyed recent election victories with extra bonus delegates.

At each party's national convention a candidate must receive a majority of the delegates' votes in order to win the nomination. Balloting is conducted by a roll call of the states, allowing the chairman of each state delegation to announce with a dramatic flourish how many votes the state casts for each candidate. If none of the contenders receives a majority on the first ballot, additional votes are taken until someone clears the magic hurdle of 50 percent plus one. Well-organized nation-wide preconvention campaigns have made it increasingly probable that the leading candidate will win on the first ballot, however, and not since 1952, when the Democrats nominated Adlai E. Stevenson on the third ballot, has it taken more than one roll call.

Nonetheless, there is always an air of excited uncertainty about a national convention, and in politicians' breasts hope springs eternal. In the first place, many of the delegates are not legally pledged to vote for any particular candidate and those informally committed may be persuaded by some last-minute break (say, a new public opinion poll) to change their minds. Furthermore, there·are usually half a dozen or more candidates seeking the nomination, making a clear majority difficult to obtain. Some of these candidates are "favorite sons" of their native states who may be running to polish their political images back home or to force one of the major candidates to make some concession, such as the promise of a cabinet appointment, in return for their withdrawal from the race. But they hope, too, for a situation in which the front-runners will be deadlocked and the convention, after three or four ballots, will turn to them as a compromise, or "dark horse" candidate. It doesn't happen often, but an obscure Ohio senator named Warren G. Harding was nominated on the tenth ballot by the 1920 Republican convention and went all the way to the White House.

Few political institutions in America have received more criticism than the national party conventions. Although polls reveal that they usually nominate the candidate favored by most members of their party, they have been indicted as unrepresentative elites, with most of the delegates chosen by undemocratic methods. In 1968, for example, only 41 percent of the delegates to the Democratic National Convention were chosen in presidential primaries. When Hubert Humphrey captured the nomination without campaigning in any primary, the demands for reform could not be contained even by the Chicago police force. In 1969 the chairman of the Democratic National Committee appointed George McGovern to head a twenty-eight member commission to devise guidelines that would be binding on all state party organizations in the selection of future convention delegates. The result was a requirement that the process of delegate selection take place the same year as the convention and involve a maximum number of Democratic voters. More important, the reform commission imposed a modified quota system on the selection of convention delegates to insure that young people, women, and some ethnic minorites would have convention representation in rough proportion to their total numbers.[6]

Although these guidelines were not enforced uniformly, they profoundly altered the power structure of the Democratic party and made a vital contribution to the nomination of Senator McGovern. Compared with the 1968 Democratic National Convention, in that of 1972 the percentage of delegates under thirty jumped from 4 to about 20, of women from 13 to 40, and of blacks, Chicanos, and Indians from less than 8 to 35. Not surprisingly, these were the very groups to which McGovern had appealed most strongly.

The winds of change are no respecter of party, and Republicans, too, felt a breeze. A special committee created by the GOP convention in 1968 made nonbinding recommendations for revised methods of delegate selection. As a result, the percentage of delegates under thirty at the 1972 Republican convention rose from 1 to nearly 10, of women, from 17 to about 30, and of racial minorities from less than 3 to approximately 6.[7] Preparations were made to extend these trends in selecting delegates for 1976.

Although the system remains imperfect, it must be assessed in terms of the available alternatives. It is surely more democratic than nomination by caucuses (meetings of members of the same party in Congress) which was the method used prior to the first major party convention in 1832. Similarly, a nominating convention has at least one advantage over a nation-wide presidential primary, which is the alternative most frequently recommended. A national primary would give an increased edge to the most well-financed candidates, since all-out campaigns throughout the country would then be necessary. Now such massive drives need be launched only in the presidential primary states, and usually only in some of these.

Besides nominating a presidential candidate, a national party convention performs other functions. It elects members of the national committee, although this simply confirms the persons nominated by

---

6 Commission on Party Structure and Delegate Selection, *Mandate for Reform* (Washington, D.C.: Democratic National Committee, 1970).
7 Ibid., pp. 26–28, and *Los Angeles Times*, July 28, 1972, pp. 14–15.

each of the state delegations. It also adopts a platform, which sometimes precipitates a convention's most exciting controversies. The platform sets forth policies the party favors, usually in a series of vaguely worded planks, but it is not binding on the candidates. Far less time is spent on another convention task, the selection of a vice-presidential candidate.

By tradition, the national convention follows the recommendation of its presidential nominee in selecting a vice-presidential running mate. But both campaign politics and the convention agenda often require that a decision on the vice-presidential nominee be made so quickly that it cannot be made very wisely, as happened in the case of Senator George McGovern's selection of Thomas Eagleton in 1972.

When McGovern was nominated on the night of June 12, he had less than twenty-four hours to pick a suitable running mate. Senator Edward Kennedy had to be asked because he would bring the most strength to the ticket. He declined. Hubert Humphrey had to be asked because his selection would strengthen both party unity and an old, but severely strained, friendship. He too declined. The other imperatives were those impersonal but contradictory ones of a balanced ticket and ideological compatibility. Since McGovern was a farm-state Protestant, he needed an urban Catholic or Jew. He must select someone who could placate union opposition, entice Chicago's Mayor Daley to back the ticket, reassure women of his support, and in addition counteract his radical image without alienating his most liberal supporters among young people and blacks. Yet a running mate would also have to share McGovern's values, his priorities, and his vision of the future.

Only five hours before the roll call was to begin for the vice-presidential nomination, George McGovern telephoned Thomas Eagleton to offer him the second spot on the ticket. Eagleton neglected to mention his electric shock treatments for depression and his three periods of hospitalization for nervous exhaustion which soon threatened to obscure the vital issues requiring campaign debate with a continued discussion of one man's mental health. Twelve days later, he withdrew from the race. In the aftermath of the 1972 controversy it seemed obvious that some change was desirable, and a Democratic party committee began studying possible future reforms.

National committees: prestige without power The national committee of each party is chosen for a four-year term and is the highest party authority during the interval between conventions. Traditionally, both the Republican and Democratic committees have been chosen by the various state delegations to the national conventions and have consisted mainly of a man and a woman from each state. The Republicans enlarged their National Committee a number of years ago to include the chairman of the Republican state committee from each state which was carried by the last Republican presidential candidate, or which has a majority of Republican congressmen, or which has a Republican governor. Starting from the same two members per state basis, the Democratic National Committee was enlarged to 303 members in 1972 to make it more representative of the entire party. The committee of each party elects a chairperson, usually on the recommendation of its presidential candidate for whom he or she acts as a major campaign coordinator and advisor. When Jean Westwood was chosen to head the Democratic National Committee in 1972, it was the first time either party had conferred this responsibility on a woman.

The national committees discharge three major responsibilities: (1) They raise money to finance the national campaign and assist in campaign research, management, and strategy planning; (2) They try to promote cooperation among party organizations in the various states; and (3) They select the city in which the next national convention will be held, appoint necessary convention officers and committees, plan the agenda, make all necessary arrangements for the housing and transportation of delegates, and arrange for TV and other media coverage. In 1972 the Democratic National Committee was required to perform a fourth function when vice-presidential candidate Thomas Eagleton withdrew from the race. When a nominee for either President or Vice President dies or resigns, the rules of both parties stipulate that a new nominee be selected by the national committee.

Although national committee membership normally carries considerable prestige and great responsibility, it entails little real power over state and local party organizations. In addition to the national conventions and national committees, each party has campaign committees for the Senate and for the House of Representatives. Their sole function is to raise funds for the candidates seeking election or reelection to Congress.

State and local organization: politics as patronage   State and local party organizations are not as powerful as they once were. In spite of this, many of them remain stronger than their counterparts at the national level. At one time, party strength was most apparent in the politics of city and county government. The boss-controlled "machines" such as those of Ed Crump of Memphis, Tom Pendergast of Kansas City, and "Boss" Tweed of New York may have been greased with corruption but they ran exceedingly well on election day. And all were examples of local organizations on which the state and national parties were largely dependent.

Most observers believe that the declining influence of political machines in the past thirty years is due to several factors. As more government jobs were awarded on the basis of civil service examinations, fewer were available as rewards for loyal service to the winning party. In addition to this decline in patronage jobs, machine influence has been weakened because more cities are electing officials on a nonpartisan basis, and are substituting primary elections for local party caucuses in the selection of candidates. The availability of welfare benefits and a general increase in the standard of living have diminished the dependence of poor people on partisan political groups and thus weakened the parties at the local level even more.[8] It is also possible that the increasing effectiveness of the mass media has made the door-to-door precinct work that is so characteristic of traditional party organization, particularly in the cities, no longer as important as it once was.

But here one must be wary of generalizations: The youthful supporters of Senator McGovern fashioned astonishingly successful campaign organizations before the primary elections which paved the way to his presidential nomination. In local politics, Albany, New Haven, and Chicago still have highly efficient party organizations, while Los Angeles, Detroit, and Seattle do not. At the county level, it would be difficult to find a more engrossing example of effective, although informal, party organization than that of Nelson County, Kentucky,[9] or one of more widespread state patronage than in Centre County, Pennsylvania.[10]

While some of the same factors that have weakened the parties at the local level are also present on a state-wide scale, many state party organizations are still held together by throngs of workers and campaign contributors motivated less by a firm belief in the party platform than by a fervent desire for government contracts or jobs. Among the variables that affect the strength of parties at the state level are the degree of party competition, the scope of the civil service system, the level of prosperity, the influence of pressure groups, the urban-rural balance, and the degree to which the traditional political culture demands a strict code of ethics.

Most states have a party organization that begins in the precinct, township, or ward—political units that usually include from a few hundred to several thousand voters. Officials at these lowest of political levels usually select city and/or county committees, which in turn choose district and/or state central committees. State party conventions are still common, and before the advent of the direct primary in the early years of this century, they nominated candidates for governor and other state offices. This was the practice in New York until 1968.

But many states have party structures that deviate widely from the general pattern. In California, for example, there are no official party organizations below the county committee level, and most members of the state committee are appointed by party nominees for Congress and various state offices.

Volunteer groups: politics as principle   As many official party organizations declined in vigor, a political void developed. Increas-

8 Fred I. Greenstein, *The American Party System and the American People,* 2nd ed. (Englewood Cliffs, N.J.: Prentice-Hall, Inc., 1970), pp. 47–54.

9 John H. Fenton, *People and Parties in Politics* (Glenview, Ill.: Scott, Foresman and Company, 1966), pp. 67–70.

10 Frank J. Sorauf, "State Patronage in a Rural County," *The American Political Science Review* 50 (December 1956): 1046–56. The situation described may be fairly typical of the entire state of Pennsylvania, where the state civil service system covers only about 20 percent of its employees.

ingly candidates looked elsewhere for support. Those with enough money often turned to professional public relations firms and to greater television exposure. Some relied more heavily upon pressure group support. More idealistic aspirants were delighted to find that new political volunteer groups were springing up around the country, more interested in policy decisions than patronage dispensation, and eager to support candidates genuinely committed to the principles in which they believed.

Much as these volunteer groups differed, their members tended to be disillusioned with established party organizations, relatively young, remarkably well educated, ideologically sophisticated, and—too often—politically naive.[11] They had one appeal that is especially alluring to millions of citizens: Being both new and opposed to "machine politics," these groups were relatively unstructured and eager for the support and encouragement of new recruits.

These groups have tended to be farther to the left (or right) than the official organizations of the parties with which they are associated. This is not difficult to explain, since moderates do not work very hard in any volunteer group (unless motivated by personal gain) because they usually don't see too much wrong with society. Ideological purists, on the other hand, exert enormous energy because they are seriously convinced that if they don't society will surely collapse.

The future of American parties   The party system in America has been a crucial force which has molded and oriented the political beliefs of the people. Yet there are some compelling reasons to suspect that the strength of the Republicans and Democrats is slipping and that we may be entering an age of party decline or realignment. Ticket splitting, for example, has reached epidemic proportions. In the 1970 off-year elections there were twenty-three states in which both U.S. senators and governors were elected and in eleven of them the voters chose a senator of one party and a governor of the other. Moreover, the number of independents has increased steadily, and according to a Gallup Poll, among college students the percentage of political independents rose by 13 between 1966 and 1970, while Republicans declined by 8 percent and Democrats by 5 percent.[12]

The major reasons for the disintegration of traditional party loyalties may be summarized:

1) Television has enhanced the importance of personal charm and charismatic leadership to the detriment of party loyalty.

2) Public relations and professional campaign management firms have assumed some of the functions of party organizations.

3) The emotional impact of social issues such as crime, abortion, and school busing, along with the growing importance of foreign policy, has eroded the economic foundations (rich Republicans

11 Greenstein, op. cit., pp. 57–59.
12 Gallup Poll, *Los Angeles Times,* Feb. 14, 1971, Sec. H., p. 5.

Figure 22   Party Affiliations of the People

	Republican	Democrat	Independent
1973	27%	42%	31%
1968	27	46	27
1960	30	47	23
1950	33	45	22
1940	38	42	20

Source: Reprinted by permission of the American Institute of Public Opinion (The Gallup Poll).

vs. poor Democrats) of party preference. This was especially apparent in the refusal of the AFL-CIO, for the first time in twenty years, to endorse the Democratic presidential candidate in 1972. Many individual unions, however, remained securely in the fold.

4) The growth of civil service systems has deprived the parties of much patronage as a reward for campaign support.

5) Nonpartisan elections and the adoption of the direct primary have diminished the influence of party leaders in choosing the candidates for public office.

6) The increasing speed of social change makes it more difficult for parents to transmit old party loyalties to their children.

7) The intensification of attitudes rooted in racial and ethnic differences has accentuated the internal divisions within both major parties.

8) Since parties are weakest in those states where pressure groups are strongest, the continuing availability of campaign contributions from generous lobbyists has perpetuated a high degree of financial independence from both major parties among candidates for office.

9) Because both Republican and Democratic candidates have provided fewer new ideas or policy innovations than either pressure groups or minor parties, increasingly sophisticated and well-educated voters may view the major parties as somewhat irrelevant to the solution of contemporary problems.

It would be both brazen and misleading to conclude that funeral arrangements should be undertaken for the two-party, broker-oriented politics of the United States. Habits die hard. Yet it is difficult to escape the feeling that both the Republican and Democratic parties are confronted with a difficult challenge: Although still strong and seldom attacked, will they be increasingly ignored?

Chapter **8**

The Price of Democracy
Campaigns and Elections

Politics is the gentle art of getting votes from the poor and campaign funds from the rich, by promising to protect each from the other.

Oscar Ameringer

A political campaign is the dramatic climax of the democratic political process. It magnifies everything we have examined in the last two chapters: Public opinion becomes more intense, pressure groups grow more active, and party candidates wither or shine under the spotlight of the mass media. Part of the fascination of a campaign is that it can be a time of changed alignments and erupting emotions. The year 1972 was no exception. Many Catholics, Jews, and important union officials refused their customary support for the Democratic presidential candidate, a former security consultant for the Republican National Committee was arrested for attempting to bug the headquarters of the Democratic National Committee, a would-be assassin crippled the governor of Alabama, and a vice-presidential candidate withdrew from his ticket for the first time in history. But campaigns also display some reasonably stable characteristics, to which we will direct our attention.

POLITICAL CAMPAIGNS

The final outcome of an election depends to a considerable extent on the candidates chosen in the primaries, the money and other resources they have at their disposal, and the skill they employ in waging their campaigns.

The Primary Process

The selection process by which parties recruit their nominees has taken several forms. During our early history, small groups of party leaders, known as caucuses, picked the party candidates. In Andrew Jackson's time, in the 1830s, larger groups of party members began meeting in conventions for the same purpose. But full democracy demanded that *all* voters be permitted to select the candidates of their party.

Primaries first appeared in Crawford County, Pennsylvania, when Democrats were allowed to vote for their party nominees as early as 1842.[1] The idea didn't catch on until Wisconsin required that candidates be chosen by a direct vote of the people in 1903.[2] Since then, these preliminary elections, or primaries, have replaced the old convention system throughout the nation. The party primary is one of America's most important contributions to democracy.

At two political levels, however, the party primary has not yet played a determining role. Ironically, they are at opposite ends of the political scale—in the selection of candidates for President and Vice President and in the nonpartisan local elections in many cities. In between, at the state level, are two interesting exceptions: In Nebraska and Minnesota candidates for the state legislatures are not chosen by party primaries nor are their party designations listed on the ballots.

Closed primaries   Most states have laws that permit only persons who are registered as members of a certain party to vote in that party's primary. Thus, the primary is closed to outsiders. In the North, the closed primary tends to produce relatively clear-cut policy differences between the nominees of the two parties since candidates for the Democratic nomination will have to appeal to most liberal voters and those seeking the Republican nomination must make themselves acceptable to a more conservative electorate.

Outside the South, the candidate who has a plurality usually wins the party's nomination even though he or she may not have a majority (over 50 percent). In the South the situation is somewhat different. Since the candidate who gets the Democratic nomination is almost certain to be elected there, the nominee is required to get a majority of the primary votes. If no one does, there is a second, or *runoff,* primary between the two leading candidates. So it is quite possible that an elected official in a southern state has been through three elections: the primary, the runoff primary, and the general election.

Open primaries   A few states have open primaries in which the voter can help select either Republican or Democratic nominees, regardless of his or her own party preference. In Wisconsin, for example,

1 Hugh A. Bone and Austin Ranney, *Politics and Voters* (N.Y.: McGraw-Hill Book Company, 1963), p. 111.
2 Howard R. Penniman, *The American Political Process* (N.Y.: Van Nostrand Reinhold Company, 1962), p. 83.

he or she may simply ask for the primary ballot of either party upon arriving at the polls. This situation often produces many *crossovers.* For instance, if a Democrat is running for reelection to the U.S. Senate with no opposition in the Democratic primary, many Democrats may ask for the Republican primary ballot and vote for the most liberal of the candidates seeking the Republican Senate nomination, or—perhaps— the one they believe would be easiest to defeat in the general election. In the state of Washington, all primary voters are confronted with a *blanket* ballot listing all candidates seeking the nominations of all parties. The voter may vote for one candidate of any party for each office.

Open primaries may produce nominees who have appealed to voters of all parties, and who consequently display relatively few policy differences. The voters in the general election in such situations are often confronted with a barely distinguishable choice between two moderate candidates.

Nonpartisan primaries In races for many local offices, and in the nonpartisan election of the state legislatures in Nebraska and Minnesota, candidates are chosen in primaries in which the party affiliations are not indicated on the ballots. Usually, if no candidate receives a majority of the total votes cast, there is a runoff election between the two front-runners, regardless of party.

Running for office What must you do if you wish to run for office? Requirements vary from state to state, but normally the process is rather simple. Whether you are seeking the nomination of a political party or are running for a nonpartisan job, all you have to do is get a nominating petition signed by a certain percentage of voters and—in some states—pay a small filing fee. If you wish to run as an independent, or to organize a new party, election laws require a far higher number of signatures on the appropriate petition. Although ballots normally permit voters to write in the names of persons not printed there, write-in candidates almost never win, because voters have the habit of deciding among names already printed on the ballot, and because any technical error, such as misspelling a name, will invalidate the vote.

Campaign Resources

A huge registration advantage for one party or the other, the long-established reputation of a popular incumbent, or some overwhelming issue can make the outcome of some campaigns a foregone conclusion. Let us assume, however, that a campaign will make the difference between victory and defeat—as is often the case. What will be needed to win?

The candidate The first ingredient in the victory recipe is a good candidate, with the following characteristics:

1) Intelligence. Americans admire common sense but are contemptuous of too much scholarship. Depending on the district, the fact that a candidate has "been an Oxford scholar may be a help or

something to be hidden."[3] The voters want someone with whom they can identify—someone who mirrors them at their best.

2) A wide acquaintance. Colonel Jacob M. Arvey, a long-time Democratic Party leader in Chicago, once remarked, "It's tough to vote against a man you know—especially if you like him."[4] At the congressional district or state level, this may be of less importance than in a race for the local school board or city council, where many political careers begin. The ideal candidate, therefore, is a joiner, since the more organizations one belongs to the more people one knows. In addition to a wide acquaintance, having many group affiliations offers subsidiary benefits: It develops skillful ease in interpersonal relations and a familiarity with parliamentary procedures and group behavior.

3) A concern for people. The successful politician is usually one who finds a certain exhilaration in handshaking, backslapping, and small talk, along with a sense of camaraderie with the person with a problem—no matter how trivial. The demands of a campaign require candidates to compromise ideals less often than emotions. Unless they genuinely like people, they will find it difficult to appear interested when bored, enthusiastic when indifferent, or hopeful when dejected.

4) Fluency. A candidate who is glib, who can talk easily and quickly, has an immense advantage, especially when answering unexpected questions from an audience, or in face-to-face exchanges with his or her opponent or news reporters.

5) Determination. What the "killer instinct" is to a boxer, determination is to a candidate. He must *want* to win with a nearly inexhaustible persistence. As a former candidate for the Indiana senate put it:

You put all your personality into a campaign. You give it your time, your effort, your money, your heart, and your soul. . . . My friends who were defeated with me knew the rules and played the game and had no regrets. Would we do it again? If we had the time and . . . the money we would.[5]

6) Good health and family support. The rigors of a campaign can be physically and emotionally exhausting. The candidate gets endless opportunities to eat and drink, but too little chance to sleep. Unfortunately, a diminished family life or even divorce are also among the occupational hazards of the chronic campaigner.

From the various attributes above, plus others intangible or unique to each candidate, come success and—in rare instances—genuinely charismatic leadership. But other factors also influence a campaign.

Money   It was Jess Unruh, former candidate for governor

---

3 Stimson Bullitt, *To Be A Politician* (Garden City, N.Y.: Anchor Books, Doubleday & Company, Inc., 1961), p. 82.
4 Quoted in Michael J. Kirwan, *How to Succeed in Politics* (N.Y.: Macfadden-Bartell Corp., 1964), p. 33.
5 James B. Kessler, "Running for State Political Office," Cornelius P. Cotter, ed., *Practical Politics in the United States* (Boston: Allyn & Bacon, Inc., 1969), p. 141.

in California, who said "money is the mother's milk of politics." Although he came to regret his candor, his observation is essentially correct.

The cost of political campaigns has skyrocketed even more rapidly than the cost of living. The presidential race in 1964 probably cost in the neighborhood of $38 million, or approximately fifty-four cents per vote,[6] while the amount spent at all levels of politics was over four times that figure. In 1968 national campaign expenditures climbed to over $62 million,[7] or eighty-five cents per vote, and total campaign outlays (national, state, and local) reached $300 million.[8] A serious presidential campaign cannot be launched for less than $15 million, and a race for governor or U.S. senator in a large state will cost well over a million.

Campaigns for the House of Representatives are less expensive, but still range from a low of $15,000 to a high of more than $125,000.[9] This wide discrepancy can be attributed to the fact that some districts are safe for the majority party incumbent, while in others there are close contests in which the opposing parties are tempted to believe that a few more dollars will convert defeat into victory. In races for the state legislature, the spread in possible campaign costs is, for the same reason, equally great. From $1000 to $50,000 would cover the vast majority.

Where does the money come from? At the national level from 25 to 75 percent came from fewer than 1 percent of the voters—the "fat cats" who contributed over $500—between 1948 and 1964. In the 1968 campaign, 424 persons contributed $10,000 or more to the party of their choice, and seventeen gave more than $30,000.[10] In most instances, the Republicans have benefited from the generosity of wealthy businessmen and conservative pressure groups, but labor contributions, mostly to Democratic coffers, reached nearly $8 million in 1968. This money was raised through appeals in union newspapers and meetings, as well as in person-to-person solicitation in plants and factories throughout the nation.

The inventiveness with which campaign funds are raised sometimes delights the imagination. The fund-raising dinner is an old standby, and entails appearances by prominent politicians and popular entertainers. The costs, depending on the fame of the attending dignitaries, may range from a few dollars to $500 per plate, and the menu—from box lunches to filet mignon—varies accordingly. On the eve of the 1972 Democratic convention, a telethon featuring dozens of entertainment, sports, and political celebrities netted over two million dollars. Both

6 *Politics in America, 1945–1966,* 2nd ed. (Washington, D.C.: Congressional Quarterly, Inc., 1967), p. 88.
7 U.S. Bureau of the Census, *Statistical Abstract of the United States: 1971,* p. 367.
8 Daniel S. Berman and Louis S. Loeb, *Laws and Men* (N.Y.: The Macmillan Company, 1970), p. 149.
9 Kirwan, op. cit., p. 10.
10 Herbert E. Alexander, "The Cost of Presidential Elections," Cotter, op. cit., pp. 281–82, and *Newsweek,* Dec. 13, 1971, pp. 23–32.

parties seem to assume public endorsements by such stars can be translated into votes and money. At the local level, rummage sales, wine-tasting parties, benefit theater performances, and raffle tickets have all been used to fatten the campaign coffers.

In spite of the variety of contribution sources, both major parties have worried about excessive dependence on a narrow financial base. Both have recognized that legislation in this field is woefully inadequate. As a result, Congress enacted early in 1972 the most sweeping campaign finance reform in half a century. It limits total spending, with the exception of postage for mass mailing and phoning by volunteer workers, to no more than ten cents per potential voter. No more than six cents of this total may be spent for radio or television advertising. Furthermore, any contributions exceeding $100 must be disclosed in periodic reports. Candidates for national office are limited in the amount of money they may contribute to their own campaign: $50,000 for presidential aspirants, $35,000 for those seeking Senate seats, and $25,000 for House candidates.

One result of the new legislation was to limit to $8.4 million the amount permitted for radio and television time to each presidential candidate in 1972, compared with the $12 million spent in Mr. Nixon's 1968 campaign. If democratic government is to reflect the desires of people rather than the demands of dollars, other reforms may be needed, such as tax-supported campaigns, shortened periods of campaigning, and free postal delivery and television time for campaign messages.[11]

The organization In addition to a good candidate and an adequate amount of money, an effective campaign organization is indispensable to most successful races. For partisan contests in states where there are strong parties, the organization may be ready-made, eager to support the party nominee. But in nonpartisan races, in states with weak parties, and in primary fights for the party nomination, a new one may have to be developed from scratch. In either case, it is here that the average citizen becomes most involved in the democratic process. The blueprint for a good organization should include the following basic components:

1) Precinct workers who will go door-to-door to find persons not yet registered to vote, distribute literature (thereby saving on mailing expense), sometimes solicit campaign contributions, and get persons to the polls on election day.

2) A headquarters staff that disseminates buttons, bumper strips, and campaign brochures; stuffs and addresses envelopes for campaign literature; makes phone calls soliciting support and reminding people to vote; and organizes and directs precinct workers. There is usually some building contractor, realtor, or other landlord who will

11 Berman and Loeb, op. cit., p. 157. In 1971, Congress passed legislation authorizing limited tax support for campaigns, but it was not to take effect until 1976.

donate a vacant store that can be used as a campaign headquarters for a few months.

3) A squad of people, often teen-agers, to put up small campaign posters along major streets. Such persons may also drive people to the polls on election day, distribute literature at shopping centers, and baby-sit for other campaign workers and voters.

4) Members of a finance committee to raise money from the "fat cats" who are potentially large contributors. Contributors worth $25 may be important at the local, grass-roots level; "fatness" is relative.

5) Occupational or special-interest committees that appeal for votes and other campaign support, usually by letter, from groups such as lawyers, teachers, veterans, farmers, ethnic organizations, and clergymen.

6) Publicity and advertising personnel to design billboards, newspaper advertisements, and campaign brochures, as well as to write stories for newspaper release.

7) Research and statistics workers who will prepare the candidate with information regarding major issues, as well as provide him or her with data regarding the opponent.[12]

A campaign manager who can pull all these together and free the candidate from personal concern with small yet often important details could be a campaign asset of incalculable value. And just what is effective campaign organization worth? One of the few relevant studies has found that in a midwestern industrial city "the increment to a party from the best, as compared with the worst, precinct workers amounted to about 5 percent in the 1956 presidential election"[13]—a figure that could make a difference in many a close contest. Yet the above question, like so many others in social science research, requires the exasperating answer: It all depends. If the candidate is well enough known and admired, money and organization may be clearly secondary. If there is enough money to promote the candidacy effectively, other factors may matter little. But all other factors being equal, organization may be decisive.

Of the three considerations—candidate, money, and organization—the candidate may be most important in the smallest electoral districts where he or she can be widely known. At the other extreme, in state-wide or national politics, there is evidence that money counts most. *The U.S. News and World Report* asserted in 1968 that "eight times out of ten, the man who spends the most money is the winner."[14] It is probable that organization is most important at the intermediate level, in the election of state legislators or members of

---

12 Some of this material is discussed in more detail in Paul P. Van Riper, *Handbook of Practical Politics,* 3rd ed. (N.Y.: Harper & Row, Publishers, 1967), pp. 45–63. I am indebted, also, to Dorothy Le Conte, a campaign manager with few peers, who taught me much regarding the material in this chapter.
13 Philips Cutright and Peter H. Rossi, "Grass Roots Politicians and the Vote," *American Sociological Review* 23 (April 1958).
14 Quoted in *We the People* (n.p.: California State Chamber of Commerce, 1970), p. 45. This Chamber of Commerce election pamphlet asserts that "One of every five United States Senators is a millionaire."

the U.S. House of Representatives. But effective organization means the recruitment of campaign workers, and it is one of the ironies of politics that legislators, to whom workers may be most important, have the fewest government jobs with which to reward the faithful.

Campaign Strategy: How to Win

Elections may be won or lost by the skill with which the candidate, money, and organization are combined for maximum effectiveness. These are questions of strategy.

Getting around   Even if a large amount of money is available, it must be budgeted carefully. One of the biggest expenditures in a national or state-wide race is apt to be the transportation cost of flying the candidate, press secretary, a few staff men, and dozens of reporters from one place to another. Buses and trains are still used occasionally, but they too require money.

TV or not TV?   Television has had a greater impact on campaign budgets than any other factor in recent history. In the course of the 1964 presidential campaign, $4.1 million was spent for time on the three national television networks, and by 1968 this figure had spiraled to $8.9 million.[15] In addition to television time itself, political commercials cost a lot of money to produce. Joseph Napolitan, former campaign manager of Pennsylvania's Governor Milton Shapp, has strong feelings on this subject:

When some candidates have, say $100,000 for television, they put maybe $5,000 into production so they can spend more on time. I'd rather spend $30,000 on production and only $70,000 on time. . . . (Y)ou just can't make good cheap films.[16]

Increasingly, political broadcasting comes in small doses—spot announcements as short as twenty seconds that are over before the viewer has time to switch channels. By the beginning of the 1970s, thirty seconds between the Jim Nabors show and the Thursday night movie cost about $3500 for a single Los Angeles channel, and a five-minute spot would go "well into six figures if bought for network use."[17]

Is it worth the price? Most of the experts seem to think so, and can provide at least a few examples to help prove it. In 1966 the first Republican ever elected to Congress from a district in Houston put 80 percent of his campaign budget into advertising, of which 59 percent went for television and only 3 percent to newspapers.[18] In 1970, however, Governor Dale Bumpers of Arkansas and Senators Lawton Chiles of Florida and Adlai Stevenson of Illinois all defeated candidates

15 *The New York Times Encyclopedic Almanac, 1970,* p. 155.
16 Quoted in Herbert M. Baus and William B. Ross, *Politics Battle Plan* (N.Y.: The Macmillan Company, 1968), pp. 331–32.
17 Bill Boyarsky, *Los Angeles Times,* Oct. 13, 1970, p. 1, and Baus and Ross, op. cit., p. 329.
18 Joe McGinniss, *The Selling of the President, 1968* (N.Y.: Pocket Books, 1970), pp. 37–40.

Paul Sequeria, Rapho Guillumette
Pictures.

Campaigning among minority groups: Senators Charles Percy and George
McGovern pass out free groceries for Reverend Jesse Jackson's Operation
Breadbasket and the Uptown People's Coalition in Chicago.

who outspent them for media time.[19] The costs of television to the
American political process may be more than monetary. Its critics say
that it substitutes images for ideas, personality for principle, glamour for
wisdom.

    The price of polls Reliable public opinion polls, developed
by George Gallup and Elmo Roper in the 1930s, serve many purposes.
Initially they are used to determine whether the potential candidate has
any chance of winning, what his strength is in various geographic
regions, and what issues the voters are most worried about. Along with
air travel and TV, the polls have pushed up the costs of modern
campaigning enormously. Louis Harris, whose fame was first established
as John F. Kennedy's private pollster, estimates that no more than
$75,000 was spent for polls in the 1946 and 1948 campaigns combined. By
1960 the figure had probably reached a million and a half, and in a single
congressional district, the minimum cost for a public opinion poll is
$2000.[20] According to one estimate, three fourths of the candidates for

19 *Newsweek,* Nov. 16, 1970, p. 77.
20 Van Riper, op. cit., p. 130.

governor, two thirds of the candidates for the U.S. Senate, and one tenth of the candidates for the House of Representatives used polls in 1962.[21] "A candidate," writes a man who was one, "now pays less attention to district leaders than to opinion polls."[22]

Professionalized campaigns   Karl von Clausewitz, a famous Prussian general, once declared that war is too important to leave to generals. Adapting this idea, two professional campaign managers have asserted that "political campaigns are too important to leave to the politicians."[23] The advent of professional public relations and advertising firms specializing in campaign management has provided candidates with help in four areas.

1) They perform many functions which in the past were commonly the responsibility of party organizations. These include the issuance of press releases, recruitment of campaign workers, fund raising, and research on issues. Political parties still assist their candidates with all these, but with the decline in patronage, the weakening of party loyalties, and the gradual elimination of corruption, the party machinery is no longer capable of doing what it once did. Professional management firms have rushed to fill the void.

2) They are knowledgeable about television technicalities, such as editing or staging, on which the old-fashioned party leader has little expertise.

3) Similarly, they are aware of the specialized knowledge required for public opinion polls, involving sampling techniques, question phraseology, demographic comparisons, computer processing, and statistical interpretation. Here, again, the politician has little competence.

4) They have the advertising skill to make the sophisticated budgeting decisions to get the most votes for the money in choosing among the ever-growing media possibilities. As Leonard Hall, former chairman of the Republican National Committee, put it, "You sell your candidates and your programs the way a business sells its products."[24]

For all its effectiveness, however, some worry about the desirability of this advertising approach to politics. Adlai E. Stevenson, a twice-defeated nominee for President, said that the "idea that you can merchandise candidates for high office like breakfast cereal . . . is the ultimate indignity to the democratic process."[25]

The use of professional campaign consultants began in San Francisco in the late 1930s, with the public relations firm of Whitaker and Baxter, a husband-and-wife team. In 1952 a New York company— Batten, Barton, Durstine and Osborn—became the first involved in a

21 Kirwan, op. cit., p. 30.
22 Bullitt, op. cit., p. 65.
23 Baus and Ross, op. cit., p. 258.
24 Quoted in McGinniss, op. cit., p. 21.
25 Quoted in Vance Packard, *The Hidden Persuaders* (N.Y.: Pocket Books, 1958), p. 172.

national race, that of Dwight D. Eisenhower.[26] It is no coincidence that this was the year when "(t)elevision and the airplane came of age as campaign agencies."[27]

Today campaign management firms have become firmly entrenched as well-paid allies of both major parties, and Madison Avenue, the New York address of many advertising and public relations firms, has become synonymous with a professionalized approach to politics. A 1969 survey revealed twenty-nine businesses classifying themselves as professional campaign management firms. They do not come cheap. A "well-known Democratic consultant" estimates that his firm asks about $80,000 for "an average campaign for a U.S. House candidate." His personal services cost $500 a day.[28]

The issues: an adventure in prophesy   The road to victory does not always lead down Madison Avenue. Most candidates for a city council or state legislature do not need and cannot afford the services of professional consultants. Those seeking the bottom rungs of the political ladder usually must rely on their own popularity and their ability to assess correctly the issues that most concern the voters.

Sometimes compelling issues arise that are beyond the immediate control of candidates for even the highest offices. The Depression in 1932, and the communist offensive in Vietnam in 1967–68 are cases in point. Yet sometimes candidates can make their own issues. In 1961 Sam Yorty was elected mayor of Los Angeles in part because he promised to end the requirement that bottles and cans be separated from other garbage for trash collection purposes. In 1958 the decision of many Republicans to support "right-to-work" proposals bitterly condemned by labor unions was believed to have caused the loss of thirteen seats in the U.S. Senate, forty-nine in the House, and control of seventeen state legislative chambers.[29] More recently, issues such as changes in land zoning and school busing have affected the outcome of many local elections. At the state and national levels, Republican losses of governorships and House seats in 1970 have been attributed to too much emphasis on the law and order "social issue" and too little stress on economic problems.[30]

Although public opinion polls help to identify the problems that most concern the people, the selection of effective campaign issues is still a challenge to even the most gifted of seers and prophets. There is some evidence that the closeness of a campaign influences the choice of issues. In a lopsided race in which the outcome is a foregone conclusion, the issues may be sharply drawn; the probable winner attempts to "educate" the voters while the opponent speaks out, even in the face of

26 By the mid-1950s, Whitaker and Baxter had managed seventy-five campaigns and won seventy of them. For a brief account of some of their successes, along with the importance of BBD&O, see Packard, ibid., pp. 155–63.
27 Jasper B. Shannon, *Money and Politics* (N.Y.: Random House, Inc., 1959), p. 61.
28 *Congressional Quarterly Guide to Current American Government* (Fall 1970), pp. 131–32.
29 Kirwan, op. cit., p. 136.
30 Jules Witcover, *Los Angeles Times*, Nov. 7, 1970, p. 10.

obvious scorn for his or her opinions. In a close contest, however, candidates have a pragmatic tendency to moderate their views, and to emphasize only those issues designed to win the crucial but undecided vote.[31]

The best time and the proper place Some candidates, notably President Nixon, believe that a campaign should begin slowly, gradually pick up momentum, and finally peak on election day. Others believe in what has been called a "scrambling" technique in which an all-out effort is made for the entire duration of the campaign.[32]

There is also the question of where the candidate should concentrate most of his attention. As a general rule, the probable winner is well advised to cultivate the most fertile fields—those counties, towns, or neighborhoods in which he or his party are strongest. The reason is simple: Supporters do no good if they stay home on election day. The candidate who is trailing, on the other hand, must spread himself a bit more thinly, campaigning where he is popular in order to motivate his supporters to get out the vote, but reaching out into opposition territory as well.

Another decision confronting every campaign organization is how to spend the limited amount of money available. Television and travel expenses have already been mentioned. There may also be newspaper ads. A basic leaflet with one or two folds is considered well-nigh essential. It can be distributed in door-to-door precinct work, at factory gates, and in shopping centers, or used in direct mailings.

A recent innovation in campaign technology is the use of computerized letters which appear to be directed to each voter personally. If material is distributed by mail, it is worth the money to send it first class, so it will not be thrown out with the junk mail. That can cost $60 or $70 per 1000 voters. In comparison, a spot radio announcement—although not as selective as mail in its coverage—costs about a dollar or two per 1000 listeners.[33] Billboards are substantially more expensive, but many observers believe a few of them are necessary especially if the candidate is not well known and needs to establish name-recognition as a major contender.

There are literally dozens of products that can gobble up a campaign budget, including cards, matchbooks, straw hats, and other gimmicks, all bearing the candidate's name. In the 1968 campaign the Nixon forces, for example, ordered over half a million balloons, over twenty million buttons, and nine million bumper strips. The latter, at a little more than three cents each, cost $300,000.[34] For some of these items, their relative cheapness may be exceeded only by their uselessness. Fifty coffee hours during which candidates appear briefly in private

31 John W. Kingdon, *Candidates for Office* (N.Y.: Random House, Inc., 1966), p. 133.
32 Kirwan, op. cit., pp. 152–67.
33 Van Riper, op. cit., pp. 185–87.
34 Dale E. Wagner, "The Relationship between Party Campaign Finance and Campaign Materials," unpublished paper prepared for delivery at the 1970 Annual Meeting of the American Political Science Association in Los Angeles, September 11, 1970.

homes to talk with twenty or thirty neighbors may be worth all the campaign buttons ever pinned to a lapel.

The incumbency factor   In 1970 over 85 percent of the 435 members of the House of Representatives won reelection. In part, this illustrates the campaign advantage possessed by the incumbents already in office. As public officials, they command more publicity than the private citizens who may run against them; they know personally many lobbyists working for influential pressure groups; and often their names appear first on the ballot. Moreover, the boundaries of their districts may have been drawn to help them, and they can stress what they have done, rather than what they promise to do. They can claim that their constituents would benefit by their experience and the power advantages which seniority often brings. As officeholders, finally, they can get speaking invitations before nonpartisan groups that would never invite a mere candidate. These are formidable assets.

What can the challenger do? He must be aggressive, even offensive, in denouncing the most vulnerable portions of the incumbent's record. And he can pray for a landslide on behalf of his party.

ELECTIONS
Voting Behavior

Many influences converge upon the voters on election day. They have been subjected to the political attitudes of family, friends, and schools; they have absorbed (or ignored) the political information dispensed by the mass media; and they have been surveyed, categorized, computerized, and analyzed by census statisticians, poll takers, news commentators, public relations experts, and political candidates. Their support has been solicited by dozens of pressure groups attempting to influence government policy; and finally, they have been counted, courted, co-opted, and occasionally even corrupted by political parties seeking election victories for a wide variety of both noble and ignoble purposes. The result of all this lavish attention is what they do when they cast their ballots. At that moment, the voters are sovereign.

How do voters vote? That is perhaps the central issue in a democracy. Yet many of them don't vote at all. In the last half-century the percentage of the voting-age population that cast ballots in presidential elections has varied between 43.5 (in 1920) and 64.0 (in 1960).[35] Of those who do vote, what influences their choices when they stand alone with their consciences in the privacy of the polling booth? In varying degrees and combinations, at least three factors are involved: the candidates (especially for the major offices), party preference, and campaign issues.

Voting for the man   Many people say that they vote for the man and not the party. Perhaps they do, but only if they know

35 U.S. Bureau of the Census, *The Statistical Abstract of the United States: 1970*, p. 368.

something about the people who are running. Yet in 1970 only 53 percent of the voters knew the name of their representative in Congress and about a fifth of them knew how he or she voted on any major bill. Seven years earlier, 91 percent could identify Elizabeth Taylor, while only 72 percent knew who Senator Barry Goldwater was.[36] Although most people are aware of the candidates for major offices, chances are they "know" them in the sense that they have a "feel" for their personalities, projected by TV, better than they "know" their intelligence, executive ability, or even their stand on important issues.

Voters seem to sense the limitations of the information available to them. Since they know less about candidates for Congress than for President, the voter turnout in off-year congressional elections has been from 13 to 23 percent less than in presidential election years.[37] Moreover, in voting for congressional and state legislative candidates, who are generally unknown, voters seem to rely primarily on party affiliation in making up their minds. While the Democratic vote in presidential elections dropped 19 percent between 1964 and 1968, the Democrats lost only 1 percent of the seats in the House of Representatives and two tenths of 1 percent of all state legislative seats as a result of the 1968 balloting.[38] It seems clear that when voters know nothing about the candidates—in spite of what they may say—they vote their party preference; they do, in other words, the best they can.

The primacy of party   Throughout the entire nation, there are more Democrats than Republicans. This is reflected by public opinion polls and by the long-standing Democratic majority in Congress. The importance of this numerical edge is somewhat offset, however, by a lower voter turnout among Democrats and independents than among Republicans. The key reason for this is probably the lower income of most Democrats; this is related to less education which is related in turn to a lack of knowledge concerning governmental affairs and little interest in political matters. Low income may also result in infrequent voting if it is tied to job changes which require people to move around a lot, making it difficult to meet voter residency requirements (although this is no longer very difficult). In most congressional or state legislative races, the importance of party affiliation is so predictable that if a district is about 52 percent Republican in voter registration (or close to 58 percent Democratic), it is assumed to be safe for the majority-party candidate.

Campaign issues   Hardest to interpret is the effect of actual issues on voting behavior. To understand this factor, we must know what issues the voter thinks important, the candidates' positions on

36 Gallup Poll, *Los Angeles Times,* Sept. 20, 1970, Sec. H, p. 7, and Fred I. Greenstein, *The American Party System and the American People,* 2nd ed. (Englewood Cliffs, N.J.: Prentice-Hall, Inc., 1970), pp. 13–14.
37 Greenstein, op. cit., p. 10.
38 Philip E. Converse, *et al.,* "Continuity and Change in American Politics: Parties and Issues in the 1968 Election," *American Political Science Review* 63 (December 1969): 1084–1085.

Figure 23   Party Identifications

National Totals	Republican	Democratic	Independent	Other or Don't Know
	24%	49%	24%	3%
Sex				
Male	23	49	26	2
Female	25	50	22	3
Age				
21–29	19	47	31	3
30–49	20	52	25	3
50 and over	31	48	19	2
Education				
Grade school	20	58	18	4
High school	22	50	26	2
College	38	34	26	2
Income				
Under $5,000	21	55	21	3
$5,000–$9,999	22	50	26	2
$10,000 and over	39	34	25	2
Class Identification				
Propertied	54	22	23	1
Middle	33	38	26	3
Working	16	62	21	1
Occupation				
Professional, business	34	37	26	3
White-collar workers	25	45	29	1
Farmers	28	44	28	under .5
Blue-collar workers	17	57	24	2
Union Member				
Yes	15	60	23	2
No	27	46	24	3

these issues, and the degree to which the voter correctly understands their positions.

The issues stressed by the candidates may not be key determinants of voter decisions. In the 1960 campaign, for example, there was much debate over the so-called missile gap between the United States and Russia, while John F. Kennedy's Catholicism, which received less comment by the candidates, was a more important consideration to most voters. It is also necessary to recognize that the "real" issues may correspond neither to those that candidates talk about nor to those that voters think about. During the 1972 campaigns, for instance, the most important issue confronting the nation *may* have been environmental pollution, although candidates stressed school busing and tax loopholes, while voters fretted most about inflation and welfare.

The obligation to vote   Much has been written about the citizen's obligation to vote. Some argue that it makes no difference for whom you vote—just so you vote. This is patently absurd. It makes a great deal of difference if the majority votes for an embezzler for state treasurer, an extortionist for sheriff, or a fool for President. If one knows or cares only about a few candidates, one should vote only in the races in

	Republican	Democratic	Independent	Other or Don't Know
Religion				
Protestant	29%	45%	24%	2%
Catholic	12	63	22	3
Jewish	9	65	22	4
Ethnic Groups				
English	35	36	27	2
German	33	38	28	1
Scandinavian	31	37	30	2
Irish (Catholic)	14	59	26	1
Italian	14	63	22	1
Eastern or Central European	15	63	20	2
Race				
White	27	45	26	2
Negro	3	87	6	4
Ideological Spectrum[1]				
Liberal, completely or predominantly	8	66	25	1
Middle-of-road	16	60	21	3
Conservative, predominantly	30	42	25	3
Conservative, completely	40	30	28	2

[1]An explanation of President Nixon's 1972 victory lies in the results of a Gallup poll taken three months before the election: 41 percent of the voters view themselves as conservative, 30 percent middle-of-the-road, and 24 percent liberal, with 5 percent holding no opinion. At the same time, Nixon was viewed as substantially more conservative than Senator McGovern, his Democratic opponent. *Los Angeles Times,* August 27, 1972, p. 7.

Source: "Party Identification by Voter Characteristics" from *The Political Beliefs of Americans, A Study of Public Opinion,* by Lloyd A. Free and Hadley Cantril, Rutgers University Press, New Brunswick, New Jersey, 1968. Reprinted by permission.

which they are involved—and then go home. Otherwise, the vote becomes a menace to good government.

Another bit of nonsense is the allegation that to vote intelligently one must spend long hours of study, attend political meetings, and become—for all practical purposes—a political science major. It just isn't that hard. An intelligent voter is simply the man or woman who cares enough about the society to decide, with some thought, what issues are most vital and which candidates can best cope with them. If one knows too little about issues or candidates, it is not necessarily stupid to vote a straight ticket for the party of one's considered choice. This increases that party's chances of controlling both the executive and legislative branches, thereby facilitating cooperation between them and allowing the party to reap the advantages of legislative committee chairmanships.

A citizen doesn't have to do the job of intelligent voting without help. If one trusts one's union or the editorial policy of a newspaper, for example, there is nothing wrong with voting for the candidates they endorse. If one wishes to know how a congressman or state legislator voted on a particular issue, pressure groups such as the Chamber of Commerce probably know. If one wants to see brief biographies of the candidates and short statements of their major views, the League of Women Voters has compiled them. But before following others' recommendations, one should consider the interests and biases of those who make them. In the final analysis, intelligent voting springs as much from the spirit as the mind. It is the most solemn sacrament of democratic politics, a symbol of our common faith in our fellow citizens.

Voting Qualifications

The history of American voting laws is marked by two long-term trends. The first is the gradual elimination of restrictive requirements based on religion, property ownership, tax payments, race, sex, and literacy. The second is the transfer of considerable authority over voting regulations from the states to the national government.

When the Constitution went into effect, states were free to set up whatever voting restrictions they wished with one exception: Article I, Section 2 allowed anyone to vote for members of the U.S. House of Representatives who was permitted to vote for members of the lower house of his state legislature. In the next half-century, most of the states, having long since abandoned religious voting requirements, also repealed laws requiring the ownership of property. In 1870 the Fifteenth Amendment stipulated that no citizen could be prohibited from voting because of race. It took ninety-five years, until the passage of the Voting Rights Act of 1965, before this amendment was uniformly enforced and racial justice was brought, finally, to polling booths throughout the nation.[39]

Shortly before the 1920 presidential election, Amendment Nineteen banned voter qualifications based on sex. Women's suffrage, earlier granted in a few states as an act of chivalry, had become a demand the nation could no longer deny. Amendment Twenty-four, added in 1964, eliminated the payment of a poll tax, or any other tax, as a voting qualification. While once a barrier to the poor in many states, all but four had voluntarily abandoned the poll tax before the Constitution required it. Finally, in 1971, the Twenty-sixth Amendment lowered the nation-wide voting age to eighteen, following the trail blazed earlier only by Georgia in 1944 and Kentucky in 1955. The result was to enfranchise over eleven million people who otherwise would have been unable to vote in the 1972 elections. Politicians were perplexed regarding its implications. Young people were clearly more liberal than their elders, but the proportion who went to the polls was far lower.

Although the preceding developments have limited the states severely, four remaining requirements still deserve mention:

1) Citizenship. While aliens were once permitted to vote in some areas, usually because local machine bosses benefited thereby, citizenship is now a requirement in all states.

2) Residency. All states once had minimum residency re-

39 See Chapter 5, p. 114.

Figure 24   Age Differences

	Young	Old
Church Attendance[1]	33%	44%
Withdrawal from Vietnam by 1971[2]	63	55
Liberal[3]	61	34
Conservative[3]	26	52

[1]*Los Angeles Times,* Dec. 27, 1969, p. 19. Figures are for an average week. Young are 21–29, old are 50 and over.
[2]Ibid., Sept. 27, 1970, Sec. H, p. 3. Young 21–29, old 50 and over.
[3]Ibid., May 31, 1970, Sec. F, p. 8. Young are college students, old are general public.
Note: In 1968, only 51.1 percent of those between 21 and 24 said they voted, compared with 67.8 percent of the entire voting-age population. U.S. Bureau of the Census, *Statistical Abstract of the United States: 1970,* p. 369.
Source: Reprinted by permission of the American Institute of Public Opinion (The Gallup Poll).

quirements, ranging from two years in Mississippi to sixty days in West Virginia. The 1970 Voting Rights Act, however, set a thirty-day maximum as sufficient for voting for President and Vice President, and court decisions have ruled this to be adequate for the election of all officials.

3) Registration. A minimum period of residency is implicit in state laws that make voters register before the first election in which they wish to vote. Registration is relatively new as voting requirements go. It emerged toward the end of the last century to guarantee honest voting, especially in large northern cities, when fraud ran rampant: People ineligible to go to the polls were urged (and sometimes paid) to do so frequently, using fictitious names and addresses. "Vote early and vote often" seemed to be the motto of the corrupt politician. To obtain a list of persons eligible to vote, most states now use a system of permanent registration, requiring people to reregister only if they have moved, changed their name, or failed to vote in the last general election. Others require everyone to register at periodic intervals.

4) Literacy. About fifteen states have some sort of literacy requirement. Rather ironically, the practice began in Connecticut and Massachusetts to deal with immigrants in the 1850s, but it has been most frequently employed in the southern states to disenfranchise blacks. Literacy may mean anything from the simple ability to read and write to the ingenious capacity to "interpret" a provision of the state constitution. New York required a fifth-grade educational level. To prevent literacy tests from being used as a mask to conceal racial discrimination, the Voting Rights Act of 1965 suspended them in counties in which less than 50 percent of the adults were registered to vote, and the 1970 law mentioned earlier suspended them in all states until 1975. The literacy test created a special problem for substantial numbers of intelligent citizens who are unable to use the English language very well. This has been particularly true of the Puerto Rican population in New York and the Mexican-Americans in California.

At the root of all disputes about voting qualifications is a fundamental dilemma: Legally, voting is a privilege, but in democratic theory, it is a right. Should only the wise, the informed, or the successful

Rhyoda Galyn, Photo Researchers, Inc.

Voter registration in New York City's Chinatown.

vote? That group, depending on its definition, might be very small. Or on the other hand, should everyone affected by government policy be permitted to vote for government officials? Consider the implications.

Balloting

What happens on election day is influenced in some degree by the voting procedures and ballot forms prescribed by the election laws of the fifty states.

Voting procedures   Prior to 1880, incredible as it seems to the modern citizen, it was relatively easy to find out how someone else voted. Ballots were printed by individual candidates or parties and varied in size or color. But the Australian or *secret ballot* is now used throughout the country and has almost eliminated the possibility that one person—a husband, employer, or creditor—can dictate the voting choices of another.

All ballots were printed on paper and marked by hand until Lockport, New York, introduced the use of voting machines in 1892. Over two thirds of the states now authorize their use, but the decision is often left to individual counties. There seems to be little doubt that voting machines, or a system of computerized punch-card ballots, help to prevent deliberate fraud or unintentional mistakes in the counting of votes. The chief objections to the use of voting machines center upon their expense and the relatively remote possibility of widespread mechanical failure.

Ballot forms   There are two basic distinctions involved in an analysis of ballot forms; one has to do with the way in which candidates' names are arranged and the other with the ballot's total length. About thirty states use the Indiana, or *party-column ballot,* with the candidates of each party listed in the same column. The voter may easily make a mark, or pull a voting machine lever, to vote a straight ticket for all candidates of one party. The remaining states use the Massachusetts, or *office-block ballot* on which candidates' names are grouped according to the offices for which they are running. Although party affiliations are listed, the voter must vote for each office individually, so it is just as time-consuming to vote a straight ticket as a split ticket.

Campaign strategy, as one might expect, is influenced by these facts. Especially in states with party-column type ballots, many lesser candidates might sweep into office on the coattail of a popular candidate for President, governor, or U.S. senator at the top of the party list. In the final analysis, the party-column ballot encourages party loyalty while the office-block ballot shifts attention to the qualifications of individual candidates. When Ohio changed to the latter form in 1950, the late Senator Taft estimated that he gained at least 100,000 votes.[40]

Partisan elections using the office-block ballot, like nonpartisan elections, present a special problem: How is the order in which names appear on the ballot to be determined? It is an important question, since many politicians believe that the top spot is worth as much as 5 percent of the vote, but state laws answer it in a variety of ways. In some places the incumbents' names are listed first, while in others the arrangement is alphabetical, or based on drawing straws, or rotated so that all candidates have their names in top position on an equal number of ballots.

The question of ballot length is important because, as indicated earlier, the average voter has neither the inclination nor the information needed for intelligent decisions among a long and bewildering array of choices. The long ballot may contain state constitutional amendments to be approved by the voters, certain proposed laws

---

40 V. O. Key Jr., *Politics, Parties, and Pressure Groups,* 5th ed. (N.Y.: Thomas Y. Crowell Company, 1964), pp. 641–44, has been very helpful for this section. A study of the 1952 and 1956 elections showed that 18 percent fewer voters who classified themselves as independents voted a straight ticket on office-block ballots than on party-column ballots. Angus E. Campbell and Warren E. Miller, "The Motivational Basis of Straight and Split Ticket Voting," *American Political Science Review* 51 (June 1957), p. 307.

required to be submitted to the electorate, and the names of candidates for numerous local, state, and national offices ranging from local coroner to President.

The antidote is simply a short ballot. The movement in that direction has concentrated on seeking two specific reforms: conversion of many state and local offices from elective to appointive ones, and the scheduling of local elections at different times of the year from state and national ones. The second, entailing what are called nonconsolidated ballots, has been the more successful.

Fewer people vote for local offices than for President or governor regardless of which system is used. On long, consolidated ballots there is ordinarily a drop-off of about 25 to 30 percent between the number of people who vote for the major candidates at the top of the ballot and those who bother to choose among local candidates at the bottom.[41] If local elections are separated from state and national ones, the turnout is often less than one quarter of those eligible to vote.

Direct Democracy: More Gods That Failed?

There was a time, around the turn of the century, when many big-city governments were in the clutches of graft-ridden, boss-controlled political machines and it was common knowledge that entire state legislatures were dominated by a few wealthy business corporations. California, it was said, had the best legislature money could buy, and the Southern Pacific Railroad had bought it. A succession of reformers under the Progressive label devised what they fervently hoped to be a solution to the problem. They proposed to take power away from the corrupt bosses and the bribed lawmakers and give it back to the people through a kind of political trinity: the initiative, referendum, and recall. Some would say these new gods have failed.

The initiative: for people or pressure groups? In 1898 South Dakota became the first state to adopt the initiative and referendum as methods of enacting state legislation. The initiative is a process whereby the registered voters can sign a petition proposing a new law or constitutional amendment. When sufficient signatures have been obtained, usually defined as a certain percentage of the vote cast at the last election, the proposal is submitted to the people as a ballot proposition at the next election. If a majority of the voters approve the measure it is adopted. The initiative therefore enables the people to enact laws whether the legislature likes them or not. It is now authorized in twenty states and in individual cities spread throughout many more.[42]

While the initiative was designed to thwart the influence of the powerful pressure groups and rich corporations that may have dominated elected legislators, there is some evidence suggesting that

41 Key, ibid., p. 646.
42 The states are Alaska, Arizona, Arkansas, California, Colorado, Idaho, Maine, Massachusetts, Michigan, Missouri, Montana, Nebraska, Nevada, North Dakota, Ohio, Oklahoma, Oregon, South Dakota, Utah, and Washington. Clyde F. Snider, *American State and Local Government*, 2nd ed. (N.Y.: Appleton-Century-Crofts, 1965), p. 169.

these same pressure groups and corporations are most skillful in utilizing the initiative process. For one thing, they have the money to pay professional petition circulators to obtain the required number of signatures, and the additional money necessary to wage highly effective campaigns to pass (or defeat) initiative measures that appear on the ballot. In the California general election of 1964, for example, four initiative propositions appeared on the ballot. Of the three that were passed, one was put there by railroads (to remove the legal requirement for a minimum number of crewmen on each train), another by theater owners (to ban pay television), and a third by the state Real Estate Association (to prevent state action eliminating racial discrimination in housing). The latter two were subsequently declared unconstitutional.

The case against the initiative, however, goes beyond the allegation that it doesn't control the influence of powerful lobbyists. It is said that it possesses certain inherent evils, including a reduction of the authority of legislative bodies, the possible enactment of poorly drafted or "crackpot" legislation, the lengthening of a ballot already too long, and the submission to the voters of highly technical and complex legislation that would baffle even the wisest of lawmakers.

On balance, however, these criticisms seem a bit too harsh. While it has not realized the idealistic hopes of its initial proponents, neither has it produced much horrible legislation. Most initiative measures, in fact, have been defeated by the voters and the process at least provides some psychic satisfaction as the purest form of direct democracy to be found in the American political system.

The referendum: limiting the legislatures In twenty-two states—all those with the initiative, plus Maryland and New Mexico—the referendum permits voters to repeal laws already passed by the legislature. There are several different varieties of the referendum. One involves the collection of signatures on a petition that will submit a state law or local ordinance to the voters for possible defeat. Another permits a state legislature or city council to place whatever proposals it wishes on the ballot, and thereby "pass the buck" to the electorate. A third requires that certain measures be put to the people, usually including amendments to state constitutions, bond issues to borrow money, and certain kinds of tax proposals. The first two types of referenda have been generally less significant than the initiative, and less frequently used. The last, however, has been important in shaping the structure of state and local governments and in granting (or denying) additional funds for schools and other publicly financed programs.

The recall: lest power corrupt Normally an elected public official can expect to serve out his prescribed term—two years, four years, or whatever—barring only death, voluntary resignation, or unlikely removal by impeachment proceedings. But officials in thirteen states, and in many cities in other states as well, face the possibility of defeat in special recall elections before their terms have expired.

The recall was first authorized at the local level in Los Angeles in 1903 and for state offices in Oregon just five years later. Like the initiative and one type of referendum, it requires the collection of signatures on a petition requesting a special election for the purpose of removing an official from office. It is rooted, perhaps, in the famous axiom of Lord Acton that power corrupts, and absolute power corrupts absolutely. If a majority of voters believe an official has indeed been corrupted, or has outrageously flouted the will of his constituents, the recall can be used to remove him promptly. While the initiative has been most important at the state level, recall elections have been confined largely to local politics and even here have been used rather sparingly. Nonetheless, mayors have been recalled in Detroit, Los Angeles, and Seattle, and the very possibility of such action, however remote, may help to keep officials on their toes.

Conclusion to Part Three

Democracy depends on a precarious balance between the power of the government and the power the people exert on the government. Unrestrained government power can produce tyranny; unrestrained popular power can produce anarchy; and both of these conditions jeopardize individual rights.

Since they have little force or authority compared to government, people must rely primarily on influence to persuade officials how to act. Here we confront a fact of overwhelming significance: Except for the vote, the political resources that can be converted into influence are distributed in a grossly unequal fashion. Money, prestige, access to the mass media, knowledge—all are concentrated in a minority of the population, although in the polling booths power is equalized.

The central thesis of Part Three is that people can remedy their relative powerlessness. First, they can organize pressure groups to advance their multiple and diverse interests. Second, they can seize, through democratic procedures and prodigious amounts of time and energy, the machinery of the major political parties. Imperfect as they are, they are the best instruments available for defining alternative solutions to the great problems confronting us. Third, the people can master the mechanics of campaign techniques and improve their skills in evaluating the candidates and issues on which they vote. Only then will election results reflect the real interests of the people rather than their manipulated preferences based on deceptive slogans, false fears, or the contrived glamor of candidate images. There are other ways average citizens can exercise influence. They can write letters to officials and editors, sign petitions, and nourish their children with the sense of participation, fair play, and respect for human dignity that are the staples of the democratic diet. But none is more important than support for pressure groups, participation in party activity, and intelligent voting.

Bibliography

Chapter 6

The People's Influence: Public Opinion and Pressure Groups

Binstock, Robert H., and Katherine Ely, eds., *The Politics of the Powerless* (Cambridge, Mass.: Winthrop Publishers, Inc., 1971).

Cirino, Robert, *Don't Blame the People* (Los Angeles: University Press, 1971).

Congressional Quarterly Service, *Legislators and the Lobbyists,* 2nd ed. (Washington, D.C.: Congressional Quarterly, Inc., 1968).

Dawson, Richard E., and Kenneth Prewitt, *Political Socialization* (Boston: Little, Brown and Company, 1969).

Graham, Hugh Davis, and Ted Robert Gurr, *Violence in America* (N.Y.: A Signet Book, New American Library, Inc., 1969).

Greenstein, Fred I., *Children and Politics* (New Haven: Yale University Press, 1965).

Report of the National Advisory Commission on Civil Disorders (N.Y.: Bantam Books, Inc., 1968).

Skolnick, Jerome H., *The Politics of Protest* (N.Y.: Ballantine Books, Inc., 1969).

Truman, David, *The Governmental Process,* 2nd ed. (N.Y.: Alfred A. Knopf, Inc., 1971).

Chapter 7

Government by the People: Political Parties

American Political Science Association, Committee on Political Parties, *Toward a More Responsible Two-Party System* (N.Y.: Holt, Rinehart & Winston, Inc., 1950).

Bone, Hugh A., and Austin Ranney, *Politics and Voters* (N.Y.: McGraw-Hill Book Company, 1963).

Campbell, Angus, *et al., The American Voter* (N.Y.: John Wiley & Sons, Inc., 1960).

Goldman, Ralph M., *The Democratic Party in American Politics* (N.Y.: The Macmillan Company, 1966).

Jones, Charles O., *The Republican Party in American Politics* (N.Y.: The Macmillan Company, 1965).

Key, V. O., Jr., *Politics, Parties, & Pressure Groups,* 5th ed. (N.Y.: Thomas Y. Crowell Company, 1964).

Chapter 8

The Price of Democracy: Campaigns and Elections

Bullitt, Stimson, *To Be a Politician,* rev. ed. (Garden City, N.Y.: Anchor Books, Doubleday & Company, Inc. 1961).

Cotter, Cornelius P., ed., *Practical Politics in the United States* (Boston: Allyn and Bacon, Inc., 1969).

Lane, Robert, *Political Life* (Glencoe, Ill.: The Free Press, 1959).

McGinniss, Joe, *The Selling of the President, 1968* (N.Y.: Pocket Books, 1970).

Van Riper, Paul P., *Handbook of Practical Politics,* 3rd ed. (N.Y.: Harper & Row, Publishers, 1967).

PART FOUR

THE PEOPLE'S GOVERNMENTS

The political influence of the people is aimed at every level of government. In the next three chapters, we shall examine the national and state governments together, to emphasize their essential similarity of structure, as well as to simplify a comparison of their differences.

Like the national government, each of the fifty states displays a separation of powers among legislative, executive, and judicial branches, the primary purpose of which is to prevent too much power from falling into the hands of too few people. The three branches are constitutionally equal and, in most instances, the system of checks and balances makes the cooperation of all three essential. It does little good for the legislative branch to pass a law if the executive fails to enforce it, and executive enforcement is useless if the judiciary declares it unconstitutional. But in avoiding excessive concentrations of power, we run the risk that no branch can act with the speed and decisiveness necessary to cope with the crises of modern life.

The three branches are not always equally effective. In time of war, the national executive attains near dominance, after which legislators energetically reassert their authority; since the mid-1950s, a number of judicial decisions have had exceptional significance for American life. In the long run, the performance of the three branches would probably have pleased the Founding Fathers.

Chapter **9**

Legislatures
Congress and State Legislatures

All government—indeed every human benefit and enjoyment, every virtue and every prudent act—is founded on compromise and barter.

Edmund Burke

Of the many roads to the White House, the winners of the last four presidential elections have traveled the same one. They all served in Congress, first in the House of Representatives and then in the Senate, before they became chief executive. The explanation is simple: Legislative bodies have a central place in American democracy and are more powerful than in any other nation in the world. To discover why the legislature is so central to democracy, we shall look first at the functions, the structure and membership, and the internal organization of these bodies, and then at dilemmas presented by the legislators' role in government.

LEGISLATIVE FUNCTIONS

The common tasks of the national and state legislatures are far more important than their differences. They all share four principal functions: (1) establishing public policy by passing laws, (2) controlling finance, (3) revising constitutions, and (4) checking the other two branches.

Policy Making

In passing laws, often known as statutes, legislatures are performing their best known and probably their most important function. By this means they formally establish official policy and the general methods by which it is to be implemented and enforced.

Congressional authority   The lawmaking authority of Congress is defined by the very first article of the Constitution and is broadly interpreted by the courts. The powers enumerated in Article I, Section 8 have spawned an astonishing array of implied powers deemed "necessary and proper" to carry them into effect.[1] On many occasions, Congress exercises its powers directly, as when it creates national parks or prohibits racial discrimination in hiring workers. Sometimes, however, Congress delegates substantial policy-making power to the executive branch, as when it authorized the President to impose wage and price freezes or the Food and Drug Administration to prohibit the sale of dangerous products.

State legislation   The legislatures of the various states can pass any laws not prohibited by the U.S. Constitution or the constitution of the state in question. The broad sweep of such authority is guaranteed by the reserved powers guaranteed to the states by the Tenth Amendment of the Constitution. State legislation, for example, may establish the scope of city and county power, determine what constitutes a crime, provide for colleges and universities, set licensing standards for people employed in numerous occupations, and regulate gambling, divorce, and abortion.

Controlling the Purse Strings

It does little good to pass a law without money to implement it. The legislature controls the purse strings through appropriation bills which allocate funds to all other agencies of government for their operating expenses. Naturally, it cannot appropriate money unless it raises it in some fashion, either by taxes or by borrowing funds through the sale of government bonds. Chief Justice John Marshall acknowledged long ago the scope of this sort of government power when he wrote that the power to tax is the power to destroy. Although the chief executive makes detailed budget recommendations, legislative bodies finally determine both where the money comes from and where it goes; in effect, they take from some what they give to others, a process that involves nothing less than the redistribution of wealth.

In bicameral legislatures, the lower house is often the most important in exercising financial controls. In Congress the House of Representatives has exclusive authority, under Article I, Section 7, to initiate bills to raise revenue. It has similar power, though only by

1 See Chapter 2, p. 35.

tradition, to introduce appropriation bills designed to spend money. Nevertheless, the Senate may exert considerable impact on money bills, and all are subject to amendment and final approval by both houses before they are sent to the chief executive.

There are two steps in the process by which Congress spends money. The first is the passage of legislation *authorizing* the expenditure of funds for a stated purpose and the second is the enactment of a bill actually *appropriating* money. Often the amount appropriated is smaller than that authorized; and in most cases the final figure is a compromise between the amounts approved by the Senate and by the normally more frugal House of Representatives. On appropriations for military aid to foreign nations, however, the Senate has threatened to cut off funds, in part as a protest against American involvement in Vietnam.

Constitutional Revision

It is normally the task of a legislature to propose whatever changes it thinks necessary in the state or national constitutions. In order to amend the United States Constitution, the proposed change is usually initiated by a two-thirds vote of Congress and takes effect only when approved, or ratified, by three quarters of the state legislatures. Alternative methods are also provided by the Constitution. In amending most state constitutions, some extraordinary vote in excess of a simple majority is also required in the state legislature, followed by the submission of the amendment to the voters in a referendum election. In Delaware, however, legislative action alone is sufficient.

Checking the Other Branches

In the system of checks and balances, legislative bodies have several ways to influence the other two branches.

Confirmation   One of the checks on the executive branch is the power of the senates to approve appointments made by the President or governor. In the national government, all top officials in the executive departments and agencies, plus all judges, are chosen by the President subject to the "advice and consent" of a Senate majority. In practice most presidential appointments are confirmed without much trouble, although there have been some notable exceptions. President Eisenhower, for example, appointed Lewis Strauss, former chairman of the Atomic Energy Commission, to be Secretary of Commerce, but the Senate failed to confirm him, and he withdrew the nomination of Mrs. Clare Booth Luce as Ambassador to Brazil after severe Senate criticism. Rather than risk Senate rejection, President Lyndon Johnson also withdrew his nomination of Abe Fortas as Chief Justice of the Supreme Court. More recently, the Senate rejected two of President Nixon's appointees to the U.S. Supreme Court.

Senatorial courtesy   There are close to a thousand posts in the national government requiring Senate confirmation, including U.S. district attorneys, judges, ambassadors, tax collectors at various ports, and many postmasters. The President cannot possibly make so many selections on the basis of his own personal evaluations. Customarily, therefore, for the federal jobs located in the various states he appoints people who have been recommended by senators of his own party from the states where the job vacancies exist. If he does not, by tradition his choice will be rejected by the Senate. This practice, known as senatorial courtesy, was illustrated when President Truman appointed two men to U.S. district court judgeships in Illinois, neither of whom had been recommended by Senator Paul Douglas, a fellow Democrat from that state. The Senate refused to confirm the appointees. The practical effect of senatorial courtesy is to give U.S. senators who belong to the President's party a certain amount of patronage.

Gubernatorial appointments   At the state level, many executive department heads are elected and thereby removed from both gubernatorial appointment and confirmation by state senates. Moreover, a big majority of states elect judges, similarly reducing executive and legislative control. Nonetheless, governors normally have some appointive power, subject to confirmation or rejection by state senates.

Impeachment   Officials already in office may be removed by the legislature through a process known as impeachment. Technically, impeachment is a formal accusation against an executive official or judge, usually leveled by a majority vote of the lower house. The upper chamber then acts as a sort of trial jury, in which a two-thirds vote is most commonly necessary to convict and thereby remove the accused official from office.

This process has several variations. If the President is faced with impeachment charges, the chief justice of the United States Supreme Court presides over the Senate. In New York the judges of the state's highest court sit with the state senate in hearing impeachment cases; in Nebraska and Missouri impeachment charges are heard only by the state supreme court; and in Alaska the upper house impeaches and the lower house convicts or acquits. The Oregon legislature has no impeachment power at all.[2]

Since Andrew Johnson was impeached on politically inspired, trumped-up charges and acquitted by a margin of just one vote in the Senate, the impeachment process has been somewhat discredited. In our entire history, the House of Representatives has impeached only twelve national officials, and of these only four—all lower-court judges—were convicted.[3] At the state level, impeachment proceedings have been almost as scarce. New York, Texas, and Oklahoma removed

2 Clyde F. Snider, *American State and Local Government,* 2nd ed. (N.Y.: Appleton-Century-Crofts, 1965), pp. 215–16.
3 Henry J. Abraham, *The Judicial Process* (N.Y.: Oxford University Press, Inc., 1962), p. 42.

governors in this fashion, most recently in 1923, and Tennessee got rid of a judge by impeachment in 1958.

Treaty approval   To some extent, the President's control over foreign policy is checked by the requirement that treaties with other nations be approved by a two-thirds vote of the United States Senate. This, along with its authority to confirm appointments, gives the Senate a larger role in limiting executive power than that possessed by the House of Representatives.

The expansion of government machinery   Legislative power over the other branches also includes the authority to create government agencies. The increasing responsibilities of modern governments have resulted in the passage of new laws, requiring in turn a rather steady expansion of executive departments and commissions to implement them. Just as these are usually answerable to the President or to state governors, so the decisions of the lower federal courts created by Congress are subject to appeal to the Supreme Court.

Investigatory power   Legislative bodies can, and often do, establish committees to look into the enforcement of the laws they pass. Usually this is done by permanent standing committees (or their subcommittees), but sometimes by special investigating committees. In any event, such inquiries enable Congress not only to supervise the executive branch but also to compete with it in getting public attention. During the 1950s, Senator Joseph McCarthy (R-Wis.) used the investigatory power as a springboard for flamboyant charges that Communists had infiltrated major executive agencies of the government, including the U.S. Army. When witnesses are required to testify before legislative committees, they may bring along a lawyer to advise them and may invoke the Fifth Amendment protection against compulsory self-incrimination. But they have no right to cross-examine earlier witnesses who may have made charges against them, nor to call other witnesses in their own behalf. Although legislative committees have no power to convict anyone of a crime, the allegations made in testimony before them can drag a good name through the dirt. It is important to note, in this connection, that *congressional immunity* protects members of Congress from being sued for what they say on the Senate or House floor or in committee hearings.

Most investigations, however, constitute a healthy examination of important problem areas in public policy. In June 1972, for example, various congressional committees held hearings on the trans-Alaska oil pipeline, health and accident insurance, the abuse of barbiturate drugs, and pesticide control. As usual, the leading witnesses were lobbyists, executive officials, and interested legislators. Such investigations are limited by two factors: First, tradition, along with the principle of separation of powers, has prohibited chief executives from appearing before legislative investigating committees; and second, questions directed to witnesses who are subpoenaed must have some relationship to facts about which there is power to pass laws. The investigating process, in other words, must not be used for the sole purpose of accusing or harassing witnesses. As former Chief Justice Earl Warren said in the case of *Watkins* v. *U.S.*, "there is no Congressional power to expose for the sake of exposure."[4]

Other checks on the courts   In addition to confirming court appointments or impeaching judges, there are two other legislative checks on the judicial branch. One is the power of Congress to change the number of judges serving on any federal court. The size of the Supreme Court has varied between five and ten, although it has remained at nine ever since 1869.

In 1937 President Franklin D. Roosevelt, unhappy over many court decisions handed down by a predominantly Republican tribunal, asked Congress to increase the number of judges from nine to a possible fifteen. The overwhelmingly Democratic Congress, usually eager to comply with Roosevelt's requests, construed this as a crude attempt to "pack" the Supreme Court and inflicted upon the President his most stinging legislative defeat in over twelve years in the White House. A nine-member Court seems destined to remain for a long time to come.

A second check on the Supreme Court is the authority of Congress to determine the kinds of cases that it can hear on appeal from lower courts. If the lawmakers don't like the decision of the Court in a certain kind of case, they can alter its appellate jurisdiction to prevent similar cases from reaching the high court in the future. Although this has not been done for more than a century, unpopular decisions involving school prayers, unequally populated legislative districts, and compulsory school busing have prompted such threats in recent years.

STRUCTURE AND MEMBERSHIP

Congress and forty-nine of the fifty state legislatures are two-house, or bicameral, bodies. Members of the lower house represent constituencies rather different from those represented by members of the upper house. Further, the way in which a state is apportioned into election districts makes a big difference in who gets elected to the legislatures.

Bicameralism

There were many reasons for the establishment of bicameral legislatures in the United States, including the example of the English Parliament and the necessity of two houses to gain the support of both the large and small states for the Constitution. But the survival of bicameralism indicates that it has some inherent advantages. The fact that a bill must pass two houses should theoretically produce better

4 354 U.S. 178 (1957).

legislation; the oversights, passions, or prejudices of one chamber can be corrected and counterbalanced by the other.

A one-house legislative body, however, is neither without precedent nor virtue in American government. Unicameralism characterized a few colonial legislatures, as well as the Continental and the Confederation Congresses. The overwhelming majority of city councils and county boards have only one house, although Nebraska, in 1937, became the only state legislature to have switched from bicameralism to unicameralism. Obviously, one house reduces costs and increases speed in the legislative process.

Some critics charge that bicameralism confers too much power on *conference committees.* When one house refuses to accept amendments that have been added to a bill by the other house, a conference committee is appointed, consisting of a few members of both chambers, whose task it is to come up with a compromise version. Sometimes entirely new provisions are added at this stage. Members of both houses usually conclude that the revised bill is better than none at all in this situation, and the conference committee compromise is enacted into law. Obviously, a one-house legislature eliminates the need for such a process.

The Allocation of Legislative Seats

Congressional apportionment For a democracy, no characteristic of a legislative body is more important than the way in which seats are divided among the people to be represented. The Founding Fathers viewed the decision to grant the people of each state two seats in the Senate as immensely significant, for this is the only provision in the Constitution which they made immune from future amendment. They also provided that membership in the U.S. House of Representatives should be reapportioned among the states every ten years on the basis of an official population census, with the stipulation that each state would have at least one seat.

As the original thirteen states grew in population, and as new ones were gradually admitted to the Union, the total size of the House grew from sixty-five members to a total of 435 after the 1910 census. Congress then decided that if the House continued to grow it would be far too large to function efficiently. As a result, a law was passed freezing the size of the House at 435. Now when a state gains additional seats because its population has grown much faster than the national average, states with slower population growth lose seats. After the 1970 census, California gained five additional members of the House, and Florida three, while New York and Pennsylvania lost two each. Ten other states each gained or lost one seat.

After each state has been informed of the number of seats to which it will be entitled for the next ten years, it is the obligation of the state legislatures to determine the boundaries of the districts from which each representative will be elected. The inevitable result is a bitter redistricting fight.

State legislative apportionment Following each census, then, state legislatures emerge to a commanding position in our political system as they draw both congressional district boundaries and the boundaries from which their own members will be elected for the next ten years.

As indicated in Chapter 5,[5] this process produced rural-dominated legislatures until 1964, when the U.S. Supreme Court required members of both houses in state legislatures, as well as members of the House of Representatives in Congress, to be elected from districts of approximately equal population. Today all states elect almost all legislators except for U.S. senators, on a one-man, one-vote basis, and reapportionments are mandatory after each census.

In the apportionment of legislative seats, the chief difference between the national House of Representatives and the state legislatures is that voters in each congressional district elect only one representative whereas some members of fifty-six of the ninety-nine state legislative chambers are elected from multimember districts. Thirty members of the Arizona legislature are chosen from the same district and there are districts in Florida, Maryland, Texas, and Vermont where voters are expected to select fifteen or more state legislators.

The politics of gerrymandering When reapportionment is inevitable, nearly every conceivable interest group attempts to influence the reshaping of district boundaries to its own advantage. This process is known as *gerrymandering.*

The most influential groups concerned with redistricting are the political parties. The majority party in a state legislature usually can draw boundaries that will improve the chances of most of its candidates by a careful analysis of past election results in every part of the state. Assume that in Figure 25 each letter represents an equal number of voters, and that *R* stands for areas predominantly Republican, while *D*

Figure 25   Republican-controlled Gerrymander

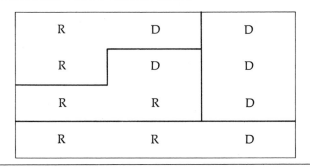

stands for areas Democratic to the same extent. If the Republicans have a majority in the state legislature, they might draw boundaries to win in three of the four districts. But if there is a Democratic majority in the state capitol, the same region might be arranged to elect only one Republican and three Democrats, as shown in Figure 26.

Figure 26   Democratic-controlled Gerrymander

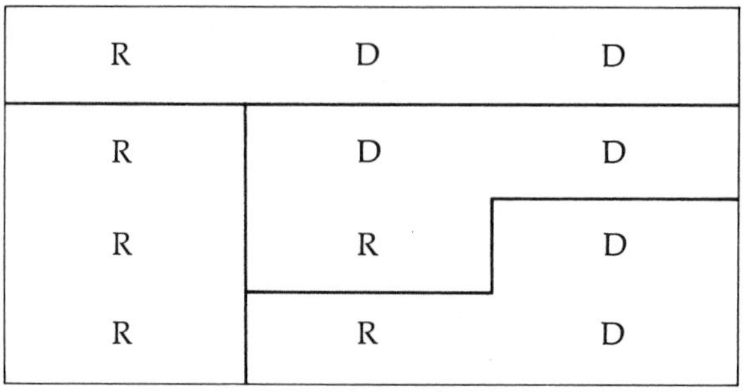

R	D	D
R	D	D
R	R	D
R	R	D

Compromise boundaries, favoring two Republicans and two Democrats, are shown in figure 27.

Figure 27   Compromise

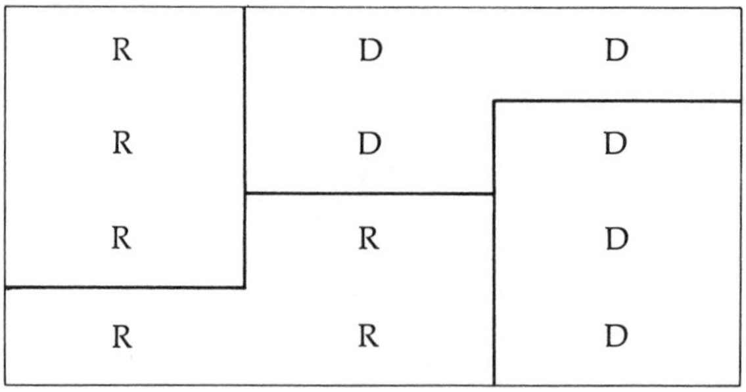

R	D	D
R	D	D
R	R	D
R	R	D

Party considerations are not the only ones which are important in apportionment deliberations, however. Racial groups, for example, have an important stake in the matter. Given a certain area, black candidates may be elected in no districts, in one, or in two, as illustrated in Figure 28.

The interplay of personal ambitions is also a major factor. Members of the lower house of a state legislature may wish to have district boundaries drawn to help get them elected to the upper house, or to Congress. At a minimum, they would like to guarantee their reelec-

Figure 28   Racial Gerrymander

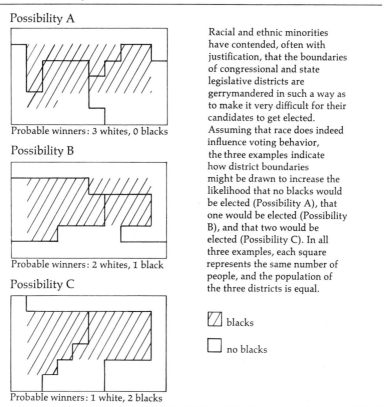

Possibility A

Probable winners: 3 whites, 0 blacks

Possibility B

Probable winners: 2 whites, 1 black

Possibility C

Probable winners: 1 white, 2 blacks

Racial and ethnic minorities have contended, often with justification, that the boundaries of congressional and state legislative districts are gerrymandered in such a way as to make it very difficult for their candidates to get elected. Assuming that race does indeed influence voting behavior, the three examples indicate how district boundaries might be drawn to increase the likelihood that no blacks would be elected (Possibility A), that one would be elected (Possibility B), and that two would be elected (Possibility C). In all three examples, each square represents the same number of people, and the population of the three districts is equal.

blacks

no blacks

tion.[6] One of the most predictable results of gerrymandering is the creation of many safe districts where incumbent legislators can hardly lose. Consequently, in congressional elections between 1950 and 1970 an average of 85 percent of the members of the House of Representatives won reelection.

City and county officials feel that they too have an interest in state legislative and congressional apportionment. In general, they believe that if units of local government are split by district boundaries a sense of community solidarity may be jeopardized and community interests inadequately represented.[7] The late Justice Frankfurter summed up the importance of the whole issue quite succinctly. The "practical significance of apportionment," he wrote, "is that the next election

6 Leroy C. Hardy and Charles P. Sohner, "Constitutional Challenge and Political Response: California Reapportionment, 1965," *Western Political Quarterly* 23 (December 1970): 733–51.
7 For a staunch defense of the community as an important and almost mystical basis of representation, see Alfred de Grazia, *Apportionment and Representative Government* (N.Y.: Praeger Publishers, Inc., 1963).

results may differ because of it."[8] So too may the kinds of legislation enacted.

Legislative Diversity

American legislatures vary enormously in membership, and from two to six years in length of legislative terms. When the term is four or six years, elections are usually staggered so that half or a third of the membership must seek reelection every two years. Another important difference among legislative bodies lies in the frequency and length of their sessions. About half the state legislatures meet every year and the other half every other year. Moreover, many states limit the length of sessions while others, especially the large industrial states, do not. The crucial distinction is that service in some state legislatures amounts to a part-time job, while membership in the rest, as well as in Congress, is a full-time occupation. Salaries and other financial reimbursements vary

Figure 29   The State Legislatures

State	Senate Size	Term	Lower House Size	Term	Sessions Years Held	Duration Limit[1]	2 Year Compensation[2]
Alabama	35	4	106	4	Odd	36 L	$11,000
Alaska	20	4	40	2	Annual	None	17,495
Arizona	30	2	60	2	Annual	None	14,800
Arkansas	35	4	100	2	Odd	60 C	3,600
California	40	4	80	2	Annual	None	48,950
Colorado	35	4	65	2	Annual[3]	None	9,600
Connecticut	36	2	177	2	Annual[3]	147 C or 154 C & 84 C or 91 C	4,000
Delaware	19	4	39	2	Annual	June 30	12,050
Florida	48	4	119	2	Annual	60 C	33,600
Georgia	56	2	195	2	Annual	45 C & 40 C	10,775
Hawaii	25	4	51	2	Annual	60 L	28,860
Idaho	35	2	70	2	Annual	60 C	10,200
Illinois	58	4	177	2	Annual	None	24,000
Indiana	50	4	100	2	Annual	61 L & 30 L	11,725
Iowa	61	4	124	2	Annual	None	13,625
Kansas	40	4	125	2	Annual	None & 60 C	7,050
Kentucky	38	4	100	2	Even	60 L	9,850
Louisiana	39	4	105	4	Annual[3]	60 C & 30 C	16,500
Maine	32	2	151	2	Odd	None	4,100
Maryland	43	4	142	4	Annual	90 C	8,300
Massachusetts	40	2	240	2	Annual	None	23,000
Michigan	38	4	110	2	Annual	None	36,000
Minnesota	67	4	135	2	Odd	120 L	12,960
Mississippi	52	4	122	4	Annual	90 C & 125 C	14,500
Missouri	34	4	163	2	Annual	June 30/& May 15	18,750

8 *Baker* v. *Carr,* 369 U.S. 186.

State	Senate Size	Term	Lower House Size	Term	Sessions Years Held	Duration Limit[1]	2 Year Compensation[2]
Montana	55	4	104	2	Odd	60 C	$ 2,100
Nebraska	49	4	. . .	. . .	Annual	90 L & 60 L	9,600
Nevada	20	4	40	2	Odd	None	3,900
N. Hampshire	24	2	400	2	Odd	None	200
New Jersey	40	4	80	2	Annual	None	20,000
New Mexico	42	4	70	2	Annual[3]	60 C & 30 C	1,800
New York	57	2	150	2	Annual	None	36,000
North Carolina	50	2	120	2	Odd	None	10,000
North Dakota	49	4	98	2	Odd	60 L	3,590
Ohio	33	4	99	2	Odd[4]	None	25,500
Oklahoma	48	4	99	2	Annual	90 L	16,800
Oregon	30	4	60	2	Odd	None	10,500
Pennsylvania	50	4	203	2	Annual	None	24,000
Rhode Island	50	2	100	2	Annual	60 L	600
South Carolina	46	4	124	2	Annual	None	9,200
South Dakota	35	2	75	2	Annual	45 L & 30 L	5,000
Tennessee	33	4	99	2	Odd[4]	90 L	8,100
Texas	31	4	150	2	Odd	140 C	11,040
Utah	28	4	69	2	Annual[3]	60 C & 20 C	3,200
Vermont	30	2	150	2	Odd[4]	None	5,400
Virginia	40	4	100	2	Annual	30 C & 60 C	4,500
Washington	49	4	99	2	Odd	60 C	9,900
West Virginia	34	4	100	2	Annual	60 C	3,000
Wisconsin	33	4	100	2	Annual	None	21,000
Wyoming	30	4	61	2	Odd	40 C	1,640

[1] Duration limit means the number of days the legislature may meet in regular session. L means legislative working days. C is the number of calendar days between convening and final adjournment. In some states with no limit, legislators' expense allotments stop after a certain period of time. In other states with a limit, such a limit may be revoked by a special (e.g., $^2/_3$) vote. Where two figures appear for the same state, one is for odd-numbered years and the other for even-numbered ones except for Mississippi, where the second figure applies every four years.

[2] For all states except Massachusetts, these figures include estimates of daily expenses for which the lawmakers were reimbursed, as well as salaries and other expense payments. The figures are based on January 1970 estimates.

[3] Every other year, the session is limited to budget and financial matters.

[4] Legislature may divide session by recess to meet in even year also; Ohio must.

Source: "The State Legislatures" from The Book of the States. Copyright © 1970 by the Council of State governments. Reprinted by permission. Information on sessions from 1972 edition, pp. 60–61.

accordingly. Figure 29 reports some of the most recent data on these and other variations.

Congress convenes each January, as required by the Constitution, and usually remains in session until the following autumn. Members of both houses receive annual salaries of $42,500, certain expense money, and the franking privilege which permits them to send postage-free mail.

What Manner of Men?

If legislatures are to represent accurately the interests and convictions of the people, as assumed in democratic theory, some have

Figure 30   Occupation of Legislators' Fathers, Legislators Themselves, U.S. Senators, and the U. S. Labor Force, 1950

Occupation	State Legislators' Fathers[1]	State Legislators[1]	U.S. Senators	Labor Force 1950
Professional, technical	18%	47%	64%	7%
Proprietors, managers, officials	29	35	29	7
Farmers, farm managers	25	10	7	16
Craftsmen, foremen, operatives	16	2	—	31
Clerical, sales	5	5	—	15
Unskilled labor, servants, farm labor	5	—	—	20
Other, not known	2	1	—	4
	100%	100%	100%	100%

[1] Data compiled from four states: California, New Jersey, Ohio, and Tennessee.
Source: "Occupational Backgrounds" from *State Legislative Systems* by Wilder Crane, Jr., and Meredith W. Watts, Jr. Englewood Cliffs, N.J.: Prentice-Hall, Inc., 1968. Reprinted by permission. Note that "less than 10 percent of state legislators held occupations that were the same as those held by the majority of wage earners in the country." Ibid., p. 45.

argued that legislators must possess certain important characteristics in the same proportion as these characteristics are found in the total population. In fact, however, lawmakers are a rather special breed, unlike their fellow citizens in certain key respects.

Sex and race   Women, to cite the most extreme example, constituted a little more than half the total population but only 2.4 percent of Congress in 1972 (13 out of 535). Blacks, comprising more than 11 percent of the population, also held only 13 seats. Furthermore, only in Ohio did the percentage of blacks in the legislature exceed the percentage of blacks in the state.[9]

Occupational background   A comparison of the occupations of state legislators, legislators' fathers, U.S. senators, and the general public is shown in Figure 30. An analysis of the 1972 Congress discloses additional information about the types of people most likely to win election to this most exalted of legislative bodies. Of the 535 members, 462 had previous experience in public office, mostly state and local, while 387 were veterans.

Occupationally, lawyers constituted fewer than 1 percent of American workers, but well over half of all members of Congress. Other well-represented occupations on Capitol Hill were business and banking, 173; teaching, 72; farming, 47; and journalism, 36.[10] It is wise, if one wishes to run for legislative office, to have a secure occupation to which to return if one loses. As Bullitt observed:

9 *Congressional Quarterly Guide to Current American Government* (Fall 1970), p. 136. See also p. 138 for the number of blacks in each of the state legislatures.
10 *The New York Times Encyclopedic Almanac 1972*, p. 108.

A private calling is essential to the politician who is brave and wishes to be free. Like Cincinnatus, he should have a plow standing ready for him in a field at home. . . . Without a happy alternative, an acrobat's net, he cannot afford the independent judgment which he must have to do his duty. Through the window he sees the old men sitting on the courthouse lawn; unless he can afford to lose he may think, "There . . . go I," and keep a wetted finger in the air.[11]

Age Practical considerations prohibit young people from gaining their proportionate share of legislative seats. One can seldom hope to accumulate the acquaintances, money, or prestige necessary for a successful campaign before reaching middle age. The Constitution requires members of the House to be at least twenty-five and senators thirty years old. The average age of congressmen in 1971 was fifty-two in the House and fifty-six in the Senate.[12] Among committee chairmen, who attain their position by party seniority, the average age was sixty-six.[13]

The unrepresentative representatives Out of the welter of statistics, an overriding conclusion emerges: Legislative representatives are not very representative. Those who make our laws are generally male, white, professionally trained, business-oriented, and middle-aged. With inevitable exceptions, this means that legislators are rarely inclined to favor major alterations in the society in which they have attained such a high socioeconomic status.

INTERNAL ORGANIZATION

Within any legislature, some members have more power than others. Generally, maximum influence is exerted by presiding officers, committee chairmen, and party leaders.

Presiding Officers

The presiding officers have the authority to recognize speakers, interpret the rules of procedure, and decide on the committee to which each bill will be sent.

The Vice President, and a note on filibusters The Constitution authorizes the Vice President to preside over the U.S. Senate. But he is not considered a member of that body, may not participate in legislative debate, and may vote on bills only in case of a tie. If the Vice President is absent, the presiding officer is the president pro tem, a senator elected by his colleagues and usually the member of the majority party with longest Senate service.

Each legislative chamber adopts its own rules of procedure,

11 Stimson Bullitt, *To Be a Politician* (Garden City, N.Y.: Anchor Books, Doubleday & Company, Inc., 1961), p. 7.
12 *The New York Times Encyclopedic Almanac* 1971, p. 154.
13 *Congressional Quarterly Guide to Current American Government* (Fall 1970), p. 63.

and as those in the Senate are relatively few and informal, the Vice President rarely must render significant interpretations. Moreover, the Senate rules provide for unlimited debate. This means that each senator can normally talk as long and as often as he or she wishes on any bill before it can be brought to a vote. In such a situation, it makes little difference who is recognized at any particular time, since each will have a chance sooner or later anyway.

Unlimited debate permits a leisurely and thoughtful consideration of a bill but it also permits a small minority of the Senate to defeat a bill favored by a clear majority. This is accomplished by a *filibuster*—a colorful series of marathon speeches that can tie up the Senate for weeks and prohibit it from considering any other pending legislation. While talking a bill to death, a senator may speak about anything and may even read—as Senator Huey Long of Louisiana once did—the Bible, the Constitution, the Sears Roebuck catalogue, or recipes for "pot likker" sent him by his constituents.

Before 1917 there was no way to end a filibuster. In that year, however, Senate Rule 22 provided for the termination of debate through a procedure known as *cloture*. Sixteen senators must first sign a petition requesting that a filibuster be ended and then two thirds of those present must vote to stop debate.

Most senators are proud of their tradition of unlimited debate, justified as a means of arousing public opinion by dramatizing the depths of conviction displayed by those opposing the bill. The filibuster is frequently denounced, however, as an impediment to majority rule. There have been thirty-six cloture votes in fifty-three years, and only seven succeeded in shutting off debate.[14]

The Speaker of the House   The House of Representatives elects its own presiding officer on a straight party-line vote. Thus, the Speaker is accorded recognition as the most influential member of the majority party in the House. When the Speaker was at the pinnacle of his power, prior to certain reforms in House rules enacted in 1910, he ruled the chamber in a nearly dictatorial fashion. Even now, a strong one, like the late Rep. Sam Rayburn of Texas, is second only to the President of the United States in general political influence.

The sources of the Speaker's power are numerous. Because rules of procedure are far more intricate in the House than in the Senate, his authority to interpret them is more significant. Similarly, his power to recognize members to speak is important because severe time limitations on House debate prevent many representatives from speaking at all. He also appoints members to certain special committees (as distinct from standing committees, discussed below), names the Speaker pro tem to preside when he is absent, and performs personal but meaningful services for House members, such as the allocation of office space.

14 Lewis A. Froman, Jr., *The Congressional Process* (Boston: Little, Brown and Company, 1967), pp. 118–22.

Moreover, if the President belongs to his party, he plays a major role in engineering congressional approval of administration proposals.

Lieutenant governors and state speakers At first glance, the presiding officers of state legislative bodies appear to have jobs patterned slavishly after their congressional counterparts. Indeed, this is often true, yet variation does exist. In more than thirty state senates the presiding officer is the popularly elected lieutenant governor, whose role is rather weak. In California and many other states, the president pro tem, a substitute presiding officer elected from among the senators, has greater influence than his national counterpart and more legislative power than the lieutenant governor. Tennessee provides an interesting deviation from the common pattern. There, whoever is elected presiding officer by the state senate becomes the lieutenant governor.

In state lower houses, as in the U.S. House of Representatives, the presiding officer is chosen from among the members and is called the Speaker. Usually, he has even more power than the House Speaker in Congress, especially in appointing the members and chairmen of legislative committees.[15] In Florida, Utah, and a few other states, however, legislative leadership is weakened and deprived of continuity by the regular rotation of the speakership among several legislators.

Standing Committees

Most of the work of modern legislative bodies is done in their standing committees. These provide for a division of labor which enables each lawmaker to acquire considerable knowledge in a particular area of public policy. Every legislator, national and state, is assigned to at least one standing committee which considers all bills dealing with its specialized field. Before he was elected President, Woodrow Wilson called the standing committees of Congress "little legislatures" with the power to bury a bill in "dim dungeons of silence whence it will never return."[16] In this respect, things haven't changed much.

Committee assignments and the seniority system in Congress In both houses, there is nothing more important to the average legislator than his or her committee assignments. A preference will be dictated by three main considerations: the major concerns of the home district, his or her own background and interests, and the influence and publicity to be derived from committee membership. However, for freshmen congressmen there may be a wide discrepancy between the committee posts they would like and those they actually get. They can blame two factors for their disappointments: the party-ratio tradition and the seniority system.

15 Wilder Crane, Jr., and Meredith W. Watts, Jr., *State Legislative Systems* (Englewood Cliffs, N.J.: Prentice-Hall, Inc., 1968), pp. 57 and 61, and William J. Keefe and Morris S. Ogul, *The American Legislative Process* (Englewood Cliffs, N.J.: Prentice-Hall, Inc., 1964), p. 42.
16 Quoted by Bertram M. Gross, *The Legislative Struggle* (N.Y.: McGraw-Hill Book Company, 1953), p. 266.

On most of the standing committees, the ratio of Republicans to Democrats is roughly the same as in the whole chamber. Thus, if there are sixty Democrats and forty Republicans in the Senate, a ten-member standing committee probably will consist of about six Democrats and four Republicans. The seniority system is a bigger obstacle to a desired committee assignment. It usually means that legislators are given their choice of committees in order of their length of continuous service in the Senate or House. The chairman of each standing committee, moreover, is invariably the member of the majority party who has served longest on that committee.

The most obvious result of the seniority system is that it produces committee chairmen of long experience, advanced age, and—sometimes—questionable competence. More important, perhaps, is that legislators who accumulate enough seniority to become chairmen often are able to do so because they come from areas where the two parties do not compete on a very equal basis. Such noncompetitive, one-party regions tend to reflect social change and shifting opinion very slowly, and hence chairmen, with a few exceptions, are more conservative than most congressmen. When the Democrats are in a majority, as they have been since 1955, the seniority system naturally tends to elevate to chairmanships a disproportionately large number of congressmen from the South, where two-party competition is weakest. In 1972, Old Dixie could claim nine of the seventeen Senate standing committee chairmen, including both senators from Mississippi, Arkansas, and Louisiana, and eight of the twenty-one chairmen (including four Texans) in the House of Representatives.[17] This is an advantage no other section of the country enjoys and has been a major obstacle to Democratic Presidents such as Truman and Kennedy in their efforts for passage of liberal legislation.

The power of the chairmen   The seniority system would be less important if the committee chairmen were less powerful. They determine the agendas of committee meetings and frequently prevent bills from reaching the floor by pigeonholing them (refusing to schedule them for committee consideration). If a bill is not discussed in committee, or if the committee refuses to report it out to the floor, it is almost certainly dead. It can be revived only by a discharge petition in the House or a discharge motion in the Senate that will take it from the committee and place it before the whole House or Senate for further action. The discharge procedure requires the approval of a majority of the entire membership of either chamber, and is rarely used.

If a committee chairman decides not to pigeonhole a bill, he may refer it to a subcommittee which he alone can create and the membership of which he appoints, or he may schedule open public hearings at which lobbyists and officials from the executive branch have

17 *Congressional Quarterly Guide to Current American Go ʒernment* (Fall 1971), pp. 61 and 63.

Paul Conklin.

Secretary of State Rogers defends the administration's foreign policy before the Senate Foreign Relations Committee.

opportunities to testify regarding the bill's alleged merits or defects. After public hearings have been concluded, the committee meets privately to consider the bill and to add whatever amendments it wishes.

Rounding out their authority, committee chairmen also play prominent roles in floor debate, participate in conference committees to iron out differences between the two houses, and hire most of the professional staff members who assist committees in their work. As the late Rep. Clem Miller once observed, "There are all sorts of ways to get things done in Congress. The best way is to live long enough to get to be a committee chairman."[18] Since the length of human life is not yet determined by majority vote, it is easy to see why reformers have worked for several decades to obtain a more democratic method than the seniority system for selecting committee chairmen.

Committees in the U.S. Senate There are seventeen standing committees of the Senate, with members chosen by party committees, which are in turn selected by the Democratic floor leader and the chairman of the Republican Senate Conference.[19] As we have seen, seniority carries great weight, although if two senators from the same party have served an equal length of time, personal and political factors are also involved. When former President Johnson was the leader of the Senate Democrats in 1953, he broke with previous tradition by persuading his party's Committee on Committees to award each new Democrat one major committee assignment.[20]

Two committees have unique importance in the Senate because they deal with matters beyond the scope of any committees in the House of Representatives. One is the Foreign Relations Committee.

18 Clem Miller, *Member of the House* (N.Y.: Charles Scribner's Sons, 1962), p. 39.
19 These party leaders are discussed below, pp. 232–233.
20 Daniel M. Berman, *In Congress Assembled* (N.Y.: The Macmillan Company, 1964), pp. 144–50.

Figure 31   Senate Standing Committees Ranked According to Desirability

1. Foreign Relations	9. Banking, Housing and Urban Affairs
2. Finance	10. Labor and Public Welfare
3. Commerce	11. Public Works
4. Judiciary	12. Government Operations
5. Appropriations	13. Rules and Administration
6. Armed Services	14. Post Office and Civil Service
7. Agriculture and Forestry	15. District of Columbia
8. Interior and Insular Affairs	* Aeronautical and Space Sciences
	* Veterans' Affairs

Source: "Senate Standing Committees Ranked According to Desirability" from "The Seniority System in Congress" by George Goodwin from *American Political Science Review,* Vol. LIII (June 1959). Reprinted by permission of the American Political Science Association. *These committees were not ranked.

Because treaties with foreign nations must be approved only by the Senate, this is the only committee that has an opportunity to review them before they are put to a vote.

Somewhat similarly, the Senate Judiciary Committee has initial jurisdiction over presidential appointments to the federal courts—a matter over which the House of Representatives has no control. The Judiciary Committees in both houses have jurisdiction over most civil rights bills and proposed constitutional amendments.

Committees in the House of Representatives   There are twenty-one standing committees in the House, with Democratic members chosen by the Democrats serving on the Ways and Means Committee and Republican assignments made by a special Committee on Committees comprised of one Republican congressman from each state. The choices of both parties are influenced by their party leaders, and the Speaker has considerable impact upon the committee assignments of members of his party. Seniority, of course, is a major factor, but considerations of popularity, competence, and ideology also may be taken into account.

The most coveted committee posts in the House are on Rules, Ways and Means, and Appropriations. The Rules Committee is unique because its major function is to determine when and for how long bills approved by other standing committees will be debated on the House floor, and whether amendments may be offered there. While the power of the Rules Committee is supposed to facilitate action on pending legislation, it is sometimes employed to prevent any floor action at all if a bill is opposed by the committee chairman or a majority of its membership. The result of this whole process is that most bills must get through two committees before they reach the floor of the House, but only one to receive consideration in the Senate. Although the power of the Rules Committee is defended on the basis of the far larger number of bills introduced in the House than in the Senate, its abuse of authority has made it, along with the Senate filibuster and the seniority system, the most frequently criticized of congressional practices.

Figure 32   Standing Committees of the House of Representatives (in alphabetical order)

Agriculture	Internal Security
Appropriations	Interstate and Foreign Commerce
Armed Services	Judiciary
Banking and Currency	Merchant Marine and Fisheries
District of Columbia	Post Office and Civil Service
Education and Labor	Public Works
Foreign Affairs	Rules
Government Operations	Science and Astronautics
House Administration	Standards of Official Conduct
Interior and Insular Affairs	Veterans' Affairs
	Ways and Means

Source: *New York Times Encyclopedic Almanac* 1972, pp. 113–114. On a few matters, notably atomic energy and defense production, there are joint standing committees consisting of both senators and representatives, rather than separate ones in each chamber.

The Ways and Means Committee derives its special influence from that provision of the Constitution (Article I, Section 7) providing that "all bills for raising revenue shall originate in the House of Representatives. . . ." Most such measures are tax bills and all are referred to this committee to recommend ways and means of raising money. Since all expenditure bills are traditionally introduced first in the House, its Appropriations Committee has an advantage comparable to that of Ways and Means. No committees receive more attention from the President, interested in getting his proposed programs approved, or interest groups, interested in obtaining subsidies or avoiding taxes.

Finally, it should be noted that either house may appoint special *select committees,* usually for a one-year period, to investigate designated problems and provide information or recommendations to the entire body. In recent years, such committees have not been of great importance.

State legislative committees   Although wide variations exist, all state legislatures employ a system of standing committees and most seem patterned after those in Congress. In a search for greater efficiency, their number has been generally reduced, although there are fifty in the Mississippi lower house.[21] In all but seventeen state senates and five lower houses, members and chairmen are appointed by the presiding officers.[22] Seniority plays a prominent role in determining committee memberships in less than half the states, although it is clearly dominant in New Mexico's senate and a few other chambers. In Iowa, it seems to be a downright liability, and in other states the presiding officer usually can make appointments on the basis of his personal political alliances, sectionalism, or other factors. The result may be the "stacking" of the most influential committees to benefit some particular group.

21 Crane and Watts, op. cit., p. 61.
22 John C. Wahlke, "Organization and Procedure," Alexander Heard, ed., *State Legislatures in American Politics* (Englewood Cliffs, N.J.: Prentice-Hall, Inc., 1966), p. 142.

In Florida, for example, rural interests known as "pork-choppers" have been notably successful in gaining prize committee assignments.[23]

By and large, committees seem to play a less important role in state legislatures than in Congress. One reason for this is a reluctance or inability to kill bad bills in the committees to which they are referred. As of 1968, both houses in fifteen states and one house in two others require committees to report out all bills.[24] A more important weakness among state legislative committees is the inadequacy of their professional staffs for such tasks as providing legal research and technical information. Joint standing committees are of considerably more significance in a few states, notably Connecticut, Maine, and Massachusetts, than in Congress. In Connecticut they are the only type of standing committees in existence.[25]

Party Leadership

It is hard to make general statements about the importance of the two major parties in determining legislative organization and procedure; too much seems to depend on the personalities of party leaders, differences between majority and minority party status, the variable degrees of competition between the two parties from state to state, the structural differences between the upper and lower houses, and the unique traditions of the Republicans and Democrats in each chamber.

Floor leaders in the U.S. Senate   About one thing, however, there can be little doubt: The *majority leader,* or floor leader of the majority party, in the United States Senate is the most powerful member of that body, and he thus ranks just below the President and the Speaker of the House in the total scheme of American politics. His preeminence stems from influence regarding committee assignments, control over the order in which the Senate will debate bills reported out of the various committees, the tradition that he will be recognized by the presiding officer whenever he wishes to speak, and his close relations with the White House—especially if the President belongs to the same party. In a sense, he has no comparable counterpart in the House of Representatives, since he combines some of the powers of the Speaker, the majority leader, and the Rules Committee in the lower chamber—all rolled into one.

The minority leader, who heads the numerically weaker party in the Senate, has only a little less power. He helps to determine committee appointments for members of his party, is consulted by the majority leader on the agenda for Senate debate, and, if the President belongs to *his* party may act as the semiofficial spokesman for the administration on pending legislation.

23 Keefe and Ogul, op. cit., pp. 164 and 171.
24 Crane and Watts, op. cit., p. 67.
25 Keefe and Ogul, op. cit., p. 151, and Wahlke, op. cit., pp. 141–42.

The majority and minority leaders are elected by a vote of all senators who belong to their respective parties, meeting in what are known as *caucuses* or (more recently) *conferences.* Although seniority may exert some influence, factors such as personality, intelligence, ideological commitment, legislative skill, and the accumulation of political debts play major roles in the final choices.

The Democratic conference allows its floor leader to accumulate more power than the Republican leader is permitted to muster. Both conferences elect an assistant leader, known as the majority or minority *whip,* to assist the leader in making sure party members are on the Senate floor when important matters come up for a vote. These positions are often a stepping-stone to bigger things. Sen. Mike Mansfield (D-Montana), the present majority leader, was previously the majority whip, and Sen. Hubert Humphrey (D-Minnesota), rose from whip to Vice President.

Party organization in the House Here, as in the Senate, congressmen meet in party caucuses (conferences) to elect majority and minority leaders and majority and minority whips. In a sense, they play the same roles as their Senate counterparts, but with two important differences. One is that the most important member of the majority party is elected Speaker, with the majority leader ranking second, and the majority whip third. The majority leader is often considered the heir apparent to the Speaker, as when Rep. John W. McCormack (D-Massachusetts) and Rep. Carl Albert (D-Oklahoma) made this rather natural transition in 1962 and 1971 respectively. Similarly, the minority leader has a good chance of becoming Speaker if congressional elections shift control of the House from one party to the other.

The second major difference in the influence of House and Senate party organizations is that—as noted earlier—the order of business in the House is determined by the Rules Committee rather than by the party leadership.

Parties in state legislatures Not much attention has been given to a systematic analysis of party organization in state legislatures, probably because it possesses so little uniformity. To cite rather extreme examples, Nebraska and Minnesota elect legislators on a nonpartisan basis, while party organization in the New York and New Jersey legislatures is normally more influential than in Congress. Available evidence indicates that the more two-party competition exists in state elections, the more important party leaders and alignments are in the legislatures.[26] Information regarding the legislative strength of the two parties is indicated in Figure 33.

Informal Power

Informal power is less easy to describe, but no less real than the various forms of formal authority. Almost every legislative body is

26 Crane and Watts, op. cit., Table 3–1, p. 42, and Keefe and Ogul, op. cit., p. 286.

Figure 33   State Legislatures Classified According to Degree of Party Competitiveness 1947–1966*

A 1   One-party States: Same party controlled the governorship and both houses throughout the period, and minority representation was negligible (all Democratic states).

Alabama   Arkansas   Louisiana   Mississippi   South Carolina

2   One-party States: Same party (Democratic) controlled the governorship and both houses throughout the period, and the minority representation was negligible (but Republicans were stronger here than in the group above, and this second group had developed a greater degree of two-party competitive politics).

Florida   Georgia   North Carolina   Tennessee   Texas   Virginia

B States with One Party Dominant: Same party controlled both houses throughout the period but did not always control governorship, and (except for Oklahoma) minority party occasionally had over one-fourth of the seats in at least one house.

Democratic: Arizona   Kentucky   Maryland   Oklahoma   West Virginia
Republican: Kansas   New Hampshire   Vermont

C 1   Limited Two-party States: Same party controlled both houses throughout most of the period and the governorship at least half the time.

South Dakota   Maine   Missouri   North Dakota   Iowa   Illinois
New Mexico   Wisconsin   Rhode Island   New York   Wyoming   Idaho

2   Limited Two-party States: Same party controlled both houses throughout most of the period but usually not the governorship.

Michigan   New Jersey   Ohio

3   Limited Two party States: Two houses controlled by different parties during most of the period.

Nevada   Connecticut

D Two-party States: Neither party had dominant legislative control, and in most cases party control of legislature approximated control of governorship.

Pennsylvania   Massachusetts   Oregon   Indiana   Delaware
California   Washington   Colorado   Utah   Montana

---

*Alaska and Hawaii are omitted because of their brief terms as states, and Nebraska and Minnesota are omitted because they have nonpartisan legislatures.
Source: Adapted from tables 6.1a. and 6.1b. in *The Legislative Process in the United States,* by Malcolm E. Jewell and Samuel C. Patterson. Copyright © 1966 by Random House, Inc. Reprinted by permission of the publisher.

characterized by informal alliances that may include the official leadership, sometimes challenge it, or simply exist as alternative centers of power.

In Congress, for example, over a hundred liberal Democrats in the House of Representatives belong to the Democratic Study Group. It raises campaign funds for its supporters, employs a small staff, and distributes pertinent information to gain support for bills important to its interests. The Wednesday Club is a somewhat similar group consisting of moderate and liberal Republicans. In addition, there is a Black Caucus in the House of Representatives which seeks to promote black interests, and the Members of Congress for Peace through Law (MCPL), a bipartisan, bicameral group that favors greater support for the United Nations, normalized relations with the People's Republic of China, and other comparable foreign policy objectives.

Sectional and economic groupings are even older among congressmen, but are less organized. There is, for example, a "farm bloc," a narrower "cotton bloc," an "oil bloc" and so on. The majority of congressmen tend to avoid frontal attacks on such groups. Representatives from the same state also meet occasionally in state caucuses. Of most importance is a loose coalition of Republicans and conservative southern Democrats which controls most major committees and has had a functional majority in Congress since World War II.

In the Senate, smaller and more intimate than the House, a kind of inner "club" has developed across party lines. It has no formal membership, consists of personal friends with considerable seniority, subtly enforces Senate traditions and behavior norms among younger members, and has considerable influence.

The sum total of formal and informal organization in the legislatures results in a considerable fragmentation of power. This decentralization creates numerous points of access for lobbyists, many obstacles to the passage of a bill into law, and hence a rather frustrating sluggishness in the legislative process described below.

THE LEGISLATIVE PROCESS

As President Kennedy observed in a 1962 television interview, "It is very easy to defeat a bill in the Congress. It is much more difficult to pass one."[27] He was neither the first nor the last President to be frustrated by that painful legislative truth. Of the "six great goals" announced in President Nixon's 1971 State of the Union address, four of them (revenue sharing, welfare reform, reorganization of the executive branch, and extended health insurance) had yet to clear Congress some twenty months later and only modest progress had been made on the other two (environmental protection and economic prosperity.) To as-

27 See Robert Sherrill, *Why They Call It Politics* (N.Y.: Harcourt Brace Jovanovich, Inc., 1972), p. 101.

certain why this can be, it is necessary to understand the obstacle course that confronts bills in Congress—and in most of the state legislatures as well. In the following sketch of a bill's passage in Congress, we see in sequence some of the procedures mentioned earlier.

Introduction of a Bill

Although congressional legislation must be introduced by either a senator or a representative, it may be suggested or even written by the President, some administration official, lobbyist, or influential constituent. (Tax, or other revenue bills, it will be remembered, can be introduced only in the House.) Occasionally, identical bills are introduced simultaneously by a senator and a representative to save time and so that both may receive whatever credit results. Important *public bills* may apply to the whole nation, but there are also *private bills* designed to admit a specific immigrant into the country or to provide some other assistance to an individual citizen. Each bill is given an identifying number and is referred by the presiding officer to the appropriate standing committee.

Committee Consideration

In ordinary circumstances, the committee has the power of life or death over bills assigned to it, and most receive the death sentence. It may never consider a bill (pigeonhole it); or refer it to a subcommittee; or consider it and then kill it; or amend it and send it on to the next pitfall awaiting it; or—in rare instances—send it on as originally introduced. In 1963–64, as an example, less than 12 percent of all bills were reported out by the committee to which they were sent.[28]

Once in awhile, as with the Civil Rights Act of 1964, a presiding officer will not send a bill to certain burial in the committee which would normally have jurisdiction over it, but will refer it instead to a committee known to be more favorably disposed toward it. If a bill is considered by the committee to which it is sent (a matter decided largely by the chairman) hearings are held at which interested persons may testify. Within a six-day period in June 1972, for example, witnesses testifying on a housing bill before the House Banking and Currency Committee included three congressmen, two lobbyists for retired persons' organizations, three housing industry lobbyists, two local government lobbyists, lobbyists for the American Bar Association and Americans for Democratic Action, and George Romney, Secretary of Housing and Urban Development.[29]

Compounding the frustrations for a President trying to get a bill passed is the fact that the enormously powerful committee chairmen

28 Froman, op. cit., p. 36.
29 *Congressional Quarterly Weekly Report,* June 24, 1972, pp. 1538–39.

support Presidents even of their own party less frequently than do most of their party colleagues in Congress.

Floor Action and Conference Committees

The relatively few bills that win a majority vote in committee (and sometimes in a subcommittee before that) usually have been subjected to grueling controversy and numerous amendments. In the House most important legislation must then go from a standing committee to the Rules Committee, which determines if and when the bill will arrive on the floor of the entire House. It is not uncommon for as many as thirty bills a year to die in the Rules Committee. In the Senate, the scheduling of debate for bills reported out of committee is primarily determined by the majority leader.

The Rules Committee normally limits debate by the entire House of Representatives to one or two hours per bill, and occasionally prohibits amendments from being proposed from the floor. In the Senate, any bill that gets out of committee may be brought to the floor by any senator, usually as scheduled by the majority leader. While it is easier to get a bill before the Senate than the House, the absence of time limits on debate make it harder to bring to a vote. If a bill's opponents resort to a filibuster—the ultimate weapon—it takes only one senator more than one third of those present to prevent cloture.

After a bill has passed one house of Congress, it is sent to the other where the procedure begins anew with a referral to a standing committee. If the second house passes the bill in the same form as the first, it is sent to the President for his signature. But if new amendments are added, the revised bill must be returned to the originating chamber for approval of the changes. Should it refuse to approve, which happens about one tenth of the time, both the Senate and House versions of the bill are sent to a conference committee. The members of this committee are usually chosen by the presiding officers from the two standing committees that had considered the bill earlier. Then, behind closed doors, about a dozen senators and representatives attempt to hammer out a compromise. When the compromise version goes back to the Senate and House of Representatives for a final vote, no further amendments are permitted and the bill is usually passed.

Presidential Action

By the time an important bill reaches the President's desk it has gone through a standing committee in each house, perhaps also subcommittees, the Rules Committee of the House, the Senate and House themselves, and often a conference committee. It may bear little resemblance to any bill the President initially requested and may indeed be a bill he never wanted at all. His options are discussed in the following

Steve Clevenger, BBM Associates.

To know the concerns of the people he or she represents, a legislator must listen. Senator Edward Kennedy hears the views of Vietnam war veterans.

chapter, but should he choose to veto it, a two-thirds vote is then required in both houses of Congress before it can become law.

LEGISLATIVE DILEMMAS
The Representative Function

There is considerable significance in the fact that one house of Congress is called the House of Representatives, for legislators are supposed to *represent* the people. As one scholar suggests, this means that lawmakers are to "stand for" or symbolize the people, just as a flag symbolizes a nation. Yet in another sense, a representative is one who "acts for" the people as well.[30] The representative's interests must be their interests, his desires their desires. The legislator, therefore, is required to play an ambivalent role: He or she is a part of the government, and at the same time a living link between the government and the people whom it is designed to serve.

The legislator as errand boy Frequently the legislator's role as a link between government and people makes him something of an errand boy. Many hours are spent helping constituents who have problems with some government agency. When the average citizen wants a visa for a relative in some foreign country, a draft deferment, a change in a proposed highway route, or reconsideration of an unemployment compensation claim, the first impulse often is to write his congress-

30 Joseph Tussman, *Obligation and the Body Politic* (N.Y.: Oxford University Press, Inc., 1960), p. 61.

man or state legislator. When a local businessman wants a government contract, he frequently does the same thing. A member of the House of Representatives in Washington, D.C., remarked that "[W]e spend too much time on errand boy activities. . . . But the real question is how we can avoid doing that. I think that . . . we cannot."[31]

Two recommendations have been made to lessen the errand boy burdens of lawmakers. One is to provide them with larger office staffs, which assume much of the responsibility for assisting constituents with their problems. The other, more drastic in nature, is for the legislature to appoint an ombudsman to investigate citizen complaints against executive agencies.

The office of ombudsman was created in Sweden over a century ago and has proved so effective in cutting bureaucratic red tape and righting administrative wrongs that it has spread to several other nations and to the state governments of Hawaii, Nebraska, and Iowa. Oregon also has an ombudsman, but appointed by the governor.[32] At least one congressman, Rep. Henry Reuss of Wisconsin, has proposed the establishment of such an office by Congress. Whether such an official would be as successful in a large and diverse country as in a small homogeneous one is problematical.

The legislator as representative But there is much more to the representative function than being an errand boy. In a mystical way, for one to be elected a representative is to be transformed into those who elected him. A legislator is expected to respond so automatically to the constituents' wants and needs that the people—through him—rule themselves.

This concept of the representative function has encountered many objections and evoked more questions than can be answered here. Does it mean that only teen-agers or machinists or blacks can faithfully represent teen-agers or machinists or blacks? Does it mean the legislator should reflect only home district views, even at the expense of the rest of the nation? Does it mean ignoring his or her own judgment, even when the constituents are thought to be wrong on a certain matter?

Conscience or Conformity?

After several centuries of representative government, there is still little agreement on what it means to represent the people. Two schools of thought provide alternative explanations.

The agency theory One view of the legislator's job, already noted, is that it is to do what the people who elected him or her would do themselves if they had the chance. Voters in Boston instructed their

31 Quoted in Charles L. Clapp, *The Congressman: His Work as He Sees It* (Garden City, N.Y.: Anchor Books, Doubleday & Company, Inc., 1963), p. 118.
32 Ed Meagher, "Ombudsman has Good 1st Year," *Los Angeles Times*, Aug. 30, 1970, Sec. B, pp. 4 and 5.

representatives how to vote as early as 1661,[33] and in his maiden speech to the House of Representatives, John Tyler, later to become President, defended such arrangements:

Is the servant to disobey the wishes of his master? How can he be regarded as representing the people when he speaks, not their language, but his own? He ceases to be their representative when he does so, and represents himself alone.[34]

Tyler expressed what is sometimes called the agency theory of representation, according to which the official is the agent of the voters and obligated to do their bidding. But whether such moral obligation exists or not, political expediency often dictates the same result. An unidentified congressman was recently quoted as saying

I take the position that "a politician's first duty is to get re-elected" and I think this sometimes requires casting votes you might prefer not to cast. The alternative to your re-election in most cases is the election of someone who would be diametrically opposed in conviction to what you stand for.[35]

The trustee theory Another concept of representation views the representative as a trustee to whom the voters have delegated the authority to act in their behalf in whatever way he or she sees fit. The classic statement of this doctrine was made by Edmund Burke, the great English scholar-politician. In a speech to the voters of Bristol in 1774, he said

Certainly, Gentlemen, . . . a representative [ought to be in] the most unreserved communication with his constituents. Their wishes ought to have great weight with him . . .; their business unremitted attention. It is his duty to . . . prefer their interests to his own. But his unbiased opinion, his mature judgement, his enlightened conscience, he ought not to sacrifice to . . . any set of men. . . . Your representative owes you not his industry only, but his judgement; and he betrays, instead of serving you, if he sacrifices it to your opinion.[36]

Legislators might well note that in the next election, Burke was defeated. Nonetheless, more than a century and a half later, a survey of congressmen found that 54 percent agreed with Burke while 37 percent believed they should vote in accordance with the consensus in their constituencies.[37] More recently, a study of four state legislatures revealed that the trustee conception was embraced by 81 percent of Tennessee lawmakers, 61 percent of those in New Jersey, 56 percent in Ohio, and 55 percent in California.[38]

Some writers impute a moral superiority to legislators who

33 Austin Ranney, *The Governing of Men* (N.Y.: Henry Holt and Co., 1958), p. 240.
34 Quoted in John F. Kennedy, *Profiles in Courage* (N.Y.: Pocket Books, 1957), p. 13.
35 Quoted in Clapp, op. cit., p. 427.
36 Reprinted in Hanna Fenichal Pitkin, ed., *Representation* (N.Y.: Atherton Press, Inc., 1969), pp. 174–75.
37 Alfred de Grazia, *Public and Republic* (N.Y.: Alfred A. Knopf, Inc., 1951), p. 158.
38 John C. Wahlke, Heinz Eulau, William Buchanan, and Leroy C. Ferguson, *The Legislative System* (N.Y.: John Wiley & Sons, Inc., 1962), p. 281.

"vote their conscience" to support an unpopular cause, rather than yielding to popular pressures. John F. Kennedy, for example, wrote a Pulitzer prize-winning book, *Profiles in Courage,* in which he lauded about a dozen such congressmen. Perhaps their rarity deserves recognition.

Legislators can most easily vote their judgment on controversial bills, disregarding possible constituency opinion, (1) if they have a few years (as in the case of U.S. senators) before reelection, (2) if last reelected by a big margin from a safe, noncompetitive district, or (3) if their judgment is strongly supported by the party or pressure groups most influential among constituents and most likely to make financial contributions to the next campaign.

Conflicting Demands

The actual behavior of a lawmaker is the product of many influences. How he or she votes on many bills, of course, reflects a general orientation (prolabor or probusiness, liberal or conservative) toward the issue at hand. Yet there are other bills (often of a somewhat technical nature) on which ideological preferences provide little guidance. In any event, the lawmaker is likely to be barraged by many cross-pressures. Constituents back home, the party leadership, powerful lobbyists, and trusted colleagues all may be clamoring for that vote—some for a bill and some against it.

The lawmaker knows exactly what vote each of these groups want with one exception: Seldom is it known for sure what a majority of the voters (the only group that controls his or her whole career) want on any given piece of legislation. Neither mail nor public opinion polls will reflect opinion accurately. Letter writers are not necessarily representative of the general population, and polls are fallible. One study showed an amazingly low relationship between what congressmen thought their constituents favored on certain issues and what their views really were.[39] Compounding this perplexity, lawmakers don't know what percentage of the voters are even aware of a particular issue, or whether the *intensity* of voters' convictions, if they are aware of it, is strong enough to cost a legislator the next election for voting the wrong way. Congressmen seem to believe that their voting records have a greater effect upon their chances of winning another term than is probably the case, even in the face of evidence that less than half of the people know anything about either candidate in most races for the House of Representatives.[40]

The importance of constituency pressure, then, lies partly in the fact that legislators are acutely conscious of it, no matter how inaccurately they may perceive it. It also lies partly in the population characteristics of the districts from which lawmakers are elected. It is

39 Warren E. Miller and Donald Stokes, "Constituency Influences in Congress," *American Political Science Review* 57 (March 1963): 45–57.
40 Loc. cit.

usually assumed, for example, that the United States Senate is more liberal than the House of Representatives because senators are elected from state-wide districts that almost invariably include some traditionally liberal voters (such as blacks or union members), while many representatives are chosen from small districts with virtually none.

It is difficult to generalize about the impact of either party leaders or lobbyists upon legislative votes, in part because legislators perceive their own roles in relation to these people in different ways. With respect to political parties, some lawmakers think of themselves as "loyalists" who place a high premium on party support while others, at the opposite extreme, are proud to be "mavericks." In spite of many exceptions, however, it is generally agreed that in Congress, party affiliation is the best single indicator of how lawmakers will vote. Similarly, with respect to pressure group lobbying, some legislators are "resistors" who believe such behavior unfortunate, while others are "facilitators" who believe it beneficial.[41]

The influence of a lawmaker's colleagues weighs heavily on the decision-making scales. Although the average legislator seems to have a local perspective, primarily concerned with the needs of his own district, the welfare of the entire state or nation is occasionally impressed upon him by legislators from other areas. Chances are that he has grown to like his colleagues and has come to realize, moreover, that unless he votes the way they wish upon occasion, he cannot expect to receive reciprocal treatment. This kind of vote trading is therefore not merely expedient, but an indication of mutual respect. In addition, a legislative body develops its own distinctive customs and behavior expectations. There is strong group pressure to remain loyal to these norms which, at least in the United States Senate, include courtesy and mutual assistance.[42]

The Legislature as Institutionalized Compromise

In conclusion, a legislative body, if truly representative, will consist of many lawmakers advancing as many conflicting interests as are found in the entire society. About the best a legislator can do for his constituents, therefore, is to fight as hard as he can for what they would like and then strike as good a bargain as possible for what they can actually get. This, of course, requires compromise among the competing interests—labor vs. business, city vs. suburb, and so forth. It is a process for which a legislative body is uniquely suited.

41 Wahlke, et al., pp. 502–503 and passim.
42 Donald R. Matthews, *United States Senators and Their World* (Chapel Hill: University of North Carolina Press, 1960). For an interesting analysis of "deviant senatorial behavior" see Ralph K. Huitt, "The Outsider in the Senate: An Alternative Role," *American Political Science Review* 55 (September 1961): 566–75.

THE NEED FOR REFORM

The first congressional reform law in twenty-four years was passed in 1970. It required that all roll call votes taken in committee be made public, that more votes on the House floor be recorded, and that committee procedures be made slightly more democratic. But it did not deal with those procedures which have received the most bitter criticism: the seniority system for selecting committee chairmen, the power of the House Rules Committee to determine what can be considered by the entire membership, and the enormous difficulty of stopping a Senate filibuster. In short, it did not redistribute congressional power more evenly among the members nor seriously impede the capacity of a minority of congressmen to thwart majority action.

If reform is needed in Congress, revolution may be required in many state legislatures. They are, as one observer noted,

Figure 34   Rank Order of the 50 State Legislatures

Overall Rank	State	Overall Rank	State
1	California	26	Tennessee
2	New York	27	Oregon
3	Illinois	28	Colorado
4	Florida	29	Massachusetts
5	Wisconsin	30	Maine
6	Iowa	31	Kentucky
7	Hawaii	32	New Jersey
8	Michigan	33	Louisiana
9	Nebraska	34	Virginia
10	Minnesota	35	Missouri
11	New Mexico	36	Rhode Island
12	Alaska	37	Vermont
13	Nevada	38	Texas
14	Oklahoma	39	New Hampshire
15	Utah	40	Indiana
16	Ohio	41	Montana
17	South Dakota	42	Mississippi
18	Idaho	43	Arizona
19	Washington	44	South Carolina
20	Maryland	45	Georgia
21	Pennsylvania	46	Arkansas
22	North Dakota	47	North Carolina
23	Kansas	48	Delaware
24	Connecticut	49	Wyoming
25	West Virginia	50	Alabama

Source: Table 1, "Rank Order of the 50 State Legislatures" from *The Sometime Governments* by John Burns. Copyright © 1971 by the Citizens Conference on State Legislatures. Reprinted by permission of Bantam Books, Inc.

poorly organized and technically ill equipped. . . . They do not meet often enough or long enough; they lack space, clerical staffing, professional assistance; they are poorly paid and overworked; they are prey to special interests, . . . ; their procedures and committee systems are outmoded.[43]

Fortunately, improvements are under way in many states, and some legislatures are functioning quite efficiently. But the discrepancy among them is enormous. A massive study was recently made of the legislatures of all fifty states. On the basis of five criteria (functionality, accountability, informedness, independence and representativeness), they were ranked from best to worst, with the results shown in Figure 34.

43 Alexander Heard, ed., *State Legislatures in American Politics* (Englewood Cliffs, N.J.: Prentice-Hall, Inc., 1966), pp. 1–2.

Chapter **10**

Executives
Presidents, Governors, and Bureaucracies

When I woke up this morning, the first thing I saw was a headline . . . that our Navy was going to spend two billion dollars on a shipbuilding program. Here I am, the Commander in Chief of the Navy having to read about that for the first time in the press. Do you know what I said to that? . . . I said: "Jesus Chr-rist!"
President Franklin D. Roosevelt

The President of the United States is the most powerful man in the world. His counterpart in each of the fifty states is a sort of minor league president, a governor who heads his own regional domain. It is these officials—and the bureaucracies that serve them—with whom this chapter is concerned.

THE PRESIDENT AND THE GOVERNORS
The Pomp and the Power

The President and the state governors have responsibilities so awesome, challenges of such magnitude, and opportunities so unique, that they are more than mere chief executives. They play many roles or—as some say—"wear many hats." Moreover, their functions must be performed simultaneously, for they overlap and each affects all of the others.

Heads of State The first executive "hat" is almost crown-like, for Presidents and governors are heads of state who play a symboli-cally patriotic role, much like that of a royal monarch. It is they who embody the ties that bind us together, the links between a proud past and a perilous future. As a head of state, the chief executive may lay a cornerstone for a new government building, award medals of honor to heroic servicemen, greet foreign royalty, or throw out the first ball at the beginning of the baseball season.

In addition to gratifying our national appetite for pomp and ceremony, this function serves a number of other purposes, both for the people and for the chief executive. For the people, it permits a view of the President and state governors in a number of different circumstances and a better assessment of their qualities of leadership. For the chief execu-tives, the head of state role keeps their thumbs on the pulse of the body politic and gives them politically priceless opportunities to improve their public images in what seem to be nonpolitical situations.

Many nations—England, West Germany, Japan, and oth-ers—have both a chief of state and a chief executive. One performs ceremonial functions; the other runs the government. In the United States, the President does both. A skillful leader exploits the prestige of the first role to enhance his power in performing the second. Thus, when a President issues a Labor Day proclamation, he is not only acting as chief of state but hopes also to be gaining additional political support from union members that will strengthen his position as head of the government.

But the ceremonial role can pose a hazard. People may confuse opposition to the chief executive's policies as a government leader with attacks upon him as a symbol of the nation itself. Although it is politically expedient for a President to encourage this confusion so as to minimize criticism, most people have learned to cherish the role of the President as head of state, while often deploring his performance as head of government. Few faulted President Nixon for conveying the congratu-lations of the nation to astronauts returning from the moon, but many criticized him for giving the space program priority over such domestic needs as improved health care.

Chief politicians　A chief executive must be, by definition, one of the most skillful politicians in the country. He has, after all, blended the ingredients of power—nomination by a major party, money, personal prestige and popularity, mastery of the mass media, and all the rest—into a consummately successful victory formula.

After his election, a President or governor does not cease to be a politician. In fact, if he does, he will seldom be an effective chief executive. To be a politician entails the skillful use of power—the ability to alter people's behavior in socially significant ways. If the leader is unable or unwilling to use the full range of his power—to threaten vetoes of extravagant appropriation bills, to promise Supreme Court appoint-ments to Southerners, or to deploy troops to Thailand, for example—progress toward his goals will be slow indeed. On the other hand, to squander these power resources in behalf of trivial objectives is to demean the dignity of his office.

Among the power resources available to a President or governor is his position as leader of his own political party. As noted earlier, tradition permits the President to choose his vice-presidential running mate and the chairman of his party's national committee. Through his influence with the national committee he can affect the allocation of campaign funds to party candidates for Congress and through speeches at fund-raising dinners he can attract campaign contributions. He can personally endorse the congressional candidates he favors, as President Nixon did in 1970 by campaigning for Republican nominees in twenty-three states. He can attract instant publicity to whatever members of his party he chooses by news releases and in press conferences. He can allow congressmen to announce government contracts awarded to plants in their districts. By judicious use of his vast patronage powers he can reward the party faithful with prestige appointments and punish the party heretics by ignoring their existence. When two supporters of the President lost Senate races in 1970, one was appointed to the White House staff (Clark MacGregor) and another named as Ambassador to the United Nations (George Busch). But a third loser who had opposed the President slipped back into the shadows of private law practice (Charles Goodell). In politics, there is no isolation so bleak as that of a man without honor in his own party.

But why should a President bother himself with such petty partisan politics? The answer is that if he wishes his legislative program to be enacted into law, his vetoes upheld, his appointments confirmed, his military excursions financed, and his treaties approved, he needs congressional support. Since he can expect relatively little from members of the opposition party, he must secure as much as possible from his own. Besides, he may wish to seek reelection, and for that the full support of his party's machinery is essential.

A governor, too, is normally the leader of his own party within the state. For many of the same reasons mentioned above, his ability to elicit its loyalty is often essential to his success.

Managers of the economy   As each level of government has expanded, so too has its impact upon the economy. The force and direction of this impact is determined largely by the executive branch— by the state governors, and especially by the President. Governments now are major employers, landowners, purchasers, stockpilers, awarders of contracts, and producers of such commodities as electric power and nuclear weapons—all functions which are authorized by legislatures but directed and implemented by the executive bureaucracy. Although it is a cruel injustice, it is also symbolically significant of the President's potential influence on the state of the economy that the squalid shacks in which many Americans lived during the Great Depression of the 1930s were known as "Hoovervilles," after the President who was in office when the Depression began.

Executive influence on the economy was strengthened enormously in 1921 when Congress gave to the President the responsibility of submitting a unified budget proposing specific expenditures for all agencies in the national government. Beginning with Illinois in 1917, all states except Arkansas have also adopted this so-called executive budget, thereby giving the governor the major role in planning the allocation of state tax funds. Most governors possess a power which even the President lacks: They have an *item veto* on appropriation bills which enables them to veto expenditures for certain purposes while signing the rest of a budget bill into law.[1] Therefore, while legislative bodies still vote the money for government programs, they rely upon the executive for overall initial planning as well as for control through the veto power.

The President's obligations in the economic arena were further broadened by the Employment Act of 1946 which created the Council of Economic Advisers and required the President to send an annual economic message to Congress recommending measures needed to move the nation closer to full employment.

One of the more dramatic examples of presidential influence on the cost of living came in 1962 when John F. Kennedy was faced with an announced price increase by the nation's leading steel companies. Sure such an increase would be dangerously inflationary, he denounced the steel executives on television, threatened to transfer government contracts, and instigated antitrust investigations. Within a week, the steel corporations revoked the price boost.[2] When President Nixon exercised power which Congress had given him a year earlier to impose direct price and wage controls, it was a startling reversal of his administration's policy. He knew, certainly, that his success as a candidate in 1972 might well depend on his success as a manager of the economy in 1971.

The chief diplomat The President determines the official attitude of the United States toward every nation on earth. Constitutionally, he may sign treaties with other countries, recognize and exchange diplomatic representatives with other governments, and, with Senate approval, appoint American ambassadors abroad. In addition, through his control of other agencies in the executive branch, he directs American espionage and the content and scope of American propaganda abroad.

In most respects, the powers of state governors are somewhat comparable to the powers of the President; in the domain of foreign affairs, however, the authority of the President is unique. As he descends the steps of *The Spirit of '76* in Peking or Moscow, Bucharest or Bonn, he carries with him, as supreme diplomat, the prospects of survival in a nuclear world.

Commanders in chief The opening words of Article II,

1 Clyde F. Snider, *American State and Local Government,* 2nd ed. (N.Y.: Appleton-Century-Crofts, 1965), pp. 694, 261.
2 Louis W. Koenig, "Kennedy and Steel: The Great Price Dispute," Alan F. Westin, ed., *The Centers of Power* (N.Y.: Harcourt Brace Jovanovich, Inc., 1964), pp. 1–52.

Section 2 of the U.S. Constitution provide that "The President shall be commander in chief of the army and navy . . . and of the militia of the several states, when called into the actual service of the United States." In effect, this means that he can order troops anywhere, anytime, to fire on any foe. It is one of the most controversial provisions of the Constitution because its utilization nullifies the significance of the clause in Article I, Section 8 which gives Congress the "power to . . . declare war."

The growth of the President's role as commander in chief, ignoring the constitutional prerogatives of Congress, has been a gradual one, but full-scale "presidential wars" made their debut when Harry S Truman ordered U.S. forces to resist aggression against South Korea in 1950. The result, sanctioned by a United Nations resolution, was a period of hostilities lasting three years and killing more than thirty thousand Americans. These losses exceeded those of the Mexican and Spanish-American Wars combined, both of which were declared by Congress. Since President Johnson committed combat forces to Vietnam in 1965, nearly fifty thousand American lives have been sacrificed in a conflict lasting longer than any in our history.

It is probable that the Founding Fathers never intended to authorize the President to send troops into battle without either a congressional declaration of war or an enemy attack on American soil. Instead, it seems likely that they made the President commander in chief in order to authorize immediate retaliation in the event of aggression against the United States, and to insure civilian supremacy over the entrenched power of career military officials. The principle of civilian control over the military is a vital one, for if government policy yields to the wishes of the people with bombers and tanks, it cannot be directed by those armed only with votes.

In an era of hostile power blocs there is no doubt that the President must have the capacity to respond rapidly and reasonably to missile-laden provocations. But we must recognize that presidential authority as commander in chief has come dangerously close to dictatorship in military matters.

The military power of a governor seems trivial in comparison, yet significant by any other standards. He is commander in chief of his state militia, or national guard, except when the President has called it into national service. When race riots, hurricanes, or other disasters require action beyond the capacity of local police officials to control, a governor's judgment in sending in the additional forces he controls may be decisive in the restoration of an orderly peace.

Checking the Other Branches

Chief executives are influenced by legislative and judicial bodies and, in the total system of checks and balances, exert reciprocal influences upon them.

The legislative initiative   As we noted in the last chapter, many laws originate in the desire of some legislator to provide benefits to his district or to assist some local citizen. Paradoxically, however, chief executives are the source of most major legislative proposals. Article II, Section 3 directs that the President shall "from time to time give to the Congress Information of the State of the Union, and recommend to their Consideration such Measures as he shall judge necessary and expedient . . ." This process has now become rather ritualized, with an annual State of the Union message usually delivered in person each January. In this address, the President spends less time describing what the state of the union is than what he would like it to be. He uses it to outline very broadly the kind of new legislation he would like to see Congress enact. This is followed in close succession by a proposed budget of more than a thousand pages requesting specific amounts of money for each govern- ment agency, and an economic report recommending congressional action to insure general prosperity. In the months that follow, the President dispatches special messages to Congress, prepared by various executive agencies, in which he requests the passage of specific bills outlined in great detail. This recommended legislation is then introduced by sympathetic congressmen. Since 1953 no President has sent fewer than 170 legislative proposals to Congress in a single year, nor have fewer than 20 percent been enacted into law.[3] As a result, it is now commonplace to speak of much recent legislation in such terms as "Johnson's war on poverty," or "Nixon's revenue-sharing program."

State legislatures have come to rely upon governors for legislative leadership even more than Congress looks to the President. They are often poorly equipped with the staff assistance or research facilities necessary to formulate the detailed legislative solutions required by increasingly complex problems. The result is that

it has become customary to call the governor "the chief legislator," in spite of the . . . principle of separation of powers. . . . (G)overnors are now judged primarily by their legislative program rather than by their administrative ability, and most voters as well as most state legislators expect the governor to have a legislative program on the major issues of public policy.[4]

A variety of vetoes   Other checks that the chief executive can exert on the legislative branch are to call special sessions, to adjourn the legislature if the two houses cannot reach agreement on a date, and to exercise the veto power. Of these, the last is by far the most important.

When a chief executive receives a bill, he may sign it,

3 *The New York Times Encyclopedic Almanac* 1970, p. 172, and *Congressional Quarterly Weekly Report,* Feb. 19, 1972, p. 375. When President Johnson won approval of 69 percent of those he submitted in 1965, he had a larger congressional majority of members of his own party than any President in over twenty-five years. By contrast, in 1971 President Nixon, scoring only 20 percent, was faced with an opposition party majority of four in the Senate and thirty-seven in the House.
4 Wilder Crane, Jr., and Meredith W. Watts, Jr., *State Legislative Systems* (Englewood Cliffs, N.J.: Prentice-Hall, Inc., 1968), p. 99.

thereby completing its enactment into law, or veto it by returning it to the house where it was introduced. He is usually given a certain number of days in which to make up his mind (the President has ten), and if he chooses to veto it, the decision is usually fatal for the bill. It takes two thirds of those voting in both houses of Congress to enact a bill by overriding a President's veto. More stringent requirements prevail in most state legislatures; in Alaska, for example, a three-quarters vote is required, and in many states two thirds of the total membership. On the other hand, in six states a simple majority of the total membership can override a veto, and in North Carolina the governor is without any veto power.[5]

Should the chief executive neither sign a bill nor veto it within the time allotted him, the bill normally becomes law automatically. But if legislators have adjourned and gone home before the time limit for the regular veto has expired, the President and a few governors may kill a bill through what is called a *pocket veto* simply by refusing to sign it. The effects of the veto on legislation passed at the national level are summarized in Figure 35.

Figure 35   Congressional Bills and Presidential Vetoes, 1953–1970

Bills Passed	Regular Vetoes	Pocket Vetoes	Overridden Vetoes
12,671	108	135	4

Source: U.S. Bureau of the Census, *Statistical Abstract of the United States: 1971*, pp. 355–56.

All but eight state governors have a kind of check on the legislature which the President lacks. This is the *item veto*, mentioned earlier, which enables them to reduce or eliminate certain expenditures in an appropriations bill while signing the others into law.[6] The item veto gives governors more control over state budgets than the President has over the national budget and makes passage of *pork barrel* legislation more difficult in state legislatures than in Congress.

Since pork barrel measures benefit a particular region or district, rather than a larger area, they are particularly helpful in getting incumbent legislators reelected. A new court house or bridge or state college for the "home folks" will provide construction jobs and looks pretty impressive in the campaign literature of the candidate who can claim credit for getting the money to build it. Proposals for such appropriations are usually attached to more important bills as amendments, or *riders*, mainly because their sponsors fear that the chief executive

5 An unusually perceptive commentary on this topic may be found in Duane Lockard, *The Politics of State and Local Government,* 2nd ed. (N.Y.: The Macmillan Company, 1969), pp. 363–66. The six states are Alabama, Arkansas, Kentucky, Indiana, Tennessee, and West Virginia. *The Book of the States,* 1970–71 (Lexington, Ky.: The Council of State Governments, 1970), p. 78.
6 The eight states are Indiana, Iowa, Maine, Nevada, New Hampshire, North Carolina, Rhode Island, and Vermont. A few state governors have the authority to reduce the amounts of money appropriated for various "items" as well as to delete them entirely.

would veto them unless they were tied to the expenditure of more vital funds. Legislators tend to vote for each other's pork barrel measures in the vote-trading process called *logrolling.*

Special sessions   The Constitution requires Congress to convene each January, and allows the President to call it into special session at his discretion. The mere suggestion that he may do so if action is not taken on certain bills is usually sufficient to prolong the regular session as long as is necessary. As a result, no President has called a special session since 1948. In over half the states, however, constitutions limit the length of regular sessions, and governors frequently resort to calling special sessions. Unlike the President, they can even limit the topics with which special sessions in about a third of the states may deal.[7]

The appointment of judges   All federal court judges are appointed by the President, subject to confirmation by the U.S. Senate. Since these judges are chosen for life, the selections may influence the judicial branch long after the President who made them has slipped into the history books. One of the nine judges on the U.S. Supreme Court in 1972, for example, had been appointed by a President who died a quarter of a century earlier. Although the governor may appoint some judges in several of the states, this power is a less significant check upon the judicial branch than that of the President in the national government. The whole matter is examined in the next chapter.

Executive clemency   Another check on the judicial process is the power of executive clemency which permits three kinds of orders: pardons, commutations, and reprieves. A pardon releases a person from further criminal punishment—usually a portion of a prison term. When whole groups of people are simultaneously pardoned, as frequently urged for draft resisters, the action is often called amnesty. A commutation is an executive order reducing a sentence imposed by the courts, and a reprieve simply postpones the time when a sentence is to begin.

The President has full powers of executive clemency over persons accused of violating national laws, but nearly half of the state governors have their authority over state law offenders curbed by constitutional restrictions, often involving approval by some pardon board. Yet the practical effects of the President's clemency powers are less significant, because most serious crimes are state, not national, offenses.

A Note on the Presidency

The similarities in the powers of the President and those of state governors have made it possible to discuss them together. In a deeper sense, however, the powers of the President are incomparable. Even if the mystique of his office can be penetrated and his authority categorized into its component elements, there is still the suspicion that

---

7 Donald R. Grant and H. C. Nixon, *State and Local Government in America* (Boston: Allyn and Bacon, Inc., 1963), p. 215.

the presidency, both as man and institution, somehow exceeds the sum of its parts.

The President's unique importance is best explained, perhaps, in terms of two curiously interrelated considerations: His authority is concentrated and his constituencies are numerous. On the first, it is well to note that Congress and the courts consist of many people, and their very multiplicity disperses the pressures brought by corporations, columnists, litigants, lobbyists, union leaders, and ordinary citizens throughout the nation. To influence national executive action, however, their ultimate target must be the man in the White House. He is the focus for the profusion of demands, desires, and fears that characterize this incredibly heterogeneous society.[8]

The President's constituencies, the groups which may affect his political future, are as varied as they are numerous. Most obviously, he is the only public official (discounting the Vice President) who is chosen by voters throughout the entire nation. This national constituency looks to him, as they have since the time of Washington, to transcend our infinite diversity by providing the moral leadership necessary to define our national purpose and attain our common goals. His international constituency, important only since World War II, sees in him the military assistance, trade concessions, or financial aid sometimes necessary for survival. Less broad but also significant are two domestic constituencies. One is the partisan coalition which supported his candidacy (campaign workers, party leaders, financial contributors, and so forth), and the other consists of congressmen and administrative officials—the bureaucracy—without whose help his efforts are doomed to failure.[9]

Taken together, these multiple constituencies impose on the President the obligation to meet an awesome array of sometimes contradictory expectations. His enormous power is scarcely commensurate with the demands made upon it, yet the very immensity of the challenge holds out a promise of greatness.

THE MAKING AND MAINTENANCE OF CHIEF EXECUTIVES
Room at the Top—for Whom?

The office of chief executive is the highest rung on the ladder of political success. What are the characteristics of those who have occupied it?

Qualifications for office The President and Vice President must meet constitutional standards set forth in Article II, Section 1. They must be citizens by birth, at least thirty-five years old, and must have resided in the United States for fourteen years or more. It seems doubtful

8 James MacGregor Burns, *Congress on Trial* (N.Y.: Harper & Bros., 1949), pp. 181–92.
9 Richard E. Neustadt, "The Presidency at Mid-Century," *Law and Contemporary Problems* 21 (Autumn 1956): 609–45.

Paul Sequeira.

His car well protected, President Nixon is acclaimed by supporters in suburbia.

that many political careers have been thwarted by these requirements. The state constitutional requirements for governors are somewhat similar, although less stringent, and are also of very little practical political consequence.

Characteristics of chief executives While millions of Americans meet the minimum legal qualifications for President, it is clear that few hurdle the informal barriers erected by an accumulation of traditions, myths, and considerations of political expediency. If the characteristics of the thirty-six persons who have become President are a guide to the kinds of people who have the best chance in the future, the field can be narrowed substantially. A composite description reveals that the "average" President is a male Caucasian, in his fifties, of English or Scotch-Irish descent. He is most often a lawyer who has previously served as a governor or U.S. senator.

The youngest ever to serve were Theodore Roosevelt at forty-two and John F. Kennedy at forty-three while the oldest were William Henry Harrison at sixty-eight and Dwight D. Eisenhower at seventy. There have been no non-Christians and only one Roman Catholic (Kennedy), although four had no formal religious affiliation. Methodists and Baptists, most numerous among Protestant denominations in the general population, have each sent only two to the White House, while among the churches of higher socioeconomic status, Episcopalians can claim nine Presidents, Presbyterians seven, and Unitarians four. All Presidents have descended from Irish, English, French,

Dutch, German, or Swiss stock.[10] Times, of course, are changing. Vice President Spiro Agnew is of Greek extraction and his opponent in 1968, Sen. Edmund Muskie, is of Polish parentage.

One can not be sure of the significance of these characteristics, or of the very similar ones shared by most congressmen and judges. It is plausible, however, that officials drawn so predominantly from the ranks of the relatively privileged may have difficulty understanding the problems, let alone the attitudes, of those less favored. Conversely, groups such as the poor, members of ethnic minorities, young people, and women may become increasingly alienated from a society that passes them by so frequently in recruiting its top leadership.

There was once considerable discussion about "availability" as a factor in choosing presidential nominees. The most available candidates were said to be those who possessed the characteristics of the previous Presidents, plus the advantage of coming from a large, politically doubtful state. The theory was that a party should nominate a man from a state with many electoral votes which the party might not win if it chose someone from somewhere else. But since television has demonstrated its ability to publicize almost anyone from anywhere in just a few weeks, this concept has been largely abandoned. Coverage by the mass media has also shifted attention from the presidential possibilities of governors, who cope mostly with state problems, to the potentialities of U.S. senators who speak out on national and international issues. Ideologically, a moderate image is an enormous asset. The "log cabin" tradition, moreover, occupies a nostalgic place in American political lore. It assumed that any boy could grow up to be President, and that a poor boy who made good had an even better chance. Recent history indicates that humble origins are neither a help nor a hindrance, as long as one can raise $25 million or so for a presidential campaign. There is another aspect of availability that still endures: the family man. No divorced man has ever been President (although this is no doubt a less serious liability than in the past), and we have elected only one bachelor.

It is reasonable to assume that many of the same characteristics that made for presidential availability also would improve one's chances for gaining a governorship. The backgrounds of governors, however, seem to reveal considerable diversity. A recent study shows that the largest number were lawyers in their late forties. Teaching ranked second as an occupational background.[11] Not surprisingly, all were males.

The Election Process

The procedures by which chief executives are chosen are sometimes complex and often controversial.

10 Most of this information came from *The New York Times Encyclopedic Almanac* 1972, pp. 62–63.
11 Grant and Nixon, op. cit., p. 213.

The electoral college   If every voter had to understand the whole process by which the President and Vice President are elected, chances are that we would never be able to choose them at all. The fact that we do is a triumph of common sense over legal technicalities, a conquest of function over form.

At the constitutional convention, a major controversy raged over who should elect the President. The compromise finally agreed upon provided that he should be chosen by an electoral college, but with the understanding that each state could select its members however it wished. It was further agreed that each state would have the same number of electors in the electoral college as it had members of Congress (two in the Senate plus as many in the House of Representatives as its population warranted).

Initially, each elector was to cast two votes. The person receiving the most votes would be President, and the person placing second would be Vice President. If no candidate received a majority, the election of the President was transferred to the House of Representatives, where all congressmen from each state were given a single vote. If the person finishing second lacked a majority in the electoral college, then the election of the Vice President became the responsibility of the U.S. Senate.

This procedure, outlined in Article II, Section 1, worked smoothly until 1800 when a tied vote in the electoral college between Thomas Jefferson and Aaron Burr (who belonged to the same party) threw the election into a long and bitter fight in the House of Representatives. After thirty-six ballots, and with the support of Alexander Hamilton, his long-time foe, Jefferson was elected President. This crisis prompted the ratification of the Twelfth Amendment which provided that each member of the electoral college should cast one vote for President and a second, separate vote for Vice President.

The actual implementation of these constitutional provisions was quite undemocratic originally. In the first place, until the ninth presidential election in 1824, members of the electoral college in most states were chosen by the state legislatures. The sequence is as follows:

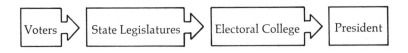

Gradually, however, state laws were changed to eliminate the state legislatures from this process and to permit the voters to elect members of the electoral college directly, as they do today in every state.

A second major change has democratized the process still more. Candidates for the electoral college are now nominated on political party tickets and pledged in advance to vote for the presidential nominee of their party. It was the rise of political parties, therefore, that transformed the role of the individual member of the electoral college from that of a free agent voting for whom he pleased to that of a political mirror, merely reflecting the voters' preference for his party's candidate. In each state, indeed, the electoral college selects the choice of the voters so automatically that in most states the ballots contain only the names of the presidential and vice presidential contenders, and not the names of the candidates for the electoral college who are committed to vote for them.

Political parties have had another effect on the process of electing the President: As a result of the two-party system, one of the major party candidates is almost certain to get a majority in the electoral college, thereby minimizing the possibility that a presidential election will be thrown into the House of Representatives. Only twice in our history, in 1800 and again in 1824, has there been a third candidate sufficiently popular to prevent an electoral college majority. It could, of course, happen again, and the third-party candidacy of George Wallace in 1968 came closer than any in more than fifty years to doing just that.

Electoral college reform   The electoral college, cumbersome and archaic as it is, might seem to be only a harmless relic of the dead past. Yet the number of reform proposals, pushed with great vigor, belies such a generous assessment. There are two major criticisms of the present system. One is that nothing can prevent a member of the electoral college, if he wishes, from voting for someone other than the candidate of his party. This has never altered the outcome of a presidential election, but to avoid this possibility, President Lyndon B. Johnson proposed that individual electors be eliminated and electoral votes be automatically awarded to the candidate with the most popular votes in each state.

The second, and more serious, accusation against the electoral college is that it permits the election of a President whose opponent received more popular votes. This objection cannot be dismissed lightly, for it actually occurred after the elections of 1824, 1876, and 1888. The voters' second choice became President. The cause of this perversion of the democratic process is that members of the electoral college are elected at large in each state. As a result, if a candidate carries a state by just one vote, he wins all of that state's electoral votes. This situation has had a profound effect on presidential campaign strategy and has enhanced the importance of populous urban areas in presidential elections, since it is the states with big cities that have many electoral votes.

Let us take a hypothetical example of how this situation might affect the next presidential election. Assume that the two candidates are running neck and neck throughout the nation as a whole, both in popular and electoral votes, and that the result will depend on the outcome of races in California and North Dakota. In California, each voter is voting for forty-five members of the electoral college and in North Dakota for three members. Finally, the vote count is completed, and results are announced:

Figure 36   How A Majority Can Lose

	Popular Vote		Electoral Vote	
	Republican	Democratic	Republican	Democratic
North Dakota	160,000	80,000	3	0
California	3,390,000	3,400,000	0	45
Total	3,550,000	3,480,000	3	45

Given such a distribution of votes, the Democratic candidate would win in the electoral college, even though his Republican opponent was favored by more people. Such an injustice can occur whenever one candidate carries the large urbanized states (*e.g.,* California) by even a few votes, while losing the small predominantly rural states (*e.g.,* North Dakota) by a substantial margin.

Several reforms have been suggested to eliminate this possibility. The Lodge-Gossett plan would split a state's electoral vote in the same proportion as the division of the popular vote. Former Senator Karl Mundt (R.-N. D.) would permit the people to elect one member of the electoral college from each congressional district and choose only two at large from every state. A final plan, already proposed as a constitutional amendment by a two-thirds vote of the House of Representatives, would abolish the electoral college completely in favor of a direct vote by the people. It includes the proviso that if no candidate receives at least 40 percent of the popular vote, a runoff election would be held between the two candidates with the most votes.

Those who favor the retention of the electoral college contend that its abolition would undermine the importance of the states and encourage the formation of minor parties. Some also suggest that since the U.S. Senate overrepresents small states in the Congress, the electoral college should be preserved because it enhances the importance of voters in the big states. People who want a direct popular vote for President rest their case chiefly on the grounds of simplicity and the assumption that it conforms most closely to the democratic theory of majority rule.

The choice of state executives   The President and the Vice President are the only officials in the entire national government who are chosen by and responsible to a nation-wide constituency. At the state level things are different. In addition to the governor and the lieutenant governor, the voters often elect four or five other state-wide executive officials, most commonly the attorney general, secretary of state, treasurer, and auditor (or controller). The number of officials appointed by the governor is correspondingly reduced.

The process by which state executives gain office is a simple one. They are nearly always nominated in party primaries and elected by a direct vote of the people. In Georgia and Vermont, however, the election is thrown into the state legislature if no candidate receives a majority of the popular vote.

Service and Succession

Many perils confront a chief executive, including death and defeat when seeking reelection. It is one measure of the hazards of the presidency that somewhat more than one in five have died in office. Four Presidents died naturally (W. H. Harrison, Taylor, Harding, and F. D. Roosevelt) and four were shot (Lincoln, Garfield, McKinley, and Kennedy). Governors seem to fare much better; they tend to be younger and make less dramatic targets.

Terms and salaries   Originally, no limit was placed on the number of four-year terms a President might serve. The examples of Washington, Jefferson, Madison, Monroe, and Jackson soon established a two-term tradition, however, and it was not until Franklin D. Roosevelt was elected to a third term in 1940 and a fourth in 1944 that this precedent was broken. Amendment Twenty-two was designed to prevent repetition of the Roosevelt example and limited the President to two terms or (if he had served a portion of his predecessor's term) no more than ten years in office.

A few state governors are elected for two-year terms, but a steadily growing majority are chosen for four. In some states, governors may be reelected without limitation, and in 1970 New York voters returned Nelson Rockefeller to an unprecedented fourth four-year term. Often governors are prohibited from seeking a second *successive* term out of fear that they may accumulate excessive power, and sometimes they face the same limitations as Presidents—no more than a two-term total. Only once, in North Dakota, was a governor removed in a recall election.

While in office, the President receives a salary of $200,000 per year, and the reimbursement for governors ranges from about $18,000 to $55,000. Housing accommodations and expense accounts are also provided.

Succession   The problem of an orderly succession process for filling vacant executive offices is still unsolved in many nations, where leadership often is seized by disgruntled military officers and consolidated by purges of all potential rivals. In the United States, the Constitution (Article II, Section 1) provides that the Vice President shall assume the powers and duties of the President in the event of his removal, death, resignation, or inability. It gives Congress the power to provide for succession if both the President and Vice President are disqualified and the Speaker of the House of Representatives is now next in line of succession, followed by the president pro tem of the Senate and cabinet officials beginning with the Secretary of State. Fortunately, only Vice Presidents have been summoned to fill a vacant presidency, and the torch has always been passed peacefully.

The presidential transition process might have proved more awkward if a President had died when the nation was without a Vice President. This situation has existed fifteen times—on the eight occasions when former Vice Presidents were forced to become Presidents, and during the periods immediately following the deaths of seven Vice Presidents. The possibility of a prolonged vice-presidential vacancy was eliminated by the Twenty-fifth Amendment, which requires the President to appoint a Vice President, should there be none, subject to the confirmation of a majority vote in the House and Senate.

When governorships become vacant before the term of office expires, the lieutenant governor fills the vacancy, except in ten states where there is no such official. In these states, the presiding officer of one of the state legislative chambers assumes the governorship.[12]

The problem of disability   Although the Constitution authorizes the Vice President to take over when the President is unable to discharge his powers and duties, it does not say what constitutes inability or who should determine whether it exists. As a result, no Vice President, no matter how sick or incapacitated the President has been, has dared to displace him. Thus, while President Garfield lay for more than two months in a coma, and again during the prolonged illnesses of Presidents Cleveland, Wilson, and Eisenhower, the ship of state drifted more or less aimlessly (although fortunately in placid waters).

The Twenty-fifth Amendment, in addition to providing a way to fill vice-presidential vacancies, establishes methods to cope with presidential disability. It permits the President to declare himself disabled, or—if he does not or cannot—it allows the Vice President and a majority of either the cabinet, or of some other body designated by Congress, to declare him disabled. Should the President object, the matter is submitted to Congress, with a two-thirds vote of both houses necessary to overrule him.

THE ADMINISTRATIVE BUREAUCRACY

Executives get their name from the fact that it has been their historic function, in the words of Article II, Section 3, to "take Care that the Laws be faithfully executed . . ." In other words, they administer, enforce, and thus carry out the laws. With thousands of statutes on the books, enormous administrative bureaucracies have been created to help them. They consist, in part, of the departments, commissions, and other agencies described below.

National Executive Organization

If the President spent just one hour a week supervising each of the agencies directly responsible to him in the executive branch, he would have about a sixty-hour work week, and would have to sign or veto bills, plan new legislative programs, grant pardons, appoint judges, discharge his ceremonial obligations, and perform all the rest of his

12 Ibid., pp. 218–19.

functions in what little time was left. Confronted with such overwhelming tasks, he does the best he can; he appoints people he trusts to head the various executive agencies, and usually intervenes personally only when troubles arise. Yet he knows that the ultimate responsibility is his.

The agencies reporting to the President may be grouped into four categories: (1) the departments headed by cabinet members; (2) agencies in the Executive Office of the President; (3) regulatory commissions; and (4) government corporations—with a substantial number left over. Only the most important can be mentioned here, but first, a few words on the vice presidency—an office too much maligned.

The vice presidency   John Adams, our first Vice President, complained that his was "the most insignificant office that ever the invention of man contrived or his imagination conceived." It has never quite recovered from that assessment. Theodore Roosevelt was put in the post to get rid of him as governor of New York, and John Garner, a salty old Texan who had the job for eight years, is said to have advised Lyndon Johnson not to take it because he believed the vice presidency wasn't "worth a bucket of warm spit."

Yet, since eight Vice Presidents (including Theodore Roosevelt and Lyndon Johnson) have assumed the presidency because of the deaths of their predecessors, the office obviously has great potential. But it is also important in itself.

In addition to presiding over the Senate and "checking the President's health," Vice Presidents have been delegated increased responsibility in the last quarter of a century. Perhaps the most powerful was Richard M. Nixon, whom President Eisenhower authorized to call cabinet meetings and exercise surveillance over the administration while he was recuperating from his several illnesses. Mr. Nixon also assumed many party campaign responsibilities for the President and represented him at a variety of ceremonial functions. The Vice President has increasingly become something of a world traveler, commissioned by the President to make various goodwill or fact-finding tours. He is also chairman of the National Space Council, director of the Office of Intergovernmental Relations, and a member of the National Security Council.

The point is not that the Vice President is an inherently powerful executive, but that he may become as important as the President wishes. His office is a largely untapped resource but one that has attained increasing public visibility in recent years. Vice President Agnew, for example, has succeeded in attracting more publicity and infuriating the political opposition to a greater degree than any Vice President in history—with the possible exception of Richard Nixon. The most important evidence of the growing stature of the vice-presidential office is its increasing effectiveness, demonstrated by both Nixon in 1960 and Hubert Humphrey in 1968, as a springboard to a presidential nomination.

The departments   The eleven departments now in the ex-

Figure 37   The Structure of the National Government

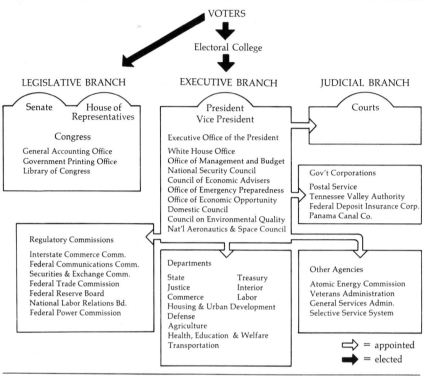

Note: Many agencies are not shown.
Source: U.S. Bureau of the Census, *Statistical Abstract of the United States: 1971*, p. 371.

ecutive branch have been created by Congress over many years. These agencies are among the most prestigious in government, and their heads, usually called secretaries, constitute the nucleus of the President's cabinet. Traditionally, four departments (State, Defense, Treasury, and Justice) have been considered more important than the others, although expanded welfare programs and increased concern with environmental pollution have focused much attention on the Department of Health, Education and Welfare and the Department of the Interior. The relative influence of all the departments depends, in part, on the people who head them, and their distinctive relationships to the President. A list of the departments, with their major functions, appears in Figure 38.

The Executive Office of the President   The Executive Office is actually a collection of agencies which provide the President with advice, assistance, and coordinated effort in various fields. Among the more important are the Council on Environmental Quality, the Cost of Living Council, the Office of Emergency Preparedness, the Office of Economic Opportunity, and the four others whose descriptions follow.

The National Security Council integrates foreign policy formulation, in this respect eclipsing the functions of the State Department to some degree. It consists of the President, Vice President,

Figure 38   Executive Departments in the National Government

Department and date established	1971 Employees[1]	Major Functions
State, 1789	39,513	Supervises diplomatic personnel; advises on foreign policy; administers foreign aid.
Defense, 1947[2]	1,145,696[2]	Coordinates budgeting, logistics, and general administration of armed services; supervises Joint Chiefs of Staff; awards military contracts.
Treasury, 1789	98,173	Collects taxes; coins money; sells bonds; runs Secret Service to enforce laws in this area and protect government leaders.
Justice, 1870[3]	40,828	Administers F.B.I. to enforce acts of Congress; prosecutes court cases for U.S. government; maintains federal prisons; investigates violations of antitrust and civil rights laws; gives legal advice to government; supervises immigration.
Health, Education and Welfare, 1953[4]	110,100	Administers social security pension and Medicare programs, federal aid to education, pure food and drug laws, and public health research and assistance.
Interior, 1849	64,577	Administers Bureau of Indian Affairs, mine safety laws, conservation of mineral resources, national parks, overseas territories, some hydroelectric power facilities.
Agriculture, 1862	105,006	Guarantees minimum prices on certain crops; stores food surpluses; provides crop insurance; administers national forests; helps finance farm services.
Commerce, 1903	37,012	Awards patents; promotes exports of U.S. products; administers Bureau of the Census and Weather Bureau.
Labor, 1913[5]	11,246	Enforces minimum wage laws; administers unemployment compensation; mediates some labor-management disputes; compiles cost-of-living statistics.
Housing and Urban Development, 1965	15,544	Directs urban renewal financial grants, government-guaranteed home purchase loans, and public housing assistance.
Transportation, 1966	68,126	Administers interstate highway programs, air safety standards, automotive safety laws, the Alaska railroad, and Coast Guard.

[1] U.S. Bureau of the Census, *Statistical Abstract of the United States: 1971*, p. 389.
[2] The Defense Department replaced the War Department, in charge of army affairs, and the Navy Department, both established in 1789. The employment figure includes civilians only.
[3] The office of Attorney General was created in 1789 but he was given no departmental responsibility until 1870.
[4] The national government performed functions in these fields through separate agencies long before the department was created.
[5] The Labor Department was once a part of a Department of Commerce and Labor.

Secretaries of State and Defense, and Director of the Office of Emergency Preparedness; others may also participate. The Central Intelligence Agency, which gathers and interprets vital information concerning security matters, reports to the NSC.

The White House Office is an organizational extension of the President himself—it helps to manage his time, fill his brain, disseminate his thoughts, and execute his commands. More than any other agency, it is a monument to the institutionalization of the presidency. The nation's highest office, in a sense, has outgrown the man who holds it. It expands inexorably, as though reaching out to grapple with each new complexity in the nation it seeks to govern. To some degree, the White House Office is molded by the personal preferences of each President. Individual titles come and go; President Nixon has employed over fifty persons variously designated as counselors, assistants, special consultants, deputy assistants, deputy counselors, special assistants, and secretaries. The purposes for which the last few Presidents have used these officials have become rather standardized. Several are speech writers, one may act almost as a junior-grade president, and another serves as a press secretary in charge of press releases and news conferences. Usually included are a chief adviser for national security matters (the invaluable Henry Kissinger in the Nixon administration) and a congressional liaison man, who acts as the President's chief lobbyist. These men are closest to the President— they accompany him to Camp David on his weekend retreats and are privy to his deepest political desires. If one wanted to understand President Nixon's view of the world in 1972, one would need to inquire into the vistas opened to him by Kissinger, H. R. Haldeman, Ronald Ziegler, John Ehrlichman, Robert Finch, and other leading figures in the White House Office.

Perhaps the most important tool available to a President in establishing national priorities is his authority to recommend allocations of money to Congress. The proposed budget is prepared primarily by the Office of Management and Budget, to which all other government agencies must submit estimates of desired expenditures.

The Council of Economic Advisers is one of the smallest agencies in the national government, employing less than sixty people. Yet its three members are charged with the responsibility of providing the President with the most able economic advice about how to curb inflation and unemployment, while increasing both the living standard and the gross national product.

Regulatory commissions   Among the many "independent" agencies of the national government—those not embraced by the eleven departments or the Executive Office of the President—are the commissions charged with protecting the public by regulating various phases of private business activity. In this area, a distinction should be made between those industries in which public policy has sanctioned monopolistic control by a single corporation, and those in which government has encouraged free and vigorous competition among many firms.

Monopoly is most common in the public utility industries whose services are vital to the entire population. If two electricity, natural gas, railroad, or telephone companies were competing in the same area, for example, there would be duplicate wires, pipes, and rails, thereby increasing costs, cutting the profits of each corporation, and resulting in higher rates for the consumer. In the radio and television industries, it is essential to grant each station a monopoly on a particular wave length so that the audience will not be plagued by two or more programs (to say nothing of commercials) simultaneously. Yet if consumer choice is limited by monopolistic control, as it often is, who is to grant the monopolies? Who is to protect the public from the abuses that may result—exorbitant rates, sloppy service, or poor programming?

The answers, presumably, are the regulatory commissions of the national and state governments which grant franchises, impose rate limitations, and establish minimum standards. Some of these agen-

Figure 39   Regulatory Commissions in the National Government

Commission and Date Established	No. of Members	Terms	Functions
Interstate Commerce Commission, 1887	11	7 yrs.	Licenses and fixes rates for railroads, trucks, buses, and domestic shipping.
Federal Reserve Board, 1913	7	14 yrs.	Controls supply of currency and certain banking policies.
Federal Trade Commission, 1914	5	7 yrs.	Assists in enforcing antitrust laws and prohibits false advertising.
Federal Power Commission, 1920	5	5 yrs.	Regulates prices and services in electric power and natural gas industries.
Federal Communications Commission, 1934	7	7 yrs.	Grants radio and television licenses and fixes rates for telegraph and telephone services.[1]
Securities and Exchange Commission, 1934	5	5 yrs.	Licenses stock and bond brokers and protects market investors.
National Labor Relations Board, 1935	5	5 yrs.	Holds elections to determine union collective bargaining rights and forbids unfair practices.
Civil Aeronautics Board, 1938	5	6 yrs.	Assigns airline routes and regulates rates and services.
Federal Maritime Commission, 1961	5	5 yrs.	Regulates dock charges and foreign routes for American merchant ships.

[1] Citing a shortage of funds and staff members, the FCC announced in December of 1971 that it was abandoning an attempt to investigate the fairness of rates charged for interstate phone calls. Its decision was widely criticized and later modified.

cies impose certain controls upon competitive industries as well. The functions of the major ones are indicated in Figure 39.

Regulatory commissions differ from most other executive agencies in four respects. First, they have what is sometimes called quasi-legislative and quasi-judicial powers, which simply means that they function somewhat like lawmaking bodies in formulating rules for the corporations they regulate, and somewhat like courts in holding hearings relative to those rules. Second, they are multiheaded agencies whose decisions, because of their complex nature, are made by groups rather than by single administrators. Third, they are bipartisan in membership to insure a representation of both parties and, it is hoped, diverse attitudes. Finally, they have considerable independence from the President, to make sure—among other things—that he cannot intimidate them into granting preferred treatment to corporations in which his friends own stock. Members of these commissions are appointed for specific terms of office and cannot be fired (except for demonstrated cause) until their terms have expired. In fact, these agencies are so independent that they are sometimes viewed as a fourth branch of the government.[13]

The major criticism levied against the regulatory commissions is that their relative independence from overall government control has allowed them to fall under the influence of the business interests from whose ranks their members are often chosen. Corporation-oriented wolves, it is argued, are sent to guard the defenseless chickens. As *Newsweek* magazine summed up the allegation, "the [regulatory] agencies seem more concerned with serving the industries they are supposed to regulate than with protecting the public."[14]

Government corporations   There are about twenty government-owned corporations in the national government created to sell some form of services that will defray all or a large part of their operating expenses. The newest of these—the U.S. Postal Service, created in 1970—is also by far the largest. Before the new corporation was established, the post office was operated as a government department whose 727,645 employees made it second only to the Defense Department among all government employers.[15]

Previously, the Tennessee Valley Authority, providing hydroelectric power, flood control, and recreation facilities in seven southeastern states,[16] was the largest government corporation, although the Federal Deposit Insurance Corporation, guaranteeing private bank de-

13 A mammoth collection of court decisions, official documents, and enlightened commentary on the regulatory commissions may be found in *Separation of Powers and the Independent Agencies: Cases and Selected Readings* (Washington, D. C.: U.S. Government Printing Office, 1970).
14 August 24, 1970, p. 45.
15 U.S. Bureau of the Census, *The Statistical Abstract of the United States: 1970,* pp. 396–97.
16 A favorable account of the TVA, often condemned as America's most socialistic enterprise, is found in David E. Lilienthal, *TVA: Democracy on the March* (Chicago: Quadrangle Books, Inc., 1944).

posits up to $20,000, and the Panama Canal Company are also important. Even more than the regulatory commissions, government corporations are largely independent of presidential control. They are also favorite targets of right-wing attacks upon socialistic programs.

Miscellaneous agencies There are many other agencies in the executive branch that cannot be squeezed into neat administrative pigeonholes. One of these, the Veterans Administration, is next only to the Defense Department and Post Office in number of employees and dispenses G.I. college benefits, administers veterans' hospitals, and allocates funds for pensions. Lest it run low on clients, another government agency, the Selective Service System, has been busily providing new ones.

The General Services Administration is also too important to be ignored. It employs over 38,000 people, yet is engaged in activities that command no headlines and little attention. It is responsible for the purchasing of supplies and the management of property for many other government agencies in order to reduce the waste of tax money and duplication of government activities.

From spoils to merit: the civil service During most of our early history, the victorious presidential candidate appointed his friends and supporters—almost always members of his own party—to public office. Although this *spoils* or *patronage* system is correctly associated with President Andrew Jackson, on a smaller scale its origins go back to 1801 when the control of the national government was first transferred from one party to another. Jackson justified the system by a principle of rotation in office, arguing that the potential corruption of government employees could be checked by replacing them with some frequency. He insisted, moreover, that almost any man had enough common sense to hold almost any job and that it was democratic, therefore, to give as many people as possible an opportunity to work for the government.

However worthy Jackson's intentions may have been, the spoils system deprived the government of experienced workers and often resulted in the appointment of men of dubious competence. An alternative system was available. The Prussian government had been hiring people on the basis of merit since late in the seventeenth century and England followed suit in 1853. In America, not until after the issue was dramatized by the assassination of President James A. Garfield by a disgruntled job seeker did any significant reform occur. In 1883 Congress passed the Pendleton Act creating a Civil Service Commission to supervise the selection of government employees on the basis of merit as demonstrated in competitive examinations. Although less than 15 percent of all jobs were initially covered, the merit system has gradually expanded to include more than 90 percent of the civilian employees of the United States government.

The Civil Service Commission consists of three persons appointed by the President, only two of whom may belong to the same party. From offices in ten cities scattered throughout the nation, it

Figure 40   Some Characteristics of Civilian Employees of the United States Government

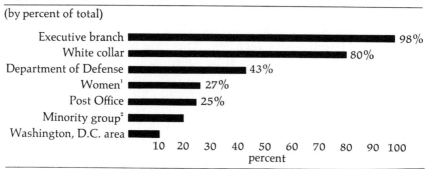

(by percent of total)

Executive branch	98%
White collar	80%
Department of Defense	43%
Women[1]	27%
Post Office	25%
Minority group[2]	
Washington, D.C. area	

10 20 30 40 50 60 70 80 90 100
percent

[1] Over half are employed in clerical, office, health, management, and library capacities.
[2] About 78 percent are blacks. Of government employees with the highest job classifications (GS 12–GS 18) 4.5 percent are members of minority groups.
Source: U.S. Bureau of the Census, *Statistical Abstract of the United States: 1971*, pp. 388–90.

coordinates employment, promotion, and dismissal procedures for most agencies in the executive branch, although some, such as the Foreign Service in the State Department, the F.B.I., and the Tennessee Valley Authority, maintain their own merit systems independently.

In 1971 there were 2,847,000 civilians employed by the national government, a number larger than the total populations of any of the twenty-six smallest states and nearly three times the number employed in 1940. These federal employees possessed a range of occupations almost as diverse as the entire economy, and included about 149,000 engineers and architects, 113,000 accountants and budget specialists, 94,000 medical personnel, 48,000 lawyers and legal assistants, 34,000 social scientists, 26,000 machine tool operators, 13,000 painters and paperhangers, and 65,000 manual laborers.[17] Related information about the federal civil service is found in Figure 40.

The overwhelming majority of government employees, after passing the appropriate examinations, are given job classifications in one of the General Schedule (GS) grades, numbered from 1 to 18 and paying, in 1971, from $4326 to $36,000 per year. Employment procedures include two important rules: The hiring officer in each bureau must fill each vacancy by employing one of the three persons scoring highest on the civil service examination, and on each examination disabled veterans, their wives, or their widows are given a ten-point bonus; any veteran receives a five-point bonus. After a probationary period, civil service employees cannot be fired without a public hearing, and under certain circumstances may appeal to the Civil Service Commission itself. All in all, government employment represents a potential career of considerable attractiveness.

17 U.S. Bureau of the Census, *The Statistical Abstract of the United States: 1971,* p. 390.

State Executive Organization

Not counting the cities, counties, and other agencies of local government, the fifty states employ over two-and-one-half million people—nearly as many as the civilians working for the national government. Even though the merit system has not gained so wide an acceptance at the state as at the national level, most employees in most states are recruited and protected by civil service procedures. State administrative organization, with few exceptions, differs most markedly from the national government in the dispersion and fragmentation of executive authority. In theory, the governor is a chief executive; in fact, there are many popularly elected "chiefs," each with his own staff of state employees.

The lieutenant governorships   Although his office is generally modeled upon the vice presidency, the lieutenant governor's usually exceeds it in power. If the governor is out of the state, for example, many states give the lieutenant governor full powers as acting governor. In Indiana and Florida he may also serve as the head of some administrative department,[18] while in California, and many other states, he is an automatic *ex-officio* member of a number of commissions dealing with such matters as the management of state lands and the administration of the state university.[19] The lieutenant governorship differs from the vice presidency in another respect. In a majority of states, the lieutenant governor is elected separately, and therefore may even belong to a different party than the governor.

Other elected executives   In forty-four of the states, the heads of five or more state agencies are chosen by the voters and in seven of them over ten agencies fall in this category.[20] At the other extreme, the governor has the widest discretion in appointing his executive subordinates in Alaska, Hawaii, Maryland, New Hampshire, New Jersey, and Pennsylvania.

The state executive posts most frequently filled by popular election, aside from governor and lieutenant governor, are secretary of state, attorney general, treasurer, and auditor. The secretary of state usually records official documents and laws, grants charters incorporating businesses, and supervises election machinery all the way from the printing of ballots to the counting of votes. The attorney general is the legal adviser to the governor, state legislature, and all executive agencies; he represents the state in court when it is suing or being sued, and usually oversees the prosecution of criminal cases. State treasurers have custody over tax receipts, allocate money to other agencies on the basis

18 Snider, op. cit., p. 269, and *The Book of the States,* 1970–71, op. cit., p. 138.
19 Winston W. Crouch, *et al., California Government and Politics,* 4th ed. (Englewood Cliffs, N.J.: Prentice-Hall, Inc.; 1967), p. 161.
20 The seven states placing the most executive positions beyond gubernatorial control are Georgia, Louisiana, Mississippi, North Carolina, North Dakota, Oklahoma, and South Carolina. *The Book of the States,* 1970–71, op. cit., pp. 146–47.

of state legislative appropriations, and, in many cases, sell bonds when the state must borrow money. Auditors, often called state controllers, have the job of checking on state expenditures, much as the head of the General Accounting Office does in the national government. They also enforce financial restrictions on cities and counties.[21] The governor's authority is further diminished in several states by the popular election of public school superintendents, agricultural commissioners, and other executive officials.

Major departments and other agencies   Most state executive departments are under the control of persons chosen by the governors, and employ a majority of the people on state payrolls. Combined employment figures for the fifty states reveal the relative significance of major state agencies:

1) Higher education	623,918
2) Hospitals	406,789
3) Highways	293,089
4) Natural resources	122,893
5) Financial administration	88,177
6) Public welfare	83,558[22]

In addition, each state has a public utility or public service commission, responsible for regulating rates and services within each state for the electric power, telephone, bus, natural gas, and similar industries. Other major state agencies license motor vehicles and drivers, enforce minimum standards for doctors, lawyers, pharmacists, barbers, morticians, and other occupations, and operate state parks and other outdoor recreational facilities.

The Problem of Bureaucratic Responsibility

At both the national and state levels of government, the central problem posed by administrative bureaucracies is how to make them accountable to the people—or to officials elected by the people. There is a widespread feeling that bureaucracies mean rule-bound, delay-filled indifference to the citizen and that they are unduly high in both operating costs and in project failures. The Federal Housing Administration has been criticized for granting mortgage insurance on "almost totally defective" homes,[23] compensatory education programs have been of little value in many instances,[24] and a subcommittee of the House of Representatives has reported that nearly $1.5 billion has been given to the states by the federal Law Enforcement Assistance Administration without any "visible impact on the incidence of crime." The

21 Snider, op. cit., pp. 277–80.
22 *The Book of the States, 1970–71,* op. cit., p. 180.
23 *Congressional Quarterly Weekly Report,* June 24, 1972, p. 1538.
24 Ibid., May 6, 1972, p. 1009.

Mary Rosenfeld, Nancy Palmer
Photo Agency.

At all levels of government, bucking bureaucracies has become a difficult problem. Here a young father complains of inaction on conditions in his rundown housing project in Somerville, Massachusetts.

report concluded that the program had been characterized by "inefficiency, waste, maladministration and, in some cases, corruption."[25] All too often, the bureaucracy seems to be a self-serving entity—too important to abolish and too complex to control.

Such charges are important because government directly touches most people's lives through the executive bureaucracies. Somewhere in an administrative office many decisions are made affecting the ordinary citizen's life—here will be granted or denied one's right to practice a profession, here will be set restrictions on where and how one can build his house, here will be determined how safe one's food will be, what textbooks one's children will read, where roads shall be constructed, and whether or not one is eligible for specific welfare grants and services. Thus, in applying general laws to concrete cases, administrators in effect have a policy-making role of great consequence.

There is no easy way for either voters or their elected officials to compel a vast bureaucracy to carry out its role in the public's interest. Random checks may be made, flagrant abuses may be investigated, but still the most constant vigilance is required. Here perhaps is one place where we rely on the pervasive influence of our political culture with its stress on the rule of law, the importance of fair treatment, and procedures for redress of grievances.

To some degree, the dozens of departments, bureaus, and commissions that make up the national and state bureaucracies can be made more efficient by reorganizing the executive branches. This was done in the early 1950s at the national level as a result of recommendations made by a commission headed by former President Herbert Hoo-

25 *Los Angeles Times,* April 10, 1972, p. 1.

ver. Many agencies that previously had reported directly to the White House were consolidated, and the President's administrative task thereby lightened. But twenty years passed, new agencies were created, and President Nixon concluded that reorganization was again required. He created a Domestic Council within the Executive Office of the President to provide better coordination among various agencies and asked Congress, to no avail, for the legislation necessary to combine eight existing departments into four new ones. At the state level, there seems little progress toward consolidating executive agencies under gubernatorial control.

But true responsibility is more than efficiency. Executive agencies are filled with thousands of experts who are inherently irresponsible because their jobs are so specialized that neither the President and governors nor the voters can understand what they are doing. When physical and social scientists testify that they need X number of new employees or X number of dollars to develop a harmless pesticide, a new weapon, or a mass rapid transit system, few have the knowledge to verify or dispute their claim. Secrecy, too, is a barrier preventing an intelligent assessment of bureaucratic performance. If the voters, or even Congress, cannot be told what the Central Intelligence Agency is doing, how can they know if it is being done well, or even if it should be done at all?

The problem of holding bureaucrats responsible for their performance and accountable to elected executive officials is thus increasingly difficult. Sheer size, specialized expertise, and secrecy may be as big a threat to genuinely democratic government as any we now encounter.

Chapter **11**

Judiciaries
Courts and Judges

*Scarcely any political question arises in the United States that
is not resolved, sooner or later, into a judicial question.*
                                                    Alexis de Tocqueville

Every government must pass laws and enforce them. These
are the functions of legislative and executive bodies, sometimes called the
political branches of government because they are inevitably subject to
group pressures and properly swayed by public opinion. But among a
people who value justice, there must be a third branch, somewhat
independent of the other two, which applies the law to specific disputes
and alleged crimes in a humane and impartial fashion. This is the work of
the courts, the presumably nonpolitical judicial branch of the national
and state governments. Yet in the 1968 presidential campaign, Richard
Nixon charged (as have many before him) that courts were actually
making policy and that this tendency should be checked by the appointment of judges humble enough to defer more often to the decisions of
legislative and executive authorities. After his election, he made precisely
the kind of judicial choices he had urged, yet these appointments proved
just as controversial as the earlier ones he had deplored. When nonpolitical offices become political issues, they deserve close examination.

COURT JURISDICTION AND
PROCEDURE
The Reach of the Judicial Arm

Judges have authority over two types of cases; they settle
disputes between citizens, and they deal with violations of the law. The

first type of controversy is a civil case, and the second, far less common, is a criminal one.

Civil cases   In judicial controversies between two private parties, the government merely provides the court room, judge, and perhaps the jury to arbitrate the dispute impartially. It stands above the battle, while decisions are often rendered on the basis of judge-made common law decided in similar cases in the past.

Civil cases are either (1) contract cases in which the opposing sides have some legally binding relationship with one another, such as an employment contract, marriage, mortgage, lease, or will—although divorce is by far the most common type of contract case, or (2) tort cases in which there is personal injury or property damage but no legal relationship between the parties. Most numerous here are cases resulting from automobile accidents.

In civil cases, a plaintiff sues a defendant. Traditionally, the law requires that each side assume equal responsibility for justifying its position and that the decision favor the one with a preponderance of evidence. The Seventh Amendment to the U.S. Constitution, guaranteeing the right to trial by jury in civil cases involving over $20, is applicable only in federal courts although even there the defendant usually waives this right and prefers to let the judge render the verdict.[1] As Amendment Seven does not apply in state courts, there an even higher ratio of civil cases is decided by judges rather than juries. Still, much time is spent in both the national and state court systems in trying to select juries for civil cases.

Criminal cases   Although there are cases in which governments sue or are sued in civil cases, their direct courtroom involvement is most important in criminal cases. These pit the government, as the prosecution, against the accused defendant.

Criminal cases involve alleged violations of law and are of two broad varieties: felonies (major crimes), usually punishable by at least a year in prison, and misdemeanors (minor crimes), entailing less severe sentences. In all criminal cases the burden of proof falls exclusively on the prosecution. The government must prove the defendant's guilt beyond a reasonable doubt. A slight edge in evidence, therefore, is not sufficient for a conviction; the defendant is presumed innocent until *proven* guilty.

The Constitution guarantees the right of trial by jury in criminal cases in state as well as federal courts. Until the Supreme Court ruled otherwise in 1972, the common law required a unanimous verdict in criminal jury trials, and even now it appears that a vote of 8 to 4 would be too narrow a margin to reach a decision. If the jurors cannot agree, there occurs a mistrial, or hung jury. The prosecution has the option of either dropping the charges or beginning the trial again with a new jury.

---

1 In U.S. district courts in 1970, civil cases outnumbered criminal ones by an almost 3 to 2 margin. Of the civil cases, over 3000 were decided by a jury and about 6000 without one.

Figure 41   Cases in Federal Courts

Courts	1950	1960	1970
U. S. District Courts			
Civil trials	5663	6002	9449
Nonjury	3648	3161	6078
Jury	2015	2841	3371
Criminal trials	2314	3040	6583
Nonjury	825	943	2357
Jury	1489	2097	4226
Total	7977	9042	16032[1]
U. S. Supreme Court			
Total cases filed	1181	1940	3405[2]

[1] This represents an increase of over 100 percent since 1950.
[2] This figure is for 1969 and is an increase of nearly 200 percent since 1950. Chief Justice Warren E. Burger places the cases filed in 1970 at 4400. *U.S. News and World Report,* Dec. 14, 1970, p. 42.
Source: U.S. Bureau of the Census, *Statistical Abstract of the United States: 1971,* pp. 150–51.

Since the Constitution, in Amendment Six, requires a speedy trial in criminal cases, they take precedence over civil cases, with the result that it may take years before a civil suit is brought to court. Also, the constitutional guarantee of the right to legal counsel is limited to criminal cases.

Crisis in the courts   While Americans may be a notoriously lawless people, they have a paradoxical reverence for the law as a potential panacea for every problem. "There oughta be a law . . .," cries a massive chorus every time a wrathful public perceives a potential threat to its safety or even to its sensibilities. The result is many laws, many lawbreakers, and a staggering number of cases brought before the courts. Too many cases and too few judges have produced a judicial crisis of unprecedented magnitude.

One of the more dramatic manifestations of this crisis occurred in New York City in October 1970, when prisoners staged a five-day jail riot and seized thirty-two guards as hostages in protesting overcrowded conditions and delays of up to a year before trial. Manhattan Criminal Court was so overburdened that some judges heard nearly three hundred cases a day. "The result," as one reporter noted, "is turnstile justice in a subway rush-hour atmosphere."[2]

In the federal courts, too, the work load has increased dramatically. Among the reasons for overcrowded court dockets is our reliance on the courts to settle an excessive variety of problems. Chief Justice Burger has expressed doubts about

whether such things as divorce, child custody, adoptions . . . belong in the

2 John J. Goldman, "New York Facing a Breakdown in Criminal Justice," *Los Angeles Times,* Dec. 7, 1970, p. 1.

courts at all. . . . (T)he chronic alcoholic, the narcotic addict, the serious mental patient—there's a . . . question whether they should be dealt with in the judicial framework.[3]

Burger indicated that such problems, in addition to automobile accident cases, might be handled instead by administrative agencies. Others have suggested that private use of marijuana and homosexual activity by consenting adults should be legalized, if only to free the police, prison officials, and judges for the more pressing business of protecting life and property.

The more rigid enforcement of defendants' rights in recent years places additional demands on court time. This is especially true with respect to the guarantee of an impartial jury. Pretrial motions seeking a change of venue and prolonged questioning of potential jurors can take as long as the trial itself. Moreover, when an appeals court reverses a conviction, it often returns the case to the lower court for a new trial.

Finally, there has been not only the well-known increase in the rate of serious crime, but also a rapid rise in the number of cases involving welfare benefits and the protection of consumers from unsafe merchandise. These two categories are especially important because they affect the interests of the middle-class and poor Americans who are generally most defenseless against abuses by government or corporation bureaucracies. The neighborhood legal services program, administered by the Office of Economic Opportunity, has instituted *class-action* suits which represent not individuals, but entire categories of affected persons. So have nonprofit public-service law firms such as "Nader's Raiders," headed by Ralph Nader. Among recent class-action suits have been those that have attempted to restrict the arbitrary repossession of cars and other merchandise bought on credit, establish fair hearing procedures for those whose welfare payments have been cut off, and protect wilderness areas from environmentally destructive commercial development.

Besides removing certain matters from the jurisdiction of the courts, judicial burdens might be eased by an increase in the number of judges and "the appointment of para-judges to deal with the enormous mass of pretrial hearings, motions, and administration of court calendars, all of which take up a major portion of a judge's time."[4] Perhaps a small step in the right direction was the creation of an Institute of Court Management at the University of Denver Law School designed to train court executives in modern management methods. It graduated its first class in December 1970.[5]

3 *U.S. News and World Report,* Dec. 14, 1970, p. 35.
4 Judge Irving R. Kaufman, U.S. Court of Appeals, 2nd Circuit, "Court Crisis: A Matter of Volume and of Money," *Los Angeles Times,* Nov. 15, 1970, Sec. F, p. 3.
5 *U.S. News and World Report,* op. cit., pp. 32–33.

The Road to Justice

Original and appellate jurisdiction   Original jurisdiction is the authority to render decisions in either criminal or civil cases that have never been tried in court before. The lowest of the state courts and the federal district courts, at the bottom of the judicial branch in the national government, have original jurisdiction only. Appellate jurisdiction is the authority of higher courts to hear cases on appeal that have been tried before in a lower court.

The adversary system: legal warfare   The American people love a good fight. That may explain the popularity of plays, television series, and novels based upon courtroom drama. For the Anglo-American legal tradition conceives of a trial as essentially a battle between two adversaries, fair and honest, fought hard and tenaciously, out of which truth will somehow emerge and the best man will finally win. This is the essence of the adversary system. A leading authority has described it well:

(T)he judge will question a witness only to avert grave injustice, not to advance the case for either side. He is not in any sense an active elicitor of truth regarding the testimony presented. . . . (H)e is an independent arbiter. . . . This is a concept basic to the common law adversary proceeding . . . that "sets the parties fighting."[6]

While there is reason to believe that the adversary system is well suited to criminal cases where a defendant is simply innocent or guilty, it is possible that it is sadly inappropriate for settling more complex civil disputes, such as divorce or accident liability cases, where both parties may be at fault. If no one is committed to the active, disinterested search for truth, truth may not be found.

It is, therefore, encouraging to note that there is growing use of pretrial conferences in which judges encourage the opposing attorneys to agree on as many facts as possible and thereby limit the issues in dispute. A somewhat similar purpose is served by the procedure of discovery, which permits one lawyer to learn what evidence is possessed by the opposition in advance of the trial. In addition, many disputes are settled by informal negotiations between the opposing attorneys. In criminal cases, such negotiation often involves *plea bargaining* in which the defendant pleads guilty to a charge less serious than that for which he was initially arrested. In civil cases, a compromise financial settlement may be hammered out in the judge's private chambers. Such out-of-court solutions no doubt fall short of perfect justice, but they represent more or less voluntary agreements which reduce court time and provide pragmatic concessions that may well be as fair as those imposed by judicial decrees. On the other hand, plea bargaining may provide society with

6 Henry J. Abraham, *The Judicial Process* (N.Y.: Oxford University Press, Inc., 1962), p. 94.

too little protection from hardened criminals or induce innocent defendants to plead guilty to avoid a long prison sentence based on circumstantial evidence. Surely justice should not be sacrificed in the interest of convenience.

COURT STRUCTURE AND PERSONNEL
National Courts

Article III of the Constitution provides for a U.S. Supreme Court and whatever lower courts Congress may wish to establish. The resulting judicial system is relatively simple.

Federal district courts The first year Congress met under the present Constitution, in 1789, it created United States district courts. There are now over three hundred judges serving on ninety-three district courts with at least one in each state and territory. In criminal cases, these courts have original jurisdiction over all acts—felonies and misdemeanors alike—prohibited by Congress. In addition, they have jurisdiction over most civil cases to which the United States government is a party, and those involving citizens of different states in which over $10,000 is at stake. In most instances, only one judge hears each case, and the defendant may claim the right to trial by jury.

Courts of Appeals In 1891 Congress created the courts of appeals. Between the district courts and the U.S. Supreme Court, they have appellate jurisdiction in both criminal and civil cases. There are now about one hundred judges distributed among eleven courts. Three judges usually hear each case. The vast majority of cases reaching these courts come from the U.S. district courts, although a few arrive from other sources such as regulatory commissions in the executive branch.

The Supreme Court The highest court in America is the United States Supreme Court. Here, at the judicial summit, nine judges (a number determined by Congress) exercise authority equaling that of the President or Congress. The Supreme Court has both original and appellate jurisdiction, although almost all of its cases fall in the latter category. Article III of the Constitution, as altered by the Eleventh Amendment, establishes original jurisdiction over suits involving foreign diplomats, those between states, or those between the national government and a state. All in all, the Court has heard an average of less than five cases a year under its original jurisdiction, mainly involving interstate disputes. The most notable in recent times have been those between Maryland and Virginia over oyster fishing and between California and Arizona concerning water from the Colorado River.[7] In 1947 a major dispute involving national versus state ownership of offshore (or tidelands) oil resources also reached the Supreme Court under its original jurisdiction.[8]

7 Ibid., pp. 157–58.
8 *United States* v. *California,* 332 U.S. 19.

Figure 42   The Judicial Branch

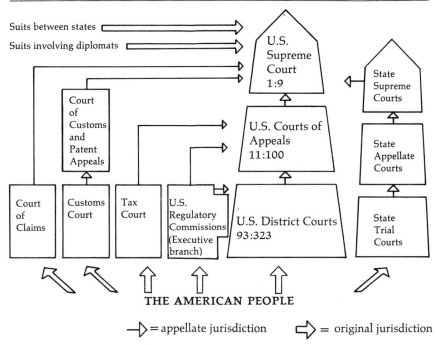

Note: In the federal pyramid, the first figure indicates number of courts, and the second indicates number of judges.**

The appellate jurisdiction of the Supreme Court consists of cases heard earlier by the various national courts of appeals, or by the state courts, although some cases involving important constitutional issues may arrive directly from the district courts. The only circumstance under which a case can be appealed from a state court is one in which someone has charged state or local officials with violating the U.S. Constitution or a law or treaty authorized by it. Such cases go directly from the highest state court to which it may be appealed to the U.S. Supreme Court.

Most cases reach the Supreme Court on *writs of certiorari*, which are court orders granting appeals from lower courts. These writs are usually issued when four Supreme Court justices feel a case to be of compelling importance. Of more than 3000 cases presented to it each year, the court renders decisions on three or four hundred, with less than half dignified by full written opinions.

Other federal courts   Various specialized courts complete the judicial branch of the national government. These are the Court of Claims, in which citizens may bring civil suits against the national government for damages of one kind or another; the U.S. Customs Court, which reviews administrative decisions on the tax to be imposed on merchandise brought into the country from foreign nations, and the Court of Customs and Patent Appeals, which hears appeals from the

Customs Court, the Patent Office in the Commerce Department, and the Tariff Commission.

State Courts

State court structures are similar to the federal one, but usually are organized in four or five levels.

Justices of the peace Justice courts, at the bottom of the judicial structure and often charged with dishonesty, are being replaced in many states. The justices of the peace (J.P.s) are often part-time, without legal training, and reimbursed only from fines and costs they themselves impose. In order to encourage more civil suits and improve their business, J.P.s have a notorious reputation for ruling for the plaintiff—in 99 percent of the cases in Michigan, 98 percent in Tennessee, and 79 percent in Indiana at various times in the past. It is no wonder J.P. was said to stand for "judgment for the plaintiff." There is little indication that the few criminal cases J.P.s are permitted to hear elicit any more fairness than the civil actions. The jurisdiction of these petty officials is normally confined to civil cases involving no more than a few hundred dollars and the most minor of misdemeanors. They usually can pick up a few dollars by performing marriage ceremonies and often have the authority to hold preliminary hearings to determine whether persons accused of more important crimes shall be held for possible later action before a major trial court.

Other trial courts In many states, the function of the J.P.s is exercised by full-time, salaried, professionally qualified judges serving on municipal courts, or similar tribunals with different names. They have original jurisdiction only.

In addition, every state has higher trial courts (generally known as county, superior, district, or circuit courts) with authority over all major cases. At this level a million-dollar damage suit or a murder case, for example, will be brought to trial. Supplementing this original jurisdiction is often appellate jurisdiction over cases heard first by J.P.s or municipal court judges.

At the trial court level, it is common to have a variety of specialized courts handling particular kinds of cases, or else general trial courts organized in specialized divisions. Either system permits judges to gain considerable experience and expertise in a certain field of law and presumably raises their level of competence. At the municipal court level, judges may specialize in traffic citations or in small claims cases, in which the plaintiff is suing for no more than a few hundred dollars and in which lawyers and juries may even be prohibited.

At the major trial court level, judges may specialize in juvenile cases, probate matters, or domestic relations. Juvenile cases are generally considered especially significant because the defendants may have a better chance of being rehabilitated. Probate matters involve wills, inheritances, and guardianship for dependent children and incompetent adults, while domestic relations cases embrace many of the traumatic disputes that pull families apart—divorce, child custody, alimony, separate maintenance, and parental visitation rights. Since the family is generally acknowledged to be the basic social unit, the highest of trial courts usually has jurisdiction over the legal battles affecting it.

Reform at the lower court levels has been sorely needed in many states, not only to root out corruption and gross incompetence, but also to reorganize courts with confusing and overlapping jurisdictions. It is heartening to note progress in that direction. Courts were reorganized in Colorado, Idaho, and Oklahoma (where J.P.s and county courts were abolished) in 1969, and significant court integration recently took place in Ohio, Pennsylvania, and Rhode Island as well.[9]

The appellate courts All states have a supreme court to hear cases appealed from the trial courts mentioned above, although it is called a supreme judicial court in Maine and Massachusetts, a supreme court of appeals in Virginia and West Virginia, and a court of appeals in Kentucky, Maryland, and New York. In addition, twenty-three states have intermediate appellate courts to help screen out and reduce the work load of the highest state court.[10] The number of state supreme court judges ranges from three (in Delaware) to nine (in seven states.)

The Selection of Judges

Judicial appointment While all federal judges are appointed by the President subject to confirmation by a majority vote of the U.S. Senate, the situation at the state level is both different and far more complex. State supreme court judges are appointed by the governor in sixteen states,[11] appointed by the legislature from nominations submitted by the governor in Connecticut, elected by the legislature in Rhode Island, South Carolina, Vermont, and Virginia, and elected by the voters in the remaining twenty-nine states. Most lower court judges are also elected, although some are chosen by higher courts, city councils or other local governing bodies.[12]

The case for appointing judges rests primarily on three arguments: (1) the voters know too little about prospective judges to be able to elect them intelligently; (2) to force a judge to seek office in an election campaign compromises the independence and integrity he needs to dispense justice impartially; and (3) good attorneys are more likely to be attracted to judgeships if they can gain them through appointment rather than through the rigors of a bitter, expensive, and acrimonious election campaign.

Even where judges are elected, the governor may appoint

9 William L. Frederick, "State Judicial Systems," *The Book of the States*, 1970–71 (Lexington, Ky.: The Council of State Governments, 1970), pp. 117–18.
10 *The Book of the States*, 1970–71, pp. 120–21.
11 Alaska, California, Colorado, Delaware, Hawaii, Iowa, Kansas, Maine, Maryland, Massachusetts, Missouri, Nebraska, New Hampshire, New Jersey, Oklahoma, and Utah.
12 *The Book of the States*, 1970–71, op. cit., pp. 124–25.

persons to fill judicial vacancies which occur between elections. This is of considerable significance, because in many states about one third of all judges die or resign before their elective terms have expired.

Judicial election   Among the states in which supreme court judges are chosen by the voters, in fifteen they are elected on a partisan basis, with candidates chosen by the opposing political parties,[13] and in fourteen they are elected on a nonpartisan ballot, with the party affiliation of the candidates unlisted.[14]

Election of judges is often justified on the grounds that judges apply the existing law to cases coming before them in a way which reflects their own values and preferences. The whole common law tradition, in fact, allows each judge to establish some legal principle whenever statutes and earlier legal precedents seem inapplicable. Hence, it is argued, democratic theory requires that judges, like all important policy-makers, be selected by the people. The discretion available to judges is indicated by a study of 298 national and state supreme court justices. It disclosed that in at least nine kinds of cases the decisions of Republican and Democratic judges differed to a statistically significant degree. This finding might seem to bolster the contention that people should be permitted to elect judges whose views are most similar to their own.

Yet the same study also revealed that judges who were appointed rendered decisions reflecting their party affiliation substantially less often than those who were elected.[15] Persons who value a politically independent judiciary more than one which is responsive to the wishes of the majority may cite this evidence, therefore, to support the case for appointed judges.

Another argument for elective judgeships is that chief executives use judicial appointments as a form of patronage to reward their supporters. As one honest, if somewhat cynical judge has admitted, "a judge is a lawyer who knew a governor."[16] And both governors and Presidents have a preference for their own party; among federal judges it is worth noting that President Franklin D. Roosevelt appointed 217 Democrats and 8 Republicans, Harry Truman 118 Democrats and 12 Republicans and Dwight Eisenhower, finally accorded the opportunity for sweet revenge, 175 Republicans and 11 Democrats.[17]

The California and Missouri plans   Out of the charges and countercharges in the debate over appointment *vs.* election have come two compromise plans promising the best of both worlds. The first plan,

---

13 Alabama, Arkansas, Florida, Georgia, Illinois, Indiana, Louisiana, Mississippi, New Mexico, New York, North Carolina, Pennsylvania, Tennessee, Texas, and West Virginia.
14 Arizona, Idaho, Kentucky, Michigan, Minnesota, Montana, Nevada, North Dakota, Ohio, Oregon, South Dakota, Washington, Wisconsin, and Wyoming.
15 Stuart S. Nagel, "Political Party Affiliation and Judges' Decisions," *American Political Science Review* 55 (December 1961): 843–50.
16 Quoted by Fred Rodell in A. N. Christensen and E. M. Kirkpatrick, eds., *The People, Politics, and the Politician* (N.Y.: Henry Holt and Company, 1941), p. 542.
17 John J. Kennelly, "Elect Judges?—Yes," *The Rotarian,* June 1961, pp. 40, 54, 56. President Kennedy chose 111 Democrats, 11 Republicans, and 1 Liberal.

adopted by California in 1934, requires that judges on the higher courts be appointed by the governor subject to the approval of a special judicial commission. At the next election the voters are permitted to vote, yes or no, on whether such judges shall have a full term in office. No opposition candidates are permitted. The voters have never rejected a judge selected in this way.

The Missouri plan works in much the same way, but requires the governor to make his initial appointment from among three persons whose names are submitted by a judicial nominating committee. A few states, including Alaska, Iowa, Kansas, and Nebraska have adopted variations of this method.[18]

The Care and Characteristics of Judges

Few jobs in our society carry the prestige and honor of a judgeship, especially on a higher court. It is well to examine some of the factors affecting the judicial life style, as well as the characteristics of the men and women who enjoy its rewards.

Judicial tenure and salaries Judges in the national court system have life-time jobs, subject only to their unlikely removal on impeachment charges. At the state level, however, few are so lucky. The vast majority of the state higher court judges have terms ranging from six to twelve years, and those on the trial courts from two to six years. However, most elected judges have relatively little difficulty getting reelected. The voters in many states, distracted by better publicized races for other offices, tend to vote for incumbent judges almost automatically unless they have been involved in some recent scandal or a highly unpopular decision.[19]

The Chief Justice of the U.S. Supreme Court receives an annual salary of $62,500; the eight associate justices get $60,000, court of appeals judges $42,500, and district court judges $40,000. At the state level, supreme court judges receive from a low of $19,000 in Mississippi and Wyoming to a high of $42,500 in New York, and major trial judges earn from $10,500 in Oklahoma, to $39,100 in New York. While judges hardly go hungry on such salaries, they earn far less than thousands of lawyers. Why, then, would one want to become a judge? There are perhaps as many reasons as there are judges, but among them are the prestige and relative security of judicial office, its usefulness as a springboard to even higher office, and a desire for public service. In addition, there are fringe benefits. Most judges do not have to pay for their office space, secretarial assistance or other professional necessities.

Characteristics of judges Except for justices of the peace,

18 Abraham, op. cit., pp. 34–39, and *The Book of the States,* 1970–71, loc. cit.
19 In Kansas, for example, of the 309 district court judges seeking reelection between 1930 and 1956, less than 40 percent were opposed and fewer than 8 percent defeated. Duane Lockard, *The Politics of State and Local Government,* 2nd ed. (N.Y.: The Macmillan Company, 1969), p. 451.

nearly all jurists are lawyers. Oddly enough, this is true in the federal courts only as a result of tradition, common sense, and the political influence of bar associations. Although the Constitution prescribes rather detailed requirements for legislative and executive officials regarding age, citizenship, and residency, it imposes none of any sort on judges. At the state level, judges untrained in the law were once rather common, but a long drive to professionalize the judiciary has diminished their number substantially and many states now make admission to the bar a constitutional requirement for judges. One effect of the attorneys' monopoly over the judicial branches is that judges have a higher socioeconomic background than the average American.

The courts are not only dominated by lawyers, but by a specific kind: male lawyers. No woman has ever served on the U.S. Supreme Court, and a survey of the names of state supreme court justices reveals only four women among the fifty states combined.[20] It is probable that this situation is less the result of deliberate discrimination than of a sort of institutionalized sexism within the legal profession. In 1970 only 9000 of 315,000 lawyers in America were females.[21]

THE SUPREME COURT AND JUDICIAL REVIEW

Courts in all countries have the job of settling disputes, acquitting the innocent, and punishing the guilty. But American courts have the unique additional power of judicial review, which means that they can declare legislative and executive acts unconstitutional and therefore invalid.

In the hands of state courts judicial review becomes a sort of two-edged sword, cutting down government actions which violate either the state or federal constitutions. But whenever any action is declared contrary to the federal constitution, it will result, almost inevitably, in an appeal to the Supreme Court of the United States.

The Court of Last Resort

The Supreme Court is well named; it is the final interpreter of the law, the ultimate watchdog of the whole governmental process, the court of last resort. It is the final arbiter of what the Constitution permits and what it prohibits. If one dislikes the Court's decision, one has but three choices: defy it, wait patiently in the hope the Court will reverse itself later, or seek a constitutional amendment nullifying its ruling.

The politics of judicial selection Many factors influence a President's nomination of Supreme Court judges. One is partisan

20 *The Book of the States,* 1970–71, op. cit., pp. 562–611. Much of the other data regarding state court systems in this chapter has come from Section III of this source.
21 U.S. Bureau of the Census, *The Statistical Abstract of the United States: 1971,* p. 153.

loyalty; another is general political philosophy. In either case, a President may be disappointed to find his appointee voting against his expectations once cloaked with black-robed independence, prestige, and life tenure on the Supreme Court. President Theodore Roosevelt was quickly angered by Justice Oliver Wendell Holmes, shortly after he had appointed him, and President Eisenhower was thought to regret his selection of Chief Justice Earl Warren. President Nixon apparently made his appointments more carefully. During the 1968 campaign, he emphasized his intention to choose justices with a preference for a "strict construction" of the Constitution. Seldom has a campaign promise been kept with such frequency or fidelity. Before he had completed three years in office, he had the rare opportunity to make four such selections. His choices have consistently justified his confidence. As a result, constitutional interpretation in the areas of police power, press freedom, trial by jury, and race relations may be altered for several decades. Ten Supreme Court justices have held their posts for more than thirty years.

Emphasis is sometimes placed on the maintenance of a balance on the Supreme Court, both in terms of geographical sections of the country and religion, but balance is a relative concept. Less than a quarter of all Supreme Court justices have come from west of the Mississippi River, and New York, Ohio, and Massachusetts have produced nearly a third of the total number.[22] President Nixon appointed three persons from the South, on the grounds that this section was underrepresented on the Court, before one of them won Senate confirmation. The concept of a religious balance has traditionally meant seven Protestants, a Catholic, and a Jew, but this tradition is a relatively recent one and has resulted in only six Catholics and five Jews out of the one hundred justices who have served on the Court. President Nixon explicitly repudiated religion as a legitimate factor in judicial recruitment, and as a result our highest court is now without a Jew (with Justice William Brennan the lone Catholic) for the first time since 1916. President Lyndon B. Johnson may have broadened the ideal of a balanced Court by selecting the first black, Justice Thurgood Marshall, to sit on that body.

In making his choice, the chief executive relies in large measure upon the recommendation of his attorney general who, in turn, has usually sounded out the Committee on the Federal Judiciary of the American Bar Association.[23] Of necessity, the likelihood of Senate opposition must be considered also, as well as pressures brought to bear by influential interest groups. The rejection of two Nixon appointees reflects the close scrutiny the Senate, especially its Judiciary Committee, gives to Supreme Court nominations. It also indicates the influence of the labor and civil rights lobbies, both strongly opposed to the Pres-

22 Much of the material in this section, somewhat updated, has come from Abraham, op. cit., pp. 47–81.
23 John R. Schmidhauser, *The Supreme Court* (N.Y.: Holt, Rinehart & Winston, Inc., 1961), pp. 77–91.

ident's choices. Another factor involved in Supreme Court appointments is prior judicial experience. Over a third of the justices throughout our history have had none at all—including such notable ones as Chief Justices John Marshall, Roger Taney, and Earl Warren.

The most likely result of all these considerations is a Supreme Court justice who is

probably Protestant; of Anglo-Saxon stock . . .; a background of upper-level social status; reared in an urban environment; a member of an economically comfortable, civic-minded, politically active family; with B.A. and LL.B. degrees; experienced in some public or civic office.[24]

In 1972, six of the nine justices were over sixty years of age.

The mystique of court procedure If majestic rituals and symbolic procedures enhance the legitimacy of government bodies, the prestige of the Supreme Court is not difficult to explain. It is big on ceremony, both public and private.

Opposing attorneys in each case present written briefs to the Court. In addition, at least eight days a month are devoted to oral arguments, in which each side of every case is usually permitted an hour to emphasize its most persuasive contentions. At the beginning of each of these sessions, a court crier intones an impressive chant: "Oyez, oyez, oyez! All persons having business before the Honorable Supreme Court of the United States are admonished to draw near and give their attention, for the Court is now sitting. God save the United States and this Honorable Court." The chief justice takes the middle chair, and the eight associate justices arrange themselves, in order of seniority, on either side of him. During these sessions, each of the nine justices may direct questions, sometimes sharp, to the opposing lawyers. Occasionally, to the delight of the press and public present, the justices exchange verbal barbs with one another.

Then, on Friday, the Court meets in secret conference, each justice first shaking hands with each of his judicial brethren. The chief justice presides and summarizes the cases on the agenda. Each of the associates, in order of seniority, makes additional comments, and then voting begins, in reverse order, with the most recently appointed associate voting first and the chief justice last.

The assignment of opinions When the votes are tallied, the chief justice assigns the responsibility of writing the majority opinion of the Court. This explains the case briefly, describes the issues it presents, and justifies the Court's decision so that it may provide guidance to lower courts in deciding similar cases and persuade the nation of its correctness. Just as the Constitution is the heart of American law, Supreme Court opinions are its lifeblood, applying constitutional principles to the gravest disputes in the nation.

If the chief justice has voted with the minority, the task of

24 Henry J. Abraham, *The Judiciary* (Boston: Allyn and Bacon, Inc., 1965), p. 96.

assigning the majority opinion falls to the senior associate justice who voted with the majority. Once written, the opinion is circulated among other members of the majority. If any justice should disagree with its reasoning, he may write a concurring opinion giving his own reasons for reaching the same conclusion as the majority. Similarly, any justice who voted with the minority may write a dissenting opinion in which he states why he believes the majority was wrong. These dissenting opinions are sometimes very influential, fanning a spark of doubt regarding the majority's wisdom that may lead the Court on some future occasion to reverse its earlier decision. This has happened about a hundred times since the adoption of the Constitution.

The Nature of Judicial Review

Although judicial review has been controversial since the doctrine was first used in the case of *Marbury* v. *Madison,* it has now become deeply entrenched in our constitutional system. Judicial review is used to declare government acts unconstitutional primarily under three circumstances: if one level of government (national or state) exercises power properly belonging only to the other; if one branch of the government exercises power properly belonging only to either of the other two; or if any government agency or official exercises power that violates the constitutional rights of an individual. But two broadly different interpretations of judicial review have staunch supporters on the Supreme Court.

Judicial self-restraint   One group of judges, now led by Chief Justice Burger, contends that the power of judicial review should be used with great restraint and only against laws or actions that are blatantly unconstitutional. They complain that too often judges interpret the Constitution to reflect their own views, thereby invalidating government acts simply because they don't like them. President Nixon clearly advocated judicial self-restraint when he asserted his intention to appoint judges who

would be strict constructionists who saw their duty as interpreting law not making law. They would see themselves as caretakers of the Constitution and servants of the people, not superlegislators with a free hand to impose their social and political viewpoints upon the American people.[25]

Perhaps the essential spirit of judicial self-restraint was best captured in a remark Justice Oliver Wendell Holmes addressed to Justice Harlan Fiske Stone:

Young man, about 75 years ago I learned that I was not God. And so, when the people . . . want to do something I can't find anything in the Constitution

---

25 Alan Barth, "Strict Constructionism—the Illusory Quality of Labels," *Los Angeles Times,* April 19, 1970, Sec. E, p. 3.

expressly forbidding them to do, I say, whether I like it or not, "Goddamit, let 'em do it."[26]

This spirit has taken flesh in the form of specific rules the Court imposed upon itself to minimize the use of judicial review. Mr. Justice Brandeis summarized them in a concurring opinion in the case of *Ashwander* v. *Tennessee Valley Authority* in 1935:

1) The Court will not pass upon the constitutionality of legislation in a friendly, non-adversary, proceeding. . . .

2) The Court will not anticipate a question of constitutional law in advance of the necessity of deciding it. . . .

3) The Court will not formulate a rule of constitutional law broader than is required by the precise facts to which it is to be applied. . . .

4) The Court will not pass upon a constitutional question . . . if there is also present some other ground upon which the case may be disposed of. . . .

5) The Court will not pass upon the validity of a statute upon complaint of one who fails to show that he is injured by its operation. . . .

6) The Court will not pass upon the constitutionality of a statute at the instance of one who has availed himself of its benefits.

7) When the validity of an act of the Congress is drawn in question, and even if a serious doubt of constitutionality is raised, it is a cardinal principle that this Court will first ascertain whether a construction of the statute is fairly possible by which the question may be avoided.[27]

To these so-called Ashwander rules, two others must be added that serve also to reduce the frequency with which government acts are declared unconstitutional: The Court will not decide "political questions" that are within the proper domain of the other two branches (although what these are is sometimes disputed), and the burden of proof rests on those claiming that a particular act is unconstitutional. Yet in spite of all these indications of reluctance, the Supreme Court has in fact declared 87 acts of Congress and 733 state laws unconstitutional between 1789 and 1969.

Judicial activism A somewhat different interpretation of the power of judicial review is held by those sometimes called judicial activists, or (to use President Nixon's preferred term) loose constructionists. This group, now including Justices William J. Brennan and William O. Douglas, contends that it is difficult to construe "strictly" such essentially "loose" terms of the Constitution as *"unreasonable* searches and seizures," *"cruel and unusual* punishments," and *"due process of law."* The broad language of the Constitution, they argue, requires broad latitude for the Court in interpreting it and in enforcing its provisions. Activists stress the importance of judicial review in protecting individual

26 Charles P. Curtis, *Lions Under the Throne* (Boston: Houghton Mifflin Company, 1947), p. 281.
27 297 U.S. 288.

rights. They see it as a refuge for minorities from oppressive government action provoked by age-old prejudices, current political pressures, or the fleeting passions of the moment.

Here it is important to note two quite different kinds of provisions in the Constitution. First, there are those that *grant* power to government officials, such as the "necessary and proper" clause concerning congressional authority, or the "commander in chief" clause conferring presidential prerogatives. To interpret these provisions broadly or loosely would *increase* governmental power and result in fewer acts declared unconstitutional.

But, secondly, there are constitutional provisions, such as the Bill of Rights, that *limit* the power of government in the interests of protecting the liberty of the individual. To interpret these broadly would *diminish* governmental power and result in more acts declared unconstitutional. Thus, judicial activism, implying a readiness to exercise judicial review, is furthered by *a strict construction of power grants and a loose construction of power limitations.* Few judges are entirely consistent on the matter, although it is generally agreed that judicial activism reached its zenith during the era of Chief Justice Earl Warren (1953–1969). It is equally clear that the Burger Court, under the impetus of the Nixon appointees, shows a dominant preference for judicial self-restraint.

Judicial politics Whether the courts pursue policies of activism or self-restraint, it seems inevitable that their decisions will have a greater political impact than has been assumed in classical legal theory or desired, perhaps, by President Nixon. The Warren Court rendered important policy decisions by interpreting the Constitution to ban prayer in the public schools, to require that criminal suspects be informed of certain rights, and to prohibit the election of lawmakers from unequally populated districts. Although such decisions have represented triumphs of judicial activism, they have also revealed disputes over legal theory and policy preferences which have pitted some judges against others.

In controversies such as these, even the long robes of judicial authority cannot obscure essentially political splits of a profound and persistent nature. Within the Supreme Court itself, attitudes coalesce, coalitions form, and ideological animosities emerge which can be measured by a quantitative analysis of judicial voting behavior. In 1957, for example, activist Justices William O. Douglas and Hugo Black voted together in 89 percent of the cases on which the Court was divided, but sided with Justice John M. Harlan, noted for his self-restraint, only 29 and 33 percent respectively.[28] In 1972 the four Nixon appointees, Chief Justice Warren Burger and Justices Harry Blackmun, Lewis Powell, Jr., and William Rehnquist, voted together in thirteen out of eighteen (or 72 percent) of the cases decided by a 5 to 4 vote.[29]

The truth is that judges could not stay out of politics, even if

28 Glendon A. Schubert, *Constitutional Politics* (N.Y.: Holt, Rinehart & Winston, Inc., 1960), p. 159.
29 *New York Times*, July 2, 1972, p. 18.

they wanted to, because politics involves making decisions about government policy. The higher the court, the more frequent and important are
the policy decisions it is required to make. For example, when judges
exercise their power of judicial review, they pass judgment on the
constitutionality of a law or executive procedure which is already
established. If they uphold the challenged action, they are *perpetuating
existing policy.* If they declare the action unconstitutional, they are
changing existing policy. A fundamental issue between activism and
self-restraint may not be, therefore, whether the courts should intervene
in the action of other government agencies, but on whose side. But,
although judicial interpretation can either affirm or invalidate existing
policy, it has its limits: It can seldom make new policy.

Even when a case involves no question of constitutionality, it
may reflect some of the enduring conflicts in our society: employers *vs.*
employees, manufacturers *vs.* consumers, whites *vs.* blacks, prudes *vs.*
pornographers. When the courts render a decision, they incorporate into
public policy a legal preference favoring the interests of one group and
opposing those of its adversary. That is a policy decision which is
profoundly political in nature.

Finally, judges are trapped in a political web woven around
them by external political pressures. Interest groups exert influence for
and against the appointment of particular judges, and their lawyers
intervene in specific cases through the submission of *amicus curiae* legal
briefs on behalf of one side or the other. Presidents and governors use
judicial appointments to reward the party faithful or to perpetuate their
own political attitudes. Courts must also be sensitive to public opinion,
puzzling as it often is. They have no armies, few jobs, and little money to
help them gain compliance with their decisions. Devoid of force and
influence, the power of judges stems from authority rooted in the faith
and confidence of the people. If these judges "follow the election
returns," as was once alleged, it is because they realize that when the
public no longer acknowledges the legitimacy of their decisions, then the
rule of law ends and barbarism begins.

Judicial review, democracy, and freedom   The chief attack
on judicial review is that it is undemocratic. And so it seems to be, if
democracy means majority rule. It is difficult to imagine anything less
democratic, in fact, than a law passed by an overwhelming majority of
elected congressmen, enthusiastically signed by the elected President,
and then declared unconstitutional by a 5 to 4 vote of the appointed
Supreme Court.

Yet the American political system is dedicated to individual
freedom as well as to democracy, and in defense of this freedom judicial
review can make its greatest contribution. Since legislative and executive
officials are elected by majorities, they are compelled both by moral
obligation and by political expediency to do what the majority wishes.
The protection of minority rights against a prejudiced and hostile
majority, therefore, is the responsibility of an independent court system,

armed with judicial review, and staffed by judges neither selected by majorities nor in danger of removal by them. The American Constitution is preeminently an experiment in the limitation and control of power—whether exercised by a majority or a minority—through the rule of law. Without the protection of judicial review, it is doubtful whether that great experiment can succeed. If it does not, both majority rule and minority rights will perish with it.

Conclusion to Part Four

Each of the three branches of government possesses a characteristic kind of power. The legislative branch wields influence, especially through the power of the purse. By appropriating or refusing to appropriate money for the vast variety of government programs it exerts not only a potent check on the other two branches but also an enormous impact on the distribution of wealth among the people and on the priorities of the government among competing demands for better health care, greater national security, more effective control of pollution, and innumerable other goals. Power is more diffuse in the legislature than in the other branches and this branch is the most accessible target for influence from the public.

The executive branch controls force: the armed forces, national guard units, state police forces, the F.B.I., the secret service, highway patrols, federal prisons, and state penetentiaries. Because coercion is the ultimate form of power, the executive is the most dangerous branch. It is also the biggest, and its bureaucracies affect the citizens most frequently. In addition, as activities have multiplied, executive agencies have developed a new influence—specialized knowledge—on which the other branches must depend. The old system of checks and balances strains to render the executive safe for a free people.

The judicial branch must rely almost exclusively on authority, especially on the Constitution, that supreme source of authority which pledges equality of legal protection. If the courts are unable to gain voluntary compliance with their orders, only the executive has the power to enforce them. If that branch refuses, races will remain segregated, contracts will be violated, alimony will be unpaid, suspects will be forced to confess, and law will be washed away in a sea of anarchy, with only the strongest or richest remaining afloat.

Bibliography

Chapter 9

Legislatures: Congress and State Legislatures

Burns, John, *The Sometime Governments: A Critical Study of the 50 American State Legislatures* (N.Y.: Bantam Books, Inc., 1971).

Clapp, Charles L., *The Congressman: His Work as He Sees It* (Garden City, N.Y.: Anchor Books, Doubleday & Company, Inc., 1963).

Crane, Wilder, Jr., and Meredith W. Watts, Jr., *State Legislative Systems* (Englewood Cliffs, N.J.: Prentice-Hall, Inc., 1968).

Davidson, Roger H., *The Role of the Congressman* (N.Y.: Pegasus, The Bobbs-Merrill Co., Inc., 1969).

Froman, Lewis A., Jr., *The Congressional Process: Strategies, Rules, and Procedures* (Boston: Little, Brown and Company, 1967).

Keefe, William J., and Morris S. Ogul, *The American Legislative Process: Congress and the States* (Englewood Cliffs, N.J.; Prentice-Hall, Inc., 1964; 2nd ed., 1968).

Wahlke, John C. *et al.*, *The Legislative System* (N.Y.: John Wiley & Sons, Inc., 1962).

Chapter 10

Executives: Presidents, Governors, and Bureaucracies

Book of the States (Lexington, Ky.: Council of State Governments, biennial).

Corwin, Edward S., *The President: Office and Powers*, 4th ed. (N.Y.: New York University Press, 1957).

Koenig, Louis W., *The Chief Executive*, rev. ed. (N.Y.: Harcourt Brace Jovanovich, Inc., 1968).

Neustadt, Richard E., *Presidential Power* (N.Y.: John Wiley & Sons, Inc., 1960).

Rossiter, Clinton, *The American Presidency*, rev. ed. (N.Y.: Harcourt Brace Jovanovich, Inc., 1960).

Sorensen, Theodore C., *Decision-Making in the White House* (N.Y.: Columbia University Press, 1963).

U.S. Government Organization Manual (Washington, D.C.: U.S. Government Printing Office, biennial).

Woll, Peter, *American Bureaucracy* (N.Y.: W. W. Norton & Company, Inc., 1963)..

Chapter 11

Judiciaries: Courts and Judges

Abraham, Henry J., *The Judicial Process* (N.Y.: Oxford University Press, Inc., 1962; 2nd ed., 1968).

Friedman, Leon, and Fred L. Israel, eds., *The Justices of the United States Supreme Court 1789–1969* (N.Y.: R. R. Bowker Co., 1969).

Jackson, Robert H., *The Supreme Court in the American System of Government* (N.Y.: Harper & Row, Publishers, 1955).

Jacob, Herbert, ed., *Law, Politics, and the Federal Courts* (Boston: Little, Brown and Company, 1967).

Roche, John P., and Leonard W. Levy, eds., *The Judiciary* (N.Y.: Harcourt Brace Jovanovich, Inc., 1964).

Schmidhauser, John R., *The Supreme Court* (N.Y.: Holt, Rinehart & Winston, Inc., 1961).

PART FIVE

THE GRASS ROOTS

Unlike national and state governments, those at the grass roots level lack a separation of powers. These local authorities, geographically closest to the people and theoretically easiest for them to control, do not have judicial branches, since all courts technically belong to national or state governments. In addition, the law-making and law-enforcing functions have been so intermingled in many cities, counties, and other local government units that legislative-executive distinctions lose much of their meaning. Chapter 13 deals with the importance of local government, its legal authority, and the roles played by counties, towns, townships, and special districts. Chapter 14 describes city governments and their political processes, and Chapter 15 discusses some of the vital problems threatening the urban-suburban complexes of our major metropolitan areas.

The President has expressed a desire to redirect political power back to the people. If they are to exercise this authority effectively, it will be through the local institutions examined in the following pages.

Chapter **12**

Localities
Variations on Popular Government

*There are many states in which even the smallest local units
could perform better if given greater discretion to choose their
own form of government and to supply themselves with
desired local services. . . . In general, the less home rule a
state allows its local units, the more the state legislature must
divert its time and energy from statewide concerns to the
details of local problems.*
The Commission on Intergovernmental Relations

During the last fifty years, government power gravitated
toward the national capital as surely as the Potomac River flowed into the
Atlantic Ocean. It was an understandable trend, for only the national
government had the money to fight the Depression in the 1930s and
World War ii in the 1940s.

At about the time older generations had adjusted their
political focus on Washington, D.C., events much closer to home forced
them to shift their attention suddenly back to governments at the local
level. Big cities exploded with racial violence, smog filled the urban air,
traffic slowed to a crawl, school boards grappled with busing crises, and
local police tried valiantly to stem the rising tide of crime. City halls and
county court houses were besieged with demands for action, yet seemed
paralyzed by confusion and financial crises.

After the spotlight swung to the local level, a new factor of
undetermined importance entered the scene. Eighteen-year-olds received the vote, and in cities and counties with large college campuses

they held a potential balance of political power. In the late summer of 1971 a newspaper headline announced "Young voters think local, not national"[1] and a few months later Newcomerstown, Ohio, elected a nineteen-year-old mayor. Local government, in various ways, was beginning to receive the closer look it had long deserved.

THE LEGACY OF LOCALISM

The significance of local government transcends the problems that have gained recent headlines. It lies both in its objective importance to the total political system and in the traditions and myths that surround it.

The Importance of Local Government

Employment   First, a very practical consideration: This is where the government jobs are. If you seek to get on the public payroll, or if you are a taxpayer concerned about meeting it, consider the fact that local governments in America employ more civilians than do the national and state governments combined—almost 9 percent of all employees in the entire nation.

Political incubator   The local level is where it all began for many of the major names in American politics. Television may permit a handful of handsome candidates to start at the top politically, but it is just as significant that Harry Truman started as a county judge, that Hubert Humphrey earned his spurs as mayor of Minneapolis, and that Spiro Agnew received his political baptism as a Baltimore County administrator. A 1955 study disclosed that twenty-nine United States senators and over one hundred representatives had had previous experience in local government.[2]

Local government is thus an agency of opportunity. While only 537 positions in the national government and some thirteen thousand at the state level are filled by popular vote, more than half a million local officials are elected by the people. Here, Herbert Kaufman cautions us that many local government jobs "are not ordinarily sought actively and may even be filled by reluctant incumbents who accept office only because they consider it a civic duty to do so." But subtracting those elective posts which may be of only marginal political utility, Kaufman still finds at least 170,000 jobs worth campaigning for in local governments.[3] Mathematically, then, the chance of being elected to a city council or school board is about fourteen times better than the possibility of being sent to Congress or the state legislature. For women and young

1 *Christian Science Monitor,* Sept. 1, 1971, p. 1.
2 Roscoe C. Martin, *Grass Roots Government* (University, Alabama: University of Alabama Press, 1957).
3 *Politics and Policies in State and Local Government* (Englewood Cliffs, N.J.: Prentice-Hall, Inc., 1963), p. 16.

Figure 43   Employment in National, State,
and Local American Governments, 1970

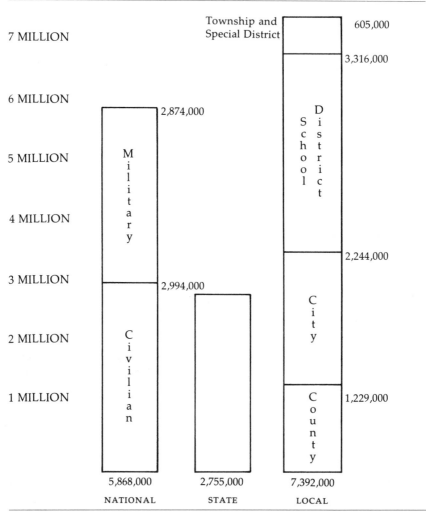

Source: U.S. Bureau of the Census, *Statistical Abstract of the United States: 1971*, pp. 250, 388, and 420.

people, so often bound to home and school, local politics may be especially attractive.

Style of life   The personality traits, the character, the value system of the average citizen are all affected far more by local agencies, particularly the public schools, than by state or national influence. Local politics are more personal, even private, than any other kind. It is a county official who records your birth and marriage, a city planning commission which may determine whether a gas station will be built on the vacant lot next door, a local school board which sets the attendance boundaries deciding how many black and white children get to know

Figure 44   Number of Governments and Their Elected Officials, 1967

	Governments	Elected Officials
National	1	537
State	50	13,038
County	3,049	74,199
City	18,048	143,927
Township	17,105	129,603
School District	21,264	107,663
Special District	21,782	56,943

Source: U.S. Bureau of the Census, *Statistical Abstract of the United States: 1971*, p. 363.

each other on the public school playgrounds. Should ill fates befall you—say, a permanently disabling injury, or poverty in old age—it is a county welfare worker who will parcel out your meager assistance. Are there "topless" bars in your part of town? Has sex education permeated your schools? Have your policemen unnecessarily abused the young black with a "natural" or the young hippie with bare feet? The answers are provided by local government.

To the dismay of many, the national government has narrowed the discretion of local officials in several of these areas. Planning commissions must sometimes make land-use decisions that are dictated by Washington guidelines for the use of urban-renewal funds; school boards must abandon forced segregation or lose federal aid to education; counties must dispense welfare money coming from the national government according to national specifications. Perhaps surrender of local control is too high a price to pay for financial assistance; where the need is acute, perhaps it isn't. It is a matter on which honest men may differ.

Ethnic integration   For members of ethnic minorities, local government is especially important. When the Irish, Italians, Poles, and other national groups began arriving in America, they were subjected to varying degrees of discrimination. In return for their votes, party machines in the cities gave them a few dollars, small favors, false promises, and a few token job appointments. The machines then took their continued loyalty for granted, but did little to earn it. To some degree, this situation still exists. As years passed, however, many of the unpopular groups developed one advantage which paid quicker dividends in local politics than it did in the social or business life of the community: They amassed large populations and voted for members of their own ethnic groups at the polls. Faced with social snobbery and economic discrimination, to them politics became the surest road to success.

Large concentrations of German-speaking peoples gained political control over such midwestern cities as St. Louis and Milwaukee. Farther north, Scandinavians dominated local government in Minnesota and the Dakotas. On both the East and West coasts, Italians played a major role, personified by men such as Senator John Pastore of Rhode Island and Mayor Joseph Alioto of San Francisco. Former New York

Mayor Fiorello La Guardia possessed the greatest of all political assets in that city, a Jewish mother and an Italian father. Still more impressive was the impact of the Irish in Boston. Once the entrenched stronghold of proper Puritans of English ancestry, the place where the "Cabots speak only to Lowells, and the Lowells speak only to God," its ethnic transformation soon gave power to such Irish Catholic families as the Fitzgeralds, McCormacks, and Curleys. The acceptability of this group was at last assured with the election of John F. Kennedy as President, aided by such assistants as Lawrence O'Brien and Kenneth O'Donnell, men promptly tabbed by political reporters as "the Irish Mafia."

When ethnic minorities voted a man into office, it was expected that he would appoint dozens of his compatriots to public jobs. Through such patronage an Irish background became an integral part of the policeman stereotype. It was primarily to counter this sort of spoils system that the civil service movement began almost a hundred years ago to insist on minimum standards and competitive examinations for would-be government employees. Members of ethnic minorities could also rise to prominence by supporting a political party organization, as well as by election or appointment to government jobs. The career of Carmine de Sapio, former boss of New York City's Democratic organization, Tammany Hall, is a case in point. A former New York official has summarized the importance of the local party in assimilating ethnic minorities:

The . . . machine *controlled* the vote. It took immigrants, made them citizens, bailed them out in Night Court, kissed their babies and took their adolescents on picnics. . . . It took various racial groups and saw to it that their most aggressive leaders were supplied with reasonably lucrative sinecures on the public payroll. Then, on election day, it took their votes in exchange. . . . The organization [now] . . . *influences* the vote. When it goes after racial and religious blocs—and both parties do—it does so by nominating a Negro to a higher office than ever before . . ., or an Italian for State-wide office, or a member of the Jewish faith for a post on the highest court of the State.[4]

No matter how much it may be deplored, politicians, especially in New York, still seek an ethnically balanced ticket. If the candidate for mayor is Irish, it is deemed imperative that the candidate for the city council presidency be Jewish, Protestant, or—if another Catholic seems inevitable—at least Italian or Polish. This is because national origins and religious preferences have a high correlation with voting behavior; bloc votes do indeed exist, and the Irish still vote for Irishmen and Italians for Italians.[5] This phenomenon has aided groups which have practiced it in sufficiently large numbers. As a result, upward mobility in American society is closer to reality in local government than

4 Warren Moscow, "Exit the Boss, Enter the Leader," *New York Times Magazine,* June 22, 1947.
5 See Duane Lockard's interesting example drawn from the Pastore and McGrath gubernatorial campaigns in Rhode Island. *The Politics of State and Local Government,* 2nd ed. (N.Y.: The Macmillan Company, 1969), p. 229.

perhaps in any other segment of our national life, with the exception of athletics and entertainment.

All this has obvious implications for blacks, who now constitute "the most important single interest in the politics of our cities today."[6] Power came to Carl Stokes of Cleveland, Kenneth Gibson of Newark, and Richard Hatcher of Gary, Indiana, because the black residents of those cities eagerly seized their opportunities to elect black mayors. This manifestation of "Black Power" would have been impossible without the bloc voting long traditional among so many other groups of Americans.[7]

Figure 45   Ethnic Composition of U.S. Cities

Rank	City	Population[1]	Foreign Stock Percentage[2]	Leading National Origin of Foreign Stock[2]	Negro Percentage[1]
1	New York	7,896,000	48.6	Italy	21.2
2	Chicago	3,369,000	35.9	Poland	32.7
3	Los Angeles	2,816,000	32.6	Mexico	17.9
4	Philadelphia	1,950,000	29.1	Italy	33.6
5	Detroit	1,513,000	32.2	Poland	43.7
6	Houston	1,233,000	9.7	Mexico	25.7
7	Baltimore	906,000	14.8	Russia	46.4
8	Dallas	844,000	6.9	Mexico	24.9
9	Washington, D.C.	757,000	12.6	Russia	71.1
10	Cleveland	751,000	30.9	Poland	38.3
11	Indianapolis	746,000	6.5	Germany	18.0
12	Milwaukee	717,000	30.0	Germany	14.7
13	San Francisco	716,000	43.5	Asia (China)	13.4
14	San Diego	697,000	21.5	Mexico	7.6
15	San Antonio	654,000	24.0	Mexico	7.6
16	Boston	641,000	45.5	Ireland	16.3

[1]Source: U.S. Bureau of the Census, *Statistical Abstract of the United States: 1971*, pp. 21–23. 1970 Census.
[2]Source: U.S. Bureau of the Census, *County and City Data Book*, 1967. 1960 Census. A person of foreign stock is one born in a foreign country or with one parent born in a foreign country.

The Myths of Local Government

Local government is more than an important political fact; it is a set of myths. Some correspond to reality quite closely while others do not, but all of them have shaped American attitudes toward local political authority.

6 C. Peter Magrath, Elmer E. Cornwall, and Jay S. Goodman, *The American Democracy* (London: The Macmillan Company, 1969), p. 158.
7 In Stokes' election as mayor of Cleveland in 1967, he received at least 88 percent of the vote in the ten wards that were at least 75 percent Negro, but no more than 30 percent in any of the fourteen wards which were more than 93 percent Caucasian. Jeffery K. Hadden, Louis H. Masotti and Victor Thiessen, "The Making of the Negro Mayors 1967," James D. Barber, ed., *Readings in Citizen Politics* (Chicago: Markham Publishing Company, 1969), p. 178.

Community In the fourth century, B.C., Plato envisioned an ideal state of only 5000 citizens. So enduring was this conception of utopia that eight hundred years later St. Augustine described perfection not in universal or even national terms but as the *City* of God. Things haven't changed much. Most of us today think of the good life in terms of a community. For some it is the tranquillity of quiet roads and for others the excitement of bustling boulevards, but few people dream of happiness on a state or national or global scale. Who cares about Vietnam when his neighbor may mug him—or bring soup to a sick wife?

The love of community leads to a preference for government at a local level. We tend to trust the authorities closest to us. We find it easiest to point the finger at those most remote, most strange, about whom we know least: Down with the U.N.; damn the Washington bureaucrat; up with the town council! Objections may be raised to this sort of local pride and community solidarity. It has seeds of narrow provincialism, says one argument. Another contends the local ties of territory are less significant than those of occupation, class, or race. But for many, the myth that the community is superior to other social units remains strong.

Democracy A second myth is the belief that local government is more democratic, more easily controlled by the people, than government at state or national levels. Facts, however, seem to weaken this faith. Voters seem to know, and care, less about local officials than national ones. In New York City, for example, those who voted for mayor were only 72 percent of presidential voters,[8] and in many elections for school board members or town councilmen the choice is made by less than half of all potential voters.[9]

Why is it so? Why should voter turnout be higher in national than in local elections? One explanation lies in the inevitable lack of concern which national magazines and television networks display toward local government. Another is the fact that increasing numbers of people move frequently from town to town, even from state to state, and thereby abandon interest in local leaders while continuing to focus on national figures. Most important, perhaps, is that Americans tend more and more to congregate in large municipalities, in which city hall is—or seems to be—as remote, impersonal, and bureaucratic as the state or national capitals.

The myth that local government is democratic government persists, nonetheless, probably because there seems high hope for its future potential. On this issue the liberals, even radicals, seem to be moving closer to what has been an essentially conservative position. In 1968 parents in the Brownsville and Oceanhill sections of New York City, mostly poor and black and liberal in their politics, fought for decentralizing control of the school system, thereby localizing it in a traditional and

8 Lockard, op. cit., pp. 28–29.
9 Robert R. Alford and Eugene C. Lee, "Voting Turnout in American Cities," *American Political Science Review* 62 (September 1968), p. 808.

very meaningful way. Indeed, the whole concept of "Black Power" came to be equated with local power: black policemen in black ghettoes, black mayors in predominantly black cities, black employees and managers in businesses selling to black customers. Among some in the New Left, "power to the people" meant power that was decentralized and thereby humanized. Their ideal of a participatory democracy required student influence in campus administration, worker influence in factory administration, and poor peoples' influence in the administration of poverty programs. All were varieties of local control, which, in a political context, was often defined as control by a community or a neighborhood rather than by a city or county.

All the while, in paradoxical agreement, the political right implored Americans to "Support your local police," and denounced the Supreme Court for usurping local control over such issues as prayer in schools and pornography in book stores. Whatever changes and inconsistencies may have occurred in the alignment of liberals and conservatives on the issue of local *vs.* central power, two conclusions may be reasonably drawn. One is that every group favors the concentration of governmental power at whatever level it can most easily influence, whether it is national, state, or local. Second, in an age of bigness, there is generally renewed interest in small units of government.

Efficiency   The advocates of decentralized power usually proclaim the superior efficiency of local government. An integral part of the stereotype of the Washington bureaucrat has been the red tape with which he nearly chokes his office. Five copies are made of documents when one would do. Needless secretaries have secretaries who have secretaries themselves. This sort of inefficiency is often thought to be less flagrant in town or city or county government.

Like many myths, this is probably a half-truth. Certain functions are probably performed most efficiently at a national level, others by states, and some by formal or informal neighborhood organizations. Two respected commentators note that "Centralized scientific research, specialized medical treatment, consolidated schools, and central depository libraries are all instances of economies that may be realized through centralization." Yet they observe shortly thereafter that "Obviously, too, there can be economies and efficiencies in decentralization."[10] Efficiency depends, then, on what is being centralized, and to what degree.

Honesty   If one believes politicians to be corrupt, it follows that the more successful they are, the more they are to be distrusted. Corruption is therefore sometimes thought to be more common in the national government than in its home town counterparts. The judgment of history indicates that obvious instances of dishonesty, *e.g.,* bribery, the lavish use of tax money for the pleasure of public officials, and

10 J. Roland Pennock and David G. Smith, *Political Science* (N.Y.: The Macmillan Company, 1964), p. 515 and 516.

kickbacks on government contracts, have occurred more often at local and state levels than at the national one. While only two presidential administrations have been badly tarnished by dishonesty—those of Grant and Harding—there are dozens of examples of corruption at local levels. In the late nineteenth and early twentieth centuries, city government was almost synonymous with corrupt government. The old "Tweed Ring" in New York was perhaps most notorious, but the later machines of Crump in Memphis, Pendergast in Kansas City, Curley in Boston, and Hague in Jersey City stirred the wrath of those pledged to morality in government. The most dishonest government America has ever seen, in all probability, was in the big cities of the North and the rural areas of the South, for these two areas were alike in their large proportions of the ignorant and the impoverished, both easily exploited by unscrupulous politicians.

The picture seems to have changed. Who could imagine a local political leader today who would publicly distinguish, as did George W. Plunkitt of Tammany Hall at the turn of the century, between "honest graft and dishonest graft."? An increase in literacy, the use of the secret ballot and the voting machine, the reform movement with its preference for professionally trained administrators, higher salaries for officials, and federally financed welfare programs to alleviate the poverty on which corruption feeds have all resulted in greater honesty. Nevertheless, much depends on the peculiar political culture of each community. Morality, like responsiveness to popular demands and administrative efficiency, in large measure reflects the traditions and expectations of the local population. For every public official who accepts a bribe, there is a private citizen who offered it.

THE BASIS OF LOCAL AUTHORITY
Legal Foundations

Local government goes totally without mention in the Constitution of the United States. As indicated in Chapter 2, our political system is characterized by a *federal* distribution of power in which only the national and state governments have independent constitutional authority. It is the states, organized as unitary systems, that delegate to local governments the only powers they possess. This legal principle, known as "Dillon's Rule," was established by John F. Dillon, a judge on the Iowa Supreme Court in the late nineteenth century. In certain respects, that rule has been modified by the substantial home rule that some states have granted to their cities and counties.

Varieties of Local Governments

Most Americans, familiar only with the region of the country in which they live, would be astonished by the more than 81,000 local governments existing in America. These include over 3000 counties, about 18,000 cities, 17,000 towns and townships, nearly 22,000 school districts, and 21,000 other special districts. This rather bewildering assortment is further confused by the differences in terminology found in various parts of the country, which result in units of government called boroughs, villages, parishes, and other names as well. We may simplify this variety of local governments by classifying them in two general categories: *quasi-municipal corporations* and *municipal corporations*. The first, of which counties are the leading example, are created by the states and are designed to function primarily as administrative subdivisions of them. The municipal corporations, among which cities are most important, operate under state law but are usually formed by local residents for the purpose of responding to local needs. In practice, many local governments fall partially into both categories, that is, they help carry out state policy and at the same time act in behalf of local interests.

The Delegation of Authority

The fifty states are free to delegate authority to local governments as they see fit. This is most frequently done in two ways, each of which has many variations.

Legislative enactment   The first method, legislative enactment, is by far the oldest and still the most common. It entails the passage of laws by the state legislature, often arranged into municipal codes, which prescribe the organizational structure for cities, counties, and other kinds of local government, along with the powers which they are permitted to exercise. Some of these laws may apply to all cities in the state, or there may be a separate statute passed for each city, as is the case in ten states.[11]

Between these two extremes are two compromise procedures. The one most widely used requires the state legislature to classify all cities according to population and to authorize particular government structures and powers for the cities in each class. This was designed to prevent the legislature from discriminating in favor of some cities and against others, but it has been abused occasionally by classification groupings into which only one city falls.[12] Sometimes, of course, the unusual size of a particular city may justify such a practice. The other compromise is an optional plan which allows cities to choose from among several different legislatively devised forms of government. This is the primary method of granting power to cities in a third of the states

11 Maine, New Hampshire, Vermont, Connecticut, Rhode Island, Delaware, Maryland, Florida, Georgia, and Tennessee. Much of the material in this section is taken from Clyde F. Snider, *American State and Local Government*, 2nd ed. (N.Y.: Appleton-Century-Crofts, 1965), pp. 26–28 and 352–55.
12 Philadelphia, Pittsburgh, and Indianapolis are examples in point. Lockard, op. cit., p. 119. At one time eleven different Ohio cities were in special classifications. Charles R. Adrian and Charles Press, *Governing Urban America*, 3rd ed. (N.Y.: McGraw-Hill Book Company, 1968), p. 168.

and obviously allows them wider discretion than the plans previously discussed.

County authority, too, is often conferred through classification systems or optional choices provided by the state legislatures. Townships, towns, and villages are empowered in this way more rarely, while public schools and special districts are almost always granted power only by the general laws applicable to all similar governmental units in the entire state.

Home rule Not surprisingly, cities and counties lost patience rather quickly with their subordinate role in the unitary structures of the states. Why, indeed, should they be controlled by state legislators who often had never set foot within their borders? The local governments answered by launching what came to be known as the home-rule movement. In essence, home rule permits cities and counties to establish their own forms of government in documents called charters. These are, in effect, local constitutions and usually require the approval of both the local voters and the state legislature.

Cities sometimes get the initial authority to draw up their own charters from laws passed by the state legislatures, but in twenty-six states, beginning with Missouri in 1875, that power has been derived directly from the state constitution, subject only to a few minor restrictions.[13] Of the approximately eighteen thousand cities in the United States, some five thousand have been permitted to write charters and about one thousand have done so.[14] It seems certain that most of these are among the 5400 cities whose populations exceed 2500. Only half as many state constitutions now make provision for county home rule as for similar city power.[15] Of the nation's three thousand counties, five hundred are permitted to draw up charters but only twenty have done so. Half of these are in California, which started it all in 1911.[16]

How important has home rule really become? Although a charter permits considerable freedom in establishing local government structure, and sometimes expands local taxing powers, it does very little to increase local authority in determining government policy. Only charter cities, for example, can usually decide whether the city clerk should be elected or appointed, or how many persons should serve on the city council. But, ordinarily, such municipalities have no more authority to legalize gambling or limit building heights than those who receive their powers through legislative enactment. Another factor to bear in mind is that some states have given local governments substantial authority whether they have adopted charters or not. In Wisconsin,

13 In addition to Missouri, these are Alaska, Arizona, California, Colorado, Hawaii, Kansas, Louisiana, Maryland, Michigan, Minnesota, Nebraska, Nevada, New Mexico, New York, Ohio, Oklahoma, Oregon, Pennsylvania, Rhode Island, Tennessee, Texas, Utah, Washington, West Virginia, and Wisconsin.
14 Snider, op. cit., p. 73.
15 These are the constitutions of California, Florida, Hawaii, Louisiana, Maryland, Michigan, Minnesota, Missouri, New York, Ohio, Oregon, Texas, and Washington.
16 Snider, op. cit., p. 74.

Oregon, and California, according to one writer, legislative enactment confers so much discretion on all cities that they may "feel no need for a locally drawn charter."[17]

Perhaps the most impressive testimony to the increasing authority of local government comes from the President's Advisory Commission on Inter-governmental Relations which has asserted that "with the spread of municipal and county home rule, local units of government are becoming residuaries of 'sovereignty' in a fashion comparable to the Federal-state relationship."[18] Whether home rule will subvert "Dillon's Rule" to the extent that state-local relations are really transformed from a unitary to a federal basis is best left for the future to determine.

COUNTY GOVERNMENT

Although county governments are less important than they once were, they still have jurisdiction over more people than city governments, and are an appropriate place to begin our consideration of the various types of grass roots political units.

The Counties: a Panoramic View

The 3049 counties in America, averaging about sixty per state, are found in all states except Rhode Island, Connecticut, and Alaska (although they are called parishes in Louisiana). They range in number from three in Delaware to 254 in Texas. In thirteen states there are small areas, usually cities, which are exempt from the jurisdiction of any county government. These include the municipalities of Baltimore, Maryland; St. Louis, Missouri; and thirty-three cities in Virginia.[19]

Significance Not only are counties the most pervasive units of local government in America, but they have a history dating back to the formation of Henrico County, Virginia, in 1611—only four years after the establishment of the first English colony. In much of colonial America, they were the principal unit of local government, and during the intervening years they have exercised more authority over more people than any other variety of local government. Even today, Los Angeles County, California, most populous in the country, has a budget exceeding that of thirty states,[20] and a population greater than forty-

17 John R. Kerstetter, "Municipal Home Rule," *The Municipal Yearbook, 1956* (Washington, D.C.: International City Managers' Association, 1956), pp. 255–66.
18 *Apportionment of State Legislatures* (Washington, D.C.: Government Printing Office, 1962), p. 44.
19 This information, and some of the other statistical data in this chapter, is taken from the U.S. Bureau of the Census, *County and City Data Book: 1967* (A Statistical Abstract Supplement). The information cited here is from p. 610.
20 The Los Angeles County budget, excluding expenditures of special districts, was $844,383,466 in the 1964–65 fiscal year. Beth Wycoff, ed., *Los Angeles County Almanac, 1968* (Los Angeles: The Republican Central Committee of Los Angeles County, 1968), p. 38. This figure more than doubled in the next six years, reaching $1,771,142,551 for the 1970–71 fiscal year.

three states. Initially strongest in the South, county government is now equally important in the West, of somewhat less significance in the Midwest and East, and remains of least consequence in New England. The following discussion focuses primarily on county governments that display considerable influence and continuing vitality.

Size   The range of population and area found in America's counties is matched only by the diversity of the problems they face. While several million people are concentrated in Los Angeles County, Cook County, Illinois (the site of Chicago), and Wayne County, Michigan (the location of Detroit), only a few hundred widely dispersed residents are to be found in Hinsdale County, Colorado, Loving County, Texas, or Alpine County, California. In 1970 the average county population was about sixty-seven thousand. No less remarkable is the disparity in area: The biggest, San Bernardino County, California, sprawls over twenty thousand square miles—larger than nine states—and the smallest, Arlington County, Virginia, embraces only twenty-four. The national average is about nine hundred square miles.

The "Dark Continent" Brightens: County Functions

Rural roots   When most Americans were farmers, the county was the brightest bloom of grass roots government. It built the roads, settled disputes over farm boundaries, often supervised the schools, and even guarded the health of the livestock. State legislators were frequently elected from county-wide districts and the national and state governments helped finance the distribution of expert agricultural advice, as they still do, through officials known as county agents. At the town honored by designation as the county seat, one did major shopping, sold crops, and enjoyed the leisure and diversion reserved usually for Saturday nights.

Dual purposes   As Americans streamed into cities and suburbs, their identification with counties weakened quickly. The counties' proper place in the total scheme of government became so uncertain that one writer called them the "Dark Continent of American Politics."[21] One reason for this confusion is that the county, as a *quasi*-municipal corporation, has long lived in a condition of limbo, partly a creature of the state government which created it, and partly a product of the local population which placed demands upon it. Consequently, counties serve two purposes: They assume state-imposed responsibilities for everyone within their borders, and they assume local responsibilities demanded by people not served by city governments.

21 The phrase was H. S. Gilbertson's. See John A. Fairlie, "County Government," *Encyclopedia of the Social Sciences*, IV, pp. 504–08.

Some of the state-imposed functions are:

1) administration of relief to the poor, and other welfare programs;
2) assessment and collection of property taxes;
3) maintenance of property-ownership records;
4) voter registration and election administration;
5) issuance of marriage licences and birth certificates;
6) road construction and repair;
7) criminal prosecution and jail operation;
8) maintenance of health and hospital facilities.

In response to urbanization and other socioeconomic changes, counties have gradually assumed the second category of responsibilities. These require state authorization, but have been assumed in part as a result of the demands of residents themselves. Such functions may not be available to all county residents because they are, in a sense, city services for people who don't live in cities. Among the more important are:

1) fire and police protection;
2) park and recreation facilities;
3) building code adoption and enforcement;
4) airport and/or harbor operation;
5) control of alcoholic beverage sales;
6) business licensing and vice legislation;
7) library facilities.

In all these respects, the differences among counties are enormous.

Future potential   Is county government worth keeping in an increasingly metropolitan age? Or is it merely, as one scholar asserted, a "weirdly archaic survival"[22] of our rural past? Most local government experts seem to have confidence in the county, although many city officials have their doubts. There are four clouds that many observers see hovering above the future path of county development. One of these is the excessive number of counties which, in the interests of efficiency, should be reduced by consolidation. Such a proposal became a major political issue in New Mexico in 1971. The other major problems currently confronting most counties are the lack of strong executive officers, the need (shared by most other local governments) for additional money, and the reluctance of many states to grant more home rule.

Yet the road ahead still looks generally bright, perhaps chiefly because quite a few counties have responded to urban needs by providing an effective substitute for city government. Of the 310 counties in metropolitan areas, all over 100,000 in population in 1960, police protection for residents living outside city boundaries was provided by 152, libraries by one hundred, street construction services by 112, and

22 Thomas H. Eliot, *Governing America,* 2nd ed. (N.Y.: Dodd, Mead & Co., 1964), p. 742.

parks by ninety-five. Even for people living within cities, over forty of these counties provided all of the above services. Twelve also assumed responsibility for fire fighting, and five even provided for garbage collection.[23] These examples have been so notable that the further strengthening of county government as a solution to urban problems has been advocated by the Committee for Economic Development, the Republican Coordinating Committee and, predictably, the National Association of Counties.[24]

One of the major obstacles to the solution of problems confronting metropolitan areas is that they are divided into ever-increasing numbers of separate cities and other governmental jurisdictions. Therefore, a chief goal of urban reformers has been to keep people with common needs within common areas of governmental authority. If they breathe the same polluted air or are stalled together in the same traffic jam, they should be able to turn to the same political agency to demand relief. Because about half of the regions defined as metropolitan areas by the Census Bureau fall within a single county, there the county government can at least help reduce the number of newly created cities in a single urban complex. In California, for example, a 1963 state law authorized a Local Agency Formation Commission in each county to pass on the incorporation of additional cities. Even more sweeping changes, as we shall see later, have come about as a result of governmental consolidation in Marion County, Indiana, Davidson County, Tennessee, and Dade and Duval Counties in Florida.

Nevertheless, there are reasons for doubting the durability, and certainly the necessity, of county governments in America. Rhode Island has fared well without them for years, Connecticut recently abolished them, and Alaska, when joining the family of states, pointedly refrained from establishing them. Hawaii, the most recent entry into the Union, established few and delegated relatively little power to them. In North Carolina, Delaware, West Virginia, and most of Virginia, control over county roads has been transferred to the state governments. The bulk of the evidence indicates, however, that the counties have survived, and in some cases facilitated, the transition from a rural to an urban America rather well.

Organizational Structure: Fusion of Power

County governments are so numerous and diverse that it is a surprise to learn that the vast majority are quite similar in one vital characteristic. This is the fusion of legislative and executive authority in the same officials, and hence the absence of the separation of powers

---

23 Victor Jones, "The Changing Role of the Urban County in Local Government," *Public Affairs Report,* June 1963 (Berkeley: Institute of Governmental Studies, University of California).
24 Hoyt Gimlin, "Local Government Modernization," *Editorial Research Reports on the Urban Environment* (Washington, D.C.: Congressional Quarterly, Inc., 1969), p. 78.

principle so characteristic of American government at other levels. The county board embodies this fusion.

The county board   Boards are the chief governing bodies in the counties and bear a wide assortment of labels—supervisors, commissions, county courts, boards of revenue, and still others. They number from three to 111 members (in Wayne County, Michigan), although five to nine is the most common size. Members are usually elected from districts of relatively equal population, but in about a fifth of the counties, all are chosen by the voters of the entire county at large.

These bodies are largely administrative agencies with responsibility for implementing policies that the states have imposed on them. Yet with the movement for local home rule, boards have gained increasing legislative power as well. They may impose certain taxes, appropriate money, and in states that have permitted local option on such matters as gambling or the sale of liquor, county boards may pass local laws (called *ordinances*) determining policy on these issues as well. Where cities also have local option, the county ordinances usually apply only to the unincorporated areas falling outside municipal boundaries.

County administrative departments   The number of agencies in a given county depends on its size and the functions it performs. The largest is often the welfare department, providing aid to the needy. Although financial assistance for this program comes from the national government, the counties must bear much of the burden of paying for its administration. The sheriff's department is also important, especially where there are no state-wide police agencies authorized to enforce the bulk of criminal law. In any event, county jails normally fall under the sheriff's jurisdiction, and their business is booming. A third vital department is the assessor's office, which has the responsibility of appraising all real estate to determine its value for property tax purposes. Traditionally, the property tax has been the main source of income for counties and all other units of local government as well.

The offices of recorder and registrar, sometimes combined, stand guard over the major milestones of life for county residents. Here one finds official acknowledgements of births, deaths, marriages, divorces, mortgages, deeds, and sometimes voter registrations. In many counties, there is also a clerk who may issue certain business licenses, grant hunting and fishing permits, prepare minutes and agendas for county board meetings, sometimes perform the functions of recorder-registrar, and—in a few instances—exert direction over other administrative and judicial functions.

Among the most colorful of county officials is the district attorney. The "fighting D.A.," firmly embedded in American legend as a fearless champion of the helpless against the ruthless, normally has the responsibility of bringing criminal defendants to trial. The political careers of Earl Warren, former Chief Justice of the United States Supreme Court, and Thomas E. Dewey, New York governor and twice the presidential nominee of the Republican party, were propelled from the launching pads of this office. In addition, many counties possess a coroner to determine the cause of death if it occurs under curious circumstances, a treasurer to maintain surveillance over the receipts and allocations of county funds, and a county highway superintendent. The heads of the departments and offices mentioned here are sometimes appointed by the county board, but too often chosen by a confused and overburdened electorate.

Executive consolidation   Mae West, the reigning sex queen of three generations of Americans, once said that too much of a good thing is wonderful. Perhaps so. But if the election of public officials is good, then most county governments are absurdly wonderful. In 1967 an average of twenty-four county officials were elected by the voters in each county.[25] The total includes many administrators with very little policy-making authority. It is clearly unlikely that the average voter will learn much about the relative merits of candidates for coroner, recorder, surveyor, or similar county offices. They are seldom discussed in the media and their functions are about as clear to most citizens as those of a Russian procurator. To put it briefly, too many county executive officials are elected by voters who know too little about them.

Three solutions to this problem have been proposed. One is to have county officials appointed by the county board and responsible to it. This plan has had discouragingly few adoptions. The second is to create a county manager to supervise and coordinate administrative departments. In Wisconsin, thirty counties permit the county clerk to assume this function and in some Alabama and Arkansas counties certain county judges have administrative powers resembling those of a chief executive. Most observers, however, advocate the selection of a separate manager by the county board, with authority similar to that of city managers in cities that possess council-manager forms of government. County managers can hire, and often fire, most department heads. This system is employed in about thirty counties in the United States located in at least ten states—North Carolina, Virginia, California, Georgia, Maryland, Florida, Nevada, Montana, New York, and Tennessee.

Even more counties have increased administrative coordination substantially, although not to the degree possible under county managers, through board-appointed chief administrative officers. These "quasi managers" now help boards to perform their executive functions in Hamilton County, Tennessee (which includes the city of Chattanooga), Cuyahoga County, Ohio (the location of Cleveland), and in certain counties in South Carolina, Oregon, and California. The government of Los Angeles County is fairly typical of these.

The third reform is more dramatic. It strips the board almost completely of its administrative authority and creates a genuine separa-

25 U.S. Bureau of the Census, *Statistical Abstract of the United States: 1971,* p. 363.

Figure 46   The Government of Los Angeles County

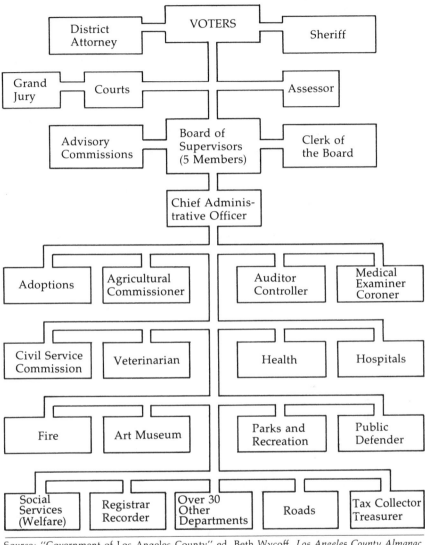

Source: "Government of Los Angeles County" ed. Beth Wycoff, *Los Angeles County Almanac 1968*. Reprinted by permission of The Republican Central Committee of Los Angeles County.

tion of powers comparable to that at the national and state levels. This is accomplished by providing for a county chief executive to be elected directly by the voters. About a dozen counties now have such a plan, including DeKalb, Georgia; Milwaukee County, Wisconsin; Jefferson Parish, Louisiana; and Westchester, Erie, Nassau, Suffolk, Oneida, and Onondaga Counties in New York. This form of government was also implemented in 1969 by King County, Washington, encompassing the city of Seattle, with a population of about a million and a quarter. It has been endorsed by Bernard F. Hillenbrand, executive director of the National Association of Counties.[26]

All these reforms have two essential objectives: to make county government more democratic and more efficient. The large number of elected officials makes both of these goals unattainable. The essence of democracy is a government whose officials are responsible to the wishes of a majority of the citizens. Yet voters can hardly hold politicians responsible if there are so many of them that they can't even remember their names.

The essence of efficiency involves clear-cut lines of administrative authority to carry out coordinated policies. Yet the existence of many elected executives, none of whom has any real power over the others, and who often have widely differing policy views, contributes more to chaos than coordination. As we have seen, this problem bedevils the executive branches of most of our state governments as well.

TOWNS, TOWNSHIPS, AND SPECIAL DISTRICTS
Towns: The Pride of New England

In informal conversation the term "town" usually refers to a small city, and it has that legal status in certain parts of the country. But in New England, where towns include rural as well as urban areas, it has a different meaning. There, as a scholar from that region has said, it is "the most local of local governments,"[27] representing the purest form of direct (as distinguished from representative) democracy to be found in the American political system. There are over 1400 such units of government performing functions normally associated with both cities and counties in other parts of the country.

The town meeting   Governmental authority in the town is centered in the town meeting—an annual assemblage which all voters are eligible to attend. It levies taxes, appropriates money, and establishes broad guidelines for town policy. It also elects a moderator who presides over the meeting itself, a board of selectmen (called town council in Rhode Island) which possesses administrative responsibility, and a clerk who issues "marriage, dog, and liquor licenses."[28]

Recent modifications   Obviously, this form of government is most appropriate for small towns, where it still functions quite satisfactorily. But as populations increase, modifications must be made. Thus, Brookline, Massachusetts, established a representative town meeting system in 1915 which is now employed in several dozen other towns as well. This entails the election of about a hundred town meeting members

26 Ray Zeman, "County Manager Plan May Be Put on Ballot," *Los Angeles Times,* Feb. 1, 1970, Sec. B, p. 2.
27 Robert S. Babcock, *State and Local Government and Politics* (N.Y.: Random House, Inc., 1956), p. 95.
28 Ibid., p. 97.

to perform the functions formerly shared by all voters interested enough to attend the meetings. The increasing complexity of local government has also prompted boards of selectmen in about two hundred towns to appoint full-time professional managers.

Townships: Midwestern Mainstays?

Form and functions   Just as the town is an important unit of local government in New England so, to a lesser extent, is the township in fifteen states of the Midwest and parts of the East.[29] In about half of these states, townships are governed by an annual meeting of interested citizens. In the remainder, governmental power is vested in a specially elected board or in a board consisting of other elected officials such as the township clerk, treasurer, and justice of the peace.

The townships' major responsibility is usually the maintenance of roads, although they frequently administer elections, collect taxes, give assistance to the poor, and engage in law enforcement. In Illinois, they serve as school districts, and in five states—Kansas, Michigan, New Jersey, New York, and Pennsylvania—urban townships may now exercise some municipal authority.

Gradual decline   Unlike the New England towns which have assumed numerous municipal functions and demonstrated considerable adaptability, most townships have remained primarily rural in character and have become increasingly expendable. They are essentially subdivisions of the county governments (which have gradually usurped many of their responsibilities), and it is generally agreed that they are too small to function economically. Consequently, when experts deplore the excessive number of local governments, townships become their leading candidates for extermination. Their total number has diminished in fact, and Oklahoma has abolished them completely.

Special Districts: Jacks-of-One-Trade

Like those at the national and state levels, most kinds of local governments are jacks-of-all-trades, each performing a variety of functions. Special districts, on the contrary, are normally limited to just one specific job. They are about equal in number to cities and counties combined, and are multiplying more rapidly than any other kind of government, having increased from just over 12,000 to more than 21,000 between 1952 and 1967.

Purposes and rationale   Why are these other local governments needed? Many authorities would snort that they are not—at least not in such profusion. Needed or not, there are several reasons why they

---

29 These are Illinois, Indiana, Kansas, Michigan, Minnesota, Missouri, Nebraska, New Jersey, New York, North Dakota, Ohio, Pennsylvania, South Dakota, Washington, and Wisconsin. In New York and Wisconsin the townships are called towns and in Washington they exist in only two counties. Snider, op. cit., pp. 347–48.

were formed. First, many special districts cope with problems common to an area that does not conform to other government boundaries. In southern California, for example, the Metropolitan Water District includes eight counties, and the Port of New York Authority encompasses parts of two states—New York and New Jersey—because its harbor facilities sprawl across state boundaries. At the other extreme, there are street lighting districts which cover areas considerably smaller than the cities in which they are located.

A second reason for the formation of special districts is the desire to evade state restrictions on the taxing and borrowing powers of other local government units. If a county has raised all the money it legally can, for example, it is tempting to form new units of government to defray expenses for such facilities as libraries or hospitals. Still another factor favoring creation of special districts is the desire to keep certain functions "out of politics," or at least beyond the realm of political party competition and the hiring of employees on a patronage basis.

The chief functions performed by these specialized governments, in order of frequency, entail fire protection, soil conservation, drainage, water supply, cemeteries, housing and urban renewal, and sewerage. Their diversity is indicated by the fact that over 3500 special districts are devoted to purposes other than these leading ones.

Operation   Sometimes the states provide for the creation of special districts by the state legislature but most often by the authorized action of cities, counties, or groups of voters using the initiative and referendum. Each district is usually permitted to levy charges for its services, to impose a property tax up to a certain maximum, and to incur some bonded indebtedness. In this way it is expected that citizens who are served by a district will pay the costs of its operation.

The governments of special districts are varied in form. Usually authority is integrated in a single body which is sometimes chosen by the state governor or a judge, but more frequently by the county boards or city councils of the area included in the district. Occasionally voters elect the governing officials.[30] Special districts are located in every state. Illinois has the most, followed by California, Pennsylvania, Kansas, Texas, New York, Nebraska, and Washington— each with over nine hundred. There are proportionately more situated in rural areas than urban ones although they are important nearly everywhere.

Criticism   It is impossible to deny that the functions performed by special districts are essential ones, but easy to argue that they should be discharged by some other unit of government instead. The chief objection to them is that they impede the integration and unified control of local affairs. More specifically, they make it difficult to transfer tax funds from one use to another, they diminish the significance of

30 The scholar who has devoted more extensive attention to special districts than any other is probably John C. Bollens. See his *Special District Governments in the United States* (Berkeley: University of California Press, 1957).

counties and cities, and they remove governmental authority from effective control by the people, who are often unaware of the existence of many special districts.

The Others: Many Brands, Few Products

Like detergents and shaving creams, local governments bear a variety of labels with essentially similar contents. Small cities, for example, often have such legal designations as "villages" (in the Midwest and New England), "boroughs" (in the East), and "towns" (in the South and West). Many state legislatures classify cities by size, and sometimes vary the terminology accordingly. Similarly, several states— mostly southern—subdivide counties into units similar to townships, but with far less authority. These are called "hundreds," "precincts," "civil districts," or "militia districts." School districts, severely affected by metropolitan problems, are discussed in Chapter 14. But first, we look at the cities.

Chapter **13**

The Cities
Structure and Politics

I resent people talking about the near-impossible job of
running New York: What do they mean by "near"?
Mayor John V. Lindsay

America is a nation of cities. According to 1970 census
figures, there are twenty-six more populous than four of our states, and
six of them—New York, Chicago, Los Angeles, Philadelphia, Detroit,
and Houston—have over a million inhabitants. In international terms,
New York City has more people than Switzerland or Sweden, Chicago
has more than Ireland or Israel, and Los Angeles more than Lebanon or
Laos. Historically, just as the county was the principal local government
of a rural America, so the municipality (legally termed city, town, or
village depending on the size and section of the country) is the dominant
political unit today.

THE FORMS OF GOVERNMENT

Cities may be classified in many different ways. For example, those with home rule charters have some control over their own
governmental structure, while for others, a structure is prescribed by
state law. More significant here, however, are the different forms of city
governments.

Mayor-Council Plan

The oldest and most common type of city government is the mayor-council form. The most distinctively American, it is based on the separation of executive and legislative powers common also to national and state governments. This form has two major variations, the strong-mayor and weak-mayor plans, but each entails the popular election of both a city council to make policy and a mayor with greater or lesser authority to carry it out.

Rather oddly, it is most entrenched in the smallest cities (under 25,000) and in the largest ones (over 250,000). The weak-mayor variety is characteristic of the former while a strong mayor is prevalent in the latter. The distinction between these two varieties rests on whether the mayor has the veto power and on how many department heads he can appoint and directly control. If he can hire and fire the city clerk, attorney, police chief, and other municipal administrators, he is "strong." If these officials are elected by the voters, or are responsible largely to the city council or to citizens' commissions appointed to oversee each department, then the mayor is relatively "weak."

Among mayor-council cities, the trend has been from the weak-mayor toward the strong-mayor variety. In 1936, 70 percent of cities over 5000 elected two or more administrative officials, thereby diminishing the mayor's power, but within thirty years this figure had dropped to 48 percent.[1] The change can be attributed to the fact that centralized executive authority promotes better coordination among the city departments and hence greater rationality in the allocation of budget funds. New York, New Orleans, Boston, Cleveland, and Detroit are among the strong-mayor cities, while Atlanta and Seattle provide weak-mayor contrasts. Mayor-council governments, strong and weak alike, prevail among ethnically and religiously diverse industrialized cities, especially in the East.[2]

Council-Manager Plan

The mayor-council form of government reigned unchallenged until early in this century when the progressive movement launched a wave of political invention of which the chief result for local government was the council-manager form of government.

Origins of the plan In 1908 the city council of Staunton, Virginia, hired a manager to coordinate the administration of city functions. This general idea was popularized by Richard S. Childs, president

[1] Charles R. Adrian and Charles Press, *Governing Urban America,* 3rd ed. (N.Y.: McGraw-Hill Book Company, 1968), p. 189. This change reflects the increased popularity of the council-manager form of government, discussed later, as well as a switch from weak to strong mayor.
[2] Robert R. Alford and Harry M. Scoble, "Political and Socioeconomic Characteristics of American Cities," *Municipal Yearbook, 1965* (Washington, D.C.: International City Managers Association, 1965), pp. 82–98.

Figure 47   The Mayor-Council Form of City Government

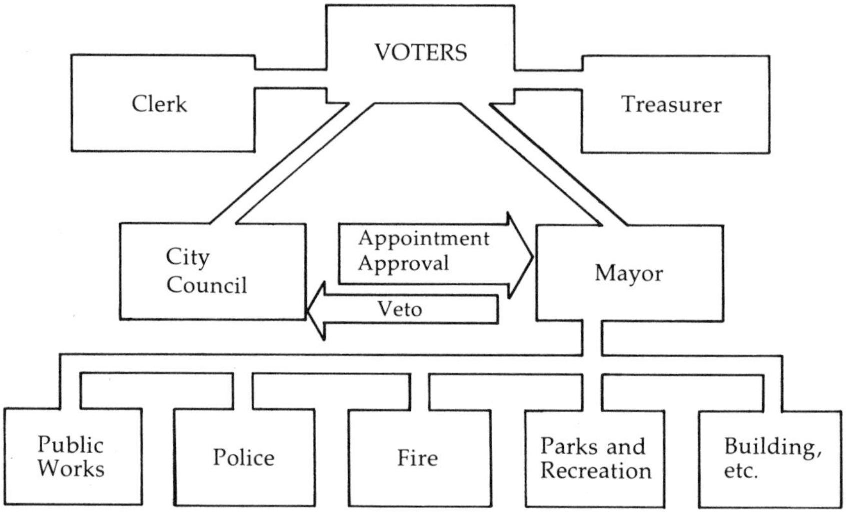

of the National Municipal League, and is still advocated by the League's
Model City Charter. Such a plan was placed in more formal operation by
Sumter, South Carolina, in 1912, but did not command national attention
until 1914 when Dayton, Ohio, devastated by a severe flood along the
Miami River, attempted to deal more effectively with such problems by
adopting a new city charter providing a council-manager form of government. Subsequently the plan spread quickly. It had been adopted by 273
cities in 1924, 613 in 1944, and over 2100 in 1972, becoming the most
commonly employed form of government in medium-sized cities with
populations from 25,000 to 250,000. It is most popular in rapidly growing
cities, in suburbs, and in the West and South. The largest cities employing it are Dallas, San Antonio, San Diego, Kansas City, Phoenix,
Cincinnati, Oklahoma City, Oakland, Long Beach, and Fort Worth—all
over 350,000 population.

Characteristics   The council-manager form of government
abolishes the traditional separation of powers. The city council both
determines policy and also appoints the manager, who supervises the
departments which carry it out. The voters, therefore, may hold the
council accountable for all of city government; the council may hold the
manager responsible for administering policy; and the manager may
hold department heads answerable for the final enforcement and implementation of city regulations and services. This particular scheme, more
closely than any other, approaches two of the most cherished goals of
professional public administrators: (1) Lines of authority and responsibility should be clear-cut and uniform, and (2) there should be a
differentiation between the "political" officials who make policy and the
"administrative" officials who carry it out.

Figure 48   The Council-Manager Form of City Government

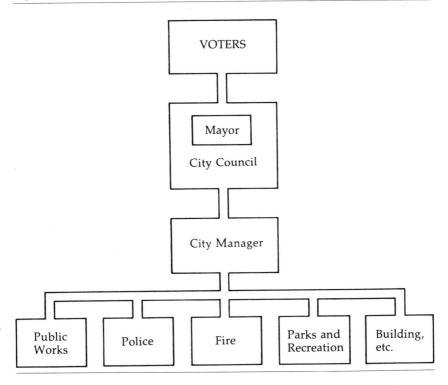

Relative merits   Is the council-manager plan better than the mayor-council one? Using a test of expertise, it would seem so. More than twenty universities have offered administrative training designed for city managers and about two thirds of all people holding that post have been recruited from other cities because of their professional success. City councils, with only rare exceptions, hire managers on the basis of their administrative qualifications. In sharp and sorry contrast, most mayors lack both the training and experience relevant to such responsibilities as effective budgeting, personnel recruitment, and the awarding of contracts for the construction of public buildings. Instead, mayors are usually elected because they have acquired considerable political influence as lawyers, realtors, or city councilmen. Many are chosen because they are well known and popular, possess a kind of flamboyant charm, and televise well.

On the other hand, while conceding the superiority of the council-manager plan in administrative expertise, many argue that in a democracy, the best form of government is not necessarily that which is best administered, but that which is most responsive to public needs. It might not be efficient or economical, for example, to reroute a major highway around a small park, at considerable expense, merely because it was important to the local children or particularly pretty. Yet considerations of service, beauty, or sentiment are no less important because they cannot be measured by adding machines or computers. In the same vein, city managers are criticized for putting so much emphasis on middle-class standards of orderliness and public frugality that it is difficult for them to compromise the conflicting interests of diverse racial and economic groups found especially in large cities.

Many believe that a strong mayor is more sensitive to community values than a city manager, in part because the mayor risks his job whenever he ignores them, while the city manager is usually secure in his preoccupation with administrative efficiency. Unfortunately, however, the same kind of political responsiveness which makes mayors keenly attuned to public opinion may also make them excessively solicitous of local pressure groups or wealthy supporters. City managers present the dilemma in reverse: While less susceptible to the political pressures of organization and money, they may also be less likely to respond to the legitimate wishes of the rank-and-file citizens. For this reason, in part, a radical slate of candidates was elected to the Berkeley, California, city council in 1971 on a platform that included the abolition of council-manager government in favor of the old mayor-council form.

Critics of the council-manager plan also argue that it really does not insulate the impersonal processes of administration from the heat of political, or policy-making, considerations. As evidence, they cite a study of eight council-manager cities in Florida which revealed that over a fifteen-year period, twenty-two changes occurred in the power factions controlling city councils, and as a result, city managers were fired on twelve of these occasions. Moreover, the same study found that "all managers . . . were involved to a greater or lesser degree in the shaping or vetoing of public policy."[3] It has also been contended that these professional administrators tend to resign their jobs too frequently when lured by a higher salary in another city, and occasionally dominate the city councils from whom they are supposed to take orders. With an amateur, part-time council, meeting only weekly or biweekly, the latter danger is especially great.[4]

Perhaps no form of government is "best," except in terms of the unique aspirations and problems of specific cities. The council-manager form holds maximum hope for honesty, efficiency, and expertise; the mayor-council form seems more democratic, humane, and responsive to the citizens. Some large cities seem to have acknowledged the advantage of a professional city manager, while still retaining a mayor-council form of government, by appointing an official who serves as a chief administrative officer. He is chosen by the mayor and usually has some authority for departmental supervision and budget preparation. New Orleans, San Francisco, New York, Philadelphia, and Los Angeles

3 Gladys M. Kammerer, et al., The Urban Political Community (Boston: Houghton Mifflin Company, 1963), pp. 193–94.
4 William T. Evjue, "Is the City-Manager Plan the Answer? No," Better Homes and Gardens, June 1957, pp. 14–18, 21–22, 191.

are among cities employing such officials, although sometimes with different titles.[5]

Commission Plan

Running a poor third among forms of city government is the commission system. Just as the council-manager plan surfaced from the flood waters in Dayton, so the commission form was conceived in the rubble of a hurricane and tidal wave that struck Galveston, Texas, in 1900. Des Moines, Iowa, was impressed by the success of the new idea in Galveston, adopted it in 1907, and thereby gave it nation-wide impetus. Although it was utilized by about five hundred cities at the peak of its popularity, this number has dropped substantially, and even Des Moines defected to the council-manager form in 1949. Although commission cities are found most frequently in the South, there are a few in all sections of the country—in total over 160, of which the largest are Memphis, Portland (Oregon), St. Paul, and Tulsa.

The commission plan obliterates the separation of powers even more than the council-manager form. It entails the election of a single body called a commission, usually consisting of five persons. Collectively, this commission acts as a legislative body, enacting ordinances and functioning as a city council. Individually, however, each commissioner is an executive official heading one or more city departments. There is thus a police (or public safety) commissioner, a public works commissioner, a recreation and parks commissioner, and so forth.

The chief advantages of the system are that it is fairly simple, permits a short ballot, and eliminates the paralysis stemming from the executive-legislative conflict often found in mayor-council cities. The disadvantages, however, seem more important, for the plan lacks the coordinated, highly visible, and sometimes inspired leadership which a strong mayor can provide in a mayor-council system, and at the same time it contributes none of the professional competence, experience, and efficiency associated with the council-manager form. Disputes among department heads (who are really the elected commissioners) about such matters as budget allocations are difficult to resolve because of the lack of overall leadership. Whatever its merits, the commission plan is historically important as the first major innovation in American city government.

THE INSTITUTIONS OF GOVERNMENT

Regardless of the varied forms that city governments may take, they have much in common. Some of their characteristic institutions and political processes can now be examined.

---

5 Wallace S. Sayre, "The General Manager Idea for Large Cities," *Public Administration Review* 14 (Autumn 1954): 253–58.

Figure 49   The Commission Form of City Government

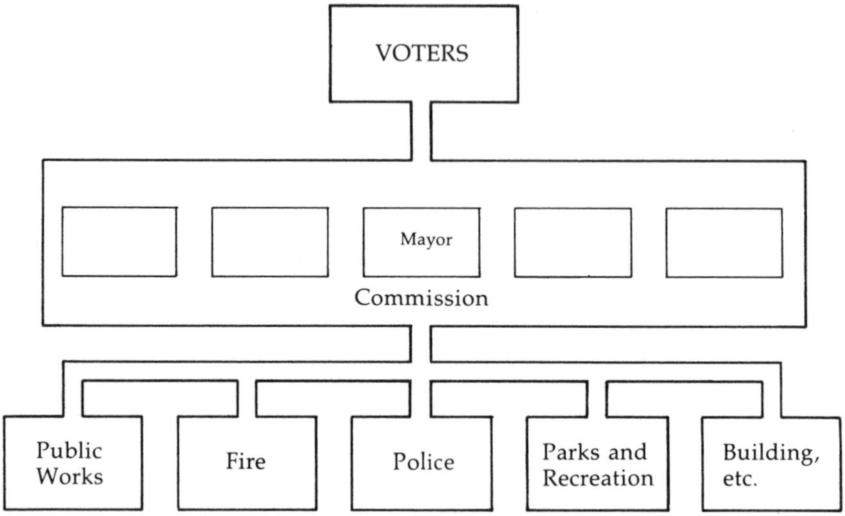

City Councils

All governments must determine public policy. In most cities, this legislative function is performed by a city council, which passes ordinances for levying taxes, spending money, building parks and police stations, zoning land for factories, stores, and homes, and generally creating, at its most enlightened level of performance, whatever the people may define as "a good community." At one time over a third of all councils were bicameral bodies, but the second house has now all but disappeared. Council size varies widely, ranging from three members to fifty (in Chicago), with an average of seven.

The job of the councilman (or alderman, as he is sometimes called) is usually part-time, involving only a few meetings a month, and it carries either no salary at all or only a nominal one. In many large cities, however, especially in those with mayor-council forms and invariably in those with the commission system, council membership entails full-time responsibilities and carries with it reimbursement which occasionally exceeds $15,000 per year. Elections are usually for four-year terms, with about half the members coming up for reelection every two years.

Election systems   A debate has raged for a long time between those who believe councilmen should be chosen from wards, or single-member districts, and those who favor election at large, from the entire city. If the ward system is used, each section of the city is guaranteed a member, it is easier for each citizen to know his or her councilman, and ballots will be shorter and less confusing. Moreover, election campaigns limited to a single district will be less costly, and hence less wealthy candidates will be encouraged to seek office. Such a system assures blacks and other ethnic or social minorities a better chance to elect a percentage of council members proportionate to their total city population. In Detroit, to cite one of the more notable examples, at a time when blacks accounted for about 30 percent of the population all of the nine councilmen, elected at large, were whites. Finally, it seems to many that only single-member districts guarantee that the average voter can find a sympathetic ear—or at least one not totally deaf—at city hall. If a neighborhood wants a stop sign erected at a dangerous intersection, for example, it needs a broker to cut through the mass of bureaucratic red tape separating its demand from the city agency equipped to meet it. The councilman *from that ward* has the sharpest knife in the neighborhood.[6] This single-member-district system is found most frequently in very large cities, where many diverse interests require an official spokesman.

Those favoring the at-large election system contend that the selection of councilmen from districts pits various wards against one another and deprives the council of members whose political survival coincides with the interests of the entire city. They insist that if all the best candidates reside in one particular section of the city, the voters should be permitted to elect all councilmen from that section. Finally, they associate ward elections with corrupt political machines, incompetent patronage appointees, and political interference with administrative functions.

In broad terms, at stake are the relative values of decentralization, simplicity, minority rights, and responsiveness to group demands, all of which seem embodied to some degree in election by wards, and, those of civic solidarity, majority rule, honesty, and competence, all advanced by at-large election. In abstract terms, it is a choice between two conceptions of politics: One, simple and somewhat cynical, tries only to compromise essentially conflicting interests; the other, more majestic and utopian, seeks the common good through rational consensus. In any case, the advocates of at-large elections seem to be winning. Of all cities with over 5000 people, 67 percent elect all councilmen at large, 20 percent choose them exclusively by wards, and 13 percent by some combination of the two methods.[7]

Characteristics Who are these city fathers who serve as councilmen? More often than in state legislatures or Congress, they might be city mothers. Although still grossly underrepresented, women held 6.7 percent of the seats on the councils of fifty-three cities in Los Angeles County in 1957, to cite but one example,[8] compared with a peak representation of less than 5 percent in the national House of Represen-

6 Arthur W. Bromage, *On the City Council* (Ann Arbor, Michigan: George Wahr Publishing Co., 1950).
7 *Municipal Yearbook, 1968* (Washington, D.C.: International City Managers Association, 1968), p. 59.
8 Robert G. Huckshorn, *BGR Observer* (Los Angeles: Bureau of Governmental Research, U.C.L.A., 1957).

tatives, 2 percent in the U.S. Senate, and less than 4 percent in the California state legislature. As in legislative bodies governing larger areas, professional people—especially lawyers—are overrepresented among councilmen, although there seems to be also an extraordinarily high ratio of businessmen, with real estate and insurance salesmen particularly numerous. The large number of realtors may be explained partially in terms of the impact of zoning or land-use laws on property values. Industrial workers, by contrast, are notably scarce among local legislators. The existence of a business and professional elite seems vividly apparent in city council politics.[9]

City Executives

Mayors   Every city has a mayor. In mayor-council cities he normally can be assumed to be the chief executive, with varying degrees of administrative authority over department heads. In the council-manager form of government, however, he is often the elected council-man whom the council has chosen as its presiding officer. Similarly, in commission cities the mayor has little more power than the other commissioners. In fact, commission governments have no chief executive in any effective sense, and therein lies their chief defect.

All mayors, however, act in ceremonial capacities, symbolizing the cities they serve. They cut ribbons to inaugurate the use of newly paved streets, lay cornerstones for new buildings, address conventions held in the city, and exert considerable influence on public opinion through access to local newspapers, radio, and television. When cities need greater aid from the state or national governments, they can become effective lobbyists in seeking it. As public relations men, they seek broad markets for locally produced goods and may try to induce new industries and commercial centers to locate in "good old Something-ville."

It is only in the strong-mayor variety of mayor-council governments that executive authority is effectively concentrated. In cities of this type the mayor can combine popular support, the veto and appointment powers, control over budget preparation, and authority to submit recommendations for new ordinances to the council into an impressive capacity for effective civic leadership. This aggregation of influence is far from universal, however. About a third of all mayors have no veto power at all, even in mayor-council cities where the veto is most common.

---

9 A survey of eighty-three councilmen in sixty-three Los Angeles County cities in 1962 revealed that 58 percent were "managers, officials, and proprietors" (nonfarm) in 1962. Edwin E. Olson, "The Occupational Orientation of Councilmen in Los Angeles County," unpublished paper delivered at the Western Political Science Association meeting, 1963. Of 283 Los Angeles County city councilmen surveyed in 1957, 34 were real estate and/or insurance salesmen, 23 lawyers, 19 engineers and scientists, and 13 laborers (about 4 percent). Huckshorn, loc. cit.

City managers While a strong mayor can augment his executive authority with considerable personal political influence, in cities with a council-manager system the city manager is less fortunate. He is hired by the city council and can be fired by it. As a result, the security of his job depends upon his efficiency in administering city agencies and his skill in maintaining favor with a majority on the council. It is a difficult dual role. He is both master of his department heads and servant of the council, and woe befalls the manager who confuses the two.

The hazards of the city manager's position are increased if he perceives his job differently than does the council to which he is responsible. A study in northern California has revealed that while 88 percent of the managers believed they should assume leadership in formulating city policies, 58 percent of the councilmen thought they should not.[10] On other aspects of the city manager's job there is more agreement. It is generally acknowledged that it should involve preparation of the city budget for the council's consideration, supervision of the enforcement of council policy, and selection and control of department heads. On the last point, three quarters of the fifty-eight councils examined in a Florida study were found to give virtually automatic approval to departmental appointments made by the city managers.[11]

For those who reach the peak of their profession, the job of city manager is often more financially rewarding than that of mayor. The managers in Cincinnati, Dallas, and San Diego, for example, receive over $38,000 per year, a larger salary than any mayor in America, except the mayor of New York, who earns $50,000.[12] To be sure, the names of city managers are not yet revealed by history books. But neither do they suffer the vilification which mayors so often face at the hands of ambitious political opponents and a sometimes fickle public.

Other executives As noted in the last chapter, the biggest structural weakness in most county governments is the excessive number of elected officials, and the weak mayor-council form of city government displays the same defect. Less frequently, so does the strong-mayor variety. Other than mayors and councilmen, city treasurers and clerks are the most commonly elected officials, with voters selecting them in over 20 percent of all cities. The election of city assessors, auditors, attorneys, controllers, and even police chiefs (in 4 percent of all cities) has not entirely disappeared, although in the overwhelming majority of cases, all these officials are appointed by the council, mayor, or manager. The selection of most police chiefs by appointment affords an intriguing example of the haphazard processes of historical evolution, since county

10 Ronald O. Loveridge, "The City Manager in Legislative Politics: A Collision of Role Conceptions," unpublished paper delivered at the Western Political Science Association meeting, 1967.
11 Gladys M. Kammerer and John M. De Grove, *Florida City Managers: Profile and Tenure* (Gainesville, Fla.: Public Administration Clearing Service, University of Florida, 1961), table 17.
12 *The New York Times Encyclopedic Almanac* 1972, pp. 209–29.

sheriffs, who usually perform similar functions, are nearly always elected.

Almost all cities have an official attorney, sometimes serving on a part-time basis. He advises various agencies and officials regarding the extent of their constitutional authority, represents the city in court when it sues or gets sued, drafts proposed ordinances for the council in legally proper language, and occasionally prosecutes persons accused of violating those ordinances. Unlike the county district attorney, he rarely has the authority to prosecute alleged violations of state law.

The departments   The number of city departments depends chiefly on the size of the city. Among the most common, known to every grade-school child, are police, fire, and recreation and parks. In addition, the public works department, sometimes headed by an official known as the city engineer, is in charge of the construction of municipal buildings, sewers, street repair, garbage disposal, bridges, sidewalks, street lights, and similar matters.

Building codes, a rather recent arrival on the civic scene, are enforced by building departments and impose minimum standards upon the work of carpenters, plumbers, electricians, and other contractors in the construction industry. Even new retaining walls for back yard gardens or the installation of an extra toilet may convert the home handyman into a lawbreaker unless he has submitted plans to, and obtained a permit from, his local building department. No precaution is too trivial when the public safety is at stake.

Health departments inspect restaurants and nursing homes, frequently provide outpatient clinics and, in large cities such as New York and Philadelphia, huge public hospitals. These hospitals may operate in conjunction with university medical schools and serve as major research centers. County health departments may eliminate the need for cities to assume some of these functions; in any event, public health facilities usually provide the urban poor who are too young for Medicare a reasonably high standard of medical care.

Civil service administration   A large and growing number of cities have established agencies to hire, promote, discipline, and discharge municipal employees. Since these number about two million people, this process is obviously of immense consequence. Cleveland, typical of cities of its size, had more than 13,000 full-time employees on its payroll in 1965.

Not until late in the last century were city jobs available on anything but a patronage basis. The merit system, begun at the national level, gradually replaced the entrenched spoils system and many cities established three-member civil service commissions to administer competitive examinations for available job vacancies. This was in keeping with the prevailing view at that time that administrative corruption could best be prevented by putting departments under the control of a multi-member board or commission rather than a single person. Although such civil service commissions are still common, there is now a tendency to replace them with a personnel department headed by a single official.

THE POLITICAL PROCESS

Political parties and pressure groups operate in various ways on the local scene. The interaction of formal city government structures with such political factors shapes the development of urban policies. City politics, then, requires a look.

Partisan and Nonpartisan Elections

Partisan elections, in which candidates are chosen in party primaries and identified by party affiliation on the ballot, are used in fewer cities than nonpartisan elections. Either way, candidates usually get their names on the ballot by obtaining a specified number of signatures and perhaps paying a filing fee.

The elimination of political partisanship is usually defended on the ground that city issues have no relevance to those on which the major parties compete nationally. There is no "Republican way" to collect trash or put out fires, it is argued, in contrast to a "Democratic way." Yet the chief explanation for the rise of nonpartisan elections is historical. Because city government was often sick with corruption at the turn of the century and was frequently dominated by party machines, the reformers of the Progressive movement concluded that the machines caused the corruption. They prescribed nonpartisanship as the cure, augmented, usually, by the commission or council-manager forms of government, civil service systems, and at-large elections. Rich in imagination and full of righteous wrath, these doctors of the body politic practiced a kind of faith healing filled more with promise than performance.

Their nonpartisan medicine, in spite of its growing popularity, may reflect an incorrect diagnosis of city ills in the first place. It is reasonable to believe that municipal corruption is caused more by economic factors than by partisan ballots or defects in governmental institutions. Poverty may tempt city dwellers to trade votes for even the smallest favors from city hall, and low salaries for civic officials may entice them to dispense government jobs, award municipal contracts, and pass certain ordinances only if there are some kickbacks to be gained in return. If this explanation is valid, the cure lies in higher living standards for the people, better salaries for officials, and an enlightened, vigilant electorate.

The advocates of nonpartisan elections made another questionable assumption: that the elimination of "politics" from the processes of city administration can be achieved by banning political parties from formal participation in campaigns. Experience indicates that candidates need not be labeled "Republican" or "Democrat" to make them vigorous and occasionally ruthless contestants in the game of municipal politics.

It is also doubtful that local disputes are without any relationship to state or national issues. Private *vs.* municipal ownership of utilities, the right of city employees to go on strike or join unions, and the relative amounts of money budgeted for parks and police have close counterparts in the larger political arena. But the case against nonpartisan elections does not rest here. Three alleged disadvantages are frequently cited: (1) Nonpartisan local elections may weaken parties at the state and national levels; (2) they maximize the importance of personalities and name recognition while minimizing the significance of platforms, programs, and issues; and (3) they may make it difficult to recruit good candidates and to solicit campaign funds.[13]

Nonetheless, partisan elections may also have liabilities in the realm of local politics. Minority party candidates (usually Republicans in big cities) have a relatively small chance of winning regardless of their abilities, and the smoke from interparty battles may obscure city issues with ones that can be resolved only at the state or national levels.

Campaign Types

It would be neat but misleading to classify all local elections into the two categories, partisan and nonpartisan. Each has many variations, some of which are sketched below.

Partisan elections, with party affiliation decisive   When machine politics dominated local government, the party affiliation of candidates was nearly always the decisive campaign factor. The party with the most tightly knit organization could not only elect its entire slate of local candidates but also exert enormous influence on the outcome of congressional and state-wide races. Party organizations this effective were usually found in cities with a mayor-council form of government. The mayor himself was often the party boss, oiling his political machine with patronage appointments and other favors dispensed to loyal campaign supporters. If he were the mayor of a big city, his influence could reach all the way to the White House. Campaigns in which the party is all powerful are fast disappearing in local politics, but "the last hurrah" has yet to be heard in Albany, Pittsburgh, and a few other cities.

Partisan elections, with party affiliation indecisive   In most cities employing partisan elections, party affiliation is somewhat important but may be counterbalanced by other campaign factors. Even the powerful Democratic organization in New York City was unable to prevent the election of Mayor Fiorello La Guardia on a local Fusion party ticket or the election, much later, of Mayor John Lindsay, first as a Republican, and then as a Liberal party candidate. Similar unpredictabili-

13 See Charles R. Adrian, "Some General Characteristics of Nonpartisan Elections," *American Political Science Review* 46 (September 1962): 766–76.

ty marks the election histories of St. Louis, Cleveland, Buffalo, Indianapolis, and New Haven.

The impact of party affiliation on the success of local party candidates is often related to far broader political trends. This is especially true if the local elections are consolidated with state and national ones—that is, if the names of candidates for all offices are on the same ballot. If so, local candidates may ride into office on the coattails of an immensely popular gubernatorial or presidential candidate of the same party. An Ohio study comparing votes for county offices with those for presidential candidates revealed a coattail influence but indicated also that voters displayed more consistent party loyalty in races for local offices than in those for the presidency.[14] If the opposing parties are equally well organized in a local campaign, each may nullify the effect of the other and the election results will hinge upon other variables. Similarly, the use of office-block rather than party-column ballots, discussed in Chapter 8, may minimize the importance of party affiliation.

Nonpartisan elections with much party activity   Chicago's Mayor Richard Daley has already established a secure spot in the folklore of American politics as one of the last of the powerful party bosses. It comes as a surprise, then, to learn that members of Chicago's city council are chosen in nonpartisan elections. This curious anomaly is explained by the fact that the mayor himself is elected on a partisan ballot and has at his disposal a Democratic party organization so powerful as to render the council nonpartisan in name only. Kansas City, Denver, and Hartford are other cities in which nonpartisan elections are little more than a mask concealing party machines which operate with great effectiveness.[15]

Nonpartisan elections with little party activity   In most nonpartisan elections, the regular organizations of the two major parties do not play major roles. Yet this generalization encompasses as many distinctive campaign styles as there are cities. Cincinnati, for example, was long characterized by a nonpartisan system which had, nevertheless, two contending factions. Although candidates are not identified on the ballot by party affiliation, many elections have seen a slate of Republicans challenged by an opposing group supported by the City Charter Committee, often called the Charter party.[16]

In other cities, election outcomes are determined by the relative strength of factions within a party. This has been particularly true of the Democratic party in Boston, Baltimore, and many southern cities including Durham, Memphis, and New Orleans.[17] These factions

14 V. O. Key, Jr., "Partisanship and County Office: The Case of Ohio," *American Political Science Review* 47 (June 1953): 525–32.
15 Duane Lockard, *The Politics of State and Local Government*, 2nd ed. (N.Y.: The Macmillan Company, 1969), p. 231.
16 Adrian and Press, op. cit., p. 103.
17 James Q. Wilson, "Politics and Reform in American Cities," Ivan Hinderaker, *et al.*, eds., *American Government Annual, 1962–1963* (N.Y.: Holt, Rinehart, & Winston, Inc., 1962). For a description of the Durham situation, see Lewis Bowman and G. R. Boynton, "Coalition as Party in a One-Party Southern Area: A Theoretical and Case Analysis," *Midwest Journal of Political Science* 8 (August 1964).

must usually form alliances with one another or with ethnic, economic, or upper-class civic reform groups in order to get candidates elected. Still more cities are characterized by freewheeling, highly personalized campaigns which one writer has called the "politics of acquaintance."[18] Racial factors, media endorsement, and business, labor, or church groups may have great influence—although usually on a temporary basis. Los Angeles, Seattle, Dallas, and most relatively small cities might be crammed into this catchall category.[19]

Local Interest Groups

Where political parties are relatively weak, as they usually are in city elections, pressure groups are ordinarily strong. These organizations make the campaign contributions that parties are unable to provide. At the level of local politics, real estate associations and government employee groups are especially important. The former are interested in zoning and building code policies and the latter in higher salaries and better working conditions. Other business organizations—notably banks, liquor interests, and public utility corporations—are also often extremely active in local politics. In company towns, where a single firm employs a large percentage of the residents, the dominant corporation can exert enormous influence by threatening to move to some other city if its particular desires (such as a tax freeze) are not indulged. An example of this sort of pressure was provided by the activity of an oil company in Bayonne, New Jersey, in 1957.[20]

A wide array of other groups deserves recognition. Churches are concerned with gambling, pornography, and welfare legislation. Racial and ethnic organizations are increasingly influential, especially in their attempts to elect some of their own members to public office and to exert some control over educational policies and police practices. The strength of labor unions is especially great in industrialized northern cities such as Milwaukee and Detroit. James Madison warned, in the tenth *Federalist* paper, that small units of government were easier for a particular faction to dominate than larger ones. His observation should be pondered long by those interested both in cities and in pressure groups.

Two Kinds of City Politics

The distinguishing characteristics of city government seem to cluster together in two broad groups. One category is marked by the mayor-council form of government, the selection of aldermen from single-member councilmanic districts, and partisan elections. Cities possessing these traits are often big, frequently old, and largely in the East.

18 Eugene C. Lee, quoted in Adrian and Press, op. cit., p. 100.
19 Edward C. Banfield, *Big City Politics* (N.Y.: Random House, Inc., 1965).
20 Lockard, op. cit., pp. 257–58.

By contrast, the other major category of cities is characterized by manager or commission forms of government and at-large nonpartisan elections. Such cities are frequently of moderate size, suburban, and most numerous in the South and West.

Some cities possess characteristics of both these types and do not fit neatly into either group. Yet the combinations indicated above are typical enough to require some explanation. One theory, already mentioned, is that city corruption elicited a series of proposed remedies that often included abandonment of the old mayor-council form of government, partisan elections, and single-member districts largely because these were typical of the cities thought to be controlled by bosses.

Another interpretation stresses the different characteristics of the people living in the two types of cities. It assumes, with some evidence, that cities with the mayor-council form and its accompanying traits have generally poor populations which are ethnically and economically diverse. These cities, it is argued, develop a "private regarding" ethos; this puts emphasis on the jobs and services which are needed by the many heterogeneous groups within it and which can be obtained most easily by partisan ward elections and a popularly chosen mayor with wide executive power. Naturally such ideals are inconsistent with a merit system, which awards city jobs on the basis of competence rather than need. By contrast, the reformed cities in the other category are said to have relatively wealthier, more homogeneous, predominantly middle-class populations which display few major social cleavages.[21] They can afford to be less concerned about jobs and services, and have a "public regarding" ethos emphasizing honesty, efficiency, and economy in government.

A final explanation rests upon the sectional differences among various parts of the nation. This theory suggests that council-manager governments and other reform characteristics are common in the West because many new cities were being formed there when these ideas were first gaining popularity. Similarly, at-large elections may be a method of minimizing the election of black or other minority group councilmen in areas where prejudice is great.[22] Actually, of course, each municipality is as unique as a finger print. The important point is that these interpretations may help citizens to understand their home towns a little better.

21 This theory, derived from Richard Hofstadter's *Age of Reform,* was promulgated most completely by Edward C. Banfield and James Q. Wilson in *City Politics* (Cambridge: Harvard University Press and Massachusetts Institute of Technology, 1963).
22 Raymond E. Wolfinger and John Osgood Field, "Political Ethos and the Structure of City Government," *American Political Science Review* 60 (June 1966): 306–26.

Chapter **14**

Metropolitan Maladies
Crisis and Response

*Human history becomes more and more a race between
education and catastrophe.*

H. G. Wells

Cities no longer exist in isolation. They soon spawn surrounding suburbs and hence become parts of vast, sprawling metropolitan areas. In these congested regions nearly seven out of every ten Americans now live. It is here that crime is most common (see Chapter 4), racial conflict most acute (Chapter 5), and pollution most poisonous (Chapter 15). Delinquency, rising divorce rates, mental illness, and the rapid spread of communicable disease stand out in bold relief on the urban horizon. Indeed, all of the threats that menace our society seem accentuated in metropolitan areas. In this chapter, we shall first focus attention on three of the many symptoms of metropolitan maladies—inadequate transportation, bad housing, and poor schools—and then examine increased revenues and governmental reform as possible cures.

TRANSPORTATION: THE CRISIS
OF MOBILITY

When most Americans were farmers, they literally lived on their jobs. When they switched their employment from farm to factory a new problem emerged—how to get people from where they lived to where they worked. At first, the solution was simple enough. Homes were built within walking distance of factories, or at least close enough to be measured in blocks and traversed quickly and cheaply by streetcar or bus. As industry grew, however, industrial noise, smoke, and congestion drove more and more workers to seek residence farther and farther from their jobs. This outward migration made the suburbs the most rapidly growing residential areas in the nation, but it also placed an ever greater strain on the transportation system needed to get people to work.

The Automobile: Servant or Master?

The first officially recorded sale of an automobile occurred on April Fool's Day, 1898. By 1920 nine million of the mechanical monsters were registered,[1] and in less than a lifetime this number had climbed more than 900 percent to over eighty-eight million, more than one car for every three persons in the United States.[2] In 1969 they accounted for nearly 87 percent of all intercity traffic in the nation.[3]

It is hard to exaggerate the impact of the automobile. Some of its effects are tragic: In 1970 alone motor vehicle accidents resulted in 55,000 deaths,[4] more than the Americans killed in all of World War I or the entire Vietnam conflict. The same year, a single accident in fogbound Orange County, California, involved 108 cars and injured fifty people.[5]

The impact of the automobile upon the economy has been just as profound. It has generated development of service stations, the tire industry, and automobile insurance companies, along with the incredible growth of the oil, gasoline, and highway construction businesses. The new technology has elicited governmental responses designed to ameliorate the transition from horse-drawn carriages to hot rods. Thus, government has built roads, licensed both vehicles and their drivers, passed traffic laws, and offered driver training in public high schools. It has installed traffic lights and parking meters, set automobile safety standards, and limited exhaust pollutants.

The chief problems resulting from automotive transportation are most obvious in the big cities. One of these is smog and, ironically, another is slowness. In downtown Philadelphia it takes as long to travel twelve miles by car as it did by horse and buggy a century ago.[6] A third difficulty is the voracious appetite of the automobile for land. It requires parking spaces, gas stations, new car show rooms, used car lots, surface streets, major highway interchange ramps, and finally junkyards. Estimates of the acreage used for automobiles run from 55 to 85 percent of the total land area in Los Angeles,[7] 50 percent in Atlanta, 40 percent in

1 John C. Bollens and Henry J. Schmandt, *The Metropolis* (N.Y.: Harper & Row, Publishers, 1965), p. 313.
2 U.S. Bureau of the Census, *Statistical Abstract of the United States: 1971,* p. 535.
3 Ibid., p. 525.
4 Ibid., p. 540.
5 *Newsweek,* Jan. 18, 1971, p. 44.
6 Loc. cit.
7 Steven V. Roberts, *Atlantic Monthly,* September 1969, p. 32, and Webb S. Fiser, *Mastery of the Metropolis* (Englewood Cliffs, N.J.: Prentice-Hall, Inc., 1962), p. 29.

Boston, and 30 percent in Denver.[8] A final indictment against the automobile is that it has driven thousands of people from their homes. In the fifteen months before January 1, 1970, federally aided highway construction displaced 27,516 housing units.[9]

Why does the network of roads and highways continue to expand in spite of the mounting evidence that it is inflicting serious damage upon urban life? Some of the answers lie in the complexities of human habit; others lie in the political clout of the highway lobby, a coalition of pressure groups representing the oil, trucking, automobile, and concrete industries. In 1970 they defeated a California referendum that sought to divert a portion of gas tax revenue from highway use to the construction of other kinds of transportation facilities, and in 1972 they were fighting congressional legislation that would permit highway trust fund money to be used for mass rapid transit. Public roads now extend 3.68 million miles in length, of which 42,000 have been constructed as a result of the 1956 Federal-Aid Highway Act. Because this commits the national government to defray 90 percent of building costs, it also encourages the states to build more highways in order to receive their share of federal money. Despite the fact that highways have been financed by a combination of governmental revenues—federal aid, state gas tax resources, toll road fees, and local funds—most are under local jurisdiction.

The routing of major highways is an explosive political issue in many communities, for ultimate decisions can not only force people from their homes and businesses, but also diminish the value of adjacent property, or—at the other extreme—increase the value of real estate just a few blocks away.[10] It can also lead to proposals for alternate methods of transportation.

Mass Rapid Transit

The idea of mobility has long captivated man's imagination and been a major component of his conception of freedom. Ironically, the airplane that makes man almost as "free as a bird" cannot transport him twenty miles to his work. There are, of course, alternatives. Streetcars, buses, commuter trains, and subways have transported millions of passengers with remarkable speed, economy, and safety. Since World War II, however, the preference for private cars has forced public transportation systems into an era of hard times, cutting the number of passengers in half between 1946 and 1960.[11] In 1969 and 1970 financial disasters forced private bus systems to be taken over by eight cities, and in the summer of 1970 the Penn Central railroad, vital to passengers for

8 Gus Tyler, "Can Anyone Run a City?" *Saturday Review,* Nov. 8, 1969, pp. 22–25.
9 *Los Angeles Times,* Nov. 25, 1971, Part XI, p. 9.
10 Charles R. Adrian and Charles Press, *Governing Urban America,* 3rd ed. (N.Y.: McGraw-Hill Book Company, 1968), p. 459.
11 Bollens and Schmandt, op. cit., p. 468.

Paul Sequeira.

Several interrelated urban problems can be detected in this scene from Cabrini Green in Chicago.

New York and carrying 140,000 commuters a day, "slid into the biggest bankruptcy in history."[12] The hardest-hit victims of deteriorating bus and rail facilities, however, are those without private cars—the young, old, and poor. For them, it means severely restricted access to the recreational facilities, medical care, shopping centers, and jobs upon which a decent level of survival depends. Yet in 1970 the national government was spending five billion dollars on highway programs and less than $200 million on urban public transportation.[13]

Although the future of urban rapid transit appears only through a haze of auto exhaust, there are signs of light ahead. In Philadelphia, a new train line to southern New Jersey is working well; in Chicago, the network of subways and buses functions with relative efficiency; in San Francisco, the Bay Area Rapid Transit System promises new and improved rail transportation. Monorails have optimistic advocates, and so do tracked air-cushion vehicles, although these are still little more than a gleam in the eyes of traffic engineers. Most encourag-

12 *Newsweek,* op. cit., p. 44.
13 George H. Favre, "Highways and Transportation," *Christian Science Monitor,* July 21, 1970, p. 16.

ing of all is the U.S. Department of Transportation, established in 1966, and the legislation passed by Congress late in 1970 giving it ten billion dollars over a twelve-year period to help finance mass rapid transit in urban areas.

Out of the crisis in urban mobility, one fact appears dominant: If public transportation is to be improved significantly, the taxpayer will have to foot a large portion of the bill. Without government contracts or subsidies, private enterprise will not run the risks involved. Moreover, without such aid the metropolis is threatened by the gradual hardening of its traffic arteries; put differently, the urban bird is caged.

HOUSING: THE CRISIS
OF HABITABLE CITIES

Since basic housing needs are affected by population changes, we must remind ourselves that the American population is a marvelously restless one, shifting continually from East to West, from the interior to the coasts, from the rural to the urban areas. In 1970 nearly one out of every five people changed their place of residence and of these, over a third moved to a different county and about a sixth to a different state.[14] This sort of massive population movement created great cities in the nineteenth century and added the suburbs surrounding them in the twentieth. Together, they have produced the metropolitan areas which continue to grow outward and which, if present trends continue, will converge with others expanding from opposite directions. Thus, by the next century giant megalopolises may be expected to stretch from Boston to Washington, D.C., from San Francisco to San Diego, all across the southern shores of the Great Lakes, and perhaps along the Gulf coast.

Already the nation's heartland is being drained of some vitality, for while the nation's population increased by 13 percent between 1960 and 1970, the populations of the Dakotas and West Virginia actually declined. Simultaneously, a steady infusion of new arrivals produced an increase of 25 percent in the Pacific states and of 18 percent in the South Atlantic states.

Redistributing the People

Housing density Although the 1960s saw a drop in the percentage of people living in central cities and an increased percentage in the suburbs, the overall impact of the population movement was to increase population density so that 70 percent of the nation's people now live on 1 percent of its land. In Manhattan there is an incredible average of 67,808 persons compacted in each square mile.[15]

14 U.S. Bureau of the Census, *Statistical Abstract of the United States: 1971,* p. 34.
15 Ibid., p. 22.

Such overcrowding intensifies smog, traffic congestion, and nearly every other problem confronting urban areas. The National Commission on Population Growth therefore recommended in 1972 that a conscious plan be formulated to redistribute the population in a less concentrated arrangement. Housing policies at both the national and local levels are indispensable components of any such plan and might involve the following programs:

1) The construction of low-density public housing projects in areas of low population concentration. This is difficult because many suburban cities have prohibited such housing projects in an attempt to prevent an influx of poor people, often of minority races.[16]

2) The use of loan guarantees from the Federal Housing Administration (FHA) and veterans' loan agencies to encourage home construction and purchase, primarily in low-density neighborhoods.

3) The construction of new government office buildings and other facilities in areas where well-spaced housing is feasible.

4) The awarding of government contracts to factories located in small or medium-sized cities.

5) The use of subsidies to develop "new towns" of low population density outside large metropolitan areas. A number of European countries have set encouraging precedents in this respect.

6) Limitations on the construction of such facilities as sewers and electric generating plants for areas where there are already too many housing units.

7) City planning and zoning policies that prohibit increased housing density. This last proposal is especially pertinent to a consideration of local government, since the authority to limit the heights of apartments and regulate space between houses is usually exercised at that level.

Through a combination of these and other measures, coordinated action by national, state, and local governments can determine to a considerable degree where housing units are to be built and hence where people will live.

Planning and zoning policy   The chief control over the type and location of housing facilities, along with commercial and industrial establishments, is imposed by local zoning policies. Permanent agencies to plan for future land use date from 1907, when Hartford, Connecticut, formed a planning commission roughly comparable to those now operating in over a thousand cities. These planning commissions, usually chosen by the city council or the chief executive, make recommendations to the council regarding land use. They often employ a full-time, professional planning staff to devise proposals for orderly civic growth. It is not an easy job. New methods of transportation, social and economic changes, and political pressures brought primarily by real estate speculators and housing developers all converge to make public policy in this

16 Sidney Wise, ed., *Issues 71–72* (N.Y.: Thomas Y. Crowell Company, 1971), pp. 15–31.

area among the most controversial issues facing the modern city. A new airport raises noise levels and thereby lowers property values in adjacent residential areas. Poor people in the old inner city press for low-cost housing in new suburbs. Building contractors seek to construct ever larger apartments on smaller parcels of land. Any change benefits some, often over the objection of others, and thereby constitutes a basic ingredient of political conflict.

Zoning ordinances determine the actual use of land. Certain areas are assigned to manufacturing; others are slated for stores and assorted commercial purposes; some are set aside for schools, parking, libraries, fire stations, parks, and similar public necessities; and much is reserved for residential use. Each of these categories is sometimes subdivided further. Land zoned for residences, for example, may be designated for single-family houses, duplexes, or multi-unit apartments.

Zoning is important both to the individual and to the city. For the individual, it protects the enjoyment he derives from his home. Assume that you have purchased a house in a quiet residential neighborhood. Imagine, then, the impact on your life when the empty field a block away is rezoned for a small airport, or the nursery across the street is sold to a fertilizer factory employing a thousand workers. Only intelligent planning implemented in wise zoning ordinances prevents this.

By the city council, hard pressed for increased revenue, wise zoning may be viewed somewhat differently. It is confronted with the twin facts that a substantial amount of money comes from property taxes, and that the value of property depends largely on how it is zoned. Property zoned for manufacturing will bring in the most revenue; that limited to single-family dwellings produces least. The temptation to rezone confronting the council is obvious, and the seduction may be complete if a particular lot is owned by someone in a position to help the council members later. Yet if a city really wishes to prevent increased population density, along with its street congestion, overcrowded schools, and loss of open spaces, a zoning policy committed to the maintenance of single-family housing is essential.

Planning involves not only zoning policy but building regulations as well. The height of apartments and the amount of space between structures, designed to maximize fresh air and sunshine, are commonly stipulated by ordinance, as are also standards meant to ensure safe construction.

More and Better Housing

In 1970, over four and a half million American homes lacked hot running water, a private toilet, or a private bathtub or shower. These substandard dwellings were equal to the total number of housing units in Chicago and Detroit combined. But ten years earlier the situation was twice as bad. The problem of inadequate housing, often accompanied by overcrowding, is especially acute in central cities. Of all housing units occupied by nonwhites in 1960, 30 percent were substandard in Detroit, 32 in Philadelphia, 42.4 in New York, 42.8 in Chicago, 45.9 in Dallas, 56.9 in New Orleans, and 58.9 in Pittsburgh.[17]

Anthony Downs has tried to capture the human suffering implicit in these figures.

Thousands of infants are attacked by rats each year; hundreds die or become mentally retarded from eating lead paint that falls off cracked walls; thousands more are ill because of . . . continuing failure of landlords to repair plumbing or provide proper heat. . . .[18]

Housing deterioration is most acute in the central cities simply because it is there that urban dwellings are oldest. As their desirability diminished, increasingly affluent white middle-class residents bought newer homes in the suburbs, thereby increasing racial segregation in the schools and inducing stores, shops, and even factories to follow them out of the city. Three other results ensued: Cities faced a severe financial crisis because of the loss of tax revenue; deteriorated housing attracted poor black migrants able to afford nothing more; and traffic congestion increased due to the number of new suburbanites who retained their city office jobs. If housing can be improved in the major urban centers, millions of human lives may be salvaged from squalor and despair, and the city itself may yet preserve its historic function as a center of science, learning, jobs, and culture.

Public and private partnership In 1934, Congress established the FHA (Federal Housing Administration) to guarantee loans made by financial institutions for the purchase of homes by certain qualified buyers, and the Veterans' Administration later assumed similar obligations for ex-service men. The people who needed decent housing most desperately, however, were rarely qualified to receive it under these programs. In 1949 Congress passed a Housing Act to provide government-constructed rental units for low-income families, and in 1965 it established the Department of Housing and Urban Development to coordinate programs. Subsequent policies have focused on mortgage and rent subsidies for the poor and on slum clearance and urban renewal projects.[19] The Johnson administration launched a "model cities" program to encourage neighborhood redevelopment by providing technical advice and financial aid to cities that had devised promising plans for a comprehensive attack on housing as well as transportation, poverty, and related problems. In 1970 construction began on about a million and a

17 *Report of the National Advisory Commission on Civil Disorders* (N.Y.: Bantam Books, Inc., 1968), p. 468.
18 Anthony Downs, "Moving Toward Realistic Housing Goals," Kermit Gordon, ed., *Agenda for the Nation* (Washington, D.C.: The Brookings Institution, 1968), p. 142.
19 More information on the role of various governments in housing improvement may be found in Reo M. Christenson, *Challenge and Decision*, 3rd ed. (N.Y.: Harper & Row, Publishers, 1970), pp. 143–53, and James L. Martin, "Housing and Community Development," *The Book of the States*, 1970–71 (Lexington, Ky.: The Council of State Governments, 1970), pp. 443–50.

Paul Sequeira.

Housing evictions—part of the vicious cycle of poverty.

half new housing units, of which some 66 percent were privately financed, 32 percent built with FHA or VA guaranteed loans, and 2 percent constructed under government housing programs.[20] "During the last three years" as Senator Jacob Javits (R-N.Y.) pointed out on the floor of the Senate in 1972, "more subsidized housing for low- and moderate-income families has been provided than in the preceding thirty years."[21]

       Government plays another type of role in this area. Cities and counties adopt building code ordinances designed to make sure that construction is safe and sturdy. Codes often specify also that off-street parking be provided and that adequate lighting, heating, and plumbing facilities be installed. Unless building regulations are frequently and fairly reviewed, they may give an unjustified advantage to the manufacturer of some particular kind of building material or prevent the use of relatively new innovations such as prefabricated construction. And the

20 Computed from U.S. Bureau of the Census, *Statistical Abstract of the United States: 1971*, p. 668.
21 *Congressional Quarterly Weekly Report*, June 17, 1972, p. 1447.

codes must be stiff enough to guarantee safety and durability without forcing costs so high that only the wealthy can afford to live in the units constructed.

Trends and issues   As we have seen, recent housing developments have been characterized by growing government involvement and a decrease in the percentage of substandard dwellings. Other significant trends are the increases in the cost of housing and in the percentage of home ownership. Between 1960 and 1970, the median value of owner-occupied homes increased by $5100 and since 1950 the overall percentage of the family budget spent for housing has gone up from 11.1 to 14.5. Perhaps in reaction to these rising costs, the number of new mobile homes has more than doubled since 1964.[22] Since 1940, more and more Americans have fulfilled the dream of "a little place of our own." The percentage of all housing units owned by their occupants has risen more than 20 percent, to 64.2 in 1970. Recent construction figures indicate that this trend may be reversed, however, since population pressures have forced more construction of new apartments and proportionately fewer of new single-family houses.[23]

As the population grows, the housing crisis embraces exceedingly complex issues. To what degree should government give financial assistance to new construction? How much assistance should be directed toward slum clearance or urban renewal projects? Where will the displaced former slum dwellers be housed? How can a sense of national unity and interracial harmony be fostered when the poor (mostly black) are consigned to the decaying inner cities, while the prosperous (mostly white) run for cover in suburbia?

THE PUBLIC SCHOOLS: CRISIS IN THE CLASSROOM

The United States, which has lagged behind other countries in areas such as civil service reform and care of the poor and aged, has been a world leader in the establishment of free, compulsory education. The American educational system represents one of the longest and strongest governmental commitments ever made by the American people. We have made school attendance compulsory, and we have contributed enormous taxes to extend it to as many people for as many years as possible. As a result, more persons are employed by all American governments combined in the field of education than in any other area, and education ranks second behind military and diplomatic outlays in total government expenditures.

Old-fashioned American pragmatism explains so much support: It pays off for the people. Figure 50 reveals that a high-school graduate earns over twice as much, on the average, as a seventh-grade

22 U.S. Bureau of the Census, *Statistical Abstract of the United States: 1971,* pp. 676, 308, and 669.
23 Ibid., pp. 677 and 669.

Figure 50   Mean 1968 Income of Males 25 Years Old
and Over, by Years of School Completed

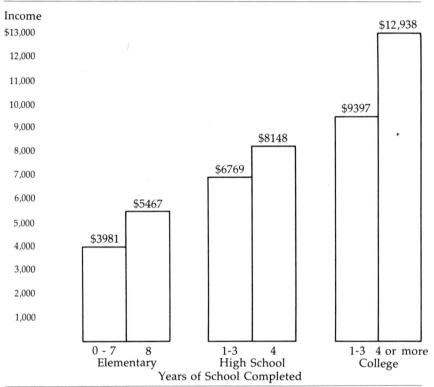

Income

$13,000	$12,938
12,000	
11,000	
10,000	$9397
9,000	
8,000	$8148
7,000	$6769
6,000	
5,000	$5467
4,000	$3981
3,000	
2,000	
1,000	

0 - 7	8	1-3	4	1-3	4 or more
Elementary		High School		College	

Years of School Completed

Source: U.S. Bureau of the Census, *Statistical Abstract of the United States: 1971*, p. 111.

dropout, and the incomes of men with four or more years of college exceed by over 50 percent the earnings of those with only a high-school education. About half the population has completed high school. Of those between twenty and twenty-four years of age, more than a third now have at least a little college experience. Public schools can claim most of the credit for this accomplishment, since about 88 percent of elementary pupils, 90 percent of high-school students, and 75 percent of college students attend government-controlled, tax-supported educational institutions.[24] The public school occupies an especially precious place in American society for another reason as well. It has provided a port of entry for immigrant children, socializing them to the customs and values of this culture. For each new generation, the public school is an incubator for the American dream.

Yet, especially in urban areas, the public schools are in trouble. Teachers are assaulted, dangerous drugs are often accessible to students, and vandalism is prevalent. Both discipline and curricula are the subjects of intense dispute. Angry parents have made school busing a

24 Ibid., pp. 110 and 107.

political issue; taxpayers display increasing reluctance to provide funds; the public demands that reading and other basic skills be taught more effectively. Dissatisfaction with public schools has mounted to such a peak that a number of economists and politicians have suggested that taxes be used to give parents pay vouchers permitting them to send their children to any school, public or private, of their choice. In order to view such issues in proper perspective, we must examine both the organization and politics of the American public school system.

Public School Organization

School districts Schools are administered by the state in Delaware and Hawaii, by counties in several southern states, and by towns or townships in New England. However, at the elementary, secondary, and community college levels, public schools are most often under the control of local school districts, of which there were 20,406 by the latest count. For maximum organizational efficiency many of these probably should be combined. Although consolidations have reduced the number of school districts by more than 70 percent in the last twenty years,[25] many are still too small, especially in rural areas, to provide either economical or high-quality education. As recently as 1968, there were about 4000 schools with only one teacher.[26] School district consolidation can take place either horizontally, by adjacent elementary districts merging with another, or vertically, by an elementary district combining with a high school district to form a unified system.

Bucking this consolidation trend, a number of big city districts are considering dismemberment or at least decentralization in order to tailor educational programs to the ethnically and economically diverse neighborhoods they serve. New York City schools have already moved in that direction, in the midst of heated debate and the biggest teachers' strike in American history.[27]

School boards The governing bodies of most school districts are local boards usually chosen by the voters in nonpartisan elections and consisting of from five to nine persons. In a few cities, including New York and Chicago, school board members are appointed by the mayor or other officials. It is the school board's responsibility to make policy on such matters as budgets, attendance boundaries, school construction, elective courses, and the employment of a chief administrator known as the superintendent. Board members usually meet once or twice a month and receive little or no compensation for their services except prestige, self-satisfaction, and perhaps free tickets to football

25 J. Allen Thomas and Russel W. Meyers, "State Public School Systems," *The Book of the States,* 1970–71 (Lexington, Ky.: The Council of State Governments, 1970), p. 295.
26 U.S. Bureau of the Census, *Statistical Abstract of the United States: 1971,* p. 100.
27 Thomas and Meyers, op. cit., p. 296, and David Selden, "School Decentralization: A Positive Approach," *The Record,* Teachers College, Columbia University 71 (September 1969).

games and school dances. While the superintendent is responsible to the board, it generally follows his recommendations.

The characteristics of most school board members follow the pattern of middle- or upper-middle-class predominance apparent among officials at higher governmental levels; about three quarters of them throughout the nation are business and professional men, and less than 20 percent of all school boards include as many as two women.[28] Racial minorities are underrepresented. A 1969 study of 165 junior college trustees in Florida revealed that 97.6 percent were white, 89.2 percent were male, and 86.1 percent Protestant.[29] The overall implications of these facts for such educational issues as ethnic studies courses, compensatory education programs, racial integration, and teachers' unions are not yet clear.

Public School Politics

The basic issue in all political controversies is who should make policy, and on what matters.

Public control   In the area of education, as in many other areas, voters have complex interests. They want to keep taxes down, yet they also want high-quality schools; they want some influence over what is taught, yet they don't want professional educators to be intimidated by political pressures. These contradictory factors may help to explain why so many potential voters stay away from the polls when school board candidates and school finance appear on the ballot.

Perhaps more than anywhere else in government, public school politics reflects the universal tension between the wishes of the people and the wisdom of the experts. If Johnny *still* can't read in the fifth grade, for example, should the public demand the scalps of the school board, principals, or teachers—or should they believe that trained educational specialists will somehow solve the problem if given more facilities, money, and time? Broadly stated, the issue involves the tough and persistent question of the proper relationship between a trained bureaucracy (represented in education by school administrators and the teaching faculty) and a concerned democracy (embodied in the voters and the board members they elect).

Interest groups   The diversity of our society is reflected in the multiplicity of pressures to which the educational system is subjected. Various church groups want the schools to offer some moral or religious training within the limits of (and sometimes in defiance of) Supreme Court decisions. Some also desire greater tax support for parochial schools, a goal toward which President Nixon has pledged his efforts.

In major cities throughout the nation, blacks, Chicanos, and other ethnic groups have insisted that the curriculum reflect both the

28 Adrian and Press, op. cit., p. 435.
29 J. Richard Gilliland and Michael Y. Nunnery, "Florida Trustees: Characteristics and Opinions," *Junior College Journal* 40 (February 1970): 26.

contributions of these groups to the total society and their unique needs with respect to such matters as bilingual instruction and remedial reading classes. Many blacks favor school busing, since it usually entails education in better schools, while other groups seem either indifferent or hostile to this method of achieving integration. In New York and elsewhere demands have been made for minority principals in schools with predominantly minority enrollment.

Then there are pressures for more (or less) sex education, corporal punishment, patriotic indoctrination, and instruction on drug dangers. Taxpayers' organizations frequently oppose the issuance of school bonds or the increase of school taxes, while Parent-Teacher Associations and labor unions work equally hard in favor of such measures. When budgets must be slashed, there is little community agreement on whether the knife should fall first on athletics, music education, or some other area of the curriculum. Perhaps the most persistent dispute is between those who favor an emphasis on vocational training and others who want the schools to provide a broad background in the liberal arts and humanities.

Schools in the big cities are usually subjected to the most frequent cross-pressures simply because they must respond to a more heterogeneous constituency than those outside metropolitan areas.

The educational establishment   The school system is expected not only to accommodate and compromise the community inputs described above, but also to resolve the power struggles that are waged within its organizational structure. Superintendents and other administrators have been confronted in recent years with faculties seeking greater participation in educational decision making. This is reflected both in the growth of the American Federation of Teachers, a union affiliated with the A.F.L.-C.I.O., and in the growing militancy of the National Education Association, a larger, more conservative organization. Collective bargaining, the right of teachers to strike, the desirability of tenure, and the selection of department chairmen are but a few of the issues on which faculty and administrative opinion may clash. From another direction the superintendent may be pressed by the school board for larger class sizes, a different selection of teaching materials, or other educational changes. Complicating matters still more, students have emerged as a new power bloc in the educational community. First in higher education and now even at the high-school level, they protest against administrative restrictions and ask for some voice in the decisions which determine the content of their education.

FINANCE: THE CRISIS OF MONEY

Early in 1971 the mayors of New York City and Newark warned a congressional committee that without increased assistance from the national government their cities faced imminent financial collapse. To avert that crisis, New York cut its police force by eight hundred men and slashed library hours from seventy-eight to forty each week. At the same time, the governor of Pennsylvania announced that the Philadelphia public schools might be forced to close early unless they could come up with $85 million.[30] Farther west Los Angeles County announced that with few exceptions county employees who resigned would not be replaced due to a budget deficit. In 1970 Wisconsin voters turned down forty-four proposed school bond issues while approving only twenty-nine.[31] Local governments are in grave financial trouble.

Urban Plight and Suburban Flight

The financial crisis can be attributed in part to the fact that the population of most major cities has declined while that of their suburbs has increased. One might assume at first glance that this was a good sign and that the distribution of the population over a wider area is something to be encouraged. The problem, however, is that the people who move to the suburbs are the middle-class residents whose tax money is most needed to solve the central-city crises they are so eager to escape. The centers of urban areas present the worst fire hazards, because their buildings are oldest, and the highest communicable disease rates, because their inhabitants live so close to one another. They also have the most crime because of a complex mixture of poverty, drug addiction, and the amoral nature of a transient, frustrated population that is frequently isolated from such restraining influences as a family, church, or genuinely concerned community. The result is that the per capita costs of local government have been about $23 a year higher in our largest central cities than in their surrounding areas.[32]

The vanishing tax dollar As big cities have lost people to the suburbs, they have also lost tax revenue produced by new business and industry. Three quarters of all new jobs and nearly two thirds of industrial construction were located outside the central cities in the 1950s and 1960s.[33] In only four years, Detroit, Washington, D.C., Cleveland, Minneapolis-St. Paul, Seattle, and Miami all lost over 6 percent of their retail sales to surrounding suburbs.[34] This not only indicates a relative decline in sales tax revenue but is also a symptom of the general reduction in the taxable wealth of our major cities. Local governments have the least revenue where local problems are most costly.

The property tax revolt While more money alone will not solve urban problems, few would deny that it is an ingredient essential to an effective solution. Yet local governments seem to be frustrated at every turn in their quest for additional revenue. In the first place, the states usually place limits on the amount and kinds of taxes that can be

30 *Los Angeles Times,* Jan. 23, 1971, p. 21.
31 Ibid., Jan. 30, 1971, p. 3, and *Time,* March 13, 1972, pp. 66–67.
32 Computed from Adrian and Press, op. cit., p. 345.
33 Tyler, loc. cit.
34 Bollens and Schmandt, op. cit., p. 133, and U.S. Bureau of the Census, *Statistical Abstract of the United States: 1971,* p. 414.

locally imposed. In addition, they have restricted the borrowing power of local governments, and have required tax exemptions for religious, charitable, and educational institutions. Finally, most properties owned by local, state, and national governments—parks, office buildings, highways, or military bases—are also beyond the legal reach of tax collectors.

Within these limitations, the property tax has long been the major source of income for local governments. Few other levies have been so reliable in yielding substantial amounts of money, but none has caused more resentment in recent years. There are valid criticisms of this source of revenue. One especially pertinent is that it tends to produce relatively fewer dollars for cities than for suburbs. Big cities devote more space to court houses, museums, police headquarters, and other nontaxable public property than small towns; the remaining taxable property is usually older and more run-down (hence producing fewer property tax dollars) than newer suburban developments. Landlords of cheap, crowded slum dwellings avoid repair or renovation because it makes their taxes soar. To remedy this situation, some have suggested that property taxes be reduced for owners who have improved their holdings, or that rental housing units be assessed for tax purposes on the basis of income derived from them rather than their actual market value.

Another objection to the property tax centers on its relationship to market value. Since industrial property is more valuable than that used for commercial purposes, commercial property more valuable than apartment units, and apartments more valuable than single-family homes, local governments are tempted to zone land for whatever use would increase its tax yield rather than for the use that would enhance its desirability as a place to live.

One more of the many criticisms of the property tax seems especially worthy of attention: It has no rational relationship to ability to pay. The owners of a small factory making a huge profit are required to pay less taxes than the owners of a large factory losing money. Similarly, an eccentric bachelor millionaire living in a $20,000 house pays less property tax than a machinist with a wife and four children living in a $30,000 home. Worst of all, the amount of property taxes paid by a home owner depends almost as much on the value of the other property in the same city as it does on the value of his own home. This is because the property tax revenue of each local government is determined by the total assessed valuation of property within its boundaries multiplied by the tax rates set by local governing bodies. An area rich in industry and business can impose a relatively low tax rate in order to pay its bills while a poor residential area must impose a high one.

The inequities of school finance   A heavy reliance on the local property tax means that rich governments can provide better services than poor ones. This fact stands out vividly with respect to school districts. The national government provides about 7 percent of the costs of elementary and secondary education in the United States, the state governments 41 percent, and the local school districts 52 percent, mostly derived from the property tax. When property within a district has a high assessed valuation for tax purposes (usually because of expensive industrial installations and shopping centers), that district can afford schools far superior to those in districts with less valuable property. There resulted in 1970, for example, per pupil expenditures in Texas ranging from $243 to $2087.[35]

This kind of disparity led courts in California and Minnesota, as well as in Texas, to rule that reliance on local property taxes for school financing violated the "equal protection of the laws" clause of the Fourteenth Amendment. Should the United States Supreme Court uphold these decisions, states would be forced to shoulder most of the educational costs. This alone would not assure equal educational standards. In 1971 all school districts in New York state spent an average of $1370 per pupil compared with an Alabama average of $489. The only way to assure equal financial resources for all schools in the country is for the national government to assume the costs. Because of the fear that more federal financing would lead to more federal control, this proposal has attracted few advocates. Nonetheless, the principle of federal support for education was strengthened enormously in 1965 when Congress appropriated money for general use by elementary and secondary schools for the first time.

The Quest for More Revenue

Although it still provides the largest local source of funds, the inequities of the property tax have led to a demand for other revenue sources. Whereas property taxes accounted for 73.1 percent of local government income in 1902, they had dropped to 43.3 in 1962.[36] To make up the difference, St. Louis, Louisville, and numerous cities in Ohio and Pennsylvania have been among those adding a local income tax. New Orleans, Denver, and many municipalities in California, Illinois, and elsewhere have imposed a sales tax.

Most importantly, however, local governments have extracted more financial aid from the state and national governments, even while pleading successfully for more home rule with respect to their independence in making local policy decisions. State aid often takes the form of subventions, which are state taxes returned to various localities from which they were collected, while most federal assistance has been in grants-in-aid, as illustrated in Chapter 2, requiring the local governments to assist in financing the programs aided. A nation-wide summary of local revenue sources appears in Figure 51.

National-local relations As their financial plight worsened, local governments looked less to the states than to the national government for additional assistance. During the Great Depression of

35 *Newsweek,* June 7, 1971, p. 101.
36 Bollens and Schmandt, op. cit., p. 348.

Figure 51   Local Government Revenue, 1967–68 (in millions of dollars)

Revenue, total	$70,171
From state governments	21,950
From federal government	1,954
Individual income taxes	1,077
Sales taxes and gross receipts	1,932
Property taxes	26,835
Other taxes	1,327
Charges and miscellaneous	9,714
Utility revenue	5,683
Liquor stores revenue	262
Insurance trust revenue	1,044

Source: "Local Government Revenue, 1967–68" from *The Book of the States,* 1970–1971. Reprinted by permission of the Council of State Governments.

the 1930s, President Franklin D. Roosevelt's New Deal began to put the national government in direct contact with cities by assisting them in constructing low-rent public housing, hospitals, sewerage systems, and other projects for the dual purpose of enriching local life and employing the jobless.

What cities first viewed as unexpected emergency assistance, they eventually made one of their most incessant demands. The national-local relationship became institutionalized at the cabinet level with the creation of the Department of Housing and Urban Development during the Johnson administration, and now "more than 100 Federal Government agencies supply more than 500 services" to cities in the United States.[37] It would be ironic if the home rule movement found that the road from state control led into a dead end of national dependency.

Big cities turned increasingly to the national government for help partly because rural-controlled state legislatures were insensitive to their problems. It seems reasonable that the court decisions requiring the election of an equitable number of representatives from urban areas will make the state capitol more sympathetic to city needs in the future than it has been in the past. In any event, the increasingly close relationship between national and local governments often bypasses the states and may foreshadow the emergence of a new variation in American federalism. President Nixon's revenue-sharing program points in this direction.

Revenue sharing   In his 1971 State of the Union address, President Nixon asked Congress to help in launching a "new American revolution." One of the most important components of that revolution was a revenue-sharing program in which the national government would give large amounts of money to state and local governments. As enacted by Congress in 1972, $30.1 billion would be allocated over a five-year period, with $5.3 disbursed during the first year. About one third of the total would go to the state governments, apportioned according to a

37 Adrian and Press, op. cit., p. 294.

Figure 52   Revenue Sharing

Under the formula agreed upon by a House-Senate conference committee, these amounts of federal money will be parceled out in 1972. (In millions of dollars)

State	State Share	Local Share	Total	State	State Share	Local Share	Total
ALA.	38.7	77.4	116.1	MONT.	6.8	13.8	20.6
ALASKA	2.0	4.0	6.0	NEB.	14.3	28.6	42.9
ARIZ.	16.7	33.4	50.1	NEV.	3.7	7.4	11.1
ARK.	18.0	37.0	55.0	N.H.	5.0	10.2	15.2
CALIF.	185.2	370.6	555.8	N.J.	54.5	109.0	163.5
COLO.	18.2	36.4	54.6	N.M.	11.0	22.2	33.2
CONN.	22.1	44.0	66.1	N.Y.	197.0	394.1	591.1
DEL.	5.2	10.5	15.7	N.C.	45.0	90.4	135.4
D.C.	7.9	15.8	23.7	N.D.	6.5	13.2	19.7
FLA.	48.6	97.3	145.9	OHIO	68.9	138.0	206.9
GA.	36.6	73.2	109.8	OKLA.	19.8	39.6	59.4
HAWAII	7.8	15.8	23.6	ORE.	18.8	37.4	56.2
IDAHO	6.6	13.2	19.8	PA.	91.2	182.6	273.8
ILL.	91.5	183.1	274.6	R.I.	7.8	15.8	23.6
IND.	34.7	69.6	104.3	S.C.	27.1	54.3	81.4
IOWA	25.6	51.4	77.0	S.D.	8.3	16.8	25.1
KANS.	17.6	35.2	52.8	TENN.	32.8	65.6	98.4
KY.	29.1	58.2	87.3	TEXAS	81.4	163.0	244.4
LA.	37.8	75.8	113.6	UTAH	10.4	21.0	31.4
MAINE	10.3	20.8	31.1	VT.	4.9	9.9	14.8
MD.	35.6	71.3	106.9	NEV.	35.0	70.2	105.2
MASS.	54.3	108.6	162.9	WASH.	28.0	56.0	84.0
MICH.	73.9	147.8	221.7	W. VA.	17.4	34.9	52.3
MINN.	34.6	69.2	103.8	WIS.	44.6	89.3	133.9
MISS.	30.2	60.4	90.6	WYO.	3.2	6.5	9.7
MO.	32.9	65.8	98.7				

Source: Chart "Slicing Up the Pie" from *Newsweek,* Sept. 25, 1972, p. 43. Reprinted by permission of *Newsweek.*

formula based on the *amount* of money collected in state income taxes and on the *percentage* of total personal income taken by all state and local taxes. In this way, the greater the tax effort a state made to help itself, the more federal aid it would receive. Assistance to local governments would amount to nearly twice as much and would be distributed primarily on the basis of population, urban concentration, and poverty.

Under dozens of separate grant-in-aid programs, state and local governments received over five times as much assistance from the national government in 1972 as in 1959. The additional money received through revenue sharing can be spent without the restrictions accompanying the older grants and carries no requirement that the governments receiving aid put up matching funds. Whether it can revitalize our cities and counties, enable them to give tax relief to the property owner, and provide sufficient resources to cope with urban problems remains to be seen.

GOVERNMENTAL REFORM

The modern metropolis has nearly as many governments as it has problems. They compete for tax funds, new industry, and competent employees. They pursue contradictory policies with respect to zoning, vice control, noise abatement, and public housing. They provide grossly unequal services in such areas as police protection, recreation, trash collection, and fire prevention. Worst of all, they disperse responsibility so thinly as to be all but invisible to the confused voters who wish to hold them accountable for their actions.

This chamber of metropolitan horrors is no figment of poetic license. It exists. In metropolitan Chicago a few years ago, there were 821 local governments including five counties, forty-two townships, 593 school districts, and sixty-six other special purpose districts.[38] In Los Angeles County there are seventy-seven incorporated cities. In King County, Washington, the city of Seattle shares authority with over two hundred other local governments. The 100,000 residents of the Highline School District, south of Seattle,

are governed, taxed, or served by King County, the school district, the Port of Seattle, four small cities . . ., eight sewer districts, eleven water districts, six fire districts, a library district, a road district, a drainage district and the County Housing Authority—thirty-six local governments, with over one hundred elected officials.[39]

There are over two hundred metropolitan areas in the United States whose residents share the same needs for good schools, rapid transportation, better housing, and all the other ingredients of a decent life in twentieth-century America. Yet all these are frustrated by a multiplicity of contiguous and sometimes overlapping local governments that provide an expensive duplication of functions. Fortunately, the political imagination of metropolitan planners has produced some encouraging ideas.

Annexation

When a city fills up, people overflow into adjacent areas. The residents of these outlying regions are then confronted with a choice. They may remain in unincorporated county territory, or seek incorpora-

38 Robert A. Walker, "Chicago," William A. Robson, ed., *Great Cities of the World* (N.Y.: The Macmillan Company, 1955), pp. 195–96.
39 Citizens Advisory Committee, Joint Committee on Urban Area Government, Legislature of the State of Washington, reprinted in Michael N. Danielson, ed., *Metropolitan Politics* (Boston: Little, Brown and Company, 1966), p. 128.

tion as a separate city, or be annexed by the expanding city to which they are adjacent.

The expansion of large core cities by annexation integrates the fringe areas under the same authority as the bulk of the metropolitan population. Inequalities in municipal services are thereby eliminated, and coordinated policies in zoning, transportation, and other fields are more easily established. But state laws vary enormously with regard to both the incorporation of new cities and the annexation of land by existing ones. Kansas City, Oklahoma City, Toledo, San Antonio, and Memphis all have grown substantially in recent years by means of annexation. This process is relatively easy in Virginia, where it may be accomplished by court order, and in Texas, which requires only the action of the city wishing to expand. Many states, however, require a vote by the people to be annexed before the process is completed. Where suburban centers are already incorporated as separate cities, or where their populations differ substantially from those of the major metropolis in economic status, ethnic background, or political attitudes, annexation prospects are so dim as to be practically invisible.

County-City Consolidation

Most of the recent efforts to reform metropolitan government focus on the attempt to integrate services in the major city with those in the surrounding suburban communities. The objectives sought by such integration are equality in facilities, efficiency in performance, and economy in costs. These goals could be attained most readily by a complete consolidation of all cities and counties in a region into a single metropolitan government. At least four obstacles block the road to so sweeping a reform. First, affluent suburbanites suspect it would mean an increase in their taxes to help provide better services for the poorer residents in the central city. Second, some people believe that a merger of municipalities would erase the unique characteristics of each city and erode a sense of civic pride. Third, local government councilmen, board members, department heads and other officials fear that integration with other local governments would cost them their jobs or at least jeopardize their status. Finally, blacks and Democrats in the central cities often see such plans as attempts to transfer political power to whites and Republicans in the suburbs. It is not surprising that progress toward consolidation has been slow.

The first major breakthrough occurred in Florida in 1957, with a partial consolidation of the city of Miami, twenty-seven suburban cities, and Dade County. The resulting metropolitan government reserves to each city the power to perform purely local functions but delegates to the county broad authority over planning, transportation, and many other matters. The system operates much like a council-manager plan with the chief governing body chosen in part by the voters of the entire county, in part by a district system, and with one additional member chosen from each city with over sixty thousand people. The Miami-Dade County innovation is an example of a kind of metropolitan area federalism, patterned somewhat after municipal government arrangements in London, England and, more recently, in Toronto, Canada.

Even greater consolidation was attained by the 1962 creation of the Metropolitan Government of Nashville and Davidson County in Tennessee, and by the 1970 merger of Indianapolis and Marion County in Indiana. Both represent a nearly total fusion of city and county governments and both employ a strong mayor-council form of government. Jacksonville and Duval County in Florida have combined their governments in similar fashion, and San Francisco, Denver, and Honolulu each have units of local government which are combined cities and counties.

Cooperative Action

Less dramatically many other local governments have embarked upon cooperative programs designed to ease the burdens of metropolitan man. In Los Angeles County, for example, the Lakewood Plan permits cities to sign contracts with the county providing them with building code enforcement, police and fire protection, and other municipal services. In other areas, major cities sometimes sell water or other necessities to outlying suburban communities and there are an increasing number of formal and informal agreements among metropolitan governments regarding such matters as reciprocal fire-fighting assistance. In the twin-cities area of Minneapolis and St. Paul, the metropolitan council appointed by the Minnesota governor has the power to veto the location of new sewers, airports, and mass transit routes. As a result, a regional guide for future development has a good chance of checking the urban sprawl that has caused chaos in so many areas.

Finally, representatives of county, city, and other local governments have formed councils of governments (COGs) in more than thirty metropolitan areas. Although COGs have little decision making power, they provide instruments for gathering data, improving region-wide communication, and facilitating cooperative planning in such matters as zoning and mass rapid transit. Leading examples are found in the Association of Bay Area Governments in the San Francisco area, the Supervisors' Inter-County Committee in the Detroit vicinity, and similar agencies with various names around New York, Philadelphia, Washington, D.C., Atlanta, Seattle, Los Angeles, and Salem, Oregon. A 1966 Act of Congress required the approval of such groups before certain federal grants could be accepted by local governments.

The Interrelationship of Metropolitan Problems

In one way or another, the awesome array of urban problems are all interrelated. Thus, some people are doomed to poor housing in central cities because they could not obtain adequate public transportation to their jobs if they moved to the suburbs. Others, more prosperous and with private cars, move to the suburbs because the schools there are financed by a broader industrial and commercial tax base—and when they move, the tax revenue for the central-city schools is diminished even more. New housing tracts are commercially profitable only if transportation facilities make them easily accessible; when constructed, they increase the demand for more schools. Basic to the solution of metropolitan problems is a more integrated and equitable system of taxation and the creation of local governments whose power and jurisdiction are commensurate with the metropolitan crises which threaten their inhabitants.

Conclusion to Part Five

The record of local grass roots government is a story of unfulfilled potential. Because it represents the most decentralized authority in the American political system, it is here that the individual citizen can most easily maximize his influence on the official decision-making process. His dollar contributed to a candidate for the county board or city council, for example, will have a far greater campaign impact than if used in a race for the United States Senate. Moreover, the average voter can actually speak personally before meetings of local legislative bodies.

These advantages are dissipated all too often, however, because citizens experience such difficulty in holding local officials accountable for their actions. There are too many elective positions for the voters to keep track of; the authority of officials is diffused and overlapping; and the media fail to provide adequate information regarding proposed local policies. Finally, the most pressing needs of the modern metropolis are compounded as a numerous array of fragmented and competitive local governments fight for, rather than share, the available tax dollars. Yet the number and diversity of local governments makes them exciting laboratories in which to experiment with new policies and unique structural forms. The serious crises they confront make continued innovations essential to the survival of modern urban life.

Bibliography

Chapter 12

Localities: Variations on Popular Government

Bollens, John C., *Special District Governments in the United States* (Berkeley: University of California Press, 1957).

Duncombe, Herbert S., *County Government in America* (Washington, D.C.: National Association of Counties Research Foundation, 1966).

Gimlin, Hoyt, "Local Government Modernization," *Editorial Research Reports on the Urban Environment* (Washington, D.C.: Congressional Quarterly, Inc., 1969).

Kotler, Milton, *Neighborhood Government* (Indianapolis: The Bobbs-Merrill Company, 1969).

Lockard, Duane, *The Politics of State and Local Government,* 2nd ed. (London: The Macmillan Company, 1969).

Morlan, Robert L., ed., *Capitol, Courthouse and City Hall,* 3rd ed. (Boston: Houghton Mifflin Company, 1966).

Chapter 13

The Cities: Structure and Politics

Adrian, Charles R., and Charles Press, *Governing Urban America,* 3rd ed. (N.Y.: McGraw-Hill Book Company, 1968).

American Political Science Review (periodical).

Banfield, Edward C., *Big City Politics* (N.Y.: Random House, 1965).

Danielson, Michael N., ed., *Metropolitan Politics* (Boston: Little, Brown and Company, 1966).

Goodman, Jay S., ed., *Perspectives on Urban Politics* (Boston: Allyn and Bacon, Inc., 1970).

Shank, Alan, ed., *Political Power and the Urban Crisis* (Boston: Hollbrook Press, Inc., 1969).

Chapter 14

Metropolitan Maladies: Crisis and Response

Bollens, John C., and Henry R. Schmandt, *The Metropolis* (N.Y.: Harper & Row, Publishers, 1965).

Christenson, Reo M., *Challenge and Decision,* 3rd ed. (N.Y.: Harper & Row, Publishers, 1970).

Flinn, Thomas A., *Local Government and Politics* (Glenview, Ill.: Scott, Foresman and Company, 1970).

Litt, Edgar, ed., "Public Policies: A Reader's Guide to Education and Politics," *The Political Imagination* (Glenview, Ill.: Scott, Foresman and Company, 1966).

McKeown, James E., and Frederick I. Tietze, *The Changing Metropolis* (Boston: Houghton Mifflin Company, 1971).

Public Administration Review (periodical).

PART SIX

THE PEOPLE
AND PUBLIC POLICY

The final payoffs, the ultimate outputs of the entire political system, are the policies made and enforced through government bodies. These policies profoundly affect the quality of our lives. Chapter 15 involves one of the oldest questions in politics: the proper relationship between law and personal morality. In large measure, its contemporary concerns are issues such as abortion, drugs, and homosexuality. Chapter 16 is about the national economy. It is an area over which governments have been exercising increasing influence and toward which the views of liberals and conservatives are most easily distinguishable. Bread-and-butter issues are involved here—minimum wages, strikes, taxes, inflation, and poverty. The effects of international affairs discussed in Chapter 17 are not only personal and national, but are also global in scope. For on a wise foreign policy may hinge the future of humanity.

In a sense, all the foregoing sections of this book are a prelude to this one, because their purpose and utility is in giving some insight into the government machinery, and the influences on it, through which future policy may be made to reflect the people's preferences.

Chapter **15**

Life Styles
Politics of Personal Morality

How small of all that human hearts endure,
That part which laws or kings can cause or cure!
Samuel Johnson

Sometimes the boundaries between what is personal and what is political are badly blurred. As a result, there is bitter controversy about what is "my own business" and what is "the government's business." The problem is aggravated by the fact that in congested urban environments, what each one of us does has an intensified impact upon everyone else.

This chapter's topics epitomize this conflict. Some might say the topics—such as pollution—are social problems that have nothing to do with "personal morality." Their adversaries would claim that unless people make individual moral decisions to have fewer children, use smog-belching cars less frequently, and boycott products in plastic containers, they will produce—and deserve—a more polluted planet. Whoever is right, the matters discussed in this chapter have in fact become political issues, whether they should be or not.

POPULATION
The Problem

By 1955 the birth rate in the United States was over 30 percent higher than it had been twenty years before. Abruptly, as though sensing impending catastrophe, the trend began to reverse itself, and in 1971 the birth rate dropped to an all-time low. Many factors contributed to the decline: the widening use of contraceptives, the tendency of women to marry later, more lenient abortion laws, money worries caused by inflation and unemployment, and the suggestion by the women's liberation movement that motherhood was neither the inevitable fate nor noblest function of every female. Yet the large number of women now of childbearing age indicates that even at a reduced birth rate the population of the nation will rise nearly 25 percent by the year 2000.[1] The implications of such growth are staggering. Every twelve months America must build the equivalent of a city the size of Philadelphia to accommodate its additional population. In 1970 President Nixon appointed a twenty-four member National Commission on Population Growth and the American Future to recommend appropriate new policies.

The picture abroad is even more ominous. The world's poorest nations are experiencing the most rapid increase in population. While it will take more than seventy years for the population to double in the United States, birth rates indicate a doubling time of thirty-one years in Indonesia, twenty-four years in Kenya, and twenty-two in Brazil.[2] For the earth as a whole, the population now exceeds 3.6 billion. It took thousands of years to produce the first billion, as President Nixon pointed out in 1969, only a hundred years to double that number, and about thirty years (1930–1960) to produce the third billion.[3] Each year in the 1970s, the world's population increases by at least seventy million, a number equal to the total inhabitants of Canada and Mexico combined. As noted in Chapter 2, it seems inevitable that the United States will feel intensified pressures to liberalize its immigration policies and perhaps to expand its foreign aid programs. While the United States accounts for only 6 percent of the global population, it uses over 40 percent of the world's most valuable (and often irreplaceable) resources.[4] Chances are very great, therefore, that the iron, aluminum, petroleum, and other raw materials that will be consumed by an American baby during its lifetime will be unavailable to an infant in some poorer nation.

Proposed Solutions

National recommendations   In the late 1950s, President Eisenhower said he did not believe birth control was a governmental responsibility. Only a decade later, President Nixon sent a special message to Congress on the problems of overpopulation. Warning that unabated population growth could seriously impair the quality of life, he

1 *Newsweek,* March 27, 1972, p. 75.
2 Paul R. Ehrlich, *The Population Bomb* (N.Y.: Ballantine Books, 1968), p. 22.
3 *Los Angeles Times,* Dec. 8, 1969, Part VII, p. 5.
4 Rudy Abramson, *Los Angeles Times,* Aug. 11, 1970, p. 1.

asserted that "[W]e should establish as a national goal the provision of adequate family planning services within the next five years to all those who want them but cannot afford them."[5] Congress responded in 1970 by appropriating $285 million over a three-year period to help local communities provide family-planning assistance (a euphemism for birth control) to those wishing it. In addition, the lawmakers authorized the President to appoint the population commission mentioned earlier. He chose as its chairman John D. Rockefeller III, the brother of Governor Nelson Rockefeller of New York.

After nearly two years of intensive investigation, the Rockefeller commission endorsed the objective of Zero Population Growth, a relatively new pressure group, by urging that population increase be halted. To bring this about, it proposed that sex education be made available to all, especially in view of the evidence that as many as 15 percent of all pregnancies are unwanted. In addition, it advocated that public and private health services pay the full costs of voluntary sterilization and contraceptives, that state laws restricting the sale, advertising, or display of contraceptives be repealed, and that a crackdown be initiated against aliens who are in the country illegally.

Its most controversial recommendations, however, were that physicians be allowed to prescribe birth control pills and intrauterine devices for teen-agers without their parents' consent, and that abortion be permitted on request.[6] The legal implications of these suggestions were far-reaching, since even the distribution of contraceptives to single adults was restricted in twenty-six states until the Supreme Court declared such laws unconstitutional in 1972, and stiff antiabortion statutes were more numerous still. President Nixon rejected the proposals on the grounds that they "would do nothing to preserve and strengthen close family relationships" and tended to "demean human life."[7]

Another Rockefeller commission recommendation, receiving far less attention, was to relieve population pressures in huge metropolitan areas by encouraging migration to cities of 25,000 to 350,000 inhabitants. Many smaller towns, it was suggested, are doomed to economic extinction.

Population and personal morality   Any policy designed to limit the population elicits passionate controversy unless it involves only a naive and ineffective reliance on self-denial in ordinary sexual relations. The bitter intensity of the argument can be explained by the following considerations:

1) Birth control involves the family, a basic institution of our society and one "intimate to the degree of being sacred," according to the United States Supreme Court.[8]

5 *Los Angeles Times,* Dec. 21, 1969, p. 1.
6 *Los Angeles Times,* March 17, 1972, pp. 1 and 15, and *Newsweek,* March 27, 1972, p. 75.
7 *Los Angeles Times,* May 6, 1972, pp. 1 and 13.
8 Justice Douglas, *Griswold* v. *Connecticut,* 381 U.S. 479.

2) It also involves sex—a basic human impulse.

3) It encounters considerations of personal morality, especially with respect to abortion, which many view as a form of murder.

4) It often offends the religious convictions of Catholics, as well as many others, although 31 percent of American Catholics have expressed disagreement with church dogma on the matter of abortion.[9]

5) Some blacks believe birth control to be a genocidal attempt by the white power structure to maintain its dominance over a growing minority.

6) Female activists in the women's liberation movement demand control over their own bodies, including the freedom to obtain abortions at their own discretion and without cost.

7) Certain corporation executives and union leaders believe that national prosperity, high profits, and full employment depend on continued population growth, in spite of contrary assurances by the Rockefeller Commission.

Obviously any program involving the family, sex, moral scruples, religious conviction, racial rivalry, personal freedom, and economic change cannot anticipate universal acclaim. In the last analysis, population restrictions are either preventive, entailing contraception, or remedial, suggesting abortion. Both depend more on state laws than on national policies.

State government action There was a time when some states totally prohibited the dispensation or use of contraceptive devices, but these prohibitions were declared unconstitutional in 1965.[10] Rigid restrictions on abortion were imposed by all states until 1970. Prior to that time, about 8000 legal abortions were performed each year, in addition to 800,000 to a million illegal ones.[11] Usually, abortions were permitted only in cases of rape or incest, or to protect the life of the mother. At opposite ends of the nation, Hawaii and New York liberalized their laws in 1970 to permit abortion at the request of the expectant woman, except in cases where the fetus may be viable—a period four or five months after the time of conception. To safeguard the health of prospective mothers, so often jeopardized by untrained abortion "butchers," the operation could be obtained only from licensed doctors. The number of legal abortions performed in 1971 rose to an estimated 420,000. In New York, which accounted for more than half the national total, there was nearly one abortion for every live birth.[12] This prompted the state legislature, under strong religious pressure, to repeal the 1970 liberalization, but its action was killed by Governor Rockefeller's veto.

Both the Republican and Democratic national conventions turned down legalized abortion planks in their 1972 platforms, but a case

9 Gallup Poll, *Los Angeles Times,* Nov. 30, 1969, Sec. H, p. 2.
10 *Griswold* v. *Connecticut,* op. cit.
11 Gallup Poll, loc. cit.
12 *Los Angeles Times,* May 4, 1971, Part II, p. 2 and Feb. 29, 1972, pp. 1 and 17.

before the Supreme Court contended that antiabortion laws were an unconstitutional denial of the liberty of women. In 1973 the Court upheld abortion on request in the first three months of pregnancy.

ECOLOGY AND POLLUTION

Ecology is the science dealing with the relationship of living things to one another and to their environment—the water, air, and land around them. Ten years ago, most people had never heard of it. They assumed that human beings were masters of all they surveyed, the world and all that dwelled within it. Rather suddenly this arrogance was challenged. Irrefutable evidence accumulated indicating that we were befouling our earth, contaminating our air, depleting our minerals, and poisoning our waters. Gradually, Americans adjusted to a new insight: We pollute our planet at our own peril, and we are partners, rather than masters, in an intricate ecological relationship upon which the survival of all species, including our own, depends.

The delicacy of ecological balance could be illustrated by many examples, but perhaps one is sufficient. Some scientists feared that if the world's tallest trees, the giant redwoods of the Pacific coast, continued to be victims of the lumberman's saw, the following sequence of events might ensue. With the trees gone, birds nesting in them might migrate elsewhere; with the birds gone, insects upon which they fed might multiply; with the insects multiplying, the crops on which they fed might be destroyed; and with the crops destroyed, the farmers who harvested them might move to the city to make their contributions to the traffic congestion, smog, and other ills of urban life. Other scientists warned also that with the redwoods gone, the moisture-laden clouds that once dropped rain when impeded by high branches might pass farther inland to change dry climates to wet ones, and wet ones to arid wastelands. This scenario projecting possible future developments may or may not be correct. Mercifully, the Redwood National Park, created by an act of Congress in the late 1960s, may prevent us from ever finding out.

The Land Abused

The most obvious of our natural resources is the land on which we live. We have despoiled it horribly, in some areas growing the same crops so often that it is drained of natural nutrition, and in other areas covering it with so many asphalt highways and roofed buildings that it can scarcely absorb rain and melting snow without the risk of floods and severe soil erosion. Of the nearly endless examples of land pollution only a few can be cited.

Waste not, want not   One of the biggest problems confronting both modern ecologists and local government officials is how to dispose of waste products most effectively. Garbage, trash, junk, and excrement total nearly a ton per person each year in the United States and disposal costs alone amount to $4.5 billion annually.[13] The price tag on human waste could reduce human want substantially. In this area, perhaps, the relationship of population growth to pollution is most apparent. People pollute, or—as Pogo of comic strip fame has put it—"we have met the enemy and he is us." A partial inventory of yearly national waste proves the point: thirty million tons of paper and paper products, four million tons of plastics, one hundred million tires, thirty billion bottles, and sixty billion cans. In addition, over fifty thousand abandoned cars were towed away in New York City alone in 1969.[14]

Some forms of waste material present greater problems than others. Paper, for example, is biodegradable, which means that it decays fairly readily. Aluminum can be melted down for reuse. Such processes, known as recycling, are not so easy with other materials, however, and many ecologists view plastic containers as major environmental villains.[15] Human waste can be recycled in sewerage treatment plants with relative ease and safety but psychological factors seem to make most people reluctant to use the water thereby produced. Glass bottles, so easy to reuse or recycle, usually end up in garbage dumps.

The conservation crusade The preservation of a decent environment requires two things: We must use restraint in dumping debris upon it, as well as in extracting its treasures from it. The dangers of squandering our natural resources first gained political recognition from President Theodore Roosevelt, who early in this century launched a conservation movement which has been invigorated by modern ecologists. Government activity has been most apparent in four areas: the protection of forests and grazing areas, the preservation of the natural beauty of wilderness regions, restraints on cheap and often wasteful extraction of mineral resources, and the prevention of soil erosion. Programs in these areas often entail land ownership and management by the national government.

Forest and grazing land is protected in part by the U.S. Department of Agriculture, which may set limits on the commercial lumber and cattle usage of land within its jurisdiction. National parks— Yosemite, Yellowstone, Everglades, and over thirty more—are under the jurisdiction of the Interior Department. They are usually restricted to hikers, sight-seers, and the commercial enterprises necessary to meet their needs. The Interior Department also enforces congressional statutes to regulate the mining, petroleum, and other extractive industries. Soil erosion has been combatted by a number of government agencies including the Agriculture Department, which encourages contour plowing on hillside areas, reforestation, and other preventive measures; the Interior Department, which operates a series of dams; and the

13 John Fischer, "Survival U: Prospects for a Really Relevant University," Garrett De Bell, ed., *The Environmental Handbook* (N.Y.: Ballantine Books, Inc., 1970), p. 140.
14 I. S. Bengelsdorf, *Los Angeles Times,* Aug. 16, 1970, Sec. F, p. 2.
15 Garrett De Bell, "Recycling," *The Environmental Handbook,* op. cit., pp. 215–16.

Army Corps of Engineers, which has straightened rivers and undertaken other construction projects. In all these areas, there are frequent exercises of concurrent powers by both the state and national governments.

Chemical suicide? Modern science, with good intentions, has developed ingenious chemical compounds to combat malaria and save crops from destruction by insect pests. But when these chemicals, for instance DDT, are used indiscriminately, their results may be as disastrous as they were unexpected. The Food and Drug Administration of the Department of Health, Education and Welfare has estimated that from eight hundred to a thousand people die annually from pesticide poisoning,[16] and farm work is becoming an increasingly hazardous occupation. Even Eskimos in the Arctic and seals in the Antarctic have been found with DDT residues in their fat deposits.[17] There is some evidence relating such pesticides to liver cancer, leukemia, high blood pressure, and calcium deficiency.[18] The brown pelican, state bird of Louisiana, is almost extinct, probably because its eggshells collapse so frequently as a result of DDT contamination.[19] In June 1972 the government announced an almost total ban on its domestic use.

There are additional indications that birth defects and even death may be caused by chemical herbicides (weed-killers) such as those used for defoliation in Vietnam. A commission of the American Association for the Advancement of Science discovered that ninety children died in a 350-person hamlet in Quang Ngai province in South Vietnam during a four-month period in late 1969. The area had been heavily sprayed with a herbicide believed to contain arsenic.[20] Rachel Carson's best selling *Silent Spring*[21] was the loudest of the early warnings against chemical pollution. A decade later, officials had begun to take her seriously.

Water and Air

Only the meanest of men would throw trash in his neighbor's yard. Yet humans have been thoughtlessly discarding their wastes into neighboring air, rivers, bays, and oceans for many years. And recently they have begun to suffer the consequences. The earth is an organic whole, and the refuse of any of its parts—land, water, and air—pollutes them all.

Liquid poison People can survive for weeks without food but only days without water. Yet pure water and the life which it sustains is being fatally polluted. For instance, about 8000 pounds of Pacific Ocean kingfish destined for human consumption were impounded by the U.S.

16 Steven H. Wodka, "Pesticides Since *Silent Spring*," *The Environmental Handbook*, op. cit., p. 76.
17 Ehrlich, op. cit., pp. 50–53.
18 Wodka, op. cit., p. 78.
19 *Newsweek*, Jan. 26, 1970, p. 31.
20 Bryce Nelson, *Los Angeles Times*, Dec. 31, 1970, p. 1.
21 Greenwich, Conn.: Fawcett Publications, 1962.

Food and Drug Administration (Department of HEW) in December 1970 due to excessive DDT concentrations. Earlier the same month FDA confirmed that some tuna and swordfish already on the market contained more mercury than was generally agreed to be safe, and in May 1971 the FDA warned the public not to eat any swordfish at all.[22] But oil produced the most dramatic examples of water pollution: In 1969 a ruptured oil well off the Santa Barbara coast killed hundreds of seabirds, blackened forty miles of California beaches, and injured countless seals and sea lions. Later, an oil spill off the shores of West Falmouth, Massachusetts, covered over 5000 acres, killed clams and snails, and contaminated oysters and scallops.

DDT, mercury, and oil are not the only villains. New York City has dumped about ten million tons of solid wastes per year into the Atlantic Ocean, with "a marked effect on the abundance and distribution of marine organisms."[23] A recent study reveals that residents of 80 percent of communities under 50,000 population drink water violating governmentally established standards.[24]

It is difficult to determine which waterways are most polluted. One source awards the dubious honors to ten rivers: the Ohio, the Houston Ship Channel, the Cuyahoga, Michigan's Rouge River, the Buffalo, the Passaic and the Arthur Kill, both in New Jersey, the Merrimack on the border between New Hampshire and Massachusetts, the Androscoggin in Maine, and the Escambia in Florida.[25] The plight of the Escambia, dumping into the bay adjacent to Pensacola, has been well documented. Among its alleged polluters are such major American corporations as Monsanto, American Cyanamid, and Westinghouse. Shrimp are among the chief victims. A 1970 account reports that on August 5, "35 small private shrimp boats put out for a day's work. They returned with only 330 pounds among them. Two years ago each would have brought in 600 to 1000 pounds."[26] Not to be outdone, the Cuyahoga in Ohio attained the ultimate in river pollution: It caught fire and burned two railroad trestles. Among the larger bodies of inland water, Lake Erie has suffered most. Discharges of acids, oil, cyanide, iron, bacteria, and other substances have consumed much of the oxygen necessary for water-based life.[27] The situation, moreover, has been getting worse. A report to Congress disclosed that there were about 5000 more miles of polluted waterways in 1971 than in 1970.[28]

Air contamination Southeast of Los Angeles, real estate developers once trumpeted the virtues of smog-free Orange County. Now, the cynics say, it is orange-free smog county. Air pollution,

22 *Los Angeles Times,* Jan. 10, 1971, Sec. B, p. 7; Dec. 31, 1970, p. 1; Dec. 18, 1970, p. 31; and May 7, 1971, p. 14.
23 *Los Angeles Times,* Dec. 12, 1969, Part VII, p. 6.
24 *Los Angeles Times,* Sept. 21, 1972, Part 1–A, p. 6.
25 *Newsweek,* Jan. 26, 1970, p. 37F.
26 Kenneth Reich, *Los Angeles Times,* Oct. 18, 1970, Sec. B, p. 6.
27 *Memo from COPE,* No. 5–70 (March 2, 1970), Committee on Political Education, AFL–CIO, pp. 1 and 3.
28 *Los Angeles Times,* Aug. 8, 1972, p. 10.

however, has ceased to be a laughing matter. Instead, it is a crying, coughing, sneezing, and sometimes dying matter. On Thanksgiving Day 1966, a layer of smog, to which 168 deaths have been attributed, descended on New York City;[29] a "fixed blanket of dirt particles" impervious to wind or rain hangs in the air over Boston;[30] the rate of lung cancer deaths is twice as high in cities as in rural areas.[31]

Air contamination comes in several forms. One is a collection of tiny particles of metals, tar, stone, ash, soot, and other substances found in such widely separated locations as Anchorage, Charleston, West Virginia, East Chicago, and Phoenix.[32] Another type is sulphur dioxide, produced by such fossil fuels as oil and coal and forming sulphuric acid when combined with smoke particles. A third variety is photochemical smog which consists of gases such as carbon monoxide and ozone. This form of pollution is frequently intensified by a "thermal inversion" in which a combination of warm sunshine and surrounding mountains traps auto exhaust near ground level. Los Angeles, perhaps, has suffered from it most severely. When various forms of smog combine, as they sometimes do in New York, the dangers to plant and animal life are increased substantially.

While air pollution is most obviously related to lung cancer, emphysema, and other respiratory ailments, there is some evidence linking it to heart and circulatory diseases, and even to cirrhosis of the liver.[33] It is just possible that if we survive poisoned foods and polluted water, we may breathe ourselves to death. Throughout the nation, the major smog contributors are auto exhaust 60 percent, industry 19 percent, generation of electric power 12.5 percent, and heating and refuse disposal 8.5 percent.[34]

Pollution of Sound and Sight

Once loud noise was a mere annoyance. Now noise levels in some areas have doubled in the last ten years and cause a serious threat to human health.[35] Doctors agree that continuous sound above eighty-five decibels (twenty-five above street traffic) can cause deafness—a volume regularly exceeded in New York City.[36] At the 1969 meeting of the American Association for the Advancement of Science noise was said to affect human beings from the period of prenatal development to the time at which it contributes to premature aging by speeding the deterioration of circulatory systems. A London study, moreover, links exces-

29 *Newsweek,* Jan. 26, 1970.
30 Associated Press dispatch, *Los Angeles Times,* Oct. 28, 1970, p. 4.
31 National Research Council, reported in *Los Angeles Times,* Sept. 11, 1972, p. 1.
32 Robert Rienow and Leona Train Rienow, *Moment in the Sun,* excerpted in *The Environmental Handbook,* op. cit., p. 114.
33 United Press International dispatch, *Los Angeles Times,* Oct. 28, 1970, p. 4.
34 *Memo from COPE,* No. 4–70 (Feb. 16, 1970), Committee on Political Education, AFL-CIO, p. 1.
35 William Zinsser, *Life,* Oct. 31, 1969, p. 12.
36 *Newsweek,* Jan. 26, 1970, p. 40.

sive noise to an increase in mental illness.[37] Residential property values have fallen in some areas adjacent to airports, and classroom procedures have had to be altered in nearby schools. Yet federal and state regulations have had relatively little impact on the problem, and only a few cities are enforcing effective antinoise ordinances.

Ugliness too has become a concern. This is because the noblest goal of ecology—like that of politics—is to improve the quality of life. Life without beauty is drab and dull, and natural beauty—the most easily polluted of all earth's resources—has been wantonly diminished. Debris and litter, gauche and gaudy billboards, junk yards, strip mining, and leveled forests are among the major signposts on the road to an ugly America. All is not lost, however. National parks help preserve the loveliness of vast wilderness areas, city planners recognize the need for more open space, and the antilitter publicity campaign has been intensified. In the mid-1960s Congress appropriated modest sums of money to help fund local beautification projects which Mrs. Lyndon B. Johnson helped to publicize.

The Political Response to Pollution

However much one might wish that governmental institutions would take the lead in identifying and solving serious problems, the truth is that they seldom do. Our recent perception of the frightening, nation-wide dimensions of the problem of pollution was not prompted by our elected leaders but by far-sighted citizens and private groups such as the Sierra Club, National Wildlife Federation, and many local organizations.

Recent progress Several government agencies, including the Departments of Interior, Agriculture, and HEW, have performed a few functions relating to ecology for many years. Recent developments have brought greater coordination in this area. In his first official action of the 1970s, President Nixon signed the National Environmental Policy Act introduced by Senator Henry Jackson (D-Wash.) to create a three-member Council on Environmental Quality in the Executive Office of the President. The law requires that before any new facility can be constructed by a federal agency or a company licensed by it, a detailed report on its environmental impact must be submitted to the Council for its evaluation. Later in 1970 the President established an Environmental Protection Agency (EPA) which has broad authority to enforce controls on air pollution, pesticides, and other ecological hazards.

Subsequently, other significant congressional action has been directed against pollution. A series of amendments to the Air Quality Act required that automotive pollutants be reduced by 90 percent by 1975, and the Water Quality Improvement Act obligated petroleum

37 *Los Angeles Times,* Dec. 29, 1969, p. 1; Jan. 6, 1970, Part II, p. 1; and April 30, 1972, Sec. G. pp. 4–5.

Chicago Tribune Photo.

Cleaning up the Des Plaines River.

companies to pay the cost of cleaning up oil spills. In what was widely
regarded as a major victory for conservationists, a combination of
legislative and executive action killed the construction of a jetport near
the Everglades National Park in Florida.[38] In 1971 President Nixon took
another major step to protect the Florida environment. Despite protests
that he had subverted congressional authorization, he cut off funds for
the completion of a 107-mile canal linking the Atlantic Ocean and the
Gulf of Mexico, because the Council on Environmental Quality believed
the project might jeopardize wildlife and endanger the "unique natural
beauty" around the Oklawaha River.[39] Of even more importance, perhaps, Congress cut off funds for a supersonic transport plane (SST) due
to concern about potential air pollution and increased noise levels.
Balancing the ledger, environmentalists suffered a major defeat with
government approval of the trans-Alaska hot oil pipeline.

       Progress at the state and local levels has resulted in the
enactment of more than a thousand pieces of environmental legislation,
some of which displayed astonishingly sharp teeth. The Illinois Pollution

38 *Congressional Quarterly Guide to Current American Government* (Fall 1970), p. 42.
39 *Los Angeles Times,* Jan. 20, 1971, p. 4.

Control Board, for example, fined an asphalt roofing plant $149,000, perhaps the highest ever imposed in the United States, for dumping untreated waste in the Des Plaines River.[40] A process has been devised for recycling bottles into "glasphalt" pavements for parking lots, and garbage can be converted into low-sulfur fuel oil. Moreover, the pollution in at least some waterways (the Houston Ship Channel and Oregon's Willamette River, for example) has been diminished as a result of proper treatment.[41] In its 1972 annual report, the Council on Environmental Quality revealed that air contamination had been cut by 16.9 percent in eighty-two metropolitan areas, although rivers were generally dirtier than ever. In hope of reversing this trend, Congress passed, over President Nixon's veto, a bill authorizing the largest nonmilitary expenditure in history, $24.6 billion, for water pollution control. Most of the money was to finance municipally constructed waste-treatment plants. The same legislation requires private industry to meet rigid waste-disposal standards by 1983 and provides low-interest loans for the purchase of necessary purification equipment.[42]

International cooperation in environmental research was launched in 1972 by an American-Soviet agreement to exchange information and a 114-nation conference in Stockholm sponsored by the United Nations. In an agreement with Canada, President Nixon committed $3 billion to a coordinated assault on pollution in the Great Lakes.

The burden of the future   Just as the stakes are high in the battle against pollution, so is the cost. Public and private expenditures exceeded $10 billion in 1970, and the annual outlay must be tripled by 1980 if significant progress is to continue. Some plants, unable or unwilling to pay the price for antipollution installations, have closed down and workers have lost their jobs.

Complicating the effort to clean up the environment is the necessity of developing new sources of energy to avert an impending power shortage.[43] While electric generating plants have enormous pollution-producing potentialities, for example, more electricity seems necessary to power the recycling procedures that are ecologically desirable. How the dilemma is resolved will have a significant impact on our future environment.

The greatest source of optimism is a heightened level of ecological consciousness. Necessary as legal and political action are, ecological progress also requires individual commitment. In the National Environmental Policy Act, Congress asserted that "each person has a responsibility to contribute to the preservation and enhancement of the environment." Unless we are willing, for example, to use biodegradable

40 Ibid., April 20, 1971, p. 12.
41 *Newsweek,* June 12, 1972, pp. 48 and 38.
42 *Los Angeles Times,* Sept. 21, 1972, Part I–A, p. 1 and Oct. 5, 1972, p. 4. In its closing hours in 1972, the ninety-second Congress also passed a noise control act that permitted the Environmental Protection Agency to set maximum noise levels for trains, trucks, jackhammers, motorcycles, and other commercial products.
43 *Congressional Quarterly Weekly Report,* May 6, 1972, pp. 1018–20.

products more and automobiles less, the righteousness of our public demands can scarcely compensate for our lack of personal responsibility.

DRUG CULTURES

Nearly all societies, ancient as well as modern, have developed drugs to seek pleasure or escape pain, and many times governments have been called upon to regulate or prohibit their use. With changing tastes and technological advances, different people have come to prefer different drugs. In contemporary America, not surprisingly, those that appeal most to the old are legal, while some favored by the young are not.

Old-fashioned Follies

Tobacco   News of the exotic American herb called tobacco reached Europe over four hundred years ago. It emerged in its most popular and dangerous variety around the turn of the century in the form of cigarettes. Annual per-person consumption grew from two-and-one-half packs in 1900 to 202 packs in 1971. Cigarettes became socially acceptable for women as well as men by the 1930s and with the endorsement of movie stars and athletes were a symbol of sophistication, adulthood, and success.

Although the health hazards of tobacco were identified in the late 1850s, no serious attempts to obtain governmental control were launched until this century. In 1964 the Surgeon General of the U.S. issued a report, *Smoking and Health,* which documented its dangers. In 1966 under the leadership of Senator Maurine Neuberger (D-Ore.), the national government required cigarette packs to bear the words, "Caution: Cigarette Smoking May Be Hazardous to Your Health." In 1971 this inscription was strengthened to read, "Warning: The Surgeon General Has Determined That Cigarette Smoking Is Dangerous to Your Health." Cigarette advertising was also banned on television, which had earned 8 percent of its revenue from this source, and many believe that it should be prohibited completely.

There is overwhelming evidence to justify such action. Abnormal lung cells have been identified in 93.2 percent of smokers and only 1.2 percent of nonsmokers. Heart disease and respiratory ailments also seem related to cigarettes, and the total death rate "for male smokers between the ages of 45 and 64 is twice as high as that for nonsmokers."[44] But governmental attempts to discourage smoking have determined enemies—the tobacco farmers, cigarette manufacturers, advertising companies, and the magazines which derive advertising revenue from them.

The percentage of cigarette smokers has dropped a little in

44 A. Lee Fritschler, *Smoking and Politics* (N.Y.: Appleton-Century-Crofts, 1969), p. 17.

recent years. In 1968, it stood at 45.9 among males over sixteen and 30.5 among females.[45] While the number of smokers continued to decline, the proportion of heavy smokers increased in 1971, thereby producing record sales and the first per capita increase in consumption since 1966.[46]

Tobacco usage glaringly illuminates the difficult distinction between personal and social morality. Its direct effects involve only the individual who is "hooked." It neither obscures his vision nor excites his passions. Yet if a nicotine addict with a dependent wife and several young children may die of lung cancer directly attributable to smoking, is he not a social menace? Does government have a responsibility to protect his family from his folly? Such questions strike at the heart of the politics of personal morality. Government policy with respect to smoking involves a variety of agencies: congressional legislation, labeling requirements by the Federal Trade Commission, scientific analysis by the Surgeon General in the Department of Health, Education and Welfare, advertising controls by the Federal Communications Commission, and—ironically—various kinds of assistance to tobacco farmers by the Department of Agriculture.

Alcohol   Beers, wines, and liquors are among the oldest and most pervasive diversions known to man. Their use is more widespread than tobacco, less addictive or habit-forming, but with far more serious social consequences. Alcoholism is a disease that plagues about four out of every hundred Americans, a number exceeding the population of New York City. Drunkenness plays a role in about half of all fatal automobile accidents, and accounts for far more arrests than any other crime.[47]

Alcohol has attracted more political attention than cigarettes, probably because its possible effects are so dramatic and its use offensive to the religious scruples of more people. The prohibition movement, designed to outlaw the sale of alcoholic beverages, was led by Methodists and Baptists, and resulted in the ratification of the Eighteenth Amendment to the Constitution shortly after World War I. By 1933, when the Twenty-first Amendment repealed the Eighteenth, Americans had participated in a classic example of a government's inability to administer public policy in the face of widespread public defiance. When a law loses too much authority, there is too little force to compel obedience to it. Prohibition, however, remained in effect in some regions as a result of state laws; many cities and counties still have the local option to remain dry.

The old-time prohibition movement has been reduced to the polite indignation expressed by such organizations as the Women's Christian Temperance Union. Yet alcoholic beverages remain an important concern of government policy. Liquor advertisements are banned from radio and television; state laws fix licensing requirements for

45 U.S. Bureau of the Census, *Statistical Abstract of the United States: 1971*, p. 79.
46 *Los Angeles Times*, June 23, 1972, p. 19 and July 27, 1972, p. 12.
47 *Los Angeles Times*, Feb. 19, 1972, p. 3.

dealers or restrict retail distribution through state-owned liquor stores; sales are limited to certain hours and in some areas forbidden entirely on Sundays and election days. All fifty states tax the sale of alcoholic beverages, and this revenue, plus the tax on tobacco products, swells their treasuries by an annual total of seventeen dollars for every human being in the nation.[48]

Turning On and Tripping Out

Marijuana Regardless of its other effects, "pot," "grass," or whatever else marijuana might be called has provoked bitter controversies. Out of these disputes, however, one can extract a few broad generalizations likely to win wide agreement, especially among those best informed on the subject.

1) Unlike tobacco and alcohol, its use is illegal. There is a trend, however, to reduce simple possession (in contrast to selling) from a felony to a misdemeanor, as recommended by the American Medical Association in a reversal of its previous, more punitive stand.[49]

2) It is not physically addictive and does not require increasingly greater amounts to feel its effect.[50]

3) "The principal danger is that one may become psychologically dependent on marijuana and, instead of coping with everyday problems, withdraw through frequent use of the drug."[51]

4) Its use is growing in popularity. Estimates of the number of Americans who have "gone to pot" at least once range from twelve to twenty-five million. The number of arrests for drug offenses, mostly involving marijuana, increased 516 percent between 1960 and 1969, a larger jump than for any other type of crime.[52] Gallup polls reveal that the percentage of students admitting they have tried marijuana rose from 5 in spring 1967 to 51 in February 1972, and the percentage for all adults increased from 4 in 1969 to 11 in 1972.[53]

Beyond this, there is little agreement regarding any aspect of marijuana usage. Public opinion on legalization showed 15 percent favoring no penalty whatever for its use, but 64 percent advocating even stiffer penalties than those currently in effect.[54] There is only a little more consensus among scientists. Some, like Dr. Luther A. Cloud, feel that alcoholism is a far greater menace and that marijuana is "(no) more a problem than going to the movies on Saturday afternoon."[55] At the other extreme, Dr. Sidney Cohen believes that "potheads" who use it daily are the most likely to get hooked on "hard" drugs and have

48 U.S. Bureau of the Census, *Statistical Abstract of the United States: 1971*, p. 400.
49 *Los Angeles Times*, Feb. 10, 1971, p. 5, and *Newsweek*, July 3, 1972, p. 50.
50 *Newsweek*, Sept. 7, 1970, p. 22.
51 James L. Goddard, *Life*, Oct. 31, 1969, p. 34. Dr. Goddard was once the director of the U.S. Food and Drug Administration.
52 U.S. Bureau of the Census, *Statistical Abstract of the United States: 1971*, p. 146.
53 *Los Angeles Times*, Feb. 10, 1972, p. 24, and March 26, 1972, p. 5.
54 Loc. cit.
55 *Los Angeles Times*, Jan. 30, 1970, Part II, p. 8.

Figure 53   Student Use of Alcoholic Beverages and Drugs

Substance	Ever used	
	1970	1972
Beer	82%	
Wine	79	
Hard liquor	75	
Marijuana	42	51%
Amphetamines	16	22
Barbiturates	15	15
LSD (and other hallucinogens)	14	18

Source: Reprinted by permission of the American Institute of Public Opinion (The Gallup Poll).

experienced temporary changes in brain waves sometimes associated with epileptic seizures.[56]

Several problems seem to complicate intelligent political action in this field. One is that early reports of the dangers of marijuana were undoubtedly exaggerated, and helped produce a "credibility gap" which led young people to disregard more accurate warnings against more deadly drugs. While pot is not a narcotic by scientific analysis, for example, it is legally classified as such. Among the users themselves, few report any ill effects. A second problem stems from a comparison of marijuana with tobacco and alcohol. Young people feel that it is hypocritical to legalize the latter, while prohibiting the former. Some older persons, on the other hand, argue that although the dangers of pot are no greater than cigarettes and liquor, two wrongs don't make a right. Why compound the existing evils, they ask, by condoning still another?

The intense controversy surrounding the drug led to the establishment of an official National Commission on Marijuana and Drug Abuse, for which President Nixon chose former Pennsylvania Governor Raymond P. Shafer as chairman. Eighteen months later its conclusion was that "Marijuana's relative potential for harm . . . does not justify a social policy designed to . . . punish those who use it." It recommended that private possession for personal use no longer be a criminal offense, and that even public possession of more than one ounce or the distribution of small amounts not involving a profit should be punishable by a fine of no more than $100. The White House was not impressed by the commission's report. A spokesman announced rather curtly that President Nixon "still opposes legalization of marijuana."[57] In November 1972 California voters also rejected a measure, placed on the ballot by the initiative process, that paralleled the recommendations of the Shafer Commission in most major respects. It seemed that for some time to come marijuana would continue to place a serious burden on the

56 *Los Angeles Times*, Oct. 13, 1970, p. 3.
57 *Los Angeles Times*, March 23, 1972, p. 1.

severely strained facilities of police departments, courts, and probation agencies throughout the nation.

The hard stuff   The new drug culture includes not only marijuana but also other, more dangerous concoctions. Many of these are neither wholly legal nor entirely illegal but available only when prescribed by a licensed physician.

The amphetamines (stimulants) are a good example. They are pep pills or "uppers" and aid in the treatment of fatigue, obesity, and certain mental disorders. "Speed," or methedrine, is a variety often used to dangerous excess. Accumulated tolerance to these drugs seems to require increased dosages to obtain the desired effect, although physical addiction does not develop. Excessive amounts can cause nervousness, insomnia, delusions, and hallucinations, especially if the drugs are injected intravenously. Barbiturates are depressant drugs, or "downers," widely used as sleeping pills. They produce physical dependence and overdoses may lead to emotional outbursts, slurred speech, and death. Hallucinogenic or psychedelic drugs are unavailable by prescription and are sometimes said to produce the wildest "turn on," the farthest "trip" of all. With the use of LSD, for example, senses are heightened, vivid colors appear, sound and perspective are distorted. Most dangerously, ego identity is often lost and acute feelings of persecution and fear may develop, along with severe mental illness.[58] Peyote and mescaline are milder varieties of hallucinogens.

By far the most serious threat is heroin. According to Stewart Alsop, "New York City . . . is being killed by heroin." After careful examination he estimates that many of the city's 100,000 addicts are hooked on an escalating and illegal habit costing upwards of $40 a day. Theft is necessary to support such a habit. In New York's twenty-fourth police precinct, he writes, almost "two-thirds of the crime . . . is now 'drug-connected'."[59] The poppy fields of Turkey produce about 80 percent of the American supply, and nothing, according to Alsop, "can be a more important . . . foreign policy objective than control of the heroin traffic that threatens to kill . . . all this country's big cities."[60]

One national survey indicates that as many as one-and-a-half million teen-agers have tried heroin at least once and other studies reveal that the total number of addicts rose from 332,000 in 1969 to 559,000 in January 1972. To meet the threat, President Nixon issued an executive order creating a National Narcotics Intelligence Office in the Justice Department to analyze and coordinate information on drug peddlers. He also asked Congress to appropriate about a third of a billion dollars (more than ten times the 1969 amount) to aid drug treatment programs.[61] The most effective method yet devised to treat heroin

58 *Report of the President's Commission on Law Enforcement and Administration of Justice* (Washington, D.C.: U.S. Government Printing Office, 1967), pp. 213–16.
59 *Newsweek,* Feb. 1, 1971, p. 76.
60 *Newsweek,* Feb. 8, 1971, p. 104.
61 *Los Angeles Times,* May 10, 1972, p. 24; August 17, 1972, p. 14; and July 28, 1972, p. 4.

addiction seems to be another drug, methadone. Although somewhat less lethal than heroin, it too is addictive, and on that basis has encountered some ethical, medical, and legal objections.

THE SEXUAL EVOLUTION

Lawmakers throughout the ages, with their fellow human beings, have had an enduring fascination with sex. When sexual attitudes change rapidly, as seems to have happened in recent years, impassioned controversy inevitably results and demands arise quickly for a reexamination of statutes involving homosexuality, pornography, and other related matters. Some have charged (or hoped) that all this constitutes a sexual revolution. While current trends challenge old values and move with accelerated speed, it seems more prudent to speak of a sexual evolution. By whatever name, problems of both personal morality and public policy are posed.

Marriage and Sex

Governmental concern about sex is often related to preservation of the family. State laws determine who can be married (only one man and one woman at one time) and what constitutes marriage (an officially certified ceremony). Only thirteen states, plus the District of Columbia, recognize common law marriages not legally registered.[62] This is especially important since sexual relations outside of marriage are illegal in many states (adultery in forty and fornication in twenty-two.)[63]

The legal importance of sex in maintaining the marriage relationship is revealed by the fact that adultery is the most widely recognized ground for divorce. Only in California, where a 1970 law provided sweeping changes, is this no longer sufficient to terminate a marriage. There, the grounds have been reduced to two, irreconcilable differences and incurable insanity, and Texas seems to be moving in this direction.[64] Divorces in most states are granted, at least nominally, for mental or physical cruelty. For all causes, the divorce rate rose over 50 percent from 1960 to 1970. In the latter year, the ratio of divorces to marriages was nearing one to three.[65]

The middle-aged American is often staggered by the degree to which contemporary sexuality challenges the comfortably familiar sex codes of his youth. Some colleges have established coeducational dormitories; many young people live together openly before marrying; prostitution (legal only in certain Nevada counties) flourishes in some cities

62 *The New York Times Encyclopedic Almanac, 1972,* p. 491. The states are Alabama, Colorado, Georgia, Idaho, Iowa, Kansas, Montana, Ohio, Oklahoma, Pennsylvania, Rhode Island, South Carolina, and Texas.
63 *Playboy,* August 1972, pp. 188–89.
64 *The Book of the States,* 1970–71 (Lexington, Ky.: The Council of State Governments, 1970), pp. 401–05.
65 U.S. Bureau of the Census, *Statistical Abstract of the United States: 1971,* p. 48.

under the guise of massage parlors. What does it all mean? The answers range from moral decay to a new dawn of frankness and freedom. In a few respects, at least, we can measure the changes in sexual behavior with some accuracy. Forcible rape increased by 56.6 percent between 1960 and 1969; the rate of illegitimate births (nearly one out of ten babies in 1968) more than tripled since 1940;[66] and a venereal disease epidemic pushed reported syphilis cases up 16 percent between 1970 and 1971 alone.[67]

Public opinion polls show a decided generation—or education—gap regarding moral codes. In 1969 Gallup reported that 68 percent of the total population believed premarital sex was wrong, but that this view was disputed by 66 percent of college students who thought it was not wrong.[68] Other research reveals that behavior reflects these attitudes. The percentage of male college students who had premarital intercourse increased from about 51 to 57 from the mid-1940s to the mid-1960s, while the increase among women was from 27 to 43 during the same period.[69] In 1971 apparently 46 percent of all unmarried females had lost their virginity by age twenty.[70]

The political implications of the evolution of sexual behavior are numerous. Divorce cases crowd court calendars; illegitimacy places additional burdens on welfare programs; prostitution crackdowns consume police resources as well as newspaper headlines; venereal disease frequently requires treatment by public health facilities; and the discrepancies are widening between the law and many kinds of sex relations, both in and out of marriage. Yet public debate has focused more on pornography than on the phenomena just discussed.

Pornography

The most blatant evidence of changing sexual mores is found in the increased frequency with which nudity and erotic material is openly available to the interested public. Topless bars and stag movies have appeared in large urban centers and total nudity has made its debut on the American stage. Much of this development with respect to books and magazines has been described in Chapter 3 in terms of its constitutional status as defined by recent court decisions. As sex depiction became more explicit, many Americans were quick to indict it as a moral menace and to demand more rigid government control. In the forefront of the antipornography forces was a pressure group called the Citizens for Decent Literature. In 1967 Congress responded to the growing controversy by creating the Commission on Obscenity and Pornography to study the problem and to make appropriate recommendations.

66 Ibid., pp. 146 and 49.
67 *Newsweek*, Jan. 24, 1972, p. 46.
68 *Los Angeles Times*, Sept. 14, 1969, Sec. F., pp. 2 and 3.
69 For a summary of early research in this area, see Vance Packard, *The Sexual Wilderness* (N.Y.: Pocket Books, 1970), pp. 127–28. He reports his own more recent findings on pp. 145–47.
70 *Time*, Aug. 21, 1972, p. 34.

The commission became nearly as controversial as its subject. President Johnson appointed the eighteen initial members, headed by William B. Lockhart, Dean of the University of Minnesota Law School, and including two sociologists, a psychiatrist, a judge, a publishing executive, several attorneys, and three clergymen. In June 1969 a resignation gave President Nixon the opportunity to select his only appointee. He chose Cincinnati attorney Charles H. Keating, Jr., head of the Citizens for Decent Literature and recognized as one of the nation's leading antismut campaigners. Three months later, Keating unsuccessfully requested the President to fire twelve of the other commissioners. In March 1970 he complained that the commission "takes the attitude that its role is to be an objective collector of fact" and stated that the President did not "send me in as an objective observer."[71]

By the end of September, Keating had already asked for a congressional investigation of the commission, and the Nixon administration had repudiated its recommendations through statements of the presidential press secretary, the Postmaster General, and the Attorney General. The Senate rejected the report by a vote of 60 to 5. On October 23 the President issued his own personal denunciation. "So long as I am in the White House," he stated, "there will be no relaxation of the national effort to . . . eliminate smut from our national life. . . . Pornography can corrupt a society. . . . It should be outlawed in every state in the union."[72] Seldom had a legally authorized scientific study been so thoroughly and promptly castigated by political leaders.

What could the commission have recommended to elicit such protest? First it urged "that a massive sex education effort be launched . . . aimed, as appropriate, to all segments of our society, adults as well as children," and that this effort "should be a joint function of several institutions . . .: family, school, church, etc." Absorbing most of the attack was its recommendation that "legislation prohibiting the sale, exhibition, or distribution of sexual materials to consenting adults should be repealed."[73] The breadth of this proposal is indicated by the fact that it would affect antipornography laws in forty-eight states as well as several congressional statutes. Extensive studies, the commission concluded, show no significant relationship between exposure to erotic materials and crime, delinquency, deviant behavior, or emotional disturbance.[74]

Homosexuality

The last but not least indicator of changing attitudes has been the recent insistence of homosexuals upon equal treatment. Although homosexuals have included an impressive number of dis-

71 Jules Witcover, Los Angeles Times, March 25, 1970, p. 4.
72 This material is taken from accounts in the Los Angeles Times, Oct. 18, 1970, Sec. G., p. 4 and Oct. 25, 1970, pp. 1 and 10. It has been corroborated and expanded by reference to Earl Kemp, ed., The Illustrated Presidential Report of the Commission on Obscenity and Pornography (San Diego: Greenleaf Classics, Inc., 1970), pp. 15–17.
73 Kemp, op. cit., pp. 52 and 53.
74 Ibid., pp. 212–17, 53.

tinguished men and women, their private lives have been subjected to criminal prosecution in most nations throughout most of recent history. By and large, they have accepted this with fearful timidity as the price they must pay for their sexual preferences. In the last few years, however, many "gay" people are demanding that legal discrimination against them be abolished. The first flamboyant protest came in New York in the summer of 1969 after a police raid on a homosexual bar. A violent counterattack ensued, followed by a decline in arrests.[75] At least six states—Connecticut, Colorado, Illinois, Idaho, Oregon, and Florida—have eased their laws regarding sex between consenting adults, heterosexual or homosexual.[76] Among the objectives of homosexual activities are an end to discrimination in government employment and the legalization of marriage between persons of the same sex. Public policy regarding "gay liberation" affects perhaps some seven million people, two-thirds male and one-third female.

MORALITY AND POLITICS

The topics of this chapter are only a few of the intersections at which government policy may collide with personal behavior codes. Many Americans would argue, for example, that war, malnutrition, and the glorification of violence in the mass media are more profoundly immoral than anything thus far outlawed. Others would select professional boxing or the use of animals for medical research as activities gruesomely appropriate for legal prohibition. Substantial numbers, on the other hand, would legalize cockfighting or racial discrimination by private landlords.

Yet another issue, gambling, has become one of increasing controversy as more and more states, hard pressed for additional revenue, begin to view it as a lucrative source of potential taxes. New Hampshire, New York, and New Jersey succumbed to the temptation by authorizing state-run lotteries in the 1960s and a few other states have followed suit. New York City legalized offtrack betting in 1971, while racetrack betting produces $500 million annually for the twenty-eight states that allow it. In Nevada, the only state with legal casinos, gambling defrays 40 percent of state expenses.[77] But here again, the stubborn and persistent voice of morality raises the question: Does this not tempt the poor to squander money they can ill afford to risk?

The theoretical case for legal restrictions on personal morality is a persuasive one: Unless law embodies moral principles, it lacks authority and invites anarchy; base impulses will be curbed only when there is fear of punishment; if the family and church decline in influence, governmental responsibility for the establishment of behavior norms must be correspondingly enlarged. The opposing position is equally

75 *Newsweek,* Oct. 27, 1969, pp. 76–81.
76 *Los Angeles Times,* Jan. 24, 1972, pp. 1 and 3.
77 *Newsweek,* April 10, 1972, pp. 46–52.

convincing: For the state to establish moral guidelines is to venture close to tyranny, usurp the functions of other social institutions, and subvert the authority of the individual conscience which constitutes the core of personal character and self-control.

The dispute will not end soon for at least two reasons. First, drunkenness, prostitution, gambling, and similar offenses are victimless crimes in the sense that injuries are inflicted, if at all, primarily on the persons who commit them. Many citizens would prefer to have the police, prosecutors, and judges devote their limited resources to protecting the potential victims of murderers, muggers, and thieves, about whose immorality there is widespread agreement. Second, ours is a heterogeneous society embracing a diversity of ethnic, economic, and religious groups. Each of these has developed, to some degree, its own subculture, its own unique and vital style of life. Even were it desirable to impose a legally coerced uniformity of life styles, there is little prospect for agreement on whose standards should be uniformly enforced. Nevertheless, one should not conclude that politics and morality are separate compartments of life, with neither affecting the other. Yet they can effectively influence one another without causing divisive friction only with respect to those few and fundamental values essential to our common democracy: respect for diversity, commitment to human dignity, and compassion for our fellow citizens. Many life styles can be accommodated to these ideals.

Chapter **16**

The General Welfare
Politics of Prosperity and Poverty

*We can have democracy in this country or we can have great
wealth concentrated in the hands of a few, but we can't have
both.*

Louis D. Brandeis

The United States is the most prosperous nation on earth,
yet one out of every eight Americans is poor. This paradox is but one of
many factors that have led to persistent demands for greater government
intervention in economic affairs. However, the kind of government
intervention that does occur is significantly affected by the distribution of
wealth, since money is a political resource of great potential power.

A serious consideration of official policy in this field requires
a recognition that any similarity between our most cherished economic
myths and the realities of the modern American economy are purely
coincidental. Myth has it that the economy is characterized by rugged
individualism, free enterprise, and laissez-faire capitalism. The facts are
that corporations are far wealthier than individually owned firms, that
economic enterprise is subjected to many legal controls, and that the
government has been of enormous assistance to business. The complex
relationship between government and the economy is symbiotic—each
needs the other—and is better understood through careful analysis than
by invoking the nostalgic phrases of a bygone era.

The private economy generates the taxable wealth and builds
the schools, roads, and missiles that American government requires.
The government, reciprocating fully, oversees the amount of money in

circulation, subsidizes businesses, establishes minimum wages, guarantees farm prices, and performs countless other services upon which a healthy economy depends. Yet the marriage between government and the economy is an uneasy one, marred by continuous disputes. Currently, these controversies center around the distribution of wealth, inflation, unemployment, poverty, health, strikes, consumer protection, and public ownership. They are the subjects to which this chapter is devoted.

THE DISTRIBUTION OF WEALTH IN AMERICA

In societies divided into rigid social classes, most people have accepted the distribution of wealth as a fixed condition beyond their control. America has been different. Millions of our people have enjoyed upward mobility because of abundant opportunities for improving their social status and increasing their incomes. Although the "rags to riches" dream may be rarely realized, enough people have attained enough prosperity to sustain the success myth and perpetuate widespread discontent with present levels of income. The "revolution of rising expectations" which has been identified in the underdeveloped nations of the world in the last thirty years has existed in America for the last two centuries.

Americans are the wealthiest people the world has ever known. Our gross national product (GNP), defined as the total value of goods and services produced in a year, is the highest on earth, both in terms of its total volume (a little over one trillion dollars) and on an average per-person basis (over $4600).[1] Per capita income has soared 30 percent in twenty years in terms of its real buying power.[2] The median family income (half higher and half lower) was $10,285 in 1971.[3]

In the 1972 presidential campaign, Senator George McGovern sought to capitalize on the belief that many people had not attained their fair share of the nation's wealth, and he proposed programs for what conservatives called a radical redistribution of income.

The incomes of American families vary so widely that average figures may be misleading. The poorest 20 percent of the people live on 3.4 percent of the total national income while the richest 20 percent receive more than 13 times as much, or 45.1 percent of the total income. The top 1 percent, moreover, receive twice as much as the bottom 20 percent.[4] In dollar amounts the differences are equally impressive. About 3000 families receive over one million dollars a year while six million families get less than $3000.[5] Furthermore, the gap is widening. According to a 1972 study released by the Joint Economic Committee of

1 U.S. Bureau of the Census, *Statistical Abstract of the United States: 1971*, p. 805.
2 U.S. Bureau of the Census, *Statistical Abstract of the United States: 1970*, p. 312.
3 *Los Angeles Times*, July 18, 1972, p. 1.
4 Richard L. Strout, *Christian Science Monitor*, Jan. 29, 1972, p. 12.
5 Ibid., p. 3.

Congress, the income spread between the richest fifth and the poorest fifth rose from $10,565 in 1947 to $19,071 in 1969 when measured in the equivalent of 1969 dollars.[6] Assuming that vast income disparities create social tensions and economic problems, what is to be done about them? According to the congressional study just cited, ". . . Practically speaking, any redistribution of wealth must come through the imposition of a system of effective wealth taxes."

Taxes

In both political rhetoric and economic reality, income redistribution is linked closely to tax policy. The distinction between progressive and regressive taxes is a crucial one in this regard.

Progressive taxes   A progressive tax takes a higher and higher percentage of earnings as income increases; it thereby reduces income differences. The graduated income tax is the most significant of progressive taxes, since it produces more revenue for the national government than any other source and, in addition, is imposed by all but ten states. The federal income tax rates are steeply progressive, ranging from 14 percent of taxable income of less than $2000 to 70 percent of income exceeding $100,000.[7] A 1972 poll found that people believed it to be the fairest of all taxes.[8]

Yet the income tax structure is less progressive than it looks because of loopholes which provide tax exemptions and which also tax

Figure 54   Principal Sources of National Government Revenue

Fiscal 1973 Estimate

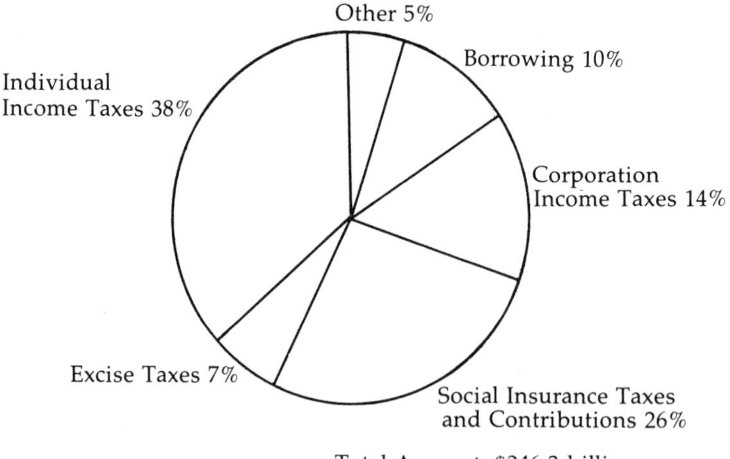

Individual Income Taxes 38%

Other 5%

Borrowing 10%

Corporation Income Taxes 14%

Excise Taxes 7%

Social Insurance Taxes and Contributions 26%

Total Amount: $246.3 billion

Source: Reprinted by permission of United Press International.

6 *Los Angeles Times,* March 19, 1972, p. 1.
7 U.S. Bureau of the Census, *Statistical Abstract of the United States: 1971,* p. 379.
8 *Los Angeles Times,* May 20, 1972, p. 14.

income from certain kinds of investments less heavily than income from wages. Amidst revelations that 156 Americans who earned over $200,000 a year had paid no income taxes in 1967, Congress passed a tax reform act in 1969.[9] In spite of the new changes, the next year there were still 112 persons in that category who paid no income taxes at all and, astonishingly, three persons who paid none on million-dollar incomes. Altogether, there were at least three thousand people in 1968 who had incomes, *after* taxes, exceeding $230,000, or approximately twenty-eight times the earnings of half the families in the nation.[10] Among the most important deductions providing tax shelters are interest on municipal bonds, exemptions for business entertainment expenses, and the bulk of capital-gains income derived from profits on the sale of stock or real estate. If this last source of potential revenue were taxed at the generally prevailing rate for wages, it would produce $7 billion of additional revenue.[11] Businesses too have enjoyed the generosity of lucrative tax exemptions. Oil and mining companies are granted depletion allowances of more than 20 percent on the assumption that the mineral resources that sustain them will someday be exhausted. Moreover, corporations which purchased new plants and equipment were granted accelerated depreciation deductions in 1971 which cost the U.S. Treasury Department about $3 billion in lost taxes.[12]

Regressive taxes   A regressive tax is just the opposite of a progressive one. It takes a higher percentage of low incomes than of high ones. The chief example is the sales tax, a revenue source providing more money for state governments than any other, and one imposed by all states but five.[13] Such taxes require a person making $4000 a year to pay as much as one earning $400,000 each time he buys a gallon of gas or a bar of soap. Put differently, a truly progressive tax is based on ability to pay; a regressive tax is not.

Other regressive taxes are the payroll deductions for social security benefits and the excise tax—a specialized sales tax levied by both national and state governments on such items as liquor, cigarettes, and cosmetics. A widely discussed new possibility, if a reform of the national tax structure is enacted into law, is a value-added tax. This would impose a levy on business at every stage in the production process and would be, in effect, another regressive sales tax passed along ultimately to the consumer.

Just as the national government relies primarily on the

9 *Labor Looks at Congress* (Washington, D.C.: An AFL-CIO Legislative Report, 1971), p. 4.
10 Computed from U.S. Bureau of the Census, *Statistical Abstract of the United States: 1970,* p. 389. See also *Los Angeles Times,* Jan. 3, 1972, p. 19. For figures from earlier years, see Ferdinand Lundberg, *The Rich and the Super-Rich,* ed. Eileen Brand (N.Y.: Lyle-Stuart, Inc., 1968).
11 Richard L. Strout, loc. cit.
12 D. J. R. Bruckner, *Los Angeles Times,* March 29, 1972, Part II, p. 7.
13 *The Book of the States,* 1970-71 (Lexington, Ky.: The Council of State Governments, 1970), p. 221. The five states without sales taxes are Alaska, Delaware, Montana, New Hampshire, and Oregon.

Figure 55   Principal Sources of State Government Tax Revenue, 1969

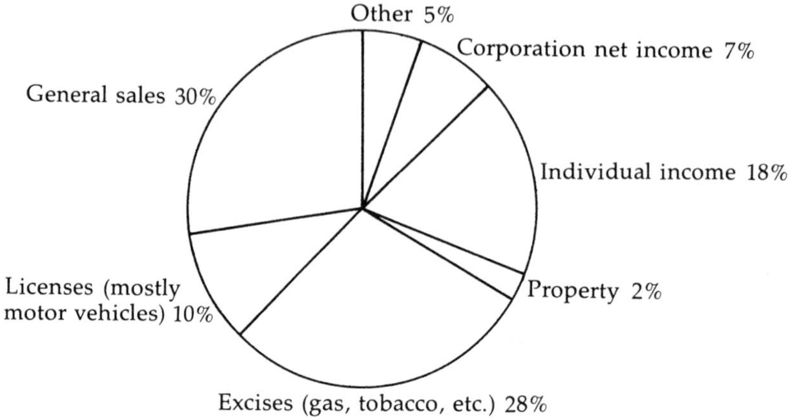

Other 5%
Corporation net income 7%
General sales 30%
Individual income 18%
Licenses (mostly motor vehicles) 10%
Property 2%
Excises (gas, tobacco, etc.) 28%

Source: "Combined State Tax Revenue, 1969" from *The Book of the States*, 1970–71. Reprinted by permission of The Council of State Governments.

income tax and state governments on the sales tax, so the financial bulwark for cities and counties is the property tax. It too is regressive in application and, among all taxes, was voted "least fair" by a landslide margin in a government-authorized public opinion poll.[14] The principle of taxation based on ability to pay is violated not only by regressive taxes but also by the differing tax burdens imposed in various parts of the nation. The amount of state and local taxes paid on each $1000 of personal income recently ranged from a low of $88.39 in Ohio to $140.96 in Hawaii.[15]

Tax reform   From city halls to the corridors of Congress, demands for tax reform reached a crescendo in the early 1970s. There are two explanations for this outcry. In the first place, the combined taxes of all levels of government nearly doubled between 1960 and 1970, rising from $711 per person to $1348.[16] About two thirds went to the United States Treasury and the remainder to state and local governments. Second, it became increasingly apparent that the middle class, the great workhorse of the American economy, was saddled with the heaviest tax burden. The poor received government benefits far exceeding the taxes they paid; the rich were reaping most of the benefits of tax loopholes and exemptions. The middle-income workers, however, had a powerful weapon that might redress their grievances: a majority of the votes. It seemed obvious that the tax load could not be reduced, for it was already lighter than in most prosperous nations. It might, nevertheless, be somewhat redistributed.

Tax objectives   It must be noted, finally, that taxes are a versatile device for purposes beyond the raising of revenue and the

14 *Los Angeles Times*, May 20, 1972, p. 14.
15 U.S. Bureau of the Census, *Statistical Abstract of the United States: 1971*, p. 406.
16 *Time*, March 13, 1972, p. 66.

Figure 56   The Tax Burden

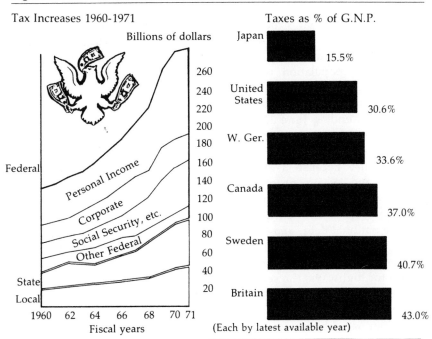

Tax Increases 1960-1971

Billions of dollars

Taxes as % of G.N.P.

Japan 15.5%

United States 30.6%

W. Ger. 33.6%

Canada 37.0%

Sweden 40.7%

Britain 43.0%

Federal

Personal Income

Corporate

Social Security, etc.

Other Federal

State

Local

1960   62   64   66   68   70 71
Fiscal years

(Each by latest available year)

Source: Charts "*Tax Increases 1960-70* and *Taxes as % of GNP in Selected Countries.* from *Time*, March 13, 1972. Reprinted by permission from *Time*, The Weekly Newsmagazine; Copyright Time Inc.

redistribution of wealth. Tax policy may discourage the purchase of certain products (such as foreign imports against which a protective tariff is levied) or encourage particular kinds of investments (such as bonds sold by local governments forced to borrow money). It is often argued also that unless tax advantages can be gained by investing in industry or contributing to worthy charities, business would have inadequate money to expand and the poor would receive little private assistance.

Appropriations

National wealth can also be redistributed by changes in government expenditures. Lawmakers have little control over some of these: Pensions must be paid to retired employees, school district revenue must be used for education, and state constitutions sometimes earmark certain funds for speci fed purposes (such as gasoline taxes for roads and highways). Nonetheless, most government spending is determined by legislative choices, which roughly reflect the priorities attached to various public needs, and which are basic issues of political disputes. Do we spend too much for submarines and not enough for medical research? Too much for subsidized housing and not enough for pollution control? Since over 30 percent of our GNP is spent by various levels of government, the answers affect every citizen. Where does the money go?

National expenditures In 1901 the federal government spent about half a million dollars. Seventy years later it spent four hundred times that much. This phenomenal change does not reflect the difference in population, which has not quite tripled, as much as it does inflation, the transformation of our domestic economy, and America's new role in world affairs. President Nixon's proposed budget for the 1973 fiscal year, ending June 30, totaled $246.3 billion. This averaged about $1100 for each person in the country and represented an increase of 37 percent above total expenditures five years earlier. The budget was notable also because it allocated 32 percent of the total to national defense and 45 percent to human resources, a ratio exactly opposite of that five years before. The most costly items were defense, income security (retirement benefits, welfare payments, and so forth), interest on the national debt, and health programs.

State and local expenditures The combined budgets of all fifty states reveal that appropriations for education are more than twice those for highways, the second-largest budget item. Public welfare runs a close third and health and hospitals a poor fourth. Total expenditures are over $80 billion annually, with individual state budgets ranging from less than half a billion to over $10 billion.

The budget totals for cities, counties, and other kinds of local governments show the same rank order as those for the state governments—education, highways, and welfare—but with educational appropriations outstripping highways by a ratio of better than five to one. For city governments, police protection moves into second place, highways drop to third, and sewerage and sanitation ranks fourth.

Deficit spending In 1970 the national, state, and local governments spent about $60 billion more than they received in taxes, a

Figure 57 Estimated Selected National Government Expenditures, 1971.

Item	Total Amount (in millions)	Percent of Budget
National defense	$76,443	35.9
Income security (welfare, pensions)	55,546	26.1
Interest (on national debt)	19,433	9.1
Health	14,928	7.0
Commerce and transportation	11,442	5.4
Veterans benefits	7,969	4.7
Education and manpower	8,300	3.9
Agriculture and rural development	5,262	2.5
International affairs and finance	3,586	1.7
Space research and technology	3,368	1.6
Community development and housing	3,858	1.8
Natural resources	2,636	1.2

Source: U.S. Bureau of the Census, *Statistical Abstract of the United States: 1971*, pp. 373–74.

Figure 58   Selected State and Local Government Expenditures, 1969

Item	Total Amount (in millions)	Percent of Combined Budget
Education	$47,238	35.9
Highways	15,417	11.7
Public welfare	12,110	9.2
Health	1,509	1.1
Hospitals	7,011	5.3
Police protection	3,901	3.0
Fire protection	1,793	1.4
Natural resources	2,552	1.9
Sanitation and sewerage	2,969	2.3
Housing and urban renewal	1,902	1.4
Local parks and recreation	1,645	1.3
Interest on general debt	3,732	2.8
Utilities and liquor stores	8,820	6.7
Employee retirement	3,221	2.4
Unemployment compensation	1,992	1.5

Source: U.S. Bureau of the Census, *Statistical Abstract of the United States: 1971*, p. 403.

process known as deficit spending. Out of the last nineteen years, the national budget has been balanced in only four, as the government debt has risen from about $271 billion to nearly $400 billion. The budget submitted by President Nixon for 1972 marked the first time that a Republican President deliberately endorsed deficit spending as a device to foster economic prosperity. The theory behind deficit spending is that if the government spends more than it receives, the effect will stimulate the economy (but perhaps raise prices) by giving people more money in military contracts, welfare payments, and so forth, than it takes from them in taxes. As the people then spend this money, demand for goods and services is increased. This policy, prominently associated with British economist John Maynard Keynes, has gained general acceptance.

Like people, governments can spend more money than they receive only by borrowing money. This they do by selling bonds. The cost of an accumulated debt is the interest that must be paid on these bonds. Some of the national government's debt is owed to the Federal Reserve System, but most of its bonds are owned by business corporations and private individuals. In one of its more futile gestures, Congress placed a legal limit on the national debt, but raises the ceiling whenever the debt approaches it.

Unlike federal deficit spending, state and local indebtedness must frequently be authorized by special procedures, such as a vote of the people. In 1969 the fifty states had a debt of over $39 billion and the figure for all local governments was nearly $94 billion.[17]

Deficit spending has long worried American conservatives,

17 U.S. Bureau of the Census, *Statistical Abstract of the United States: 1971*, p. 396.

Figure 59   Federal Budget Surpluses and Deficits, 1954-1972

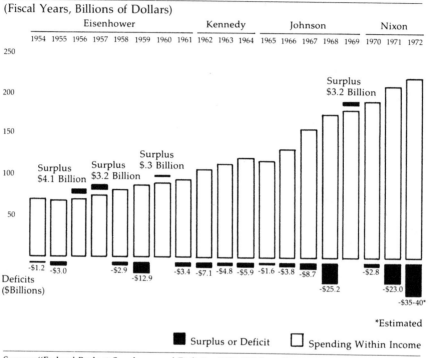

*Estimated

■ Surplus or Deficit   □ Spending Within Income

Source: "Federal Budget Surpluses and Deficits, 1954-72" from *Los Angeles Times*, Jan. 19, 1972.
Reprinted by permission of the Los Angeles Times and the Congressional Quarterly, Inc.

and few would deny that there is a point at which the total debt might
become dangerous. Most economists, however, seem to believe that as
long as the government can pay the yearly interest on the debt and still
finance necessary programs there is no cause for anxiety. Its ability to do
this depends on tax revenue, and tax revenue, in turn, depends on the
health of the economy, measured usually by the size of the GNP. This
view is somewhat reassuring, since interest on the national debt has
remained rather constantly at 8 to 14 percent of the total budget for the
last twenty years and the national budget has held steadily to about 20
percent of the GNP during the last decade.

Keeping the books   We have noted earlier that only legislative bodies can impose taxes or appropriate money. We observed also
that they usually do this on the basis of recommendations submitted by
the President or, in most states, the governor. But what happens then?
Who are the bookkeepers who make sure that these nearly incom-
prehensible sums of money flow in and out as prescribed by law?

Federal tax money is collected by the Treasury Department.
After it is appropriated and spent, the "watchdog of the Treasury," the
General Accounting Office headed by the Comptroller General, audits
the expenditures and reports its accounting to Congress. At the state
level, different taxes may be collected by different administrative of-

ficials, but the state treasurer maintains supervision over the funds until they are spent. A state auditor or controller then acts as an accountant to make sure expenditures were only for authorized purposes.

Sometimes there is a legislative-executive deadlock over fiscal (financial) policies in Washington. What happens when Congress appropriates money which the President refuses to spend? Two months before the end of the 1972 fiscal year there were $12.3 billion in appropriated but unspent funds impounded by the Office of Management and Budget. Some denounce this as an unconstitutional defiance of congressional authority designed to scuttle programs the President doesn't like. Others argue that an appropriation bill merely makes funds available unless accompanied by a direct legislative command that they be spent. They insist, further, that the full expenditure of certain appropriations would require the administration to disregard considerations of efficiency, prudence, changed circumstances, and the need to limit total government spending.[18] The issue gained a new dimension in October 1972 when President Nixon unsuccessfully asked Congress for the formal power to cut whatever programs he wished, to keep total expenditures under $250 billion for the 1973 fiscal year.

Government as Benefactor

A substantial amount of tax money is appropriated to generate economic prosperity. There is scarcely a product in America that is produced without some form of direct or indirect government help. Although this assistance is classified according to the sector of the economy that benefits most directly from it, the economic system is a machine of such intricately interdependent gears that anything which turns one of them will affect the others as well. A government contract awarded to an aerospace firm, for example, is usually considered an aid to business, although it also provides more jobs for workers. Similarly, if government price guarantees raise the price of corn in Kansas, farmers will be able to buy more cars made in Michigan. In fact, the division between business and agriculture is fading fast as large corporations buy up more and more farm land, while the unionization of farm workers obscures the difference between agriculture and labor. Yet in spite of their interaction and overlapping, the organization of the national government makes it convenient to consider the economy in the traditional categories of agriculture, business, and labor. In 1971 it was chiefly through the U.S. Departments of Agriculture, Commerce, and Labor that direct financial subsidies of $5.4 billion, $2.6 billion, and $924 million were dispensed to farmers, business firms, and workers respectively.[19]

Aid to agriculture   Why is it that although business is the

---

18 *Los Angeles Times*, May 10, 1972, Part VI, pp. 1, 2, and 7.
19 U.S. Bureau of the Census, *Statistical Abstract of the United States: 1971*, p. 377.

richest sector of the economy and labor the most numerous, it is the farmers who receive the most money from the government? Among the possible explanations is the fact that business and labor often stand in an adversary relationship to one another; what one favors, the other opposes. But no powerful lobby systematically resists agricultural demands. Additionally, rural states are overrepresented in the U.S. Senate, relative to their populations, and until the Supreme Court intervened with its one-man, one-vote formula, farm areas were overrepresented in the House of Representatives as well. Finally, a combination of seniority and leadership skills has given men from the smaller, nonindustrial states the most important posts in both houses of Congress: In 1972, the Senate majority leader came from Montana, the Speaker of the House from Oklahoma, and the chairman of the House Rules Committee from Mississippi. If such persons show favoritism toward their rural constituents, many would argue that it is justified by the unique perils of the farmer who cannot easily control the price of his products or the weather on which the harvest depends. Farm incomes historically have shown exceptionally great fluctuations between boom and bust.

Justifiable or not, agriculture has long received special assistance. Current policy dates particularly from the New Deal's Agricultural Adjustment Act of 1938. It guaranteed to farmers minimum prices for certain crops if they agreed to certain production limitations. Price guarantees were based on a formula known as *parity*: the ratio of prices received by farmers to prices paid by them for production and living costs during some period in the past. Congressional programs have also provided low-interest loans for the purchase of farms, funds for agricultural research, services for improved marketing of crops, and low-premium insurance against disasters such as floods and insect epidemics.

The price-support legislation stems from a cruel economic paradox: Agricultural overproduction can easily result in agricultural poverty. Using mechanized techniques, farmers can produce a surplus of food so large as to force normal market prices too low to provide the income for an adequate standard of living. Without government action to curtail farm output, an excess of supply in relation to demand might make wheat and other basic farm commodities almost as plentiful as water, and nearly as cheap. Consequently, government price guarantees for farm products are normally contingent on the acceptance of acreage limitations. This program, however, has not been notably successful in reducing output, because farmers might plant fewer acres but fertilize more heavily or plant rows of grain closer together. Beginning in the 1950s, the soil-bank program somewhat more successfully cut production by paying farmers for acres not planted at all.

When the market price of certain crops fell below the government parity guarantee, prior to the 1960s the Commodity Credit Corporation in the Department of Agriculture purchased and stored the harvest, and the taxpayers shouldered the cost. Much of that food went to relieve famines in other countries or to school-lunch and food-stamp programs for the American poor. In 1965 the government curtailed its purchase and storage programs and gave the farmers who accepted acreage limitations direct payments to make up the difference between the market prices at which they sold their crops and the level of parity guarantees. As a result, government-stored surpluses dropped drastically and the export of farm produce to foreign nations, sold at prevailing prices, increased substantially.

Figure 60   Top Farm Subsidies, 1969

Cotton	$ 828,000,000
Wheat	$ 857,000,000
Feed Grains	$1,643,000,000
Total	$3,328,000,000

Source: Reprinted by permission from *The Christian Science Monitor.* © 1970 The Christian Science Publishing Society. All rights reserved.

A major criticism of agricultural legislation is that it has benefited rich farmers most and poor farmers least. By 1969 so much farm land had been purchased by large corporations that twenty-one companies received over half a million dollars each for not growing crops.[20] At the other extreme, 1.1 million farmers (about a third of the total) get less than $500 a year for crops they don't plant and the national average is about $1500. In response to growing criticism of the program, legislation passed in 1970 limits each farm owner to no more than $55,000 a year in government subsidies.

State governments aid farmers by animal vaccination and programs to control plant disease. With grants-in-aid from the national government, they also supervise the work of county agricultural agents who give technical advice on farm problems.

The future of American agriculture remains uncertain, except for a few established trends: Improved scientific techniques will enable more and more crops to be produced by fewer and fewer farmers, corporate ownership of land will continue to increase, the unionization of farm workers will proceed, and limitations on food production in the face of widespread world famine will make government assistance to agriculture among the most controversial areas of public policy.

Aid to business   Government assistance to private business is nearly as old as the republic, beginning with the establishment of a national bank to grant low-interest loans during the administration of President Washington. It is sometimes justified on the grounds that this aid will trickle down from the business firms receiving it to the workers they employ, the consumers they supply, and ultimately to the entire economy. Often assistance has meant outright gifts, as when millions of acres of land were given to railroad corporations in the middle of the last

20 Richard L. Strout, *Christian Science Monitor,* July 14, 1970, p. 3.

Figure 61   Amtrak Passenger Routes

Source: Reprinted by permission of the National Railroad Passenger Corporation.

century, or when the government initiated subsidies for the construction of privately owned merchant ships in 1936. This latter program reached a peak in 1972 when $659 million was allocated to build sixteen new ships in five shipyards employing thirty-six thousand additional workers.[21] The same year, $65 million was granted to nine feeder airlines to provide local service to small cities. The Brookings Institution estimated that such subsidies have amounted to nearly one billion dollars in the past twenty-five years and questioned their necessity.[22]

In 1970 Congress created Amtrak, a semipublic railroad corporation to assist in providing passenger transportation. Private railroads, operating about three hundred and fifty passenger trains, had lost $200 million a year in competition with heavily subsidized airlines and highways. Under the new system, the railroads pay Amtrak about $66 million a year and sign contracts to provide it with employees and operating equipment. In return, Amtrak operates the passenger trains, reduced to nearly two hundred, with the assistance of congressional appropriations of $265 million through June 30, 1973. Although the losses of private railroads have been cut and the quality of passenger service improved, Amtrak estimates an operating deficit of $152 million for 1972 and $124 million for 1973. Whether trains can be restored to a competitive position with other methods of transportation remains a matter of dispute.[23]

21 *Los Angeles Times,* July 2, 1972, p. 1.
22 Ibid., July 3, 1972.
23 *Congressional Quarterly Weekly Report,* Dec. 18, 1971, pp. 2622–26; Ibid., June 17, 1972, pp. 1450–51; and *Christian Science Monitor,* Jan. 26, 1972, p. 4.

The programs providing indirect assistance to business, sometimes defraying costs it would otherwise have to shoulder alone, are more numerous. They include constructing airports, mapping coastal waters, gathering economic statistics, conducting job-training programs, permitting reduced postal rates for publishers and advertisers, providing assistance in finding foreign markets, and diplomatic intervention in behalf of investments threatened in foreign nations. In 1971 Congress authorized a quarter-billion-dollar loan guarantee to salvage Lockheed Aircraft from impending bankruptcy.

Dwarfing all the above are government contracts for military equipment which averaged over $30 billion a year between 1968 and 1971. Such expenditures may well be necessary for national defense, but they also produced over a billion dollars worth of contracts for each of thirty-eight corporations between 1961 and 1967.[24] A high level of defense spending is encouraged by one of the most powerful interest group coalitions in America—the so-called military-industrial complex. Both the armed forces and large manufacturing corporations have a direct interest in the production of modern weaponry, and both have powerful friends on Capitol Hill. Their closely knit relationships are indicated by the 993 high-ranking ex-officers who accepted jobs with private defense contractors between 1969 and 1971, and the 232 former defense industry executives who took jobs in the Defense Department during the same period.[25] Moreover, fifty-nine members of the House of Representatives owned stock in companies with major defense contracts in 1971.[26]

State and local governments also contribute to business prosperity, but usually in less dramatic ways. Tax concessions and contracts for construction of roads, schools, harbors, and hospitals are examples of this sort of assistance.

It often has been argued that without government contracts, especially for military equipment, the economy would collapse and additional millions would be thrown out of work. The available industrial capacity might produce more consumer goods than the people need if a substantial portion of it were not diverted to the construction of bridges, prisons, tanks, and other government necessities. Automation, both on the farm and in the factory, has enabled fewer and fewer workers to fulfill private needs. Without public expenditures for something—schools and medical equipment as well as missiles and battleships—the market might be flooded with unwanted television sets and automobiles, with widespread unemployment sure to follow. In the long run, economic prosperity does not depend on the government purchase of war weapons; it does rely on government contracts for the production of something, almost anything, that lies beyond the realm of personal expendi-

24 Congressional Quarterly Service, *Legislators and the Lobbyists,* 2nd ed. (Washington, D.C.: Congressional Quarterly Inc., 1968), p. 56.
25 *Los Angeles Times,* Jan. 9, 1972, p. 12.
26 *Congressional Quarterly Weekly Report,* June 17, 1972, p. 1384.

ture. In no other way is government assistance to the economy more important.

Aid to labor   Government support for labor is comparatively recent. Attempts to regulate child labor had begun by the mid-nineteenth century, but not until 1938 was child labor prohibited throughout the nation. Unfortunately, the prohibition has not been totally effective. In 1970 the Labor Department uncovered 13,000 violations of the law—in a Detroit motel, a New York chemical enterprise, Oregon berry fields, and Texas vegetable farms.[27] Concern for the welfare of children was followed by attempts to protect women from excessively long hours of sweatshop labor; in 1908 the Supreme Court upheld an Oregon law regulating hours for working women.

The struggle to afford workingmen some of the same protection was difficult, in part because of opposition by the Supreme Court. Not until the 1930s was the goal of an eight-hour day finally attained. In addition to a shorter workday, the major objective of industrial workers was decent pay. Massachusetts adopted a minimum wage law for women in 1912, but the Supreme Court, clinging to a laissez-faire interpretation of the Constitution, invalidated such legislation in 1923.[28]

Finally, in one of the most significant bills ever enacted by Congress, the Fair Labor Standards Act of 1938 incorporated all three of labor's major objectives: Child labor was outlawed, payment of time-and-a-half for work over forty hours a week was required, and a minimum hourly wage was established. The Supreme Court, under heavy public pressure, surrendered to the needs of the twentieth century and upheld the legislation three years later.[29] It was an important beginning which laid the basis for future legislation embracing more workers and increasing the minimum wage, in many stages, to $1.60 an hour.

The most important direct financial assistance from the government is that which aids workers and their families when death, advanced age, or disabling illness deprive them of an income. Such programs began in Germany in 1888, Britain in 1908, and France in 1910, but it was not until a quarter of a century later that Congress came to the aid of retired Americans by passing the Social Security Act of 1935. It provides monthly pensions to retired workers and to their surviving dependents (whether death occurs before or after retirement age). The program is financed by a payroll tax paid by employers plus an equal amount deducted from employees' wages. Numerous amendments to the original Social Security Act have increased old age and survivors' benefits, and brought additional workers under its umbrella. More than 90 percent of all employees are now covered by social security, while

27 Lloyd D. Musolf, *Government and the Economy* (Glenview, Ill.: Scott, Foresman and Company, 1965), p. 80, and *Newsweek*, April 12, 1971, p. 83.
28 *Adkins* v. *Children's Hospital*, 261 U.S. 525.
29 *U.S.* v. *Darby Lumber Co.*, 312 U.S. 100.

benefits go to over twenty-six million persons, including many who were self-employed. Retirement pensions, computed on the basis of previous earnings, averaged about $146 a month in 1972, when Congress boosted benefits by 20 percent and provided for future automatic increases linked to rises in the cost of living.

The social security program was supplemented in 1956 with a provision for payments to eligible workers who become totally disabled before the age of retirement, and in 1965 with the program of Medicare for hospital and health insurance for those over sixty-five. Financial outlays under all these social security programs now aid more than one out of every four families in America.

A major state government aid to labor takes the form of compulsory workmen's compensation laws to benefit employees injured on their jobs. The responsibility for costs incurred due to industrial accidents now falls heavily upon the employer.[30] Additional programs assisting labor, including unemployment compensation and legislation protecting labor unions, are discussed later in this chapter.

Federal Assistance to the States

The grant-in-aid programs, by which federal aid goes to state and local governments, are another means of redistributing the national wealth. A 1972 comparison of the amount of taxes paid by each state with the dollars received in grants reveals which states were being helped and at whose expense. Alaska, paying only thirty-three cents in taxes for each dollar of aid, benefited most, with Mississippi, at thirty-four cents per dollar, a close second. At the other extreme, Connecticut subsidized federal grants most generously, paying $1.70 in taxes for each dollar received in aid, followed by Illinois with a ratio of $1.65 per dollar. Altogether, twenty states paid more than they received while the remaining thirty enjoyed a net profit. With few exceptions states in the West and South fared best, primarily at the expense of states in the Midwest and East.[31] Throughout the country, twenty-three of the thirty states with a net benefit from grants-in-aid were also among the thirty with the lowest per capita income.[32] Like Robin Hood, the program takes from the rich and gives to the poor. In this respect, it is typical of the total effect of government financial policy, as indicated in Figure 62.

INFLATION AND UNEMPLOYMENT

Among the most perplexing problems plaguing the American economy in the early 1970s was a rather unusual combination of rising prices and increasing unemployment. The Nixon administration was confronted with a difficult dilemma, for the medicine used to cure

30 Musolf, op. cit., pp. 81–82.
31 *The New York Times Encyclopedic Almanac 1972,* p. 121.
32 U.S. Bureau of the Census, *Statistical Abstract of the United States: 1971,* p. 314.

Figure 62   Redistribution of Income Resulting from
Government Taxing and Spending

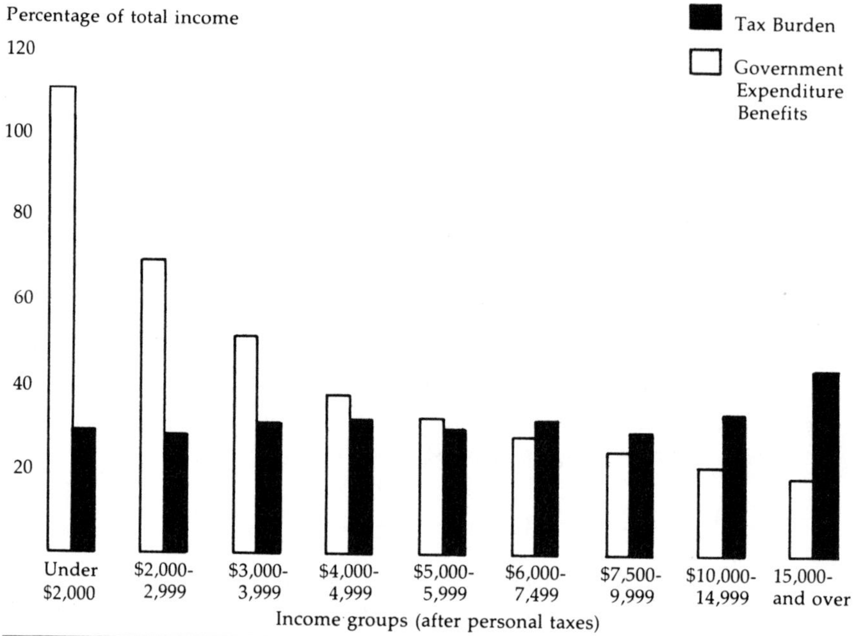

Percentage of total income

■ Tax Burden

☐ Government
    Expenditure
    Benefits

Income groups (after personal taxes)

one usually tended to make the other worse. A cut in spending tended to
keep prices down but throw people dependent on government contracts
out of work. An increase in spending tended to create more jobs but force
prices up.

Inflation

In the seven-year period from 1959 through 1965, consumer
prices rose an average of 1.3 percent per year. Suddenly the rate of
increase spurted to 2.9 percent in 1966–67, 4.2 percent in 1968, 5.4
percent in 1969, and 5.9 percent in 1970—the highest in nineteen years.[33]
Wage increases were swallowed up by higher living costs, the purchasing
power of pensions and saving accounts were diminished, and by 1971,
when President Nixon imposed price and wage controls, drastic action
was obviously required. The causes of inflation, and methods of curtailing it, became topics of vital concern. There are two general methods of
combating inflation indirectly—through monetary controls or through
fiscal policy.
     Monetary and fiscal policy In a free market economy

[33] Ibid., p. 333. See Chapter 14 for distribution of funds under revenue sharing.

prices are determined by the ratio of money in circulation to the amount of merchandise for sale. High prices result from too many dollars "chasing" a limited amount of goods. The price level can be stabilized either by decreasing the amount of available money (purchasing power) or by increasing the amount of goods for sale.

The Federal Reserve Board controls the supply of available currency largely in two ways. First, it raises or lowers the *discount rate,* which is the interest rate at which private banks can borrow money, and second, it sets the *reserve rate* determining the percentage of a bank's assets which may not be loaned to private borrowers. In times of rising prices, most economists favor a "tight money" plan in which the discount and reserve rates are raised. Theoretically, this means that private banks will be forced to raise their interest rates and make fewer loans, thereby discouraging people from borrowing money to spend on new investments or purchases. With less money available to buy goods, prices should therefore decline. Conversely, when the economy is sluggish, a lower discount rate will permit banks to loan money at lower, more attractive interest rates, and a reduced reserve rate will enlarge the total funds available for borrowing. The resulting increase in buying power will usually force prices up. Because members of the Federal Reserve Board are appointed by the President for fourteen-year terms, it is hard for the President or Congress to exert much political control over monetary policy.

The other method of inflation control is fiscal policy, referring to the amounts of money injected into the economy by government spending or taken out of circulation by taxation. If the government increases expenditures, it also increases buying power and thereby tends to inflate prices; if it raises taxes, it reduces buying power and therefore tends to lower them.

Government regulation If inflation cannot be curbed by monetary and fiscal policies, the government may, as a last resort, try to curb it directly by putting legal limits on prices. Under normal circumstances, the inflation of the late 1960s and early 1970s might have been controlled by monetary restrictions reducing the amount of borrowed money and by fiscal restraints cutting government expenditures below the level of tax revenues. But the resulting decrease of buying power was potentially dangerous at that time because of the high level of unemployment. Cutting the money in circulation would diminish the demand for more goods necessary to put the jobless back to work. As a result, in 1971 President Nixon repudiated his long-standing opposition to direct legal controls by utilizing authority given him by Congress a year earlier. He established a Pay Board to limit wage raises, a Price Commission to regulate price increases, and a Cost of Living Council to supervise the total program. In the face of considerable criticism from organized labor, corporate profits and stock dividends were largely exempt from these sweeping legal controls. Although controversy continued to surround it, "Nixonomics," or the "New Economic Policy" as the President preferred to call it, had slowed the rate of inflation a year later while unemployment dropped slightly.

Unemployment

Work is deeply ingrained in the American character. The early New England Puritans imputed to it a dignity, even a moral virtue, which has permeated the nation. People identify with their jobs, so one thinks of oneself as "a carpenter," "an engineer," or "a housewife." President Nixon stressed this "work ethic" in his acceptance speech at the Republican National Convention in 1972. "Here in America," he said, "a person should get what he works for, and work for what he gets."

It was an embarrassment, therefore, that unemployment in the United States hovered near 5 percent of the labor force in 1970 compared with 3 percent in France and less than 2 percent in Japan, West Germany, and Sweden.[34] Worse, it rose to over 6 percent in 1971 and fell back only a little (to 5.5) by mid-1972. Traditional solutions to the problem, including reduced interest rates and massive increases in government spending, threatened to intensify the inflationary pressures which many perceived to be at least as dangerous as a high rate of unemployment. If joblessness could not be significantly reduced without fueling the fires of inflation, there was at least a well-established government program to ease the financial pain.

Unemployment compensation   The Social Security Act of 1935 provided unemployment insurance benefits for jobless workers, to be implemented largely by state legislation. The cost of unemployment compensation is shouldered primarily by state taxes imposed on employers. Over the years benefits have increased and a higher percentage of workers have been covered. In 1970 unemployed persons throughout the nation received an average compensation of 37.5 percent of their former wages for an average of twelve weeks. Average benefits varied from over $60 per week in Connecticut to less than $34 in West Virginia and Puerto Rico.[35] Congress passed legislation in 1970 and again in 1972 extending unemployment grants for thirteen weeks beyond that provided by state laws in areas where the unemployment rate remained unusually high.

Toward full employment   While payments to the unemployed were launched during the Depression, Congress did not acknowledge responsibility for an adequate number of jobs until a decade later. Then, although it made few specific commitments, the Employment Act of 1946 pledged the government to use its resources to promote general prosperity, and created a three-member Council of Economic Advisers, located in the Executive Office of the President, to analyze available data

34 Ibid., p. 803.
35 Ibid., p. 286.

and make recommendations regarding economic problems. It also obligated the President to send an economic report to Congress each year outlining proposals for ensuring the general health of the economy.

There are few indications that the problem of recurrent unemployment will disappear in the near future. The tendency of American corporations to establish plants in other countries where wages are lower, the growing competition from foreign-owned industries, and the impact of automation in replacing workers with machines have all made the creation of a sufficient number of jobs a formidable challenge. The Nixon administration has recognized this by urging the expansion of job-training programs and defining full employment, for practical purposes, as an unemployment rate lower than 4 percent. In the 1972 presidential campaign, Senator McGovern urged that the government itself become an employer of last resort for those who could not be hired by private enterprise. The proposal was viewed as less than radical by those who remembered the jobs provided by such New Deal agencies as the Works Progress Administration and Civilian Conservation Corps nearly forty years before.

THE PERSISTENCE OF POVERTY

"Poor Americans" may seem to be a contradiction in terms, yet in this wealthiest of nations nearly 13 percent of the population was living in poverty in 1971. While this was about 9 percent less than in 1960, it included some twenty-five million poor people—more than the residents of Texas, Illinois, Maine, and Hawaii combined. The poor were defined by the Census Bureau in 1971 as those living on the equivalent of incomes lower than $4,137 for a non-farm family of four. Who were they, and why was their persistent poverty so stubborn a problem?

The Poor and Their Problems

The evidence indicates that those trapped by poverty were not simply random losers, but were concentrated in certain groups as indicated in Figure 63. While the public correctly associates poverty with unemployment, the working poor constitute a significant share of the total problem. The lowest-paid fourth of American workers (earning two dollars an hour or less in 1970) displayed several noteworthy characteristics: 86 percent were not unionized, about 70 percent were employed in retail trade and services (stores, hotels), 48 percent worked fewer than thirty-five hours a week, and 39 percent lived in the South.[36] From this and other data a profile of the poor emerges with considerable clarity. More frequently than their percentage of the population, they are either relatively young or old, black, members of female-headed households,

36 Steven Sternlieb and Alvin Bauman, "Employment Characteristics of Low-wage Workers," *Monthly Labor Review*, U.S. Department of Labor, July 1972, pp. 9–14.

Figure 63 Who Are the Poor?

Children, Elderly Make Up Majority of the Poor	Number	Percentage of All Poor
Under age 16	9,917,000	38.8%
Ages 16–64	10,990,000	43.0%
Over age 64	4,652,000	18.2%

Poverty Is Most Common in Central Cities, Rural Areas	Number of Families	Percentage of All Poor
In central cities	1,781,000	33.6%
In suburbs	1,189,000	22.4%
Outside metropolitan areas	2,333,000	44.0%

The South Leads in Number of Poor	Number of Families	Percentage of All Poor
Northeast	916,000	17.3%
North Central	1,191,000	22.4%
South	2,356,000	44.4%
West	840,000	15.8%

7 Out of 10 Poor Are White	Number	Percentage of All Poor
Whites	17,780,000	69.6%
Nonwhites	7,780,000	30.4%

The Poor Trail in Education

Among Heads of Household Over Age 25 With—	Per Cent of Poor	Percentage of People Above the Poverty Line
1 to 8 years of schooling	50.0%	22.6%
9 to 11 years of schooling	20.7%	16.4%
High-school graduates	20.4%	33.6%
College—1 year or more	8.9%	27.4%

Source: U.S. Bureau of the Census. Reprinted from *U.S. News & World Report* (August 14, 1972). Copyright 1972 U.S. News & World Report Inc.

from the South, and poorly educated. If they have jobs, they are part-time ones, without union protection, in retail and service industries.

One might then infer that poverty can best be combated by remedying such problems as inadequate pensions, racial discrimination, marital instability, and school dropouts. Yet a recent public opinion survey indicates that most Americans blame poverty on the poor themselves, and attribute it to such personal faults as laziness, lack of thrift, loose morals, and drunkenness.[37] This provides an ideal rationalization for opposing any organized antipoverty program.

37 *Los Angeles Times*, June 24, 1971, p. 19.

Whatever its causes, the effects of poverty are numerous, tragic, and sometimes surprising. Studies of British children indicate a significant relationship between family income and both height and reading skill.[38] Moreover, a prominent medical expert contends that even with "the most expert medical attention" the poor would "remain unhealthy, contending daily with rat-infested, garbage-strewn slums."[39] The poverty-stricken are also afflicted with malnutrition. A survey revealed that anemia was eight times as prevalent in Louisiana as in Honduras—one of Latin America's poorest countries—and vitamin A deficiency among poor people in Washington state was placed at 23 percent.

Michael Harrington, who played a major role in focusing national attention on the scope of American poverty, drew its connection with poor nutrition and health very clearly in discussing what he calls "the vicious circle of poverty."

The poor get sick more often than anyone else in society. . . . Because they are sick more often and longer than anyone else, they lose wages and work, and find it difficult to hold a steady job. And because of this, they cannot pay for good housing, for a nutritious diet, for doctors. At any given point in the circle, particularly when there is a major illness, their prospect is to move to an even lower level and to begin the cycle, round and round, toward even more suffering.[40]

In spite of such evidence, some have taken comfort from the assumption that the less fortunate Americans are poor but happy. This comforting illusion was shattered by a Gallup survey disclosing that 56 percent of those who earn over $15,000 a year say they are "very happy," compared with only 33 percent of those who earn from three to five thousand.[41]

The War on Poverty

In his 1964 State of the Union address, President Lyndon B. Johnson declared a symbolic war on poverty. The result, later that same year, was congressional passage of the Economic Opportunity Act, which created the Office of Economic Opportunity and gave it responsibility for the coordination of a series of new antipoverty programs. Among the OEO projects were the Job Corps, Neighborhood Youth Corps, Community Action Programs, and Head Start. The Job Corps enrolls persons from sixteen to twenty-one years of age in general and vocational education programs in centers usually far removed from the "culture of poverty" from which they came. While training for a useful occupation, each of the participants—more than 196,000 by 1970—

38 Alex Gerber, *Los Angeles Times,* July 2, 1972, Sec. E, pp. 3 and 6.
39 Ibid., p. 3.
40 *The Other America* (Baltimore: Penguin Books, Inc., 1964) p. 22.
41 *Los Angeles Times,* January 15, 1971, Part IV, p. 4.

Marion Bernstein.

Job training for neighborhood unemployed, in the East Harlem Environmental
Extension Program, New York.

receives room, board, and a small cash allotment. The Neighborhood
Youth Corps has served two-and-a-half million people. It provides work
and educational opportunities to young persons who have dropped out of
school, or might do so without outside help, and permits them to remain
at home. Community Action Programs, varied in nature and under local
direction, provide legal aid, child-care facilities, recreational centers,
birth-control clinics, and similar services. The Head Start project has

conducted preschool classes for more than three million children whose home environments lack the educational toys, picture books, and other learning tools that the middle class takes for granted.

The antipoverty law included many other provisions—a work-study program to help poor college students, adult education assistance, and loans for poor farm families (up to $2500) as well as small businesses (up to $25,000). How successful it all has been is a matter of dispute. Many of its programs have been transferred from the OEO to other government agencies by President Nixon or sabotaged by controversies among local groups fighting for administrative control.[42]

Welfare: the "Monstrous Outrage"?

Newsweek magazine called it "the Shame of a Nation" and President Nixon labeled it "a monstrous, consuming outrage." They were talking about government welfare programs, presumably motivated by the compassionate generosity of a rich nation. What went wrong?

The answer must go back to 1935, with the passage of the Social Security Act which authorized three categories of assistance for those unable to work: old-age assistance (OAA), aid to families with dependent children (AFDC), and aid to the blind (AB). Later a fourth category, aid to the permanently and totally disabled (ATD), was added. For each of these, the national government puts up about half the money; the remainder comes from state and local governments and hence varies widely throughout the country. In December 1970 the average recipient received $104 per month under AB, $97 under ATD, $78 under OAA, and $187 per family under AFDC.

By 1972 popular criticism of these welfare programs rose to the level of a major political issue. Over fifteen million people were receiving assistance of some sort—a jump of more than 40 percent in less than three years. The major increase came in the AFDC category, now embracing nearly eleven million people and constituting seven out of ten welfare recipients. In May 1972 total welfare costs reached an annual rate of nearly $20 billion, more than the combined total budgets of California and New York, or about one fourth of the money spent on national defense.[43]

The causes of the "dependency explosion" were obscure and probably numerous. Some involve basic changes taking place in American society—the move of displaced farm families into the cities in search of nonexistent jobs, increased unemployment, the rising rate of illegitimacy, and a wider knowledge of the existence of welfare benefits. The formation of the National Welfare Rights Organization, organizing

42 A summary of the Economic Opportunity Act of 1964 may be found in Leon H. Keyserling, *Progress or Poverty* (Washington, D.C.: Conference on Economic Progress, 1964), pp. 147–50. Figures reflecting its implementation are in U.S. Bureau of the Census, *Statistical Abstract of the United States: 1971*, pp. 325–26.
43 *Los Angeles Times*, Sept. 15, 1972, p. 21.

many of the previously unorganized poor, has helped dispense this information more widely than ever before. The Supreme Court also must bear some of the responsibility. It has ruled that states may not impose residency requirements (commonly one year) before granting aid to needy persons coming from another state, prohibited aid termination because an unrelated man is living with a mother and her children, and held that welfare recipients have a right to a full administrative hearing before assistance is cut off.

Whatever the reasons, and however necessary welfare payments may be to alleviate grinding poverty, the rapid increase in total costs has led to charges of fraud, generally unsubstantiated except in a few unusually bizarre and widely publicized cases. It has also led to very real financial crises for the state and local governments which pay the 85,000 social workers needed to administer the aid.[44]

Figure 64   Welfare Recipients in Major Cities

Recipients to Population	Atlanta 1 in 10	Baltimore 1 in 7	Boston 1 in 5	Chicago 1 in 12
	Cleveland 1 in 13	Dallas 1 in 23	Detroit 1 in 8	Los Angeles 1 in 8
Recipients to Population	Memphis 1 in 12	Miami 1 in 25	New York City 1 in 7	Philadelphia 1 in 8
	Pittsburgh 1 in 14	St. Louis 1 in 7	San Francisco 1 in 7	Washington, D.C. 1 in 11

In some cases, calculations are based on the population figures for the county in which the city is located

Source: Chart "Welfare Recipients in Major Cities" from *Newsweek*, Feb. 8, 1971, p. 23. Reprinted by permission of Newsweek.

Conservative misgivings about welfare sink deeper than money. They spring from a profound commitment to the ideas that it is wrong to get something for nothing and that dependence on the government erodes self-reliance and individual initiative. More surprising are welfare critics on the left end of the political spectrum, who indict the present system on grounds that it is inadequate to provide a decent standard of living and that the stigma attached to it is humiliating. They tend to believe that any person should be guaranteed, as a fundamental right, an income necessary to meet physical needs. Whatever the philosophical or sociological merits of these divergent arguments, the economics of the matter seem indisputable: No one gets rich on welfare. In the AFDC program, clearly the most controversial, Mississippi paid a family of four $840 a year in 1970 and half the states paid less than $2652.[45] State differentials are shown in Figure 65.

44 *Newsweek*, Feb. 8, 1971, pp. 22–30.
45 Much statistical data on welfare may be found in U.S. Bureau of the Census, *Statistical Abstract of the United States: 1971*, pp. 291–295; *Newsweek*, loc. cit.; and in Vincent J. Burke, *Los Angeles Times*, Nov. 26, 1970, p. 3.

Figure 65   What The States Pay

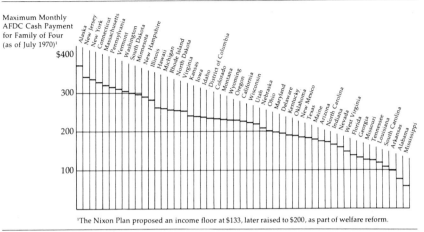

¹The Nixon Plan proposed an income floor at $133, later raised to $200, as part of welfare reform.

Source: Chart "What the States Pay in Welfare" from *Newsweek*, Feb. 8, 1971, p. 29. Reprinted by permission of Newsweek.

In addition to the categories of people assisted by grants-in-aid from the national government, the states maintain general assistance programs, averaging $112 per month in 1970, for poor persons who are not aged, blind, disabled, or supporting dependent children. As with the recipients of federally aided programs, any income they receive normally reduces the money to which they are entitled.

The Family Assistance Plan advocated by President Nixon (FAP) was a major antipoverty reform proposal. It would have abolished the AFDC program and provided, for the first time, a guaranteed minimum family income throughout the nation. The proposal was to pay each four-person family with no outside income $2400 a year, plus a portion of each additional dollar the states agreed to provide. This is more than that provided by several states in 1970. The most intriguing feature of the FAP was that it also would help the working poor and provide a strong incentive to find jobs. Elliot L. Richardson, Secretary of HEW at the time, explained that the "family wage earner could keep the first $60 a month of outside earnings and beyond that he could keep 50 cents of every dollar earned while he is still eligible."[46] The string attached—and a sturdy one at that—was that anyone accepting aid (except for children, old people, the disabled, and mothers of children under six) would have to get a job or accept job training. The proposal would even open new day care centers so that mothers of young children could go to work if they wished.

Significant AFDC reform was delayed indefinitely in 1972 when Congress declined even to authorize the testing of several different programs for a trial period. Some still favor the Nixon FAP; others prefer a negative income tax which would give cash payments to the poor,

46 "In Search of Fairness in Welfare," *Los Angeles Times*, Nov. 15, 1970, Sec. F, p. 3.

graduated on the basis of need, but without corresponding work requirements; still others believe both to be too expensive or favor other
approaches. Congress did reform other welfare categories, however, by
removing aid to aged, blind, and disabled persons from state and local
administration, effective January 1, 1974, and placing it under the social
security program. In the process, it established a guaranteed minimum
income of $130 a month for recipients falling within those three groups.

THE HEALTH CRISIS

There is no constitutional right to adequate medical treatment or hospital care, and only in recent years have health problems
become a major concern of all levels of government. For poor people, the
problems of disease and sickness are related to unsanitary housing
conditions and inadequate diets. But for almost all Americans, good
health depends on the availability of medical care they can afford. The
health bill for the average family more than doubled between 1960 and
1970, due largely to better salaries for hospital employees, higher doctors' fees, and the use of new, more expensive medical equipment. The
problem affected not only the poor, but the vast middle class as well, and
posed a particular threat to older people who are sick most frequently.

Special medical attention to our senior citizens was an out-
growth of a broader plan unsuccessfully advocated by President Truman
in 1949. He asked Congress to create a system of national health
insurance, such as had prevailed in many Western European countries
for a long time, which would pay most medical costs for all Americans.
The well-financed lobbying of the American Medical Association killed
the proposal. It took sixteen years to revive it, and then it was in the
emaciated form of President Johnson's 1965 Medicare program for the
aged. This provided hospitalization and certain posthospitalization benefits for the elderly, to be financed by an increase in social security payroll
taxes. In addition, senior citizens were permitted to buy $50 deductible
medical insurance covering treatment in doctors' offices. At the same
time Congress provided for grants-in-aid to the states to help finance the
Medicaid program which defrays a substantial portion of the cost of
medical care for persons of any age whose incomes fall below a level
established by each state. In 1972 Medicare coverage was broadened to
include the totally disabled as well as the elderly.

Amid still-rising health costs and renewed agitation for a
system of general health insurance such as proposed by Senator Edward
Kennedy, President Nixon responded with his own comprehensive
health program in a special message to Congress, in February 1971. It
encompassed a multiple approach to the problem: Employers would be
required to provide private group insurance for their employees; free
Medicare for the aged would be expanded; and Medicaid would be
replaced for poor parents by a family health insurance program financed

Bob Fitch, Black Star.

Blacks take action to combat sickle cell anemia, a disease to which they may be hereditarily susceptible.

by general tax revenue. It is too early to predict the outcome of congressional action on these proposals.

An equally perplexing difficulty is the shortage of doctors, estimated at about fifty thousand. The U.S. ranks behind several countries in the number of physicians per hundred thousand people,[47] and the future looks no brighter. The Nixon administration slashed federal loans for medical students to such a degree that by 1971 the number aided had dropped from 13,251 to 5191.[48]

Medical research is another area of health in which the government is involved. Much of this is conducted through nearly a dozen National Institutes of Health (in the Department of Health, Education and Welfare) which specialize in various kinds of illness. In the early 1970s, particular attention was focused on health problems of infants and children—such as crib death and sickle cell anemia—and on cancer.

47 U.S. Bureau of the Census, *Statistical Abstract of the United States: 1971,* pp. 799–800.
48 *Los Angeles Times,* Dec. 25, 1970, Part VII, p. 17.

STRIKES AND INDUSTRIAL DISPUTES

Strikes are among the most dramatic and controversial episodes in American economic life because they interrupt the production process on which national prosperity depends. Yet there is such misunderstanding about their role in the economy that their immediate effects are often exaggerated while their historical significance is underrated.

Unions and Strikes

Since a strike is a simultaneous work stoppage by a group of employees, it is clearly impossible unless those employees are organized, formally or informally, in some sort of labor union. Until 1842, however, unions were considered illegal conspiracies, and long after that strikes were often broken by viciously enforced court injunctions. To prohibit strikes was to deprive workers of their only influence—the ability to withhold their labor—and hence to subject them to whatever terms their employers might dictate. As a result, union influence was diminished drastically as long as antistrike injunctions could be justified as necessary to protect corporation property or eliminate a "restraint of trade."

The Norris-La Guardia Act, passed by Congress in 1932, represented the first important protection for the union movement in America. It forbade "yellow dog" job contracts, which required workers to forfeit their right to join a union, and also prohibited the use of court injunctions in most labor-management disputes. Three years later, this was reinforced by the passage of the Wagner Act (the National Labor Relations Act). It required that whenever a majority of the employees of a company wished to be represented by a labor union in bargaining for better wages or working conditions, the company had to recognize that union as the agent legally empowered to sign contracts for all the workers collectively. (It is important to note that stockholders were bargaining collectively, through corporation management, well before workers balanced the industrial scales by bargaining collectively through unions.)

The Wagner Act also created a National Labor Relations Board to enforce union membership rights and to conduct elections to determine which union, if any, the workers wished to designate as their bargaining agent. As a result of this legislation many contracts were signed, often after tumultuous strikes, that provided for a *union shop* in which workers were required to join the union within several months after they had been hired. Occasionally, contracts established a *closed shop* instead, requiring the employer to hire only those who were already union members.

After World War II, several unpopular strikes led a Republican controlled Congress to pass the Taft-Hartley Act over President Truman's veto. It authorized the President to obtain a court injunction to prevent workers from striking for eighty days if he felt a strike would create a national emergency. The law also declared collective bargaining contracts providing for a closed shop to be unenforceable in the courts, and permitted the states (in its heatedly controversial Section 14b) to forbid union shop contracts as well. On the assumption that no one should be forced to join a union, twenty states exercised this option by banning the union shop through "right to work" laws. Opponents of these laws contend that union membership is not too much to require of those benefiting from union negotiations. The Taft-Hartley Act also prohibited contribution of union dues to political campaigns. In 1959, in the wake of publicity over labor-racketeering scandals, the Landrum-Griffin Act required unions to submit annual financial reports to the Department of Labor and to guarantee a secret ballot in the election of union officers.

The Settlement of Industrial Disputes

Several decades of experience in industrial relations reveal seven basic methods by which labor-management disputes may be resolved. Some are clearly more satisfactory than others.

1) In *open shop* companies, in which no one is required to join a labor organization, unions are usually not recognized as the legal bargaining agent for the employees. In such situations, each worker must bargain individually with the management for the best wage he can get. Unless he possesses some specialized skill at a time of relatively full employment, with competing companies eager to hire him, chances are he will have little negotiating leverage and must either accept or reject the employer's offer. Sometimes nonunion companies provide relatively desirable job benefits, but this is often because it is necessary to compete for workers with companies that are unionized.

2) Since the passage of the Wagner Act, most disputes in such basic industries as mining, steel, automobiles, and trucking are settled through collective bargaining between union and company officials. The result is a contract covering wages, hours, and working conditions for the employees, usually for a two- or three-year period. For the duration of the contract, of which there are about 300,000 now in effect, strikes and other work stoppages are prohibited by mutual agreement.

3) If grievances occur while a contract is in force, they are usually settled by binding arbitration in which both sides agree to abide by the decision of some impartial third party. Disputes involving firing, promotion, and other such matters are handled in this fashion.

4) It has often been suggested that if labor and management cannot resolve a dispute voluntarily, laws should compel them to accept the decision of an outside arbitrator regarding the issues involved. Although generally opposed by both unions and industry, compulsory

arbitration has been employed during time of war, at the national level and by a number of states, in settling disputes in such public utilities as the electric and gas industries.

5) Both the state and national governments have established agencies to act as intermediaries between labor and management in order to encourage them to compromise their differences. Although such agencies have no authority to compel the parties to agree, the Federal Mediation and Conciliation Service has an enviable record in helping to settle disputes. The National Mediation Board serves a similar purpose for the air transport and railway industries, aided for the latter by the National Railroad Adjustment Board.

6) The Taft-Hartley Act provision preventing certain strikes for a period of eighty days has been employed, on the average, a little more than once a year. When the injunction period has elapsed, if no agreement has been reached nothing can prevent a work stoppage unless new laws are passed. In 1970 and 1971 Congress enacted special legislation to cope with rail strikes. The most drastic measure government can take is to seize ownership of a plant or an entire industry. As a result, workers become government employees who are legally prohibited from striking. In both World Wars and the Korean conflict this was occasionally done.

7) When all else fails, or has not been utilized, labor-management disputes result in strikes, or occasionally in lockouts, which are plant closures barring workers from their jobs unless they accept company terms. Since lockouts are rather rare, the question then arises, why strikes? The answer in most instances is that they settle the disputes, one way or another. But strikes have served other functions as well. Few would deny that prevailing wage rates would be lower today if workers had never struck for higher ones. But sometimes strikes have also been necessary to establish the procedures of collective bargaining, thus giving workers some influence over the job conditions that affect their lives. For the employer strikes may be less undesirable than government intervention and control. Many employers recognize that the right to strike encourages free collective bargaining, and that this, in turn, promotes a stable work force with high morale, as well as a guarantee that during the period of a labor contract production will not be interrupted.

The public may have less to fear from strikes than is commonly supposed, since they exert strong pressure on both labor and management to reach a rapid and equitable settlement. During 1970, however, when more workers went out on strike than at any time since 1952, the most damaging work stoppage was the ten-week automobile strike against General Motors, and that alone was estimated to have reduced the GNP by nearly 2 percent. Strikes contribute also, no doubt, to inflation. But there is considerable evidence that even massive strikes by longshoremen and steel workers have had no crippling effects on the national economy.[49] Not since 1946 has as much as 1 percent of national work time been lost as a result of all work stoppages combined.

Few would claim that strikes are inherently desirable, yet they have served on occasion to bring the labor-management scales into better balance and are often preferable to settlements dictated by either governmental or corporate decrees.

CONSUMER PROTECTION

Modern technology has made us more dependent upon men and women we have never seen than any generation since time began. Each day we place ourselves at the mercy of meat packers, bridge builders, pharmaceutical chemists, and manufacturers of everything from automobiles to hairpieces, paying more and more for all their products and knowing not even their names. We are all consumers and hence all victims of those anonymous technological specialists upon whom we rely. It is not surprising, then, that "consumer protection" has become one of the louder demands of the early 1970s. Actually, for nearly a century, various groups of Americans have been calling upon government to shield them from business enterprises that were guilty of exploitation, carelessness, or deception.

Varieties of Consumer Protection

The first demands for significant controls on American business were either ignored or ridiculed. Periodic attempts to regulate it were denounced as attempts to kill the goose that lay the golden eggs. But in the 1880s Congress yielded to farm pressure by establishing the Interstate Commerce Commission to control the allegedly exorbitant rates charged by American railroads for hauling crops to market. This was followed by the creation of additional regulatory commissions, briefly summarized in Chapter 10, for the purpose of controlling consumer rates charged by other businesses, especially those engaged in providing public utilities such as telephone service and electric power.[50]

Antitrust legislation Another form of business regulation is exemplified by the long-standing efforts to protect the consumer by stimulating business competition. When an entire industry is dominated by fewer and fewer companies, a situation is created in which it may be easier for them to control the market by forming trusts or agreements to set excessively high prices. Although the number of corporations in America more than doubled since 1950, now exceeding a million and a

---

49 *Impact of Longshore Strikes on the National Economy* (Washington, D.C.: U.S. Department of Labor, 1970); E. Robert Livernash, *Collective Bargaining in the Basic Steel Industry* (Washington, D.C.: U.S. Department of Labor, January 1961), p. 18; and Thomas E. Mullaney, "The U.S. Economy in 1970," supplement to *The New York Times Encyclopedic Almanac*, 1971, p. 5.
50 See pp. 265–66.

Figure 66   Corporation Mergers and Acquisitions

Number

				8213

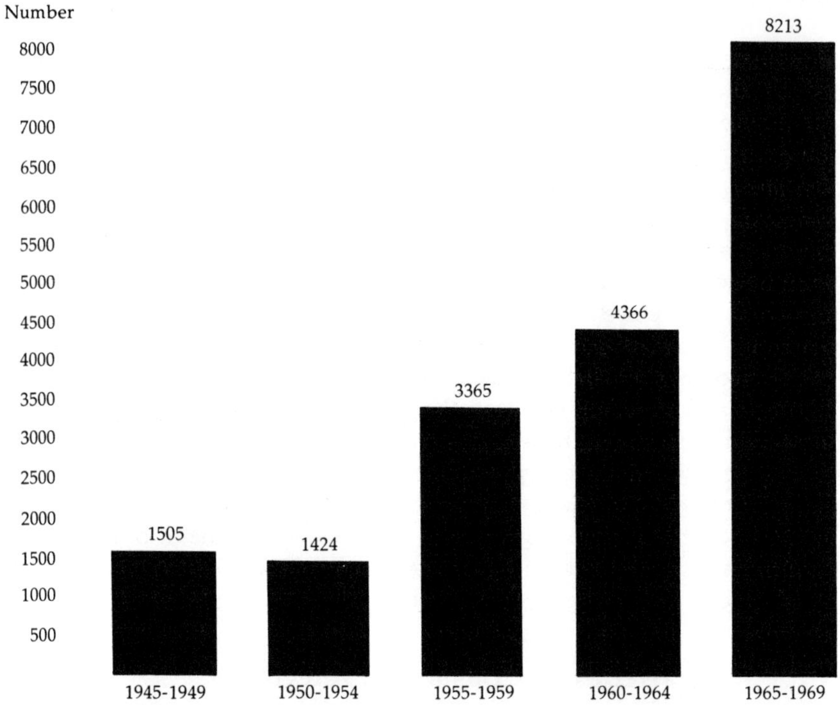

Source: U.S. Bureau of the Census, *Statistical Abstract of the United States: 1971*, p. 474.

half, the percentage of total corporate assets owned by the two hundred
largest ones jumped from 47.7 in 1950 to 60.1 in 1969.[51]

    The result of this increased concentration of corporate power
appears to be decreased competition, higher profits, inefficiency, and
deception. That, at least, was the conclusion of a study of one hundred
large industries authorized by the Federal Trade Commission. It estimated that waste or excess profits (above 5 percent) consumed up to 11
cents of every sales dollar in the photographic equipment and supplies
industry, 9.1 cents in the auto industry, 8 cents in the drug industry and
6.4 cents in the steel industry.[52] It is the consumer, of course, who pays
the extra cost. Accelerating the increased concentration of industrial
wealth is the rapid increase of corporation mergers and acquisitions of
small firms by large ones.

    It is clear that the 1890 Sherman and the 1914 Clayton
Antitrust Acts have not enjoyed notable success in preventing a concentration of power in a relatively few large corporations. Nevertheless,
there is undoubtedly more competition today in such industries as oil,

51 U.S. Bureau of the Census, *Statistical Abstract of the United States: 1971*, p. 467.
52 *Los Angeles Times,* April 26, 1972, p. 17.

tobacco, aluminum, and chemicals than there would be had no such legislation been passed.

Food and drug controls As long ago as 1906 Congress began passing legislation to safeguard the public against sawdust in their sausages and harmful powders in their pills. Modern chemistry has made this task more difficult, but legislation was enacted in 1962 giving the Food and Drug Administration in the Department of Health, Education and Welfare the responsibility of approving new drugs before their sale to the public. Five years later, the Wholesome Meat Act extended federal inspection standards to meat packing firms that had previously been controlled by less stringent state regulations. State governments remain vitally involved in this field through the fair-trade laws limiting price competition in dairy and other industries where it might result in a dangerous deterioration of product quality, while local governments enforce health and sanitation laws regarding restaurants, nursing homes, and hospitals.

Product safety If the current consumer crusade can be said to have begun with a particular event, it was perhaps the 1965 publication of *Unsafe at Any Speed,* by a thirty-one-year-old attorney named Ralph Nader. It gained immediate popularity, and its attack on the dangers of American cars was instrumental in the passage of the Automobile Safety Act the next year. The consumer is not safe, however, even in his home. One expert estimates that unsafe school or household products cause six thousand deaths and four million injuries each year.[53] Television sets have ignited into flames, microwave ovens have leaked radiation, and infants have strangled on improperly designed baby furniture.[54] There are, however, a few encouraging signs of progress. In 1972, for example, the Food and Drug Administration recalled 200,000 hazardous toys and announced that it would forbid the sale of pesticides and other household poisons in containers that could easily be opened by children.[55] The same year, Congress created a five-member Consumer Product Safety Commission to impose safety standards the violation of which might be punishable by imprisonment.

Telling the truth to the consumer The Federal Trade Commission, in addition to its responsibility in the antitrust field, has long had the authority to ban fraudulent advertising from the channels of interstate commerce. Nonetheless, much special legislation has been necessary, such as that involving wool and fur products, to prevent misleading labeling. Perhaps the most important contribution to the cause of business candor was the "truth-in-lending" bill passed by

---

53 Arnold B. Elkind, Chairman of the National Commission on Product Safety. This advisory body, created by Congress in 1967, has recommended a sweeping safety law covering all consumer products and the creation of a new independent agency to administer it. *Congressional Quarterly Weekly Report,* Dec. 18, 1971, p. 2627.
54 Sidney Margolius, "Labor's Stake in Product Safety," *Viewpoint* 1 (Fall 1971): 11–12. This is an official publication of the Industrial Union Department of the AFL-CIO, and this issue is devoted entirely to consumer concerns.
55 *LosAngeles Times,* June 30, 1972, p. 14 and Sept. 14, 1972, p. 29.

Congress in 1968. This was designed to make sure borrowers are told just how much interest they will really have to pay if they buy that new refrigerator on "twenty-four easy payments."

In 1971 Massachusetts became the first state in the nation to enact legislation requiring unit pricing by markets to permit shoppers to compare the pound-for-pound cost of goods sold in different-sized packages. This law, like one passed in Maryland which permits customers to sue a manufacturer directly for faulty merchandise, was based on a model consumer protection statute prepared by attorneys working for the National Consumer Law Center, an antipoverty agency established in 1969 by the Office of Economic Opportunity.

No-fault auto insurance Dissatisfaction with auto insurance has mounted steadily in recent years due to its rising cost and apparent uncertainty of protection. Only about half of the $14 billion which insurance companies collected in premiums in 1970 was paid out in claims or returned to policyholders. Such conditions created an unusually receptive public attitude when the proposal for no-fault insurance first attracted widespread attention, and President Nixon hailed it as "an idea whose time has come" in a message to the National Governors Conference in 1972.[56] Although it appears in many variations, the simplicity of the essential concept has unmistakable appeal: A motorist injured in an accident is paid for medical care, income loss, and certain other expenses by his or her own insurance company, regardless of who was at fault. The advocates of this form of insurance contend that it would drastically reduce the number of lawsuits arising out of auto accidents, and thereby reduce both the time needed to settle claims and the cost of insurance premiums. Their opponents argue that it benefits negligent drivers at the expense of innocent accident victims and would actually increase premium costs. By late 1972, however, the growing popularity of the no-fault idea had shifted the issue: The question was no longer whether or not such legislation should be passed, but whether it should be enacted by the state legislatures in various and often severely restricted versions, or by Congress in a bill providing broad coverage.

The Bureaucracy of Consumer Protection

While consumer-oriented pressure groups continue to press for the passage of more effective laws, they are equally concerned with the administrative machinery by which existing legislation is enforced. One problem was mentioned in Chapter 10—regulatory commissions are often staffed by people more sympathetic to the industries they regulate than to the public they were created to serve. Another is the vast number of uncoordinated agencies that are involved in the task of consumer protection. To cite only a few examples, the Department of Agriculture determines the maximum fat content of sausage products, the Depart-

56 *Congressional Quarterly Weekly Report,* June 24, 1972, p. 1530.

ment of Transportation enforces highway and automobile safety standards, the Civil Aeronautics Board controls airline fares, and in the Executive Office of the President there are both a National Business Council for Consumer Affairs and a consumer counselor to render whatever advice they see fit. A third administrative difficulty, caused in part by inadequate budgets, is delay in enforcement action. It took the Food and Drug Administration more than nine months to begin implementation of the Poison Prevention Packaging Act of 1970, and three-and-a-half years after Congress directed the Commerce Department to tighten flammability controls, no new standards for clothing had been put into effect.[57]

A possible solution to some of these problems is the creation of a consumer protection agency both to coordinate programs and to advocate consumer interests before other regulatory bodies. Bills to accomplish this were introduced in Congress in 1971. But even the approach favored by President Nixon—to place the new agency in the Department of Health, Education and Welfare and confer rather restricted powers upon it—attracted a filibuster in the Senate. Since nearly all consumer protection proposals involve protection from commercial interests, business organizations such as the National Association of Manufacturers and the Chamber of Commerce support milder measures. Aligned against them were Ralph Nader, the Consumer Federation, and their traditional allies.[58]

GOVERNMENT OWNERSHIP: CREEPING SOCIALISM?

For the most part, this chapter has been devoted to government's role in economic aid and regulation—redistributing wealth; seeking to control inflation, unemployment, and poverty; promoting better health; facilitating the settlement of labor-management disputes; and protecting the consumer. But the government also owns and operates a substantial portion of the economy, a role less extensive in its range of activity, yet more direct and, when added to its regulatory roles, providing the basis for the controversy over "creeping socialism."

American conservatives tend to regard government-owned production of goods and services as a socialist blasphemy to the capitalist creed. American liberals, on the other hand, are haunted by nightmares of greedy and unscrupulous "robber barons," the private capitalists who once dominated substantial segments of American business. They are willing to admit—in their more candid moments—that government ownership is indeed socialistic and that, in small doses, it isn't such a bad idea at that. Most Americans take a characteristically pragmatic view.

---

57 Erma Angevine, "Defenseless in the Market Place," *Viewpoint,* op. cit., pp. 2–4. The author is the executive director of the Consumer Federation of America, one of the leading consumer pressure groups.
58 *Congressional Quarterly Weekly Report,* Dec. 18, 1971, p. 2629.

They accept the virtues of a mixed economy, owned part privately and part publicly. Regardless of its desirability, one must note the degree to which government ownership has intruded on an essentially capitalist economy.

To begin with, the national government owns a little over one out of three acres of land in the United States, devoted mostly to forests, wildlife, and grazing; and the postal service has been a major federal responsibility since the beginning of the republic. In more recent times, the national government broadened its commercial ownership to include the Alaska railroad, the Panama Canal Company (which operates restaurants and bowling alleys as well as the canal), and the Tennessee Valley Authority. The TVA, created in 1935, is perhaps the most controversial of these enterprises, because it involves the production of electricity—a profitable industry largely dominated by private power companies. Along with the Bonneville Power Administration and other dams administered by the Interior Department, it produces about a fifth of the electric power manufactured in the United States.

Other national business enterprises include government-owned naval shipyards (existing in conjunction with private installations), army post exchanges, and Federal Prison Industries, Incorporated, which uses convicts to manufacture products such as mail sacks. Altogether, the national government operates thousands of facilities paralleling those provided by private firms, employs nearly three million civilians, and owns property assets worth nearly $400 billion.

By and large, there has been less resistance to government-owned businesses at the state and local levels than to similar national enterprises. Many city governments own water, sewage treatment, airport, and other facilities. Municipalities own about thirty bus lines, along with streetcar systems in San Francisco, Pittsburgh, Philadelphia, and Boston. Among our largest cities, Los Angeles and Cleveland operate electric power systems and Philadelphia and Houston are in the natural gas business. The Port of New York Authority, a special local government agency created by an interstate compact between New York and New Jersey, operates docks, bridges, airports, and terminals for buses, trucks, and grain.

State governments thrust themselves into business ownership in varying degrees. North Dakota, perhaps, has led the way with the operation of a flour mill, terminal elevator, state bank, and an insurance program covering fires, tornadoes, and hailstorms. Alabama, Louisiana, Maine, Georgia, South Carolina, and Virginia maintain docks and other port facilities, while over a dozen states own airports and retail liquor stores.[59]

There are two major advantages to government ownership of businesses operating in most of these areas. One is that private

59 Clyde F. Snider, *American State and Local Government,* 2nd ed. (N.Y.: Appleton-Century-Crofts, 1965), pp. 618–21.

corporations often are not interested. Public utilities providing services that are essential to a modern, industrialized economy require an immense capital outlay, which investors may be reluctant to risk, before any income is earned. It is tempting, therefore, to ask various governments to defray the initial construction costs either out of tax revenue or through the sale of bonds.

Second, governments can sell goods or services cheaper than private corporations, given a reasonable degree of efficiency, because they do not have to return a profit to stockholders. Rates, therefore, need be only high enough to defray costs. As a result, it is to the advantage of a privately owned steel company, for example, to buy water or electricity from the city rather than from another private corporation. Whatever the merits of the opposing arguments, the forseeable future reveals little indication that government ownership will either expand or diminish to any appreciable degree.

Chapter 17

The Global Village
Politics of War and Peace

I make American foreign policy.
> *—President Harry S Truman*

A major irony confronting the world's people in the 1970s is that the issue on which their survival depends, the issue of war and peace, is the very one over which they have least control. This state of affairs stems from three conditions. First, as long as the peoples of the world are grouped into nations, each must deal officially with the others through the single, unified voice of the chief executive. Second, foreign policy is difficult to formulate democratically because much of it must be done with maximum secrecy, and what the people—or Congress—do not know about, they cannot control. Finally, the people would find it difficult to direct foreign policy democratically, even without intentionally imposed secrecy, because it involves so much that is literally foreign to their experience. Most Americans know whether they want the government to "do something" about unemployment or air pollution because these matters have affected them or people they know. But they have no knowledge (and often no interest) as to whether the government should do something about clashes between Indians and Pakistanis or the left-wing government of Chile.

Nonetheless, recent years have seen policy decisions made by the "experts" fall under heavy criticism from millions of citizens. Many argue that democracy requires that the general goals of *all* government action—both at home and abroad—be popularly approved. No one would deny that the intricate tactics of foreign policy implementation should spring from the specialized knowledge of professional experts. But the broad objectives, the global strategy, should be set by those who pay the price in both money and lives.

THE FORMULATION OF FOREIGN POLICY

Many agencies have a hand in developing and implementing international policy, but the President has the preeminent position.

The President

In his first inaugural address, Thomas Jefferson, carrying on a policy established by George Washington, pledged "peace, commerce, and honest friendship with all nations,—entangling alliances with none." Since then, the relative peace of the nineteenth century has been followed by the total wars of the twentieth; honest friendship with all nations has given way to profound hostility toward some; and nonentanglement has been replaced by perhaps the most intricate web of international commitments ever woven. The role of the White House in these changes is clear in several areas.

Treaties   Article II, Section 2 of the Constitution gives the President power "to make Treaties" subject to the approval of a two-thirds vote of the Senate. For many decades we needed no pacts with other countries to insure our security. But with the advent of aircraft and long-range missiles, the two great oceans no longer provided the invulnerable shields of earlier times, and American Presidents sought treaties establishing military alliances. Such treaties have linked the United States to forty-three nations.

President Truman began the process in 1948 by leading the country into the Organization of American States (OAS), designed to facilitate the military and nonmilitary cooperation of twenty-two nations in the Western Hemisphere. The next year he launched the fifteen-member North Atlantic Treaty Organization (NATO), a collective self-defense pact which provided that an armed attack against one or more of them in Europe or North America should be considered an attack against them all.[1] President Eisenhower added the Southeast Asia Treaty Organization (SEATO), modeled after NATO, and initially including the U.S., Great Britain, France, Australia, New Zealand, Pakistan, Thailand, and the Philippines. Somewhat similar bilateral treaties have been negotiated with Japan, China (the Formosan government of Chiang Kai-shek), South Korea, the Philippines, and a few other countries. Most of these pacts were designed to deter possible Communist aggression by strengthening and unifying the non-Communist world.

The vast bulk of American treaties, however, have little to do

---

1 The initial members were the United States, Canada, Belgium, Denmark, France, Great Britain, Iceland, Italy, Luxembourg, the Netherlands, Norway, and Portugal. Greece and Turkey joined in 1951 and West Germany in 1955.

with military alliances. Of these, some of the most notable established the United Nations in 1945, banned the testing of nuclear weapons in the atmosphere (thus curtailing radioactive contamination) in 1963, and limited strategic nuclear weapons in 1972.

Executive agreements The President may also negotiate executive agreements with foreign governments. These differ from treaties in that they do not require Senate approval, they are usually less important than treaties, and they may deal only with subjects over which the President has been granted authority by some provision of the Constitution, a law, or an earlier treaty. In this century, there have been far more executive agreements than treaties. These have included secret military commitments with allied powers against a common foe, authorized by the President's constitutional power as commander in chief of the armed forces, and tariff-cutting agreements sanctioned by acts of Congress. By the beginning of 1972, the United States was a party to 947 treaties and 4359 executive agreements.[2]

Recognition Nations make official contacts with one another through a reciprocal agreement known as recognition. This involves the exchange of ambassadors and the establishment of embassies in each other's capital cities through which the governments carry on diplomatic relations. Foreign consulates may be established in a few other cities to help tourists from "back home" who get in legal troubles, to assist in immigration matters, and to promote business and similar relationships between the two countries. In contrast to such *de jure* recognition, a condition known as *de facto* recognition exists if two nations have not exchanged ambassadors but have entered into trade negotiations, peace talks, or other relationships of a short-term nature. The President decides if, when, and to what degree (*de facto* or *de jure*) the United States will recognize every other nation on earth. At one extreme, President Wilson believed that no government should be recognized which had not come to power legally. At the other, President Franklin D. Roosevelt returned to the practice that had prevailed in the nineteenth century and recognized any government that was in effective control of its nation. In 1972 our government maintained formal diplomatic relations with most nations, with the notable exceptions of the People's Republic of (Communist) China, Cuba, East Germany, North Korea, and North Vietnam.

Diplomatic appointment The President has constitutional authority to appoint diplomatic personnel, subject to Senate confirmation; traditionally the most important of these has been the Secretary of State, first in rank among cabinet officials. In recent years, however, the advisory role of the Secretary seems to have declined. Several recent Presidents, including Franklin Roosevelt, Kennedy, and Nixon, have acted more or less as their own Secretaries of State, relegating the persons who held that post largely to administrative functions. Others,

2 *Congressional Quarterly Weekly Report,* June 24, 1972, p. 1551.

like Truman, Eisenhower, and Johnson, have relied heavily on their Secretaries (Dean Acheson, John Foster Dulles, and Dean Rusk, respectively) for formulating major policy suggestions.[3] Paralleling the Secretary's decline has been the rising significance of foreign policy advisers who serve as assistants to the President in the White House Office. Notable among these have been McGeorge Bundy serving under Kennedy, Walt Rostow under Johnson, and Henry Kissinger under Nixon.

There are also dozens of ambassadors and other administrators who are expected to impart a steady stream of accurate information to the President. During most of our history, ambassadorships have been dispensed as patronage. The result has been few ambassadors of distinction, although lower-echelon career men in the State Department's Foreign Service have often been experienced experts. During the last two decades, however, nearly 70 percent of the ambassadors have come from the ranks of career diplomats.

War leader Recently the lives of many citizens have been touched by the power of the President as commander in chief of the armed forces. The Indochina conflict, initiated and perpetuated by presidential directives, leaves no doubt as to his decisive impact on the extent and intensity of military action. Nevertheless, the Constitution confers the power to declare war on Congress and there has been important disagreement about the scope of legitimate presidential authority in his exercise of war-making discretion. The chief executive also controls the men who wage our wars. In a dramatic example of civilian control over field commanders, President Truman fired the popular General Douglas MacArthur at the height of Korean hostilities some twenty years ago.

Adding together the powers to make treaties and executive agreements, to recognize foreign governments, to appoint diplomatic personnel, and to command the armed forces, the sum total of the President's influence makes him, in the words of a Supreme Court justice, "the sole organ of the federal government in the field of international relations."[4] And, as we shall now see, he has substantial help.

The executive establishment Over the years, an elaborate foreign policy bureaucracy has developed, of which the State Department is the most venerable part. It supervises the work of American diplomats, negotiates treaties and executive agreements at the direction of the President, grants passports to Americans traveling abroad, and administers nonmilitary economic assistance to foreign countries through the Agency for International Development (AID).

Headquartered in the massive Pentagon, where twenty-five thousand of its employees roam seventeen miles of corridors, the Department of Defense is entrusted with the supervision of the armed forces. The major function of the DOD is to award contracts for military

---

3 Norman L. Hill, *Mr. Secretary of State* (N.Y.: Random House, Inc., 1963), pp. 33–5.
4 Justice Sutherland, *U.S. v. Curtiss-Wright Export Corp.*, 299 U.S. 304 (1936).

equipment to private corporations. Within the armed forces, the highest body is the Joint Chiefs of Staff, consisting of the Army and Air Force Chiefs of Staff, the Chief of Naval Operations, the Commandant of the Marine Corps (by custom), and the Chairman of the Joint Chiefs, a high-ranking officer who may be chosen from any branch. On administrative matters, such as budgeting and procurement of supplies, the Joint Chiefs are responsible to the Secretary of Defense, but when the President acts as commander in chief, they serve as his chief advisory body on matters pertaining to strategy and tactics.

We have already mentioned the National Security Council in Chapter 10. It was created by Congress in 1947, as a part of the Executive Office of the President, and its importance is indicated by its membership. While the NSC was often bypassed during the Kennedy and Johnson administrations, it attained a preeminent position in national security planning under President Nixon. During his first three years in office, it met more than seventy times to provide him with what he termed "a clear statement of the issues, realistic options for dealing with them, and the implications of each option for our long-term objectives."[5]

The importance of the NSC is augmented by the Central Intelligence Agency, a body responsible to it. The CIA coordinates intelligence data gathered by all government agencies and collects additional information as well. Intelligence means information about any developments throughout the world that may affect American security. It can be overt, relying on newspapers and open observation, or clandestine, requiring acquisition of secret information, if necessary by spying.[6] Each of the armed services also maintains an intelligence unit. In mid-1970 their combined payrolls totaled over 136,000 persons and they expended $2.9 billion—an amount exceeding the revenue of forty-five state governments in 1968.[7] In addition, there is the Defense Department's National Security Agency and intelligence activity carried on by the State Department.

The first task of the CIA is to gather information from these sources, as well as from journalists, businessmen traveling in foreign nations, and other private citizens. It supplements data from these contacts by its own espionage efforts, including the use of aerial surveillance by such means as the U-2 planes flying over Cuba which detected the installation of Russian offensive missiles in 1962. Finally, its job is an interpretive one. It must decide, for example, the significance of a possible cut in the price of Soviet refrigerators. Does it mean that Russians are demanding more consumer goods? Is it a reflection of increased steel production? Are metals being diverted from military to nonmilitary production? The correct answers may hold the key to the future of Soviet-American relations.

5 Richard Nixon, *U.S. Foreign Policy for the 1970s,* A Report to the Congress, February 9, 1972 (Washington, D.C.: U.S. Government Printing Office, 1972), pp. 208–09.
6 Allen W. Dulles, *The Craft of Intelligence* (N.Y.: Harper & Row, Publishers, 1963), p. 58. Mr. Dulles was once the director of the CIA.
7 UPI dispatch, *Los Angeles Times,* May 19, 1970, p. 8, and Bureau of the Census, *Statistical Abstract of the United States: 1970,* p. 418.

The use of espionage seems to be as old as recorded history, but the CIA has evoked controversy principally because of its other activity. In 1970 it was revealed that CIA agents in Laos masqueraded as rural development workers, ostensibly employed by the Agency for International Development.[8] Far more importantly, the CIA was responsible for organizing the disastrous Bay of Pigs invasion of Cuba in 1962 and the successful overthrow of President Jacob Arbenz Guzman of Guatemala in 1954.[9] Its secret financial subsidies to domestic groups such as the National Student Association have elicited additional criticism. Some are concerned that behind its necessary mantle of secrecy, the CIA wields irresponsible power in a multitude of ways beyond the effective control of the American people. Even influential congressmen have bemoaned their lack of knowledge concerning the agency. Speaking of its role in the war in Laos, Senator Stuart Symington, a member of the Armed Services Committee's subcommittee on CIA oversight, charged that "Nobody knows the amounts the CIA is spending. . . . When we ask about specific operations, they say they are too secret."[10]

There are many other agencies deeply immersed in world affairs. The Office of Emergency Preparedness, in the Executive Office of the President, is responsible for stockpiling reserve supplies of crucial raw materials and for coordinating civil defense planning. In addition, President Nixon gave it temporary responsibility for administering the wage and price freeze that he imposed in August 1971. The United States Information Agency, organizationally independent but operating under State Department guidelines, is in charge of the nation's international propaganda program. It administers the Voice of America radio network, libraries in other nations, and various facilities designed to project a favorable national image. Another independent agency, the Atomic Energy Commission, is responsible for the development and manufacture of nuclear weapons, while the F.B.I., in the Justice Department, bears the burden of counterespionage activity designed to thwart the work of spies employed by other countries. The Peace Corps, finally, provides technical and educational assistance to help raise living standards in underdeveloped nations.

Congressional Influence

Executive dominance in foreign policy is not absolute, thanks largely to the authority vested in Congress. The Senate has a secure preeminence in this field because of its constitutional prerogatives of confirming diplomatic appointments and approving treaties. Yet the Senate has made scant use of its powers. Few ill-qualified nominees have been rejected. The confirmation power can also be used to stymie diplomatic recognition of a foreign government, but this too is seldom

8 *Los Angeles Times,* June 8, 1970, p. 15.
9 David Wise and Thomas B. Ross, *The Invisible Government* (N.Y.: Bantam Books, Inc., 1965), pp. 6–77 and 177–96.
10 *Congressional Quarterly Guide to Current American Government* (Spring 1972), p. 69.

done; the Senate's refusal to confirm President Truman's selection of Myron Taylor as America's representative to the Vatican stemmed far more from opposition to formal diplomatic ties than from displeasure with Mr. Taylor. Finally, the Senate has seldom repudiated treaties, in part because of the feeling that to do so would undermine America's international credibility on a matter on which a presidential commitment had already been made. Yet no chief executive can afford to forget the Senate's rejection of membership in the League of Nations following World War I, and the humiliation it brought to President Wilson. Since then, Presidents have consulted influential senators, especially the chairman of the Foreign Relations Committee, early in the process of treaty negotiation.

The Constitution gives Congress as a whole the authority to declare war, yet the last fifty years have made it abundantly clear that the President can initiate war-sized hostilities at his own discretion. The result is a constitutional contradiction of the most profound proportions. Unhappiness with this situation is not a recent phenomenon, for over a century ago Congress passed a resolution condemning the Mexican War (which had been formally, if reluctantly, declared), as one "unnecessarily and unconstitutionally begun by the President."[11] Resentment over the Vietnam venture has led to the most thorough reexamination of the war power since President Polk ordered aggression against Mexico. In 1970 Senators John Sherman Cooper (R-Ky.) and Frank Church (D-Idaho) sponsored a proposal, approved by both houses, prohibiting the reentry of American combat forces into Cambodia. In 1971 Senators Mark Hatfield (R-Oregon) and George McGovern (D-S.D.) attempted to cut off all money for Indochinese hostilities, and Senator Jacob Javits (R-N.Y.) introduced legislation limiting the President's ability to authorize belligerent military action to a thirty-day period unless Congress approved its continuation.[12] The President has steadfastly opposed all such restrictions on his role as commander in chief; as Secretary of State William P. Rogers put it before the Senate Foreign Relations Committee, "Unlike the presidency, the institutional characteristics of Congress have not lent themselves as well to the requirements of speed and secrecy in times of recurrent crises and rapid change."[13]

Both houses of Congress are also involved in appropriating money for international activities. Military appropriations have not been a very effective tool for restricting presidential discretion with respect to the armed forces. When Theodore Roosevelt, for example, met with congressional reluctance to finance his proposal to send a naval fleet around the world, he announced that there was already enough money to start the trip, and that if Congress wanted the ships to return it would appropriate the rest. That is exactly what happened. On the Vietnam issue, even congressional "doves" have been reluctant to vote against

---

11 *Newsweek,* June 1, 1970, p. 29.
12 Ibid., April 19, 1971, p. 28.
13 *Congressional Quarterly Weekly Report,* March 25, 1972, p. 660.

military funds necessary to permit American troops, having been committed to battle by the President, to fight that thankless battle effectively. On the other hand, Congress has frequently appropriated less than the President's full budget requests for aid to foreign nations.[14]

In addition to regulating the flow of money for the conduct of world affairs, Congress controls the method of getting men into the armed forces. According to Article I, Section 8 of the Constitution, the military power of Congress includes the authority to "raise and support Armies. . . . [and] provide and maintain a Navy. . . . " From this, the legislators in Washington have derived the implied powers to conscript men into the armed services and to prohibit the burning of draft cards.[15] Other congressional powers relating to the field of foreign affairs include the authority to limit immigration, discussed in Chapter 2, and to impose tariffs (taxes on imports).

Court Adjudication

In foreign policy, as in domestic matters, disputes between national and state governments and between presidential and congressional authority may be settled by the U.S. Supreme Court. In *Missouri v. Holland*,[16] the Supreme Court ruled that a treaty entered into under the authority of the President (with Senate approval) superseded a conflicting state law that would have been constitutional without such a treaty.

In 1936 the Supreme Court decided another important case, *U.S. v. Curtiss-Wright Export Corp.*[17] Congress had passed a resolution permitting the President to prohibit the shipment of arms to foreign nations if, in his judgment, such an action would contribute to international peace. President Franklin D. Roosevelt was quick to exercise this authority, and Curtiss-Wright, finding its shipment of machine guns to Bolivia thwarted, contested the power of Congress to transfer its control over foreign trade to the President. With only one dissent, the Supreme Court upheld executive supremacy in foreign affairs as an inherent and essential part of the sovereignty of an independent nation.

A third case was decided during the height of the conflict in Korea. President Truman had authorized his Secretary of Commerce, Charles Sawyer, to seize the nation's steel mills to prevent a strike that threatened to curtail the production of military equipment. A divided court ruled in *Youngstown Sheet and Tube Co. v. Sawyer*[18] that the President's power in foreign affairs was by no means unlimited, and that he had no inherent power to nationalize the steel industry, regardless of

14 William P. Gerberding, "The Foreign Aid Controversy," Donald G. Herzberg, ed., *American Government Annual, 1964–1965* (N.Y.: Holt, Rinehart & Winston, Inc., 1964), p. 48.
15 *U.S.* v. *O'Brien*, 391 U.S. 367 (1968).
16 252 U.S. 346 (1920).
17 299 U.S. 304.
18 343 U.S. 579 (1952).

its military implications. In declaring such action unconstitutional, the Court took a major step in expanding the power of judicial review to limit executive authority at the highest level. It has resolutely avoided any decision, however, relating to the constitutionality of the Vietnam war.

THE WORLD OF FOREIGN POLICY

The various agencies involved in the formulation of foreign policy have just been described. What we need now is a picture of the world within which a foreign policy operates.

International Politics

International power entails the capacity of one nation to alter the behavior of another nation. As a result, such power relationships as coercion, influence through economic aid, and appeals to traditional authority are as characteristic of world affairs as of domestic political processes.[19] The principal difference is that the international scene lacks the domestic agency for ultimate peaceful settlement of disputes— government.

The players in the international power game are the nation-states. In the politics of internal affairs, individual citizens increase their relative influence by banding together into groups—political parties, unions, corporations, and associations. Similarly in foreign affairs, when nations associate with one another in alliances and power blocs, their influence is enhanced. Yet legally each country is independent and sovereign, an autonomous entity answerable only to itself. Like each citizen, each nation pursues its self-interest and attempts to maximize its power—its capacity to affect the behavior of others. Foreign policy thus becomes the pursuit of the national interest.

The maximization of a nation's power depends on the resources available to it. Among these resources, geographic factors (location, size, and the existence of natural boundaries such as oceans and mountain ranges) are probably less important now than in the past, as a result of the development of long-range bombers and intercontinental ballistic missiles (ICBMs). Yet in fighting an enemy far from home, distance itself remains an obstacle in moving troops and supplies. There is little doubt that such logistical problems help to explain the failure of the United States to defend Czechoslovakia in 1968 or Hungary in 1956 from ruthless repression by armed Soviet intervention. Population may also be of diminishing importance if land wars between massive armies are replaced by nuclear wars requiring only small numbers of highly trained technicians. But this is only a dim possibility, and if demographic

19 Hans J. Morgenthau, *Politics Among Nations,* 4th ed. (N.Y.: Alfred A. Knopf, Inc., 1967), p. 5.

characteristics such as scientific skill and morale are added to sheer numbers they can total a decisive weight on the scales of international power. High morale, the least tangible of these factors, was an ingredient that made the Japanese and North Vietnamese among the most formidable foes ever faced by American troops. Natural resources, governmental stability, industrial development, advanced weaponry, accurate intelligence, and diplomatic skill—these and others are also significant components of power in the dynamic and precarious milieu of international relations.[20]

Besides doing what it can to maximize its power, a nation-state must define its national interest—in other words, decide the goals toward which to apply its power. The task of its foreign policy is to achieve as many of these as possible, by appropriate strategy and tactics. As an example, we may mention a few alternative strategies that might be followed by a country with the goal of ensuring peace for itself.

To begin with, world domination sometimes has been rationalized as a strategy designed to guarantee peace through the invincible power of the dominating nation. In such a situation, peace also contributes to the maintenance of *status quo* power relationships in which the strong stay on top and the weak remain on the bottom. The "Pax Romana" and "Pax Britannica" of the Roman and British empires provide historical examples. At the end of World War II it seemed to some that American military preponderance stemming from our monopoly of nuclear weapons was so great as to ensure a "Pax Americana" should we wish to exercise our strength toward that end. Whatever may have been the case then, the truth is that today American power relative to the rest of the world is simply inadequate to such a grandiose goal.

A second strategy sometimes proposed to secure peace is isolationism. In the United States, this policy has roots in our historical preference for neutrality toward conflicts in the rest of the world; it assumes that this country can and should abnegate its alleged international responsibilities and ought to "quit meddling in other people's business." This attitude became more or less official policy between World Wars I and II, and had its defenders as late as the 1950s when some urged that we establish a "Fortress America," impervious to attack but aloof from foreign conflicts. In the 1972 presidential campaign, Senator McGovern was accused of "neo-isolationism."

Somewhere between domination and isolationism is a third strategy, collective security. This rests on the belief that aggression against *any* nation is less likely to occur if *many* nations have collectively pledged themselves in advance to its defense. If such an attack occurs anyway, collective security proponents argue that it can be more easily repelled by the joint action of the many than by the valor of the victim acting alone. The underlying assumption is that should an aggressor

20 John G. Stoessinger, *The Might of Nations*, 3rd ed. (N.Y.: Random House, Inc., 1969), pp. 15–27.

conquer another nation, its strength (and appetite) would be enhanced and the power of the rest of the world to oppose successfully its further conquests would be diminished.

The maintenance of a balance of power is another strategy that has been followed to preserve peace. While the term covers a variety of situations, there are generally a small number of major nations whose roughly equal power resources counterbalance one another. This potential counterforce may deter each from aggression. In nineteenth-century Europe, often considered an outstanding example of the operation of a balance of power system, England played a special role as balancer with some success, shifting her weight against whatever nation or alliance of nations seemed most powerful or aggressive. After World War II, a bipolar world emerged, in which only the United States and the U.S.S.R. had predominant power. Since the United Nations collective security system was inoperative, both the Americans and Russians relied on a security system comprised of regional defense pacts. This concept lies at the heart of the NATO treaty commitment that an attack on one is an attack on all. The situation was simply a variation of the balance of power, a confrontation of alliances, in which, however, the crucial balance was that between the two superpowers. Both of these pursued a policy of nuclear deterrence, and the relative impotence of the other nations enhanced the rigidity of the resulting balance of terror. By the 1970s, however, there was some loosening of this rigid bipolarity. The international balance of power became ever more intricate as the uncommitted "third world" nations remained independent of both superpowers, France developed its own "nuclear shield" to reduce its reliance on American defense promises, China established a position as a significant weight on the scales, and each superpower faced restlessness within its own treaty system.

In any case, whatever goals or strategies a nation chooses for its foreign policy, it must employ its resources to persuade, influence, or force other nation-states to cooperate with it. Some bargaining is usually inevitable. However, some would argue that the enormous disparity in strength between the United States and Guatemala, or between the U.S.S.R. and Czechoslovakia, makes the sovereignty of the smaller nations a legal fiction which obscures the realities of international power relationships. When a weak country lies within the sphere of influence of a stronger one, the former becomes little more than a "satellite" or "client" of the latter. All nations may be sovereign but, to paraphrase George Orwell, some are more sovereign than others.

The principal attack on the nation-state system comes from those who view national sovereignty as the very source of the world anarchy that jeopardizes human survival. The nation-state, they believe, is a political anachronism better suited to government in the eighteenth century than the twentieth. They contend that sovereignty must be transferred from the national to the supranational level, and be vested in a world body such as the United Nations. The "realists" indict this as "idealistic" and impractical. Yet in an age threatened by nuclear war, some idealism may be man's only realistic hope.[21]

International Organization

In the early 1970s, the world presents a striking contrast. A number of countries are threatened with dismemberment into smaller units. People in Quebec cry for independence from Canada, Basques want to disassociate from Spain, Bangla Desh attained freedom from Pakistan, and Biafra fought a valiant but losing struggle for separation from Nigeria. Simultaneously, these centrifugal forces, pulling nations apart, are countered with centripetal ones, impelling them to join with one another in international organizations designed to promote their common futures.

There seems to be an increasing sense of regionalism among the world's people, acting as an antidote to narrower nationalism and constituting either a step toward universalism or another barrier against it. Such regionalism is manifested in military treaties such as NATO in Western Europe and the Soviet-sponsored Warsaw Pact in Eastern Europe, as well as in economic alliances such as the phenomenally successful European Economic Community (EEC or Common Market) and the Council for Mutual Economic Assistance (COMECON), its rough counterpart among Communist nations to the east. Other efforts toward regional economic integration include the European Free Trade Association (consisting of several nations outside the EEO and COMECON) and the Latin American Free Trade Association. The Arab League, founded in 1945, and the Organization of African Unity, founded in 1963, have generally fallen short of their initial promise for economic and political cooperation.[22] The British Commonwealth is too unique a pattern for general adoption.

The most ambitious attempt at world unity launched thus far is the United Nations, established in 1945 during the closing months of World War II. It consists of six major organs. The General Assembly is the heart of the UN, with more than 130 member nations. It is a sort of "town meeting of the world" which provides a propaganda forum, at least, in which nations can air their divergent views on international disputes, but it can only make recommendations on courses of action. The purse strings of the entire organization are in its hands, so it can dispense funds and impose assessments, which are, however, unenforceable.

Such enforcement powers as the Security Council was to have had are yet to be realized. The UN Charter (its constitution) gives it

21 For a survey of early plans for peace through world organization, see Herbert Hoover and Hugh Gibson, "The Problems of Lasting Peace," reprinted in *Prefaces to Peace* (N.Y.: Doubleday & Company, Inc., 1943), pp. 172–77.
22 Karl W. Deutsch, *The Analysis of International Relations* (Englewood Cliffs, N.J.: Prentice-Hall, Inc., 1968), pp. 181–90.

"primary responsibility for the maintenance of international peace and security."[23] It consists of five permanent members and ten elected by the General Assembly for two-year terms. Each of the permanent members (the U.S., U.S.S.R., France, Great Britain, and China) has a veto over any matter of substantive importance. In one sense this veto power is a realistic acknowledgement that peace is impossible if any major nation is intent upon war, yet at the same time it has been a major stumbling block to effective action against international aggression. As a result, the General Assembly approved the American-sponsored "Uniting for Peace" resolution in 1952, authorizing itself to recommend action against aggression if the Security Council is immobilized by a veto. The Security Council was able to authorize action against North Korea's attack on South Korea in 1950 because of a temporary Soviet boycott, but the UN role in establishing peace around the Suez Canal and in the Congo resulted from action by the General Assembly.

The Economic and Social Council coordinates about a dozen specialized agencies working to promote international cooperation in such fields as health, adult education, and advanced agricultural methods. Working quietly and undramatically it may have contributed to more human progress than the other five organs combined.

Perhaps the Trusteeship Council and the International Court of Justice have been least significant of the major UN organs. The former was created primarily to oversee the administration of colonies taken from the countries defeated in World Wars I and II, and many of these have now become independent nations. The latter consists of fifteen judges from as many countries but has authority to hear only those cases submitted to it voluntarily. It has handed down few decisions, of which fewer still have involved important world conflicts. Its significance lies more in its potential than in its record.

The Secretariat, finally, is the administrative organ of the UN, providing the thousands of international civil servants—clerks, translators, economists, and many others—needed to keep the organization functioning. It is headed by the Secretary-General, whose office has grown substantially in importance since Trygve Lie of Norway became the first to assume it in 1945. Credit for this must go to Lie's successor, Sweden's Dag Hammarskjold, whose diplomatic initiatives and personal grace enhanced the prestige of his position. The peacekeeping missions of the Secretariat have facilitated the resolution of conflicts in the Congo, on the island of Cyprus, in Indonesia, and even—for a number of years—in the Middle East. Although his powers are still quite limited, the Secretary-General, now Kurt Waldheim of Austria, has emerged as an active executive. He is nominated by the Security Council and elected by the General Assembly for a five-year term.

Although the UN has helped to alleviate a number of critical situations, its future remains in doubt, especially for three reasons. In the

23 Article 24.

first place, the United Nations is a confederation and suffers, like all such governmental forms, from the fact that it has only those few powers which its member nations choose to give it. It has no standing army to enforce either its own decisions or the body of international law laboriously developed through the years by custom, treaties, and the decisions of international tribunals. Like the American national government under the Articles of Confederation, it lacks the power to tax and is dependent on voluntary payments by its members. France and the Soviet Union have been notable for their failure to pay their assessed shares.

From this derives the second problem confronting the UN—inadequate money. Including the specialized agencies, its total operating budget for 1971 was $1.1 billion, or about the same as that of the state of Iowa. The United States contributed over a third of the budget, $441 million, which was somewhat less than the city budget of Philadelphia.[24] In 1972 the U.S. sought to get its assessment, based principally on capacity to pay, reduced to 25 percent of regular UN expenditures.

A third criticism of the UN centers around the increasingly unrepresentative nature of the General Assembly, where each country has one vote. The result is that nations representing a small fraction of the world's population and power, and contributing a small percentage of the UN budget, can produce a majority of votes. Yet the UN has already survived longer than its predecessor, the League of Nations, and its flexibility was demonstrated when after twenty-three years of exclusion, the People's Republic of China was admitted in 1972.

THE FOUNDATIONS OF MODERN U.S. FOREIGN POLICY

Many historians feel that American policy between World Wars I and II was a failure. We will never know whether the second of these two tragedies would have occurred if we had joined the League of Nations, or if we had maintained strong armed forces, or if we had resisted the first indications of Fascist military ambitions, but there are reasons to believe that these policies might have been wiser than the alternatives we adopted. Having done none of these things, however, with the attack on Pearl Harbor on December 7, 1941, we were engulfed by World War II. The hope of avoiding a repetition of past mistakes largely shaped American foreign policy for the next quarter of a century.

Hemispheric Supremacy

The oldest and most consistent of American policies toward other nations, and perhaps the one involving our safety most directly, is maintenance of a dominant position in the Western Hemisphere. Rela-

---

24 *Los Angeles Times,* Dec. 23, 1971, p. 4, and Bureau of the Census, *Statistical Abstract of the United States: 1971,* pp. 411 and 416.

tions with Canada have been generally placid, but with many nations to the south they have been more erratic. The cornerstone of our Latin American policy is the Monroe Doctrine, enunciated in 1823, according to which any expansion of European influence in this hemisphere would be interpreted as an act hostile to the United States. In 1930 President Hoover revoked President Theodore Roosevelt's corollary to the Monroe Doctrine, which had justified armed intervention in Latin American countries, and Hoover's successor, Franklin D. Roosevelt, implemented a "Good Neighbor" policy toward those nations. Despite this policy, after World War II President Eisenhower felt that the left-wing government of tiny Guatemala was a sufficient threat to warrant its overthrow and President Johnson sent marines into the Dominican Republic, presumably to protect American lives and to ensure the defeat of what he called "a band of Communist conspirators."

But the most important development in Latin American relations in the postwar period followed the triumph of Fidel Castro in Cuba in 1959. Castro entrenched himself as a Communist dictator some ninety miles off the coast of Florida and President John F. Kennedy authorized the abortive "Bay of Pigs" invasion attempt. Fearing future attacks from U.S. soil, Castro turned increasingly to the Soviet Union for economic and military assistance, and by the autumn of 1962 the installation of intermediate-range ballistic missiles was well under way. Having learned of this development through the CIA espionage apparatus, President Kennedy summoned the spirit of the Monroe Doctrine on nation-wide television and warned of this "explicit threat to the peace and security of all the Americas, in flagrant and deliberate defiance of . . . the traditions of this nation and hemisphere." He perceived this as a dangerous change in the international balance of power, announced a "quarantine" on the shipment of offensive weapons to Cuba (enforced by naval inspection), and urged Soviet Premier Nikita Khrushchev to withdraw the missiles in question.[25] It was a bold commitment of American strength, although less extreme than such alternatives as bombardment or another invasion. In the end, the young President was successful, and the most reckless challenge to U.S. hemispheric supremacy in this century was thwarted.

Internationalism

Since isolationism was so often associated with World War II, the United States Senate, which had rejected President Wilson's League of Nations proposal nearly thirty years earlier, overwhelmingly approved America's participation in the United Nations and its specialized agencies. Further, we gave immense amounts of economic assis-

25 The text of the President's address may be found in *The Department of State Bulletin,* 47, No. 1220 (November 12, 1962), pp. 715–20. Reprinted in Walter C. Clemens, Jr., ed., *World Perspectives in International Politics* (Boston: Little, Brown and Company, 1965), pp. 331–38.

tance to our former allies and even our old foes following World War II. Our foreign aid program was the most generous ever accorded by one nation to others. Its nonmilitary European phase was launched by the enormously successful Marshall Plan (named after President Truman's Secretary of State) in 1948, and it was expanded in the next two years by Truman's "Point Four" Program designed to assist the economically underdeveloped countries. There were and are three primary motivations for this foreign assistance: (1) a genuine desire to alleviate human suffering; (2) a general recognition that better living conditions would reduce the appeal of communism; and (3) an attempt to bolster American business by the stipulation that much foreign aid be used to purchase American-made products. The magnitude of this program is revealed in Figure 67. The internationalism implicit in American policy in recent times also found outlets in military alliances such as NATO and various cultural exchange programs involving students, teachers, artists, and entertainers.

　　　　The isolationism of the 1920s and 1930s has been supplanted not only by a resumption of international cooperation but also by what critics of American foreign policy have called a refined variety of imperialism. This no longer takes the form of territorial expansion, since the

Figure 67   U.S. Foreign Economic Assistance

(in millions of dollars)		
Area	1948–69	1970
Near East and South Asia	$10,976.4	$330.3
Latin America	4,964.2	377.7
Vietnam	3,687.1	308.4
Other East Asia	7,360.5	180.3
Africa	2,266.2	138.6
Europe	15,228.9	none
All other (nonregional)	3,703.6	333.6
Total	$48,194.8	$1,668.9
Major National Recipients		
United Kingdom (Great Britain)	3,834.9	none
Vietnam	3,687.1	308.4
India	3,405.7	159.0
France	3,190.3	none
Korea (South)	2,874.7	16.6
Pakistan	2,161.9	118.7
Turkey	1,983.2	40.4
Italy	1,650.3	none
Germany (West)	1,472.4	none
China (Taiwan)	1,367.0	none
Brazil	1,265.8	61.2

Source: *New York Times Encyclopedic Almanac* 1971, p. 691, and U.S. Bureau of the Census, *Statistical Abstract of the United States: 1971*, pp. 763–64.

only areas obtained by the United States in the last half-century have been a few small, sparsely populated islands in the Pacific that were former Japanese colonies. More than compensating for these acquisitions, the United States voluntarily relinquished colonial control over the Philippines in 1945 and returned Okinawa to Japan in 1972.

The most significant form of alleged imperialism in recent years has been the result of economic growth and the activities of American enterprises abroad. Over a third of the petroleum in West Germany, half of the cars in Britain, and two thirds of the sewing machines and razor blades in France were sold by U.S. firms in 1963,[26] and American private investments abroad more than tripled (from over $29 billion to $110 billion) between 1955 and 1969.[27]

Communist Containment

The containment policy can best be understood by a quick look at the power relationships that rose out of the rubble of World War II. Only two nations emerged stronger after the war. They were the United States, committed to political democracy and economic capitalism, and the Soviet Union, ensnared by political dictatorship and dedicated to a communist economy. The decision to "contain" Communism (*i.e.,* to confine it to its existing domain) was made in 1947 when the United States sent military aid to suppress a Communist-provoked civil war in Greece and to bolster the defenses of neighboring Turkey. The Truman Doctrine proclaimed America's determination to give similar assistance wherever needed and this containment policy has been reaffirmed by each succeeding administration. It stems not only from the Soviet challenge to American military superiority, Russian imperialism in Eastern Europe, and Communist aggression in Korea, but also from domestic pressures in the United States. It has been politically profitable to accuse one's critics—rightly or not—of being Communist "dupes," "sympathizers," "appeasers," or just plain Communists. Liberals and leftists in America have charged that the policy of Communist containment has subverted our moral purpose because we have supported oppressive, right-wing dictatorships in Spain, Greece, Korea, Taiwan, and Latin America simply because they were anti-Communist.

Nonetheless, much opposition to Russian imperialism in the postwar world seems justified in terms of either our military security or the protection of human freedom. Perhaps the most obvious examples are the defense of West Berlin during the Soviet blockade in 1948, our reaction to the Cuban missile crisis in 1962, and our continuing military assistance to Israel. It should be noted also that development of the

26 Christopher Layton, Trans-Atlantic Investments (Boulogne-sur-Seine, France: The Atlantic Institute, 1966), p. 19. These statistics are reported in Harry Magdoff, *The Age of Imperialism* (N.Y.: Modern Reader, Monthly Review Press, 1969), p. 61.
27 Bureau of the Census, *Statistical Abstract of the United States: 1971*, p. 754.

containment policy seemed a reasonable application of the lessons of World War ɪɪ. Had Germany and Italy been "contained" when they first began their territorial expansion, that war might never have occurred.

Vietnam

The most dubious and costly response to communism has been in Vietnam. There we perceived a quest for independence from colonial control as a movement directed by Moscow or Peking, and assessed a civil war as one involving international aggression. Regardless of its merits, none can dispute the awful price that both Americans and Vietnamese have paid since the massive intervention of U.S. combat troops in 1965.[28]

America's military commitment in Vietnam moved with a slow but seemingly inexorable momentum. Prior to World War ɪɪ, Vietnam, along with Cambodia and Laos, had been part of a colonial empire known as French Indochina. Led by a Communist, Ho Chi Minh, Vietnamese forces opposing imperialist control proclaimed their independence in 1945. A nine-year civil war culminated in 1954 with a French military defeat and a series of agreements reached in Geneva. Among other things, these agreements provided for a cease-fire, prohibited the establishment of foreign bases in Vietnam, and divided the nation temporarily into a northern sector under the leadership of Ho and a southern one supported by the French and Americans. Elections were to be held during 1956 in both parts of the country for the purpose of unifying the nation under a single government. Fearing a victory by candidates most sympathetic to the northern regime, South Vietnam, with the encouragement of the United States, refused to permit such elections.

During the next decade, civil strife intensified in the South. The government, largely Catholic and formerly pro-French, was repressive yet unstable, and unpopular with large numbers of Buddhists. An American military assistance group which began training the South Vietnamese army in 1955, had grown to twenty-three thousand men by 1964. It seemed apparent that the North Vietnamese were supplying the insurgent rebels in the South, an activity which to American officials justified U.S. intervention under the 1954 SEATO treaty.

In August 1964, President Johnson reported (perhaps erroneously) that two American destroyers in international waters off the coast of North Vietnam had been fired upon without provocation. At his request, Congress passed the "Gulf of Tonkin" resolution authorizing

---

28 The literature on the Indochina war is too extensive to cite in detail. See, for example, John R. Boettiger, ed., *Vietnam and American Foreign Policy* (Boston: D. C. Heath & Company, 1968), Marvin E. Gettleman, ed., *Vietnam* (N.Y.: A Fawcett-Crest Book, Fawcett World Library, 1965), and Neil Sheehan, *The Pentagon Papers* (Toronto: Bantam Books, Inc., 1971).

the President to take action necessary to defend American armed forces or prevent aggression. The next year, Johnson ordered the bombing of North Vietnam and sent American forces into combat. By 1968 there were over 543 thousand troops in Vietnam and more than 33,000 had been killed.

After taking office in 1969, President Nixon authorized the gradual removal of American ground combat troops and launched a "Vietnamization" program designed to turn most of the fighting over to the Vietnamese. In 1972, however, he resumed and intensified aerial bombardment of the North and mined harbor facilities near the coast. While insisting that the United States keep the commitment his predecessors made to the defense of South Vietnam, the President also accelerated efforts to reach a negotiated settlement and secure the release of American prisoners of war.

Whatever its outcome, the struggle inflicted wounds on the American conscience that will take a long time to heal: a bitterly divided nation, dead student protesters, a distrust of our own government, the massacre of civilians at My Lai, and increased use of drugs among military personnel. In 1969 the $28 billion expended on the Vietnam war exceeded the total amount spent for health and medical care by all levels of government in America. The losses incurred by the Vietnamese people were larger still. Whole villages were destroyed to try to save them from Communist control, farms and forests were defoliated, and twice as much tonnage fell from U.S. bombers over Vietnam as had been dropped on all targets during World War ii.

By 1972 the long Cold War between the non-Communist and Communist spheres of the world seemed to be entering an uneasy truce. Perhaps the major explanation for this change lies in the increasing evidence that communism is no longer a single, monolithic force controlled by the Kremlin in Moscow. Yugoslavia broke from the Russian orbit in 1948, Stalin's paranoid dictatorship was replaced by the still repressive but more reasonable rule of a party elite, and the Soviet Union and China became bitter rivals for international Communist leadership. Finally, President Nixon's 1972 summit conferences with Communist leaders bore promise of more normal diplomatic relations. It is too early, however, to write the epitaph for the containment policy.

Military Dominance

Prior to the second World War, the United States relied on its productive capacity, the great oceans on either side, and its strength relative to other nations in the hemisphere to ensure its safety. Since then, however, it has attempted for the first time to maintain at least a global parity, if not an actual superiority, in military might. In 1970 its armed forces stood at 3.2 million compared with 3.3 for the Soviet Union and 2.8 for China. Its total expenditures for military purposes were about twice those of the Soviet Union, though both spent a similar percentage of their GNP.[29] The relative strength of America's nuclear arsenal was more difficult to assess. The London-based International Institute for Strategic Studies reported in 1972 that the Soviet Union had a missile armory with far greater explosive punch than America's and a slight lead in the number of strategic rockets. This was offset, however, by America's superior nuclear delivery capacity. As a result of multiple independently targeted reentry vehicles (MIRVs) that carry several bombs, each capable of hitting a different target, the Institute estimated that the United States could strike about 2710 targets and the Soviet Union about 1750.[30]

In the realm of military policy, there has been continuing debate during the last decade on the relative importance of conventional forces *vs.* nuclear weapons, the advisability of maintaining present troop levels in Europe, and the significance of growing Soviet naval power. On top of these strategic questions, there has been a growing concern over controversial cost overruns by leading defense contractors which forced up the price of weapons and led to charges of mismanagement by corporate officials. In the 1972 campaign, Senator McGovern argued that waste abounded in both the military and civilian sectors of the defense establishment and that substantial budget cuts would not imperil national security.

The armed forces themselves were plagued by problems of poor discipline and low morale. Between 1967 and 1971 the desertion rate more than doubled, servicemen who were absent without leave increased by 34 percent, and military bases were beset by rising friction between black and white troops. Various reforms were undertaken to improve the situation, the most important of which was President Nixon's announced intention to end the draft by July 1973. To attract enlistments in the new all-volunteer army, pay rates were increased, troops were relieved of many kitchen duties and other nonmilitary tasks, and an attempt was made to improve living conditions in the barracks.[31] Although the abolition of the draft met overwhelming popular approval, some believed that a professional military establishment was not consistent with democracy, while others feared that it would result in the poor and racial minorities undertaking most of the risks entailed in military service.

A Generation of Peace?

American foreign policy rests principally upon the cornerstones just described: hemispheric supremacy, internationalism, Communist containment, and military dominance. The question of the mid-1970s involves the degree to which these must be altered to attain President Nixon's goal of "a generation of peace." Several modifications

29 Bureau of the Census, *Statistical Abstract of the United States: 1971*, p. 823.
30 *Los Angeles Times,* Sept. 8, 1972, p. 27.
31 *Congressional Quarterly Weekly Report,* Feb. 19, 1972, pp. 391–95.

are already apparent and problems that lie ahead may well require others.

At Guam in July 1969, President Nixon set forth what was to be known as the Nixon Doctrine. While reaffirming our treaty commitments and the value of our nuclear power as a deterrent to attack upon our allies, the doctrine emphasized that in the future the United States would rely more heavily upon other nations to provide troops for their own defense. It was a recognition of the limits of American power resources and the growing strength of its allies. It was also an implicit assurance that future Vietnams would be avoided.

Strategic arms limitation treaty (SALT) talks between the United States and the Soviet Union extended over a two-year period before they bore fruit during President Nixon's visit to Moscow in May 1972. The resultant treaty limited each nation to two antiballistic missile sites for defensive purposes and a five-year agreement to suspend starts on the construction of new offensive missiles. It was the first brake applied to the accelerating arms race, a basis for further negotiations that resumed several months later, and an indication that both sides might settle for a rough balance of power rather than press for decisive military superiority. In any event, each nation already possessed the capacity to survive an attack long enough to obliterate the other.

The SALT agreements were but one indication of a changing pattern of relationships between the United States and Communist nations. The President who had jumped to political prominence from a springboard of implacable anticommunism had launched negotiations with Communist nations that took him not only to Russia but to China, Romania, and Poland as well. With China, the ground work was laid for cultural exchange (beginning with ping-pong teams), trade, and eventual diplomatic recognition. With Russia, arms agreements were augmented by arrangements for the exchange of information and personnel in medical research, a spaceship rendezvous, and the largest wheat sale in history. The containment policy was not necessarily abandoned but the world was moving into a post-Cold War period in which mere coexistence was accompanied by active cooperation.

The Unsolved Problems

Sources of friction with Communist countries still remained, especially in Asia and the Middle East. If conflicts arise, however, chances are good that they can be localized if the resulting casualties are sustained only by weak nations (no matter where they get their guns) as they were in the encounters between India and Pakistan or Egypt and Israel. But if a confrontation occurs between the big powers that supply most of the world's weapons, then the specter of global catastrophe could be transformed into vivid reality. To minimize this possibility, the Soviet Union, the People's Republic of China, and the United States have displayed a prudent if somewhat cynical willingness to abandon their small allies rather than risk a nuclear showdown. The Soviets thus withdrew missiles from Cuba, the Communist Chinese sent no combat troops to aid the North Vietnamese, and President Nixon agreed to the eventual withdrawal of American forces from the Nationalist Chinese garrison in Taiwan. Each of the major nations, it seems, was laying claim to a particular sphere of influence in its own portion of the world with the acquiescence of its chief rivals. Thus, if the great powers accepted a *modus vivendi* in which each realistically acknowledged the vital interests of the others, the prospects for peace might be enhanced. If ideological consistency and the interests of small countries were sacrificed in the process, it appeared to be a small price to pay. Future danger lurked in the possibilities that one great nation might misinterpret the interests of another, or that these interests might conflict.

Even as the fate of much of the world appears to be negotiated by Moscow, Peking, and Washington, at the same time Tokyo and the capitals of Western Europe have accumulated sufficient strength to determine their own roles in world affairs. Japan and the European Common Market have experienced such rapid economic growth that their exports to the United States in 1971 helped produce America's first international trade deficit since 1893, a devaluation of the dollar, and a growing concern that American-owned factories abroad might substantially increase unemployment at home.

The world had become, in Marshall McLuhan's phrase, a global village in which the nations that comprised it were interacting more frequently than ever before in a wide array of relationships—military, economic, and cultural. The weak remained pawns of the strong, but power was distributed far more widely than in the world dominated two decades earlier by the United States and the Soviet Union. That in itself produced perils, for valuable as the United Nations might become, the global village was still ungoverned.

Conclusion to Part Six

Whenever people with a substantial amount of political power decide that they want some level of American government to do something, chances are good that the government will do it. The last three chapters describe government policies in three different areas, each marked by distinguishing characteristics related to one of the major varieties of power—authority, influence, and force—to which reference has frequently been made.

Government policy concerning moral issues depends largely on voluntary compliance. Unless laws pertaining to abortion and marijuana, for example, are buttressed by the support of the family, church, and other social institutions, they often can be secretly and successfully evaded. The effective exercise of government power in this realm depends on its *authority,* that elusive legitimacy that is based on public opinion—on what the people think is "right."

Economic policy is easier to enforce than moral policy because it requires government intrusion into offices or factories rather than into bedrooms or dens. Moreover, it encounters religious or ethical objections less frequently and can be implemented by *influence* in the form of many kinds of rewards (contracts, subsidies, and social security payments) and deprivations (taxes, fines, and wage controls). Influence also largely determines economic policy. Here money is a major political resource, but as it is distributed unequally, government economic policy may be subject to minority control more easily than policy regarding personal morality.

The conduct of international relations, in contrast, often relies on war—the ultimate utilization of *force.* Foreign policy is unique also in two other aspects: The power to make it is concentrated largely in the President, and often it must respond to global pressures beyond the control of domestic politics. If the United States can employ its power in behalf of an international acceptance of world-wide authority, it will have fulfilled a mission of historic magnitude. If it should fail, there may be no historians left to assess the blame.

Bibliography

Chapter 15

Life Styles: Politics of Personal Morality

Davies, J. Clarence III, *The Politics of Pollution* (N.Y.: Pegasus, 1970).
DeBell, Garret, ed. *The Environmental Handbook* (N.Y.: Ballantine Books, Inc., 1970).
Ehrlich, Paul R., *The Population Bomb* (N.Y.: Ballantine Books, 1968).
Fritschler, A. Lee, *Smoking and Politics* (N.Y.: Appleton-Century-Crofts, 1969).
Packard, Vance, *The Sexual Wilderness* (N.Y.: Pocket Books, 1970).
Report of the Commission on Obscenity and Pornography (Washington, D.C.: U.S. Government Printing Office, 1970).
Roos, Leslie L. Jr., ed., *The Politics of Ecosuicide* (N.Y.: Holt, Rinehart and Winston, Inc., 1971).

Chapter 16

The General Welfare: Politics of Prosperity and Poverty

Banfield, Edward C., *The Unheavenly City* (Boston: Little, Brown and Company, 1968).
Congressional Quarterly Weekly Report
Domhoff, G. William, *Who Rules America?* (Englewood Cliffs, N.J.: Prentice-Hall, Inc., 1967).
Harrington, Michael, *The Other America* (Baltimore: Penguin Books, 1964).
Keyserling, Leon H., *Progress or Poverty* (Washington, D.C.: Conference on Economic Progress, 1964).
Lundberg, *The Rich and the Super Rich* (N.Y.: Bantam Books, 1969).
Redford, Emmett S., *The Role of Government in the American Economy* (N.Y.: The Macmillan Company, 1966).

Chapter 17

The Global Village: Politics of War and Peace

Cohen, Bernard C., ed., *Foreign Policy in American Government* (Boston: Little, Brown and Company, 1965).
Cole, Wayne S., *An Interpretive History of American Foreign Relations* (Homewood, Ill.: The Dorsey Press, 1968).
Deutsch, *The Analysis of International Relations* (Englewood Cliffs, N.J.: Prentice-Hall, Inc., 1968).
Hill, Norman L., *Mr. Secretary of State* (N.Y.: Random House, 1963).
Kaplan, Lawrence S., ed., *Recent American Foreign Policy,* rev. ed. (Homewood, Ill.: The Dorsey Press, 1972).
Sheehan, Neil, *et al., The Pentagon Papers* (Toronto: Bantam Books, Inc., 1971).
Stoessinger, John G., *The Might of Nations,* 3rd ed. (N.Y.: Random House, 1969).

Epilogue
Where Do We Go from Here?

"If I were dying my last words would be: Have faith and pursue the unknown end."
Justice Oliver Wendell Holmes

Is the people's power sufficient to control the government's power? In an age of rapid change, the answer to that question (like so many others) is always tentative, for every year, nearly every day, issues emerge which demand that it be answered anew. It has been common and even fashionable in academic circles to view the future of representative government with some skepticism. Moreover, the people themselves seem to have lost faith in their own power to influence official policy. A recent survey reveals that within only six years the number of Americans who distrusted their government had nearly doubled, reaching 39 percent of the population.[1]

It is far too early, however, for the people to throw in the towel. There is little reason for them either to accept the loss of their power with resigned despair or to burn the system down. On the contrary, the survival of American political institutions for nearly two centuries displays a resilience and flexibility, a capacity for change and regeneration, too great to be abandoned now. If government is remote and secretive, callous to considerations of moral decency, or insensitive to the concerns of a troubled people, it is not because something is wrong with our basic political

1 *Los Angeles Times,* Sept. 21, 1972, p. 3. The survey results were reported by Professor Arthur Miller of Ohio State University in a paper presented to the 1972 convention of the American Political Science Association.

principles but because we have permitted their perversion or distortion. Chapter 2 identified four of those central ideas which now require rededication and revitalization.

1) *Federalism.* The states and the communities within each state must resume their historic function of pursuing the varied policies demanded by their diverse populations and unique needs. Perhaps a vastly expanded program of revenue sharing by the federal government will make that financially possible, but administratively it may require that local governments be consolidated or at least reorganized to permit more simplified control by the voters. At the same time, we must recognize that at every level of government—city, county, state, and national—there is a different coalition of groups, a majority comprised of different interests, that will attempt to shape official policy to its own advantage. It is a risk as necessary as government itself.

2) *Separation of Powers.* The three branches of government must be required to respect the roles and prerogatives of the other two. Legislators, especially, have been weakened by subservience to wealthy interests, a lack of expert assistance and specialized knowledge, undemocratic procedures, fragmentation of authority among powerful and independent committees, and at the level of Congress, a surrender of their influence over foreign affairs to the encroachments of an ambitious and ever stronger presidency.

3) *Freedom.* Slowly, awkwardly, sometimes reluctantly, American government has usually done what a majority of the people want it to do. Minorities have fared less well, generally because they lack sufficient votes, money, or other basic political resources. Occasionally, however, a minority is powerless because an intolerant majority has restricted its freedom. Minority rights must be protected, then, if only because new ideas, by definition, are at first propounded only by a minority—initially, perhaps, by a minority of one. Ironically, the freedom to advocate those new ideas on which progress depends, those that are unpopular, is the very freedom that is most often in jeopardy. No regime in human history has threatened the freedom to praise its wisdom. Yet when freedom for the critics of society is abridged, the validity of their criticism can never be fairly judged. In that event, freedom for the rest of us is neither very significant nor, in the long run, very safe.

4) *Democracy.* The people's power must rest its hopes on majority rule—though a majority consisting of, and enlightened by, the many minorities that uneasily coexist in this wondrously diverse society. That is the essence of democracy. But if a majority is to exert political power, it must

muster the resources and master the skills (which are perhaps the most important resource of all) that are essential to democratic politics. This requires some intelligence and considerable work. It means going to meetings, distributing literature, and contributing money. It demands that the people organize in pressure groups to advance their interests, that they learn to control the political parties that vie for governmental office, that they demand election laws that give the poor candidate a fighting chance against the rich one. At minimum, it demands that before they vote they identify the policies they most want, their own basic interests, and the candidates most likely to advance both.

Will it do any good? If all these prescriptions are filled, or others that may be offered by wiser heads, can the people's power prevail over that concentrated in the elites whose political resources so far exceed their own?

These are variations of the same question with which this epilogue began. No one knows the answers, but if they are affirmative, if American democracy can realize its promise, it will require that the people have confidence that it can. When black leaders of the 1960s admonished their followers to "keep the faith, baby" they were expressing a fundamental psychological truth: There is no progress without faith that progress is possible.

While faith in the perfectability of ancient political principles has no sure reward, three things seem certain. One is that experience justifies more faith in democracy than in aristocracy or dictatorship. A second is that American government is already more democratic than many of the social and economic institutions it sometimes seeks to regulate. A third is that the only alternative to faith is the cynicism and despair that become self-fulfilling prophesies of doom, destroying hope and paralyzing action. But if the people define a vision of the society they want, if they learn all they can about controlling the government that may help bring it about, if they work diligently to improve the mechanisms of that government, if they demand decency and honor in their officials, and if they treat one another with the compassion and dignity necessary for concerted action, then there is cause for optimism. Spiritual salvation, according to some Christian theologians, comes from faith and good works. The former inspires the latter. So it must be if the people's power is to prevail.

The Constitution
of the United States

We the People of the United States, in Order to form a more perfect Union, establish Justice, insure domestic Tranquility, provide for the common defence, promote the general Welfare, and secure the Blessings of Liberty to ourselves and our Posterity, do ordain and establish this Constitution for the United States of America.

ARTICLE I

Section 1. All legislative Powers herein granted shall be vested in a Congress of the United States, which shall consist of a Senate and House of Representatives.

Section 2. The House of Representatives shall be composed of Members chosen every second Year by the People of the several States, and the Electors in each State shall have the Qualifications requisite for Electors of the most numerous Branch of the State Legislature.

No Person shall be a Representative who shall not have attained to the Age of twenty five Years, and been seven Years a Citizen of the United States, and who shall not, when elected, be an Inhabitant of that State in which he shall be chosen.

Representatives and direct Taxes shall be apportioned among the several States which may be included within this Union, according to their respective Numbers, which shall be determined by adding to the whole Number of free Persons, including those bound to Service for a Term of Years, and excluding Indians not taxed, three fifths of all other Persons. The actual Enumeration shall be made within three Years after the first Meeting of the Congress of the United States, and within every subsequent Term of ten Years, in such Manner as they shall by Law direct. The Number of Representatives shall not exceed one for every thirty Thousand, but each State shall have at Least one Representative; and until such enumeration shall be made, the State of New Hampshire shall be entitled to chuse three, Massachusetts eight,

Rhode-Island and Providence Plantations one, Connecticut five, New-York six, New Jersey four, Pennsylvania eight, Delaware one, Maryland six, Virginia ten, North Carolina five, South Carolina five, and Georgia three.

When vacancies happen in the Representation from any State, the Executive Authority thereof shall issue Writs of Election to fill such Vacancies.

The House of Representatives shall chuse their speaker and other Officers; and shall have the sole Power of Impeachment.

Section 3. The Senate of the United States shall be composed of two Senators from each State, chosen by the Legislature thereof, for six Years; and each Senator shall have one Vote.

Immediately after they shall be aseembled in Consequence of the first Election, they shall be divided as equally as may be into three Classes. The Seats of the Senators of the first Class shall be vacated at the Expiration of the second Year, of the second Class at the Expiration of the fourth Year, and of the third Class at the Expiration of the sixth Year, so that one third may be chosen every second Year; and if Vacancies happen by Resignation, or otherwise, during the Recess of the Legislature of any State, the Executive thereof may make temporary Appointments until the next Meeting of the Legislature, which shall then fill such Vacancies.

No Person shall be a Senator who shall not have attained to the Age of thirty Years, and been nine Years a Citizen of the United States, and who shall not, when elected, be an Inhabitant of that State for which he shall be chosen.

The Vice President of the United States shall be President of the Senate, but shall have no Vote, unless they be equally divided.

The Senate shall chuse their other Officers, and also a President pro tempore, in the Absence of the Vice President, or when he shall exercise the Office of President of the United States.

The Senate shall have the sole Power to try all Impeachments. When sitting for that Purpose, they shall be on Oath or Affirmation. When the President of the United States is tried, the Chief Justice shall preside: And no Person shall be convicted without the Concurrence of two thirds of the Members present.

Judgment in Cases of Impeachment shall not extend further than to removal from Office, and disqualification to hold and enjoy any Office of honor, Trust or Profit under the United States: but the Party convicted shall nevertheless be liable and subject to Indictment, Trial, Judgment and Punishment, according to law.

Section 4. The Times, Places and Manner of holding Elections for Senators and Representatives, shall be prescribed in each State by the Legislature thereof; but the Congress may at any time by Law make or alter such Regulations, except as to the Places of chusing Senators.

The Congress shall assemble at least once in every Year, and such Meeting shall be on the first Monday in December, unless they shall by Law appoint a different Day.

Section 5. Each House shall be the Judge of the Elections, Returns and Qualifications of its own Members, and a Majority of each shall constitute a Quorum to do Business; but a smaller Number may adjourn from day to day, and may be authorized to compel the Attendance of absent Members, in such Manner, and under such Penalties as each House may provide.

Each House may determine the Rules of its Proceedings, punish its Members for disorderly Behaviour, and, with the Concurrence of two thirds, expel a Member.

Each House shall keep a Journal of its Proceedings, and from time to time publish the same, excepting such Parts as may in their Judgment require Secrecy; and the Yeas and Nays of the Members of either House on any question shall, at the Desire of one fifth of those Present, be entered on the Journal.

Neither House, during the Session of Congress, shall, without the Consent of the other, adjourn for more than three days, nor to any other Place than that in which the two Houses shall be sitting.

Section 6. The Senators and Representatives shall receive a Compensation for their Services, to be ascertained by Law, and paid out of the Treasury of the United States. They shall in all Cases, except Treason, Felony and Breach of the Peace, be privileged from Arrest during their Attendance at the Session of their respective Houses, and in going to and returning from the same; and for any Speech or Debate in either House, they shall not be questioned in any other Place.

No Senator or Representative shall, during the Time for which he was elected, be appointed to any civil Office under the Authority of the United States, which shall have been created, or the Emoluments whereof shall have been encreased during such time; and no Person holding any Office under the United States, shall be a Member of either House during his Continuance in Office.

Section 7. All Bills for raising Revenue shall originate in the House of Representatives; but the Senate may propose or concur with Amendments as on other Bills.

Every Bill which shall have passed the House of Representatives and the Senate, shall, before it become a Law, be presented to the President of the United States; If he approve he shall sign it, but if not he shall return it, with his Objections to that House in which it shall have originated, who shall enter the Objections at large on their Journal, and proceed to reconsider it. If after such Reconsideration two thirds of that House shall agree to pass the Bill, it shall be sent, together with the Objections, to the other House, by which it shall likewise be reconsidered, and if approved by two thirds of that House, it shall become a Law. But in all such Cases the Votes of both Houses shall be determined by Yeas and Nays, and the Names of the Persons voting for and against the Bill shall be entered on the Journal of each House respectively. If any Bill shall not be returned by the President within ten Days (Sundays excepted) after it shall have been presented to him, the Same shall be a Law, in like Manner as if he had signed it, unless the Congress by their Adjournment prevent its Return, in which Case it shall not be a Law.

Every Order, Resolution, or Vote to which the Concurrence of the Senate and House of Representatives may be necessary (except on a question of Adjournment) shall be presented to the President of the United States; and before the Same shall take Effect, shall be approved by him, or being disapproved by him, shall be repassed by two thirds of the Senate and House of Representatives, according to the Rules and Limitations prescribed in the Case of a Bill.

Section 8. The Congress shall have Power To lay and collect Taxes, Duties, Imposts and Excises, to pay the Debts and provide for the common Defence and general Welfare of the United States; but all Duties, Imposts and Excises shall be uniform throughout the United States;

To borrow Money on the Credit of the United States;

To regulate Commerce with foreign Nations, and among the several States, and with the Indian Tribes;

To establish an uniform Rule of Naturalization, and uniform Laws on the subject of Bankruptcies throughout the United States;

To coin Money, regulate the Value thereof, and of foreign Coin, and fix the Standard of Weights and Measures;

To provide for the Punishment of counterfeiting the Securities and current Coin of the United States;

To establish Post Offices and post Roads;

To promote the Progress of Science and useful Arts, by securing for limited Times to Authors and Inventors the exclusive Right to their respective Writings and Discoveries;

To constitute Tribunals inferior to the supreme Court;

To define and punish Piracies and Felonies committed on the high Seas, and Offences against the Law of Nations;

To declare War, grant Letters of Marque and Reprisal, and make Rules concerning Captures on Land and Water;

To raise and support Armies, but no Appropriation of Money to that Use shall be for a longer Term than two Years;

To provide and maintain a Navy;

To make Rules for the Government and Regulation of the land and naval Forces;

To provide for calling forth the Militia to execute the Laws of the Union, suppress Insurrections and repel Invasions;

To provide for organizing, arming, and disciplining, the Militia, and for governing such Part of them as may be employed in the Service of the United States, reserving to the States respectively, the Appointment of the Officers, and the Authority of training the Militia according to the discipline prescribed by Congress;

To exercise exclusive Legislation in all Cases whatsoever, over such District (not exceeding ten Miles square) as may, by Cession of particular States, and the Acceptance of Congress, become the Seat of the Government of the United States, and to exercise like Authority over all Places purchased by the Consent of the Legislature of the State in which the Same shall be for the Erection of Forts, Magazines, Arsenals, dock-Yards, and other needful Buildings;—And

To make all Laws which shall be necessary and proper for carrying into Execution the foregoing Powers, and all other Powers vested by this Constitution in the Government of the United States, or in any Department or Officer thereof.

Section 9. The Migration or Importation of such Persons as any of the States now existing shall think proper to admit, shall not be prohibited by the Congress prior to the Year one thousand eight hundred and eight, but a Tax or duty may be imposed on such Importation, not exceeding ten dollars for each Person.

The Privilege of the Writ of Habeas Corpus shall not be suspended, unless when in Cases of Rebellion or Invasion the public Safety may require it.

No Bill of Attainder or ex post facto Law shall be passed.

No Capitation, or other direct, Tax shall be laid, unless in Proportion to the Census or Enumeration herein before directed to be taken.

No Tax or Duty shall be laid on Articles exported from any State.

No Preference shall be given by any Regulation of Commerce or Revenue to the Ports of one State over those of another: nor shall Vessels bound to, or from, one State, be obliged to enter, clear, or pay Duties in another.

No Money shall be drawn from the Treasury, but in Consequence of Appropriations made by Law; and a regular Statement and Account of the Receipts and Expenditures of all public Money shall be published from time to time.

No Title of Nobility shall be granted by the United States: And no Person holding any Office of Profit or Trust under them, shall, without the Consent of the Congress, accept of any present, Emolument, Office, or Title, of any kind whatever, from any King, Prince, or foreign State.

Section 10. No State shall enter into any Treaty, Alliance, or Confederation; grant Letters of Marque and Reprisal; coin Money; emit Bills of Credit; make any Thing but gold and silver Coin a Tender in Payment of Debts; pass any Bill of Attainder, ex post facto Law, or Law impairing the Obligation of Contracts, or grant any Title of Nobility.

No State shall, without the Consent of the Congress, lay any Imposts or Duties on Imports or Exports, except what may be absolutely necessary for executing its inspection Laws: and the net Produce of all Duties and Imposts, laid by any State on Imports or Exports, shall be for the Use of the Treasury of the United States; and all such Laws shall be subject to the Revision and Controul of the Congress.

No State shall, without the Consent of Congress, lay any Duty of Tonnage, keep Troops, or Ships of War in time of Peace, enter into any Agreement or Compact with another State, or with a foreign Power, or engage in War, unless actually invaded, or in such imminent Danger as will not admit of delay.

ARTICLE II

Section 1. The executive Power shall be vested in a President of the United States of America. He shall hold his Office during the Term of four Years, and, together with the Vice President, chosen for the same term, be elected, as follows

Each State shall appoint, in such Manner as the Legislature thereof may direct, a Number of Electors, equal to the whole Number of Senators and Representatives to which the State may be entitled in the Congress: but no Senator or

Representative, or Person holding an Office of Trust or Profit under the United States, shall be appointed an Elector.

The Electors shall meet in their respective States, and vote by Ballot for two Persons, of whom one at least shall not be an Inhabitant of the same State with themselves. And they shall make a List of all the Persons voted for, and of the Number of Votes for each; which List they shall sign and certify, and transmit sealed to the Seat of the Government of the United States, directed to the President of the Senate. The President of the Senate shall, in the Presence of the Senate and House of Representatives, open all the Certificates, and the Votes shall then be counted. The Person having the greatest Number of Votes shall be the President, if such Number be a Majority of the whole Number of Electors appointed; and if there be more than one who have such Majority, and have an equal Number of Votes, then the House of Representatives shall immediately chuse by Ballot one of them for President: and if no Person have a Majority, then from the five highest on the List the said House shall in like Manner chuse the President. But in chusing the President, the Votes shall be taken by States, the Representation from each State having one Vote; A quorum for this Purpose shall consist of a Member or Members from two thirds of the States, and a Majority of all the States shall be necessary to a Choice. In every Case, after the Choice of the President, the Person having the greatest Number of Votes of the Electors shall be the Vice President. But if there should remain two or more who have equal Votes, the Senate shall chuse from them by Ballot the Vice President.

The Congress may determine the Time of chusing the Electors, and the Day on which they shall give their Votes; which Day shall be the same throughout the United States.

No Person except a natural born Citizen, or a Citizen of the United States, at the time of the Adoption of this Constitution, shall be eligible to the Office of President; neither shall any Person be eligible to that Office who shall not have attained to the Age of thirty Five Years, and been fourteen Years a Resident within the United States.

In Case of the Removal of the President from Office, or of his Death, Resignation, or Inability to discharge the Powers and Duties of the said Office, the Same shall devolve on the Vice President, and the Congress may by Law provide for the Case of Removal, Death, Resignation or Inability, both of the President and Vice President, declaring what Officer shall then act as President, and such Officer shall act accordingly, until the Disability be removed, or a President shall be elected.

The President shall, at stated Times, receive for his Services a Compensation, which shall neither be encreased nor diminished during the Period for which he shall have been elected, and he shall not receive within that Period any other Emolument from the United States, or any of them.

Before he enter on the Execution of his Office, he shall take the following Oath or Affirmation:—"I do solemnly swear (or affirm) that I will faithfully execute the Office of President of the United States, and will to the best of my Ability, preserve, protect and defend the Constitution of the United States."

Section 2. The President shall be Commander in Chief of the Army and Navy of the United States, and of the Militia of the several States, when called into the actual Service of the United States; he may require the Opinion, in writing, of the principal Officer in each of the executive Departments, upon any Subject relating to the Duties of their respective Offices, and he shall have Power to grant Reprieves and Pardons for Offences against the United States, except in Cases of Impeachment.

He shall have Power, by and with the Advice and Consent of the Senate, to make Treaties, provided two thirds of the Senators present concur; and he shall nominate, and by and with the Advice and Consent of the Senate, shall appoint Ambassadors, other public Ministers and Consuls, Judges of the supreme Court, and all other Officers of the United States, whose Appointments are not herein otherwise provided for, and which shall be established by Law; but the Congress may by Law vest the Appointment of such inferior Officers, as they think proper, in the President alone, in the Courts of Law, or in the Heads of Departments.

The President shall have Power to fill up all Vacancies that may happen during the Recess of the Senate, by granting Commissions which shall expire at the End of their next Session.

Section 3. He shall from time to time give to the Congress Information of the State of the Union, and recommend to their Consideration such Measures as he shall judge necessary and expedient; he may, on extraordinary Occasions, convene both Houses, or either of them, and in Case of Disagreement between them, with Respect to the Time of Adjournment, he may adjourn them to such Time as he shall think proper; he shall receive Ambassadors and other public Ministers; he shall take Care that the Laws be faithfully executed, and shall Commission all the Officers of the United States.

Section 4. The President, Vice President and all civil Officers of the United States, shall be removed from Office on Impeachment for, and Conviction of, Treason, Bribery, or other High Crimes and Misdemeanors.

ARTICLE III

Section 1. The judicial Power of the United States, shall be vested in one supreme Court, and in such inferior Courts as the Congress may from time to time ordain and establish. The

Judges, both of the supreme and inferior Courts, shall hold their Offices during good Behaviour, and shall, at stated Times, receive for their Services, a Compensation, which shall not be diminished during their Continuance in Office.

Section 2. The judicial Power shall extend to all Cases, in Law and Equity, arising under this Constitution, the Laws of the United States, and Treaties made, or which shall be made, under their Authority;—to all Cases affecting Ambassadors, other public Ministers and Consuls;—to all Cases of admiralty and maritime Jurisdiction;—to Controversies to which the United States shall be a Party;—to Controversies between two or more States; between a State and Citizens of another State;—between Citizens of different States;—between Citizens of the same State claiming Lands under Grants of different States, and between a State, or the Citizens thereof, and foreign States, Citizens or Subjects.

In all Cases affecting Ambassadors, other public Ministers and Consuls, and those in which a State shall be Party, the supreme Court shall have original Jurisdiction. In all the other Cases before mentioned, the supreme Court shall have appellate Jurisdiction, both as to Law and Fact, with such Exceptions, and under such Regulations as the Congress shall make.

The Trial of all Crimes, except in Cases of Impeachment, shall be by Jury; and such Trial shall be held in the State where the said Crimes shall have been committed; but when not committed within any State, the Trial shall be at such Place or Places as the Congress may by Law have directed.

Section 3. Treason against the United States, shall consist only in levying War against them, or in adhering to their Enemies, giving them Aid and Comfort. No Person shall be convicted of Treason unless on the Testimony of two Witnesses to the same overt Act, or on Confession in open Court.

The Congress shall have Power to declare the Punishment of Treason, but no Attainder of Treason shall work Corruption of Blood, or Forfeiture except during the Life of the Person attainted.

ARTICLE IV

Section 1. Full Faith and Credit shall be given in each State to the public Acts, Records, and judicial Proceedings of every other State. And the Congress may by general Laws prescribe the Manner in which such Acts, Records and Proceedings shall be proved, and the Effect thereof.

Section 2. The Citizens of each State shall be entitled to all Privileges and Immunities of Citizens in the several States.

A Person charged in any State with Treason, Felony, or other Crime, who shall flee from Justice, and be found in another State, shall on Demand of the executive Authority of the State from which he fled, be delivered up, to be removed to the State having Jurisdiction of the Crime.

No Person held to Service or Labour in one State, under the Laws thereof, escaping into another, shall, in Consequence of any Law or Regulation therein, be discharged from such service or Labour, but shall be delivered up on Claim of the Party to whom such Service or Labour may be due.

Section 3. New States may be admitted by the Congress into this Union; but no new State shall be formed or erected within the Jurisdiction of any other State; nor any State be formed by the Junction of two or more States, or Parts of States, without the Consent of the Legislatures of the States concerned as well as of the Congress.

The Congress shall have Power to dispose of and make all needful Rules and Regulations respecting the Territory or other Property belonging to the United States; and nothing in this Constitution shall be so construed as to Prejudice any Claims of the United States, or of any particular State.

Section 4. The United States shall guarantee to every State in this Union a Republican Form of Government, and shall protect each of them against Invasion; and on Application of the Legislature, or of the Executive (when the Legislature cannot be convened) against domestic Violence.

ARTICLE V

The Congress, whenever two thirds of both Houses shall deem it necessary, shall propose Amendments to this Constitution, or, on the Application of the Legislatures of two thirds of the several States, shall call a Convention for Proposing Amendments, which, in either Case, shall be valid to all Intents and Purposes, as Part of this Constitution, when ratified by the Legislatures of three fourths of the several States, or by Conventions in three fourths thereof, as the one or the other Mode of Ratification may be proposed by the Congress; Provided that no Amendment which may be made prior to the Year One thousand eight hundred and eight shall in any Manner affect the first and fourth Clauses in the Ninth Section of the first Article; and that no State, without its Consent, shall be deprived of its equal Suffrage in the Senate.

ARTICLE VI

All Debts contracted and Engagements entered into, before the Adoption of this Constitution, shall be as valid against the United States under this Constitution, as under the Confederation.

This Constitution, and the Laws of the United States which shall be made in Pursuance thereof; and all Treaties made, or which shall be made, under the Authority of the United States, shall be the supreme Law of the Land; and the Judges in every State shall be bound thereby, any Thing in the Constitution or Laws of any State to the Contrary notwithstanding.

The Senators and Representatives before mentioned, and the Members of the several State Legislatures, and all executive and judicial Officers, both of the United States and of the several States, shall be bound by Oath or Affirmation, to support this Constitution; but no religious Test shall ever be required as a Qualification to any Office or public Trust under the United States.

ARTICLE VII

The Ratification of the Conventions of nine States, shall be sufficient for the Establishment of this Constitution between the States so ratifying the Same.

Done in Convention by the Unanimous Consent of the States present the Seventeenth Day of September in the Year of our Lord one thousand seven hundred and eighty seven and of the Independence of the United States of America the twelfth. In witness whereof We have hereunto subscribed our Names.

(The first 10 Amendments were ratified December 15, 1791, and form what is known as the "Bill of Rights.")

AMENDMENT 1

Congress shall make no law respecting an establishment of religion, or prohibiting the free exercise thereof; or abridging the freedom of speech, or of the press; or the right of the people peaceably to assemble, and to petition the Government for a redress of grievances.

AMENDMENT 2

A well regulated Militia, being necessary to the security of a free State, the right of the people to keep and bear Arms, shall not be infringed.

AMENDMENT 3

No Soldier shall, in time of peace be quartered in any house, without the consent of the Owner, nor in time of war, but in a manner to be prescribed by law.

AMENDMENT 4

The right of the people to be secure in their persons, houses, papers, and effects, against unreasonable searches and seizures, shall not be violated, and no Warrants shall issue, but upon probable cause, supported by Oath or affirmation, and particularly describing the place to be searched, and the persons or things to be seized.

AMENDMENT 5

No person shall be held to answer for a capital, or otherwise infamous crime, unless on a presentment or indictment of a Grand Jury, except in cases arising in the land or naval forces, or in the Militia, when in actual service in time of War or public danger; nor shall any person be subject for the same offence to be twice put in jeopardy of life or limb; nor shall be compelled in any criminal case to be a witness against himself, nor be deprived of life, liberty, or property, without due process of law; nor shall private property be taken for public use, without just compensation.

AMENDMENT 6

In all criminal prosecutions, the accused shall enjoy the right to a speedy and public trial, by an impartial jury of the State and district wherein the crime shall have been committed, which district shall have been previously ascertained by law, and to be informed of the nature and cause of the accusation; to be confronted with the witnesses against him; to have compulsory process for obtaining witnesses in his favor, and to have the Assistance of Counsel for his defence.

AMENDMENT 7

In Suits at common law, where the value in controversy shall exceed twenty dollars, the right of trial by jury shall be preserved, and no fact tried by a jury, shall be otherwise re-examined in any Court of the United States, than according to the rules of the common law.

AMENDMENT 8

Excessive bail shall not be required, nor excessive fines imposed, nor cruel and unusual punishments inflicted.

AMENDMENT 9

The enumeration in the Constitution, of certain rights, shall not be construed to deny or disparage others retained by the people.

AMENDMENT 10

The powers not delegated to the United States by the Constitution, nor prohibited by it to the States, are reserved to the States respectively, or to the people.

AMENDMENT 11
[RATIFIED FEBRUARY 7, 1795]

The Judicial power of the United States shall not be construed to extend to any suit in law or equity, commenced or prosecuted against one of the United States by Citizens of another State, or by Citizens or Subjects of any Foreign State.

AMENDMENT 12
[RATIFIED JULY 27, 1804]

The Electors shall meet in their respective states and vote by ballot for President and Vice-President, one of whom, at least, shall not be an inhabitant of the same state with themselves; they shall name in their ballots the person voted for as President, and in distinct ballots the person voted for as Vice-President, and they shall make distinct lists of all persons voted for as President, and of all persons voted for as Vice-President, and of the number of votes for each, which lists they shall sign and certify, and transmit sealed to the seat of the government of the United States, directed to the President of the Senate;—The President of the Senate shall, in the presence of the Senate and House of Representatives, open all the certificates and the votes shall then be counted;—The person having the greatest number of votes for President, shall be the President, if such number be a majority of the whole number of Electors appointed; and if no person have such majority, then from the persons having the highest numbers not exceeding three on the list of those voted for as President, the House of Representatives shall choose immediately, by ballot, the President. But in choosing the President, the votes shall be taken by states, the representation from each state having one vote; a quorum for this purpose shall consist of a member or members from two-thirds of the states, and a majority of all the states shall be necessary to a choice. And if the House of Representatives shall not choose a President whenever the right of choice shall devolve upon them, before the fourth day of March next following, then the Vice-President shall act as President, as in the case of the death or other constitutional disability of the President.—The person having the greatest number of votes as Vice-President, shall be the Vice-President, if such number be a majority of the whole number of Electors appointed, and if no person have a majority, then from the two highest numbers on the list, the Senate shall choose the Vice-President; a quorum for the purpose shall consist of two-thirds of the whole number of Senators, and a majority of the whole number shall be necessary to a choice. But no person consti-

tutionally ineligible to the office of President shall be eligible to that of Vice-President of the United States.

AMENDMENT 13
[RATIFIED DECEMBER 6, 1865]

Section 1. Neither slavery nor involuntary servitude, except as a punishment for crime whereof the party shall have been duly convicted, shall exist within the United States, or any place subject to their jurisdiction.

Section 2. Congress shall have power to enforce this article by appropriate legislation.

AMENDMENT 14
[RATIFIED JULY 9, 1868]

Section 1. All persons born or naturalized in the United States, and subject to the jurisdiction thereof, are citizens of the United States and of the State wherein they reside. No State shall make or enforce any law which shall abridge the privileges or immunities of citizens of the United States; nor shall any State deprive any person of life, liberty, or property, without due process of law; nor deny to any person within its jurisdiction the equal protection of the laws.

Section 2. Representatives shall be apportioned among the several States according to their respective numbers, counting the whole number of persons in each State, excluding Indians not taxed. But when the right to vote at any election for the choice of electors for President and Vice President of the United States, Representatives in Congress, the Executive and Judicial officers of a State, or the members of the Legislature thereof, is denied to any of the male inhabitants of such State, being twenty-one years of age, and citizens of the United States, or in any way abridged, except for participation in rebellion, or other crime, the basis of representation therein shall be reduced in the proportion which the number of such male citizens shall bear to the whole number of male citizens twenty-one years of age in such State.

Section 3. No person shall be a Senator or Representaive in Congress, or elector of President and Vice President, or hold any office, civil or military, under the United States, or under any State, who, having previously taken an oath, as a member of Congress, or as an officer of the United States, or as a member of any State legislature, or as an executive or judicial officer of any State, to support the Constitution of the United States, shall have engaged in insurrection or rebellion against the same, or given aid or comfort to the enemies thereof. But Congress may by a vote of two-thirds of each House, remove such disability.

Section 4. The validity of the public debt of the United States, authorized by law, including debts incurred for payment of pensions and bounties for services in suppressing insurrection or rebellion, shall not be questioned. But neither the United States nor any State shall assume or pay any debt or obligation incurred in aid of insurrection or rebellion against the United States, or any claim for the loss or emancipation of any slave; but all such debts, obligations and claims shall be held illegal and void.

Section 5. The Congress shall have power to enforce, by appropriate legislation, the provisions of this article.

AMENDMENT 15
[RATIFIED FEBRUARY 3, 1870]

Section 1. The right of citizens of the United States to vote shall not be denied or abridged by the United States or by any State on account of race, color, or previous condition of servitude.

Section 2. The Congress shall have power to enforce this article by appropriate legislation.

AMENDMENT 16
[RATIFIED FEBRUARY 3, 1913]

The Congress shall have power to lay and collect taxes on incomes, from whatever source derived, without apportionment among the several States, and without regard to any census or enumeration.

AMENDMENT 17
[RATIFIED APRIL 8, 1913]

The Senate of the United States shall be composed of two Senators from each State, elected by the people thereof for six years; and each Senator shall have one vote. The electors in each State shall have the qualifications requisite for electors of the most numerous branch of the State legislatures.

When vacancies happen in the representation of any State in the Senate, the executive authority of such State shall issue writs of election to fill such vacancies: *Provided,* That the legislature of any State may empower the executive thereof to make temporary appointments until the people fill the vacancies by election as the legislature may direct.

This amendment shall not be so construed as to affect the election or term of any Senator chosen before it becomes valid as part of the Constitution.

AMENDMENT 18
[RATIFIED JANUARY 16, 1919]

Section 1. After one year from the ratification of this article the manufacture, sale, or transportation of intoxicating liquors within, the importation thereof into, or the exportation thereof from the United States and all territory subject to the jurisdiction thereof for beverage purposes is hereby prohibited.

Section 2. The Congress and the several States shall have concurrent power to enforce this article by appropriate legislation.

Section 3. This article shall be inoperative unless it shall have been ratified as an amendment to the Constitution by the legislatures of the several States, as provided in the Constitution, within seven years from the date of the submission hereof to the States by the Congress.

AMENDMENT 19
[RATIFIED AUGUST 18, 1920]

The right of citizens of the United States to vote shall not be denied or abridged by the United States or by any State on account of sex.

Congress shall have power to enforce this article by appropriate legislation.

AMENDMENT 20
[RATIFIED JANUARY 23, 1933]

Section 1. The terms of the President and Vice President shall end at noon on the 20th day of January, and the terms of Senators and Representatives at noon on the 3d day of January, of the years in which such terms would have ended if this article had not been ratified; and the terms of their successors shall then begin.

Section 2. The Congress shall assemble at least once in every year, and such meeting shall begin at noon on the 3d day of January, unless they shall by law appoint a different day.

Section 3. If, at the time fixed for the beginning of the term of the President, the President elect shall have died, the Vice President elect shall become President. If a President shall not have been chosen before the time fixed for the beginning of his term, or if the President elect shall have failed to qualify, then the Vice President elect shall act as President until a President shall have qualified; and the Congress may by law provide for the case wherein neither a President elect nor a Vice President elect shall have qualified, declaring who shall then act as President, or the manner in which one who is to act shall be selected, and such person shall act accordingly until a President or Vice President shall have qualified.

Section 4. The Congress may by law provide for the case of the death of any of the persons from whom the House of Representatives may choose a President whenever the right of choice shall have devolved upon them, and for the case of the death of any of the persons from whom the Senate may choose a Vice President whenever the right of choice shall have devolved upon them.

Section 5. Sections 1 and 2 shall take effect on the 15th day of October following the ratification of this article.

Section 6. This article shall be inoperative

unless it shall have been ratified as an amendment to the Constitution by the legislatures of three-fourths of the several States within seven years from the date of its submission.

AMENDMENT 21
[RATIFIED DECEMBER 5, 1933]

Section 1. The eighteenth article of amendment to the Constitution of the United States is hereby repealed.

Section 2. The transportation or importation into any State, Territory, or possession of the United States for delivery or use therein of intoxicating liquors, in violation of the laws thereof, is hereby prohibited.

Section 3. This article shall be inoperative unless it shall have been ratified as an amendment to the Constitution by conventions in the several States, as provided in the Constitution, within seven years from the date of the submission hereof to the States by the Congress.

AMENDMENT 22
[RATIFIED FEBRUARY 27, 1951]

Section 1. No person shall be elected to the office of the President more than twice, and no person who has held the office of President, or acted as President, for more than two years of a term to which some other person was elected President shall be elected to the office of the President more than once. But this Article shall not apply to any person holding the office of President when this Article was proposed by the Congress, and shall not prevent any person who may be holding the office of President, or acting as President, during the term within which this Article becomes operative from holding the office of President or acting as President during the remainder of such term.

Section 2. This article shall be inoperative unless it shall have been ratified as an amendment to the Constitution by the legislatures of three-fourths of the several States within seven years from the date of its submission to the States by the Congress.

AMENDMENT 23
[RATIFIED MARCH 29, 1961]

Section 1. The District constituting the seat of Government of the United States shall appoint in such manner as the Congress may direct:

A number of electors of President and Vice President equal to the whole number of Senators and Representatives in Congress to which the District would be entitled if it were a State, but in no event more than the least populous State; they shall be in addition to those appointed by the States, but they shall be considered, for the purposes of the election of President and Vice President, to be electors appointed by a State; and they shall meet in the District and perform such duties as provided by the twelfth article of amendment.

Section 2. The Congress shall have power to enforce this article by appropriate legislation.

AMENDMENT 24
[RATIFIED JANUARY 23, 1964]

Section 1. The right of citizens of the United States to vote in any primary or other election for President or Vice President, for electors for President or Vice President, or for Senator or Representative in Congress, shall not be denied or abridged by the United States or any State by reason of failure to pay any poll tax or other tax.

Section 2. The Congress shall have power to enforce this article by appropriate legislation.

AMENDMENT 25
[RATIFIED FEBRUARY 10, 1967]

Section 1. In case of the removal of the President from office or of his death or resignation, the Vice President shall become President.

Section 2. Whenever there is a vacancy in the office of the Vice President, the President shall nominate a Vice President who shall take office upon confirmation by a majority vote of both Houses of Congress.

Section 3. Whenever the President transmits to the President pro tempore of the Senate and the Speaker of the House of Representatives his written declaration that he is unable to discharge the powers and duties of his office, and until he transmits to them a written declaration to the contrary, such powers and duties shall be discharged by the Vice President as Acting President.

Section 4. Whenever the Vice President and a majority of either the principal officers of the executive departments or of such other body as Congress may by law provide, transmit to the President pro tempore of the Senate and the Speaker of the House of Representatives their written declaration that the President is unable to discharge the powers and duties of his office, the Vice President shall immediately assume the powers and duties of the office as Acting President.

Thereafter, when the President transmits to the President pro tempore of the Senate and the Speaker of the House of Representatives his written declaration that no inability exists, he shall resume the powers and duties of his office unless the Vice President and a majority of either the principal officers of the executive department or of such other body as Congress may by law provide, transmit within four days to the President pro tempore of the Senate and the Speaker of the House of Representatives their written declaration that the President is unable to discharge the powers and duties of his office. Thereupon Congress shall decide the issue, assembling within forty-eight hours for that purpose if not in session. If the Congress, within twenty-one days after receipt of the latter written declaration, or, if Congress is not in session, within twenty-one days after Congress is required to assemble, determines by two-thirds vote of both Houses that the President is unable to discharge the powers and duties of his office, the Vice President shall continue to discharge the same as Acting President; otherwise, the President shall resume the powers and duties of his office.

AMENDMENT 26

[RATIFIED JUNE 30, 1971]

Section 1. The right of citizens of the United States, who are eighteen years of age or older, to vote shall not be denied or abridged by the United States or by any State on account of age.

Section 2. The Congress shall have power to enforce this article by appropriate legislation.

Index of States, Counties, and Cities

General Index

Gross National Product (GNP), 22, 23, 383, 387, 390, 412
Groups: types defined, 134–137. *See also* Lobbying, Pressure groups
Guatemala, 425, 430, 434
Gulf of Mexico, 370
"Gulf of Tonkin" resolution, 437
Gun control, 100–101, 164
Guzman, Jacob Arbenz, 425

H
Habeas corpus, 86
Haiti, 14
Haldeman, H. R., 264
Hall, Leonard, 195
Hamilton, Alexander, 30, 39, 59, 256
Hammarskjold, Dag, 432
Harding, Warren G., 179, 259
Harlan, John Marshall, 98 n, 106, 289
Harrington, Michael, 403
Harris, La Donna, 147
Harris, Louis, 194. *See also* Polls
Harrison, William Henry, 254, 259
Hatch Act, 160
Hatcher, Richard, 301
Hatfield, Mark, 426
Head Start program, 403, 404–405
Heads of State, 245
Health: appropriations, 388, 389; departments (city), 328; local facilities, 309; medical research, 409; national government programs, 408–409; of the poor, 403. *See also* Medicare
Health, Education and Welfare, U.S. Department of, 159, 262, 263, 366, 369, 373, 409, 415
Hearings (congressional committee), 228–229, 236
Hearst, William Randolph, 132
Heroin, 376–377
Hicklin obscenity test, 78
Hicks, Louise Day, 110
Highway construction, 335, 336, 389
Highway superintendent, county, 312
Hillenbrand, Bernard F., 314
Hitler, Adolf, 13, 55
Ho Chi Minh, 26, 437
Hoffman, Julius, 97
Holmes, Oliver W., 57, 64, 72, 73, 74, 285, 287, 444
Home rule, 296, 304, 306–307, 311, 318, 350, 351. *See also* Government (local)
Homosexuality, 276, 379–380
Honduras, 403
Hong Kong, 149
Hoover, Herbert, 247, 271–272, 433
Hospitals, 309, 389
House of Representatives, 29, 42, 46, 111, 113, 121–123, 151, 153, 173, 190, 198, 199, 231, 241–242, 258, 325, 395; apportionment, 218; committees in, 230–231; election of President, 257; impeachment, 215; party leaders in, 233; raising revenue, 213; Speaker of the House, 226, 259. *See also* Congress, Legislative branch of government, Senate
Housing, 118–119, 263, 270, 316; appropriations, 388, 389; building codes, 342–343; discrimination, 110, 150; fair, 114–115, 176; population distribution, 338–339; subsidized, 341–342; and taxation, 348–350; zoning, 339–340
Housing and Urban Development, U.S. Department of, 107, 115, 263, 341, 351
Houston Ship Channel, 367, 371
Humphrey, Hubert, 178, 179, 181, 233, 261, 297
Hungary, 428

I
Ideology, 16–18, 135, 155, 170–171, 183–184. *See also* Political culture
Illegitimacy, 378, 405
Illinois Pollution Control Board, 370–371
Immigration, 48–51, 150, 263, 361; Restriction Act (1921), 49, 50; 1965 Act, 50, 150; and schools, 344. *See also* Ethnic groups
Impeachment, 215
Imperialism, 435–436
Implied powers, 35
Imprisonment, 102–103
Income: median family, 120; distribution, 383; guaranteed minimum, 407; related to party preference, 199–200; and schooling, 344
Incumbent, 158, 198
Independence, 25–26. *See also* Freedom
Independent voters, 184–185, 199–200
India, 15, 44, 163, 169, 435, 440
Indian Affairs, Bureau of, 147, 263
Indian Patrol, 147
Indians, American, 46, 47, 48, 49, 54, 55, 107, 118, 144, 147–148, 150, 164, 180
Indictment, 95
Individualism, 18, 43, 44, 47, 51, 53–54, 72, 171, 382. *See also* Democracy, Freedom
Indochina, 423, 437. *See also* Vietnam
Indonesia, 361, 432
Industrial Revolution, 51
Inflation, 200, 397–400
Influence, 4–5, 208, 241–242, 292. *See also* Power, Pressure groups
Initiative, 206–207; and referendum, 316
Institute of Court Management, 276
Integration, 108, 116–118, 145, 146, 347
Intercontinental ballistic missiles (ICBMs), 428
Interest on government debt, 388, 389
Interior, U.S. Department of, 262, 263, 365, 369, 418
Intermarriage (miscegenation), 109, 150
Internal Revenue Service, 93
Internal Security Act (1950), 72, 74
International Brotherhood of Electrical Workers, 138
International Court of Justice (UN), 432
International Institute for Strategic Studies, 439
International Longshoremen's Union, 139
International politics, 428–433
Interstate commerce, 28, 35
Interstate Commerce Commission, 137, 265, 413
Investments, U.S. abroad, 436
Ireland, 301
Irish, 55; -Americans, 142, 254, 301
Isolationism, 21, 25, 429, 434
Israel, 66, 163, 176, 436, 440
Italian-American War Veterans, 155
Italians, 55, 301